SECOND EDITION

Dyslexia and Reading Difficulties

Research and Resource Guide for Working with All Struggling Readers

Carol A. Spafford

Literacy Coordinator and Specialist for the
Springfield, Massachusetts School System

George S. Grosser

Lead Researcher and Consultant for the
Springfield, Massachusetts School System

PEARSON

Boston   New York   San Francisco
Mexico City   Montreal   London   Madrid   Munich   Paris
Hong Kong   Singapore   Tokyo   Cape Town   Sydney

Executive Editor: Virginia Lanigan
Editorial Assistant: Scott Blaszak
Production Editor: Greg Erb
Editorial-Production Service: Walsh & Associates, Inc.
Composition and Prepress Buyer: Linda Cox
Manufacturing Buyer: Andrew Turso
Cover Administrator: Kristina Mose-Libon

For related titles and support materials, visit our online catalog at www.ablongman.com

Between the time Web site information is gathered and published, some sites may have been closed. The publisher would appreciate notification where these occur so that they may be corrected in subsequent editions.

Library of Congress Cataloging-in-Publication Data

Spafford, Carol A.
   Dyslexia and reading difficulties : research and resource guide for working with all struggling readers / Carol A. Spafford, George S. Grosser. — 2nd ed.
      p. cm.
   Include bibliographical records and index.
   ISBN 0-205-42856-8
   1. Dyslexia. 2. Reading—Remedial teaching. I. Grosser, George S. II. Title.
RC394.W6S63 2005
371.91'44—dc22

                                                                    2004057339

Printed in the United States of America

10 9 8 7 6 5 4 3 2 1   09 08 07 06 05 04

Carol Spafford would like to dedicate this book to Ken, Kenny, Rich, Monica, and Irene Spafford, all of the students and families who helped her along the way, and to M.H. Yin and Yoko.

George Grosser dedicates this book to Eleanor Grosser, family, and all of the students he was priviledged to serve.

CONTENTS

8 Fluency   181

PREFACE

Dyslexia, the most prevalent reading disability, is a mystifying problem that affects 2 to 20 percent of the population.

> Dyslexia definition = *dys* and *lexia*, or inability to effectively read words, the most prevalent specific learning disability (at least 50% of the LD population). It is thought to have a neurological basis, and the disability is unexpected in relation to other cognitive abilities and access to effective classroom instruction. There are specific difficulties with fluent reading and the phonological components of language. Secondary issues may include other academic problems (e.g., reading comprehension), difficulties in socialization (e.g., more negative peer interactions), and co-existing disabilities or disorders (e.g., ADD or ADHD in 25% of those with dyslexia). With intensive literacy support in reading and writing, a social-academic network of support, and the development of individual resiliency, individuals with dyslexia can lead successful and fulfilling lives.

Although dyslexia cannot be cured, it can be helped to the extent that the individual can live a fulfilling life. Dyslexia has been addressed by a number of authors in various ways because a definitive "cure" or "remedy" for this disorder has not been found. Therefore, one will encounter many approaches to the problem in popular and professional journals. Currently, balanced/intensive literacy instructional blocks (see Chapter 11) that actually work well for students seem to dominate the professional literature with causation attributed to neurophysiological anomalies in the left hemisphere of the brain (see Chapter 1).

The format of this book is intended to reach families and professionals to include diagnosticians, researchers, teachers, school administrators, college students, and anyone interested in learning more about dyslexia and how to support dyslexia from early childhood to adulthood.

The following questions are frequently asked by parents, classroom teachers, and other professionals. While some tentative answers can be given at this time, answers are subject to further refinements as relevant data continue to be gathered and the dyslexia knowledge base increased. These questions include:

What is dyslexia?

What is it like to be dyslexic?

How did the term *dyslexia* originate?

Do individuals with dyslexia "mirror write" and read backwards?

What are some other forms of learning disabilities?

What is the cause of dyslexia?

Is there dyslexia in languages other than English?

What is important in a dyslexia assessment?

What is the role of resiliency?

Are there gifted dyslexics?

What can the regular classroom teacher do to assist the learning of students with dyslexia?

What study skills techniques are most effective?

What can parents do to help their dyslexic children study and learn more?

What does a literacy block for students with dyslexia look like?

What VAK-T programs are currently being used with students who experience moderate to severe dyslexia?

How can we help second-language learners who are dyslexic?

What is the current focus on professional development for schools that serve students with learning disabilities or other disabilities?

Do dyslexics have optimistic chances of completing college and having fulfilling professional careers?

This book is meant to present a comprehensive overview of one of the most puzzling problems educators confront—that is, why do dyslexics have reading problems and what do we do to help them? We will try to provide some insights into this problem with the hope that with further research and study, the nature and causes of dyslexia can further be refined. We carefully document all material with research in the field.

As you will see, we have chosen an eclectic perspective. We are recommending that professionals have many strategic social and academic interventions to rely on, with families involved as "literacy partners." Common sense should always prevail. Be wary of approaches and treatments that claim to have the cures and the definite answers to this reading problem. We are taken by Janet W. Lerner's words from 1971: "The search for the perfect package to teach academic skills and foolproof programmed materials can be viewed as an attempt to minimize the teacher's need to make decisions." The teacher should always assist in determining any interventions for students with disabilities because they must implement and evaluate such efforts. It is incumbent upon all who are involved with dyslexia to *Read, Review,* and *Reason* with "care" and "careful" review.

It is our hope to better the life situation of any person with a learning disability by providing one of the most comprehensive and up-to-date sources on the subject.

Acknowledgments

A project of this magnitude necessarily entails solicitation of advice, resources, and time from colleagues. First, we wish to thank our friends from Allyn and Bacon publishing. Foremost, we were extremely privileged to have had the input and wise counsel of Virginia Lanigan, Executive Editor, and Erin K. Liedel, Development Editor. Additionally, Allyn and Bacon staff Greg Erb (Production Editor) and Scott Blaszak (Editorial Assistant) provided timely feedback and assistance. Kathy Whittier of Walsh & Associates, Inc. superbly handled day-to-day production details, including meticulously reviewing and editing the manuscript from start to finish. Publishers' Design and Production Services, Inc. created outstanding page layouts and graphics. We would also like to thank the reviewers of this edition for their time and input: Penny Chiappe, California State University, Fullerton, and Faith Christiansen, Harris-Stowe State College.

Many of the graphics for the reproducibles throughout the book were expertly created by graphic artist Pat Barfield from Advanced Print & Copy, with managers Rick and Ann Martin. Steven Beshara assisted with page layouts and organization.

Diann Cohen, Director of Reading for the City of Springfield, Massachusetts, and her staff provided superlative professional development information.

Special acknowledgment is also extended to Eleanor Balboni and Benjamin Swan, mentors and teachers of teachers. Finally, we thank Ken Spafford, Kenny Spafford, Richard and Monica Spafford, Irene Spafford, and Eleanor Grosser for their support, patience, and guidance.

1

Introduction to Dyslexia and Other Learning Disabilities

The Challenge . . .

In every school there are children who do not learn to read and spell satisfactorily. . . . increasingly, however, conscientious and discerning teachers and anxious parents are realizing that these students are intelligent non-readers (and troubled readers) who try very hard, and that such children present a challenge . . .
—(GILLINGHAM & STILLMAN, 1966, P. 1).

Anna Gillingham and Bessie Stillman, 1930s to 1960s early pioneers in the study of dyslexia, challenge us to identify children who are dyslexic and plan effective instructional programs for them.

Definition

What Is Dyslexia?

I am not exactly sure, but I think dyslexia is a reading or learning disability. It might make it hard for people to understand things or learn them as quickly as other people.

Grade 5 high honor student

Warbs that you can not conect that you are not learning fast enovgh

Generally, if you ask the question, "What is dyslexia?" there is a degree of uncertainty regarding its prevalence, nature, and causes. Data cited by the United States National Institute of Child Health and Human Development (NICHD) shows 20 percent of elementary school students are at risk for reading failure and of that number, 5 to 10 percent have difficulty learning to read despite exposure to research-based reading instruction that is successful for most students. However, these figures may underrepresent the prevalence of dyslexia because of a general underdiagnosis of reading problems. In the well-known and highly regarded Connecticut study of Sally Shaywitz (2003) and her colleagues from Yale University, these researchers determined that as many as 20 percent of all children are reading disabled with less than one-third of these identified and receiving services. There is still that "mystique" associated with dyslexia, probably due to changing terminology, speculations regarding causation, and no one "remedy" to the problem. As our fifth-grade student with dyslexia notes, there is the widespread belief that there is something wrong with how individuals with dyslexia read words. The word identification problems of individuals with dyslexia relate to specific difficulties with the phonological components of language, central to the definition of dyslexia offered below.

The following definition is provided after an exhaustive review of several hundred research studies and published articles and books on the subject of dyslexia:

"Dyslexia" definition = *dys* and *lexia,* or inability to effectively read words, is the most prevalent specific learning disability (at least 50% of the LD population). It is thought to have a neurological basis, and the disability is unexpected in relation to other cognitive abilities and access to effective classroom instruction. There are specific difficulties with fluent reading and the phonological components of language (i.e., phonemic awareness). Secondary issues may or may not include other academic problems (e.g., reading comprehension); difficulties in socialization (e.g., more negative peer interactions) and co-existing disabilities or disorders (e.g., ADD or ADHD with 25% of those with dyslexia). With intensive literacy support in reading and writing, a social–academic network of support, and the development of individual resiliency, individuals with dyslexia can lead successful and fulfilling lives. (Spafford & Grosser, 2005)

"Jumbled Up" Letters

Often, as our grade 5 high honor student states, there is the belief that individuals who are dyslexic see "jumbled words" or read backwards.

at a reading book, Some people when they book or very blurry, it might look all jumbled up

Grade 5 student with severe dyslexia

Our honor student is representative of students and adults alike in her view of dyslexia—she's not quite sure but knows that dyslexia relates to reading or learning disabilities and that learning is more difficult for individuals with dyslexia. It seems as though people with dyslexia read backwards or reverse or "jumble up" letters. Although many individuals with dyslexia have reading reversals (e.g., "b" for "d"), this is a normal phenomenon for beginning or emerging readers. With individuals who experience dyslexia, reading reversals may persist but are not the primary problem in word recognition—phonemic awareness or phonological knowledge deficiencies are at the root of word problems for dyslexics. Individuals who are dyslexic know that word reading is difficult and is also a primary obstacle to "desired" reading proficiency and "reading speed."

To summarize, for dyslexics, specific difficulties with reading and written language center on fluent reading and the phonological components of language (i.e., phonemic awareness) and not reading backwards. The National Reading Panel (NRP) (2000) reviewed a large body of research and confirms that children who are disabled readers have relatively poor phonemic awareness, and this deficiency "underlies and explains (in large part) their difficulty in learning to read" (pp. 2–14).

A grade 5 student with severe dyslexia also understands that dyslexia can originate from genetic causes. Dyslexia does have a strong familial connection with high percentages of children with dyslexic parents also dyslexic (see Chapter 2).

What Causes Dyslexia?

it happins when your born

Neurological evidence cited on page 8 shows where specific cortical dysfunctioning occurs. Developmentally, this learning disability originates at birth or by acquired injuries through accident, trauma, or disease.

Prevalence

It is estimated that at least 2.19 to 20 percent of the entire population suffers from dyslexia, the most prevalent type of learning disability (see Figure 1.1). In regard to numbers of students who are learning disabled, 4.39 percent have been identified as learning disabled of a total of 8.75 percent disabled students being served in our schools (U.S. Dept. of Education, 2002). We estimate at least half of these students would be classified as dyslexic. As a specific type of learning disability, dyslexia falls

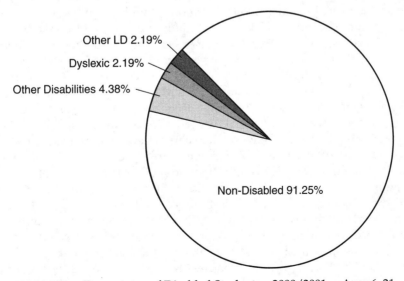

FIGURE 1.1 Percentages of Disabled Students—2000/2001— Ages 6–21

under Part B of the Individuals with Disabilities Education Act (IDEA) of 1990, P.L. 101–476:

> ...a disorder in one or more of basic psychological processes involved in using language, spoken or written, which may manifest itself in an imperfect ability to listen, think, speak, read, write, spell, or do mathematical calculations. The term includes such conditions as perceptual handicaps, brain injury, minimal brain dysfunction, dyslexia, and developmental aphasia. The term does not include children who have learning problems which are primarily the result of visual, hearing, or motor handicaps, of mental retardation, of emotional disturbance, or of environmental, cultural, or economic disadvantage . . . (USDOE, 2002)

The Individuals with Disabilities Education Act (IDEA) (P.L. 101-476) of 1990 and 1997 (P.L. 105-17) is a reauthorization of the more familiar P.L. 94-142 (1975) federal legislation, which was called the Education of All Handicapped Children Act (EOAHC). IDEA includes 1983 (P.L. 98-199) (provided funds for planning state services for young children with disabilities ages birth to 5 years of age) and 1986 (P.L. 99-457) (required states to provide services for preschool children) amendments to P.L. 94-142 and a USDOE 2003 reauthorization (see Chapter 2). Essentially, IDEA is a federal law that provides detailed specifications as to how special services will be administered to disabled children. All disabled children are guaranteed a free and appropriate education under this act. The Federal Office of Special Education Programs, directed by the Deputy Assistant Secretary, is responsible for its implementation. A major change in the P.L. 94-142 (USDOE, 1977) legislation involved deletion of the use of the term *handicapped*, replacing it with the term *disabilities*. Additionally, IDEA now requires the transition services for students leaving high school be written into a student's individual education plan (IEP). Typically, sections 617 and 618 of the regulations are referred to by professionals when looking at EOAHC (P.L. 94-142), and sections 1417 and 1418 are referenced with IDEA (P.L. 101-476, 1990).

Federal and International Dyslexia Association Descriptions

It is necessary to distinguish the problem of dyslexia from other learning disabilities. Learning disabilities in general can refer to a number of problems including difficulties in reading (dyslexia) and language, math, memory, and nonverbal communication problems. However, in most instances learning disabilities are almost always diagnosed with the use of a reading assessment battery and almost always refer to some type of reading disability or dyslexia (Aaron & Baker, 1991). Many writers use the term *learning disability* interchangeably with *dyslexia, reading disability (RD), severe reading disability (SRD),* and *severe reading disorder (SRD).* There are no firm figures regarding the percentage of individuals experiencing learning disabilities who are identified specifically as dyslexic. However, a majority would indicate at least 50 percent or 2.185 percent out of the total 4.37 percent learning disabled identified in our schools (USDOE, 2002). The USDOE (2002) reports 4.37 percent out of all disabled students as having specific learning disabilities, covering a wide range of LD categories (including reading, math, and language disabilities). We have estimated 2.185 percent of these students to be dyslexic. Of the total 8.75 percent disabled being served (see Figure 1.2), the specific learning disabled comprise the largest category, followed by speech and language impairments (1.66%), mental retardation (.92%), severely emotionally disturbed (.72%), other health impairments (.44%), multiple disabilities (.19%), autism (.12%), hearing impairments, (.11%), orthopedic impairments (.11%), visual problems (.04%), developmental delays (.04%), traumatic brain injury (.02%), and deaf-blindness (< .001%).

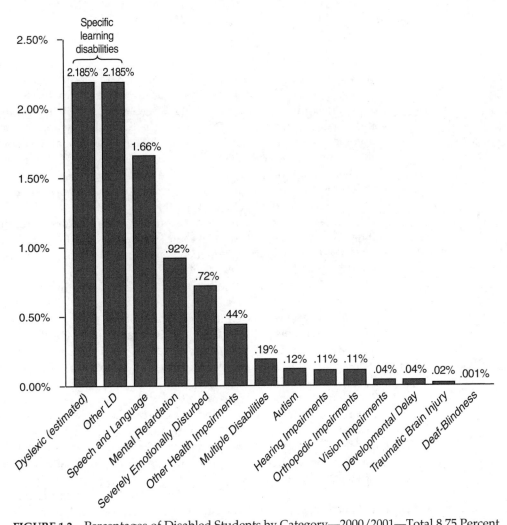

FIGURE 1.2 Percentages of Disabled Students by Category—2000/2001—Total 8.75 Percent of School-Age Population in the United States—Ages 6–21 (USDOE, 2002)

Your authors' definition of dyslexia is consistent with that of the *International Dyslexia Association* (IDA) (2003):

International Dyslexia Association (IDA) (2003) Definition:

Dyslexia is a specific learning disability that is neurological in origin. It is characterized by difficulties with accurate and/or fluent word recognition and by poor spelling and decoding abilities. These difficulties typically result from a deficit in the phonological component of language that is often unexpected in relation to other cognitive abilities and the provision of effective classroom instruction. Secondary consequences may include problems in reading comprehension and reduced reading experience that can impede growth of vocabulary and background knowledge. (Hennessy, 2003)

In 2000, the IDA published identifying characteristics that focus not just on the deficiencies in reading and other language forms but on observed strengths as well. IDA stated what dyslexia is not, as there are publications and programs that show a lack of understanding of what can be a debilitating learning problem if appropriate interventions are not in place.

*Identifying Characteristics of Dyslexia Incorporating
IDA (*) Criteria (2000, 2003):*

- Dyslexia is a strongly inherited trait. Muter (2003) has reviewed a body of research that shows estimated heritability is moderately high—0.4 to 0.7 with multiple genes implicated because reading is a complex process.
- Dyslexia is a learning disability characterized primarily by reading difficulties at the word level (specifically the phonology of language and fluency) that usually involves expressive and receptive language involvement. Concomitant and subtle comprehension difficulties may exist as well (*).
- Dyslexia is not the result of low intellectual ability. Intelligence is not a factor (*).
- Problems often emerge in spelling, writing, speaking, or listening (*).
- Dyslexia is not a disease; therefore, it has no cure (*).
- Individuals with dyslexia learn differently (*) or require differentiated or more intense instruction to best meet their learning needs.
- An unexpected gap exists between learning aptitude or intelligence and achievement in school (*).
- The problem is not behavioral, psychological, motivational, or psychosocial (*).
- It is not a problem of "seeing backward" (*) but may involve the visual system (see section on visual system implication, pp. 10–11).
- Many individuals with dyslexia are gifted and creative and have talents in areas such as art, athletics, architecture, drama, electronics, engineering, graphics, mechanics, music, or creative writing with strengths seen in visual, spatial, and motor integration (*).
- The language processing difficulties of individuals with dyslexia (*) (primary presenting problem = acquiring reading proficiency commensurate with age and developmental level) distinguish them as a group.
- The individual with dyslexia then experiences difficulties translating language to thought (as in reading and listening) and thought to language (as in writing or speaking) (*).
- Individuals with dyslexia can and do learn how to read and write proficiently with adequate support systems, but remnants of the language problems will be seen in adulthood (e.g., slower reading rates, the need to use a word processor with spell/grammar checks, and so on).
- Successful individuals with dyslexia have developed *resilient personalities* with the ability to quickly bounce back or recover from stressors, frustrations, and failures due to a personal resolve to persevere in spite of academic/social obstacles.
- Dyslexia results from differences probably in the structure and function (*) of the brain (see pp. 8–10). To best understand the neurological implications of dyslexia, one first has to picture or understand reading at the cortical level of involvement.

Summary of Important IDEA and NCLB Information Impacting Individuals with Dyslexia.   Beginning in 1994, Congress began to focus on addressing the important practice of including students with disabilities within regular classroom programs. Ensuring that all children with disabilities have available to them a free appropriate public education that emphasizes special education and related services designed to meet their unique needs and prepare them for further education, employment, and independent living under The Individuals with Disabilities Education Act (IDEA) (USDOE, 2003a), means access to the same high-quality literacy resources and instructional research-based practices as in "regular education."

IDEA may be cited as the *Improving Education Results for Children with Disabilities Act of 2003* (USDOE, 2003a) and legislates authorized formula grants to states, and discretionary grants to institutions of higher education and other nonprofit organizations to support research, demonstrations, technical assistance and dissemination, technology and personnel development, and parent training and information centers. These programs are structured to ensure that in addition to quality education programs, the rights of infants, toddlers, children, and youth with disabilities and their families are protected.

How school systems and other professionals diagnose or assess learning disabilities to include dyslexia will be significantly impacted in years to come with changes to Sections 614(b)(6) of this (IDEA) Individuals with Disabilities Education Act (20 U.S.C. 1400-1402):

> Sec. 614(b)(6)—Specific Learning Disabilities: In determining whether a child has a specific learning disability (SLD), the district "shall not be required to take into consideration whether the child has a severe discrepancy between achievement and intellectual ability . . ." In determining whether a child has an SLD, the district "may use a process which determines if a child responds to scientific, research-based intervention." (USDOE, 2003a)

Discrepancy Differences and Dyslexia

This 2003 IDEA language amendment to the definition of learning disabilities departs significantly from the common practice in the 1980s and early 1990s to look at the difference between IQ (intelligence quotients) scores and academic achievement to determine the presence of a learning disability (LD). IQ testing was considered a routine component to the psychological portion of a comprehensive LD assessment. States used prescribed discrepancy formulas to establish LD norms following the testing. Additionally, Verbal IQ and Performance IQ differences were further reviewed as significant differences between the two (especially when performance IQ was high) were considered LD indicators. Profile patterns for various IQ subtests (e.g., on the WISC-IIIR) emerged with different population subgroups such as AVID (see Spafford, 1989) with female dyslexics (low arithmetic, coding, information, and digit span subtests).

There has been growing criticism in the new millennium of the use of discrepancy differences between IQ and achievement as critical indicators for learning disabilities. Rourke (1998) and other researchers have suggested in more recent times that the use of IQ profile patterns is also of little diagnostic utility for children with learning disabilities, attributing prior research findings to inconsistencies in the use of LD terminology and study designs.

Juan E. Jiménez, Linda S. Siegel, and Mercedes Rodrigo López (2003) looked at the relationship between IQ and achievement in English-speaking Canadian and Spanish children and found differences in reading tasks as a function of Performance IQ in English but not in Spanish. These researchers point to the orthographies themselves as accounting for this finding. Spanish, with consistent orthographic features by nature, fosters the early use of phonological processing in early reading. English has a relatively inconsistent orthography where words are less reliably decoded with reference to phoneme–grapheme correspondences alone (see page 51). Therefore, the lack of reading experience has greater impact on an opaque orthography such as English where IQ performance has been previously found to significantly correlate with reading achievement for LD children. Jiménez and his colleagues cite additional research that shows low IQ scores do not necessarily equate to lower reading achievement, raising the question, Should IQ scores be used as predictors of reading achievement? Angiulli and Siegel (2003) recommend concentrating future research efforts on ascertaining *patterns of achievement scores* for LD children versus patterns of IQ scores. Future research will help to clarify this issue.

Student Outcomes and NCLB

The No Child Left Behind Act (NCLB) of 2001 was signed into law on January 8, 2002. NCLB takes IDEA one step further—student outcomes need to be structured so that students with disabilities are held to high academic expectations *and*, long-term, (1) the percentage of students with disabilities who drop out of school needs to be reduced from the current rate of about 30%, (2) the percentage of students with disabilities who graduate from high school with a diploma instead of a certificate of attendance needs to increase (currently around 56%), and (3) there needs to be increased availability of services and strategies for students with disabilities who graduate from high school to help keep them connected with postsecondary education. The National Council on Disability (NCD) (Frieden, 2004) holds critical the idea that students with disabilities need to be held to the highest expectations as the NCD review of the research shows improved outcomes when this happens.

The National Council on Disability (NCD) (Frieden, 2004) advises policymakers and practitioners alike to remain committed to closing the achievement gap between disabled students and their nondisabled peers. In addition to teaching high standards, the NCD says this can be accomplished by setting "higher" expectations, providing "more" instructional personalization, providing ongoing counseling and mentoring, nurturing and developing of self-advocacy, finding ways to "increase" parental involvement, and maintaining connections to the community with postsecondary learning options for high school graduates.

How do we put all of this together so that we best serve and meet the needs of students with dyslexia and other learning disabilities? According to the National Center on Educational Outcomes (2003), the focus should be on (1) establishing or making good use of established, research-driven *academic content standards* or the specific content students should learn; (2) *achievement standards* or levels of performance students should be expected to achieve; and (3) *assessments* or measurements of how well students achieve mastery of the standards (see Chapter 9). Students with dyslexia and other learning disabilities need to have access to and teaching related to the same academic standards as students without disabilities. The U.S. Department of Education (2003b) reports over 90 percent of the states complying with this policy, which is a departure from previous thinking in which students with disabilities were held to "different" and "not-as-rigorous" standards. Additionally, the present authors believe the level of engagement students will have in their academic studies needs to be continually considered requiring practitioners to have a large repertoire of strategies and instructional methods to keep the motivation for learning at the highest levels (Chapters 6 through 11).

Neurophysiological Evidence

Reading and the Brain

The processing of individual visual stimuli (i.e., the printed word) into more complex wholes seems to be carried out with different functions assumed by the left hemisphere and the right cerebral cortex. The left hemisphere integrates stimuli over time, as in language, deductive logic, and mathematical reasoning, whereas the right hemisphere deals with complex spatial gestalts (Grosser & Spafford, 2000). The primary means of communication is by neurons, the specialized cells for communicating messages in the brain. You may be astounded to learn that one given brain neuron (we have perhaps hundreds of billions of these) may communicate with thousands of others, creating infinite pathways for messages to follow.

During the 1990s, a technique called functional magnetic resonance imaging (fMRI) allowed researchers to discover which areas of the brain receive the most blood, revealing which areas are the most stimulated at the level of the neuron during particular tasks. During the reading process, researchers were able to establish three key activated areas on the left side of the brain (Shaywitz, 2003): (1) the left inferior frontal gyrus, (2) the left parieto-temporal lobe area, and (3) the left occipito-temporal lobe area.

As seen in Figure 1.3, the cerebral cortex (cortex = bark = protective covering) is convoluted and covers most of the brain or the uppermost part of the forebrain called the cerebrum. The cerebrum is divided into the left and right hemispheres. The cerebral cortex that covers each hemisphere is divided into four lobes: frontal, parietal, temporal, and occipital lobes. When reference is made to left and right hemispheric functioning, the left and right halves of the cerebrum are the areas of focus. The frontal lobe of the cerebral cortex is mainly responsible for higher level thought processes and motor control. The parietal lobe involves the perception of spatial relations and body sensations. The temporal lobe is primarily responsible for hearing or audition, and the occipital lobe is responsible for vision. Keep in mind that there is interactive involvement between the hemispheres and lobes for any perceived action/reflex or thought process, but there is definitely a major "division of labor."

Shaywitz's Work on Neurophysiological Causes of Dyslexia

The work of Shaywitz (2003) on the location of neurological breakdown for individuals who are dyslexic was summarized by Gorman (2003). According to Shaywitz (2003), the automatic detector in the left occipito-temporal area of the brain breaks down in children with dyslexia. A neurological anomaly prevents their brains from

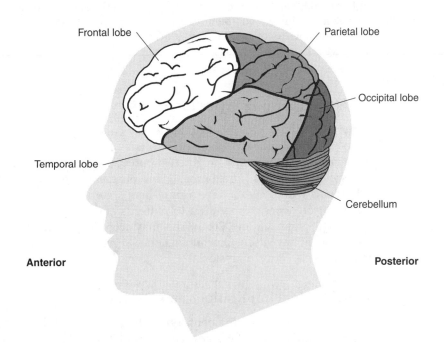

FIGURE 1.3   Four Lobes of the Cerebral Cortex

gaining automatic access to the word analyzer and phoneme producer areas of the brain. To compensate, dyslexics may rely more heavily on the phoneme producer area or by engaging in right hemispheric functions (e.g., processing visual cues from pictures). The following terminology provides clarification.

(1) Left inferior (= below or bottom end) frontal gyrus (gyrus = an outward convolution of brain tissue) = Phoneme Producer Area. This area of the brain is activated when an individual vocalizes words either silently or aloud. Phonemic analysis is initiated here (phonemes = smallest units of sounds that comprise words). "Kind," as an example, has four phonemes: /k/ /i/ /n/ /d/. For beginning readers, this section of the brain is particularly active.

(2) Left parieto-temporal area (= parietal-temporal lobe area) = Word Analyzer Area. More extensive word analysis is done here with words broken into phonemes and syllables and grapheme (smallest component of written language that can represent a phoneme)–phoneme (smallest units of sound) connections are made.

(3) Left occipito-temporal area (= occipital-temporal lobe area) = Automatic Detector Area. In this area of the brain, word recognition is automatized (fluency in word recognition is achieved). Proficient readers utilize this area extensively—automaticity occurs when word reading is fast and effortless.

Some major divisions of processing duties between hemispheres are summarized as follows:

Cognitive Processing by Hemisphere

Left Hemisphere: Responds to verbal feedback and instruction; relies on words and language for meaning; prefers a step-by-step (sequential) approach where details and facts build logically upon the other.

Right Hemisphere: Responds to visual, kinesthetic, and instruction involving demonstrations; relies on images and pictures for meaning; prefers a holistic overview and learning by exploration and discovery. (Freeley, 1987, p. 68)

Cognitive Learning Styles for Some Dyslexics

Many individuals with dyslexia have particular talents (e.g., art and design) in the visuospatial field that involve such traits as multidimensional thinking, originality, awareness of patterns, and heightened perception (Mortimore, 2003, pp. 88–89), right-hemispheric types of functioning. There is research to support the view that many individuals with dyslexia have a right-hemispheric processing style, preferring more holistic approaches, responding to patterns and images, and choosing synthesis to analysis (Morgan & Klein, 2003). This may account for some of the reasons why VAK-T approaches have been determined to be successful with some individuals with moderate to severe forms of dyslexia.

Visual System Implications and Dyslexia

Most of the research on the neurophysiological bases of dyslexia has focused on language-related areas of the brain. The present authors (Grosser, 2005; Grosser & Spafford, 1989, 1990, 1993a, b, 2000; Grosser, Spafford, Donatelle, Squillace, & Dana, 1995; Grosser & Trzeciak, 1981; Spafford & Grosser, 1991, 1995; Spafford, Grosser, Donatelle, Squillace, & Dana, 1995) along with many others (e.g., Geiger & Lettvin, 1987; Livingstone, 1993; Lovegrove, Martin, & Slaghuis, 1986; Ridder et al., 1997) describe disruptive neuroanatomical aberrations/behavioral manifestations in the visual nervous system. The visuospatial and visuomotor functions attributed to reading can be traced specifically to Brodmann area 8* and the premotor cortex (Brodmann area 6) in the frontal lobe of the brain (Cheng et al., 1995), substantiating the present authors' hypothesis that the left occipital-temporal lobe involvement described by Shaywitz (2003) could involve some neuronal dysfunctioning specific to visuospatial/visuomotor functions involving the occipital lobe along with the previously mentioned regions of the frontal, parietal, and temporal lobes.

Additional Visual System Considerations.   Specifically, research in the visual realm continues to substantiate the correlation between dyslexia and an impoverished if not absent magnocellular (transient) visual nervous system. The lower-level processing (e.g., decoding) of visual information has been referred to as "parvo" or "magno," for which several researchers have discussed two distinct visual processing systems, "the magnocellular or transient visual system" (responsible for detection of visual motion and of gross details) and the "parvocellular or sustained visual system" (responsible for the resolution of fine details as in a page of print and color vision). Decoding the printed page (fluently) is considered the most important lower-level processing requirement in the achievement of comprehension or deriving meaning from the printed page (Perfetti, 1985).

Currently, the present authors do not have a research-based hypothesis about how the low or absent transient system activity leads to disruption of processes required for proficient reading. While a good explanation is lacking, the fact (of a correlation) remains well established (see, e.g., Eden & Zeffiro, 1998; Talcott et al., 1998). The end result is that individuals with dyslexia may not be able to process incoming visual sensory information efficiently.

Summary

To summarize, for the individual with dyslexia, there are specific and significant difficulties with fluent reading and the phonological components of language—left-hemispheric types of functioning. Many prominent researchers have linked dyslexia to cortical anomalies and neurophysiological dysfunctioning particular to areas of the brain impacting language functioning (e.g., Duane, 1991; Galaburda, 1988, 1999; Geschwind, 1982; Geschwind & Levitsky, 1968; Hynd & Cohen, 1983; Hynd & Semrud-Clikeman, 1989; Livingstone & Hubel, 1988; Obrzut, 1989; Ojemann, 1991; Orton, 1928; Rourke, 1985). Recent functional MRI (fMRI) and other evidence provide insights into the neurological bases for these problems, pointing to visuospatial/visuomotor functions in the occipital lobe along with some regions of the frontal, parietal, and temporal lobes. Although it is acknowledged that the "core" of the reading problems shown by individuals with dyslexia involves the phonology of language and fluency, there are other concomitant and subtle comprehension difficulties as well. There could also be

---

*Note: Brodmann's area 8 is a part of the so-called "prefrontal area" (the "frontmost" part of the frontal lobe), while Brodmann area 6 (immediately posterior to area 8) comprises the premotor cortex. Both the prefrontal area and the premotor cortex belong to the frontal lobe. Just posterior to area 6 is the motor cortex, Brodmann area 4.

some neuronal dysfunctioning specific to visuospatial/visuomotor functions in the cerebral cortex for the dyslexic. What does all of this research bring us in terms of academic and social interventions?

No One Remedy or Cure for Dyslexia

Based on current research, there is no one program or remedy for optimizing the learning or school and life successes for individuals with dyslexia, but there are many current best methods/practices/strategies and research-based programs that have shown documented successes. The fact that there is a consensus in the field indicating that most individuals with dyslexia display a phonologic deficit (Bradley & Bryant, 1983; Schulte-Korne et al., 1998; Stanovich et al., 1997) with a concomitant lack of fluency (Johns & Berglund, 2002a; LaBerge & Samuels, 1974; Samuels, 2003) would indicate that academic programming needs to include intensive support in these areas. Chapters 6 and 8 discuss this in more depth with other important reading program components. Chapter 4 delves into developing resiliency in individuals with dyslexia with Chapters 6 through 11 focused on literacy support. Chapter 5 discusses some controversial theories, keeping in mind that some may work because of the **Hawthorne Effect**. In any case, efforts need to be placed on literacy supports/interventions because the primary presenting problem for the dyslexic is the lack of reading proficiency commensurate with age/grade/development expectations.

After presenting an overview of the nature and causes of dyslexia as well as some correlating symptoms and strengths, it is important now to mention and dispel some of the common myths about this most prevalent learning disability.

Dyslexia Myths

There are a number of "controversial" treatments or interventions (some mentioned in Chapter 5) that have little supporting empirical or research bases but are validated by a number of myths in the field. Frequently, teachers and parents are looking for a "cure" or intervention program that will help alleviate the academic and/or social difficulties experienced by the dyslexic. When valuable instructional time in school and at home is lost to ineffective interventions or treatments, dyslexics fall further and further behind their peers in literacy development. Some of the more common myths are described in Table 1.1.

One persistent, prevalent myth is that dyslexics "mirror write." Many emerging writers (K–1) will mirror write or make reversals. This is common for very young or emerging writers. In grade K, as an example, Selena and Natashe "mirror wrote." Now in grade 2, both students are considered "above average" readers and writers according to grade two literacy benchmarks.

TABLE 1.1 Dyslexia Myths

Myth	Fact
Dyslexia is a disease.	Dyslexia is a life-long learning problem or disability (not a disease) that causes the individual to learn differently. Although dyslexics have difficulties in the language area, talents and abilities can emerge in other areas.
Dyslexics only have average to above average intelligence and no other debilitating conditions.	IQ is not a factor. Sometimes dyslexics have other disabilities such as ADHD (25% of the time), physical disabilities, etc.
Most dyslexics are males.	Current research is inconclusive: Some research shows that dyslexia occurs in almost equal numbers in males and females with females frequently underdiagnosed; other research shows dyslexia rates significantly higher in boys.
Dyslexics "mirror write."	Dyslexics don't "mirror write" with any greater frequency than nondisabled peers.
Dyslexics "reverse letters all the time."	Dyslexics don't "reverse letters" with any greater frequency than nondisabled peers.
Dyslexics are always born with their language/reading difficulties.	Dyslexia can either be acquired at birth or acquired through various environmental conditions after birth such as in the case of disease or brain injury caused by an accident.
Gifted individuals are not dyslexic.	Contrary to this belief, many highly intelligent and talented individuals are dyslexic.
Dyslexics are "too clumsy" to do well in sports.	Dyslexics can play sports and many go on to play competitive/pro sports.
Dyslexics don't have many friends.	Dyslexics can have many friends.
Dyslexics don't do well in college.	Dyslexics can and do perform well in college but many times require academic support services; many colleges have learning disabilities programs.
Dyslexics never learn how to read or write.	Dyslexics can and do learn how to read, spell, and write effectively. However, reading rates tend to be slower than nondisabled peers and compensating strategies such as spell checkers and poor speller's dictionaries may need to be used as adults.
Dyslexia can be cured.	Dyslexia is a life-long condition that can be significantly improved with appropriate support services and use of compensating strategies; there is no "cure" for dyslexia.

Source: Koenig and Spafford (2001).

Dyslexia Subtypes

Remediating dyslexia can involve "fine-tuning" the match between assessment and treatment based on the type of dyslexia observed (Lyon, 1985, 1988). There is currently a lack of consensus in the field regarding a unitary subtype scheme with classification systems specifying one to several dyslexia types.

The present authors (Grosser & Spafford, 2000) have proposed three basic subtypes of dyslexia similar to those presented by Boder (1970, 1973) and Manzo and Manzo (1993). The identification of Grosser and Spafford's (a) *visual dysphonetic type* (individuals display a poor or unsatisfactory understanding of phoneme-grapheme correspondences and poor phonological awareness knowledge), (b) *dyseidetic type* (individuals show poor or unsatisfactory ability to recognize sight words with some intact phonological processing abilities), and (c) *dysphonetic-dyseidetic type* (exhibit poor or unsatisfactory phonological processing/sight word knowledge), is based on specific word recognition deficits observed for each type. In determining dyslexia subtypes, the nature of word recognition deficits needs to be considered.

The Nature of Word Recognition Deficits Determines Three Subtypes

(1) Does the primary problem appear to be phonetic? (i.e., Grosser & Spafford's *visual-dysphonetic* type)

Yes,   if   a) auditory analysis ability is impaired (i.e., segmenting and blending aurally presented words)

  and b) nonwords or pseudowords cannot be decoded phonetically

  and c) spelling errors have no relation to phonics principles

  and d) irregularly spelled words do not provide additional problems ·

  and e) comprehension is impaired

(2) (i.e., Grosser & Spafford's *dyseidetic* type)

No,   if   a) auditory analysis ability is adequate (i.e., can segment and blend aurally presented words)

  and b) nonwords or pseudowords can be decoded phonetically

  and c) spelling errors do have a relation to phonics principles

  and d) irregularly spelled words are misspelled due to the misapplication of phonic principles

  and e) reading accuracy is improved when large-type font is used

(3) If patterns in both (1) and (2) appear to be equally present, with a concomitant comprehension (severe) deficit, this type of dyslexia is referred to as a *combined* or *dysphonetic-dyseidetic* type.

Source: Grosser & Spafford (2000).

Dysphonetic Dyslexia

The most prevalent type of dyslexia is the visual-dysphonetic or dysphonetic type. Grosser and Spafford (1998) and Spafford et al. (1995) have found that individuals who demonstrated a dysphonetic type of dyslexia showed poorer contrast sensitivity—the ability to detect sine-wave gratings of both high (thick black and white lines) and low (thin black and white lines) spatial frequencies on a wall chart when either clear or colored lenses were used. Carroll, Mullaney, and Eustace (1994) explain related findings by proposing that the visual deficit observed in some individuals with dyslexia begins "... at the retinal rod photoreceptor level, involves the magnocellular pathway, and extends to the visual cortex" (p. 140).

Grosser and Spafford's research suggests that visual screening with gratings charts might at some future point in time (with substantial, validating research) be useful in a comprehensive diagnostic assessment, although some research (e.g., Demb et al., 1998) proposes that motion discrimination tasks might be more sensitive psychophysical predictors of dyslexia than contrast sensitivity tasks. Grosser and Spafford's gratings findings were similar to those of Lovegrove, Martin, and Slaghuis (1986). The gratings results may be a result of deficits in dyslexics in the visual "magno" pathway, whereas the "parvo" visual system appears to be intact (Raymond & Sorensen, 1998). However, Ridder et al. (1997) and others infer that the apparent magnocellular deficiency affects only some individuals with dyslexia, the dysphonetic dyslexics.

Subtyping Instructional Implications

The ability to differentiate subtypes of dyslexia such as the types mentioned in the box on page 14 assists practitioners in more closely refining interventions, as seen in Table 1.2. More research is needed to (1) build a consensus as to definitive subtypes and (2) identify screening procedures that will assist in differentially diagnosing dyslexia subtypes.

TABLE 1.2   Grosser and Spafford's Dyslexia Subtyping Instructional Implications

---

The recommendations below are made assuming program efforts are inclusive, except in the case of students with moderate to severe disabilities who may require some 1:1 and small group instruction outside of the regular classroom setting; curriculum content requirements/school standards should be the same—only curriculum adaptations/additional support are required. Some schools specialize in working with students who have moderate to severe dyslexia but maintain state and district curriculum standards as well. The five essential teaching of reading elements cited in the research and in the National Reading Panel Report (2000) need to be addressed for all subtypes within a balanced and comprehensive reading–writing program (Chapter 11): (1) phonemic awareness (Chapters 6 and 9), (2) phonics (Chapters 6 and 7), (3) fluency (Chapter 8), (4) vocabulary development (Chapter 6), and (5) text comprehension/strategic reading (Chapter 7).

(1) If Visual-**Dysphonetic Type**,
- training in speedier processing of consonants may be required
- explicit phonetics instruction is needed (e.g., direct teaching of sound separations, phonemic matching, finding sound/word differences, etc.)
- incorporating direct teaching of vocabulary in lessons: analogize to known words and use sentence context (Ehri, 1991)
- using multisensory instruction such as in the Orton-Gillingham and Slingerland programs, especially programs that use both visual and auditory modalities (i.e., paired oral reading)
- writing process programs with access to word processors/spell checks/poor spellers' dictionaries (peer/teacher editing)
- explicit spelling instruction with a strong phonetic base

(2) If the **Dyseidetic Type**
- training in coordinating all of the senses is in order so that in the recognition of letters, phonological processing can be as fast as lexical processing
- using multisensory instruction such as in the Orton-Gillingham and Slingerland programs (work on phonemic segmentation, sound blending, and so on)
- writing process programs with access to word processors/spell checks/poor spellers' dictionaries (peer/teacher editing)
- explicit spelling instruction with a focus on irregular English spellings; incorporate phonics instruction
- use of larger-type fonts to provide more success in reading

(3) If **Dysphonetic-Dyseidetic Type,**
- both sets of instructional programming discussed in (1) and (2)
- the student has a relatively severe disability and will require some 1:1 instruction and on a daily basis
- books on tape/access to tutors/individuals who can transcribe dictated materials
- access to tutors or individuals who can prepare/clarify/review/reinforce/extend content for both classroom assignments and tests/quizzes

---

Source: Grosser & Spafford (2000).

Because the visual-dysphonic or dysphonetic type of dyslexia is most prevalent and most learning disabilities screenings do not factor in subtypes, academic recommendations throughout the book will address the primary presenting problems for most individuals with dyslexia (dysphonetic dyslexia)—that is, specific difficulties with fluent reading and the phonological components of language (i.e., phonemic awareness). Individuals with dyseidetic dyslexia and the combined dysphonetic-dyseidetic type of dyslexia benefit from the same recommendations. In all instances, teachers or parents should see if reading accuracy is improved when large-type font is used especially at the beginning stages of reading instruction (important for the individual with dyseidetic dyslexia).

Other Types of Learning Disabilities

Memory Disorders

Memory disorders are characterized by the inability to recall what was experienced in terms of sensory stimulation (i.e., what is seen and what is heard). Memory dysfunctioning can interfere with language development, and individuals with dyslexia and other learning disabilities have been shown to display less efficient short-term and long-term memories and the ability to efficiently utilize memory strategies. Short-term memory (also called working memory) and long-term memory systems for tasks that require the processing of information appear to be clearly deficient in individuals with learning disabilities as compared to that of non-learning disabled peers (see Swanson, 1989; Swanson, Cochran, & Ewers, 1990). The relatively poor memory performances of individuals with learning disabilities have been attributed to a number of problems, including difficulties in phonological encoding of information (Torgesen, 1988), the use of rehearsal strategies and retrieval cues (Wong, 1980), and organizational and evaluative strategies (Palinscar & Brown, 1984; Pressley & Levin, 1987). Thus, there is the failure of the individual with dyslexia to reflectively monitor cognitive progress and growth as well as nondisabled readers do. Swanson (1988) believes that there are particular memory subtypes that can characterize the learning-disabled population. Swanson's theoretical premise is that particular subtypes of children with learning disabilities will consistently evidence poor performance on verbal and nonverbal memory tasks and on material that requires the encoding of information for short-term memory recall.

Mathematics Disabilities

Definition of Terms.   It would appear that there are individuals with **mathematics disabilities** alone (without reading/language disabilities and involving some type of right hemispheric dysfunctioning) (Geary, 1993) and other individuals with reading and language disabilities who have math disabilities as well (with left hemispheric dysfunctioning) (Ozols & Rourke, 1988; Rourke & Strang, 1983). The entire study of math disabilities and math problems has been an area of sparse research study for years. Spafford (1995) reported that 61 percent of an eighth-grade population studied (N = 210) displayed math performance below the 45th percentile on the Wide Range Achievement Test-Revised. Certainly the math problems of our youth are a cause for intense and continued study.

Math disabilities are developmental or acquired problems in one or more of the general areas of number sense or numeration, computational ability, problem solving, symbol interpretation, algorithm application, and visual-motoric-task completion (i.e., alignment problems). Math disabilities can occur alone or concurrently with other reading/language disabilities and are presumed to be due to central nervous system dysfunctioning in either/or both the visual and verbal realms. Math disabilities occur on a continuum with severity ranging from mild to severe.

Major Categories. There have been inconsistencies in the terminology used when defining various types of math disabilities (Sharma, 1986). However, there appear to be two major types of math disabilities supported by the neurophysiological school of thought—**acalculia** and **dyscalculia** (Keller & Sutton, 1991).

Acalculia. Acalculia is an acquired math disorder resulting from brain trauma or injury after birth. It involves a failure in math ability in many areas (Kosc, 1974). Specific subtypes of acalculia have been described in the literature. The first of these is **primary acalculia,** also called **anarithmetia** and/or **true acalculia** (Benton, 1987; Gaddes, 1985; Speirs, 1987). This math disability involves difficulties in applying algorithms to basic math operations, although memory and language skills appear relatively intact. In other words, calculating abilities are impaired across the board. A second form of acalculia is also called **aphasic acalculia.** The third variety is **acalculia with alexia,** visual-spatial acalculia. This disorder involves problems related to the visual placement and alignment of numbers resulting in math errors. A fourth type is Gerstmann's acalculia. This is a mathematics disability that has been frequently described in the literature since 1940. Individuals with **Gerstmann's syndrome** have been described as disabled in mathematics calculations, lacking in the ability to identify which finger was stimulated (finger **agnosia**), lacking in the ability to distinguish between left and right, and having **dysgraphia.** Some authorities insist that one type of Gerstmann's system can be an innate, developmental condition. Kinsbourne and Warrington (1963) have found that these individuals evidence higher incidences of left-handedness, with Verbal IQs higher than Performance IQs, and with females outnumbering males.

Dyscalculia. Kosc (1974), Novick and Arnold (1988) and others discuss developmental math disabilities they designate as *dyscalculia* whereby the individual lacks math proficiency in one or several areas. Specific types of dyscalculia have been identified in the literature:

1. **verbal dyscalculia** (oral language)—a math disorder in retrieving mathematics labels, terms, and symbols
2. **practognostic dyscalculia**—(*practo* = doing; *gnostic* = knowing; i.e., knowing by doing) a math disorder in applying math concepts when using manipulative objects in the environment (either visual or three-dimensional)
3. **lexical dyscalculia** (reading)—a math disorder that involves impaired reading of math vocabulary and symbols.
4. **graphical dyscalculia** (writing)—a math disorder that is an impairment in the writing of mathematics symbols, equations, and other relevant language terms
5. **ideognostical dyscalculia** (ideas)—a math disorder that centers on impaired mathematical thinking or impaired conceptualizations (the ideas) in mathematics
6. **operational dyscalculia** (operations)—a math disorder focusing on impaired applications of algorithms to the four basic math operations (e.g., addition) (Major source: Kosc, 1974).

Mathematics Learning Disability (MLD) Prevalence.   Globally, it is estimated that between 5 and 10 percent of school-age children evidence some mathematics disability (see Table 1.3). Yet, between the years 1974 and 1997, only 28 articles on math disabilities were cited in Psyc-Info, compared to 747 articles on reading disabilities or dyslexia (Desoete, Roeyers, & De Clercq, 2004).

Shalev et al. (2001) studied familial patterns of mathematics learning disabilities in Israel and found that family members (e.g., parents and siblings) of children who had been diagnosed as MLD (mathematics learning disabled) were ten times more likely to also be MLD than members of the general population.

During the 1990s, research involving the Third International Mathematics and Science Study (TIMSS) has shown a globalized approach to the teaching of mathematics—teachers review material from prior lessons and homework, plan direct instruction for new concepts, provide students with practice examples, and assign homework with time allocated to start homework assignments (Schmidt et al., 1999). There are many commonalities through the world in regard to mathematics approaches and how to teach students with mathematics learning disabilities. Montague, Woodward, and Bryant (2004) requested that noted researchers in six TIMSS countries describe how their educational systems evaluate and accommodate students with mathematics disabilities. As seen in Table 1.3, Australia, Belgium, Italy, Japan, Spain, and the United States all incorporate cognitive/metacognitive strategy training within mathematics programs and identify specific characteristics for students with math difficulties or disabilities.

Math Subtyping Based on Limited Study.   "We believe a stronger case is made for the heterogeneous presence of math-disability subtypes than against them" (Keller & Sutton, 1991, p. 561). However, the little available research in this area has many methodological weaknesses, ". . . [and math measures are used which] are often of unknown quality psychometrically" (Keller & Sutton, 1991, p. 561).

Geary (1993) proposes (1) visuospatial, (2) semantic memory, and (3) procedural mathematics subtypes. There are other subtype structures found in the literature and within the MLD international perspectives literature cited. Previously, the present authors (Spafford & Grosser, 1995) proposed (1) visual, (2) verbal, and (3) combined visual-verbal mathematics subtypes. Based on current trends in data analysis, the present authors offer the following subtypes.

Five-Typology Mathematics Disability Framework

(1) Dysnumeria
  - impairment in applying numerical knowledge such as math symbols, equations, relevant language
(2) Visuospatial
  - impairment in spatially representing math information and relationships on paper or misinterpreting math representations
(3) Operational Dyscalculia
  - impaired applications of four basic operations
(4) Procedural Dyscalculia
  - impaired applications of math strategies or procedures
(5) Acalculia
  - many impaired areas in mathematics

Source: Spafford & Grosser (2005).

TABLE 1.3   Mathematics Learning Disabilities (MLD): International Perspectives

Country	Prevalence	Types	Identifying Characteristics	Examples of Approaches, Interventions, Strategies	Researchers
Australia	10% to 30% of students had difficulty in mathematics.	In schools: The term *learning difficulties* is used *vs. learning disabilities.* Some researchers reserve LD terminology for children with severe learning difficulties.	Teachers: Define as children who need extra assistance with schooling because they lack or fail to use knowledge and skills associated with numeracy. Researchers: Define as a small group of students with severe, pervasive, and long-term learning difficulties.	*Constructivist approaches* dominate—emphasis on developing concepts rather than procedures and a student's ability to construct meaning and solve problems. "Discovery Learning" (see United States block)	Munroe (1977) Milton (2000) Doig (2001) Elkins (2002) vanKraayenoord & Elkins (2004)
Belgium	2.27% to 7.70%	MLD defined by DSM-IV (APA, 1994)—three criteria →	DSM-IV (1994) 1. Discrepancy between math performance and IQ 2. Severity—math test two or more standard deviations below norm 3. Resistance—Difficulties persist with regular instruction	*Cognitive/metacognitive/task analytical therapy* based on learning algorithms and heuristics.	Hellinckx & Ghesquière (1999) Desoete (2001) Ruijssenaars (2001) Kroesbergen (2002) Desoete, Roeyers, & DeClercq (2004)
Italy	1.3% to 5.00%	1. Dysnumeria (difficulties with numerical knowledge). 2. Procedural subtype. 3. Dyscalculic subtype (difficulty with mental and automatized calculation).	Difficulty acquiring a specific ability as indicated by the specific subtypes (3) ←	*Cognitive/task analytical/strategy training* focused on flexible and varying strategy usage.	Castelnuovo (1965) Lucangeli & Passolunghi (1995) Arzarello (1996) Malara, Menghini, & Reggiani (1996) Cornoldi & Lucangeli (2004)

(continues)

TABLE 1.3 *(Continued)*

Country	Prevalence	Types	Identifying Characteristics	Examples of Approaches, Interventions, Strategies	Researchers
Japan	6%	General math disability in either calculations (dyscalculia) or numeration reasoning (dysnumeria).	Difficulty acquiring a specific ability, like calculating or reasoning, with no basic delay in general intellectual development.	Three areas of emphasis using constructivist approaches. 1. The relationship between cognitive and written calcuations. 2. Relations between numeration concepts and the basic operations of +, −, ×, ÷. 3. Guiding principles for calculations cognitive/metacognitive strategies.	Ginbayashi (1984) Sato (1993) Okano & Tsuchiya (1999) Tsuge (2001) Woodward & Ono (2004)
Spain	4% with no association to reading and writing problems; up to 12% with language difficulties	Dyscalculia with and without language difficulties.	Student has special educational needs because he/she cannot learn in the context of the classroom with peers using typical resources.	*Cognitive/metacognitive strategies* for generalizing and maintaining skills.	Miranda, Arlandis, & Soriano (1997) Jimenez & García (2002) Luque et al. (2002) Bermejo et al. (2002) Casas & Castellar (2004)
United States	5 to 8% of school-age children	Subtypes: Dysnumeria Visuospatial Operational dyscalculia Procedural dyscalculia Acalculia	DSM-IV 1994 criteria or a score lower than the 20th or 25th percentile on a math achievement test and low average to above IQ scores with typically a memory or cognitive deficit.	*Constructivism* *Discovery learning*—Children are led to discover fundamental mathematical relationships after analyzing situations for patterns and structure often using manipulatives. *Anchored instruction*—systematic skills practice by embedding facts, concepts, and procedures within authentic and socioculturally relevant problem-solving examples.	Kosc (1974) Ginsburg (1977) Baroody (1991) Goldman et al. (1997) Geary (2004) Spafford & Grosser (2005)

(Spafford & Grosser, 2005)

The five-typology MLD framework offered by the present authors incorporates the (1) *Dysnumeria Subtype* found by Woodward and Ono (2004) and others; (2) *Visuospatial Subtype* discussed by Geary (1993) and others; (3) *Operational Dyscalculia Subtype* (type) shown in the research of Kosc (1974), van Kraayenoord and Elkins (2004), Casas and Castellar (2004), and others; (4) *Procedural Dyscalculia Subtype* shown by Cornoldi and Lucangeli (2004) and others; and (5) *Acalculia Subtype*, characterized by overall and severe math difficulties, a type shown by Desoete, Roeyers, and DeClercq (2004) and others where students perform more than two standard deviations below the norm in mathematics on standardized tests.

Attention Deficit/Hyperactivity Disorder (ADHD)

Attention deficit disorders should not be confused with dyslexia. Many individuals with dyslexia *do not* have attention deficits. Approximately 3 to 5 percent of school-age children have ADD or ADHD (Morrison, 2000). Fowler (1992) estimates that 25 percent of children with learning disabilities have attention deficits. Further, Lerner, Lowenthal, and Lerner (1995) suggest that *most* children with learning disabilities who experience attention deficits *do not display hyperactivity* (the *H* in ADHD). Attention deficits can be correlating behaviors for a number of disorders including dyslexia. ADHD will be described as a separate syndrome with the primary presenting problems of attention deficits and hyperactivity. Individuals with dyslexia can have attention deficits; however, these deficits would be considered secondary manifestations of the primary problem, which is reading. Stanford and Hynd (1994) caution that children with learning disabilities have distinct symptomatologies from those children with ADHD.

Attention deficit/hyperactivity disorders generally follow three types according to the American Psychiatric Association's *Diagnostic and Statistical Manual* (*DSM-IV*, American Psychiatric Association, 1994): (1) attention deficit/hyperactivity (ADHD) inattention type, (2) attention-deficit/hyperactivity impulsive type, and (3) a mixed type containing symptoms noted in (1) and (2).

ADHD Inattention Type (ADHD-IA) (Formerly called Undifferentiated ADD and ADD without hyperactivity). The ADHD Inattention type involves at least six of the following symptoms, which have persisted for at least six months:

1. exhibits carelessness in schoolwork or other work activities
2. has difficulty in maintaining attention during play activities
3. often cannot listen to others for sustained periods of time
4. does not follow through with assigned tasks to include schoolwork (not due to oppositional behaviors)
5. experiences difficulty in organizing tasks and assignments
6. will avoid or strongly dislike tasks that require sustained attention (e.g., schoolwork, job requirements)
7. will lose necessary learning tools required for task completion (e.g., pens, books)
8. is easily distracted by environmental stimuli
9. forgets to complete expected tasks during daily routines both in and out of the school setting

ADHD Hyperactivity Impulsive Type. The *DSM-IV* (American Psychiatric Association, 1994) states that the ADHD Hyperactive Impulsive type must display at least four of the following symptoms over a period of six months:

1. fidgets with arms or legs or constantly moves in his/her seat
2. leaves the classroom or other situations unexpectedly

3. will run, jump, or climb in situations where such behavior is inappropriate and unwanted
4. has difficulty becoming involved in leisure activities
5. will blurt out answers in class to questions inappropriately
6. will often have difficulty waiting his/her turn or waiting in line

ADHD Mixed Type.   According to DSM-IV, a combined type of attention-deficit/hyperactivity disorder would involve symptoms from the first two types listed (i.e., inattentive and impulsive).

Ross (1976, p. 61) suggests that attention deficit disorders are "the result of delayed development in the capacity to employ and sustain selective attention." There are a substantial number of children who are diagnosed as ADHD with some estimates keying in on 5 percent of all elementary school-age children (Wolraich et al., 1990). It is important to stress that ADHD and academic learning disabilities are not synonymous. There are many learning disabled children who do not have attention deficits or hyperactive symptoms (Samuels & Miller, 1985). "Likewise, numerous children who display impulsivity, inattention, and/or hyperactivity do well in school" (Heward & Orlanski, 1992, p. 142).

Complete Evaluation for ADHD and ADD.   The following evaluation structure is commonly used by healthcare professionals in the evaluation process: (1) parent interview, (2) teacher interview, (3) classroom observations, (4) student interview, (5) behavior rating scales (completed by teacher and parents), (6) medical evaluation, and (7) testing (intelligence, achievement, and fine motor skills) (Morrison, 2000).

Interventions for Individuals with ADHD.   All ADHD types occur before the child is 7 years of age with behaviors noted previously occurring both in an out of the school situation. ADHD students do have impaired social, academic, and emotional functioning that might require medication and/or behavioral interventions. Generally, two types of interventions are used with individuals who experience ADD or ADHD: medical and educational. Medically speaking, medication is recommended only as a last resort and generally takes the form of psychostimulants or antidepressants, which are used less frequently (Reid, Maag, Vasa, & Wright, 1994). Educationally, teachers can work cooperatively with families and school counselors on attention focusing, developing learning strategies and organizational skills, and social skills acquisition. "Part of their school acculturation is [will be] to reduce impulsivity, avoiding classroom interruptions. They need to learn a variety of behaviors, ranging from staying in their seats to listening to others as they speak" (Waldron, 1996, p. 262). Side effects of all medications need to be monitored by teachers and the school nurse. These include but are not limited to sleepiness, irritability, hypersensitivity, and depression.

Language Learning Disabilities

The Education for All Handicapped Children Act specifies that written language disorders be considered as a type of learning disability. Alley and Deshler (1979) report that children with such problems also experience difficulties in speaking and listening. Language disabilities can be either in the written or oral realms.

Aphasia.   The term **aphasia** refers to a "breakdown in the ability to formulate, or to retrieve, and to decode the arbitrary symbols of language" (Holland & Reinmuth, 1982, p. 428). Aphasia can involve both expressive (verbal encoding) and receptive problems (auditory decoding). Kleffner (1964) described disorders in understanding receptive language or the understanding of verbal symbols (Spradlin, 1967) as **receptive aphasia.**

Problems in spoken language or expressing oneself in writing are called **expressive aphasia.** The reading act is different from these specific language components. As examples, "the reader can regulate his [her] speed, going slower or faster as his [her] purpose and the difficulty of the material dictate, while the listener's speed of listening [receptive language] is set by the speaker. The listener has additional clues of voice, gesture, and appearance, and emphasis of the speaker, while the reader cannot derive such supporting information fro the printed page . . . the term reading implies comprehension of the reading act" (Lerner, 1971, p. 161). Generally, individuals who are considered to be dyslexic do not have severe receptive and expressive language problems. The term **dyslexia** is reserved for those individuals who experience primary deficits in the reading area.

Expressive Aphasia.   Expressive aphasia is characterized by difficulties in using oral or written language. Agraphia is a type of expressive aphasia that involves an impaired ability to express language in writing; dysgraphia, a specific form of agraphia, involves underachievement in spelling ability. Dysgraphia many times occurs with the condition of dyslexia. This co-existing phenomenon appears to occur across language cultures (Duane, 1991).

Receptive Aphasia.   Receptive aphasia refers to an impaired ability to understand or receive the components of our written or spoken language. Two other types of general aphasia include agnosia, or the inability to understand or recognize certain sensory stimuli, and apraxia, the inability to execute learned motor movements not due to sensory or motor disturbances. Strokes frequently induce aphasia in adults, with children acquiring such a disorder after a head injury. Individuals with mild aphasia typically have word-finding difficulties with more severe instances characterized by communication and language dysfunctioning. Language disabilities range from the relatively minor language dysfunctioning of dysgraphia to severe language comprehension impairments as in the instance of autism.

Hyperlexia.   A very rare comprehension disability despite advanced word recognition (see Table 1.4, p. 25).

Autism.   A severe language disability as noted under the 1990 (P.L. 101-476) amendments to P.L. 94-142 is the condition of **autism.** Besides severe language problems, autistic individuals display abnormal behavior patterns. Autistic individuals lack the language comprehension and awareness necessary for successful adaptation to school, home, and the environment. Autistic children can learn to read words quite well but have been shown to lack appropriate comprehension skills for sufficient understanding of presented reading material. Individuals with dyslexia, when presented with the same material as individuals with autism, will exceed the comprehension performance of the individuals with autism even though the autistics' phonological decoding skills are intact (Frith & Snowling, 1983).

Nonverbal Learning Disabilities

Johnson and Myklebust (1967) were one of the first research teams to describe nonverbal types of learning disabilities. The term *nonverbal learning disabilities* implies intact language functioning. Nonverbal learning disabilities (NVLD) are also known as developmental right-hemisphere syndrome (DRHS) because right-hemispheric brain lesions are thought to precipitate this disorder. Gross-Tsur, Shalev, Manor, and Amir (1995) cite the core symptoms of "emotional difficulties and disturbances in interpersonal skills; poor visuospatial ability; academic failure, especially in arithmetic; and left-sided neurological findings" (p. 80). Social knowledge of conventional behavior, the language of gestures, and facial expressions are lacking in this population. This is a relatively infrequently cited syndrome with few diagnostic criteria available for differentially diagnosing this population. A majority of researchers would probably agree that nonverbal learning disabilities such as **social misperception** are concurrent symptoms to other types of problems or disabilities (Spafford & Grosser, 1993). Sometimes children who have physical impairments experience nonverbal learning disabilities.

Physical Impairments and Learning Disabilities

Morsink (1984) has noted that there are hundreds of conditions within the term *physical impairment*, and the more common physical impairments can be classified within an orthopedic category (.11% of the population). Cerebral palsy, scoliosis, spina bifida, spinal cord injuries, and muscular dystrophy are included, and these students experience skeletal or muscular or joint diseases that impede mobility, coordination, and posture and sometimes include communication difficulties and learning disabilities. Often, children born with spina bifida have learning disabilities (e.g., nonverbal learning disabilities—see Table 1.4).

Summary

Dyslexia (*dys* and *lexia* = *inability* to effectively read *words*) is the most prevalent specific learning disability (at least 50% of the LD population) with prevalence figures varying from 2.185 to 20 percent. Accounting for differences in prevalence is a complex issue because there is a lack of uniformity in definition and assessment. Some researchers estimate that only one-third of students with dyslexia are identified and receive services for their disability. Discussion in this chapter also focused on an overview of the identifying characteristics of dyslexia, causation, and some of the more common myths and misconceptions.

Other types of learning disabilities were summarized, including two relatively rare disabilities, hyperlexia and nonverbal learning disabilities. Although math learning disabilities may affect 5 to 10 percent of the population, there is a sparcity of research in this area as compared to dyslexia and reading disabilities. A review of six TIMSS countries' descriptions of how their educational systems evaluate and accommodate students with mathematical disabilities showed many commonalities. Your present authors relied on this research and several other studies to determine a five-typology mathematics subtyping framework. The subtypes are listed as follows: (1) dysnumeria, (2) visuospatial, (3) operational dyscalculia, (4) procedural dyscalculia, and (5) acalculia.

Dyslexia is thought to have a neurological basis, and the disability is unexpected in relation to other cognitive abilities and access to effective classroom instruction. As discussed in this chapter, researchers (e.g., Shaywitz, 2003) have been able to show neuronal abnormalities in the brains of dyslexics with a new type of magnetic resonance imaging (fMRI) pinpointing three distinct areas of involvement: (1) the left inferior frontal gyrus (Phoneme Producer Area), (2) the left parieto-temporal lobe area (Word Analyzer Area), and (3) the left occipito-temporal lobe area (Automatic Detector Area). Brain studies (e.g., Muter, 2003) show that brain regions important in analyzing phonological information may not be defective but fail in some way to work in a coordinated way.

There are specific difficulties with fluent reading and the phonological components of language (i.e., phonemic awareness) for the dyslexic. Secondary issues may or may not include other academic problems (e.g., reading comprehension), difficulties in

TABLE 1.4 Rare Disabilities: <.01 of the Learning Disabled Population (Spafford & Grosser, 2005)

Disability	Defining Characteristics	Reading/Language Ability	Recommended Education/ Social Supports/Interventions	Resources
Hyperlexia—comprehension learning disability despite advanced word identification abilities	■ intelligent, often gifted ■ intense interest in learning * precocious word and phrase reading development; extensive sight word vocabulary * significant difficulty in understanding and using spoken language * social behavioral deficits (*Sources: Silberberg & Silberberg, 1967, 1971; Mehegan & Dreifus, 1972; Murdick, Gartin, & Rao, 2004*)	■ excellent visual approach to word analysis and word recognition abilities ■ spontaneously learns to read between the ages of 18 and 24 months of age ■ often learns to read before using spoken language ■ rote learners with comprehension difficulties (*Sources: Healy, 1982; Aram, 1997; Murdick, Gartin, & Rao, 2004*)	■ build on reading strengths and visual cues to develop child's language ■ model language usage especially how to ask questions and then how to appropriately respond ■ build on rote learning abilities with songs, memorization of poems, learning of play parts, and choral recitations ■ provide learning opportunities when the child can be paired with a language proficient peer—a strong role model (*Sources: Sparks, 1995; Aram, 1997*)	■ American Hyperlexia Association (AHA) (*AHA requires these three defining characteristics for identification of hyperlexia disorder)
Nonverbal Learning Disabilities (NLD)—social learning disability thought to originate from head injuries, radiation/brain treatments or brain trauma, treatment for hydrocephalus, or removal of brain tissue from the right hemisphere; often NLD are seen in children with spina bifida	* difficulty understanding or comprehending nonverbal communications such as body language and facial expressions; substantially impaired social judgment and interactions * lack of motor coordination for both fine and gross motor skills * slow in performing routine tasks ■ has difficulty with transitions or novel situations (*Sources: Myklebust, 1975; Little, 1993; Thompson, 1997* three identifying criteria for the disorder; *Russell, 2004*)	* difficulty with visual-spatial-organization and placing thoughts in writing ■ often precocious verbal expression and strengths in language development during preschool years ■ memory, sequencing, and organization problems in learning as curriculum becomes more challenging during the elementary school years (*Sources: Myklebust, 1975; Brumback, 1996; Thompson, 1997*)	■ build on early verbal language strengths to develop child's reading proficiency ■ teach and model problem solving skills across the curriculum ■ teach and model coping strategies ■ teach study skills and memory strategies ■ provide learning opportunities when the child can be paired with a socially "perceptive" and empathic peer—a strong role model (*Sources: Thompson, 1997; Russell, 2004*)	■ Specialists who work with children with social misperception difficulties; often children with learning disabilities experience the "social misperception syndrome" but to a lesser degree than children with nonverbal learning disabilities ■ SANDI Project (Spina Bifida Assessment of Neurobehavioral Development International: http://ped1.med .uth.tmc.edu/spinabifida); this is a collaborative medical and educational consortium

*American Hyperlexia Association criteria

25

socialization (e.g., more negative peer interactions), and co-existing disabilities or disorders (e.g., ADD or ADHD with 25% of those with dyslexia). These co-existing conditions were discussed in more detail in addition to other types of learning disabilities.

The present authors have proposed three basic subtypes of dyslexia similar to those presented by Boder (1973) and Manzo and Manzo (1993) with recommendations for teaching support based upon a current review of the literature (see Chapters 6 to 11). The identification of Grosser and Spafford's (2000) (a) *visual dysphonetic type* (individuals display a poor or unsatisfactory understanding of phoneme-grapheme correspondences and poor phonological awareness knowledge), (b) *dyseidetic type* (individuals show poor or unsatisfactory ability to recognize sight words with some intact phonological processing abilities), and (c) *dysphonetic-dyseidetic type* (exhibit poor or unsatisfactory phonological processing/sight word knowledge) is based on specific word recognition deficits observed for each type.

Although the language problems of dyslexics center on phonemic awareness and fluency, Carmelita Williams, international literacy specialist, cautions, "... phonemic awareness needs to be an active part of instructional programs for those who need it, but alone is not sufficient to foster reading proficiency" (Williams, 2000). Individuals with dyslexia will require intensive and comprehensive reading programs that balance all of the five essential teaching of reading elements cited in the research and in the *Reading First* legislation (Chapters 6 to 11): (1) phonemic awareness, (2) phonics (with systematic explicit instruction), (3) fluency, (4) vocabulary development, and (5) text comprehension/strategic reading.

To bring all students to high levels of proficiency, the National Center on Educational Outcomes (2003) recommends a focus on the 3 "As" when planning comprehensive and balanced reading programs:

(1) *Academic content standards* or the specific content students should learn.
(2) *Achievement standards* or levels of performance students should be expected to achieve.
(3) *Assessments* or measurements of how well students achieve mastery of the standards.

The present authors added:

(4) *Learning engagement and motivation* or How well are students engaged in the learning process and motivated to achieve?

Legislation such as the *Individuals with Disabilities Education Act* (IDEA) and the well-known No Child Left Behind Act (NCLB) include support grants to states and institutions of higher education and other nonprofit organizations for research, demonstrations, assistance, personnel development, and parent training to improve academic outcomes and close the achievement gap for various groups to include students with learning disabilities versus nondisabled individuals. These legislative mandates provide "... a solid foundation for major improvements in every public school in America. The enduring challenge is to do all we can in the years ahead to achieve its [the legislations] full potential for all children. ... (Our) nation, and our nation's children, deserve no less" (the Honorable Senator Edward Kennedy cited in Berg & McCarthy, 2002/2003).

We are brought full circle from the work of important dyslexia pioneers Anna Gillingham and Bessie Stillman, who in the 1930s challenged educators to identify and plan effective instructional programs for dyslexics, to a similar challenge from Senator Edward Kennedy—the challenge to realize the full learning potential of all children. Today we are looking primarily at the question, What can we do to make it better?

(Paratore, 2001) because there is an abundance of research to guide us with frameworks for comprehensive and balanced literacy programs. There is no one best way; rather, there is a multitude of successful, evidence-based methods, resources, and programs available to educators and practitioners who work with individuals who experience dyslexia and their families. Choice often depends on what works best according to district, state, and national standards and requirements, resources, developmental levels, and individual learning styles and needs.

Chapter 2 will present a historical timeline of dyslexia with an overview of how current conceptualizations of this disability are connected to the contributions of eminent pioneers. The reader will also experience through a first-person narrative some of the challenges of this sometimes debilitating learning disability creates for individuals and their families. Although we refine and further develop our approaches and methods, what it feels like to be dyslexic does not change. Please keep in mind that with intensive literacy support in reading and writing, a social-academic network of support, and the development of individual *resiliency*, individuals with dyslexia can lead very successful and fulfilling lives.

2

Historical Overview
Terminology, Legislation, Identification, and Treatment

Dyslexia pioneer and neurologist Samuel T. Orton recognized that reading problems of people with dyslexia could be traced to problems at the level of the word:

It is this process of synthesizing the word as a spoken unit from its component sounds that often makes more difficulty for the strephosymbolic [dyslexic] child than do the static reversals and letter confusions. (1937, p. 162)

Awareness of the neurological causal factors associated with dyslexia can be traced to the works of Dejerine (1892), Bastian (1898), and other researchers who linked neurological injury with reading disabilities, inferring that the corpus callosum and the visual cortex of the dominant hemisphere were implicated. Hinshelwood (1917) looked at genetic involvement with dyslexics and used the term *congenital dyslexia* to describe a familial component.

Samuel Orton, for whom the Orton Dyslexia Society was named (since renamed the International Dyslexia Association), studied individuals with reading disabilities for several decades and is best known for his classic "word-blindness" study (1925) and subsequently for initiating effecting teaching methods still in use today in cases of severe dyslexia, known as VAK-T approaches. Tables 2.1 and 2.2 summarize the work of Orton and his colleagues in developing VAK-T training methods with supporting research cited by the National Reading Panel Report (2000).

The word *dyslexia* derives from the Greek *dys* (inadequate or poor) and *lexis* (words or language). The term *dyslexia* has been known in many forms since the late 1800s . . . amnesia visualis, analfabetia partialis, congenital alexia, congenital word blindness or congenital symbolamblyopia, congenital typholexia, constitutional dyslexia, visual-spatial perceptual disorder, primary reading retardation, specific dyslexia, minimal neurological dysfunction dyslexia, specific reading disability, reading disorder, and strephosymbolia (Drew, 1956; Hynd & Cohen, 1983; Pirozzolo, 1979). Now, the term *dyslexia* is more commonly and interchangeably used with "reading disability," "learning disability," and "struggling reader." Prevalence is estimated to be in the range of 2.19 to 10 percent.

The Role of Genetics

Pennington et al. (1991) and others have found that dyslexia tends to run in families inferring a genetic link. Between 25 and 65 percent of children with a dyslexic parent become dyslexic themselves (Scarborough, 1990). Grigorenko et al. (1997) indicated that a gene for dyslexia may occur on chromosome 15 and another gene related to reading disability may be found on chromosome 6. The gene on chromosome 6 was related to two common symptoms of dyslexia, (a) a lack of phonological awareness and (b) poor

TABLE 2.1 Historical Timeline of Dyslexia Pioneers—VAK-T Multisensory Approaches: [V(Visual) A(Auditory) K(Kinesthetic) T(Tactile)] (Bases for Many Current Education/Literacy Interventions)

Dyslexia Pioneers	Area of Study	Reference	Contributions
Samuel T. Orton, neurologist, (1925) published "Word-blindness in school children." *Archives of Neurological Psychology.*	One of first scientific investigators of dyslexia. VAK-T Approach to teaching students with learning disabilities—worked with Anna Gillingham to refine teaching method which became known as the Orton-Gillingham Reading Method.	Orton S.T. (1937). *Reading, writing and speech problems in children.* New York: W.W. Norton.	Described and published defining characteristics of dyslexia: 1. Average or "normal" intelligence; 2. word reading and short-term memory difficulties; 3. phoneme confusions, substitutions, omissions, insertions; 4. letter and number reversals (b, d; 6 for 9); 5. spelling and writing deficits; 6. delayed language deficits; 7. directionality difficulties; 8. familial history; 9. higher prevalence with males.
Orton Dyslexia Society	Now the International Dyslexia Association (IDA)—Nonprofit organization committed to assist individuals with dyslexia, their families, and community support systems.	Orton, J.L. (1966). The Orton-Gillingham approach. In J. Money, (Ed.), *The disabled reader: Education of the dyslexic child* (pp. 119–145). Baltimore, MD: Johns Hopkins Press.	Two major teaching emphases proposed: 1. Multisensory Approach (VAK-T)—tactile and kinesthetic senses used simultaneously with visual and auditory modalities. 2. Teach reading with small units of language and build to larger more complex units. Orton and Gillingham's Reading Method = Teach letter and sound correspondences with VAK-T program 1. Trace letter and say its name and sound, 2. blend letters to form words and sentences, 3. read short stories with known words. Spelling reading words that are dictated is part of this method.
International Dyslexia Association (IDA)	Founded in 1949 in memory of Dr. Samuel T. Orton.		
Marian Monroe (1930s)	"Systematic Phonetic Approach"	Monroe, M. (1932). *Children who cannot read.* Chicago: University of Chicago Press.	Marian Monroe was one of Samuel T. Orton's research assistants who worked to develop his research ideas into teaching practice. Monroe created a synthetic phonetic approach with the following sequence of instruction: 1. picture presentations, 2. children identify consonants and then vowels with kinesthetic activities such as forming letters with arm movements, 3. children are taught to blend consonants after learning a few phonemes, 4. gradually students are introduced to full stories.

(continues)

TABLE 2.1 (Continued)

Dyslexia Pioneers	Area of Study	Reference	Contributions
Anna Gillingham & Bessie Stillman beginning in 1930s (1936 edition of book published by Hackett & Wilhelms, New York)	Remedial VAK training for children with reading disabilities based on Orton's methods. **Language Triangle** *Triangle diagram: **A**uditory, Visual, Kinesthetic Modalities, "All phonograms taught by VAK linkages"*	Gillingham, A., & Stillman, B. (1940, 1966). *Remedial training for children with specific disability in reading, spelling and penmanship.* Cambridge, MA: Educators Publishing Service.	1. Language triangle links V-A-K modalities, and phonograms are taught by these associations in a writing-to-read structure: Phonograms linked to **letters** and keywords and phonic associations → **writing** incorporates association procedures for letters → blending to make **words** after 10 letter names and sounds are known and can be written → sentence and **story reading** work with consonant blends, diagraphs, and dipthongs. 2. Phonetic associations = Building blocks to reading; Level I (V-A, A-K); visual symbols linked to letter names via repetition, overlearning, use of kinesthetic cueing (tracing); Level II (A-A); teacher makes letter sound—without visual cues, student names—basis for oral spelling; Level III (V-K, K-V); teacher modeling; students trace, copy, write letters from memory; A-K association basis for spelling.
Grace Fernald, beginning in 1940s	"VAK T Whole Word Method" for disabled readers with at least average intelligence who are also poor spellers.	Fernald, G. (1943, 1988). *Remedial techniques in basic school subjects.* New York: McGraw Hill (published again in 1988 by PRO-Ed, Austin, TX).	Students write words from their speaking vocabulary and compose stories using these words. Basal readers precede literature selection. **Stage 1.** Teacher scribes words in large cursive or manuscript writing; Student traces, pronounces syllable by syllable and then blends whole words. Student writes words from memory. Student reads words in a story, then files and reviews words periodically. **Stage 2.** No tracing. Student looks at word, says the word and then writes from memory. The word is repeated aloud. Then the words are filed and reviewed to mastery. **Stage 3.** Students work on three- and four-syllable words by studying them first and then writing from memory. Students read books and practice studying, writing, and filing new words. The teacher provides meanings for unfamiliar words. **Stage 4.** Fluency and comprehension are stressed. Students read and recognize words based on similarity to known words. New words are studied and written from memory and then are filed. Fluency is improved by repetition and use of tachistoscopes and metronomes.

Beth Slingerland 1950s +	VAK approach to use in speech, reading, writing spelling, concept building (literacy) to (a) reach grade level achievement in literacy, (b) automatically recall language information, and (c) guide to independence in literacy.	(1) Slingerland, B.H. (1962). *A public school system recognizes specific language disability.* Address given at the Orton Society Annual Meeting, New York. (2) Slingerland, B.H., & Alto, M. (1985). *Learning to use cursive handwriting.* Cambridge, MA: Educators Publishing.	Beth Slingerland incorporated the VAK-T teaching method of Samuel T. Orton and Anna Gillingham within Seattle classrooms, extending this approach beyond the clinic setting. Slingerland developed a direct phonics teaching method where students developed "thought patterns" to apply phonics in word recognition. Multisensory approach to teach manuscript or cursive handwriting (with letter forms and lined and patterned writing paper). Slingerland Institute for Literacy; Bellevue, Washington (www.slingerland.com)
Other VAK or VAK-T Approaches: 1960s to current	**Spalding Approach:** Spalding, R.B., & Spalding W.T. (1957, 1990). *The writing road to reading: A modern method of phonics for teaching children to read.* New York: William Morrow. (www.spalding.org)	**Recipe for Reading:** Traub, N., & Bloom, F. (1992). *Recipe for reading* (3rd ed.). Cambridge, MA: Educators Publishing.	**Alphabetic Phonics** Developed at the Scottish Rite Hospital in Dallas, Texas (www.sofdesign.com/dyslexia)

VAK or VAK-T Supporting Research: Linnea Ehri, Chair (2000), Alphabetics subsections of the **National Reading Panel Report: Teaching Children to Read** (An evidence-based assessment of the scientific research literature on reading and it implications for reading instruction: Report of the subgroups). Phonics instruction based on Orton-Gillingham VAK-T methods was significantly more effective than reading instruction without such instruction in several cited studies: For main effect sizes statistically greater than zero (showing significant impact for Orton-Gillingham phonics instruction), (d=0.63) for third-grade low achievers, (d=0.27) for grade 2 and 3 reading-disabled (children with average IQs but poor reading) and (d=0.61) for fourth- and (d=0.43) for fifth-grade proficient readers.

Sources: (1) Buchanan, M., Weller, C., & Buchanan, M. (1997). *Special education desk references.* San Diego, CA: Singular Publishing Group. (2) Spafford, C., Pesce, A. J. I., & Grosser, G. S. (1998). *The cyclopedia education dictionary.* New York: Delmar.

TABLE 2.2   Orton-Gillingham (VAK-T) Programs for Adults with Dyslexia

Sally Shaywitz (2003), *international researcher and dyslexia expert, documents that adults dyslexics need:*
(1) placement tests to determine reading levels as with younger readers, (2) assessments that pinpoint learning gaps,
(3) research-based, systematic, and small-group instruction, and (4) consistent literacy instruction—optimally at least
four times per week for 1½ to 2 hours per session or twice weekly for longer sessions (e.g., 3 hours).

Name of Program	Authors/Contact Information	Program Components
Language! A Literacy Intervention Curriculum	Sopris West, Longman, CO (2002) www.language-usa.net	■ students are given a "readability" code based on the Degrees of Reading Power (DRP) formula ■ a student's reading level is linked to a DRP score and number of recommended books (Language! program has access to 10,000+ books covering all genres)
Starting Over: A Combined Teaching Manual and Student Workbook for Reading, Writing, Spelling, Vocabulary, and Handwriting	J. Knight Educators Publishing Services, Cambridge, MA www.epsbooks.com	■ was created for adults attending basic adult education programs (1- to 3-year program) ■ phonological awareness training and letter-sound relationships are emphasized ■ instruction is provided in handwriting, crafting writing pieces, spelling, vocabulary, and comprehension ■ teachers make use of various text types including the newspaper
Wilson Reading System	Millbury, MA www.wilsonlanguage.com	■ manipulatives with letters and a finger-tapping procedure are used in the teaching of word analysis (i.e., phonics); many rules are taught ■ phonemic awareness, decoding, spelling and fluency are emphasized ■ priority is placed on using high-interest reading materials

reading of single words. The gene on chromosome 15 was related to symptom (b). DeFries, Alarcon, and Olson (1997) have shown heritability for both reading and spelling abilities with reading deficits emerging earlier on than spelling problems.

Gender Differences?

During the 1990s there was the widespread understanding that boys outnumber girls 3-, 4-, or 5-to-1 as having dyslexia. Lubs et al. (1991) found sex ratios to be equal within families of dyslexics and suggest that one factor in the overreferral or overdiagnosis of males in the classroom is the more overt behavior of male pupils. Shaywitz and other researchers reported a 1990 study (Shaywitz, Shaywitz, Fletcher, & Escobar, 1990) in which 445 Connecticut children were studied from kindergarten to third grade. The schools had identified the incidence of dyslexia in the ratio of 4:1 boys to girls for the second grade. However, these researchers independently tested the school population, and they found that equal numbers of boys and girls could be objectively classified as dyslexic.

DeFries, Olson, Pennington, and Smith (1991) have been connected with the Colorado Reading Project, which has been funded by the NICHD (National Institute of

Child Health and Human Development) continuously for several years. Their data show equal numbers of female and male dyslexics.

Current Research on Gender.   Some additional research on the gender issue was reported by Michael Rutter, Caspi Avshalom, David Gergusson, Robert Goodman, Barbara Maughan, Terrie Moffitt, Howard Meltzer, Julie Carroll, and John Horwood in the *Journal of the American Medical Association* (JAMA) on April 28, 2004. New evidence from four independent epidemiological studies points to reading disabilities being more frequent in boys than in girls, contrary to many of the studies published in the 1990s that showed statistically negligible gender differences. Rutter and his colleagues (2004) relied on the (1) Dunedin Multidisciplinary Health and Development Study of 989 individuals (52.1% male) as part of a cohort born between April 1972 and March 1973 in New Zealand and followed up from age 3; (2) the Christchurch Health and Development Study in New Zealand of 895 individuals (50% males) for a cohort studied in 1977; (3) the Office of National Statistics Study of a UK sample of 5,752 children (50.1% male) from 1999; and (4) the Environmental Risk Longitudinal Twin Study of 216 children from England and Wales (49.1% male) identified in 1994 and 1995. In all four studies, the reading disabilities rates were higher for boys than girls ranging from 21.6 percent in boys versus 7.9 percent in girls for the Dunedin study to 17.6 percent in boys and 13.0 percent in girls for the Office of National Statistics Study.

Conclusion on Gender Ratios and Dyslexia.   The research is unclear at this point in time on this issue. More clarifying research needs to be done.

Handedness: Inconclusive Findings

Another commonly held belief is that left-handedness is more frequently associated with reading difficulties (Benton & Pearl, 1978). As far back as 1925, Orton saw an elevated rate of left-handedness in dyslexics and their families. More recently, Geschwind and Behan (1982) linked left-handedness with developmental dyslexia and other disorders associated with certain immune-related disorders. However, there have been some challenges to this premise since the 1950s with Malmquist as early as 1958, Belmont and Birch in 1965, and Helveston, Billips, and Weber in 1970. These researchers concluded that non-right-handedness is *not* associated with reading problems to a significantly higher degree than it appears in the general population. The research is not conclusive on this issue as well.

Before further exploring current and prior conceptualizations of dyslexia and how these relate to ways in which this most prevalent learning disability has been identified and treated, the reader will "feel" what it is like to be dyslexic.

CASE STUDY

What It Feels Like to Be Dyslexic

Self-Realization of the Problem

Jill is a 45-year-old successful businesswoman who was a founding manager of a family business. Her expertise and business acumen have assisted her husband in increasing their small company's earnings forty-fold. As part of her responsibilities, Jill proofs many of the jobs in press. A few years ago, she had to approve the final copy of a booklet on dyslexia for a local college. In reading this booklet, Jill confirmed that she, too, was dyslexic. She describes experiencing "fear" and "excitement" as well as a "sense of relief" for she had in writing, "a description of me—that's the easiest way to put it."

Frequent Misinterpretations of Symptoms

Jill now could come to terms with her problem as she went through life unsure of why she encountered so many problems in learning how to read. She was frequently told as a child that she was "lazy," "stupid," "unmotivated," and that she "just didn't work hard enough."

Coping

Effects of Positive Reinforcement in Building Resiliency Jill vividly remembers being "super-good" in the classroom so that she could obtain an *A* in something—classroom behavior. She remembers little positive reinforcement and when praised "would hold on to the praise for dear life and not let go of it." Jill vividly recalls an incident in science class in the third grade that involved a teacher stating in front of the entire class, "Jill, you asked an excellent and intelligent question." Jill recalls that, "I was so thrilled to be called intelligent that I didn't shut up for the rest of the class—I remember that incident like it was yesterday."

The Heart of the Problem

According to Jill, reading problems were at the heart of her struggling school career.

> I always remember having trouble with reading. I would have difficulty sounding out words—I couldn't sound out words—the words never fit together right. If I heard the word said first, then I could learn the words. I did best in classes like science when the material was presented verbally. I had a hard time comprehending because I had a hard time sounding out words. I remember making reversals like "96" for "69" and "dod for bob." Spelling was my best subject if I could memorize the words just before the test. Afterwards I would forget the spellings and start all over again. For years, I spelled, "*those*" as "*thoughs*" and anything with a "*f*" sound incorrectly, like "*phone*" as "*fone*." I remember never learning how to spell "spaghetti." I would have to use a dictionary to assist me in spelling "spaghetti" even today. I don't write anything without a dictionary next to me.

Peer Relations: A Few Close Friends

Lack of Confidence When under pressure, my spelling and reading abilities get much worse. I remember becoming frustrated when discussing test scores with my peers all through my school years. This is because I remember working harder than the other kids. So I withdrew from people because I was ashamed—I would try to hide my test scores. However, I was never teased by kids and I always had a few close friends. In my family, some family members didn't think I was intellectual enough. It was never anything verbal, but it was in the way they related to me.

Lowered Self-Esteem I remember being made fun of in a cute way in school at times. For example, I had trouble with the words "subscription" and "prescription." I made the comment one time that I had to go to the pharmacy and have a "subscription filled." They told me that you get a subscription for a magazine and a prescription for medicine. Boy, that dredged up memories.

Depressed School Performance I can remember in high school I paid a lot of attention in class. As long as it was presented verbally and placed on the chalkboard, I could get Cs. When I had to read and study without that verbal help, I was lost. It just didn't make any sense to me. I think that's why I had so much trouble in math, chemistry, English, term papers, and just about everything else. But I loved French and had a tutor in French. I couldn't get any higher than a C because I had so much trouble conjugating verbs and things like that. I did best in class when the teachers talked a lot and put work on the board and summarized our books. I had a lot of trouble with classes when we had to do the readings all on our own. I would panic and freeze up. My biggest frustration came with my greatest love—my figure skating.

Dyslexia Affects All Facets of Life

Outside Interests Figure skating was my love. I spent four to five hours every day skating—before school, after school, weekends—you name it, I was skating. But figure skating was an overwhelming frustration. I mean being left-handed and having problems with directions did it. (An aside: My Dad was left-handed but he didn't have any learning problems. He went to an Ivy League college.) When you learn how to skate you learn to jump and spin in the same direction because you should be spinning in the same direction whether you are on the ground or in the air.

Orientation and Directional Problems I never learned how to spin and jump in the same direction, which is alien to the nature of figure skating. I learned how to jump in what was alien to me—in the wrong direction. Although I learned how to spin turning to the right, which was normal for me, I was taught jumping rotating to the left. This caused problems as the jumps got more difficult because the rotation became confusing to me—rotating in the direction that was confusing to me, I became disorientated when landing. It wasn't until I was older that I could understand why I never became a good jumper. Looking back on that, anything more than $1\frac{1}{2}$ rotations in the air I couldn't do.

Building Resiliency through Individual Protective Factors

Developing Reading Strategies Boosts Self-Confidence I always thought there was something wrong with me. I didn't realize until I was about 40 years old that there was nothing wrong with me. In fact, I'm glad to know that the more I try to read and understand, the better I get. When I read, if I have to comprehend, I make sure there is complete silence and that I'm not too tired. There can't be any confusing things going on in the room. Then I look at each word—word for word. I'm proud of that. I'm working hard to force myself to do things right in reading like reading from left to right.

Persistence I wish I knew at 8 years old what I know now. I'm extremely proud of what I have done on my own. I hope people who are dyslexic reading this and don't know it will learn about their problem before the age of 40 like me. I've not given up and have taken the attitude: I can do it! I got this attitude from my parents. They always told me I could do it. I hope this helps someone else to become more confident. That's the reason I'm dredging up so many painful memories.

Empathy I hope people can relate to what I'm saying because there are a lot of people out there like me and they don't have to reach the age of 40 before understanding that they aren't stupid. It might not just be them. It could be another family member. My brother has reading and spelling problems like me and it took him six years to go through a two-year college. He is extremely successful now. I give him encouragement when needed.

Building Resiliency with Environmental Supports

Support Systems Some family members have been extremely supportive and they encouraged me to improve my reading. This kind of support is critical in order to go on. From the standpoint of someone else reading this, the most paralyzing thing for a dyslexic is to be handed something to read and then try to make sense of that in front of other people. I have learned that if I take this material on my own and then read and reread it and then share it with someone, I can be successful. *Dyslexics need someone to lean on who understands them.* I've also learned to say, "I'll get back to you." For the dyslexic, there is a lot of panic when confronted with something to read and possibly not knowing what's there—the fear, the anger.

But now I also have to look to my future. I would love a tutor to help me to read better. Dyslexics need to seek that help and not be ashamed. Do you know a tutor that can help me? I guess I can say that I love to read now because I know that I'm not stupid and I'm a successful businesswoman. If I can manage twenty people and a small business, I can learn how to read better.

Summing It Up

To summarize in Jill's words the personal experiences of dyslexia, "... I was so thrilled to be called intelligent that I didn't shut up .... I would hold on to praise for dear life and not let go ... the most paralyzing thing for a dyslexic is to be handed something to read and then try to make sense of that in front of other people ... dyslexics need someone to lean on—someone who understands them ..." With a social-academic network of support, and the development of individual *resiliency*, individuals with dyslexia, as shown by Jill, can lead successful and fulfilling lives.

Resiliency and Dyslexia

In the case study mentioned, Jill's success as a businesswoman was due, in great part, to her resilient personality. The development of resiliency, or the ability to quickly bounce back or recover from stressors, frustrations, and failures due to a personal resolve to persevere in spite of academic/social obstacles, is impacted by individual protective factors, environmental factors, stressors, and coping styles. Every person is impacted differently by the individual or collective impact of these factors. Younger individuals with dyslexia (as seen in Figures 2.1 and 2.2) vary in the degree to which resiliency factors have been developed with self-esteem an issue and the need to learn to advocate for self and seek critical support systems as needed. The QUART (Qualitative Analysis of Resilient Traits) is a quick resiliency screening for all ages. Chapter 4 fully discusses the development of resiliency in relation to the aforementioned factors.

The discussion of the successes of resilient dyslexics in the popular press helps to diminish or dispel negative stereotypes or misconceptions about this sometimes debilitating learning disability.

Famous Resilient Individuals with Dyslexia

There is an ever-growing list of famous individuals who have been described as dyslexic and who have been extremely successful in the reading world. These include Cher, Whoopi Goldberg, Winston Churchill, Nelson Rockefeller, Neil Bush, Ennis Cosby, George Patton, Thomas Edison, Emile Zola, Hans Christian Andersen, Steven Spielberg, Avi, Patricia Polacco, Albert Einstein, Isaac Newton, Jackie Stewart, Jay Leno, Galileo, Leonardo da Vinci, Carl Jung, and Michelangelo. These individuals were considered gifted and also dyslexic. Certain identifying characteristics portray this population (see Table 2.3).

QUalitative Analysis of Resilient Traits (QUART)

General Instructions: Check the degree to which the student displays behaviors in the following areas. Space has been added for additional observations.

Name of Student ___R___ (severely dyslexic) _____ Date _Now in grade 4_

Evaluator _____ Grade _____ DOB _____

NOTE: Passed the Grade 3 MCAS (Massachusetts Comprehensive Assessment System) High Stakes Reading Test (top 50%)

Individual Protective Factors	Strong			Diminished or Not Evident	
• persistent (stick-to-it-ness)	5	④	3	2	1
• self-efficacy (beliefs about one's ability to plan and complete actions to reach a goal or desired level of performance)	5	④	3	2	1
• positive self-esteem (positive evaluation of oneself)	5	4	③	2	1
• optimistic (anticipates the best, hopeful)	5	④	3	2	1
• confident learner (self assured learner)	⑤	4	3	2	1
• overall positive temperament (characteristic "frame of mind" is positive)	5	④	3	2	1
• socially perceptive (accurate evaluates social situations and determines appropriate actions).	5	4	③	2	1
• good reasoning ability (able to make inferences, draw conclusions and problem solve)	5	4	③	2	1
• advocates for self (works in an informed manner to obtain better academic or social opportunities or services)	5	4	3	②	1
• arena of talent or performance valued by others _____	5	4	3	2	1
Coping Style (additional)					
• self-starter (takes the initiative when needed)	5	④	3	2	1
• internal locus of control (assumes responsibility for learning/achievement and attributes many successes to motivation, effort, resourcefulness)	5	4	③	2	1
• flexible (adaptable and accommodating when appropriate)	5	4	3	②	1
• self reflective (able to plan, self-monitor and evaluate one's own thinking, learning, comprehension, and social actions)	5	4	③	2	1
• seeks critical support systems (support from peers, teachers, family. and other community members)	5	4	3	②	1
• able to advocate for others (understands needs, feelings of peer group)	5	4	③	2	1

Major strengths _____

Major weaknesses _____

FIGURE 2.1   *QUalitative Analysis of Resilient Traits (QUART)*   (Spafford & Grosser, 2005)

QUalitative Analysis of Resilient Traits (QUART)

General Instructions: Check the degree to which the student displays behaviors in the following areas. Space has been added for additional observations.

Name of Student ____A____ (severely dyslexic)_____ Date __Now in grade 5_____

Evaluator _____ Grade _____ DOB _____

NOTE: Lowest Quartile standing on Grade 4 High Stakes Language Arts Test - Massachusetts Comprehensive Assessment
System (MCAS) - Warning Category

	Strong			Diminished or Not Evident	

Individual Protective Factors

• persistent (stick-to-it-ness)	5	4	3	②	1
• self-efficacy (beliefs about one's ability to plan and complete actions to reach a goal or desired level of performance)	5	4	③	2	1
• positive self-esteem (positive evaluation of oneself)	5	4	3	②	1
• optimistic (anticipates the best, hopeful)	5	4	3	②	1
• confident learner (self assured learner)	5	4	③	2	1
• overall positive temperament (characteristic "frame of mind" is positive)	5	4	③	2	1
• socially perceptive (accurate evaluates social situations and determines appropriate actions).	5	4	3	②	1
• good reasoning ability (able to make inferences, draw conclusions and problem solve)	5	4	③	2	1
• advocates for self (works in an informed manner to obtain better academic or social opportunities or services)	5	4	③	2	1
• arena of talent or performance valued by others _Persistency or "stick-to-it-ness"_	5	4	3	2	1

Coping Style (additional)

• self-starter (takes the initiative when needed)	5	4	③	2	1
• internal locus of control (assumes responsibility for learning/ achievement and attributes many successes to motivation, effort, resourcefulness)	5	4	③	2	1
• flexible (adaptable and accommodating when appropriate)	5	4	③	2	1
• self reflective (able to plan, self-monitor and evaluate one's own thinking, learning, comprehension, and social actions)	5	4	③	2	1
• seeks critical support systems (support from peers, teachers, family, and other community members)	5	4	3	②	1
• able to advocate for others (understands needs, feelings of peer group)	5	4	③	2	1

Major strengths _____

Major weaknesses _____

FIGURE 2.2   *QUalitative Analysis of Resilient Traits (QUART)*   (Spafford & Grosser, 2005)

TABLE 2.3   **Identifying Characteristics of Gifted Resilient Dyslexics**

I. Learning/Cognitive
1. Generally, Full Scale IQ = 110 or above
2. There are Performance–Verbal IQ discrepancies in some cases
3. Oral vocabulary advanced for age or grade level; reading average or below grade level
4. Quick thinkers; able to reason through a problem; analytical thinking excellent
5. Inquisitive and constantly questioning (can be misinterpreted as a challenge to the teacher)
6. Reading/writing/spelling skills are not commensurate with intellectual potential
7. Math skills frequently above average
8. Has a particular hobby (e.g., playing a musical instrument that she/he will thoroughly research)

II. Creativity
1. Creates novel or original solutions to problems
2. Risk taker—willingly enters into adventurous situations
3. Sensitive to others, the environment, and the fine arts
4. Understands subtle humor
5. Can be unconventional and/or nonconforming to standard expectations

III. Social
1. Tends to be independent with a small circle of friends; generally introverted, quiet, and shy
2. Is persistent and can be stubborn
3. Can irritate others by frequent questions
4. Self-critical and easily frustrated by unfinished and incorrect work
5. Can have low self-esteem, low self-concept but will persist and develop areas of giftedness
6. When placed in leadership positions, can excel with good problem-solving ability.

Determining the Presence of Dyslexia or Learning Disabilities

Definitional Legislation

There are a number of federal laws in the United States that have established frameworks for defining learning and other disabilities and related service delivery both in and out of the classroom. The most far-reaching legislation has been the Education of All Handicapped Children Act **P.L. 94-142** or Public Law 94-142 (1975, 1977). Determining the presence of learning disabilities in the United States requires adherence to the provisions initially stated in P.L. 94-142, since renamed IDEA or the Individuals with Disabilities Education Act.

Public Law 94-142 (USDOE, 2004).   Congress enacted the Education of All Handicapped Children Act (Public Law 94-142 or P.L. 94-142) in 1975 to support states and localities in protecting the rights of, meeting the individual needs of, and improving the education results for infants, toddlers, children, and youth with disabilities and their families. Public Law 94-142 was a response to Congressional concern for two groups of children: the more than 1 million children with disabilities who were excluded from the education system and children with disabilities who had limited access to the education system and were therefore not provided a "free and appropriate education." Public Law 94-142, once enacted, guaranteed a free, appropriate public education to each child with a disability in every state and locality across the country.

Four Purposes of P.L. 94-142 (USDOE, 1975) (renamed IDEA in 1990, Individuals with Disabilities Education Act, P.L. 101-476)

- "To assure that all children with disabilities have available to them . . . a free appropriate public education which emphasizes special education and related services designed to meet their unique needs."
- "To assure that the rights of children with disabilities and their parents . . . are protected."
- "To assist states and localities to provide for the education of all children with disabilities."
- "To assess and assure the effectiveness of efforts to educate all children with disabilities."

Individuals with Disabilities Education Act (IDEA) or P.L. 101-476.   P.L. 94-142, renamed, is currently known as the *Individuals with Disabilities Education Act* (IDEA), as amended in 1997 and 2003. With the reauthorization of IDEA in 2003, in determining whether a child has a specific learning disability (SLD), a district "may use a process which determines if a child responds to scientific, research-based intervention." This district shall not be required to take into consideration whether the child has a severe discrepancy between achievement and intellectual ability (USDOE, 2003). This is a significant departure from the decades-long requirement of showing discrepancies between achievement and ability. Your authors' current definition of dyslexia states that the disability is unexpected in relation to other cognitive abilities and access to effective classroom instruction. Although districts aren't required to show severe discrepancies between achievement and intellectual ability, it is expected that many districts will continue to use discrepancy differences in determining the presence of a learning disability.

Discrepancies between Achievement and Intellectual Ability

G. Emerson Dickman, Nancy L. Hennessy, Louisa Cook Moats, Karen J. Rooney, and Harley A. Tomey, III (IDA, 2002, pp. 3-4) concur that determining a discrepancy difference between achievement and intellectual ability is not useful information in a differential diagnosis model. According to Dickman et al. (IDA, 2002),

> The term *learning disability* refers to a class of specific disorders. They are due to cognitive deficits intrinsic to the individual and are often unexpected in relation to other cognitive abilities. Such disorders result in performance deficits in spite of quality instruction and predict anomalies in the development of adaptive functions having consequences across the life span . . . "*Unexpected*"—refers to "cognitive deficits" in the presence of "other cognitive abilities," all of which are *core* to the development of "*adaptive functions*" (behaviors) identified as having "*consequences across the life span.*" IQ, aptitude, or potential as compared to achievement is not a meaningful consideration and plays no role in the proposed definition. As an indication of failure, a discrepancy between aptitude and achievement provides only circumstantial and *ex post facto* evidence of a learning disability; it is not useful in identifying individuals with a learning disability. (pp. 3–4)

IDEA 2003 reauthorization (USDOE, 2003) specifics

IDEA Section 602 (2003). Definition
(3) CHILD WITH A DISABILITY—
   (A) IN GENERAL—The term 'child with a disability' means a child—
      (i) with mental retardation, hearing impairments (including deafness), speech or language impairments, visual impairments (including blindness), serious emotional disturbance (hereinafter referred to as 'emotional disturbance'), orthopedic impairments, autism, traumatic brain injury, other health impairments, or *specific learning disabilities*; and
      (ii) who, by reason thereof, needs special education and related services.
   (B) CHILD AGED 3 THROUGH 9—The term 'child with a disability' for a child aged 3 through 9 or any subset of that age range, including ages 3 through 5, may, at the discretion of the State and the local educational agency, include a child—
      (i) experiencing developmental delays, as defined by the State and as measured by appropriate diagnostic instruments and procedures, in one or more of the following areas: physical development, cognitive development, communication development, social or emotional development, or adaptive development; and
      (ii) who, by reason thereof, needs special education and related services.

Sec. 614(b)(6) — Specific Learning Disabilities:

> In determining whether a child has a specific learning disability (SLD), the district "shall not be required to take into consideration whether the child has a severe discrepancy between achievement and intellectual ability . . . ."

> In determining whether a child has an SLD, the district "may use a process which determines if a child responds to scientific, research-based intervention."

IDEA 2003 recommendations applicable to the teaching of individuals with dyslexia

SUBPART 3—SUPPORTS TO IMPROVE RESULTS FOR CHILDREN WITH DISABILITIES
(c) FINDINGS—Congress finds the following (partial sections):
   (4) Over 25 years of research and experience has demonstrated that the education of children with disabilities can be made more effective by—

(A) having high expectations for such children and ensuring their access to the general education curriculum in the regular classroom to the maximum extent possible in order . . .

(B) . . . ensuring that families of such children have meaningful opportunities to participate in the education of their children at school and at home;

(D) supporting high-quality, intensive professional development for personnel who work with children with disabilities;

(E) providing incentives for scientifically based reading programs and prereferral intervention services to reduce the need to label children as disabled in order to address their learning needs.

Summary of Relevant Legislation for Individuals with Learning and Other Disabilities to Include Dyslexia

There are three relevant U.S. laws that provide for the identification of learning and other disabilities and related services while also protecting adults and children alike from discrimination in school and in the workplace (1) **IDEA** or the *Individuals with Disabilities Education Act* (P.L. 101-476), (2) **Section 504** of the Rehabilitation Act (P.L. 93-112), and (3) **ADA** or the Americans with Disabilities Act (P.L. 101-336).

IDEA of 1990, formerly the well-known *Education of All Handicapped Children Act* of 1975, or P.L. 94-142, was discussed in detail with reference to criteria that should be used when differentially diagnosing students with learning disabilities—this includes reading disabilities or dyslexia. Before P.L. 94-142 was renamed IDEA in 1990, two crucial amendments, P.L. 98-199 in 1984 and in P.L. 99-457 in 1986, widened service delivery for children at risk for learning or other disabilities from birth through 5 years. IDEA was amended in 1997 (P.L. 105-17) and again in 2003. Your authors' definitions of dyslexia and learning disabilities are consistent with IDEA requirements. Additionally, Sec. 614(b)(6) of IDEA indicates that school districts "shall not be required to take into consideration whether the child has a severe discrepancy between achievement and intellectual ability" . . . but "may use a process which determines if a child responds to scientific, research-based intervention." In determining scientific-research-based interventions, both testing and the programs or teaching methods themselves need to be evidence-based. Chapter 9 provides in-depth guidelines for school administrators and teachers to use when considering evidence-based literacy programs, program components, or testing.

The due process provisions of IDEA permit families to be integrally involved in the provisions of educational services for their children with learning or other disabilities. Chapter 9 (pp. 262–265) brings teachers and families through the steps in developing IEPs. A checklist for the types of accommodations students can receive under all testing situations is available in both Spanish and English on page 254. This will assist families and advocates in preparing for important IEP meetings. The advocacy process is mentioned in Chapter 11 with information regarding how to be an effective advocate.

The Americans with Disabilities Act (ADA) of 1990 (P.L. 101-336) was created to protect both children and adults with disabilities from discrimination in employment, public, and private settings. There is the continued concern for the welfare and well-being of adults with dyslexia and other disabilities, and ADA helps in this regard. The National Council on Disability (NCD) (2004) cites disproportionately high dropout rates for students with learning disabilities (LD) with more LD students receiving certificates of attendance versus diplomas than nondisabled peers. These factors significantly impact life and employment outcomes for adults with disabilities. Chapter 11 (pp. 326–327) provides information on how adults with dyslexia can be supported in high school and beyond. Personal *resiliency* or the ability to quickly bounce back or recover from stressors, frustrations, and failures due to a personal resolve to persevere in spite of academic/social obstacles becomes even more critical for the adult with dyslexia. Chapter 9 outlines characteristics found in resilient adults with a case study of a severely dyslexic high school student providing insights for educators and families regarding how to support secondary-age students with disabilities (p. 258).

Dyslexia and Learning Disabilities: Origin of Word Terminology

The word *dyslexia* can be broken down into the letter-groups *dys* and *lexia,* or *distorted words* in reading and writing. The literature in the 1890s and early 1900s tended to focus on the terms **word blindness** or "alexia," which would indicate a total lack of reading and/or writing skills (Spache, 1976a, p. 179). Hinshelwood (1896) reported that Kussmaul in 1877 identified adults who had an acquired inability to read or word blindness and that a similar phenomenon was cited in Hinshelwood (1896). The term *dyslexia* was coined somewhere in the late 1800s.

Word Blindness: Focus on Word Recognition Problems (1896)

W.P. Morgan (1896) is many times credited with introducing the concept of word blindness and his description of a typical dyslexic helped to build the foundation for our current definition. In 1892, Dejerine published a case study of an individual who, after a stroke, developed an inability to read. Dejerine described this condition as alexia and, after the death of the patient, discovered a lesion in the left angular gyrus that might have caused the reading problem. Orton's 1925 critical paper entitled " 'Word-blindness' in School Children," brought this focus on neurological implications to the forefront and his report of the neurological correlates of childhood dyslexia remains "one of the best clinical descriptions of the disorder" (Shaywitz et al., 1991, p. 29).

Causation Linked to Cerebral Dysfunctioning (1802 to Present)

According to Wiederholt (1974), Franz Joseph Gall in 1802 and Bouillaud in 1825 attempted to link certain brain activities with specific loci in the brain, which led to the hypothesis by an ophthalmologist named Berlin that cerebral disease was the culprit for a group of patients who experienced great difficulties in the reading area. He, like many other medical practitioners, saw dyslexia as a type of aphasia. Today, causation is thought to be linked to some type of cerebral hemispheric dysfunction either in the language area, the vision area, or both.

Dyslexia-Aphasia Link (1874).   The term *aphasia* refers to a loss of speech/language functions that can usually be traced to cerebral disease or damage of some type. Wiig and Semel (1980) define the aphasic individual as one who has "an acquired language disorder caused by brain damage with complete or partial impairment of language comprehension, formulation and use" (p. 443). Historically, there have been two primary types of aphasia that have been studied for over a century: (1) Broca's (1865) aphasia implicates the posterior portion of the left frontal lobe, which is involved in speech production (the individual understands speech but is unable to reproduce accurately intended communications); there are articulation difficulties and a paucity of speech; and (2) Wernicke's (1874) aphasia is a type of receptive disorder characterized by faulty speech comprehension seen in the "nonsensical" speech uttered by the afflicted individual.

Speech Dysfunctioning in Aphasia (1874).   Jackson (1874) was one of the first to trace the hemispheric functioning of speech production and comprehension to specific hemispheres; he assigned speech production to the left hemisphere and speech comprehension to the right hemisphere. Certainly, the speech dysfunctioning of the aphasic individual would be expected to impact the reading process. However, there is no type of consensual agreement that dyslexia is a type of aphasia. The view that defects localized in specific brain regions such as Broca's and Wernicke's areas result specifically in motor or sensory language abnormalities, respectively, in turn causing dyslexia, is in itself open to debate. This localization position has been supplemented by a more comprehensive view of language.

For dyslexics, causation does not appear to be consistent with the apparent brain damage incurred by aphasic individuals and their subsequent speech production and comprehension problems. Although some dyslexics may exhibit aphasic symptoms, the primary presenting problem is a reading deficiency, not a speech and language disorder.

Kirk Introduces "LD" Terminology (1963)

Although dyslexia has been described in various forms since the late 1800s, it wasn't until the 1960s that this condition was called a learning disability. Mercer (1987) describes the frustration parents experienced during the 1950s and 1960s when some reading/language-disabled children weren't permitted to attend special education classes because they weren't blind, retarded, physically impaired, or named in some other special needs category. A 1963 national conference was held in order to address this problem. Samuel A. Kirk introduced the term *learning disability* at the conference as one that could be used as a special needs category for children who didn't acquire language/reading skills commensurate with their age and ability levels. According to Kirk and Kirk (1976), there are children "... who are not receptive to language but are not deaf, some are not able to perceive visually but are not blind, and some cannot learn by ordinary methods of instruction but are not mentally retarded ... [this group of children] come under the heading of 'specific learning disabilities' ..." (pp. 3–4).

World Federation of Neurology Definition (1970)

Critchley's Influence.   The Research Group on Developmental Dyslexia of the World Federation of Neurology provides a basic definition that is still embraced in most education circles today. "Dyslexia is a disorder manifested by difficulty in learning to read despite conventional instruction, adequate intelligence, and socio-cultural opportunity. It is dependent upon fundamental cognitive disabilities which are frequently of constitutional origin" (Critchley, 1970). The reader will have noticed that the hardest, basic aspects of this definition are the exclusionary ones; in other words, dyslexia is being defined on the basis that it is not a matter of poor instruction, low intelligence, or sociocultural deprivation. In addition to not being linked to IQ, dyslexia is not the result of lack of a print-rich environment outside the schools setting. This definition does not venture into subtypes nor does it point to a definitive cause. Critchley (1981) refocused this definition in the 1980s to what he termed **developmental dyslexia,** which he defined as follows:

> Developmental dyslexia; a learning disability which initially shows itself by difficulty in learning to read, and later by erratic spelling and by lack of facility in manipulating written as opposed to spoken words. The condition is cognitive in essence, and usually genetically determined. It is not due to intellectual inadequacy or to lack of socio-

cultural opportunity, or to faults in the technique of teaching, or to any known structural brain defect. It probably represents a specific maturational defect which tends to lessen as the child gets older, and is capable of considerable improvement, especially when appropriate remedial help is offered at the earliest opportunity (pp. 1–2).

Critchley's 1970 Definition Preferred

We would prefer the more general definition Critchley offered in 1970 as opposed to his 1981 conceptualization. Recent neurophysiological evidence would indicate that some dyslexics do indeed evidence different anatomical brain structures and this condition appears to have a physiological basis. Additionally, the symptoms associated with dyslexia do not lessen and continue through to adulthood.

Exclusionary Focus: P.L. 94-142 Definition (1975)

(Note: This law has been renamed the Individuals with Disabilities Education Act [IDEA] of 1990 under P.L. 101-476.)

> "Specific learning disability" means a disorder in one or more of the basic psychological processes involved in understanding or in using language, spoken or written, which may manifest itself in an imperfect ability to listen, think, speak, read, write, spell, or to do mathematical calculations. The term includes such conditions as perceptual handicaps, brain injury, minimal brain dysfunction, dyslexia, and developmental aphasia. The term does not include children who have learning problems which are primarily the result of visual, hearing, or motor handicaps, of mental retardation, of emotional disturbance, or of environmental, cultural, or economic disadvantage (Federal Register, December 19, 1977, p. 65083).

Inclusionary Focus—NJCLD Definition (1988)

NJCLD—whose membership includes representatives from the Speech-Language-Hearing Association, the Association for Children and Adults with LD, the International Reading Association, the Orton Dyslexia Association, and others—proposed an *inclusionary* definition (not to be confused with *inclusionary classrooms*):

> Learning disabilities is a general term that refers to a heterogeneous group of disorders manifested by significant difficulties in the acquisition and use of listening, speaking, reading, writing, reasoning, or mathematical abilities. These disorders are intrinsic to the individual, presumed to be due to central nervous system dysfunction, and may occur across the life span. Problems in self-regulatory behaviors, social perceptions and social interaction may exist with learning disabilities but do not by themselves constitute a learning disability. Although learning disabilities may occur concomitantly with other handicapping conditions (for example, sensory impairment, mental retardation [MR], serious emotional disturbance [ED]) or with extrinsic influences (such as cultural differences, insufficient or inappropriate instruction), they are not the result of those conditions or influences.

The NJCLD definition presented several advantages according to Hammill, Leigh, McNutt, and Larsen (1981). It (1) included adults over a life span, which is an improvement inasmuch as traditional emphases have been with children; (2) avoided the wording of "basic psychological processes," "minimal brain dysfunction," and "perceptual handicaps" because these terms lack specificity; (3) eliminated spelling disabilities because these are actually one segment of written language disabilities and dyslexia; and (4) clearly articulated that LD may occur with other handicapping conditions. Hammill (1990) asserted that the NJCLD 1988 definition more clearly artic-ulated LD symptomatology.

DSM-IV Criteria (1994)

The DSM-IV (American Psychiatric Association, 1994) doesn't define the term dyslexia as such but rather discusses reading disorders under subsection 315.00 of Learning Disorders (Academic Skills Disorders). Three conditions are listed that parallel the NJCLD (1988) definition and in a general sense, Critchley's basic premises:

A. Reading achievement, as measured by an individually administered standard-ized test of reading accuracy or comprehension, is substantially below that expected given the person's chronological age, measured intelligence, and age-appropriate education.
B. The disturbance in A significantly interferes with academic achievement or activ-ities of daily living that require reading skills.
C. If a sensory deficit is present, the learning difficulties are in excess of those usu-ally associated with it. (DSM-IV, 1994, p. E:1)

International Dyslexia Association (IDA) Definition (2003)

Dyslexia is a specific learning disability that is neurological in origin. It is characterized by difficulties with accurate and/or fluent word recognition and by poor spelling and decoding abilities. These difficulties typically result from a deficit in the phonological component of language that is often unexpected in relation to other cognitive abilities and the provision of effective classroom instruction. Secondary consequences may include problems in reading comprehension and reduced reading experience that can impede growth of vocabulary and background knowledge. (Hennessy, 2003)

Spafford and Grosser's Definition (2005)

The current authors define dyslexia, with a prevalence rate estimated to be from 2.19 to 10 percent of the entire population, as *the inability to effectively read words with specific difficulties in fluent reading and the phonological components of language (i.e., phonemic awareness). Dyslexia is thought to have a neurological basis, and the disability is unexpected in relation to other cognitive abilities and access to effective classroom instruction. Secondary issues may or may not include other academic problems (e.g., reading comprehension), difficul-ties in socialization (e.g., more negative peer interactions), and coexisting disabilities or disor-ders (e.g., ADD or ADHD with 25% of those which dyslexia). With intensive literacy support in reading and writing, a social-academic network of support, and the development of individ-ual resiliency, individuals with dyslexia can lead successful and fulfilling lives.*

Summary

The primary presenting problem of word recognition difficulties for people with dyslexia can be traced back to the concept of "word blindness" in the late 1800s with causation connected from that time forward to neurophysiological reasons. The most recent research has uncovered neurological anomalies in three areas on the left side of the brain that impede the reading process for dyslexics (Shaywitz, 2003): (1) left infe-rior frontal gyrus, (2) the left parieto-temporal lobe area, and (3) left occipito-temporal lobe area. As far back as the late 1800s, neurologists were also looking at language cen-ters of the brain such as Broca's and Wernicke's areas because injuries to these areas result in impaired verbal communications. It wasn't until the development of sophisticated MRI (magnetic resonance imaging) technology in the 1990s that researchers could pinpoint with more accuracy exactly what areas of the brain are activated for proficient readers during the reading process and which areas are underactivated for struggling readers. This is because reading, as a complex, multidimensional task, involves the activation of several areas of the cerebral cortex (see p. 9).

The Reading Process

Reading or the social construction of meaning from print is a complex process and actively involves the reader, who must interact with the printed page to derive meaning. Good teaching, background knowledge or schema, motivation, interest, prior experiences with reading, exposure to print, and resiliency all influence how efficient and effective one is during the reading process.

No two readers are alike and no two dyslexics experience the same difficulties with language in the same way. However, there are commonalities that both good and struggling readers show that when identified, provide important information for instructional planning purposes. All students, for example, can acquire the skills and motivation to become effective or successful lifelong readers. Motivation involves wanting to "pick up that book or reading" consistently if not daily and for two major reasons: (1) because reading personally satisfies a need, curiosity, or interest and (2) reading will provide the means to acquire the knowledge and skills necessary to live successful and fulfilling lives. According to Jerry Johns and Susan Lenski (2001), motivating readers is also a complex task that needs to involve modeling for students the desire and love for reading and good reading habits so that students develop positive "motivational dispositions" toward reading.

Reading Is Multidimensional

Learning to read is a very difficult task since it is multidimensional in nature. Effective readers need to consistently and efficiently (rapidly) apply their knowledge of the phonology of language to words during readings while constructing meaning. Short-term (e.g., remembering what was just read) and long-term memories (i.e., schemata) are activated while the reader is interacting with text, linking new information to what is known and what was just read. During all of this, readers continuously make and then confirm or disconfirm text predictions, summarize, make inferences, and draw conclusions. Metacognitive monitoring of one's own accuracy with regard to word identification and comprehension is constant. Depending on the reading purpose, readers are also adjusting their reading rates (relatively fast rates when skimming is needed; slower rates when attending to details for exam preparations) while organizing the information they commit to long-term memory.

Dyslexics Experience Difficulties with Fluency and the Phonology of Language. With regard to specific subcomponents of the reading task that pose difficulties for individuals with dyslexia, deficiencies in fluency and the phonology of language (e.g., phonemic awareness) have been well documented as beginning at a young age (Grosser & Spafford, 2000). Phonemic awareness is strongly correlated to word recognition and spelling (Adams, 1991; Goswani & Bryant, 1990) and therefore is requisite to developing reading proficiency.

Figure 2.3 provides a "small" window of understanding into the complexity of the reading process.

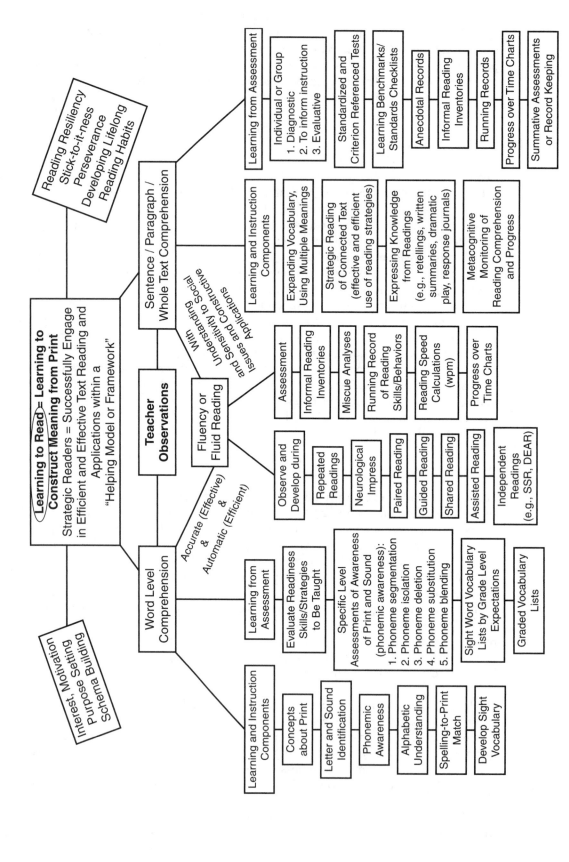

FIGURE 2.3 The Complexity of the Reading Process

Establish a Reading Purpose

Readers need to be meaningfully engaged or have a purpose for reading. According to Fernando, grade 3 gifted reader, ". . . I used to hate reading . . . then I read Spanish and English books . . . that showed me how fun reading could be. . . ." It wasn't until Fernando could make some language and cultural connections with his home language, Spanish, that reading in English became fun and purposeful.

Why Is Reading So Important?

According to Marion Sanders (2001), "everyone believes in the importance and value of reading. Reading competency is essential for school success and almost all employment; inadequate reading ability puts youths at high risk for school dropout followed by failure to develop satisfying, self-sufficient, and productive lives" (p. 1).

Y, grade 2 fluent reader, shares, "I like to read . . . if you don't read now, when you grow up, you won't know how to read."

According to J, grade 2 struggling reader, "I'll get smart—that's the best part of reading."

But J, who is struggling with fluency and word recognition says the hardest part of reading is "when you don't know the words." This is where reading breaks down for individuals with dyslexia.

Individuals with Dyslexia Have Specific Difficulties with Fluent Reading and the Phonological Components of Language

According to L, grade 2 student who evidences many correlating symptoms of dyslexia, "the hardest part about reading is the words; I don't like to read because I don't know how to read."

L is "stuck" at the word level because he lacks a basic sight vocabulary and phonological skills/awareness of the alphabetic principle. For L, problems also emerge in spelling, writing, and listening. ADHD also seems to be a presenting problem. However, L has excellent interpersonal skills with age- and grade-appropriate verbal communications. He is also particularly adept in art. How can it be that L is virtually a nonreader, probably dyslexic, but gifted in other areas? With extraordinary advances in medical technology and refined research methodologies during the decade of the 1990s continuing into the twenty-first century, we can now answer this question with a high level of certainty—-there is a neurological dysfunctioning in the brain. Understanding the reading process at the cortical level, and how dyslexic brain functioning differs from that of proficient readers, will lead us to better interventions.

Balanced Literacy Programs

Students with dyslexia, then, require comprehensive, balanced, and intensive literacy support programs that cover all of the five essential components of good reading instruction:

1. Phonemic awareness
2. Phonics (with systematic/explicit instruction)
3. Vocabulary development
4. Reading fluency, including oral reading skills
5. Text comprehension/strategic reading. (*Guidance for the Reading First Program,* 2002)

Intervention program recommendations found in this book then will address all elements of good reading instruction while consistent with the learning disabilities and dyslexia research and the No Child Left Behind Act of 2001 (P.L. 107-110) with its legislative mandates/initiatives.

The goal of No Child Left Behind is to ensure that all students read by grade 3 and then advance through the grades achieving their full academic potentials. This includes students with reading disabilities.

Summary

Dyslexia definition = *dys* and *lexia,* or inability to effectively read words, is the most prevalent specific learning disability (at least 50% of the LD population). It is thought to have a neurological basis, and the disability is unexpected in relation to other cognitive abilities and access to effective classroom instruction. There are specific difficulties with fluent reading and the phonological components of language (i.e., phonemic awareness). Secondary issues may or may not include other academic problems (e.g., reading comprehension), difficulties in socialization (e.g., more negative peer interactions), and co-existing disabilities or disorders (e.g., ADD or ADHD with 25% of those with dyslexia). With intensive literacy support in reading and writing, a social-academic network of support, and the development of individual resiliency, individuals with dyslexia can lead successful and fulfilling lives. Resiliency is the ability to quickly bounce back or recover from stressors, frustrations, and failures due to a personal resolve to persevere in spite of academic/social obstacles.

Approximately 20 percent of elementary school students are at risk for reading failure and of that number, 2.19 to 10 percent have difficulty learning to read despite exposure to research-based reading instruction that is successful for most students. The Individuals with Disabilities Education Act (IDEA) has been reauthorized under the Improving Education Results for Children With Disabilities Act of 2003 (USDOE) and recommendations applicable to the identifying and teaching of individuals with dyslexia were provided.

A summary of relevant legislation for individuals with learning and other disabilities focused on IDEA, Section 504 of the Rehabilitation Act, and ADA, or the Americans with Disabilities Act. Concern for the adult with dyslexia, covered under ADA (especially for high school students and students transitioning to post-secondary programs and colleges), was mentioned and will be a focus of attention throughout the book.

A historical perspective was presented that detailed how current definitions of dyslexia evolved. One of the earliest and most influential practitioners to study dyslexia was Samuel T. Orton, beginning in the 1920s. He influenced the development of many successful VAK-T or visual-auditory-kinesthetic-tactile approaches still in use today, and a table summarizing many of the more commonly used VAK-T methods was included. The National Reading Panel report *Teaching Children to Read* (2000) provides compelling scientifically based evidence to support their continued use in a well-balanced literacy program. Samuel Kirk introduced "LD" or learning disabilities terminology in 1963 and advanced the need for such specialized programs.

The chapter case study of Jill provided the reader with an opportunity to see first-hand some of the academic and social difficulties experienced by some individuals with dyslexia along with individual protective and environmental factors that contribute to the development of a resilient personality and personal successes.

Chapter 3 looks at international perspectives and dyslexia.

3

Dyslexia
International Perspectives

A physician in the United Kingdom, W.P. Morgan (1896), was concerned about a student of his who, despite average intelligence and good motivation, experienced difficulty in learning to read and write adequately. From the late 1800s on, there has been concern across languages and cultures for struggling readers and how to best meet their unique learning needs.

One of the main missions in dyslexia research should be the understanding of dyslexia and literacy acquisition and development in a cross-linguistic context. While much of our current knowledge . . . derives from cumulative studies of the English language, much more remains to be learned from processes of reading/spelling acquisition and development . . . from other alphabetic language(s) . . . [and] from other language systems . . .

Regarding teaching programs which help train phonemic awareness subskills . . . these teaching programs owe much of their theoretical underpinning to the work of Elkonin (1963, 1973) on teaching beginning reading to Russian children . . . children's reflection on the components of words (syllables and phonemes) . . . facilitates the reading process.

(Che Kan Leong, 1986, 2004, University of Saskatchewan and Chinese University of Hong Kong)

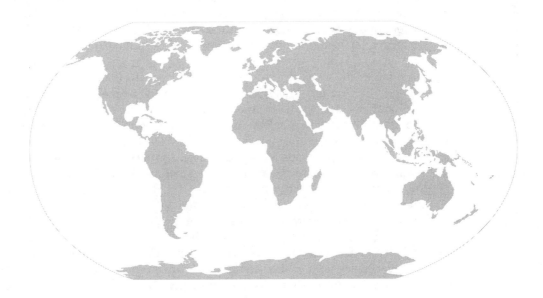

Dyslexia in Languages Other Than English?

The phonological type of dyslexia well known in the English speaking language is reported in other languages, including Chinese, Dutch, French, Japanese, and Spanish. All seem to have in common some level of *deficient* **phonemic awareness** or processing during the reading task. Goulandris notes, "With the emergence of cross-linguistic studies of dyslexia, it has become increasingly evident that it is essential to consider developmental dyslexia in terms of the specific language of instruction because the behavioural manifestations of the disorder cannot be identified without reference to the core characteristics of the spoken and written language in use" (2003, p. 1).

Deficiencies in the "phonological loop" for individuals with dyslexia have been described internationally by Lundberg of Sweden (2002), Papagno and Vallar of Italy (1995), Yin of China and Weekes of the United Kingdom (2003), and many others. Strong language predictors of dyslexia and learning difficulties—phonemic awareness and rapid naming of words—seem to be evident in languages other than English, especially for second-language learners who are dyslexic. For example, DaFontoura and Siegel (1995) identified phonological processing difficulties with Portuguese-English second-language learners with learning difficulties. Geva, Yaghoub-Zadeh, and Schuster (2000) found similar findings after studying second-language learners from varying Asian backgrounds. The term "learning difficulties" is used synonymously with "learning disabilities" and "dyslexia" in many instances at the international level.

Universal Developmental Sequence of Phonological Awareness

Durgunoglu (2002) suggests that depending on the orthography, any differences in phonemic awareness can be attributed to differences in rates of development. There is a developmental sequence of **phonological awareness** across languages at three linguistic levels: (1) syllable, (2) onset and rime, and (3) word. The phonological awareness of syllables and onset and rime (onset = the sounds of the letter or letters before the first vowel in a one syllable word; rime = the rest of the word to include the vowel) generally precedes learning to read words across languages (Goswami, 2002).

Goulandris (2003) believes it to be essential "to consider developmental dyslexia in terms of the specific language of instruction . . . and to appreciate the relevant linguistic features of that language . . . how normal reading and spelling acquisition develop and what cognitive skills underpin this development" (p. 1). For example, languages differ in regard to the linguistic (sound) units that represent graphemic (written) units and can be categorized three ways: (1) *logographic* (scripts represent units of meaning at the level of the morpheme and word—Chinese and Japanese Kanji are logographic scripts), (2) *syllabic* (scripts or symbols represent syllables—Hindi, Japanese Katakana, and Kannada are syllabic scripts), and (3) *alphabetic* (symbols or letters represent phonemes—English and other European languages are alphabetic scripts) (Goulandris, 2003).

Although problems with **phonological processing** and **fluency** characterize the reading of dyslexics across languages and cultures, some past and current research has shown that the difficulties experienced by dyslexics are metalinguistically more involved. Chinese researchers Zhang et al. (1996) and others (e.g., Stanovich, 1986b) who adhere to an interactive model of reading (see p. 93) believe there are higher level **metalinguistic** and cognitive processes that mediate not only comprehension but word recognition as well. Séverine Casalis, Pascale Colé, and Delphine Sopo (2004) found that French-speaking children with dyslexia who displayed difficulty with phonemic segmentation and fluency also had difficulty with morphological segmentation, suggesting the problem with morphemes resides at the **lexical** level of processing. Rachel

Schiff and Dorit Ravid (2004) have shown for dyslexics who speak Hebrew, ambiguous letters are orthographically represented last and weakest in long-term memory. These dyslexics generally had relatively weak internal orthographic representations for letters that had multiple relationships with the spoken form. The problems with storage and then manipulation of the phonological-orthographic patterns for some letter-sound correspondences probably reside at several metalinguistic levels to include morphological processing.

Why Is Learning an Alphabetic Orthography So Difficult?

Emerging readers face difficulties in an alphabetic **orthography** because in alphabetic orthographies, the segmentation of sound does not have an absolute 1:1 correspondence to the segmentation of letters. It is difficult for beginning readers in English to understand the relationship between spelling and sound (Liberman, 1983; Liberman, Shankweiler, Fischer, & Carter, 1974). "The wealth of phonetic information that our natural speech-perceiving mechanisms can use creates serious problems when, as in reading and writing, we try to put all that information through the eye" (Gray & Kavanaugh, 1985, p. 166).

In English alphabetic orthography, the segmentation of sound does not absolutely correspond to the segmentation of letters.

There has been much research regarding the English language (alphabetic script) and dyslexia. English does not have as predictable a mapping system for print to meaning as do other languages (Yin & Weekes, 2003). In the English alphabetic orthography, words represent the morpho (phonological) (i.e., the meaning phonology) structure of spoken words and not their individual isolated sounds (i.e., what Gray and Kavanaugh in 1985 described as the phonetic surface). For example, in trying to learn the word *kind*, a child would try to isolate four sounds but in the process will produce four syllables instead of phonemes: "kuh" "ih" "nn" "duh." Combined, these syllables form "kuhihnnduh," a written nonsense four-syllable word instead of the monosyllable word *kind*. The major point in this discussion is one that Gray and Kavanaugh (1985) emphasize in that, "the segmentation of sound does not correspond to the segmentation of letters" (p. 165) in an alphabetic orthography such as English. As another example, one can take word pairs like *music* and *musician*, where morphophonological relations are intact but the print-to-speech match is more difficult to discern. For individuals with dyslexia who need to "decipher the code," the type of phonological maturity or sophistication needed to identify *music* and *musician* would be lacking as in the case of young children (see Liberman, Liberman, Mattingly, & Shankweiler, 1980). This lack of phonological maturity or sophisticated phonological awareness appears to have a neurophysiological basis.

Specifically, Muter (2003) states brain studies show that brain regions important in analyzing phonological information may fail in some way to work in a coordinated way. As discussed in Chapter 1, researchers (e.g., Shaywitz, 2003) have been able to show where this occurs with three distinct areas of involvement: (1) left inferior frontal gyrus (Phoneme Producer Area), (2) the left parieto-temporal lobe area (Word Analyzer Area), and (3) left occipito-temporal lobe area (Automatic Detector Area). The good news is that phonological awareness can be taught (see pp. 189, 228).

Speech-Print Vocabulary Differential in English

Also relevant to English language usage, and problematic for struggling readers, would be the *speech-print vocabulary differential*. It is commonly known that the majority, or approximately 60 percent of English words in print derive from Latin and Greek sources. Less commonly known would be the findings of Corson (1995) and others who have shown that most words in daily English conversations derive from the

Anglo-Saxon lexicon. The Anglo-Saxon words are high-frequency words, usually one or two syllables in length, whereas the Latin and Greek words in written text are of lesser frequency and tend to be multisyllabic, problematic for the individual with dyslexia. Also, in the English language there are irregular words (e.g., *bread*) that make acquisition of reading and spelling skills, again, difficult for individuals with dyslexia. For individuals learning the English language, this means more teaching support is needed for academics versus conversational speech (Lundberg, 2002).

The consistency of orthographic features is what the reader relies on when encountering new words. As examples, Czech, German, Italian, Spanish, and Greek have consistent orthographic features and are relatively easy for children to learn. Because English is a relatively inconsistent orthography (and Danish, French, and Polish to a lesser degree), it is more difficult to acquire and problematic for individuals with learning disabilities.

Dyslexia across the Globe

Prevalence figures for dyslexia differ from country to country in a range of 1 to 11 percent. Ian Smythe, John Everatt, and Robin Salter (2000/2004), in *The International Book of Dyslexia: A Guide to Practice and Resources*, cite prevalence for several countries. As examples:

- Belgium 5%
- Britain 4%
- Czech Republic 2–3%
- Finland 10%
- Greece 5%
- Italy 1.3–5.0%
- Japan 6%
- Norway 3%
- Poland 4%
- Russia 10%
- Nigeria 11%
- Singapore 3.3%
- Slovakia 1–2%

To obtain a sense of how countries around the world view dyslexia and other learning disabilities and interventions to support literacy development and attainment of reading and writing proficiency, some sample countries were selected that are currently involved in identifying individuals with dyslexia or other learning disabilities/difficulties (Australia, Belgium, Canada, China, The Czech Republic, England and Wales, France, India, Ireland, Israel, Italy, Japan, Kenya, New Zealand, and Sweden). See Chapter 1 for international perspectives related to mathematics and other learning disabilities for Australia, Belgium, Italy, Japan, Spain, and the United States.

Australia

[summarized from Van Kraayenoord (2001); see pp. 19–20 for mathematics disabilities]

The term *learning difficulties* is used in Australia rather than *learning disabilities* and refers to those students who are underachieving in school. A national study conducted in 2000 showed that on the average 16 percent of children throughout the nation experienced learning difficulties. Private providers estimated 10 percent, and the school sectors and systems believed 20 percent of the children are learning disabled. Students are most likely to be identified as having a learning difficulty in literacy (reading and writing).

The terminology used to name the teachers who work with students with learning difficulties varies from Australian state to state. For example, in Queensland the terminology "support teacher of learning difficulties" at the primary level and "resource teacher" at the secondary level are used. The Australian federal government and the state education departments have formally adopted a policy of inclusion, recommending that learning disabilities staff work in regular classrooms with teachers and/or students. There are also pull-out options with students receiving ancillary services for 40 minutes one or more times per week.

Belgium

[summarized by Grammaticos & Cooreman, 2004; see also p. 19]

Dyslexia in Belgium is also referred to as *specific learning disability* with incidence cited by some researchers at 5 percent. There are three official languages in Belgium—French, Flemish, and German.

Centers in Belgium, called psycho-medical-social centers (or centers PMS in French and CLB in Dutch) or Guidance Centres, evaluate referred children. Educational psychologists diagnose dyslexia and prescribe recommendations for educational interventions based on the child's strengths and weaknesses.

The remediation program for children with dyslexia is carried out by speech therapists who work in the schools, hospitals, private practice, or the child's home one or two times per week. Families are able to choose a speech therapist who lives close to them. Typically, children in Belgium who are not progressing according to grade expectations are educated in specialized schools that include schools for children with specific learning disabilities.

Canada

[Government of British Columbia, Ministry of Education, August 2002, http://www.bced.gov.bc.ca/specialed/ppandg/planning_4.htm downloaded, Special Education Services: A Manual of Policies, Procedures and Guidelines, 3/10/04]

The Learning Disabilities Association of Canada (LDAC) and its Provincial and Territorial Associations in 2002 ratified a new definition of learning disabilities for national purposes. It resulted from a comprehensive review of learning disabilities research and feedback from hundreds of individuals in all provinces and territories, the LDAC National Legal Committee, and the LDAC Think Tank. LDAC acknowledged the support of The Burns Family Memorial Fund and the contributions of the Learning Disabilities Association of Ontario and its Definition Working Group (funded by the Government of Ontario as part of the Promoting Early Intervention Initiative), in addition to the efforts of the Association Québécoise pour les Troubles d'Apprentissage on the translation of the full document.

Official Definition of Learning Disabilities (adopted by the Learning Disabilities Association of Canada on January 30, 2002):

> Learning disabilities refers to a number of disorders that may affect the acquisition, organization, retention, understanding or use of verbal or nonverbal information. These disorders affect learning in individuals who otherwise demonstrate at least average abilities essential for thinking and/or reasoning. As such, learning disabilities are distinct from global intellectual disabilities. Learning disabilities result from impairments in one or more processes related to perceiving, thinking, remembering or learning. These include, but are not limited to: language processing, phonological processing, visual spatial processing, processing speed, memory and attention, and executive functions (e.g., planning and decision making). Learning disabilities range in severity and may interfere with the acquisition and use of one or more of the following:
>
> - Oral language (e.g., listening, speaking, understanding)
> - Reading (e.g., decoding, phonetic knowledge, word recognition, comprehension)
> - Written language (e.g., spelling and written expression)
> - Mathematics (e.g., computation, problem solving)
>
> Learning disabilities may also involve difficulties with organizational skills, social perception, social interaction and perspective taking.

In Canada, students classified as dyslexic would be identified by school systems through a system of progressive assessment and documentation. Two main approaches for supporting students with learning disabilities are recommended: (1) intense direct instruction and (2) instruction in learning and compensatory strategies. Additionally, social skills training and instruction and practice in self-advocacy skills are considered priorities.

China

[summarized from Chan, Suk-Han Ho, Tsang, Lee, & Chung, 2003; Yin & Weekes, 2003]

Zhang, Zhang, Yin, Zhou, and Chang (1996) report that 5 to 8 percent of schoolchildren in China are dyslexic. Children are diagnosed as dyslexic if they are two or more years behind grade level in reading and of average intelligence. Hua Shu in Eakle and Garber (2004) notes that morphological awareness is the most important factor in reading Chinese.

Dyslexia in Chinese (nonalphabetic script) is thought to originate from psycholinguistic impairments at multiple levels to include orthographic, semantic, and phonological processing. Specifically, dyslexia is thought to originate from the failure to develop connections between orthographic and phonological representations through the morphographic features unique to nonalphabetic scripts (Leong, 1999). Chinese characters are comprised of strokes formed into components that are square in shape: Each one represents a single character. In order to become literate, an individual can learn the most common 3,000 characters from over 40,000 characters. The Chinese system is a complex logographic system where each written form is associated with a morpheme (meaning unit), in contrast to letters in an alphabetic system (e.g., English) that in and of themselves do not convey meaning. A unique feature of Chinese languages is there are no consonant blends or clusters before or after a nuclear vowel. This means "homophony" is predominant in Chinese languages. There are suprasegmental changes in tone at the level of the vowel and tones change the morphemic content of each syllable. The skill, then, of phonological awareness at the level of the onset and rime is critical to learning spoken and written Chinese words (Leong & Tan, 2002). One method of instruction in mainland China is a method of teaching words with an alphabetic script called *Pinyin.* The Pinyin script relies on the Roman alphabet with inflectional symbols used to represent multiple pronunciations of Chinese syllables. Pinyin is thought to enhance character learning and is a routine method of instruction in China (not Hong Kong). Dyslexia with individuals who learn Chinese with Pinyin words probably involves processing in the same brain regions as alphabetic scripts (e.g., English). Phonological awareness, then, is a predictor of vocabulary development and literacy in Beijing children. Dyslexia is treated within the framework of mainstream schooling with behavior checklists such as the Hong Kong Specific Learning Disabilities Behaviour Checklist (HKSLDBC) informing instructional practice (e.g., fluency factors of misusing punctuation or using wrong verbal expression).

The Czech Republic

[summarized from Matejcek, 2002]

The term *specific learning disabilities,* as it is used in the Czech Republic, most often refers to the condition of dyslexia. The first article about the specific "inability to learn to read" in the Czech Republic was written by Antonín Heveroch, professor of neurology and psychiatry, in 1904. Formal diagnosis and treatment for dyslexics began around 1952 within the framework of child psychiatry, and in 1967, remedial services for dyslexic children were instituted within the state school system. Beginning in 1967, a dyslexia seminar has been offered in Prague for practitioners who work with individuals with dyslexia. From this seminar, the Czech Dyslexia Association was created and in 2001 became a branch of the IDA (International Dyslexia Society).

The Czech orthography is phonetically very consistent, so that phoneme-grapheme correspondences are almost always 1:1. The reading and language difficulties seen with dyslexics are similar to that in other languages; however, there is one specific difficulty found in Czech dyslexics, that being the ability to acoustically differentiate between sounds acoustically close to one another.

Private Dys-Centres offer services for students with dyslexia, and in some towns parents have founded their own Dys-Clubs. In 1992, the Czech Ministry of Education issued a special decree that defines the diagnosis of children with dyslexia, extends some "protective" measures, and advises those who care for children with dyslexia to do so with care and understanding.

England

[summarized by Carol Orton, 2004]

In England, the term *learning difficulty* is used synonymously with dyslexia. In 1996, Section 312 of the Education Act for England and Wales says,

> A child has special educational needs if the child has a learning difficulty which calls for special educational provision to be made. A child has a learning difficulty if (a) the child has a significantly greater difficulty in learning than the majority of children of the same age. (b) The child has a disability which either prevents or hinders use of educational facilities of a kind generally provided for children of the same age in schools within the area of the LEA (local education association). Special education provision means: educational provision which is additional to or otherwise different from the educational provision made generally for children of the same age in schools maintained by the LEA (other than special schools) in the area.

Schools are required to provide appropriate education programs for students based on learning needs. If a child has exceptionally severe or complex needs, the LEA assists with assessment and recommendations. The provision of services for children with special needs applies to 1 to 5 percent of the school population. Schools have "Accessibility Plans" that detail how they will (1) increase the extent to which disabled students participate in the regular curriculum, (2) improve the physical environment to increase the extent to which disabled students participate in regular programming efforts, and (3) improve the educational experiences for disabled students in collaboration with families.

The British Dyslexia Association (http://www.bda-dyslexia.org.uk) was created in 1972 and is the major organization for families and educators who work with dyslexic children.

France

[summarized from Casalis, Colé, & Sopo, 2004]

The Education Ministry in France issued an action plan in March 2001 regarding the education of dyslexic children. Several researchers are studying the nature, causes, and teaching methods for students with dyslexia.

Séverine Casalis, Pascale Colé, and Delphine Sopo (2004), for example, are currently studying metalinguistic awareness in children with developmental dyslexia. Their dyslexic children (French-speaking) have shown phonological deficiencies and fluency problems, similar to students with dyslexia in other countries. Specifically, Casalis, Colé, and Sopo (2004) are looking at the role of phonological deficiencies in larger language units or morphemes. They have found that children with dyslexia who had difficulty with phonemic segmentation also had difficulty with morphological segmentation. However, the dyslexics they worked with were able to read affixed words better than pseudo-affixed words (similar to their peers), suggesting the problem with morphemes resides at the lexical level of processing.

Reading assessments for dyslexics include fluency measures to assess accuracy and speed in word recognition, also providing information about a child's phonological processing ability. To be considered dyslexic, a child must evidence a reading delay of 18 months under the age of 9, and a delay of 24 months for older children. A child must have low average to average ability and show no language impairments, hearing problems, or neurological and emotional disorders. The child must have been enrolled in long-term reading remediation program without achieving reading proficiency commensurate with peers. This is similar to the current U.S. 2003 IDEA reauthorization language in which a school district "may use a process which determines if a child responds to scientific, research-based intervention" in determining the presence of a specific learning disability.

India

[summarized by John, George, & Mampilli, 2004]

Dyslexia in India is referred to as *learning disorders*. The Special Educational Needs (SEN), the Persons with Disabilities Act (PWD) was passed by the Indian Parliament in 1995 to serve children with learning disorders. Approximately 20 to 25 percent of the students are not achieving to the grade-level standards. India is multilingual and multicultural with several dialects spoken throughout the country—interventions differ when children experience poor school performance.

Students with dyslexia in India have alternative curriculum choices to meet their learning needs and are provided curriculum accommodations similar to those in Western cultures—e.g., extra time, the use of calculators, and "consideration of content" versus spelling in written work. There is a movement in India toward training teachers as educational diagnosticians within a multidisciplinary diagnostic model.

Ireland

[summarized by Hughes, 2004]

In Ireland, dyslexia is also known as a *learning difficulty*. The *Dyslexia Association in Ireland* (http://www.dyslexia.ie) was formally established in 2000, having been previously known as the *Association for Children and Adults with Learning Disabilities* (ACLD). The *Dyslexia Association* provides in-service training for teachers in both assessment and intervention. The Association also provides a forum to express the needs of children and their families as well as the needs of adults with dyslexia.

NEPS, or the National Educational Psychological Service (NEPS), was created in 1999 to provide psychoeducational assessment for students with learning difficulties. Special reading units within the primary schools serve students with learning disabilities or difficulties in small classes (11:1) with partial integration into mainstream classes. Most of the schools have these classes and are staffed by "Learning Support Teachers." Students served generally fall at the lowest 10th percentile in reading performance.

Israel

[summarized from Tur-Kaspa & Margalit, 2001]

The Ministry of Education in Israel adapted the 1994 National Joint Committee on Learning Disabilities (NJCLD) definition using the discrepancy paradigm for identification. Prevalence rates are commonly accepted within the 10 percent range. The identification of students with learning disabilities (LD) emerged in Israel during the 1970s when parents' groups actively promoted recognition and early identification of learning disabilities. The implementation of the Israeli Special Education Law (1988) specified inclusion program policies.

A collaboration between the Ministers of Science and of Education and the support of parent groups and researchers resulted in the appointment of a National Committee to study educating students with learning disabilities. The completed Margalit Report in 1997 resulted in the development of assessment procedures, school-based support systems, teacher training, and public awareness within an equal opportunities framework for students with learning disabilities. A National Supervisor for LD (within the Ministry of Education) coordinates systemic support approaches within the schools.

In 2000, a scientific forum for learning disabilities was founded at the School of Education at Tel-Aviv University. This forum promotes basic research, conferences, and professional development training. Comprehensive intervention programs are developed that address social, cognitive, and affective processing skills for individuals with learning disabilities.

Some researchers are currently investigating differences in how proficient readers and dyslexics use phonological, orthographic, and morphological cues. Rachel Schiff and Dorit Ravid (2004) have adopted the view of some other researchers that reading and spelling both "interface in their dependence on both graphemic and phonological information rather than on one to the exclusion of the other." The students, who were university students, in the Schiff and Ravid (2004) study did less well than proficient-reading peers effectively employing orthographic and morphological cues during the reading process.

Italy

[summarized by Stella, 2004; see also p. 19]

The movement for recognition of learning disabilities in Italy was formalized during the 1980s. The incidence reported in the literature ranges from 1.5 percent to 5.5 percent. Due to the fact that the Italian orthography is considered a predictable orthography in that graphemes closely match phonemes, Italian children learn to read and spell relatively quickly. This would also account for a lower incidence rate than countries with irregular orthographies (e.g., English).

Diagnosis of dyslexia in Italy is the responsibility of psychologists and physicians. Similar to many Western countries, a psychological evaluation, language and reading tests, memory and attention functioning, and math performance are assessed. Speech and language therapists sometimes conduct a portion of the evaluation.

Speech and language therapists working within the national health system prescribe treatment for dyslexia. The school committee of the Associazione Italiana Dislessia works with schools to ensure an adequate education for dyslexic children.

Japan

[summarized by Todo, 2004; see also p. 20]

The movement for recognition of learning disabilities was formalized during the 1990s. The incidence of dyslexia in Japan is low compared to Western countries, 3 to 4 percent.

Dyslexia diagnosis in Japan relates to the Western term *alexia*, a medical term. The terminology *learning disabilities* is widely used in Japan in the context of reading, mathematics, and writing (dysgraphia) disabilities.

The Japan Dyslexia Society provides various forms of support for children and adults with dyslexia that includes but is not limited to individualized academic instruction based on assessments given similar to those in Western countries. The Japan Dyslexia Society also suggests academic accommodations with direct work in the classroom; prepares students for exams; and transitions adults into the workplace.

Kenya

[summarized by Ferguson, 2004]

Dyslexia in Kenya is diagnosed similar to that of England and the British Dyslexia Association (BDA) (see section on England, p. 55). Specific learning difficulties teachers do some of the initial assessments and provide differentiated instruction for students with dyslexia to include work with word processors. Some schools use the services of educational psychologists. A website has been created for parents and teachers to discuss issues related to students who have dyslexia: http://www.wefer-dyslexia.8m.net.

New Zealand

[summarized from Chapman, 2002]

Neither the term *learning disability* nor *dyslexia* has been officially adopted by the New Zealand Education Ministry, but both are used in the private sector. LD, based on the United States P.L. 94-142 definition (but without the "exclusion clause") has been seen by Parliament as problematic within the New Zealand educational system. Therefore, the term *learning difficulties* is used. Support for learning difficulties occurs within literature-based, whole-language classrooms. Prevention is emphasized through programs like Reading Recovery (RR).

The well-regarded and much-researched *Reading Recovery (RR) Program* developed by Marie Clay was piloted in New Zealand during the 1970s and early 1980s. This program was made available in 1983 for children at risk for developing reading problems after one year of formal schooling (i.e., at age 6) and is currently used throughout the world. The aim of Reading Recovery is to substantially reduce the number of children who develop ongoing reading and writing difficulties by intensifying services in grades 1 and 2 (see p. 110 for a more in-depth description of Reading Recovery) when children show early signs of reading problems. The Reading Recovery program was designed for all poor readers, and according to Marie Clay, RR should assist children who do not learn to read for many life-event produced reasons (i.e., environmental, sociocultural, or economic causes) and all children who have medically based problems but who can learn to achieve in reading and writing to proficiency. In 2000, 69 percent of New Zealand schools used the Reading Recovery program.

In New Zealand resource teachers and learning and behavior specialists (RT:LB) work with students who experience difficulties in learning and/or behavior within the public schooling sector. The nationwide remedial reading service available specifically for children (and adults) with learning disabilities has been privately supported by the Federation of Specific Learning Disabilities Associations (SPELD). SPELD was created during the 1970s and offers assessment and remedial services for children with learning disabilities by registered teachers who receive special training in the concept and remediation of learning disabilities. Information from annual reports shows that since 1974, an average of 2,000 to 3,000 students have been assisted by SPELD-trained teachers in New Zealand each year.

Sweden

[summarized by Lundberg, 2002]

Individuals who are diagnosed dyslexic in Sweden show a paradox—that is, the dyslexics find it easier to read and understand the English language than the Swedish language. It would be expected that a dyslexic would have more difficulty reading and using a second language, which is not the case in Sweden. The orthographic differences between the Swedish and English languages may account for some of this phenomenon. Specifically, the Swedish language has 1:1 mapping between letters and sounds, and most consonants have two or more orthographic representations. Phonological discriminations particular to vowel length and syllable stress are necessary for spelling proficiency in Swedish. The compound words and complex phoneme-grapheme relationships found in the Swedish language may be difficult for individuals with dyslexia (Goulandris, 2003).

Wales (see England, p. 55)

Second-Language Learners and Dyslexia

What was once a perplexing issue for educators—that is, how to determine if second-language learners are at risk for learning disabilities or dyslexia—is no longer an issue. The research is clear in this area: If second-language learners are strong in their first language or home language (HL), then educators can expect that the linguistic strengths will transfer to the language of the school (SL) (e.g., Durgunoglu, 2002). Ojemann (1989) has speculated that the languages of an individual who is bilingual may be located at different cortical sites. The second language may be represented in a wider brain area for some aspects of language (e.g., naming objects). If second-language learners experience fluency and phonemic awareness/phonological decoding difficulties, then there may be a learning disability or dyslexia and the student should be tested in the home language. See Chapter 9 for a recommended screening adaptable for all students.

The learning of the sound structures of novel words (as in another language for second-language learners) requires adequate representations of the sounds and patterns in phonological short-term memory with ready accessibility to the second-language learner. For some bilingual dyslexics with developmentally appropriate vocabulary in their first language, the second-language vocabulary may be very deficient because an adequate phonological short-term memory would be requisite to learning the second language, and this may be difficult. The home language may be proficient with phonological processing difficulties in the second language.

Why Is Learning a Second Language Especially Problematic for Dyslexics?

The learning of the sound structures of novel words (as in another language for second-language learners) requires adequate representations of the sounds and patterns in phonological short-term memory with ready accessibility of these representations for use by the second-language learner. For dyslexics who experience difficulties with the phonology of language, learning a second language with an alphabetic script (e.g., English) can be especially problematic. Syntax may also be problematic.

Lundberg (2002) mentions the possibility that the acquisition of syntax may be related to the "phonological loop." Because the syntactic rules of language are abstracted from language patterns, word strings must be held in phonological short-term memory. A diminished phonological short-term memory (i.e., as with many dyslexics) would impact creation of permanent long-term memory representations. As discussed in Chapter 1, the automatic detector in the left occipito-temporal area of the brain "breaks down" in children with dyslexia. A neurological anomaly prevents their brains from gaining automatic access to the word analyzer and phoneme producer areas of the brain (Shaywitz, 2003).

The Intervention Process for Second-Language Learners with Dyslexia

Generally, the guiding principle for teaching second-language learners is to provide them with the same continuum of strategic approaches used with other struggling readers (e.g., students with dyslexia) such as guided reading, teacher read-alouds, shared reading, and literature (circles) discussion groups (Au, 2002) and to supplement these approaches with evidenced-based practices particular to a language (e.g., Sheltered English Strategies—see pp. 315–317). These various instructional approaches are mentioned throughout the book.

Background Building.   Goodman and Goodman (1978) underscore the value of background building in acquiring literacy in a second language. These researchers studied Arabic, Navaho, Samoan, and Spanish children and found background knowledge to be one of the most critical factors in the ability to read stories and then retell the story. Krashen (1987) says that for optimal instruction, teachers need to build such language acquisition in a low-risk and low-anxiety learning environment, keeping the "affective filter" low.

Additional Classroom Dynamics.   Students who are second-language learners need to be immersed in classroom environments with context-rich, interactive, and supportive collaborations where there is much language exploration and conversational use in literacy interactions among peers (Ruddell & Ruddell, 1995).

Build on Strengths of Home Language: Families as Literacy Partners.   Research has shown that initial literacy instruction should build on the strengths of the home language with families considered to be the school's literacy partners for all children who have a home language (HL) different from the language of the school. Past and current research makes clear that culture plays an important role in a child's approach to the learning environment with either positive or negative performance outcomes reflected in assessment results. As such, the infusion of culture into lesson presentations will help invest students into the learning process with relevant and personal language connections transitioning them into higher levels of performance (Stanley & Spafford, 2002).

If initial literacy instruction builds on the strengths of the home language, learning and achievement can be greatly facilitated. Literacy skills developed in the home language can be applied more readily to learning to read and write in the dominant language in school. In fact, Snow, Burns, and Griffin (1998) completed an extensive study of the factors that put children at risk for poor reading and found that beginning reading instruction with the national language for children whose parents have not had educational or economical advantages is not as advantageous as starting with the home language (HL).

However, there is the reality that many of our schools face—there are not bilingual education programs or support for each language represented in today's schools.

ESL or ELL children without access to education programs in their home language face even greater challenges. It is incumbent upon schools to provide professional development opportunities for educators to best meet the needs of these children.

International Reading Association Position Statement on Second-Language Literacy Instruction. The International Reading Association's (IRA) position statement (2001), "Second-Language Literacy Instruction," affirms the right of families to have options in regard to their children's initial literacy instruction whether it be in the home language or in the primary language of the school. Some recent initiatives in the United States are focused on eliminating bilingual education, thus moving schools away from the flexibility they need to use children's native language in their education if needed. Most second-language learners need more than one year to learn English. One year may not give both the conversational English and the English acquisition ELL students will need to succeed academically. According to the IRA, educators will need to collaboratively seek out as many ways as possible to support access to initial literacy development in both home and school languages.

In summary, educational programs that provide second language learners with opportunities to access initial literacy instruction in the home language whenever possible would be relevant for students with dyslexia. According to second-language learner (home language is Spanish; school language is English), grade 1 student Glaritza, personal connections are made this way. Glaritza states, "... I like to read books about Spanish people ... I can make personal connections ... I can even make books about Spanish people ..."

QUalitative Analysis of Resilient Traits (QUART)

General Instructions: Check the degree to which the student displays behaviors in the following areas. Space has been added for additional observations.

Name of Student ____C____ (struggling student - not learning disabled) _____ Date _____

(previously repeated a grade)

Evaluator _____ Grade ___5___ DOB _____

NOTE: Second Language Learner - Transitioning to English (second language spoken in the home)

	Strong				Diminished or Not Evident
Individual Protective Factors					
• persistent (stick-to-it-ness)	5	④	3	2	1
• self-efficacy (beliefs about one's ability to plan and complete actions to reach a goal or desired level of performance)	5	④	3	2	1
• positive self-esteem (positive evaluation of oneself)	5	4	③	2	1
• optimistic (anticipates the best, hopeful)	5	4	③	2	1
• confident learner (self assured learner)	5	4	3	②	1
• overall positive temperament (characteristic "frame of mind" is positive)	5	④	3	2	1
• socially perceptive (accurate evaluates social situations and determines appropriate actions).	5	4	③	2	1
• good reasoning ability (able to make inferences, draw conclusions and problem solve)	5	4	③	2	1
• advocates for self (works in an informed manner to obtain better academic or social opportunities or services)	5	4	3	②	1
• arena of talent or performance valued by others _Persistency or "stick-to-it-ness"_	5	4	③	2	1
Coping Style (additional)					
• self-starter (takes the initiative when needed)	5	4	③	2	1
• internal locus of control (assumes responsibility for learning/ achievement and attributes many successes to motivation, effort, resourcefulness)	5	④	3	2	1
• flexible (adaptable and accommodating when appropriate)	⑤	4	3	2	1
• self reflective (able to plan, self-monitor and evaluate one's own thinking, learning, comprehension, and social actions)	5	4	③	2	1
• seeks critical support systems (support from peers, teachers, family, and other community members)	5	4	③	2	1
• able to advocate for others (understands needs, feelings of peer group)	5	④	3	2	1

Major strengths _____

Major weaknesses _____

FIGURE 3.1 *QUalitative Analysis of Resilient Traits (QUART)*

Research by the current authors found many second-language learners to be persistent and self-efficacious but not "confident" learners, often requiring structured English teaching and a concerted effort to help build their individual protective factors and a more resilient coping style. The QUART profile shown in Figure 3.1 is that of a second-language learner transitioning to English.

An adaptive instructional literacy block with other recommendations can be found in Chapter 11 with screening information in Chapter 9.

Summary

In this chapter, the understanding of dyslexia was presented in cross-linguistic contexts with the finding that many languages seem to have in common some level of phonemic awareness or processing required during the reading task; hence, individuals with dyslexia in various countries around the world display the fluency and phonological processing difficulties reported in Western countries. However, research is this area is relatively new. Che Kan Leong (2004) and many other international literacy/dyslexia specialists believe much more can be learned about reading and spelling processes and dyslexia from an international perspective.

Goulandris (2003) believes it to be essential to consider dyslexia in terms of the specific language of instruction and to appreciate the relevant linguistic features of that language. Languages differ in regard to the linguistic (sound) units that represent graphemic (written) units and can be categorized three ways: (1) logographic (scripts represent units of meaning at the level of the morpheme and word—Chinese and Japanese Kanji are logographic scripts), (2) syllabic (scripts or symbols represent syllables—Hindi, Japanese Katakana, and Kannada are syllabic scripts), and alphabetic (symbols or letters represent phonemes—English and other European languages are alphabetic scripts).

Difficulties are faced by emerging readers and individuals with dyslexia particularly in alphabetic orthographies because the segmentation of the speech stream does not have a 1:1 correspondence to the segmentation of letters. In other words, an alphabetic orthography represents the morphophonological (i.e., the meaning phonology) structure of spoken words and not its individual isolated sounds per se.

Deficiencies in the "phonological loop" for individuals with dyslexia have been described internationally by Lundberg of Sweden (2002), Papagno and Vallar of Italy (1995), Yin of China and Weekes of the United Kingdom (2003), and many others. The phonological type of dyslexia well known in the English language is reported in other languages to include Chinese, Dutch, French, Japanese, and Spanish. Research findings in Israel and in other countries suggest that dyslexics not only experience difficulty identifying and manipulating phonemes, but there are memory problems related to how dyslexics store phonologicalorthographic patterns for some letter-sound correspondences.

There are unique problems for dyslexics who are second-language learners, one being the screening process. If second-language learners experience difficulties with phonemic awareness in the home language (HL) and other correlating symptoms of a learning disability, testing should be done in the HL to determine the possible presence of dyslexia or other learning disabilities. Educational programs that provide second-language learners with opportunities to access initial literacy instruction in the home language whenever possible would be relevant for students with dyslexia. The International Reading Association's (IRA) position statement (2001), "Second-Language Literacy Instruction," affirms the right of families to have options in regard to their children's initial literacy instruction whether it be in the home language or in the primary language of the school.

Goodman and Goodman (1978) point to the importance of background building as a critical preteaching element to facilitate the acquisition of literacy in a second language after working with Arabic, Navaho, Samoan, and Spanish children. Generally, the guiding principle for teaching second-language learners is to provide them with the same continuum of strategic approaches used with dyslexics and other struggling readers but to supplement with evidence-based practices particular to the language being taught. An adaptive instructional literacy block for second-language learners with other recommendations will be found in Chapter 11 with screening information in Chapter 9.

Chapter 4 will now delve into resiliency, or the ability to quickly bounce back or recover from stressors, frustrations, and failures due to a personal resolve to persevere in spite of academic/social obstacles. Persistent academic and social difficulties that emanate from learning problems experienced by all individuals with dyslexia necessitate the development of strong resilient personalities to achieve optimal academic, social, and career successes.

4 Developing Resiliency in Individuals with Dyslexia

The Third "R"—Reading, 'Riting, Resiliency

Resiliency Defined

What?

There has been more of a focus on the academic deficiencies and negative social implications associated with individuals who experience dyslexia and less emphasis placed on the positive characteristics shown by resilient (i.e., resiliency = the ability to quickly bounce back or recover from stressors, frustrations, and failures due to a personal resolve to persevere in spite of academic/social obstacles) and successful individuals with dyslexia. Typically, individuals with dyslexia who show strong resilient personalities, "sing at their work," "do it better," and "persevere longer." They often have good temperaments and positive self-concepts and self-esteems.

Why Identify Resiliency?

The present authors have identified "resiliency" as the third "R" in the "Reading, 'Riting, *Resiliency*" intervention program equation, believing it to be the critical link to successful academic and social adjustments for individuals with dyslexia. Individuals with dyslexia are continuously confronted with academic difficulties and often with social challenges.

Dyslexics do experience reading and writing difficulties, and literacy programs naturally focus on developing proficiency in these areas. It is a given that children and adults who experience dyslexia vary in quantity and quality of manifest academic and social characteristics and require to some extent individualized literacy programs; there is no "magic cure-all" for dyslexia. Although dyslexia is considered a reading disability, repeated academic failures and apparent reading/language deficits can diminish feelings of positive self-worth and self-esteem (Grosser & Spafford, 2000).

Persistent academic and social difficulties that emanate from learning problems experienced by *all* dyslexics necessitate the development of strong resilient personalities for *all* to achieve optimal academic, social, and career successes.

Who?

In studying the lives of some highly visible individuals with dyslexia—to name a few, Barbara and George H. W. Bush's son Neil, Baruj Benacerraf (Nobel Prize winner), Cher, Winston Churchill, Ennis Cosby (son of Dr. Bill and Camille Cosby), Whoopi Goldberg, Jay Leno, Greg Louganis, Ann Bancroft (Antarctic explorer-scientist), Edgar Allen Poe, Nelson Rockefeller, August Rodin, and Steven Spielberg (Koenig & Spafford, 2001), all shared the tenacity or perseverance to succeed despite academic and life obstacles—strong resilient personalities. The development of resilient personalities requires an understanding of the different factors or variables that contribute to its development.

Factors Impacting Resiliency

Some researchers (e.g., Fink, 1998) have conducted extensive research to determine how individuals with dyslexia who achieved high levels of literacy and occupational/school/social successes as judged by peers overcame both academic and social obstacles. Personal *resiliency* with a *network of support* emerge as common factors for many successful dyslexics described by Fink (1998) and others.

An individual's resiliency changes over the course of a lifetime and is impacted by (1) individual protective factors (traits or characteristics), (2) positive environmental factors (familial and community-oriented), (3) stressors, and (4) coping styles. Resulting outcomes can be positive (i.e., a resilient dyslexic) or negative (i.e., a dyslexic who lacks the resiliency to reach optimal life and career successes).

Individual Protective Factors

Hauser (1999) cites several individual protective factors that contribute to how resilient an individual becomes:

- Self-efficacy
- Positive temperament
- Positive self-esteem (self-concept)
- Arena of talent or performance valued by others
- Faith
- Hopefulness (optimism)
- Good cognitive reasoning ability

Other research cites the following individual qualities in people who possess strongly resilient personalities.

- Persistence (stick-to-it-ness)
- Learning motivation
- Effective learning styles
- Social perceptiveness
- Self-advocacy
- Participation in service learning and advocating for others

Positive Environmental Factors

These factors relate to an individual's participation in various social groups where significant others can nurture a person's resolve to persevere in spite of academic and/or social obstacles (e.g., having dyslexia or other disabilities).

- Connections to competent others
- Positive relations with extended family members
- Effective parenting
- Good teaching
- Words of encouragement and inspiration from others
- Second-chance situations from significant others
- Early diagnosis of dyslexia with appropriate interventions both in and out of the classroom

Stressors (see Figure 4.1 on p. 68)

These are situations or stimuli that create discomfort and such feelings as anxiety, tension, frustration, and fear. According to Coon (1994), the best way to reduce stress is to leave the source of the stress. Often, this is not possible, so individuals develop counterbalancing strategies or ways to alleviate or eliminate the stress. Stress can relate to the hassles of everyday life, learning problems, and significant life events.

- Examples of everyday life stressors: too much to do, losing or misplacing something, not liking the clothes I'm wearing today or the way I look
- Examples of learning problems stressors: failed a test, received a lower than expected grade, "tried but couldn't learn to do that"
- Examples of significant life stressors: first day in a new school, change in a family circumstance, illness

Weighting Environmental Factors and Individual Protective Factors

Individual protective and environmental factors are identified for consideration during instructional planning efforts and professional development planning. Please keep in mind that each individual will be impacted differently by the collective impact of some or all of these factors. Some thought needs to be given to the degree of importance each factor has on each individual's resiliency.

Early Diagnosis of Dyslexia and Other Learning Disabilities.   Early diagnosis of learning problems/learning disabilities with accompanying effective early interventions are critical to future academic and social successes and adjustments (Strickland, 2002). Often second-language learners with dyslexia and other learning disabilities are diagnosed later than their peers in the dominant culture (e.g., English-speaking) or not until they obtain some linguistic competence in the dominant language before being tested. This is a cause for concern because there are growing numbers of second-language learners in schools (e.g., United States) whose academic test performance in the dominant language (English) is relatively poor compared to peers.

The current authors recommend initial testing/intervention services in the home language (HL) for second-language learners who are emerging readers, when phonemic awareness and reading fluency are impaired, assuming that there would be evidence of other correlating symptoms of dyslexia. Genest (1996) emphasizes the importance of building self-esteem and notes that early diagnosis of learning disabilities and appropriate interventions might aid in the development of positive self-esteems possibly leading to more resilient personalities.

Intelligence and Ability Not Heavily Weighted Individual Protective Factors.   Overall intelligence (IQ) apparently does not account significantly for the degree to which successful dyslexics compensate for academic difficulties (Lefly & Pennington, 1991). However, cognitive styles do impact compensatory actions. Cognitive styles that include self-monitoring of performance (e.g., monitoring comprehension) and progress contribute to a more internal locus of control and self-efficacy. Zhang (2000) mentions the importance of weighting variables other than ability when evaluating student successes and failures with an emphasis on self-concept, self-confidence, learning motivation, cognitive styles, and home environment and family support.

"Stick-to-it-ness" or Persistence and Motivation: Critical Individual Protective Factors.   It would appear that "stick-to-it-ness" or persistence and motivation are significant individual protective factors. Fink (1998) found that despite ongoing struggles with basic, lower level skills typically experienced by successful adult dyslexics she

interviewed (i.e., letter identification, decoding strategies, and word recognition), many of these successful adult dyslexics reported persistently seeking out books throughout their lives in order to learn. They also were persistent in seeking help when needed. Literacy development was furthered by a strong learning motivation to know more about a content area of passionate personal interest. The "stick-to-it-ness" or persistence observed facilitated the development of effective coping strategies or styles to help deal with the stressors encountered in everyday life.

Cultural Relatedness to Development of Persistence. Some cultures place great importance on developing the character trait of persistence. For example, in Japan, two character traits considered to be of significant relevance to academic growth and performance, *gambaru* (effort) and *gaman* (persistence). These are collaboratively nurtured and developed by teachers and families as children progress through the grades (Singleton, 1989). There is comparative research that shows a substantive correlation between these two factors (*gambaru* and *gaman*) and academic success across a range of students (Blinco, 1991).

Coping Styles

Effective coping styles involve several learned responses to stressors, with the following characteristics seen in resilient individuals.

- The ability to recognize learning abilities and set realistic goals and time limits to achieve those goals
- Flexibility, especially open-mindedness toward change situations
- Tolerance
- Empathy
- The ability to regroup or reorganize or take a "new look" at a situation
- The desire to contribute positively to "the group" (e.g., peer group, family, a club or sports team, the school environment, a church group, and so on)
- Self-reflective learning style both in and out of the classroom
- The ability to seek academic and social support as needed
- The ability to use a variety of ways to relax or manage stress (e.g., exercise, meditation, hobbies, listening to music, taking a nature walk and so on)
- Knowing when it's OK and appropriate to "slow down" to relax, rest, or recreate

Coping styles (characteristic learned responses to stressors) evidenced by flexibility, tolerance, self-reflection, empathy, or support for others with the desire to contribute to the group are most likely to contribute to resilient personalities. Individuals with dyslexia frequently encounter situations in which academic and social difficulties result in frustration or failure; they need assistance in developing coping strategies that bypass learned helplessness, negativism, less than satisfactory social interactions, and an external locus of control (Grosser & Spafford, 2000; Spafford & Grosser, 1993).

All individuals need to develop various ways to relax to manage anxiety, fear, anger, or frustration in response to stress. The discomfort one feels in reaction to stress naturally is caused by the body's fight-or-flight emotional response. The body prepares to act with tight muscles and a pounding heart. When an action is not appropriate, the individual remains "uptight" (Coon, 1994, p. 442).

Wheeler and Frank (1988) suggest any full body exercise such as swimming, dancing, yoga, most sports, and walking to reduce stress. When exercise is used for stress mannagement, a daily routine is recommended. The effects of stress are diminished because the body has an outlet.

Coon (1994) also recommends meditation to "quiet" the body and "promote relaxation." According to Coon, "listening to or playing music, taking nature walks, enjoying hobbies, and the like can be meditations of sorts" (p. 443).

Dyslexics who persistently assume responsibility for learning/achievement (internal locus of control), seek support systems as needed, and stick to tasks are more apt to have effective coping styles and resilient personalities when stressors (medical, educational, familial, community) present themselves.

Figure 4.1 identifies positive resilient outcomes that in part are determined by coping style—this information can assist in planning social and academic support strategies.

Implications for Educators. The aforementioned information, among other factors, leads educators to Zhang's (2000) question, "How can we as educators use this information in the enhancement of teaching and learning?" (p. 51). The QUART (**QU**alitative **A**nalysis of **R**esilient **T**raits assessment (Spafford & Grosser, 2005; Spafford, 2004a) shown in Figure 4.2 was developed to evaluate an individual's resiliency with specific instructional implications for educators to consider as assessment terminology is operationalized.

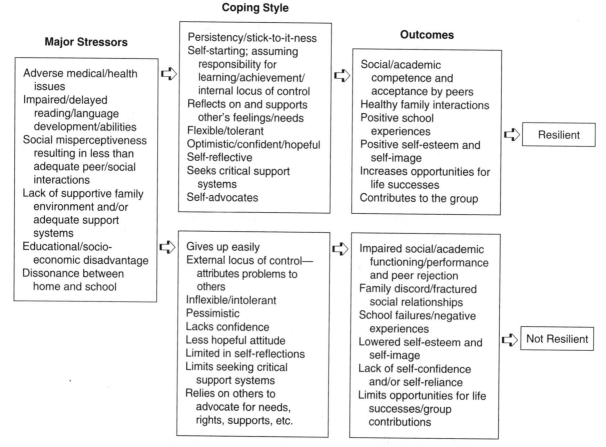

FIGURE 4.1   Identifying Positive Resilient Outcomes Assists in Planning Social and Academic Support Strategies

QUalitative Analysis of Resilient Traits (QUART)

General Instructions: Check the degree to which the student displays behaviors in the following areas. Space has been added for additional observations.

Name of Student _____

Evaluator _____   Grade _____   DOB _____   Date _____

	Strong				Diminished or Not Evident
Individual Protective Factors					
• persistent (stick-to-it-ness)	5	4	3	2	1
• self-efficacy (beliefs about one's ability to plan and complete actions to reach a goal or desired level of performance)	5	4	3	2	1
• positive self-esteem (positive evaluation of oneself)	5	4	3	2	1
• optimistic (anticipates the best, hopeful)	5	4	3	2	1
• confident learner (self assured learner)	5	4	3	2	1
• overall positive temperament (characteristic "frame of mind" is positive)	5	4	3	2	1
• socially perceptive (accurate evaluates social situations and determines appropriate actions).	5	4	3	2	1
• good reasoning ability (able to make inferences, draw conclusions and problem solve)	5	4	3	2	1
• advocates for self (works in an informed manner to obtain better academic or social opportunities or services)	5	4	3	2	1
• arena of talent or performance valued by others	5	4	3	2	1
Coping Style (additional)					
• self-starter (takes the initiative when needed)	5	4	3	2	1
• internal locus of control (assumes responsibility for learning/ achievement and attributes many successes to motivation, effort, resourcefulness)	5	4	3	2	1
• flexible (adaptable and accommodating when appropriate)	5	4	3	2	1
• self reflective (able to plan, self-monitor and evaluate one's own thinking, learning, comprehension, and social actions)	5	4	3	2	1
• seeks critical support systems (support from peers, teachers, family, and other community members)	5	4	3	2	1
• able to advocate for others (understands needs, feelings of peer group)	5	4	3	2	1

Major strengths _____

Major weaknesses _____

FIGURE 4.2 *QUalitative Analysis of Resilient Traits (QUART)*

Source: Carol A. Spafford & George S. Grosser, *Dyslexia and Reading Difficulties: Research and Resource Guide for Working with All Struggling Readers.* Copyright © 2005 by Pearson Education. May be reproduced for noncommercial purposes.

Teachers' Role Pivotal in Nurturing
Positive Resilient Behaviors

Make Wonderful What?   "You, as teachers, may provide the only chance children will have—to dream and make wonderful . . ." (Polacco, 2001, p. 31). *Make wonderful— what?* Patricia Polacco is referring to nurturing to fruition some of the special gifts and talents all students with dyslexia have by tapping into alternative expressive communicative styles (e.g., art, music, dance, and so on) discoverable by teachers when children are given opportunities to explore (e.g., keep drawing paper available so children can "retreat into their imaginations" when inspired).

Rosalie Fink (1998) confirms that teachers and tutors play pivotal roles in developing resiliency especially the qualities of persistence and tenacity while dyslexics struggle to learn to read and write. Words of inspiration, encouragement not to give up, appeals to others, and "second-chance situations" provided by understanding significant adults helped contribute to the resiliency observed in the dyslexic adults (n=60) studied by Fink.

The Role of Culture

There are fewer opportunities for some of our students to develop the necessary resiliency they need to achieve. Culture plays a role here. Some research, for example, shows that students of color experience greater levels of dissonance involving expectations and values between their lives at home and at school with this discord adversely impacting emotional and academic well-being (Nieto, 1996; Ogbu, 1987; Tatum, 1997). The home-school dissonance experienced can impact how resilient these students will be when confronted with learning challenges, struggles, and disabilities. Ladson-Billings (1994) suggests "culturally relevant teaching," where knowledge is "re-created, recycled, and shared by teachers and students alike (p. 25)."

Instructional Application: Knowing about Culturally Relevant Learning Styles

There are specific cognitive learning style preferences within the various cultural groups and subgroups within diverse societies. The Native American population in the United States, as an example, represents 500 diverse groups who do share some commonalities. There is often a disparity between the cognitive learning style preferences of the various Native American groups and the teaching style preferences of the dominant culture. Levasseur (1997) discussed commonalities in cognitive or learning style preferences for Native Americans as a group with the following characteristics providing important and relevant background for instructional preparations:

■ Many Native Americans use imagery as a primary tool for understanding new concepts.
■ Many Native Americans report a preference for modeling and demonstration versus trial and error.
■ Many Native Americans prefer to use legends and stories with symbolism, anthropomorphism, and metaphors to teach values and attitudes.

Ladson-Billings (1994) further states that culturally relevant teaching requires teachers to positively connect with students and their families with relationships grounded in equity and flexibility. Culturally responsive teaching practices as described by Knapp et al. (1995) need to be in place (with other personal and environmental factors as well): (1) be aware of students' backgrounds, (2) hold high expectations for students regardless of background, (3) design instruction to meet the needs of each student, and (4) show a recognition and appreciation for the knowledge and strengths students bring to the classrooms.

As an example, Heriberto immigrated to the United States from Puerto Rico in second grade. He was placed in a Sheltered-English immersion literacy program (see Chapter 11). His teacher, fluent in Spanish, held high expectations for Heriberto, providing him with grade-level content and support in his home language as needed. Clarifications were periodically provided in the home language to ensure Heriberto was making strong language connections. He also engaged in daily journal writing and read several books per week. Additionally, Heriberto had access to a word-to-word translation dictionary, language word walls, and a personal vocabulary ring of "new words." Heriberto benefited from optimal family cohesiveness and positive parental involvement in school studies. After receiving daily intensive literacy instruction in a three-hour block and after being evaluated as proficient in reading and writing in the language of the school, Heriberto was judged to be strongly resilient on all QUART factors. Second-language learners will typically not be strong in all QUART factors if not proficient in the language of the school.

The Role of the Family

The level of family cohesiveness and communication skills between family members are critical factors impacting adjustments for individuals with dyslexia and other learning disabilities (Grosser & Spafford, 2000; Spafford & Grosser, 1993). It would naturally follow that positive, nurturing cohesive family units that initially "lift" children during times of stress and then empower them to confidently overcome obstacles through their own efforts create critical opportunities to develop resilience.

According to Rostain, Power, and Atkins (1993), early diagnosis and intervention of learning disabilities typically results from some type of parent/family involvement and acceptance of the child's disability adding to resilience and later life successes. Families can be viewed as "literacy partners" because they can facilitate acquisition of good problem-solving behaviors, the development of respect and trust in the educational process, and the acquisition of insightful understandings that help to create successful learning experiences (Matlock, 1999).

Age or Developmental Levels and Familial Factors.   Does age or developmental level impact the degree or amount of resiliency a child will have or exhibit? Preliminary findings by the current authors (see Spafford & Grosser, 2004; Spafford, 2004a) found surprising results to this question. It was expected that children in earliest elementary grades would show less resiliency on the QUART profile than upper elementary or older students who would have had more opportunities to develop individual protective factors and a resilient coping style. However, preliminary findings (see Spafford & Grosser, 2004; Spafford, 2004a) show that even some children at the youngest grade levels show strongly resilient personalities similar to students in the upper grades.

As examples, Steve in grade 1 and Amy in grade 5 demonstrate identical QUART profiles (rated "5" in all categories). Both are strong students and class leaders. Both consistently display individual protective factors and a resilient coping style relative to other first and fifth graders, respectively. Both have siblings in the same school, strong students as well and rated similarly by teachers. The positive environmental factors of connections to competent others, positive relationships with extended family members, effective parenting, and good schooling (Hauser, 1999) are considered significant factors in Steve's and Amy's situations. Additionally, family cohesiveness and communication skills between family members have positively impacted their development of resilient personalities.

Strongly Resilient Kindergarten Students?   Is it possible for an entering kindergarten (K) student to have a strongly resilient QUART profile? As expected, preliminary research (see Spafford & Grosser, 2004; Spafford, 2004a) indicates that K students need time to develop individual protective factors and strongly resilient coping styles but many kindergarten students show strong signs of resiliency. In the K profile of Victor, an average student, confidence building continues to be a priority as for many other K students, because as emerging readers there is sometimes the element of uncertainty when approaching the printed page. What may be surprising to the reader is the fact that many K students, as with Victor, show strong advocacy skills for others.

The K profile of a struggling reader (Figure 4.3) shows a student with a positive attitude who is able to advocate for others but is unable to advocate for himself and plan and complete actions to achieve goals. The struggling K reader is transitioning into English and does not yet have the conversation proficiency needed to make strong connections to the printed page. Struggling K students transitioning into the language of the school are able to acquire individual protective factors and resilient coping styles but need time to acquire (second) language and reading proficiency to build resiliency, which is strongly related to literacy (Spafford & Grosser, 2004). The QUART profile of an average K student is shown for comparison in Figure 4.4.

Some K students are given in the highest ratings in all individual protective factors and coping style categories, but this is not the norm. As an example, Kindred, age 5, was reading on a third-grade level upon entering kindergarten and was placed in an

QUalitative Analysis of Resilient Traits (QUART)

General Instructions: Check the degree to which the student displays behaviors in the following areas. Space has been added for additional observations.

Name of Student _____ struggling reader _____ Date _____

Evaluator _____ Grade ___K___ DOB _____
                NOTE: Second Language Learner - Transitioning into English

	Strong			Diminished or Not Evident	
Individual Protective Factors					
• persistent (stick-to-it-ness)	5	4	3	②	1
• self-efficacy (beliefs about one's ability to plan and complete actions to reach a goal or desired level of performance)	5	4	3	2	①
• positive self-esteem (positive evaluation of oneself)	5	4	3	②	1
• optimistic (anticipates the best, hopeful)	5	4	3	②	1
• confident learner (self assured learner)	5	4	3	②	1
• overall positive temperament (characteristic "frame of mind" is positive)	5	4	③	2	1
• socially perceptive (accurate evaluates social situations and determines appropriate actions).	5	4	3	②	1
• good reasoning ability (able to make inferences, draw conclusions and problem solve)	5	4	3	②	1
• advocates for self (works in an informed manner to obtain better academic or social opportunities or services)	5	4	3	②	1
• arena of talent or performance valued by others _____ positive attitude _____	⑤	4	3	2	1
Coping Style (additional)					
• self-starter (takes the initiative when needed)	5	4	3	2	①
• internal locus of control (assumes responsibility for learning/ achievement and attributes many successes to motivation, effort, resourcefulness)	5	4	3	2	①
• flexible (adaptable and accommodating when appropriate)	5	4	③	2	1
• self reflective (able to plan, self-monitor and evaluate one's own thinking, learning, comprehension, and social actions)	5	4	3	2	①
• seeks critical support systems (support from peers, teachers, family. and other community members)	5	4	③	2	1
• able to advocate for others (understands needs, feelings of peer group)	5	④	3	2	1

Major strengths _____

Major weaknesses _____

FIGURE 4.3   *QUalitative Analysis of Resilient Traits (QUART)*

QUalitative Analysis of Resilient Traits (QUART)

General Instructions: Check the degree to which the student displays behaviors in the following areas. Space has been added for additional observations.

Name of Student ___average student_____ Date _After 8 months of schooling_

Evaluator _____ Grade ___K___ DOB _____

	Strong				Diminished or Not Evident
Individual Protective Factors					
• persistent (stick-to-it-ness)	5	④	3	2	1
• self-efficacy (beliefs about one's ability to plan and complete actions to reach a goal or desired level of performance)	5	④	3	2	1
• positive self-esteem (positive evaluation of oneself)	5	④	3	2	1
• optimistic (anticipates the best, hopeful)	5	④	3	2	1
• confident learner (self assured learner)	5	4	③	2	1
• overall positive temperament (characteristic "frame of mind" is positive)	5	④	3	2	1
• socially perceptive (accurate evaluates social situations and determines appropriate actions).	5	④	3	2	1
• good reasoning ability (able to make inferences, draw conclusions and problem solve)	5	④	3	2	1
• advocates for self (works in an informed manner to obtain better academic or social opportunities or services)	5	④	3	2	1
• arena of talent or performance valued by others _Puts others first_	⑤	4	3	2	1
Coping Style (additional)					
• self-starter (takes the initiative when needed)	5	④	3	2	1
• internal locus of control (assumes responsibility for learning/ achievement and attributes many successes to motivation, effort, resourcefulness)	⑤	4	3	2	1
• flexible (adaptable and accommodating when appropriate)	⑤	4	3	2	1
• self reflective (able to plan, self-monitor and evaluate one's own thinking, learning, comprehension, and social actions)	5	④	3	2	1
• seeks critical support systems (support from peers, teachers, family, and other community members)	⑤	4	3	2	1
• able to advocate for others (understands needs, feelings of peer group)	⑤	4	3	2	1

Major strengths _____

Major weaknesses _____

FIGURE 4.4 *QUalitative Analysis of Resilient Traits (QUART)*

accelerated literacy program. She was rated as strongly resilient in all categories (all 5s). Being an avid reader before entering kindergarten helped Kindred develop confidence as a reader and learner. A class leader, self-efficacious, and a self-starter, Kindred was a strong advocate for herself and others. Kindred's family was actively involved in many school activities, including the PTO and other school activities. They are considered a positive, cohesive family unit—during those times of natural stress for young children, Kindred's parents have made a point to empower her to confidently overcome obstacles through her own efforts (internal locus of control), creating critical opportunities to develop resilience and confidence as a learner. Kindred has access to many books from a wide range of genres. Her mother (a teacher) and father have facilitated the development of flexibility, empathy, tolerance, and "advocating for others" by example and through literature "book chats."

Literature Studies and Resiliency

According to Bernice Cullinan and Lee Galda (1998), good literature allows children to "explore their own feelings, shape their own values, and imagine lives beyond the one they live . . . they gain insight into human experience and begin to understand themselves better" (pp. 5–6). Themed literature materials similar to the ones mentioned that key in on "loving kindness," "caring," and "outreach" to others fosters positive coping styles and the building of self-efficacy and positive self-esteems—*important to building resilient personalities.*

Choosing the Right Books to Nurture Resiliency

Teachers need to carefully choose books after evaluating a student's strengths, prior knowledge, skills, and interests—these considerations help to engage the reader (Fink, 1995/1996, 1998) with the goal of fostering the development of lifelong reading (Fischer & Thompson, 2002/2003). Additionally, authentic books that present opportunities for deeper cultural understandings should be available for even the youngest students (Walker-Dalhouse, 1992). Teachers can use these readings to help children make connections to their own cultural and linguistic experiences (Opitz, 1998), thus building important individual protective factors and resilient readers. At the same time, teachers need to find those "anchor" points or connections (Pearson & Johnson, 1978) for students with dyslexia who by nature of their reading disability have read less resulting in comparatively less background knowledge to use when they interact with text.

Many journals/magazines and education organizations publish recommended books with resources and learning activities/lessons that merge research with appropriate cultural and linguistic practices while building resiliency.

For example, noted author and Newbery Award reviewer Judy Freeman (2001) recommended the following culturally and linguistically diverse literature K–8 titles with accompanying learning activities to teach children about sharing and caring—all about love in its many forms: *Subira Subira* by Tololwa M. Mollel (grades 1–6); *Gloria's Way* by Ann Cameron (grades 1–3); *My Very Own Room/Mi Proprio cuartito* by Amada Irma Pèrez (grades K–4); *The Girl Who Spun Gold* by Virginia Hamilton (grades 2–6); *Satchel Paige* by Lesa Cline-Ransome (grades 2–5); *The Girl Who Struck Out Babe Ruth* by Jean L. S. Patrick (grades 1–4); *Adaline Falling Star* by Mary Pope Osborne (grades 4–8); *Sacajawea* by Joseph Bruchac (grades 5–8); *The Graduation of Jake Moon* by Barbara Park (grades 5–8); *A Year Down Yonder* by Richard Peck (grades 5–8); *The Raft* by Jim LaMarche (grades K–5); *Michelangelo* by Diane Stanley (grades 4–8); *Lucky Pennies and Hot Chocolate with Grandpa* by Carol Diggery Shields (grades PK–1).

Instructional Application: The Work of Yoko Kawashima Watkins

Books That Help Build Resilient Personalities

Biographies that depict real people who developed resilient coping styles under times of extreme duress or stress allow readers to more fully develop empathy and reflect on important growth or survival characteristics. The dialogue between book characters is particularly helpful in modeling individual protective factors such as:

- Self-efficacy
- Positive temperament
- Positive self-esteem (self-concept)
- Faith
- Hopefulness (optimism)
- Self-advocacy (also, advocacy for others)

For examples, for middle school and high school students, the biography, *My Brother, My Sister, and I* by Yoko Kawashima Watkins (1986) provides a true story of courage and survival for 11-year-old Yoko, her mother, and sister who are forced to flee their beautiful home in Korea during World War II. Sample dialogue in the book shows how Yoko and her family developed the resiliency they needed to survive the harshest of conditions. Each quote on page 75 could be a point of discussion considering the context or situation involved. Role-playing and discussing how to generalize concepts presented to other life situations provide opportunities for teacher and peer role modeling.

"Be kind to everyone—spread your goodness wherever you go." (Yoko's father's last words—p. 228)

"The Kawashima children can become a few drops of water in the ocean and make ripples that will spread humanity." (Hideyo, p. 212)

"Each one of us has a purpose on this earth. We were put here to develop ourselves." (Hideyo, p. 51)

"Go at your own pace. You will eventually achieve." (Yoko's father's words of encouragement, p. 7)

"War robs everyone's gentle heart." (Yoko, p. 150)

(surviving war) "Our mental wounds will never heal—you have to learn to develop inner strength." (Ko, p. 63)

(surviving war) "I realize our togetherness each day was precious in minutes, hours and moments." (Yoko, p. 97)

"Bound by ties of love and family honor, they never lose faith." (backcover)

"If you share your worries with me, it will be only half the burden on your back—if you share your joy it will make us doubly joyful." (Ko to Yoko, p. 132)

Summary

Our review of the literature suggests definite advantages to adding "resiliency" as the third "r" to all intervention programs for students with dyslexia resulting in an intervention equation, "Reading, 'Riting, Resiliency." When students learn the ability to quickly bounce back or recover from stressors, frustrations, and failures due to a personal resolve to persevere in spite of academic/social obstacles, they develop more positive self-concepts and feelings of self-efficacy, enhancing the motivation to learn and succeed. An individual's resiliency changes over the course of a lifetime and is impacted by (1) individual protective (positive traits or characteristics) factors, (2) environmental (familial and community-oriented) factors, (3) stressors, and (4) coping styles. It would appear that "stick-to-it-ness," or persistence and motivation, are critical individual protective factors. Resulting outcomes can be positive (i.e., a resilient dyslexic) or negative (i.e., a dyslexic who lacks the resiliency to reach optimal life and career successes).

Stressors related to the goings on in everyday life (too much to do), learning (tried but I can't learn that), and significant life events (first day in a new school) can create feelings of frustration, fear, and anxiety for the dyslexic.

Coping styles (characteristic learned responses to stressors) evidenced by flexibility, tolerance, self-reflection, empathy, or support for others with the desire to contribute to the group are most likely to contribute to resilient personalities. In this regard, we need to create many different kinds of literacy opportunities for all individuals to develop their potentials, aptitudes, abilities, and interests (Aksornkool, 2002). The ability to use a variety of ways to relax or manage stress (e.g., exercise, meditation, enjoying a hobby, listening to music, taking a nature walk) can be modeled and taught. Self-efficacy (individual protective factor), or our feelings or thoughts about how competent we are in various areas, determines in large part how resilient one is to life's stressors. Individuals with positive self-efficacy are empathic and intolerant of injustice, with a sense of fairness and a social conscience—these can be nurtured through literature and thought-provoking discussions where one continually reevaluates opinions and prejudices (Watkins, 2001). The QUART (*QUalitative Analysis of Resilient Traits*) assessment was developed to evaluate an individual's resiliency with specific instructional implications for educators to consider as the assessment terminology is operationalized.

Does age or developmental level impact the degree or amount of resiliency a child will have or exhibit? Preliminary findings by the current authors (Spafford & Grosser, 2004) found surprising results to this question. Even some children at the youngest grade levels show strongly resilient personalities similar to students in the upper grades. Kindergarten students can have strongly resilient personalities as well, but generally need more time to strengthen necessary individual protective factors and a resilient coping style because as emerging readers, K students are often problem solving with text as they develop reading proficiency. Second-language learners will typically not be strong in all QUART factors if not proficient in the language of the school.

With consistent or intensive personally relevant and culturally sensitive reading and writing support and practice, confident, engaged, and enthusiastic readers and writers emerge. More opportunities to apply reading and writing strategies and interact with text mean that the percentage of reading and writing errors or problems decreases, producing more effective/strategic and **resilient** readers and writers. These all contribute to the development of literate, socially sensitive, and fulfilled individuals who can self-advocate when needed and advocate for others as well. Chapter 5 will next present a review of controversial intervention approaches.

CHAPTER

5   Controversial Theories

Most educators and researchers in the field would agree upon the importance of research in searching out the cause(s) of dyslexia. This necessarily means we'll make mistakes along the way; that is, some treatments or interventions might be initially recommended that further research will not bear out as constructive endeavors.

Many practitioners would agree that the causal link to dyslexia is rooted in some type of neurological dysfunctioning that emanates from specific areas of the brain. We will present some controversial perspectives, because it is important to read, reason, and review so that reasonable and well-grounded educational planning results. It is critical to be well informed regarding those approaches that might not work or might not even directly impact the learning/social problems of individuals with dyslexia.

The Hawthorne Effect

The field of dyslexia research and the study of learning disabilities has experienced some provocative, unusual, and inconsistent findings. Often, parents, teachers, and other concerned persons will search for miracle cures to relieve the reading disability of the dyslexic child. First and foremost, we must stress that no conclusive research has been provided by anyone to substantiate the idea that a final cure for dyslexia is at hand. The best we can hope for with our present knowledge and available technology is to produce a combination of alleviating measures, using an eclectic approach that will be keyed to the most effective instructional methods. This process can allow us to assist the dyslexic in acquiring compensatory approaches to reading and writing. In some of the following chapters, we will be discussing some helpful procedures and methods for dealing with academic and social problems. Many disorders and deficits can be positively affected regardless of the type of intervention efforts. This is partly due to the **Hawthorne Effect,** or a positive change in behavior not due to the treatment mode, but rather to the individual's sense of participation in important research or desire to please an important supervisor, mentor, teacher, and so on. In a condition that has behavioral components, it may well be the case that the person's strivings and earnest efforts to do better may carry more weight than a treatment for the problem.

Treatment Considerations

Several controversial approaches, cures, intervention measures, and cures will be discussed in this chapter. Our intention is to enable concerned professionals and parents, as well as learning disabled individuals themselves, to make wise decisions among the many possible modes of treatment being available. Table 5.1 lists criteria to consider when selecting a treatment for a dyslexic or learning-disabled (LD) student.

TABLE 5.1   Criteria for Choosing an Intervention for a Learning Disability

---

- Weigh the likely positive and/or negative outcomes.
- Consider the theoretical support for the suggested approach or therapy.
- Take into account the expense involved in using the intervention.
- Consider the feasibility of implementing the intervention.
- Apply your own common sense. To help deal with a reading problem, the intervention *must* be reading-related. (Worrall, 1990a, 1990b)

Cerebellar-Vestibular Dysmetria (CVD) (Unproven Treatment)

According to Frank and Levinson (1977), the neural pathway from the balance organs of the inner ear to the cerebellum and the external eye muscle control nuclei of the midbrain are involved in cerebellar vestibular (CV) balance functions. Abnormal functioning in this part of the brain, however, will not be revealed in any test of cerebral cortical malfunction.

Blurring and Reversals Linked to CV System

Frank and Levinson (1977) say that the dyslexics' problems with ocular fixation and sequential scanning are analogous to the tracking difficulty we all have when trying to read signs from a rapidly moving vehicle. The impaired cerebellar-vestibular system, they claim, normally inhibits the rate at which sensory information is fed to the cerebral cortex. With a malfunctioning cerebellar-vestibular system, the rapid influx of data leads to the subjective experiences of blurring and reversals.

Internal Releasing Mechanism (IRM)

Motion sickness is hypothesized to be the result of an **internal releasing mechanism (IRM)** triggered by the excessively rapid inflow of sensory information to the cortex. This condition warns the organism that something is wrong. Frank and Levinson report that seasickness medications such as Dramamine can restore the cerebellum to normal functioning so that it can perform its task of inhibiting and thereby slowing down the flow of sensory information into cerebral sensory areas. Accordingly, Dramamine is hypothesized to relieve dyslexia (Frank & Levinson, 1977). Confirming evidence by other researchers regarding the efficacy of this approach has not been forthcoming.

Levinson (1988) also argues that his dyslexic patients nearly all showed attention deficits, and that ADD (Attention Deficit Disorder) is to be expected in all dyslexics. Wilsher and Taylor (1987) have criticized Levinson's work on several accounts.

First, there are many persons with cerebellar-vestibular difficulties who have no problems with reading. Second, a study of dyslexics by Brown et al. (1983) showed that this population had no greater percentage of people with cerebellar-vestibular dysfunctions than the general public. Third, Levinson's research involved the administration of anti-seasickness drugs to all his reading-disabled patients. There were no placebo controls, because Levinson contends, it would be unethical to deny treatment to any patient (Levinson, 1980). Fourth, he claimed positive results for his treatment on the basis of the self-reports of the research subjects. This fourth point emphasizes the vital importance of the third: Children given prescribed treatment from a qualified medical doctor may show either or both a placebo effect (faith in the treatment) or a Hawthorne Effect (a strong desire to produce an interesting result for the important person doing research on them).

Neural Organization Technique (NOT) (Unproven Method)

Ocular Lock Syndrome

Ferreri and Wainwright (1984) proposed a treatment for dyslexia that entails the manual manipulation of the skull bones in order to cure the problem. They attribute reading disability to a sphenoid wing malfunction (p. 79). This bone problem prevents the eye muscles from working freely, resulting, they say, in an **ocular lock.** The two important skull bones for this condition are the sphenoid and the temporal bones, according to Ferreri and Wainwright.

Chiropractic Interventions

Ferreri and Wainwright (1984) believe that the muscles of the eyes are attached to bones that have been "subluxed" for long periods of time. Since the eye muscles have been altered in length, they eyes can only work under "stress" involving "neural deficit" (p. 80). They hold that the key to treatment is intervention involving the eye muscles. Part of the therapy involves locating indicator muscles and then strengthening those muscles by having the patient view stimuli in the direction of the "greatest weakness." Cranial manipulations are utilized that supposedly correct difficulties with cranial faults and eye muscle imbalances.

Physiological and Psychological Inconsistencies with NOT

Some researchers (Worrall, 1990a, 1990b; Silver, 1987) have refuted the basic premise of the Ferreri-Wainwright approach by pointing out the physiological and psychological inconsistencies with this theory. For example, Ferreri and Wainwright (1984) claim that cranial bones move; this does not appear to be the case. According to Worrall, any attempt to manipulate the skull bones may produce injury to the dyslexic child (for example, pressure on the eye may be transmitted to the brain via the optic nerve, bringing on seizures). Clearly, this is one remedy that should *be avoided.*

Megavitamins (Unproven Approach)

Cott (1977, 1985) is one of the best known proponents of the use of massive doses of vitamins in the treatment of children with learning disabilities. The orthomolecular school of psychology holds that any behavioral or emotional abnormality is due to the existence of a chemical disorder in the brain. **Megavitamins** (and often, megaminerals) are said by the proponents of this view to have the capability of reordering the brain's chemistry and restoring neurological health. There is limited research to support this viewpoint.

Hypoglycemia, Hyperinsulinism, and Dysinsulinism

The basis for Cott's (1977) vitamin supplements is traced to his basic premise that, "many learning-disabled children are found to have either hypoglycemia, hyperinsulinism, or dysinsulinism; cane sugar and rapidly absorbed carbohydrate foods should be eliminated from their diets" (p. 31). Cott maintains that wheat products and milk frequently occur in foods containing sugar and are the culprits for producing what he has coined the "cerebral allergies" seen in the behavior of overactive and learning disabled children.

Diet Elimination and Supplements

Cott has recommended an elimination diet of wheat, eggs, corn and corn products, and beef. This diet is similar in theory to the one suggested by Feingold (discussed later in this chapter) recommending elimination of foods with naturally occurring salicylates, artificial flavors, and colors that occur in foods like sodas, frankfurters, apples, oranges, cucumbers, and so on. Cott also believes in a type of diet supplement whereby megavitamins are used to maintain the body's chemistry. His research has pointed to biochemical causes of learning disabilities, especially among low-income families.

Basis for Megavitamin Treatment

The basis for megavitamin treatment is rooted in the belief that minerals provided in megavitamin capsules such as zinc and selenium, for example, protect the individual against accumulating lethal doses of another mineral, in this case, cadmium. The accumulation of toxic metals, Cott contends, interferes with pyruvic acid levels and the subsequent curtailing of energy to the brain. We would agree that in some cases—e.g., lead overdoses—research has shown that toxic levels interfere with learning and normal everyday functioning. However, the use of mineral supplements *has not* been shown to be an effective preventive measure against the acquisition of physical conditions or dyslexia/learning disabilities.

American Psychiatric Association Task Force on Vitamin Therapy in Psychiatry

American Psychiatric Association Task Force on Vitamin Therapy in Psychiatry (1973) issued a report on the validity of megavitamin therapies. The report states that such treatments *are not supported* by scientific data. The unrestricted use of megaminerals and of the fat-soluble vitamins (vitamins A, D, and E), at least, may be damaging to one's health. Arnold, Christopher, Huestis, and Smeltzer (1978) found that in a sample of children with learning problems, there were no noticeable gains in academic performance with this treatment.

Feingold K-P (Kaiser Permanente) Diet (Unproven Approach)

Ben Feingold (1976), creator of the "Feingold K-P Diet" has proposed that the learning disabled and hyperkinetic child has been affected by additives placed into our processed foods to sweeten the taste of the food or to dye it with an appealing color. Feingold first used his diet in 1965 to assist a woman with an acute case of hives. Salicylates (natural compounds found in some fruits and vegetables) were removed from her diet and supposedly cured the hives (Feingold, 1976). According to Feingold (1976), "The K-P diet, which eliminates all artificial food colors and flavors as well as foods with a natural salicylate radical, will control the behavioral disturbance in 30% to 50% (depending on the sample) of both normal and neurologically damaged children" (p. 558). In essence, Feingold is linking the ingestion of food colors and flavorings to learning disabilities and hyperactivity.

Feingold insists that since drugs should be the last treatment mode for learning disabilities and hyperkinesis, certainly improving the diet should be the initial treatment choice.

Elimination Diet Program

Some cases of learning disabilities and most cases of hyperactivity should be approached with the **elimination diet** program, according to Feingold (1975, 1976, 1977; Feingold & Feingold, 1979). Synthetic chemicals, particularly those added to soft drinks, hot dogs, luncheon meats, and candies, for example, are the suspect items to be eliminated from the diet. Feingold presents recipes for homemade mayonnaise and candy, even for meat dishes, salads, cakes, soups, and other main dishes. When discussing some cereal manufacturers, Feingold says, "I find it hard to believe that they are not aware of the dangers of high sugar content; or that the paint pot of colors inside many boxes is of absolutely no benefit and of no possible harm" (Feingold, 1975, p. 79). The K-P diet eliminates these food items along with natural salicylates.

Dietary Approaches and Cognition

Some case studies have supported Feingold's basic tenets, but these have been criticized for methodological problems, especially the lack of adequate controls (Sieben, 1977; Spring & Sandoval, 1976). Kavale and Forness (1985) have established that dietary approaches have little impact on cognitive functioning. However, face validity would tell us that excessive amounts of sugar or caffeine would overstimulate (Powers, 1975) or understimulate central nervous system functioning. Harris and Sipay (1990) suggest that the key, in the instance of caffeine, appears to be the amount ingested in determining whether a child would be overstimulated or understimulated.

Healthy Diets Commonsensible for All

Much research needs to be done in the areas of diet and basic nutrition; it would be difficult for us to recommend any kind of dietary restrictions because of the limited and somewhat flawed research presented thus far. Although Feingold claims that his K-P diet is harmless (Feingold & Feingold, 1979), Connors et al. (1976) have found the diet to be nutritionally lacking.

Analysis of Mineral Levels

The analysis of levels of minerals, particularly heavy metals (i.e., lead, cadmium, aluminum, arsenic, and mercury) has been linked by a handful of researchers (Marlowe, Cossairt, Welch, & Errera, 1984; Perino & Ernhart, 1974; Struempler, Larson, & Rimland, 1985; Thatcher & Lester, 1985) to reading problems. High levels of cadmium have been linked to behavioral problems and high levels of magnesium and lead to both reading and behavioral difficulties.

Proven Toxigen—Lead

Lead has been the most researched toxigen, which when even in small amounts has been hypothesized to have a negative impact on learning ability (David et al., 1976; Dubey, 1932; Marlowe, Cossairt, Welch, & Errera, 1984). Needleman et al. (1979) studied first- and second-grade children from two suburban school systems and found that children with higher lead concentrations in the blood performed significantly more poorly on the Wechsler Intelligence Scale for Children (WISC) than children with similar socioeconomic backgrounds and lower lead blood levels. Perino and Ernhart (1974) similarly found a negative correlation between cognitive and sensorimotor abilities, and lead blood levels with 3- and 6-year-old children. Although the Centers for Disease Control established in 1970 that lead in "30 micrograms (30/1,000,000ths of a gram) per 100 cc (cubic centimeter = 1/1000th of a liter) of blood" be considered biologically toxic for children (as cited in Marlowe et al., 1984, p. 421), there is a *shortage* of research sufficient to link dyslexia or learning disabilities specifically to toxic lead levels.

Lead Levels Considered Toxic for Children

A 1991 study of over 1,000 Mexican American children persuaded the Centers for Disease Control to lower the critical lead concentration to 10 micrograms (only 10/1,000,000ths of a gram) (remember that a gram is as small a weight as .035 ounces) per deciliter (100 cc) of blood. The expected age-related increase in height was decreased for children with above-average lead levels in their blood. The height loss averaged four-tenths of an inch, and, in extreme cases, was as great as a full inch, according to A.R. Frisancho, one of the investigators (*Science News*, 1991, p. 189).

Landesman-Dwyer, Ragozin, and Little (1981) found *no relationship* between blood lead levels and reading problems, lowered intelligence, and behavior disorders. These researchers studied several children in a factory area where lead was released into the environment. They determined that social factors were more related to the learning and behavioral problems observed than was the released lead.

Chelation Treatment.   **Chelation treatment** has been found to reverse the negative effects of lead poisoning (David et al., 1976). The relationship between lead and learning disabilities is far from clear, and too few studies are available to draw any conclusions at this point in time.

Link between Hair Mineral Concentrations and Learning Questioned.   Silver (1987) doubts that hair mineral analysis results can be generalized to the amount of mineral trace elements in the body itself. Certainly internal excesses would have to be assessed in relation to cerebral metabolic functioning, as brain functioning *has never been* causally linked to hair composition. Thatcher and Lester (1985) found that higher lead and cadmium concentrations were associated with a decrease in EEG amplitude. Regardless, Sieben (1977) has reported that there are *no concrete data* to support the link between mineral concentrations and learning. Struempler, Larson, and Rimland (1985) admit that "the state of the art (associations between mineral concentration and learning and behavioral problems) does not allow firm conclusions to be drawn" (p. 611).

Tomatis Audiological-Psycho-Phonology (APP)
Method (Unproven)

Based on audiometric test results, A.A. Tomatis (1978) developed a new theory of hearing, according to which the ear continuously undergoes retraining in response to stimuli of various tones. He has found that loss of hearing for high-frequency sound impairs the ability of sopranos to sing high notes. Children with ear infections become poor listeners and may develop language problems and learning disorders. Tomatis has a remedial treatment of playing higher frequency sounds to a young child with dyslexia via earphones. He claims that autistic children can be stirred to remove the high walls that they have erected to protect themselves from the language world.

Ontogenetic Perspective—APP

Kershner et al. (1986) conducted a one-year and two-year evaluation of the Tomatis Listening Training Program (LTP) with learning-disabled children. These authors found only a single group effect—that is, children who were in the placebo group were superior in performance on a Seashore Rhythm test, which is a measure of auditory discrimination. Essentially, these researchers report *negative findings* regarding achievement gains from the use of the Tomatis method. In fact, Kershner et al. (1986) are rather harsh in their assessment of this program, ". . . such programs [as the Tomatis Listening Training Program] promise what readily available procedures cannot—optimism about reversing the academic deficiencies of LD children . . . [p. 43] . . . the LTP may delay or interfere with LD children's progress toward acquiring certain fundamental auditory skills . . ." (p. 50).

Postural Rehabilitation—the Delacato System (Unproven Method)

Establishing Cerebral Dominance

Delacato's (1963) training procedures include creeping, walking, visual targeting, focusing the gaze at various distances, balancing oneself on a narrow beam, jumping up and down on the trampoline, among others, to establish cerebral dominance, which he says is lacking in dyslexics. The establishment of cerebral dominance, according to Delacato, requires that many parts of the body should be given practice simultaneously. For example, do not train the poorly developed, learning-disabled children just to be right-handed. To quote Delacato, "we are not training a foot, an eye or a hand, but . . . we are in fact retraining a hemisphere of the brain. The retraining of one area alone cannot result in the establishment of hemispheric dominance" (Delacato, 1963, p. 122).

Delacato Theory and the Test of Time

The original Delacato theory was based on a study of brain-injured children by Doman et al. (1960); the entire report is reprinted in Delacato's (1963) book. No other empirical evidence has been presented since. Overall, the Delacato system *does not* seem to have passed the test of time.

Delacato System's Revival in the 1980s: Confirming Research Lacking

Cathexis School of Transactional Analysis (TA). The Delacato system was partially revived in the 1980s in the work of the Australian researcher, Maggie White (1988), who adheres to the Cathexis School of Transactional Analysis (TA). TA refers to the "I'm OK" school of psychological counseling. White (1988) cites Robert Lefroy of Western Australia, a remedial teacher, as having modified the Delacato training system.

Lefroy–Delacato Program.   Lefroy (1975) (as cited by White, 1988) has retrained children with dyslexia with a set of basic physical "patterning" exercises that reenact the crawling or creeping stage of development. Seven dyslexics, Lefroy claims, all showed disturbances in that developmental stage, and training improved dyslexia.

Ayres Program of Sensory-Integration Therapy.   White (1988) also cites the Ayres Program of Sensory-Integration Therapy. The Ayres program, White claims, works with 5- to 7-year-olds, while the Lefroy-Delacato program is successful for older children (ages 8 to 16). White also supports the Strauss-Lehtinen (1947) recommendation of a well-structured and stimulus-reduced school environment.

The present authors do not recommend any of these approaches as presented because of limited evidence-based research that confirms usefulness in alleviating problems typically associated with dyslexia or other learning disabilities.

Unconditional Positive Regard.   A further recommendation by White (1988), which is positively embraced by the authors, is for therapeutic tutoring to occur in a nurturing environment or showing, in Carl Roger's phrase, "unconditional positive regard." Creative curriculum planning that keys in on the learning-disabled child's strengths is also a substantive recommendation.

Perceptual-Motor Approaches Linked to IQ/Academic Progress (Unproven)

It is true that many children with dyslexia exhibit lags in motor development and could benefit from motor training programs. However, not all children with dyslexia have motor problems. Therefore, administering motor programs routinely to children and individuals with learning disabilities *is not* warranted. As Janet W. Lerner so aptly stated, "Motor training alone will not teach a child to read, any more than eyeglasses alone will instantly transform a nonreader into a bookworm" (1971, p. 107). Frostig (1968) also cautions against delaying academic remedial procedures in favor of motor-training programs alone. There are some perceptual-motor theories that directly link the learning problems and IQ/academic progress of individuals with learning disabilities to inadequate perceptual-motor skills development.

Kephart's Influence

A perceptual-motor theory of learning disabilities was offered by Kephart (1960, 1971), who believed that perceptual-development activities allow children to develop stable and reliable conceptualizations about the world. Normally developing children exhibit adequate perceptual-motor patterns by age 6, according to Kephart (1963). For the learning disabled child, the dimensions of time and space are unstable and interfere with school learning. Learning-disabled children are supposedly disorganized cognitively, motorically, and perceptually.

Motor Generalizations and LD According to Kephart.   Kephart believes that there are four motor generalizations that children must master in order to achieve academically in school: maintenance of posture and balance, contact, locomotion, and receipt and propulsion. When a child fails to integrate perceptual information with motor information, distorted perceptions result that can interfere with stored cognitive information. In this instance, Kephart states that a perceptual-motor match cannot be made.

Perceptual-Motor Training Programs—Academically Inefficient Alone

Kephart's teaching program focuses on ameliorating perceptual-motor deficiencies of children with learning disabilities by using walking boards and balance beams, jumping and hopping activities, identifying body parts, mimicking body movements, moving through physical obstacle courses, visual-ocular pursuit activities, copying geometric shapes, and other activities. Lerner's (1971) basic assessment that "there has thus far been little research evidence to indicate that practice in motor training directly results in increased academic achievement" (p. 100) is still true today. The research of Hammill, Goodman, and Wiederholt (1974) and Kavale and Mattison (1983) would confirm the *inefficiency* of such motor programs alone on learning to read.

Barsch and Movigenics

The Movigenic Theory was proposed by Barsch in the late 1960s as another theory of movement related to the problems of children with learning disabilities. Barsch (1965, 1967, 1968) looks at several dimensions that are thought to impact learning in general: (1) children acquire information through their percepto-cognitive systems; (2) movement occurs within space and children must learn to move efficiently through space; (3) motor skills are acquired in a developmental sequential manner; and (4) language skills are derived from visual-spatial grounding (with movement efficiency being the key).

The Movigenic Curriculum—Lack of Research Support. According to Barsch, a motor curriculum must be developed for the child with learning disabilities in order to bridge the gap between motor skill development and academic skills acquisition. The child is initially supposed to develop a state of proprioceptive awareness, or an awareness of the environment and his or her movements in relation to the environment. Children are directed to touch objects in the environment and to locate and move body parts around environmental objects. The mechanics of movement are then relearned properly so that children can relate time to movement to learning. An example would be to teach children how to posture themselves so that they move their bodies in relation to gravity. Planned kneeling, sitting, standing, and walking activities are involved. More complex motor acts are introduced that develop shifting capacities in rates and patterns of movement. For example, children are instructed to walk and then hop, but to continue hopping after every fifth clap. As in the case of Kephart's program, there is *little research* to substantiate the Movigenic Curriculum on learning to read.

The Eye Patch Treatment (Unproven Method)

Unstable Eye Movements

Unstable eye movement control is the prevailing deficit in dyslexia, according to Stein and Fowler (1985). In view of this hypothesis, they advocate the use of an eye patch to occlude the problem eye so that the dyslexic child can attain reliable "ocular motor/macular associations by eliminating the possibility of discrepant retinal signals being projected by the two eyes" (p. 72). Stein and Fowler suggest that the reading problems of dyslexics are characterized by letters and words that "move around, reverse themselves, or jump over each other" (p. 70). According to Stein and Fowler (1985), all reading problems involve errors in locating letters within words, letter reversals, letter rotations, etc. Even attempts by normal readers to read under difficult conditions can produce such errors (Grosser & Trzeciak, 1981). It is possible that a very few individuals are called dyslexics when their reading disability results from disorders of the external eye muscles, but they are probably the exception rather than the rule.

Eye Vergence (or the Zen of Oculomotor Maintenance)

Stein and Fowler (1985) report that 68 percent of a large sample of dyslexic children had unstable **vergence** eye movement control (unfixed reference) on the Dunlop test, which measures the level of an individual's eye movement control. Almost all of a set of proficient readers (matched for age and intelligence with the dyslexic subjects) showed good eye movement control.

They hypothesized that the dyslexic child could perform visual tracking successfully by having one eye occluded, so that confusion of the two retinal images is prevented. The experiment done to test the hypothesis was only partly successful. Stein and Fowler (1985) argued that the dyslexics who were not helped might have suffered from a nonvisual subtype of dyslexia.

Dunlop Test

Stein (1989) postulates that the right posterior parietal cortex has the special function of associating sensory and motor inputs in order to maintain a representation of objects in three-dimensional spaces. Stein (1989) added to the use of the Dunlop test. He measures the child's ability to hold fixation upon a small target during convergence at the child's own reading distance. Children with dyslexia are less adept at this task than good readers of the same age. Riddell, Fowler, and Stein (1990) also compared the accuracy of spatial localization on a nonlinguistic computer game by children having good and poor vergence control. Children with poor vergence control made significantly more errors than other children did.

Normal and Dyslexic Readers—Negligible Convergence and Stereopsis Differences

Wilsher and Taylor (1987) point out that proficient readers are just as likely to suffer poor vergence control as dyslexics, citing a study by Newman et al. (1985). Another study, by Bishop, Jancey, and Steel (1979), took the opposite tack by examining a large sample of dyslexics. Bishop et al. (1979) found *no evidence* of an extra convergence deficiency or poor stereopsis in their dyslexic subjects. Both the Newman and Bishop studies found that the Dunlop test (used as an important response measure by Stein and his colleagues) *failed* to differentiate between good and poor readers (Wilsher & Taylor, 1987).

The Scotopic Sensitivity Syndrome and Irlen Lenses (Unproven Alone without Education Interventions)

The Scotopic Sensitivity Syndrome (SSS) is Helen Irlen's conception of the condition that most of us refer to as dyslexia. It is characterized by difficulties in reading and writing, painful sensitivity to light, and problems with perceptions of wave-length and black-white contrast. SSS is not identical with dyslexia; rather, it is a complex state that can coexist with dyslexia, dysgraphia, dyscalculia, attention deficit disorder, or hyperactivity (Irlen Institute brochure).

Treating the Scotopic Sensitivity Syndrome

The Irlen Institute, headed by Executive Director Helen L. Irlen, has a number of treatment centers in several states. It is dedicated to the treatment of the Scotopic Sensitivity Syndrome, which has five major kinds of symptoms:

1. Photophobia (sensitivity to glare, discomfort with fluorescent lights, etc.).
2. Background distortion (an inability to work with sharp black-white contrast such as sheet music or pages of print).
3. Visual resolution (problems with printed matter that moves or that alternates between turning on and turning off, as in advertising signs).
4. Scope of focus (difficulty maintaining focus, with frequent blinking, squinting, or ceasing to read).
5. Depth perception/gross motor (difficulty using stairs, tailgating when driving, poor at coping with a moving ball in sports, poor at height or depth judgment). (Irlen, n.d.)

The Institute's method for treating SSS is to provide the patient with a color filter to be either worn over the eyes like sunglasses or placed over a page of print. Each corrective color is said to be unique to the particular individual. The treatment is thought to lead to improved accuracy and comprehension in reading, as well as an number of side benefits (Irlen, n.d.). The technique for treating SSS essentially involves altering the wavelength of the light entering the eyes of the individual through the use of colored filters either worn as lenses or placed over a page of print. The exact color prescribed for the individual is as unique to the person as his or her fingerprint would be. It can only be selected by intense diagnostic testing (Irlen, n.d.). This treatment is not equivalent to teaching the patient to read but is said to rectify a condition that impeded progress in reading.

Scientific Support Inconclusive: More Research Is Needed

Harold Solan (1990) has stated that Irlen has offered insufficient scientific evidence to support the idea that SSS symptoms are related to reading disorder. Testing for SSS is by the Irlen Differential Perceptual Schedule (IDPS), a test that has not been extensively standardized. Some research has not supported the benefits of the Irlen lens treatment with individuals experiencing dyslexia (Cardinal, Griffin, & Christenson, 1993; Lopez et al., 1994). For the individuals who benefit from this treatment, there may be the Hawthorne Effect.

The Blue-Gray Lens Approach

Mary Williams and her collaborators have reported that blue or gray lenses (or blue or gray transparent overlays placed over a page of print) result in improved reading on the part of reading-disabled subjects (Williams & LeCluyse, 1990). This differs from Irlen's premise that there is a unique preferred color for each individual SSS patient. Williams and other members of her school of thought hold that dyslexics have a poorly functioning transient visual nervous system. The task of this visual system in reading is to erase afterimages of past visual stimuli after a saccade, when the eyes have moved quickly to a new focal point on the printed page. The resolution of fine details needed for recognizing letters is the task of the sustained visual system. With a nonfunctional or even poorly functioning transient system, the words being read may get jumbled with words seen at the previous fixation (stopping-place) preceding the saccade. Blue or gray lenses slow down the sustained visual system, thereby providing an artificial equivalent for transient system functioning.

Research Related to the Irlen and Williams Viewpoint

Solman, Dain, and Keech (1991) used the Williams theory as the basis for their experiment on reading-disabled and normal readers. They tested for sensitivity (i.e., low threshold discriminations) at low-, medium-, and high-frequency sine-wave brightness gratings. A brightness grating is a set of parallel dark and light lines of equal thickness. A sine-wave grating has fuzzy transitions between dark and light. The term for a grating with sharp, sudden changeovers from light to dark would be a square-wave grating. A low-frequency grating has very wide dark and light lines (few changes of brightness per degree of visual angle); a high-frequency grating consists of thin lines, hence many changes from light to dark and dark to light per degree.

Why use degree of visual angle instead of inches or decimeters? Because the optical size of a visual stimulus depends on both the size of the stimulus and the distance that stimulus is away from our eyes. The visual angle measure accounts for the result of both factors, size and distance. The data obtained by Solman et al. differentiated proficient readers from disabled readers in a complex way that is hard to interpret as either supporting the Williams theory or refuting it. The color of lens that produced the best contrast sensitivity to the brightness gratings yielded the poorest visual search performance. Note that this concept of a "best" lens seems to be more relevant to the Irlen approach than the Williams.

Other Grating Data

Spafford, Grosser, Donatelle, Squillace, and Dana (1995) performed an experiment along roughly the same lines as that of Solman et al., but they presented the gratings on a stationary wall chart rather than in a continuously moving format as the Solman group did. These researchers found that the sine-wave gratings did lead to very different performances by reading-disabled subjects from those of normal-reading subjects. The poor readers had inferior sensitivity (i.e., higher thresholds) for both low-frequency and high-frequency gratings. Although various lens colors were used, each subject performed about the same with each pair of lenses worn. One of the pairs of lenses was clear. All the lenses were optically neutral. Their finding that lens color made no difference differs from both the Irlen and the Williams theories, but particularly the Irlen view. In summary, the impact of colored lenses or overlays during the reading process has yet to be conclusively determined. *If prescribed by optometrists or ophthalmologists, concurrent educational interventions need to be in place within a comprehensive or well-balanced literacy program.*

Syntonics (Unproven Treatment)

Two optometrists (Kaplan, 1983; J. Liberman, 1986) advocate syntonics as a system for the treatment of learning disabilities. Syntonics, according to J. Liberman (1986), "is that branch of ocular science dealing with the application of selected visible light frequencies through the eyes" (p. 6). According to this viewpoint, an autonomic nervous system imbalance will lead to learning disability. The sympathetic nervous system, when activated, puts us in a "fight-or-flight" readiness mode, hence it goes with a negative mood, or exophoria, in the jargon of the syntonic school. The other part of the autonomic nervous system, the parasympathetic, will, when activated, allow us to feel well-rested and satisfied. We find ourselves in a positive mood or esophoria, according to this theory. Either too much exophoria or too much esophoria will give us a restricted visual field, so we need to have a well-balanced middle-of-the-road mood. Now, red light makes us exophoric and blue light makes us esophoric, so that we are dominated by the sympathetic or the parasympathetic nervous system, respectively.

The Effect of Blue and Red Lights

Visible light frequencies are thought by the proponents of the syntonics school of thought to interact differently with the endocrine system, which is inhibited or stimulated based on the frequency of the light. Light frequencies that produce blue light are thought to elicit feelings of relaxation and lowered anxiety and hostility. Frequencies that produce the color red supposedly encourage tension and excitement. Wolfarth and Sam (1982) report that even blind subjects' behaviors are affected by selected colors. Individuals are exposed to different color filters based on the nature of the subject's autonomic imbalance. A sympathetic nervous system (SNS) predominance (i.e., exophoria) requires a treatment by a parasympathetic stimulant (blue light). A parasympathetic (PNS) predominance (i.e., esophoria) requires sympathetic NS stimulation with red light.

Theoretical Rationale for Syntonics

The theoretical rationale for the syntonics treatments is based on a visual NS pathway (not involved in visual functioning) that follows the inferior accessory optic tract via the midbrain's transpeduncular nucleus to the superior cortical ganglion, thence to the pineal gland, chemicals from which enter the cerebrospinal fluid of the third ventricle. This in turn affects the hypothalamus, which connects to the pituitary gland.

Confirmative Research Weak in Methodology

The effects of syntonic treatment may have occurred from *an inadequate scientific methodology* that is summarized as follows:

How the Experimental Subjects Were Treated.

1. Participants with constricted visual fields with minimal phoric deviation were given yellow-green light (500–590 nanometers [nm]) to normalize the visual field.
2. Participants with constricted visual fields and moderate phoric deviations first got yellow-green followed by either red (620–770 nm) or indigo (400–500 nm), the former if subject was excessively esophoric, and indigo if subject was excessively exophoric.
3. Participants with constricted visual fields and moderate to large phoric deviations got either red or indigo as appropriate.

Comparisons Questionable in Syntonics Study

"Control" participants were not exposed to the viewer at all, as either blackness or white light would have some phoric effect in the J. Liberman 1986 study as an example.

Howell and Stanley (1988) point out that there were a number of *design errors* and *procedural inadequacies* in both the Kaplan and Liberman studies. The gains reported for the experimental participants might have involved mood and motivational factors rather than perceptual ones.

Current Neurophysiological Evidence

The work of Shaywitz (2003) was summarized by Gorman (2003) in Chapter 1 in regard to where the neurological breakdown is for individuals who are dyslexic. According to Shaywitz (2003), the automatic detector in the left occipito-temporal area of the brain "breaks down" in children with dyslexia. A neurological anomaly prevents their brains from gaining automatic access to the word analyzer and phoneme producer areas of the brain. To compensate, dyslexics may rely more heavily on the phoneme producer area or engaging in right hemispheric functions (e.g., processing visual cues from pictures).

This research supports educational interventions directly related to reading and language development. Until very recent times and sophisticated MRI equipment, this research wasn't available. The treatments mentioned previously in the chapter with recommended but unproven or unsubstantiated supporting research are too far removed causally to be considered by current practitioners in the field.

Summary

Determining the causative factors of dyslexia and the various subtypes of dyslexia is not an easy task. Cerebellar-vestibular dysfunctioning, unstable eye movement control, exophoria/esophoria excesses, ocular lock syndrome, hair mineral excesses, etc. are all interesting views of why dyslexics experience difficulties in oral and written language. However, at this point these hypotheses continue to be speculative and, accordingly, adhering to any related recommended treatment would be questionable, especially when substances are ingested.

Theory should always beget practice and vice versa. It is our belief that intervention procedures should always include input from the medical and educational realms and that treatments follow a conservative and scientific route. *Educational* components should be a priority. If and when these don't suffice to alleviate the problem, interventions in the medical field can be considered only if and when the causation appears to be rooted in some physiological problem or dysfunctioning. The use of colored lenses, if prescribed by optometrists or ophthalmologists, should occur concurrently with appropriate educational interventions within a comprehensive or well-balanced literacy program. Prescribing drugs, extra vitamins, or altering bone structures are avenues that can negatively impact a child's physical well-being if done to improve reading academics. Keeping that in mind, conservatism should prevail; there should be no medical interventions to improve reading proficiency without good solid empirical evidence based on theory. The following chapters deal with educational support, interventions, and resources.

6 Developing Vocabulary and Word Recognition Skills and Strategies

According to Samuel A. Kirk, who first introduced the term *learning disabilities* at the first meeting of the Association for Children with Learning Disabilities in Chicago, Illinois, on April 6, 1963, the introduction of the learning disabilities terminology "is not as important as the . . . programming of learning material that will ameliorate . . . basic . . . deficits." Kirk replaced the widely used "strephosymbolia" (twisted symbols) with the general LD designation. Problems for individuals who are dyslexic start at the level of the word.

If you don't know a lot of words, you can go to reading. If you go to a book and read, do what I do, sound out the word parts, and the words will pop out of your mouth (grade 2 student).

Word Analysis by a Second-Grade Proficient Reader:

Look-study the word "together"
You could see the "to"
You could see the "get"
You could see the "her"
You could hear "et" in get—remember that
If you have problems with "gether,"
Put "th" with "er"
Look at it
Realize it—it's "ther"
It will pop out of your mouth—"to-get-her"

In addition to the "pop-out-of-your-mouth" word strategy, A acquired several other word strategies during his second-grade year that gave him the confidence and skills needed for reading proficiency. At the beginning of his second-grade year A was reading on a Developmental Reading Assessment (DRA) (Beaver, 1997) level of 6 (beginning first-grade level). Six months later, he was reading on a DRA Level of 24 (end of second-grade level). A attributes his reading gains to excellent teaching that helped him acquire word strategies. However, A and his family also need to take some credit for his progress—the individual protective factors characteristic of resilient students have been nurtured at home as well as school—"stick-to-it-ness," "self-efficacy" (beliefs about one's ability to plan and complete actions to reach a goal), "positive self-esteem," "optimistic/hopeful person," "confident learner," "overall positive temperament," "socially perceptive person," "good reasoning ability," and "advocate for self."

The repertoire of word analysis strategies available to A needs to be readily accessible to students with dyslexia. Word strategy bookmarks can be used and referenced during text readings to facilitate independent problem solving and build word fluency, resulting in the acquisition of new vocabulary.

Vocabulary Instruction

What Does Evidence-Based Research Inform Us about Vocabulary and Vocabulary Instruction?

The Center for the Improvement of Early Reading Achievement (CIERA), sponsored by the National Institute for Literacy (NIFL) of the Educational Research and Development Centers Program (PR/Award Number R305R70004) of the Office of Educational Research and Improvement (OERI), U.S. Department of Education, conducted an extensive study of the research building blocks for teaching children to read (Armbruster & Osborn, 2001), relying heavily on the National Reading Panel Report (2000). Vocabulary, or the words we must know to communicate effectively or read in print, was determined to be of major importance to our overall listening and reading comprehension. Four types of vocabulary were cited: (a) *listening vocabulary,* or the words needed to comprehend what one hears; (b) *speaking vocabulary,* or the words one needs to use when speaking; (c) *reading vocabulary,* or the words one needs to know when interacting with text (see *Essential 500 Reading List* on p. 232); and (d) *writing vocabulary,* or the words one uses in writing.

Indirect and Direct Acquisition of Vocabulary or Words

According to Armbruster and Osborn (2001), children learn most words *indirectly* and in three ways: (1) through oral communications or conversations with others, (2) listening to others read aloud to them (see p. 101), and (3) independent readings. Children also learn words *directly* when adults provide specific word instruction and teach word recognition and word-learning strategies.

Direct Vocabulary Instruction

Specific Word Instruction.   This involves teaching individual words to increase a student's listening, speaking, reading, or writing vocabularies, realizing that many words are included across categories.

Word Recognition and Word Learning.   Students need to have a repertoire of word recognition strategies when encountering new words in text (see p. 187). *Word learning* includes learning about a new meaning(s) for a previously learned word or term, learning the meaning for a new word that can be identified with a known or unknown concept, or clarifying or extending the meaning of a previously encountered word. Learning about new words associated with unknown concepts is particularly difficult, especially in mathematics, science, computer science, social studies, or fields where a vocabulary is domain specific (e.g., psychology).

Developing "Word-Conscious" Behaviors.   Armbruster and Osborn (2001) suggest nurturing word-conscious behaviors. This is especially important for students with dyslexia who need to extend and deepen vocabulary knowledge. According to these researchers, word consciousness is "an awareness of and interest in words, their meanings, and their power. Word conscious students know many words and use them well. They enjoy words and are eager to learn new words" (p. 44).

Teachers and parents can develop word-conscious behaviors by (1) making children aware of "why" speakers and authors make certain word choices and "how" authors and speakers find those "rich" and "colorful" vocabulary words, and (2) explicitly teaching "how" to use language tools such as poor speller's dictionaries; dictionaries that translate words from a home language to a second language being acquired; thesauruses for synonyms and antonyms; and traditional dictionaries for pronunciations, word origins, synonyms and antonyms, multiple uses, and phrase and sentence examples for correct usage (tools are available on computer word processing programs). For students with dyslexia, the dictionary can sometimes present a problem when multiple definitions are listed and the student is looking to determine a meaning based on context in reading. Students need practice determining the best definition fit for a word within a particular context.

Practice with new words should involve the repeated use of new words in a variety of contexts—identifying words in readings and using them in writings and conversations, recognizing words in listening tasks, and having fun with new words in word work. The major point here is that students need lots of "word practice" so that new words are readily identified and understood in readings and also extend speaking and writing vocabularies. Dyslexics experience difficulty at the word level with some aspects of decoding, especially with identifying and segmenting, and synthesizing phonemes. The ability to identify and manipulate phonemes in words is basic to word recognition and problematic for most struggling readers. Word recognition in itself is a complex process. The Interactive Reading Model explains why.

The Interactive Reading Model

Theoretical models underpin our teaching of reading with current emphasis on *interactive approaches* (e.g., Buehl, 2001), based on the work of David Rumelhart (1977). Models, as structures or designs, are intended to show how something is formed or how it functions by analyzing structural parts and their relation to the whole (Harris & Hodges, 1981). The interactive approach to reading views the act of reading as a complex behavior with various processes working simultaneously. Rumelhart's interactive model suggests that when readers decode, both *phonological processing* (mapping speech sounds to print) and *orthographic processing* (recognizing the visual-spelling patterns in words or word parts from previously encountered words) occur. In other words, *graphophonic analysis* is occurring.

Rumelhart built the foundation to an interactive model of reading by combining the preeminent contributions of two prior reading models: (1) bottom-up or traditional phonic approaches and (2) top-down methods as exemplified in whole language approaches.

Bottom-Up Models

The bottom-up model of teaching reading or skills approach (e.g., pioneering work of Gough, 1972; Samuels, 1973) adheres to the belief that beginning readers should begin work with the smallest elements of language starting from the learning of sounds and letters (to acquire phonological skills), then word work, sentence processing, text-level reading, and text-level processing (comprehension).

The Skills Perspective.   The skills perspective described by Cheek, Flippo, and Lindsey (1989) considers reading acquisition to be a sequential collection of skills and subskills that culminate in designated reading levels based on grade-by-grade scope and sequence data. This approach has become known as a bottom-up theoretical perspective in that we start with sounds/letters and work up to the top (comprehension). Guthrie (1973) and Samuels (1979) are just two of those researchers associated with this type of perspective. Typically, students are taught how to recognize letters and words before they read sentences, paragraphs, and stories. Becoming skilled at decoding is necessary before comprehension skills can be learned. Word recognition approaches discussed on pages 109 to 114 (e.g., Fernald-Keller, Gillingham-Stillman) focus on the basic skills that so many students with dyslexia lack. Basal texts also follow a skills perspective but incorporate whole language activities.

Working with Basal Texts.   Schwartz and Sheff (1975) specify a directed teaching format when guiding students with comprehension problems through basal texts. The Schwartz-Sheff approach involves having the teacher pose questions based on the story title and predictions made by the students. The students use critical thinking skills while reading and actively seek to confirm or revise text predictions.

Prediction is one activity that lends itself to establishing fluency, confidence in reading, critical thinking skills, discovering patterns and relationships, and relating prior knowledge to new learning across the curriculum.

When using basal readers, the teacher should assume the role of a coach. He or she needs to focus students on important cues in the story for information recall, reinforce the generation of original ideas and interpretations, and guide students toward a conceptual integration of story ideas, character, and plot development. Students should be asked both literal and inferential comprehension questions in order to stimulate their reasoning skills and establish a mindset for a basal questioning format. Teachers can also set up graphic organizers such as anticipation guides, Guide-O-Ramas, Marginal Glosses, and semantic maps (see pp. 138–139 for semantic maps) when using basal texts and other content area texts.

Top-Down Models

Top-down models or information processing approaches propose readers first work with higher level text processes (e.g., predicting meaning from readings) followed by attention to text structure, sentence-level processing, and then word work (e.g., pioneering work of Goodman & Goodman, 1982).

The Whole Language Approach.   The whole language thrust is really a philosophical position or view as to how reading should be taught. The 1970s brought several research practitioners (e.g., Goodman, 1976; Goodman & Goodman, 1982; Levin & Kaplan, 1970; Smith & Goodman, 1971) to this position because they believed reading to be ". . . a natural process and as part of the other language processes, and within these contexts there was considerable interest in students' psycholinguistic experiences. . . . [Reading] begins with the reader's experience and predictions about meaning . . ." (Cheek, Flippo, & Lindsey, 1989). This approach is known as a top-down theory in that the highest level of cognition (e.g., schema-based comprehension) is stressed more than lower level skills (e.g., decoding). Those who adhere to this perspective believe that children learn best to read by reading and should be (1) given many opportunities for reading stories or in context, (2) involved in a learning environment that encourages risk taking, and (3) focused on a meaning-based curriculum as opposed to a skills approach (Goodman, Bird, & Goodman, 1992; Goodman & Goodman, 1982).

For students who are skilled, expert, or proficient readers, the whole language approach offers an inductive and challenging way to discover phonics rules and generalizations while at the same time receiving skills-based (e.g., phonics) instruction to optimize learning. As we saw in the previous chapter, many students with dyslexia are not independent, reflective, and self-monitoring. They will need instruction in skills acquisition or bottom-up processing, but at the same time they can benefit from "whole language" teaching.

Whole language activities include sustained silent reading, the writing process and guided study skills approaches. Of these, dyslexics would not benefit from extended sustained silent reading times until proficiency in both word reading and comprehension is attained. The writing process and guided study skills are widely used and for all learners.

Rumelhart (1977) hypothesized that readers respond to graphemic input (printed word) with a type of pattern synthesis in the brain where syntactical (structural elements of sentences or sentence case), semantic (meaning knowledge), orthographic (visual-spelling patterns that identify individual words or word parts), and lexical knowledge structures (knowledge of words) are accessed before a word is discerned. The reader uses this knowledge to hypothesis test, seek information, confirm or disconfirm predictions, or even form new hypotheses to complete a new cycle of analysis before a word is recognized. All of this is occurring automatically for proficient readers.

Interactive-Compensatory Model of Reading: How Dyslexics Process Text

Keith Stanovich (1980) built on the interactive descriptive model of Rumelhart and others to propose an interactive-compensatory model of reading with disabled readers. Stanovich observed in struggling readers deficits in some areas of text processing resulting in the reader's favoring limited ways to process text (i.e., with decoding deficits, relying on the use of context cues over phonological processing), or *compensatory strategies*. Proficient readers, on the other hand, through much reading practice and interactions with text, internalize and make automatic orthographic, syntactic, lexical, and semantic knowledge. Reading words then becomes a rather automatic and effortless process with comprehension then the focus of the reader's attention.

Decoding text or recognizing words in print requires the ability to (1) map speech sounds to print (phonological processing) and (2) orthographic processing (accessing prior knowledge of letters, sounds, and spelling patterns). The word identification problems of dyslexics are rooted in insufficient phonemic awareness knowledge and the ability to read text fluently. Although the purpose of reading would center on comprehension or understanding the printed page, intensive decoding word work (bottom-up processing) needs to occur to make the reading process more automatic to improve reading fluency and comprehension. Word work alone will not be sufficient for the beginning struggling reader or dyslexic. All struggling readers have the need of much practice and exposure to connected text, especially stories, to assist with the acquisition of word knowledge. McKeown, Beck, Omanson, and Pople (1985) found that the number of times a child encounters a word is one of the strongest predictors of how well the child will learn the word—reading practice does make a difference and for all readers.

The interactive models of reading provide teachers with the knowledge that orthographic, lexical, syntactic, and semantic cueing systems are automatically used and in combination with good readers. If struggling readers are to become proficient readers, they need to focus on those aspects of word cueing systems that present a problem. For the student with dyslexia, special attention needs to be given to *graphophonic analysis* within the orthographic cueing system and at the level of the phoneme.

Engaging the Reader

"No object is more important than to gain the love and good will of those who are [to be taught] . . . In no way is this more easily accomplished than by a kind interest manifested in the student's welfare; an interest which is exhibited by actions as well as words. This cannot fail of being attended with desirable results . . ." (Hall, 1829, p. 67). Hall sets the stage for the "how to" in establishing caring communities of learners. In schools with diverse student populations there can be incongruities between the culture of the school and the culture of the home.

Culturally Responsive Instructional Practices

According to James P. Comer (1993), one of the most effective ways to engage children from culturally diverse backgrounds is to provide them with many opportunities to experience success in a number of areas—academic, artistic, athletic, as community service givers, and so on. This gives children the message that they can achieve at high levels, and they will.

A Pervasive Multicultural Approach to Education.   Sonia Nieto (1996) believes a pervasive multicultural approach to education that permeates school climate, the physical environment, curriculum, and relationships among teachers and students and the community will engage more learners from diverse backgrounds in the literacy of the school. One of the major goals of such culturally response pedagogy is to improve the achievement of low-income children and that of students of color (Banks, 2000). There continues to be an achievement gap between high-income students and low-income students and between students of color and white students.

Building on a Student's Home Language.   Robert T. Jiménez (2004) is concerned about the disconnectedness some Latino students feel as they struggle to learn English. This is a problem in the United States because Latino youth during high school are more likely to have limited English proficiency, experience grade retention, and drop out than white peers (Swail, Cabrera, & Lee, 2004). It is estimated that by the year 2025, the Spanish-speaking population in the United States will reach 51 million people or approximately 18 percent of the total population (U.S. Census Bureau, 1995). By the year 2050, it is expected that Latinos will be the majority ethnic group in the United States, making the educational experiences for Latino students a national priority. Although there is an emphasis on developing English proficiency for second-language learners as quickly as possible in the United States, Jiménez suggests also assessing and building on a student's home language (e.g., Spanish).

Learning More about a Student's Literacy Identity.   Jiménez (2004) recommends using dictations, cloze tests, retellings, and think-alouds to evaluate a Latino student's home language to learn more about the student's literacy identity. Latino students who perform well in school more often view their home language as a source of strength in literacy learning than Latino students who are struggling in school. Jiménez cites the importance of conversing with students so they can discuss relationships between their home language and English—students may need to be guided to the realization that their home language will be an extremely valuable link to English literacy. These conversations can occur on an informal basis (e.g., between classes, during afterschool clubs, and so on).

Using Nonschool-Based Literacies to Motivate Second-Language Learners.   Some of the "nonschool-based literacies" students bring to the classroom can be incorporated within curricula planning efforts. These may be more motivating and purposeful for some students. Some nonschool-based literacies may involve writing letters to distant relatives, studying popular musicians from a particular country, using handmade texts that communicate interests found in the student's community, and so on.

Modeling a Genuine Love of Reading for All Learners.   Motivated readers are better readers (Guthrie, Wigfield, Metsala, & Cox, 1999). According to Jerry L. Johns and

Susan Davis Lenski (2001), for students to be effective, lifelong readers, they must possess both the skill and the motivation to read. Johns and Lenski have found that one of the most powerful ways teachers can make a difference in the motivational disposition of students is to model for their them a genuine love of reading and the desire to read. Teachers can discuss books and printed materials they have enjoyed reading, favorite authors, when they like to read, and so on.

Classroom Management

The way in which a classroom is arranged and managed can impact student motivation. The classroom itself needs to show reading is valued. This can be done with literacy centers, inviting independent reading areas with comfortable chairs, and many book choices. Marjorie Lipson and her colleagues (2004) examined 256 schools in the state of Vermont and found that schools with successful literacy programs provided extensive experiences for students to read and write, classroom libraries averaging 500 books, and books that were accessible to all students. Students read often and extensively, averaging 20 minutes of independent reading a day (outside the reading group) at the elementary level and 50 minutes per day in the intermediate grades.

Goal Setting

Students need to take "ownership" for their own learning by establishing (or collaboratively establishing) learning goals with specific progress indicators. If the student maintains running records of learning progress over time, this creates an opportunity to monitor and regulate his or her own reading and writing.

Building Resiliency

Prolonged school difficulties or failures seem to reinforce the belief that successes are out of reach for the student with dyslexia (Spafford & Grosser, 1993). This can result in negative self-concepts and less resilient personalities. Resiliency, or the ability to quickly bounce back or recover from stressors, frustrations, and failures due to a personal resolve to persevere in spite of academic/social obstacles, can be nurtured in a number of ways. Chapter 4 covers this topic in depth.

Exploring Reading Interests

One way to increase interest in reading is *jigsaw* reading groupings (Aronson, Blaney, Sikes, Stephan, & Snapp, 1975). Each student joins two different cooperative learning groups. The first cooperative group joined may involve the reading of a topic of interest (e.g., the history of basketball or a popular music group). Groups read independently about their topics and then discuss what they learned. A group outline is generated with major points from the discussion. After the outlines are completed, new groups are formed. One member from each of the interest groups joins a new group. Each member of the new group shares information from the previous group using the outline generated from their group discussion. Tapping into students' reading interests can also be done through forming literature circles (p. 146), encouraging buddy reading, and using books students have chosen for read-alouds (p. 101).

Nurturing Metacognitive Monitoring

The classroom environment needs to nurture the development of each student's awareness of his or her own abilities, learning styles and needs. Cognitive awareness and control over one's thoughts and strategies is known as **metacognition** and is requisite to proficient reading. Good readers are metacognitively aware of what to do when confronted with challenging material and able to independently access a variety of strategies when needed (Mason & Au, 1990). Students with dyslexia, on the other hand, are not as effective in monitoring their own learning and need explicit teaching in doing so especially in regard to how to fix reading problems (see pp. 128, 134 as examples).

In conclusion, students with dyslexia tend to read less, less frequently than their peers, and often consider reading to be tedious because it is! Motivation then becomes an issue. A student's attitude toward reading and writing will impact performance. According to Mason and Au (1990), children who have positive reading attitudes are more likely to develop reading as a lifelong habit. These authors suggest observation checklists to assess reading attitudes with special attention to whether children read voluntarily in class or for enjoyment. Teachers can develop their own surveys or use a reading attitude survey from one of the many commercial informal reading inventories. Generally, positive affirmation of what a student is doing "right" versus what needs to be corrected helps to establish a positive learning attitude and motivation for learning.

Purpose Setting and Schema Building

As soon as words are learned they should be used in the context of personalized, meaningful sentences to foster a real purpose for the reading experience. There has to be background building in reading for purpose setting (Ausubel, 1960; Bartlett, 1932) especially in the case of the student with dyslexia.

In addition to purpose setting, **schema** building needs to occur. Schema theory originated with Frederick Bartlett (1932), who proposed that long-term memories are stored as parts of schemas. Schemas represent elaborate knowledge structures or networks in long-term memory that we activate when encountering stimuli and situations in our environment. According to Rumelhart (1977), these are the building blocks of cognition, how we make sense of the world. For example, most individuals have a general "school schema" with the concepts of "education," "learning," "classrooms," "students," "teachers," "books," "paper," "chalkboard," and so on activated upon encountering the word, "school." There are specific knowledge structures about each of these terms. For "books," additional general schema come to mind—the cover, pages, print, drawings, and so on. Individuals will have varying "school schema" based on experiential backgrounds, but most will possess the same general concepts mentioned. In regard to reading, schemas are continually activated by the reader (semantic cueing) during encounters with the printed page. For students with dyslexia who are struggling with the printed page, schema building beforehand will further establish a purpose for reading. It will also help to fill in knowledge gaps, thus positively impacting the ability to make inferences and draw conclusions during and after the reading.

In summary, learning to construct meaning from print involves many dimensions with interest, culturally responsive teaching, motivation, purpose setting, the building of resiliency, and schema activation necessary for engaging readers.

Vocabulary and Word Recognition Difficulties for Dyslexics

Many students with dyslexia have limited vocabularies. The word recognition difficulties experienced by dyslexics inhibit, to some extent, vocabulary acquisition. Typically, individuals with dyslexia

---

TABLE 6.1   Word Recognition Characteristics for Dyslexics and Proficient Readers

Dyslexics	Proficient Readers
Lack of sufficient phonemic awareness	Good phonemic awareness
Lack automaticity in word recognition	Automaticity in word recognition
Limited sight vocabulary	Good sight vocabulary
Ineffective metacognitive awareness at word level	Monitors comprehension of word meaning
Limited vocabularies	Good expansive vocabularies
Passive learners—low self-esteem	Confident—interact with print
Extreme cases—severely dyslexic	Extreme cases—gifted readers

1. Experience difficulty with the phonological components of language.
2. Lack reading fluency.

Table 6.1 provides a word recognition summary of "typical" word deficiencies with dyslexics.

The diagnostic word checklist shown in Table 6.2 includes attention to fluency, phonetic analysis, structural analysis, sight word recognition, and syllabication. Evaluators can key in on specific word strengths and weaknesses for individuals with dyslexia or other learning disabilities.

TABLE 6.2   Diagnostic Word Recognition Checklist

Write "Yes" or "No" if Mastered or "✓"

Use of Graded Word List for *Vocabulary Level*

List used: _____

_____   Independent Level (no more than one error in ten words)

_____   Instructional Level (no more than two errors in ten words)

_____   Frustration Level (more than two errors in ten words)

Automaticity in Reading

(see comprehension checklist to calculate)

Reading Rate _____ words per minute

Word Identification Errors or Miscues

_____   guesses that distort meaning ("grass" for "snow")

_____   misuses context clues

_____   fails to self-correct

_____   substitutes meaning words ("grass" for "lawn")

_____   repeats letters, words, or phrases ("the nice, nice person")

_____   inserts words that don't belong ("and so" after each sentence)

_____   mispronunciations

_____   letter(s) or word reversals ("b" for "d," "dan" for "and")

Phonetic Analysis

Consonants (one)

_____   initial position (**m**an)

_____   medial position (na**m**e)

_____   final position (Pa**m**)

Consonants (clusters)

_____   two-letter blends (**pl**)

_____   three-letter blends (**spl**)

_____   digraphs (**sh**)

_____   hard and soft sounds of c and g (**c**ity, **c**are, **g**iant, **g**oat)

Consonants (silent letter)

_____   (**kn**ow) Circle troublesome silent letters: wr, kn, gn, gh, mb

Vowels (one)

short   a ___ e ___ i ___ o ___ u ___

long   a ___ e ___ i ___ o ___ u ___

y (cry) _____   y (yellow) _____   y (lady) _____

Vowels (two)

_____   digraphs (ea in leap)

_____   diphthongs (oy in boy)

_____   final silent e (bike)

_____   vowel controlled by "r" (her)

(continued)

TABLE 6.2 (*Continued*)

Structural Analysis

_____ Prefixes (initial syllables; **re**set): a, ab, ad, al, anti, be, com, con, de, en, for, fore, ex, im, in, inter, intra, mid, mis, non, out, per, pre, pro, re, sub, tele, trans, un

_____ Suffixes (word endings; love**ly**): age, al, able, an ance, ant, ation, en, ence, ent, er, est, ey, full, fully, ian, ier, ible, ily, ion, ious, ish, ist, ity, ive, less, ling, ly, ment, ness, or, ous, th, ty, ure, ward, y

Compound Words _____ Possessives _____

Contractions _____

Syllabication

_____ VC/CV rule example: but/ter

_____ V/CV rule example: e/ven

_____ VC/V rule example: lim/it

_____ V/CLE or VC/CLE example: mar/ble

_____ prefix/suffix as separate syllables examples: re/set; love/ly

Sight Word Recognition

_____ List used (e.g., Essential 500 Word Reading List)

List troublesome words

_____

_____

_____

_____

_____

Context Clues

_____ use of word length

_____ use of pictures, diagrams

_____ use of graphs, charts

_____ use of maps, atlases

Dictionary Skills

_____ finds words quickly

_____ knows a, b, c order

_____ alphabetizes to second and third letters

_____ uses guide words

_____ uses pronunciation guide

_____ understands parts of speech

_____ interprets multiple definitions

_____ uses cross references

_____ understands word origins

_____ after definition can use word in a sentence or in context

Oral Reading Behaviors: Fluency

_____ observes punctuation

_____ reads in phrases

_____ uses expression/appropriate tonal qualities

_____ uses word recognition strategies

_____ adjusts rate to task at hand (e.g., reading poetry versus narrative text)

Behaviors/Attitudes during Observations

_____

_____

_____

_____

_____

Additional Comments

_____

_____

_____

_____

_____

_____

Preschoolers At Risk for Dyslexia—What to Look For

Children with speech-language impairments are at risk early on for dyslexia. Catts, Hu, Larrivee, and Swank (1994) suggest that children with semantic (e.g., knowing multiple meanings of the word "run"; filling in the blank with a reasonable word choice)–syntactic (e.g., ability to imitate sentences; grammar understanding) deficits or specific language impairments are at higher risk than those students with speech articulation impairments. These authors believe that the mean length of utterances (e.g., average length of sentences or responses to sentence prompts) and preschool school measures of receptive semantic-syntactic abilities (e.g., use a picture-vocabulary test) are good predictors of future reading problems. Good predictors of future reading successes and dyslexia are the *rapid naming* of objects, colors, letters, and words and **phonemic awareness** at the preschool level.

Reading and the Emergent Reader

Schatschneider et al. (1999) offer the following sequence of phonemic awareness tasks to follow for the emergent reader, from easiest to most difficult: (1) first-sound identifications to include pictures, (2) blending onset-rime units into real words, (3) blending phonemes into real words, (4) deleting phonemes from words and pronouncing a word that remains, (5) segmenting words into individual phonemes, and (6) blending phonemes into nonwords. The Dyslexia Checklist in Chapter 9 (p. 225) offers specific phonemic awareness checks based upon the National Reading Panel (2000) Report.

Marie Clay's (1979, 1988) *Concepts of Print* can be used to diagnose students at risk for reading disabilities. Clay's books *Sand* or *Stones* are used, while the teacher or tester asks twenty-four questions about the features of books that cover the general areas of (1) book orientation; (2) print orientation and directionality; (3) knowing that print, not pictures, tells the story; (4) print conventions (knowing upper- and lowercase letters); and (5) knowing basic punctuation marks and what they're used for. The "Emergent Reader Checklist" in Table 6.3 can also be used to evaluate print awareness.

Reading Aloud

Reading Aloud by Jim Trelease (2001): Suggestions for Families

In 1985, *Becoming a Nation of Readers: The Report of the Commission on Reading* (Anderson, Hiebert, Scott, & Wilkinson, 1985) was published with the much-cited finding: "The single most important activity for the building of knowledge required for eventual success in reading is reading aloud to children." Trelease invites families to take this finding to heart and find the time to read aloud together for enjoyment on a daily basis.

A comprehensive international reading study was done in 1990 and 1991 and involved thirty-two countries (Elley, 1992) with the overriding question, "Which country had the most proficient readers?" Finland had the most proficient 9-year-old readers, even though Finnish children are introduced to formal reading instruction at age 7.

TABLE 6.3 Emergent Reader Checklist

Print Awareness

The emergent reader or young reader needs to use text at the basic levels of print concepts and story sense. Print concepts help students make vital connections between language and the printed page. Print concepts students need to know include:

_____	■ how to hold a book
_____	■ how and what letters, words, and sentences represent
_____	■ the beginning, end, and middle of a story
_____	■ how to match the spoken word to the printed word
_____	■ when to use pictures to help understanding
_____	■ basic story sense (the who, what, why, where, when of a story)
_____	■ the different purposes for reading
_____	■ why reading is important
_____	■ sequencing skills (from letters to sentences)
_____	■ how to make reading-writing connections

Trelease (2001) reports two of the factors that accounted for the higher reading proficiency of the Finnish children: (1) the amount of time the teachers spent reading aloud to the children and (2) the amount of SSR (sustained silent reading/pleasure reading in school). Students who had daily SSR times performed better on the reading tests than children who had SSR once per week. Trelease talks about the importance of reading aloud to children: children who are read to on a consistent basis tend to develop "a passion for reading." Students who are passionate readers are more proficient readers and better students, do well on high-stakes tests, and have more expansive vocabularies.

Trelease points to the 5,000 common vocabulary words we use all the time—our "Basic Lexicon." There are approximately 5,000 other words we use in conversation but less often. Trelease argues the strength of our vocabulary is determined then by how many *rare* words we understand (about 10,000 rare words are encountered in conversation), and printed text has most of the rare words we would infrequently hear in conversations. When parents read to their children, they expose them to words not typically found in conversational exchanges—important words needed for school and formal learning.

When parents are reading to their children, three important things are occurring:

1. Children are making a positive or pleasurable connection to a book.
2. Both the parent and child are learning something (double learning).
3. The adult "is pouring sounds and syllables called words into the child's ear" (Trelease, 2001, p. 39).

Trelease's Read-Aloud Suggestions:

1. Read aloud for enjoyment on a daily basis.
2. Obtain read-aloud books the child will actually own. Trelease cited a study of Israeli children (Feitelson & Goldstein, 1986) who were high achievers and they owned ten times as many books as low achievers.
3. Provide a book basket or magazine rack in a strategic place where it can be used often. Place another book basket on the kitchen table with newspapers and other recreational reading material.
4. Read aloud to your children of all ages—even preteens and teens (series books and high-quality literature books).
5. For children's favorites, read the same books over and over again.
6. When children interrupt the reading with questions involving background knowledge, try to stop and respond immediately. For extraneous questions, Trelease recommends responding by, "Good question! Let's come back to that when we're done" (p. 68).
7. Make time to talk about books—"animatedly, passionately, and sincerely" (p. 171).
8. Make use of a treasury of books—wordless books, fairytales, picture books, poetry books, short novels, novels, and anthologies. Use recommended resources (including Internet sites) for specific titles and books that would be of interest to your children.
9. Limit the amount of writing associated with the read-alouds for enjoyment because this may lessen the pleasure of the reading experience.
10. Make sure your child has a bed lamp or reading light. After read-aloud, children may want to stay up an extra 15 minutes to continue reading under the bed lamp.

Repeated Readings: S. Jay Samuels

Samuels (1979, 2003) describes the use of repeated readings for students with dyslexia in order to improve reading fluency and accuracy, which are critical to word and comprehension proficiency. As noted in the previous chapter, if too much cognitive efforts are expended on word identification, fewer resources are available for comprehension.

Samuels (1979, 2003) suggests first reading passages with the student with dyslexia (with or to them) and then have the student reread until word identification is automatic. Samuels suggests providing a tape recording of the teacher's reading if necessary for the student to follow until independence is achieved. It is important to begin with short passages (up to 50 words) and to *gradually* increase length with experience. After each rereading, discussions can be held regarding various aspects of the text as well as retellings of what was read. According to Lauritzen (1982), the emerging reader would need some passages that rhyme and follow oral literature patterns (e.g., "Henny Penny"). The rereadings can be done in small groups or a group type of echo reading (echoing the teacher's reading after a few words or sentences). Mason and Au (1990) encourage the use of text to develop word identification by putting words, sentences, or verses on paper strips of oaktag. Certainly words used could enter a student's word bank.

Literacy connections made through the introduction of stories can be enriched early on with the use of story books, nursery rhymes, predictable books, wordless books, placing words in a,b,c order, language games, singing songs, reciting short poems, telling and retelling stories to each other, having puppet shows, using repeated readings, labeling objects around a classroom with words and phrases, and reading aloud to children (see Trelease, 2001).

Phonemic Awareness

Building Word Recognition Foundations

An initial milestone in the development of word recognition abilities is reached when students can successfully decode or use phonetic cues. Phonetic decoding (recognizing sound/symbol correspondences as meaningful units for use in speech, listening, writing, and reading) requires mastery of 40 phonemes (phoneme = smallest unit of sound in the English language—*ea,* for example) or sound units to several letters and letter combinations. By themselves, phonemes have little meaning, and they must be combined to form morphemes (morpheme = smallest meaningful unit in the English language—*ful,* for example) and words. The decoding problems of many students with dyslexia stem from poor phonemic awareness. The development of decoding proficiency begins with phonemic awareness proficiency.

Developing Decoding Proficiency

Phonemic awareness involves the ability to isolate the different sound elements in a word and then analyze and interpret these sounds (e.g., look = /l/u/k/) and is a problem area for children and adults with dyslexia (Liberman, Rubin, Duques, & Carlisle, 1985).

Teaching Phonemic Awareness

In regard to the teaching of phonemic awareness, the National Reading Panel Report (2000) emphasizes that phonemic awareness instruction is most effective when instruction focuses on one or two skills versus a multiskilled approach. The ability to *segment and blend phonemes* is directly related to effective word identification—these are probably the most important phonemic awareness skills that need to be taught.

Teach all the letters of the alphabet and how letters can be used to manipulate phonemes (e.g., segmenting and blending phonemes). The names and sounds of letters need to be overlearned. Running records of students' progress in acquiring phonemic awareness skills can be done using a literacy running record. For students who are struggling readers, difficulties can be identified through a checklist (*Dyslexia Checklist* on p. 225) with focused teaching to follow. Students also need practice breaking words into onset (beginning consonant sounds) and rimes (the vowel sounds and the rest of the word). In written work, teachers and parents can promote the use of invented spellings before guiding students to conventional rules. This allows students to practice using their knowledge of phonemes. Encouraging students to read back their work with invented spellings to reinforce the print-to-speech match should be modeled.

Phonetic Awareness Programs

The Lindamood Phonemic Sequencing Program.   The Lindamood Phonemic Sequencing® (LiPS®, 2002, www.lblp.com) Program (formerly called the *ADD Program, Auditory Discrimination in Depth*) has proven to successfully stimulate phonemic awareness. One primary decoding and spelling problem for dyslexics is difficulty judging or validating sounds within words—weak phonemic awareness. This may result in omissions, substitutions, and reversals of sounds and letters, within words presenting difficulty in learning a second language. According to Lindamood and Lindamood, "individuals with weak phonological processing cannot get the words off the page—they cannot judge whether what they say matches what they see." With LiPS, a sequence of oral motor formations for speech sounds are taught—children "feel" how the word "looks." Using the lips, tongue, and palate, students learn how to form the various speech sounds. Often a speech and language specialist administers the training—this is intensive and occurs on a daily basis. LiPS phoneme sequencing is taught 1:1 or in small-group situations. According to Lindamood and Lindamood, this awareness becomes the means of checking sounds within words and enables individuals to self-correct in reading, spelling, and speech. Individuals have been reported to gain several grade levels in decoding ability in four weeks to six weeks of intensive treatment, or to make further gains in speech-language after reaching a plateau under traditional speech therapy. The National Reading Panel Report (2000) cited supportive studies for this approach with effect sizes ranging from 1.22 for first graders to .15 for older students.

The Lindamood Auditory Discrimination In-Depth Program (ADD).   At the elementary level, the Auditory Discrimination In-Depth Program (ADD) (now LiPS®, 2002) (Lindamood & Lindamood, 1975) has been used in several research studies. Kennedy and Backman (1994) noted that with 10 students they studied with severe learning disabilities who received the ADD program on an intensive basis, significant gains were achieved in phonological awareness and phonetic spelling strategies. The training proceeds in small steps, involving both discovery and manipulation activities, until the student becomes able to discriminate among speech sounds, perceive transitions between successive syllables, associate spoken sounds with their alphabetic symbols, use the learned sound-to-symbol associations in learning to spell (as well as to use symbol-to-sound associations in learning to read), and generalize this training to the reading of prose passages. The ADD program has several applications, depending on the type of students with whom it is used: (1) Kindergarten pupils can be given a basic set of skills; (2) beginning readers or students of English as a second language can be given the chance to experience the sound and syllable patterns of the English language; and (3) students with learning disabilities can be given instruction in very small, easy-to-handle steps, with the opportunity to experience frequent reinforcement.

Phonics Approaches

Phonics instruction is not to be interchanged with phonemic awareness teaching. Phonics instruction involves the teaching of how to use grapheme-phoneme correspondences to decode and spell words. According to Marilyn Jager Adams (1991), "the goal of teaching phonics is to develop students' ability to read connected text independently." **Phonemic awareness** is just one component to the **phonology** of language and phonics teaching.

Reading from Scratch

At the secondary level, one program that is strongly phonetically based is the *Reading from Scratch (RfS)* by D. van den Honert (1985). This program was developed specifically for adolescents and adults with learning disabilities who need to begin phonics training from "scratch." It is essentially a two-year program for students with dyslexia, concentrating on providing assistance for three basic problems: (1) impaired ability to analyze a sequence of sounds and match it to a sequence of written symbols; (2) impaired ability to process written language through auditory channels; and (3) impaired sense of syntax and grammar, which produces reading without comprehension as well as spelling problems (Honert, 1985, p. 7). The Reading from Scratch program is essentially a series of two books (RfS Phonics and RfS Spelling) that contain phonics facts and consistent spelling rules. In regard to reading, words are to be sounded out so that the reader does not rely on context cues or visual assists (i.e., configuration cues). A column format for practice exercises assists in setting up word families and word groupings (e.g., by similar prefixes). Words are presented in the context of practice sentences and are constructed so that context cues do not provide much word predictability. The teacher must check pronunciations by listening to the student pronounce all words aloud. A companion spelling book presents phonics facts and generalizations in the same order as the reading book so as to maintain consistency between theory and practice.

Note that in RfS Phonics, the student receives a visual sequence and has to produce an auditory sequence, whereas, in RfS Spelling, the student receives an auditory sequence and produces a matching visual one (Honert, 1985, p. 9). The Reading from Scratch program is very suitable for older students (grade 7 to adult). Drill and practice exercises are emphasized to develop automaticity of reading. This approach, as well as the methods listed under techniques for students with severe dyslexia, are generally synthetic ways to reinforce decoding skills as opposed to analytic techniques.

Analytic Phonics Approaches

Analytic phonics approaches (also called implicit phonics approaches) introduce students first to a number of sight words or easily learned words. Then phonics instruction begins. For example, students might be introduced to the words *cake, lake, rake,* and *bake.* The student is then asked to discover what sound the *a* makes in these words. Letter sounds are not learned in isolation, and phonics rules and generalizations are discovered through inductive reasoning. These approaches are generally useful for beginning readers and those readers who experience little difficulty with word identification skills acquisition.

Harnois and Furdyna (1994) strongly suggest reading and reviewing vowel sounds and rules in the context of different sounds and spellings. These authors have found that an analytic phonetic approach can be useful with students who are dyslexic. Harnois and Furdyna (1994) recommend first breaking words down into sound components for vowel and sound analysis of two basic rules, followed by the blending of letter combinations and then structural analysis. Phonemic tasks are done in the context of stories or meaning-based written material.

The Writing Road to Reading/Spalding Method

The Spalding Method is analytic phonics approach successfully used with students with dyslexia. Romalda Spalding (1957, 1962, 1969, 1986, 1990), a teacher and associate of Samuel T. Orton, developed a phonetic approach to alleviate reading/language difficulties. According to Spalding (1990), the writing road to reading involves using "only paper and pencil, and their [the students'] minds" (p. 29). Phonics instruction involves teaching first-grade or disabled readers the first 54 phonograms. As these phonograms are learned, students immediately transfer this knowledge to written vocabulary terms in "language" notebooks. Approximately 1,500 of the most commonly used spelling/reading words are taught in the order of frequency used as they present all variations of spelling problems. Daily practice (three hours per day) consists of spelling/reading previously learned phonograms in isolation and in words. As students become proficient, they are expected to write sentences, followed by paragraphs and stories in their language notebooks. This notebook is the student's personalized reading–writing connection to the world of phonics/word knowledge/new vocabulary.

The reading to nonreaders of quality Newbery and Caldecott award-winning literature books should accompany phonics instruction after 150 of the most used words are studied first in written spelling lessons. The reading of connected text usually begins around the end of October or November. The teacher always serves as a coach and role model for students by demonstrating his or her own analytical processes while reading/writing. Farnham-Diggory (1987) describes the interactive process between teacher and student as one "giant scaffold" because the teacher must become well versed in and use scaffolding techniques. Aukerman (1984) cites positive reading/language gains for students with dyslexia after use of this approach. These authors believe that the Spalding method (see Table 6.4) stresses skills parallel to important prerequisites to skilled reading: decoding proficiency, vocabulary development, and syntactic/grammatical knowledge.

Synthetic Phonics Approaches

According to Walker (1992), synthetic phonics activities can teach "sound-symbol relationships to facilitate word identification. The student is systematically instructed to

---

TABLE 6.4   Spalding Method—The Writing Road to Reading

	Method	Speech Spelling	Writing Reading
Objective:	To use phonogram learning, sequential word analysis, and graphic markers to acquire necessary phonics skills for decoding proficiency.		
Time Frame:	3 hours per day		
Approach:	(1) Present detailed techniques for lowercase manuscript letters using a clock face. (2) Teach pronunciation of most commonly used phonograms by saying them aloud as a class (26 letters in 54 [two, three, four] letter combinations). (3) Teach spelling of 1,700 words in order of frequency use. (4) Teach marking system or underlining of phonograms studied (i.e., *th*). (5) Twenty-nine spelling rules are mastered and practiced through written exercises to include dictation in spelling notebooks. (6) Reading begins with stories (especially classics) after 150 spelling words have been entered into notebooks.		
Followup Activities:	(1) Emphasis on comprehension. (2) Written stories, plays, poems, and research.		

Source: Spalding, R.B., with Spalding, W.T. (1957, 1962, 1969, 1986, 1990). *The writing road to reading.*

say letter sounds in words and then blend the sounds together to decode the unknown word. Rules for the phonic relationships are presented with examples" (p. 243). Essentially the teacher selects a phonic rule to be taught [short *i* in the middle of a short word or consonant-vowel-consonant (C-V-C) combination], selects text and words to illustrate the rule, and then directly teaches the letter sound(s). For example, the letter *s* sounds like /s-s-s/; the letter *t* sounds like /t-t-t; the letter *i* in the middle of a short word with two consonants sounds like /i-i-i/. S-i-t sounds like sit. Look at the word *sit* in the sentence, "I sit." Students then read short sentences about people sitting and perhaps a story about a person sitting on a chair in school. Synthetic phonic approaches (also called explicit phonics approaches) are not useful if students cannot segment (i.e., separate out) the sound segments that comprise the words or hold a sequence of letter sounds in memory long enough to then blend them together. However, the Monroe, Fernald, and Gillingham-Stillman synthetic phonics methods (in part) have been shown to be successful with some students with more severe disabilities (Pesce, 1995).

In summary, Berger (1994) suggests that students with dyslexia who receive specific training in phonological awareness tasks make progress in word recognition performance. Berger's study confirms that the impact of phonetic training can be positive if given in conjunction with other word analysis training, regardless of whether the program is synthetic or analytic in focus.

Systematic Phonics Instruction

According to the National Reading Panel (2000), there is no one best phonics method. Rather, the teaching of phonics needs to be systematic, inclusive to reading programs for emerging or beginning readers and struggling readers with the explicit teaching of phonics.

Systematic Phonics Instruction versus Whole Language Instruction without Systematic Phonics Instruction? Yes and No.   Whole language theorists integrate the teaching of phonics within the context of meaningful reading and writing activities. According to Reggie Routman (1996), in the whole language approach, phonics instruction is not systematic and occurs incidentally in context as needed. All three cueing systems are emphasized within whole language teaching: (1) graphophonemics (letter-sound correspondences), (2) syntax (language structures), and (3) semantics (meaning).

Individuals with dyslexia need the systematic teaching of phonics, as one component to a balanced or comprehensive reading program that would also include the teaching of fluency, vocabulary, and comprehension. Chall's (1967) well-regarded finding that the early and systematic teaching of phonics results in greater reading achievement than later and less systematic phonics instruction has endured the test of time.

Shankweiler and Liberman (1972) point out that systematic phonics approaches place a strong emphasis on the teaching of vowels, essential for teaching children in learning to decode. According to the National Reading Panel Report (2000), current research supports the use of systematic phonics teaching approaches over alternative forms of instruction (e.g., versus whole language approaches if systematic phonics instruction is not part of the program) for all struggling readers. There are strong positive effects to teaching alphabetic knowledge and word reading skills for students who do not possess adequate **phonological awareness** of written and spoken language as in the case of most struggling readers. Evidence-based phonics programs should be considered (pp. 214–219).

For proficient readers who have internalized language **phonology,** phonics instruction would then be de-emphasized, and whole language approaches with some emphases on word analysis would be very appropriate.

Word Recognition Procedures for Severe
Cases of Dyslexia

For the severe case of dyslexia, traditional vocabulary approaches might not be sufficient (Pesce, 1995). Certainly, all reading interventions are best implemented at the earliest states possible. It will be apparent to educators and parents when young children are considered to have severe reading disabilities or to be severely dyslexic. The following is a selection of multisensory approaches that have been developed over the past several years and have been proven to be effective by some researchers. There is no consensus as to what would be the best approach.

Multisensory techniques are best implemented in the early elementary years (Pesce, 1995). These include the Monroe approach, the Fernald-Keller Kinesthetic Method, the Gillingham-Stillman Approach, the Reading Recovery Approach, the Traub Recipe for Reading program, and the Slingerland system. These approaches can be viewed at least in part as synthetic methods. They are best used when traditional methods have not been successful, and they are most effective in a one-to-one setting. These differ from analytic phonics methods or sight-word approaches.

Multisensory approaches and methods that are discussed include VAK (visual-auditory-kinesthetic), VAK-T (visual-auditory-kinesthetic-tactile), and VA (visual-auditory) (see Tables 2.3 and 2.4 in Chapter 2, pp. 29–32).

Monroe Approach

The **Monroe Method** was developed in 1932 as a way to reduce oral reading errors by eliminating incorrect pronunciations of vowels and consonants and such miscues as sound and word omissions, substitutions, reversals, and repetitions. Synthetic phonics teaching is used with correct motoric response training. The Monroe Method (Monroe, 1932) employs a three-step approach that involves (1) developing the student's ability to discriminate various speech sounds by presenting various pictures of objects, (2) forming associations between letters and their most commonly used sounds, and (3) presenting stories with phonetically controlled language.

As an example, a student might be presented with a picture of a bag (for the *b* sound) and a picture of a duck (for the *d* sound). The student has to articulate the correct sound that the picture represents. Both cards might be shown so that the student can discriminate between the *b* and *d* sounds. The student is then asked to generate words with similar initial sounds. The teacher then can proceed to write the letters *b* and *d* with the student tracing over each letter while simultaneously articulating the sound. Then the consonants are blended with vowels to form words. Students continue to articulate and trace words (e.g., say *bag* slowly, b-a-g, while you trace the word). Word families are presented, and recall is frequently checked with word flashcards. Sound-dictation can be used to replace the tracing method. This involves having the student write words as the teacher dictates each sound and then reading the list aloud.

The Monroe approach is a synthetic type of reading method that emphasizes word recognition in isolation. Goodman (1976) and others caution teachers who present letters and words primarily in isolation: It is to the student's best advantage to present learned sounds and words in a reading context as soon as possible. If the Monroe method is used, application to actual reading material is recommended. Fernald (1943) and Gillingham and Stillman (1966) have offered similar approaches to Monroe.

Fernald-Keller Kinesthetic (VAK-T) Approach

Over eighty years ago (1921), Grace M. Fernald and Helen B. Keller (cited in Gillingham & Stillman, 1966) created what has become known as the VAK-T approach for readers with severe disabilities. This method utilizes four sense modalities in the process of teaching word recognition and reading skills. For example, the child will see (visual) the word, *bell,* will hear the word said aloud (auditory) and perhaps even hear a bell ringing, will trace (kinesthetic) the word *bell* with a finger, and will feel the word as it is traced (tactile). Fernald (1943) extensively outlined a four-stage process from which Fernald and Keller developed their system.

Fernald (1943) believed that a multisensory approach was helpful for severely impaired readers with four stages necessary to the development of adequate word identification skills. Stage one involves students selecting words they wish to learn, with each word being written on a paper strip. Students trace each word to be learned with a finger while pronouncing each sound or word part as it is being traced. This procedure is repeated until the student can write the word from memory. After several words are learned, students are introduced to story-writing activities with the learned words. The teacher then types the student's work and the student maintains a word file of all the learned words. This stage involves about two months of instruction.

The student is ready to enter stage two when he or she can master words by saying the word(s) repeatedly without tracing. Words are then presented to students in list or flashcard form. Students memorize words to be learned by orally repeating each word over and over until a word can be written from memory.

During stage three the student glances at a word, says it once, and then writes it from memory. Stage three also involves having the student read text of his or her choice; when an unknown word is encountered, it is pronounced for the student. Students can learn the unknown words by looking at the words and saying them aloud several times. Then the student writes the words from memory. Again, learned words are filed in a word box.

Stage four involves having the student attempt to pronounce unknown words by looking at word parts or any resemblance to words already mastered. It is during this stage that the child is expected to generalize; that is, to be able to read new words based upon his or her knowledge of words previously learned.

This method does reinforce word recognition. However, it is noteworthy that meaning cannot be extracted when word identification skills are poor. For those students with severe reading disabilities who need an alternative to traditional teaching methods, Rupley and Blair (1989) suggest selecting words from a child's speaking vocabulary when using this approach to ensure the child has a referent for the words used. Connected text (e.g., stories) should be paired with the learned words as soon as possible.

Gillingham-Stillman (VAK) Approach

Gillingham and Stillman (1966) offer a type of phonetic method that they believe is consistent with the evolution of language abilities. This method teaches the child both the names and the sounds of letters; the names for spelling and the sounds for reading. Visual, auditory, and kinesthetic reinforcements are used. The method is intended for children at the middle elementary level but can be adapted for older students. Gillingham and Stillman (1966) suggest four levels of phonetic training that are intended to develop word identification proficiency.

This method begins with level one, the presentation of sounds that are represented by letters. The teacher shows a student a letter and then says the name of the letter. The student models this behavior. Then the teacher identifies a common sound represented by the letter and the student again models the teacher. Following this step, the teacher writes the letter with the student tracing the teacher's lines until he or she can copy the letter from memory. The same key word is always associated with a letter (e.g., a = apple).

Level two involves blending letters into words after 10 letters have been mastered (e.g., h-a-t, h-a-d). After the student is able to blend sounds into words, he or she must then analyze words into sounds. As an example, the teacher might say the word h-a-t slowly, and the students must then find the appropriate letter cards for each sound. Word families are drilled and words are sometimes traced and written after dictation.

Level three involves writing sentences and stories after students can read and write three-letter words that can be easily identified phonetically. Students prepare for sentence and story reading silently and are encouraged to avoid guessing.

Level four includes reinforcement types of activities that address phonetically irregular words, dictionary usage, and structural analysis (looking at prefixes, suffixes, and root words). This type of sequential study carries over into how these authors believe spelling should be taught.

Gillingham-Stillman System of Spelling.   This method of teaching spelling is similar to reading in that it is based on a systematic training of sound-to-symbol correspondence using both oral and written spelling formats. Supplementary dictionary work and handwriting practice round out this total language arts program.

The Gillingham and Stillman approach as well as the Fernald method stress a multisensory perspective by emphasizing letter and word repetition through visual, auditory, and kinesthetic modalities. Gillingham and Stillman place more stress on using a highly structured phonetic letter-by-letter approach, while Fernald has the students selecting whole words to be learned and then proceeding to learn specific letter-sound correspondences. Both approaches do place more emphasis on word identification than on reading for understanding. On the positive side, both approaches reinforce the acquisition of sound-symbol correspondences and their application to words and word parts. Regardless, either approach in conjunction with other literature-based and phonics programs might be necessary for the reader with a severe form of reading disability or dyslexia.

Reading Recovery (VA) Approach

The Reading Recovery Method was designed by Marie Clay of New Zealand in the 1970s for first graders at risk for reading failure (see Table 6.5). This approach particularly emphasizes the importance of listening to the sound sequences in words and seems to blend word and analytic/synthetic phonics principles into one approach. According to Clay, the teacher has to work with children individually and act as an analyzer of words into sounds. The teacher must articulate words very slowly and gradually develop the same skill in her or his pupils (Clay, 1979, p. 5).

The Reading Recovery method (see Clay, 1988) is essentially an intense tutorial method of reading instruction for first graders and involves (1) ongoing diagnoses of reading problems, (2) an initial screening, (3) lesson frameworks, (4) intense reading instruction for twelve to fourteen weeks (usually in 30-minute sessions), (5) placement in a regular reading class after "reading recovery" of important reading skills, and (6) teacher training.

The initial Reading Recovery screening is done using a ranking system by the classroom teacher on six basic measures: (1) Dolch sight word list, (2) upper- and lowercase letter identification, (3) Clay's Concepts About Print (e.g., how to hold a book, reading from left to right, and so on), (4) writing samples of a child's known words, (5) dictation sample of 37 phonemes presented in a sentence, and (6) text reading to identify level at which 90 percent accuracy is achieved. These data are used to establish a baseline by which reading growth can be measured and as a starting point for instructional efforts. Tierney, Readence, and Dishner (1990) describe a typical tutoring session as involving, ". . . rereading two or more familiar books, writing messages and stories, then rereading them, hearing sounds, cutting up stories, and introducing, then attempting, new books . . ." (pp. 373–374).

TABLE 6.5   **Reading Recovery Approach**

Staff:

1. Two full-time teachers for grade 1: One or both become "Reading Recovery" teachers two hours per day.

2. Chapter I teacher becomes a "Reading Recovery" teacher: Two hours per day devoted to Reading Recovery.

3. Reading Recovering Team: Chapter I teacher and at least one classroom teacher.

Approach:

1. First ten lessons = "Roaming in the Known"; reading/writing emphases—children . . .
   a. Write books in own language.
   b. Write down known sounds.
   c. Apply problem-solving strategies.
   d. Practice reading with books they wrote.
   e. Use sentence structure to predict meaning.
   f. Use picture clues.
   g. Relate sounds to symbols.

2. Followup lessons to develop reading independence
   a. Reread several small books to develop fluency and automaticity.
   b. Teacher records oral reading progress.
   c. Write self-created sentences in story writing—listen to the sounds of words and write the sounds.
   d. Cut up a story that was self-written, rearrange sentences, and self-correct using the original to self-check.
   e. Read a new book and focus on meaning—the teacher can help make predictions that can be confirmed or disconfirmed.
   f. Read a new book independently.

Source: Marie Clay. (1988). *The early detection of reading difficulties.* Auckland, NZ: Heineman Educational Books.

The Reading Recovery Program typically lasts twelve to fourteen weeks. Teacher leaders are required to undertake an intensive training program so that they can work with Reading Recovery teachers within a school. Research has shown that Reading Recovery Programs, and modified Reading Recovery Programs, when implemented by Reading Recovery–trained teachers, accomplish the program goal to accelerate a child's reading development at a rate faster than without such instruction. Greaney, Tunmer, and Chapman (1987) and Pinnell (1985) have documented the success of this program. Tunmer and Hoover (1993) modified the format of the original Reading Recovery Program with more **systematic phonics instruction** using a metacognitive strategy training approach. These authors report an overall program **effect size** of $d = 3.71$ (considered to be a large effect size), favoring this approach for at-risk beginning readers.

Recipe for Reading (VAK) Approach

This is a structured VAK (visual, auditory, and kinesthetic) approach to intensive reading instruction developed by Nina Traub in 1972 (latest revision, 1992). In essence, a reading text guides the teacher to introduce phonetic sounds and principles sequentially from lessons on specific letter sounds to more complex vowel digraphs, consonant blends, spelling rules, and word families. According to Traub (1992), in order to use any recipe, one must ". . . (1) know what ingredients are needed, (2) understand how they are to be combined, and (3) [be] . . . able to adapt the recipe to individual needs . . ." (preface). The first nine letters taught in this approach are c, o, a, d, g, m, l, h, and t. The child learns to use these nine letters to make, spell, and read words by reading, hearing, and feeling (tracing) letters/sound correspondences. Required materials to reinforce mastery include phonetic sound cards, word cards, phrase cards, sentence cards, storybooks, word games, sequence charts, and writing paper.

Slingerland (VAK) Approach

The Slingerland Approach was developed by B.H. Slingerland in 1971 as a daily remedial procedure for children with severe written language problems to provide a daily approach to spelling and reading lessons in the primary and intermediate grades (Slingerland, 1976). There is a set of ninety-four 8 × 10-inch photographs with games and exercises that give young children practice in speech; visual, kinesthetic, and auditory recall; and left-right orientation. *Learning to read* involves both auditory and visual components. The auditory component (e.g., the auditory perception of a vowel position), visual perception (e.g., pronouncing words on word lists from pocket charts), and discrimination (e.g., different letter/sound combinations) tasks are structured for the reader. The sequence in *learning to write* is (1) teaching new letters of the alphabet with lowercase preceding uppercase, (2) practicing new letters as presented, (3) reviewing letters taught on a daily basis, and (4) learning how to connect cursive letter forms. The ultimate goal of independent reading and writing is facilitated by both encoding (auditory blending) and decoding (unlocking new words) exercises. Guidance charts provide students with handheld learning assists. As an example, to reinforce word discrimination skills, the Slingerland Guidance Chart reads: ". . . (1) You will identify which letters and sounds are the same and different in these words, (2) Read each word as I point to it, (3) What letters are the same in these words? (4) What sounds are the same in these words? (5) What letters are different in these words? (6) What sounds are different in these words? (7) Spell and read each word as I point to it. (8) Read each word as I point to it . . ." (as cited in White, 1989, p. 67). This method is supplemented with connected reading material.

Some vocabulary programs with an emphasis on structural analysis for students with prior structured phonics instruction are shown in Table 6.6.

Vocabulary Development

With phonemic awareness programs or any other intervention program, vocabulary development needs to be ongoing. Of the following five essential teaching of reading elements cited in the research and in the National Reading Panel Report (2000), (1) phonemic awareness, (2) phonics, (3) fluency, (4) vocabulary development, and (5) text comprehension/strategic reading, *vocabulary development* is considered "crucial to academic development." Not only do students need a rich body of word knowledge to comprehend text, develop knowledge of new concepts and succeed in basic skills areas, "they also need a specialized vocabulary to learn content area materials" (Baker, Simmons, & Kameenui, 1995). Learning activities then will need to provide opportunities for students to acquire appropriate and challenging vocabularies (Stotsky, 1999), considering the following vocabulary foundations:

Vocabulary Development Foundations

- Connect words to the lives of students.
- Make associations to deepen understandings.
- Define words and use in a variety of contexts.
- Chart characteristics.
- Describe words' visuals and give tactile examples.
- Compare and contrast words.

- Rephrase or paraphrase words and meanings.
- Give examples of correct and incorrect usage.
- Formulate questions to extend word knowledge.
- Use new vocabulary to improve one's repertoire of words to use in writing. (Allen, 1999)

Reading in content area subjects can be especially problematic for students with dyslexia, because content textbooks are typically more difficult in terms of vocabulary, structure, and familiarity than basal readers or library books. Skilled readers typically have expansive vocabularies. Nagy and Anderson (1984) estimate that good readers add up to 3,000 words per year to their reading vocabularies between the third and twelfth grades. This is because proficient readers encounter an average of 1,000,000 words per year on the printed page while the poorest readers are exposed to only approximately 100,000 words per year (Nagy & Anderson, 1984). Because vocabulary acquisition is strongly tied to the development of comprehension abilities (Farr, 1969) and writing quality (Duin & Graves, 1987), effective vocabulary instruction is needed

TABLE 6.6   Sample Vocabulary Building Programs for Students with Moderate to Severe Dyslexia: Structural Analysis Emphases

Name of Program	Contact/Website	Program Focus
Benchmark School Word Identification/Vocabulary Development Program and *Benchmark Word Detectives Program*	**Benchmark School, Media, Pennsylvania;** Publications by Irene W. Gaskins, Staff, and Collaborators www.benchmarkschool.org	For dyslexic students ages 5 to 11, there is an emphasis on developing phonemic awareness. Key Words are learned by fully analyzing them and then are used to decode unknown words. Students read predictable rhymes from the Story Sheets. The Intermediate A lessons review and extend concepts introduced at the Beginning and Transition Levels with the amount of text read increasing. More emphasis is placed on spelling at this level than on decoding as students see how acquired alphabetic and word structure knowledge is connected to both decoding and spelling (165 lessons, 30 minutes each).
Spelling Through Morphographs (section of REACH)	**SRA/McGraw-Hill, Columbus, Ohio** Author: Bonnie Grossen http://www.sraonline.com/index.php/home/curriculumsolutions/di/reachsystem/reachsystem	The REACH system is structured with four lesson plan strands, two plans for students in grades 4 to 6 and two for grades 6 to 8. A Placement Test establishes the entry point for each student. There are four entry points depending on the skill level of the student—teachers begin where students are experiencing problems and end where students need to be: "up-to-speed" and "ready" for future learning. In the spelling program, students have much practice with affixes.
REWARDS (Reading Excellence: Word Attack and Rate Development Strategies)	**Sopris West** (Also see Glencoe/McGraw-Hill) 4093 Specialty Place Longmont, CO, 80504	A program that includes helping students acquire strategies to analyze words beyond decoding—this is helpful for dyslexics who tend to have difficulty with multisyllabic words above grade 3.

for individuals with dyslexia (Beck, McKeown, & Omanson, 1987). Carlisle (1993) stresses considering ". . . such problems as which words to select, how many words to teach in a unit, how much practice to give, and how much exposure to different meanings and different contexts to include . . ." (p. 100). One expands vocabulary knowledge through reading and conversation. Because individuals with dyslexia find reading to be "tedious" and "difficult," involving or engaging the reader will be a challenge.

Vocabulary-Building Activities

The vocabulary overview guide, vocabulary concept circles, vocabulary maps (list-group-label or LGL and semantic mapping), and vocabulary self-collection strategy (VSS) listed in the following pages provide organized and easily managed ways of scaffolding vocabulary acquisition to meaning structures. The visuals can also be used as study guides and references for writing pieces.

Vocabulary Overview Guide.   There is another approach available for the improvement of word-analysis skills among college-age individuals. Carr (1985) has offered three steps to improve vocabulary understanding, interest, and involvement in learning:

1. Before reading—(a) Define vocabulary by using familiar context after surveying material titles and headings. (b) Underline unknown words. (c) Try to help students use context first in determining meaning. (d) Use the dictionary to help with meaning. (e) Write definitions to reinforce concepts and usage.
2. During reading—Reinforce vocabulary comprehension by keying in on prereading words.
3. After reading—Complete a vocabulary overview guide by having students write (a) titles and category titles, (b) vocabulary terms, (c) definitions a long with synonyms and antonyms, and (d) clues to meaning.
4. Study—Have students read titles and categories. Students use clues and predict words in pairs, continually review learned terms, and add synonyms and antonyms to previously learned terms.

Vocabulary Concept Circles.   One practice format for vocabulary involves development of categorization skills through the use of vocabulary circles divided in fourths. This technique allows students with dyslexia to receive visual assists when trying to determine essential features or relationships among vocabulary terms. There are a variety of ways in which vocabulary circles can be used (see Figure 6.1).

Vocabulary Maps/Word Maps.   **Semantic mapping,** also known as **list-group-label (LGL),** was developed by Taba in 1967. Taba developed this method of categorizing vocabulary terms in order to assist students with technical vocabulary in science and social studies texts. Students use three basic strategies: 1) listing stimulus words from the lesson; 2) making group/label lists, with a main topic as well as various subtopics; and 3) doing a followup, with reinforcement and checking. Students must have prior knowledge of the words to be classified for these techniques to be successful. LGL can be used to review material for tests and can assist a teacher in a prereading situation in determining where further instruction is needed. In a postreading situation, LGL can help a teacher assess what learning has taken place.

Word analysis skills training needs to be continued at the college and university levels for students with learning disabilities. Figure 6.2 depicts how teachers of students with dyslexia at the college level can use vocabulary maps for higher level concepts.

Vocabulary Self-Collection Strategy (VSS).   Another approach that can be used with the college-age student is Haggard's (1986a, 1986b) **Vocabulary Self-Collection Strategy (VSS).** This approach was developed for students at all levels to help them create

Name the Concept That Labels the Terms in Each Circle

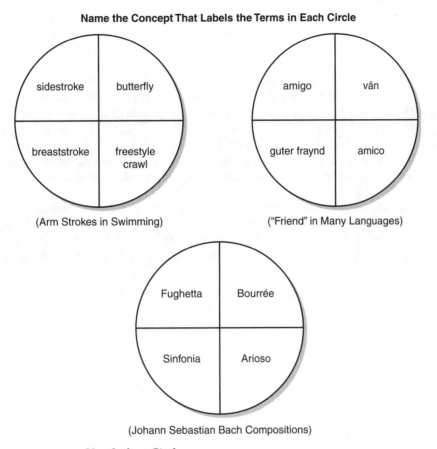

FIGURE 6.1 Vocabulary Circles

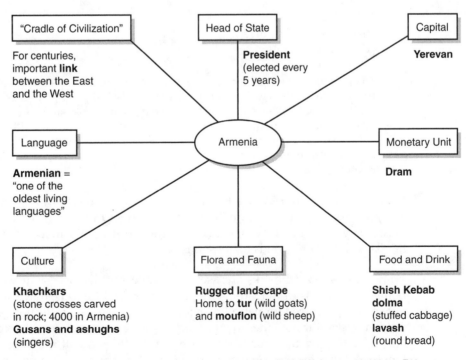

FIGURE 6.2 Illustration of a Social Studies Vocabulary Map

vocabulary lists that need to be learned based on interest levels and prior schemata. The four steps are as follows: (1) select words to be learned, (2) define words, (3) finalize word list(s), and (4) extend word knowledge. Students survey material and select words to be learned. (This can be a team effort.) In a class situation, students can nominate words to be learned, with students contributing in a discussion format as to the meaning(s) of the word(s) presented. Followup activities include using the chosen words in other activities, such as in composition writing with review providing opportunities for reinforcement. According to Haggard (1986b), the VSS approach provides "... an internal motivation ... [for] vocabulary acquisition and development ... allows one to develop systematic, personalized strategies for word learning ... [and] increases sensitivity to new words and enjoyment in word learning ..." (p. 640).

Using Vocabulary Phrases in a Chain-of-Events Outline.   Students with dyslexia can list a "chain of events" in an outline format versus using a graphic organizer before writing. The following example demonstrates how "chaining" helps connect sequences of discrete thought elements as well as establish cause-and-effect relationships.

Topic: How to Scramble Eggs
Chain of Events:

get ingredients
turn on stove
preheat pan with a little margarine or butter
crack open eggs
stir in milk
stir ingredients in pan
cook until liquid is gone
flavor
serve with toast
eat

How to Cook Scrambled Eggs
by Kenny Spafford

To make the best scrambled eggs, gather two eggs and a half cup of milk. Then preheat the stove to medium with a pan on top of it. Add enough butter or margarine to the pan and heat until melted. Next, crack the two eggs in the pan and add a half cup of milk. Later, stir the eggs until well cooked and very soft. If the eggs are still like a liquid, cook for a few more minutes until the liquid is gone. Finally, put the eggs on a plate and add pepper with onions on top for flavor. This makes two servings. Serve with toast. Eat and enjoy.

Charting Characteristics and Word Features.   Table 6.7 shows a combined feature analysis and charting of information related to dinosaurs. Characteristics (+) or examples and nonexamples (–) can be charted with narrative information that clarifies identified concepts or responds to questions.

Word Banks.   Word banks are useful for collecting learned sight words and word families. As words from reading are mastered as sight words, they can be printed on note cards and stored for periodic review and practice. The collection of words can be used in classifying activities in which words are grouped or sorted according to similar phonetic or visual properties. For example, the student might assemble a word family utilizing the silent e pattern or a common structural ending (e.g., *tion, ed, ful*). Visual patterns are also studied (e.g., *bridge, fudge, badge*). The development of vocab-

TABLE 6.7   Middle School and Elementary Levels Combined Feature Analysis and Informational Charting

Kind of Dinosaur	Plant Eater	Meat Eater	Teeth	Lived in Region	Identifying Characteristics
Tuojiangosaurus	+	−	+	Szechuan, China	bony back plates
Parasaurolophus	+	−	+	New Mexico, USA, and Alberta, Canada	snorkel-like snout
Gallimimus	+	+	−	Mongolia	long neck and limbs
Styracosaurus	+	−	+	—	large horns on head
Brachiosaurus	+	−	+	USA, Algeria, Tanzania, Portugal	82 feet long—small head

Sources: Willis, P. (Ed.). (2003). *Dinosaurs.* San Francisco, CA: Fog City Press; Yolen, J. (2003) *How do dinosaurs get well soon?* Illustrator, Mark Teague. New York: Blue Sky Press (Scholastic).

ulary through word banks and other instructional methods has been shown to increase both word knowledge and comprehension (Adams, 1990). Vocabulary words in word banks can be used in high-interest word games.

Keyword Strategies.   Keyword strategies are essentially memory strategies that combine familiar concepts with unfamiliar terms by some unusual but memorable linkage(s). For example, one could try to remember the meaning on the term *radiant* by picturing radii extending from the center of an animated and smiling circle. For younger children, memory for the meaning of the word *"loud"* could involve picturing someone holding their ears while saying *"ou[ch]."* However, we would agree with Manzo and Manzo (1993) that the memory demands of this method on students preclude its use to any great extent with children under the age of 11. These authors do stress a few potential pluses of the keyword method with adolescents: (1) The uniqueness of the keyword method provides a high-interest challenge to the learner and (2) the use of a particular keyword allows teachers to obtain another look at a student's thought processes. Pressley, Levin, and Miller (1981); Mastropieri, Scruggs, and Levin (1985); and Konopak and Williams (1988) have successfully used keyword strategies for teaching vocabulary to students with dyslexia and other learning disabilities. Essentially, students use a keyword mediator to represent information to be learned. (see Chapter 10 for study skills applications).

Using the Dictionary as a Learning Aid.   Manzo and Manzo (1993) suggest that dictionary usage is a necessary component to intervention programs because word pronunciations, meaning vocabulary, allusions, etymologies, facts, word structures, and word spellings gleaned from dictionaries can support vital word-literacy development. There are various types of dictionaries available to the student with dyslexia. There are *poor spellers' dictionaries* that allow students to find entry words by a phonetic pronunciation with correct spellings to follow; *picture dictionaries* for nonreaders; and *computer-driven dictionaries* on many word-processing programs to include spell checks, the finding of synonyms and antonyms, and multiple word meanings.

Summary

Some linguistic concepts that underlie reading success at the word level include print awareness, or understanding that print conveys meaning; graphic awareness, or knowing that words are composed of certain letters; phonemic awareness, or the ability to discriminate and recognize sound units; and the understanding and application of grapheme/phoneme correspondences. Students with dyslexia often lack basic phonemic awareness or phonological processing ability (Bradley & Bryant, 1983; Perfetti, 1985; Stanovich, 1986a, 1986b). That is, these individuals are not able to effectively use basic sound units (phonemes) to access the sound sequence of words.

The complexity of the reading task itself requires that the more basic reading processes involved in word identification, such as letter and word identification, occur with little effort and with little strain on short-term memory capacity. Research has shown that when word identification is not automatic and requires slow and laborious processing, comprehension suffers. This is because cognitive efforts are spent on word identification, leaving fewer resources available for comprehension. Several word identification techniques that impact automaticity and the development of comprehension strategies were mentioned in this chapter, with VAK-T methods recommended for those with severe disabilities. The Monroe, Fernald-Keller, Gillingham-Stillman, Reading Recovery, Recipe for Reading (Traub), Slingerland, RfS (Reading from Scratch), and Writing to Read (Spalding) methods are tried and proven methods for those individuals with poor phonemic awareness that inhibits rapid and accurate word-identification abilities. Caution has to be exercised if undue stress is placed on letter and word identification at the expense of meaning. Whether analytic or synthetic approaches are used, application of phonetic understandings must be extended to reading text itself. We learn best to read by reading, and reading should be a meaningful process for everyone.

Of the following five essential teaching-of-reading elements cited in the research and in the National Reading Panel Report (2000)—(1) phonemic awareness, (2) phonics, (3) fluency, (4) vocabulary development, and (5) text comprehension/strategic reading—vocabulary development is considered "crucial to academic development." Not only do students need a rich body of word knowledge to comprehend text, develop knowledge of new concepts and succeed in basic skills areas, "they also need a specialized vocabulary to learn content area materials."

Vocabulary-building suggestions were made based on a careful review of the literature, keeping in mind that some techniques will work better with some individuals than with others. Many of the approaches offered would be useful with all students. Such factors as the nature or cause of the reading problem, background knowledge, motivation, attention capacity, and developmental level are especially relevant when deciding what to use. The key is to be flexible (i.e., eclectic and variable) in program planning. Chapter 7 deals with comprehension and developing strategic readers and writers.

CHAPTER

7

Comprehension and Writing Proficiency
Developing Strategic Readers and Writers

Dyslexia pioneer Doris J. Johnson spoke at the fifth annual international conference of the ACLD (Association for Children with Learning Disabilities) in 1968 "suggesting that we look carefully at the criteria by which we select our materials and procedures . . . with attention given to helping children interpret "meaningful material." The focus for this chapter is just that—helping students and adults interpret or make sense of the printed page and then using reading to make writing connections.

P. David Pearson (see Pearson & Dole, 1987), Michael Pressley (see Pressley, Johnson, Symons, McGoldrick, & Kurita, 1989), and several other preeminent researchers have shown that students benefit from instruction in comprehension stategy use, especially in grades 3 through 8, and for nondisabled readers, this can be accomplished in ten hours or less (including time to practice the strategies). Ellin Oliver Keene and Susan Zimmermann (1997) cite critical comprehension monitoring strategies teachers need to emphasize in grades K through 12—activating relevant prior knowledge or schema, creating visual and sensory images, making inferences, asking questions, synthesizing, determining important ideas and themes, and utilizing fix-up strategies to repair comprehension problems.

Where to Begin

According to international literacy expert and former president of the International Reading Association (IRA) Carmelita Williams (2002), we begin with realizing how special each child is and "let joy keep pace with growing." Williams speaks of the commitment teachers and parents need to make before all of the specifics are worked out:

Teachers will be committed to . . .

1. Students and their learning
2. Knowing the content of what is taught and how to teach it
3. Taking responsibility for managing and monitoring each student's learning
4. Thinking systematically about teaching practices and learning from these experiences
5. Serving as members of learning communities

In reading, parents will be committed to . . .

1. Reading to their children often
2. Expanding their children's experiences
3. Asking their children to retell stories
4. Letting their children tell them all about their reading
5. Letting their children see them enjoy reading
6. Yielding to their children's interest in reading

Defining Comprehension: Student Experts

According to a group of second-grade proficient readers, our school experts (the majority of whom are second language learners), comprehension is . . .

comprehension means reading Deeply and understand what is the
authors is trying to tell you. comprehension also means creating
my own picture in my head.

—K

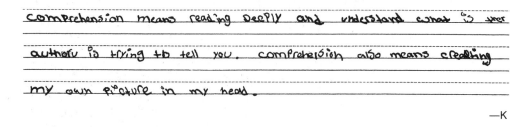

Use questions to help me
Understand what the author is
trying to say.

—R

You connect it to your life
and a book and to the world.

—A

Comprehension is like when
you do not No haw
to read you san aught
The wherds.

—C

R, K, A, and C understand what national literacy expert Dolores Durkin (1993) refers to as the "essence of reading—comprehension." According to Durkin, the act of reading is intentional thinking during the reading process in which meaning is constructed through interactions between the text and reader—meaning is abstracted as the reader problem-solves and uses what second-grade literacy expert K refers to as "deep thinking," or metacognitive processing. According to R, comprehension also means "understanding what the author is trying to tell you." This can only be done if the reader can accurately and efficiently read words so that cognitive "energies" are focused on understanding and not decoding or trying to problem-solve words. For students who are dyslexic, word recognition difficulties are a primary presenting problem. Comprehension may suffer when too much time is spent on word analysis, leaving less "thinking time" to develop understandings. The explicit teaching of effective comprehension strategies will be critical to empower students to do what D, grade 1 student, refers to as learning or knowing about something. J reminds us of the importance of using comprehension skills in reading during conversational speech to understand another person. V, fifth-grade student with severe dyslexia, has also learned that self-monitoring of comprehension involves asking the question, "Do you understand?"

douyou understand.

—V

Comprehension means that I understand you

—J

It meds when you how about sumting.

—D

Neurologists, physicians, neurophysiologists, and neuropsychologists have been telling educators for over a century when teaching strategies to students who experience what was previously known as (see Chapter 2) amnesia visualis, analfabetia partialis, bradylexia, congenital alexia, congenital word blindness or congenital symbolamblyopia, congenital typholexia, constitutional dyslexia, visual-spatial perceptual disorder, primary reading retardation, minimal neurological dysfunction dyslexia, and strephosymbolia, and now known as DYSLEXIA, that we need to consider the learning styles also known as the "neuropsychological strengths" of the learner before teaching reading, which begins at the level of the word. A dyslexia subtyping system will be introduced allowing practitioners to make additional observations about how dyslexics process words. However, there is a lack of consensus regarding a framework for subtypes with previous subtypes such as **auditory dyslexia, auditory-linguistic dyslexia, deep dyslexia, dysnemkinesia, genetic subtype, global dyslexia subtype, L-type dyslexia, P-type dyslexia, phonological dyslexia, surface dyslexia, visual dyslexia,** and **visual-spatial subtype** mentioned in the literature as well. The current authors favor the **visual-dysphonetic, dyseidetic,** and **combined dysphonetic-dyseidetic** subtyping categories (see pp. 13–14).

Teaching Comprehension

Comprehension Begins at the Word Level

It was previously thought if an individual with dyslexia had a strength in auditory and phonetic processing (Grosser and Spafford's dyseidetic type of dyslexia), *synthetic approaches* would work best (synthetic = working from part to whole; isolated letters are introduced first and later blended to make whole words). For dyslexics who showed weaknesses in auditory processing (Grosser and Spafford's dysphonic type of dyslexia), more *analytic* phonics approaches were previously recommended (analytic = working from the whole to part; letters sounds are not learned in isolation). Presently, there is more of an emphasis on *systematic phonics instruction* that incorporates both synthetic and analytic types of phonics instruction. Although learning styles still need to be considered in teaching (see example below), current research informs us that *systematic phonics approaches work best,* regardless of emphasis (analytic versus synthetic). Most current phonics instruction programs incorporate both analytic and synthetic phonic teaching elements into a direct, explicit, systematic way of teaching.

Systematic Phonics Instruction

The National Reading Panel (2000) found that "systematic phonics instruction provides beginning readers, at-risk readers, disabled readers, and low-achieving readers with a substantial edge in learning to read" (p. 2-137) over alternative forms of instruction with little focus on phonics instruction. According to the National Research Panel (2000), systematic phonics instruction involves the explicit teaching of a predetermined set of letter-sound relations. Students then practice using this knowledge of letter-sound relations to identify words in connected text. Systematic phonics programs vary greatly, however. They typically will differ in the amount of emphasis placed on controlled vocabulary or vocabulary that is used for repeated practice in connected text (decodable text). An important finding is that specific systematic approaches "do not appear to differ significantly from each other in their effectiveness" (p. 2-132). It is clear from the research, however, that reading programs that do not have a systematic phonics approach (whole word approaches or whole language approaches without a phonics component) are NOT as effective as those programs that do have a systematic phonics approach.

The National Research Panel (2000) determined that although systematic phonics approaches show positive effects on reading acquisition and proficiency, regardless of emphasis (analytic versus synthetic methods), there needs to be (1) the explicit teaching of a predetermined set of letter-sound relations, and it advantageous to have (2) specific guidance in the program regarding how to place students in flexible groups, and (3) how to pace instruction. The VAK-T approaches (see pp. 29–32), based more on a synthetic phonics model, however, have worked well with students with severe forms of dyslexia for several decades, and the National Reading Panel (2000) concurs these approaches are effective (as compared with other approaches). VAK-T methods typically have **systematic approaches** with more intense work with word study, which is what students with severe forms of dyslexia require.

Decodable Texts

What does the research say on decodable texts? Research is limited. Some phonics programs teach letter-sound correspondences and then provide "little books" that have been written to contain the letter-sound relations taught. Some systematic phonics programs make use of decodable texts and others do not; some use decodable texts to a greater extent than others. Some teachers object to the "artificial" sequence of language and "boring" story lines. However, for teachers who work with students with severe dyslexia and who are practically "nonreaders," decodable books can create an excitement for reading when the student can suddenly read a book because of the sequential nature of the vocabulary building! The research is far from clear on this issue—what is clear is that a phonics program must be direct, explicit, or systematic and used within a well-balanced literacy program (including good literature where students can "try out" their word knowledge and word-problem-solve in the context of connected print). Typically, a "phonics" sequence would move from the easiest to the most difficulty letter-sound relationships. The good news is that many researchers (see as examples: Beck & McCaslin, 1978; Schatschneider, Francis, Foorman, Fletcher, & Mehta, 1999; Yopp & Yopp, 2000) have worked out such detailed sequences.

Dyslexia Subtypes: A Major Factor in the Teaching of Phonics?

Grosser and Spafford's dyslexia subtypes allow practitioners to make additional observations about abilities related to word reading and the phonology of language: (a) **visual dysphonetic type** (individuals display a poor or unsatisfactory understanding of phoneme-grapheme correspondences and poor phonological awareness knowledge), (b) **dyseidetic type** (individuals show poor or unsatisfactory ability to recognize words with some intact phonological processing abilities), and (c) **dysphonetic-dyseidetic type** (exhibit poor or unsatisfactory phonological processing/sight word knowledge). Specific word recognition deficiencies are observed for each type. The three-type dyslexia conceptualization can be used to plan additional teaching strategies as seen in Table 7.1.

TABLE 7.1 Issues to Check for Assessment: Considerations for Teaching Based on Diagnosed Subtypes

---

(1) Does the primary problem appear to be phonetic? (i.e., Grosser & Spafford's *visual-dysphonetic* type)

Yes, if a) auditory analysis ability is impaired (i.e., segmenting and blending aurally presented words)
and b) nonwords or pseudowords cannot be decoded phonetically
and c) spelling errors have no relation to phonics principles
and d) irregularly spelled words do not provide additional problems
and e) comprehension is impaired

(2) (i.e., Grosser & Spafford's *dyseidetic* type)

No, if a) auditory analysis ability is adequate (i.e., can segment and blend aurally presented words)
and b) nonwords or pseudowords can be decoded phonetically
and c) spelling errors do have a relation to phonics principles
and d) irregularly spelled words are misspelled due to the misapplication of phonic principles
and e) reading accuracy is improved when large-type font is used

(3) If patterns in both (1) and (2) appear to be equally present, with a concomitant comprehension (severe) deficit, this type of dyslexia is referred to as a *combined* or *dysphonetic-dyseidetic* type.

Source: Grosser & Spafford (2000).

According to the subtypes listed, if the dyslexic has extreme difficulty decoding nonwords (dysphonetic dyslexics), then the individual requires *more* work with phonics instruction than dyslexics who can decode nonwords phonetically (dysdeidetic dyslexics). In all instances, the present authors recommend a systematic approach as discussed above. Remember phonics instruction is not a total reading program and is only one component to a well-balanced reading program that includes attention to vocabulary development, fluency, and comprehension. Individuals with dyslexia need extensive comprehension strategy work because, typically, word recognition has been the area of focus, as the dyslexic's major presenting problem.

Strategy Instruction

How Important Is the Teaching of Strategies or Strategy Instruction?

P. David Pearson and Richard T. Vacca (2003) tell us "the message is simple"—teaching reading with strategy instruction is vital, *but* turning this message into reality is a challenge and hard work. Pearson and Vacca stress "teachers" and not "programs" will make the difference in developing proficient, strategic readers—caring teachers who are able to combine deep knowledge of their subject matter with evidence-based reading and strategy instruction while considering knowledge of children's histories.

Strategy Instruction Begins with Teacher Preparation Programs and Ongoing Professional Development

According to the National Council for Accreditation of Teacher Education (NCATE) (1989) Approved Curriculum Guidelines of the ACEI (Association for Childhood Education International), basic teacher programs need to include "the flexible use of a variety of strategies for recognizing words in print" (Literacy Standard 13.3) and "the strategies readers can use to discover meaning from print and to monitor their own comprehension" (Literacy Standard 13.5). These inclusions have been consistently integrated within most program standards for teacher preparation and *also* within learning standards for students at all levels (e.g., state education frameworks or standards). Teachers continue the process of acquiring the best methods for strategy instruction through professional development, peer collaborations, coaching or mentorships, professional readings, book study groups, and conference participation (see pp. 270–275).

A Complex Task   The teaching of strategies is not an easy endeavor even for the most accomplished or exemplary teacher. Miniquestions such as the following are continuously raised: "What strategies?" "What teaching steps?" "When to teach?" "How do I facilitate acquisition of strategies for proficient readers?" "For struggling readers?" "For second-language learners?" "How do I assess mastery?" and "How do students self-reflect on their strategy usage?" "This didn't work—what's next?" "This worked well—when can we apply this knowledge again?" All such questions need to be connected to specific content and pedagogy. The National Reading Panel (2000) has grappled with these *no-one-best-answer* questions and published one of the most comprehensive evidence-based compendiums of the scientific research literature on reading and its implications for strategy instruction. The recommendations on strategy instruction found in this book are consistent with the National Reading Panel Report (2000) findings.

Good readers have a repertoire of strategies available to use when interacting with the printed page. Therefore, recommendations for strategy usage should be made within the context of "building a repertoire of strategies for multiple strategy usage" when approaching the printed page (Allen, 2000; Block & Pressley, 2002; Harvey & Goudvis, 2000; Miller, 2002; Tovani, 2000).

Establishing a Purpose for Strategy Usage   "Comprehension strategies are conscious plans—sets of steps that good readers use to make sense of text . . . Students who are good at monitoring their comprehension know when they understand what they read and when they do not" (Armbruster & Osborn, 2001, p. 49). For students who are dyslexic and struggling readers, the teaching of strategies needs to be purposeful, direct, and explicit with daily assisted or supported reading opportunities to "practice" strategies (Spafford, 2001). Students need to understand that the use of strategies is helping them to word-problem-solve and comprehend/study better.

P. David Pearson (2000) tells teachers and parents to "share cognitive strategies used for successful reading performance as well as the secrets of cognitive successes and failures; share the toil of learning how to read; provide enough [cognitive scaffolding] to help students attain what is just within their reach." Scaffolding to independent use of strategies is important (where children can successfully apply strategies without adult supervision or affirmation). Although much of the time students spend reading/writing and applying strategies is within the school setting or at home, Robert Frank (2002) reminds us about those times all students have to "navigate the world" without adult support—this may be a frightening experience for students who are dyslexic and used to receiving much structured support and affirmation.

Specific Comprehension Strategies/Skills That Need to Be Taught

According to the National Reading Panel (2000) Report, the following individual comprehension strategies appear to be most effective and promising for classroom instruction: comprehension monitoring (pp. 125–128), cooperative learning (pp. 301–302), graphic and semantic organizer use including story maps (pp. 134–142), question generation (pp. 127, 148), question answering (pp. 128, 131, 283), and summarization (pp. 144–146). When readers apply these strategies in combination, or multiple strategy use, reading skills improve as well as overall academic achievement. Metacomprehension, or the ability to monitor one's own comprehension, is most vital because "it allows the reader to notice when a particular strategy should come into play" (Mason & Au, 1990, p. 53).

Comprehension Monitoring or Metacomprehension   According to the National Research Panel (2000), monitoring one's own comprehension (i.e., when readers monitor how well they understand or comprehend) can be learned but within the context of other strategies. Often, students with dyslexia who are still struggling with the printed word lack an awareness of how well they comprehend text because their cognitive energies are focused on decoding or word identification. Baker and Brown (1984) stress that individuals may know how to use a particular strategy (e.g., question generation) but may not know *when* to use the strategy because comprehension monitoring is not occurring. Comprehension monitoring then needs to be ongoing and practiced within the context of other comprehension strategy usage. Question-generating approaches that require the reader to reflect on understanding develops an awareness of and ability for readers to monitor their own comprehension.

Metacomprehension Strategy Instruction   Bernice Wong (1979) was one of the first researchers to suggest the teaching of comprehension must include direct, explicit teaching of comprehension monitoring to improve information retention and understandings. The teaching steps for a study skills method, as an example, and shown on page 282, illustrates how *modified self-questioning instruction* (Wong & Jones, 1982) helps to develop an awareness of, and ability to, monitor comprehension. In this approach, students practice finding main ideas or concepts, vital to schema building. Roger Farr (1988), along with Bernice Wong and other researchers, has shown that "strategy instruction" and not teaching "to skills" produces better thinkers, readers, and writers.

Schema Building   Comprehension monitoring also involves schema building. Schema (plural = *schemata*) is a "packet" or structure of knowledge in the mind (Rumelhart, 1981). Schemata are an integrative means to bring together concepts. Think about it— you have schemata or mental snapshots (concepts that tell you about a subject or part of a subject) for graduations, an example we can all relate to (from the initial school experience to the ceremony to the post-ceremonial celebration and beyond). People may have individual schemas about graduation based on experiences (e.g., the practice of throwing one's graduation hat in the air following the ceremony) but most of us have the schema segments of a "cap and gown" and "ceremony with a diploma awarded" as images related to graduation. When readers use their schemata, they can make text-to-self connections and text-to-world connections.

As a complex, strategic process, reading involves a search for meaning by relying heavily on these knowledge structures or schemata. Philip G. Zimbardo and Richard J. Gerrig (1996) point out that we use schemata and concepts when we classify, explain, predict, reason, and communicate. Since metacomprehension is vitally involved in schema building, readers need to become good "metacomprehenders" to continuously refine, redefine, and expand schemata with the acquisition of new knowledge and experiences. More reading equals additional opportunities to build knowledge structures and "practice" in using and acquiring comprehension strategies. Metacomprehension, as a form of metacognition (thinking about one's own thinking processes), can be taught and there are additional specific teaching approaches that focus on improving or developing metacomprehension. Self-questioning is a powerful metacomprehension strategy.

Self-Questioning: A Powerful Metacomprehension Strategy

Jerry L. Johns and Susan Davis Lenski (2001) believe that self-questioning (a type of question-generation and question-answering approach) directed toward self-monitoring of comprehension and *and* "fix-ups" for comprehension problems can occur before, during, and after readings of text (see Tables 7.2 and 7.3). For students with dyslexia who experience word recognition difficulties, the question "How will I word-problem-solve?" needs to be ongoing until word recognition is no longer an issue. A laminated bookmark or card of questions could be referenced during readings. The teacher identifies those questions a student needs practice with. Teacher and peer modeling (posing and answering questions during an actual text reading) followed by guided and repeated practice will eventually lead to independent self-questioning strategy use. *It needs to be emphasized that individuals with dyslexia need to work with one or two self-questioning strategies at a time and to learn those well (in addition to "How will I word-problem-solve?" "Am I using my word-problem-solving strategies?" "What word-problem strategies worked best?").* Reading for enjoyment, fun, to learn about something of interest, to deepen an understanding about a hobby, and so on, will motivate even the most reluctant of readers.

TABLE 7.2   Goal: Self-Generating of Questions During All Phases of Reading: Strategic Self-Monitoring of Comprehension

---

(Teacher chooses one or two questions in each category for students to work on at a time *in addition to* *** questions. Students check after reading and responding. After mastery, students could have a more extensive listing for reference.)

Before Reading

***■ How will I word-problem-solve? _____
  ■ Do I have my word strategy bookmark? (or dictionary) _____ (see below)
  ■ What do I need to do to read _____ (fluently)? (substitute word phrases depending on a particularly fluency issue or problem—e.g., "in phrases," "watching my punctuation" "with expression")
  ■ What is my reading purpose? _____
  ■ What do I already know about this topic? _____
  ■ How is the text organized to help me comprehend? _____
  ■ What do I think I will learn based on my book or reading preview? _____
  ■ Can I make some reading predictions? _____
  ■ Do I need to take notes? _____ How? _____ (graphic organizer, marginal notes, use a highlighter)

During Reading

***■ Am I using my word-problem-solving strategies? _____
  ■ Am I reading _____ (fluently)? (substitute word phrases depending on a particular fluency issue or problem—e.g., "in phrases," "watching my punctuation" "with expression")
  ■ Do I keep asking myself as I read, "Does this make sense?" _____
  ■ Can I visualize or picture what this is all about? _____
  ■ When I read ahead, what parts are like my reading prediction? _____
  ■ When I read ahead, what parts are different from my reading prediction? _____

After Reading

***■ What word-problem-solving strategies worked best? _____
  ■ What did I learn? _____ What more do I need to learn? _____
  ■ What can I say about my reading predictions? _____
  ■ Do I need to go back and reread any part of the book to help me better understand? _____ with the teacher? _____ with a buddy? _____
  ■ Did I reread my notes? _____
  ■ How does what I learned fit in with what I already know? _____
  ■ Can I summarize or retell what happened from memory (or my notes)? _____ If not, should I reread the selection? _____
  ■ Did I achieve my reading purpose? _____
  ■ How did I feel about the reading? _____ Why? _____
  ■ Did I make any personal-to-text connections? _____ Text-to-text connections? _____
  ■ Did I agree with the author's point of view? _____ Why or why not? _____
  ■ Did I try my best? _____
  ■ What's next? _____

Resource: Johns & Lenski (2001), pp. 366, 372.

TABLE 7.3   Strategic Self-Monitoring of Comprehension Sample

---

(Teacher and student create individual self-reporting checklist; journal writing is helpful as the teacher and student can review progress in using strategies over time; checklists change over time to reflect new strategies used; the teacher can scribe answers for the student but needs to review *all* prompts or questions before the reading)

Before Reading

- How will I word-problem-solve? *Use my word strategy bookmark*
- What do I need to do when I encounter ending punctuation? *Pause or take a breath*
- What is my reading purpose? *To read for fun*

During Reading

- Am I using my word-problem-solving strategies? *Yes, but sometimes it's ok to skip words*
- Am I, "Watching my ending punctuation?" "Did I pause?" ✔
- Do I keep asking myself as I read, "Does this make sense?" ✔

After the Reading

- What word-problem-solving strategies worked best? *Going on and then going back to reread the word I didn't know*
- Can I summarize or retell the story to a buddy? ✔
- What was my favorite part of the story? Why? *My favorite part was when I read about Mulberry Street because I made a personal connection. My friends Aleyda and Matilda live on Mulberry Street—the teacher told us before we read the book that Dr. Seuss lived on Mulberry Street.*

Metacomprehension and Reciprocal Teaching

Ann Brown and AnnMarie Palinscar (1984) offer a program of comprehension instruction proven to be effective in improving metacomprehension or comprehension monitoring (see p. 303). The four major program components—self-questioning, summarizing, predicting, and evaluating—all require comprehension monitoring and involve group discussions, teacher modeling, guided practice, and corrective feedback. The reader will notice that many of the other approaches offered throughout the book incorporate some aspect of comprehension monitoring in conjunction with other strategies (multiple strategy usage). As students become more skilled in using multiple strategies to discern meaning, the present authors suggest making use of more independent inquiry-based learning activities and episodes such as "The Inquiry Reading and Writing Approach" created by Jack Cassidy (1981) (see p. 172). Although originally developed for gifted children, this approach has been utilized across grade levels and with all ages.

Remember Gardner's Multiple Intelligences When Teaching All Reading Strategies

Howard Gardner (1999), in *The Disciplined Mind: What All Students Should Understand,* reminds educators to consider the theory of multiple intelligences (see Table 7.4) as we nurture learners to proficiency in a number of areas. According to Gardner (pp. 76–77), "people may be motivated to learn when they undertake activities for which they have some talent. In pursuing such activities they are likely to make progress and avoid undue frustration." For students with dyslexia, who often experience reading as a slow, laborious task, the motivation to read has to be driven, in large part, by intrinsic factors (the internal desire to read). Educators and parents can provide that motivation by identifying those intelligences or frames of mind that are strengths—these readily emerge as children develop and progress through school.

Parents, as keen observers of their children, need to discuss intellectual strengths and interest areas with teachers and encourage their children to read and write (e.g., journals) extensively about their passions. As an example, Nancy Cabana, a highly regarded exemplary teacher, observed that her daughter Mia was gifted musically and encouraged her to write about this "favorite extracurricular activity." Mia extended journal writings to multiple attempts to publish her work. In high school Mia published "There But for the Grace" in *Merlyn's Pen: Fiction, Essays, and Poems by America's Teens*, expressing her passion about her music—"I play the clarinet. I feel like shouting that from a rooftop sometimes. My band director has a little framed card on his desk that says I MAKE MY LIVING TEACHING MUSIC . . . IS THERE ANY BETTER WAY TO SPEND A LIFE?" Mia continued her journalism studies in college.

Diagnosing and alleviating comprehension difficulties remains one of the most challenging aspects of the reading process. Because the teacher cannot enter the mind

---

TABLE 7.4   Gardner's Theory of Multiple Intelligences

Gardner identified the first seven major forms of intelligence in 1983; these have been referred to as "types of thinking." Gardner added an eighth intelligence, naturalistic intelligence, in 1993. Students who show strengths in one (or more) of these intelligences usually do well in the careers mentioned as examples. However, in the careers listed as examples, all require *not* one, but *many* other kinds of intelligences—one type of intelligence, however, emerges more so than the others.

(1) **Logical-Mathematical** (e.g., mathematicians, scientists, computer analysts): *Good reasoning and problem-solving skills; ability to analyze and formulate testable hypotheses.*

(2) **Verbal-Linguistic** (e.g., authors, journalists, screenplay writers): *Ability to communicate effectively both orally and in writing.*

(3) **Musical** (e.g., instrumentalists, composers, conductors): *Strong sense of pitch, rhythm, and memory for sounds, melodies.*

(4) **Visual-Spatial** (e.g., artists, engineers, architects): *Use of mental imagery, creativity to design and build.*

(5) **Bodily-Kinesthetic** (e.g., athletes, drama and dance performers): *Excellence in physical activities and ability to communicate effectively through the performing arts.*

(6) **Interpersonal** (e.g., service industry workers, salespersons, social workers, teachers): *Good leadership and people skills.*

(7) **Intrapersonal** (e.g., entrepreneurs): *Independent workers with detailed self-knowledge of strengths and weaknesses.*

(8) **Naturalistic Intelligence** (e.g., conservationists, environmental scientists): *Workers in natural settings with ability to analyze and problem solve ecological situations.*

Source: Gardner (1983, 1993)

of the reader, there is no access to the cognitive processes or strategies used by the learner. Typically, it is not until students answer comprehension questions after reading that problems are revealed and suggestions made. Comprehension checklists allow teachers to key in on important comprehension areas. Experienced teachers have learned that the best opportunities for successful intervention occur *before* reading actually takes place. Instructional procedures that set a purpose for reading and activate background knowledge have been shown to enhance reading comprehension by actively engaging learners in the reading process.

Establishing a Purpose for Reading

Students need to know that they can read for different purposes as this helps to create a "flexible reader." If students read for pleasure, they can skim the text or read slowly depending on how they feel or what assignments they receive. If students are reading content area subjects such as science or social studies, they will probably want to read slowly. With library books and literature offerings, reading rate can be accelerated. More difficult reading materials require a focused attention and concentrated cognitive efforts on the task at hand. The classroom atmosphere must provide an environment that will allow and encourage students to exert sustained attention on difficult reading tasks. For the student with dyslexia, sustained attention is a must. More cognitive attention and resources must be expended by students with dyslexia than by proficient readers to achieve and sustain satisfactory reading behaviors.

Student interest and affective dimensions impact the level of "text coherence and background knowledge" (Wade, Schraw, Buxton, & Hayes, 1993, p. 108) acquired by the reader. Just what is considered interesting information? According to Anderson, Shirley, Wilson, and Fielding (1984) and Schank (1979), interesting material is usually emotionally involving for the reader, suspenseful, and/or personalized. Certainly providing culturally relevant materials allows teachers to expand the interest levels of our students.

Wade and Adams (1990) have shown that textual material that was considered interesting and important was recalled best and that details supporting main ideas were also remembered better when the material was considered interesting. In fact, Wade et al. (1993) present evidence for improved long-term and short-term memory recall of information that is highly interesting to the reader. These authors also add that ". . . background knowledge clearly affects whether readers find a text segment interesting, easy to read, and memorable . . ." (Wade et al., 1993, p. 110). Additionally, the text material must allow for interaction between the reader and author.

Activities that set up real purposes for reading and model explicit strategies for managing the text can be expected to enhance the reading-learning process. For example, if complete understanding of material is needed, students might ". . . preview it, take notes, and question themselves about it . . ." (Moore, Moore, Cunningham, & Cunningham, 1994, p. 89). The example shown in Figure 7.1 demonstrates how teachers can set a purpose for reading.

Preview guides with dialogue or information from stories (see Figure 7.2) can be used to establish a reading purpose. The teacher provides dialogue from a story to preview some of the content. Students make predictions and look for story clues as they read. This helps to create a reading purpose by establishing background for the reading and actively engaging the reader to interact with the text.

The comprehension checklist in Assessment Chart 7.1 overviews many components critical to developing strategic readers and writers.

Prior to actual reading, it is important to establish a framework of prior knowledge by activating concepts, ideas, or feelings related to the topic. Once background knowledge is activated, learning takes place as new concepts are associated with and integrated into existing knowledge.

Before a reading on "Spain," background knowledge is activated by the teacher's questions and classroom discussion.

1. Did you know Spain is located in the Iberian Peninsula in southwestern Europe and includes the Canary and Balearic Islands?
2. Although the official language of Spain is the dialect of Castile, what other languages are spoken in Spain?
3. What is the predominant religion of Spain?
4. Why is the core terrain of Spain called the "Meseta"?
5. The largest city in Spain is its capital, Madrid. Compare and contrast the traditions and historic sites in Barcelona, the second largest city in Spain, to Madrid.
6. Spain has undergone several changes in government. How can you outline the structure of government beginning from the 1800s?
7. Where would you visit in Spain? Why?

FIGURE 7.1 Setting a Purpose for Reading: Activating Background Knowledge

Comprehension Through Dialogue

To prepare for a full lesson on a particular topic, the teacher can select dialogue that represents important characters, settings, and events keying in on the main plot or theme of the story. The students can preview this dialogue before the major reading and make predictions about the story. The student with dyslexia will need repeated readings and vocabulary enrichment beforehand. Students with dyslexia should be encouraged to obtain enough information possible so that they can make good predictions. Giving clues or reasons for predictions engages the learner to logically connect the predictions to the story.

Story Dialogue	Prediction	Clues
Then he handed the book to a young girl. "Taste!"	The young girl is going to enjoy the book.	We learned that tasting something can mean to enjoy it.
"In first grade, you'll learn to read," her brother said.	Someone is going to learn to read in first grade.	I can make a personal connection—I learned how to read in first grade.
When Trisha looked at a page, all she saw were wiggling shapes. Trisha asked Gramma, "Do you think I'm . . . different?"	Maybe Trisha is having trouble reading.	Trisha felt different.
At her next school it was the same. When Trisha tried to read, she stumbled over words. For "ran" she said "rrr,rrr"	Trisha is having trouble reading.	Trisha can't put all the sounds together in the word "ran."
"What was he teasing you about, little one?" "I don't know," Trisha shrugged.	Maybe the kids are teasing Trisha because she is having trouble reading.	Trisha was having a lot of trouble learning how to read.
Mr. Falker said, "You're going to read—I promise you that."	Mr. Falker will find a way to teach Trisha how to read.	My teacher finds different ways for kids to learn.

Source: Information from *Thank you, Mr. Falker* by Patricia Polacco (1998). New York: Philomel Books.

FIGURE 7.2 Comprehension Through Dialogue Preview Guide

ASSESSMENT CHART 7.1   Comprehension Checklist

Name: _____   Date: _____

Write "Yes" or "No" to Indicate Mastery

Affective Dimensions
_____ Sees a reading purpose
_____ Motivated to read/learn
_____ Good attitude
_____ Self-confident
_____ Good attention
_____ Able to focus on task at hand
_____ Good listening skills
_____ Can follow directions

Fluency

Compute by counting the:

$$\frac{\text{Number of correct answers}}{\text{total number of questions asked}} = \text{answer}$$

Answer $(\times) \times 100 = \%$ correct (comprehension level)

_____ Independent Comprehension Level
(Word recognition 95–99% > 90% comprehension)
_____ Instruction Comprehension Level
(Word recognition 90–95% > 75–80% comprehension)
_____ Frustration Comprehension Level (below 75%
comprehension and below 90% word recognition)

READING RATE (Automaticity/Fluency)

Compute by:

$$\frac{\text{Number of correct words}}{\text{in selection } (\times 60)} = \text{words per minute}$$
$$\frac{}{\text{number of seconds}}$$

Determine Reading Rate

_____ Below average for grade
_____ Average
_____ Above average

Oral

Gr 1 (50–80 wpm)   Gr 2 (50–90 wpm)
Gr 3 (80–115 wpm)   Gr 4 (100–120 wpm)
Gr 5 (100–130 wpm)

Silent

Gr 1 (< 80 wpm)   Gr 5 (150–160)   Gr 9 (200–210)
Gr 2 (80–110)   Gr 6 (160–175)   Gr 10 (210–225)
Gr 3 (110–130)   Gr 7 (175–185)   Gr 11 (225–240)
Gr 4 (130–150)   Gr 8 (185–200)   Gr 12 (240–255)

_____ Uses correct phrasing in oral reading
_____ Uses correct expression in oral reading

Writing/Reading Connection

_____ Prewriting activities include careful topic selection,
webbing and organizing ideas, locating necessary
references and materials, and organizing time
frames
_____ Writing activities include enough drafts and
revisions for a quality product
_____ Post-writing activities include self-editing, editing
from teachers/peers

Reference Usage

_____ Uses library to obtain books and references
_____ Can use a dictionary for pronunciations,
synonyms, and word meanings
_____ Can use a map and atlas
_____ Can use a thesaurus
_____ Can use a library card catalog system
_____ Can use an encyclopedia
_____ Knows where to find resources
_____ Demonstrates responsible and efficient Internet
usage

Story Grammar Knowledge

_____ Follows character development
_____ Identifies setting—time/place
_____ Identifies major problem(s) or plots
_____ Identifies minor problem(s) or subplots
_____ Identifies story resolution
_____ Identifies themes/morals/purposes

Metacognitive Awareness

_____ Understands the gist of a selection
_____ Can make predictions/confirm/revise
_____ Can summarize
_____ Can make cause-and-effect relations
_____ Can draw conclusions
_____ Can make generalizations
_____ Problem-solves while reading
_____ Self-monitors comprehension
_____ Self-monitors reading rate
_____ Adjusts (flexibility) to task at hand

Study Skills

_____ Completes school assignments
_____ Completes homework assignments
_____ Has daily study time
_____ Plans ahead of time to complete large
assignments/projects/reports
_____ Can take notes from oral presentations
_____ Can take notes from text presentations
_____ Can summarize oral presentations
_____ Can summarize written presentations
_____ Can outline/use graphic organizers
_____ Can use visual aids
_____ Selects appropriate exam material
_____ Organizes and reviews notes for exams
_____ Self-questions/monitors learning
_____ Can take multiple-choice, short essay, fill-in the
blank, and long essay exams

Compensatory Strategies

Compensatory strategies are *thinking strategies* that *empower* the reader to have a *reflective cognitive learning style* that renders *interactive* and *meaningful* dialogue between the reader and the printed page.

Individuals with dyslexia and other learning disabilities may sometimes have an impulsive cognitive style (Walker, 1985) or learning/thinking styles that are reactive (and reactions are too quick) as opposed to interactive. Adequate considerations are not given to hypothesis testing, weighing alternatives, and strategic planning. A reflective cognitive learning style is one that is paced to the requirements of a reading task with metacognitive (thinking) skills and self-monitoring in place. Having a reflective cognitive learning style allows the reader to respond purposively and meaningfully to the printed page. Compensatory strategies are those activities that promote the acquisition of reflective cognitive learning styles. A cognitive strategy-instruction approach is one way to develop reflective cognitive learning styles.

Swanson's Cognitive Strategy Instruction Guidelines

Swanson (1989, 1993) proposes three principles for effective cognitive strategy instruction for individuals who are dyslexic: (1) Always keep in mind that there is no one best strategy to use—different strategies can effect different cognitive outcomes; (2) consider the individual—what works for one individual may not work for another; and (3) be parsimonious—use only the strategies necessary to accomplish your goal and that's all!

Deshler's Strategies Intervention Model

One cognitive strategies model that has been used successfully with adolescents with dyslexia is that of Deshler and his colleagues, developed at the University of Kansas Institute for Research in Learning Disabilities (KU-IRLD) (Deshler, Alley, & Carlson, 1980; Deshler, Schumaker, Lenz, & Ellis, 1984; Deshler & Schumaker, 1986; Schumaker, Deshler, Alley, Warner, & Denton, 1982). Deshler and his associates propose that the teacher or appropriate professional establish a student's current level of reading/language functioning through testing. The teacher would then model appropriate cognitive learning strategies with verbal rehearsal/practice. Positive and corrective feedback is used when the teacher monitors the student implementing a strategy. Post-testing assesses growth in learning and effectiveness of strategies usage. According to the National Reading Panel Report (2000), comprehension monitoring, cooperative learning, the use of semantic organizers, question generation, and question answering are the most effective comprehensive strategies.

Comprehension of text requires strategic reading or the purposeful and flexible thinking person who is engaged in the task itself (Palinscar & David, 1992; Pressley et al., 1989; Ruddell, 1993; Searfoss & Readance, 1994). The comprehension of subject matter material in science, social studies, or other content areas in large measure rests on the student's ability to perceive the organization of ideas and utilize text structure to facilitate comprehension. Determining areas of need for the student with dyslexia would be a priority, and the methods/techniques chosen should be matched accordingly. Assessment Chart 7.1 (p. 132) serves as a guide for teachers in determining the strengths and comprehension weaknesses for the student with dyslexia.

Using Context Clues

Students can bridge the gap between word recognition and comprehension of text by developing strategies that allow discerning word meaning from context clues. The SCANR acronym developed by Jenkins, Matlock, and Slocum (1989) instructs students to substitute a word(s) for the problem word, **c**heck the surrounding context to confirm the reasonableness of the substitution(s), **a**sk or self-monitor to see if the new word actually fits, readjust if a new word(s) is **n**eeded, and **r**evise if necessary. This type of technique encourages flexibility on the part of the reader and self-monitoring and checking of ideas. Because individuals with dyslexia tend to overrely on context clues or cues when decoding, teachers need to ensure students are balancing their repertoire of word identification strategies with phonics, structural analysis, and the overstudy of sight words.

Think-Alouds—A Diagnostic/Teaching Tool

A general rule would be to present any technique first through modeling. Davey (1983) believes that modeling behaviors allows teachers to demonstrate how comprehension problems can be overcome. Davey (1983) recommends using think-alouds, predictions and hypothesis testing, visual imagery (let's picture . . .), analogies (like a . . .), and verbalizing problem areas and how to correct (fix by . . .). Think-alouds begin at the level of the emerging reader and continue through all stages of reading. Strategic interventions can be accomplished individually and in a group format. Troutman and Lichtenberg (1987, 1995) also carefully note that the teacher should observe each group as the students work through problems encountered and, especially, key in on students with learning problems.

Graphic Organizers

Graphic organizers allow the reader to organize and summarize information from think-alouds and text readings. Struggling readers have limited awareness of what external organizational devices will improve their memory and comprehension. The National Reading Panel Report (2000) found the main effect or benefit to the use of graphic organizers was on the reader's memory of content read.

Graphic organizers are diagrams or outlines that depict the main structure of the material to be read. Key terms and concepts are used to create an outline that depicts the order and organization of the textual material. Graphic organizers assist students in making those cause-and-effect relationships relevant to reading comprehension. Through the visual format, they are able to see the relationship between ideas and concepts. Traditional outlining procedures might not be sufficient for the student with dyslexia because their organizational/study skills are frequently lacking. Varnhagen and Goldman (1986) conclude from their research that individuals who experience comprehension problems also benefit from instructional techniques that focus on the causal connections/events/relationships in stories. The use of story grammar via story maps (Reutzel, 1985) and other such techniques seems to help students with comprehension difficulties (Tierney & Cunningham, 1984).

The following graphic organizers are presented: anticipation guides, guide-o-ramas and reading road maps, marginal glosses, semantic maps, story grammar structures, concept webbing with semantic maps, and text structure guides. See also Chapter 10, page 293.

Anticipation Guides: Text Previews and Reviews   A type of previewing method is to look at certain parts of the book in order to generate anticipation on the part of the reader. The use of an anticipation guide can introduce students to text concepts by having them respond to statements prior to reading. Following the reading, students review their earlier responses to revise or support prior views. Figures 7.3 and 7.4 provide examples for both the elementary and secondary levels. Valeri-Gold (1987) suggests assisting students in estimating how long it will take to read a book and then break the time required for the reading into manageable chunks. Students can read the book title, subheadings, pre-and post-chapter questions, chapter introductions and conclusions, graphs, charts, and pictures in order to make guesses or predictions about story content that can be confirmed or disconfirmed after the reading.

A pre-reading strategy that sets a purpose for reading.

Directions: Before you read *Gentleman of Rio en Medio* by Juan A.A. Sedillo, think about what you already know. Read each statement and write YES or NO on the line to show what you believe. After your reading go back to each statement and decide if you still want the same answer. Be ready to tell why you changed your mind in some cases.

Before		**After**
_____	1. The main character is a gentleman.	_____
_____	2. Land near a river (*rio*) must be valuable.	_____
_____	3. *Sobrinos* and *nietos* can be descendants.	_____
_____	4. A faded coat can look princely.	_____
_____	5. Trees can be expensive gifts.	_____
_____	6. When one signs a deed, one sells everything that grows on the land.	_____

Anticipation Guide—Elementary Example

Name ___N___ (student with dyslexia) _____ Date _____

Teacher _____ Grade ___3___

Text or Story: *Shadow Dance* by Tololwa M. Mollel; Illustrated by Donna Perrone (1998); New York: Houghton Mifflin.

Directions: Predict before your reading what might happen based on the information or questions listed in each box. After your reading, please comment on your prediction.

Before Reading	**After Reading**	**Look at the pictures in the story on pages (*notes wouldn't be written for students):**
SHe got a creaKaDYol. (She got a crocodile.)	SHe HyerThe craoDYol. (She helped the crocodile.)	8 & 9 (*note: pictures show Salome, a young girl, helping to pull a crocodile from some bushes with a rope)
The gRol Tol The BRed to go gethalp oR The BeRd IS The mom of The cerKoDYol. (The girl told the bird to go get help or the bird is the mom of the crocodile)	The piaia HelPt The gRol the pigeon helped the girl.	26 & 27 (*note: pictures show the crocodile still holding Salome but the crocodile is on land; a pigeon is talking to both Salome and the crocodile)

FIGURE 7.3 Anticipation Guide (Elementary)

Anticipation Guide—Secondary Example

Students can use prior knowledge to predict story events, effects in cause-and-effect relationships, "what's next," and so on. This establishes a purpose for reading and engages the reader to interact with text.

Secondary Example: [*Source:* Appenzeller, T. (February 2004). "The carbon cycle: A delicate balancing act for life's vital element." *National Geographic, 205*(2), 88–117]

Directions: Use your prior knowledge to predict the effect of the carbon infusion mentioned before reading "The Carbon Cycle: A Delicate Balancing Act for Life's Vital Element." Just jot some notes or phrases. After your reading, comment on your prediction

Before Reading   **After Reading**

_____   _____

_____   _____ | What happens when . . .
_____   _____ | humans dispose of 8 billion tons of carbon into the atmosphere yearly?

_____   _____

_____   _____ | What happens to the average global temperature when there is a 30% increase
_____   _____ | in atmospheric CO_2?

_____   _____

_____   _____ | What happens to the sun's heat when water vapor, billions of tons of CO_2, and methane
_____   _____ | gases combine in the atmosphere?

Followup: Research how frequent car and vehicle tuneups and regular maintenance by all owners in a country can substantially impact global warming. How do cars emit CO_2 into the atmosphere?

FIGURE 7.4   Anticipation Guide (Secondary)

Adjusting to Reading Text or Basal and Content Text Requirements

Guide-O-Ramas/Reading Road Maps.   **Guide-o-ramas** (Cunningham & Shablack, 1975) are reading guides teachers develop that *guide* the reader to note certain information while reading. The teacher can create personal messages for the student that will even refer the student to certain key pages while reading. A variation of the guide-o-rama idea is the reading road map. Figure 7.5 demonstrates how to develop a Reading Road Map.

Marginal Glosses.   **Marginal glosses** are comments authors make in margins to readers as asides, notes of clarification, vocabulary highlights, interpretations, trivia notes, and so on. These marginal glosses are sometimes printed. Teachers can also create marginal glosses with personalized notes for the student with dyslexia who might benefit from additional comments and interpretations. Marginal glosses can be used in any content area (Table 7.5).

Semantic Maps   These are graphic displays of text in which the organization and relationship of generated ideas can be seen. Cooperative activities that encourage group brainstorming result in more ideas and topics. Semantic maps can be used by students and teachers alike. The semantic map in Figure 7.6 organizes learning standards and important topics for teaching. Figure 7.7 shows an example of a semantic map completed for a biography.

Story Grammar   A **story grammar** is a structure or framework that describes consistent text features (Mandler, 1984; Moreau & Fidrych-Puzzo, 1994). At the elementary level, story grammar can focus on the basic setting, story plot, and story resolution, inasmuch as these are basic to many stories (Schmidt & O'Brien, 1986). Stein and Trabasso (1981) offer a comprehensive story grammar structure that can be used at the

Topic: World Respected Humanitarian Leaders: Dr. Martin Luther King Jr.

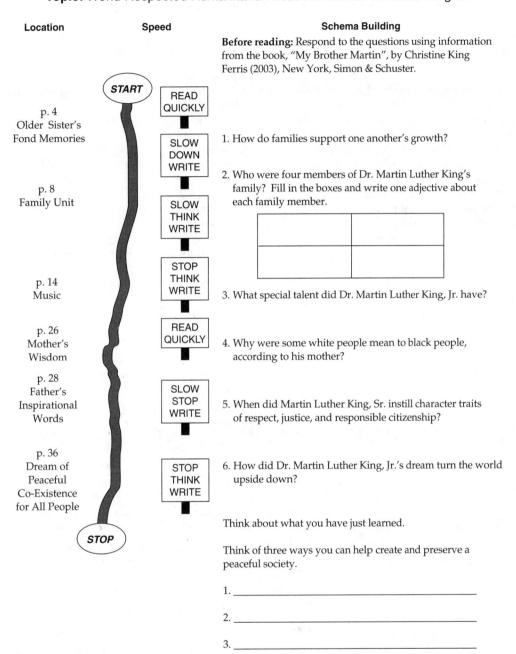

FIGURE 7.5 Reading Road Map

upper elementary and high school levels. Their story grammar identifies specific components of narrative structure, such as a setting or time frame for the story, an episode that has an initiating event to begin the episode, an internal response by the main characters that initiates actions, an attempt to carry out those actions to reach a goal(s), a consequence(s) of actions taken, and a reaction(s) of the main character(s), including their feelings, either about successfully reaching a goal(s) or failing to attain the goal(s). Students are taught to utilize story grammar by following teacher modeling in which story elements are identified and recorded. Figures 7.8 and 7.9 provide frameworks for organizing story grammar with examples. For students with reading disabilities,

TABLE 7.5   Marginal Gloss Regarding "The Chinese New Year"

Students can use sticky notes to record notes on either side of the printed page, or the teacher or student can write questions, notes, or responses in the margins of the printed page if the book is consumable.

Samples

The day of the first new moon of the lunar new year begins the Chinese New Year. A lunar year is about 354 days long, except during a leap year when an extra month is added.

The Chinese New Year is considered an important holiday because this is a time for new beginnings, hopes, and dreams. Families and communities celebrate with time-honored customs.

During mealtimes, as an example, fish is traditionally served. Peaches and tangerines are gathered and are placed in special containers.

Paragraph 1

The Chinese celebrate a new year at a different time than January 1.
When will the Chinese New Year begin this year?

Paragraph 2

I wonder what traditions are celebrated by the Chinese?

Paragraph 3

Food = Symbolic
Fish = Wealth
Tangerines = Good luck and a house full of warmth and happiness
Peaches = Bring long life

Source: Based on *This Next New Year* by Janet S. Wong; pictures by Yangsook Choi (2000). New York: Farrar, Straus & Giroux.

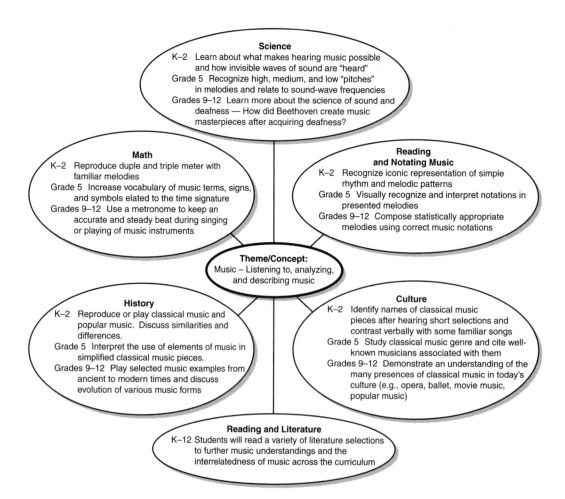

FIGURE 7.6   Integrated Theme and Concept Webbing for Teaching Music Appreciation, K–12

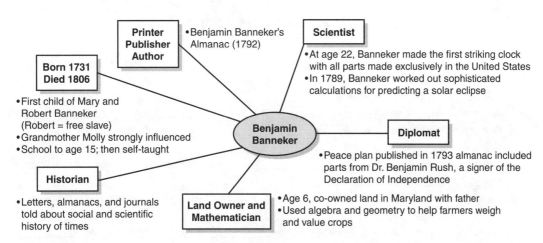

Source: Information from *Benjamin Banneker: Genius of Early America* (1978). Author: Lillie Patterson, Nashville, Tennessee: Parthenon Press.

FIGURE 7.7   Semantic Map Summarizing a Biography

Some basic story grammar elements can be found in narratives written in various countries and cultures throughout the world. These are story setting, time, main characters, story problem, and story problem resolution. There will be a chain of events that leads to the story problem resolution. Typically, a story theme is evident and is often connected to the story problem resolution.

Sample Story Grammar Frameworks

Story resource: *Thank you, Mr. Falker* by Patricia Polacco (1998), Philomel Books (division of The Putnam and Grosset Group, New York); **Genre:** autobiographical narrative; **Book Level:** All age groups—can be used as a read aloud.

> **Setting:** Michigan and California (school classrooms).
> **Time:** When Patricia Polacco was in elementary school.
> **Main Characters:** "Trisha" Polacco, Mr. Falker, Gramma
> **Problem:** Trisha is promoted to fifth grade and still can't read.
> **Resolution of the Problem:** Trisha was motivated to learn how to read and willing to work hard with her teacher Mr. Falker, who provided Trisha with the "letter and word knowledge" she needed.
> **Restated as the Theme:** One can overcome dyslexia or a reading disability with the motivation to learn how to read, hard work, and good teaching.

Episode Chain of Events to Solve the Problem (when Trisha was in fifth grade)

Initiating Event: Trisha got to fifth grade and still couldn't read.

Internal Response: Trisha feels "dumb."

1st Attempt:	*Trisha stumbles through a page in* Charlotte's Web *in grade 5.* **Consequence:** Children begin to laugh out loud.
2nd Attempt:	*Trisha hides during recess so the children can't find and tease her.* **Consequence:** Eric and Mr. Falker find Trisha's hiding spot. Mr. Falker understands why Trisha is hiding—she can't read.
3rd Attempt or Resolution:	*Mr. Falker teaches Trisha how to sound out words and put letters together to make words.* **Consequence:** For Trisha, "light poured into her brain . . . the words and sentences started to take shape." Trisha learned how to read.
Internal Response:	*Trisha was "so happy, so very happy."*

Additional books about overcoming obstacles (*source—Creative Classroom Magazine,* editor: Meg A. Bozzone, May/June 1999, p.4): *Tuesdays with Morrie* by Mitch Albom (Doubleday, 1997); *To Every Thing There Is a Season* by Leo and Diane Dillon (Scholastic, 1998); *The Circle of Days* by Reeve Lindbergh (Candlewick Press, 1998); *My Great Aunt Arizona* by Gloria Houston (Harper Collins, 1992); *Lou Gehrig: The Luckiest Man* by David Adler (Gulliver, 1997); *What a Wonderful World* by George David Weiss and Bob Thiele (Atheneum, 1995).

FIGURE 7.8   Story Grammar (= Structure of a Story)

Story Grammar Example

Name _____ Date _____

Story Title _*The Paper Dragon*_ Author _*Marguerite W. Davol*_

Illustrator _*Robert Sabuda*_ Genre _*Fairytale*_

This story takes place in _*China*_.

during or when _*Long, long ago*_.

One of the main characters is _*Mi Fei*_, and two words that describe this character are _*humble artist*_.

Another character is _*Sui Jen*_, and two words that describe this character are _*fierce dragon*_.

Another character is _*Mu Wang*_, and two words that describe this character are _*messenger*_.

There is a problem. It is _*Sui Jen, great dragon of Lung Mountain, awakened from 100 years' sleep and is loose upon the land.*_

Before the problem is solved, these things happened:

(1) _*Mi Fei went to Lung Mountain and begged dragon to return to sleep.*_

(2) _*The dragon gave Mi Fei three tasks to perform.*_

(3) _*Mi Fei brought the dragon the strongest thing in the world on paper—"love."*_

The problem is solved when _*The dragon received "the love of a village" on paper— Mi Fei's painting of his people—the dragon shrinks and disappears.*_

The story ends when _*Mi Fei found a paper dragon in place of Sui Jen and brings it back to his people.*_

The theme of the story is _*"Love can move mountains, stretch the sky, calm the sea. Love brings light and love."*_

Illustrate or tell about your favorite part of the story: _*My favorite part of the story is when Mi Fei held out the picture of his people in the village. I also enjoyed tracing these four Chinese characters and learning what they meant.*_

英 Courage   忠 Loyalty   愛 Love   誠 Sincerity

Source: Carol A. Spafford & George S. Grosser, *Dyslexia and Reading Difficulties: Research and Resource Guide for Working with All Struggling Readers.* Copyright © 2005 by Pearson Education. May be reproduced for noncommercial purposes.

FIGURE 7.9 Story Grammar Example

having a sense of a typical story structure helps both understanding and recall of story elements (McCormick, 1995).

Text Structure Guides

Questions and predictions about the reading can be developed from text structure guides that in essence outline key concepts and points to focus in on. Outlining textual material can also be done with graphic organizers. The teacher may provide instruction on specific text structures (pp. 141, 142) by selecting certain paragraphs or segments that illustrate five common text patterns: (1) descriptive, (2) sequential, (3) compare and contrast, (4) cause and effect, and (5) problem-solution.

Descriptive or Enumerative. This text pattern is designed to inform the reader about particular attributes or features of the topic (Figure 7.10).

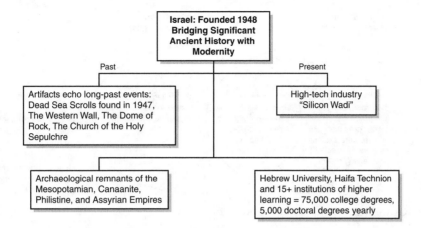

Source: Based on *Spectacular Israel* (1998) edited by Shai Ginott; Text by Amotz Asa-El; Hong Kong, China; Hugh Lauter Levin Associates, Inc.

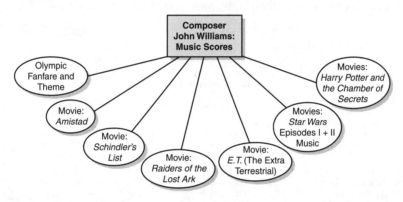

FIGURE 7.10   Descriptive or Enumerative

Sequential.   This text pattern designates the time-order of events (Figure 7.11).

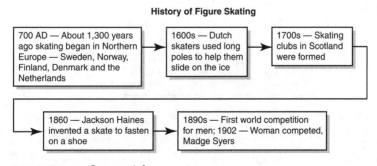

FIGURE 7.11   Sequential

Compare-and-Contrast.   This text pattern based on Venn diagrams is constructed to illustrate similarities and differences between two concepts (Figure 7.12).

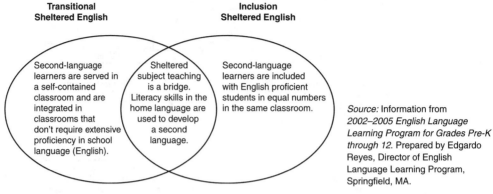

FIGURE 7.12   Compare-and-Contrast

Cause-and-Effect.   This text pattern is organized around relating the causes of certain events or conditions to their outcomes or consequences (Figure 7.13).

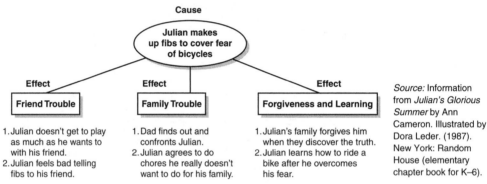

FIGURE 7.13   Cause-and-Effect

Problem-Solution.   This text pattern presents the factors associated with a particular problem and links them to possible solutions (Figure 7.14).

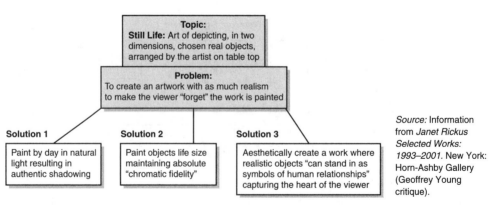

FIGURE 7.14   Problem-Solution (all three solutions were used in this example)

Strategic Reading of Expository (Informational) Text

The student with dyslexia may require repeated explicit instruction and practice to develop the awareness and strategies that support effective comprehension of expository text. Skimming, scanning, paraphrasing, surveying, and summarizing are proven ways to facilitate comprehension of expository text.

Skimming

Skimming is the rapid reading of text in order to get a sense of text structure, organization, and gist. Chapter titles, bolded type, marginal glosses, chapter previews, and chapter conclusions give the reader a cursory understanding of what the reading content involves. Teachers can instruct students with dyslexia to look for specific text components (e.g., chapter titles and headings, introduction and conclusion sections, pictures and graphics) when skimming to get a global picture of the reading at hand. Although skimming is part of the SQ3R study method mentioned in Chapter 10, Rubin (1991a) cautions that students be aware that skimming behaviors are not the same as studying, which requires "much slower and more concentrated reading" (p. 304). If students learn to paraphrase or summarize information as they adjust their reading rates, comprehension can be enhanced.

Scanning

Scanning is the rapid reading of text in order to locate needed information after a reading purpose has been established. Students who need to find information quickly, such as a phone number, an author in an index, a topic in a newspaper, and so on, can be guided to look for the keyword(s) wanted. Teachers need to point out that once the information is located, students need to read more slowly.

Paraphrasing

In studying the reading behaviors of struggling readers, Winograd (1984) has found that these readers have difficulty abstracting key ideas and summarizing or paraphrasing key concepts and information. Similarly, Taylor (1984) states that individuals who are poor readers will not actively think to paraphrase information before writing about what they read. Maggart and Zintz (1990) suggest that with poor readers, teachers first concentrate on having students paraphrase their ideas orally before written expressive tasks are assigned. These authors also indicate that discussions should follow reading assignments where students can brainstorm and share ideas regarding the summary of contextual material. Teachers can assist students with dyslexia in paraphrasing what they read by alternating with students as to who will paraphrase a paragraph, page, or story.

Immediate and positive feedback should be given to the student. The teacher should be quick to point out why the summary statement(s) are good and then add/delete obviously incorrect/irrelevant information. In this way, teachers actively model good paraphrasing or summary skills.

Paraphrasing skills can be applied to "fun" writing formats. For example, students could work on paraphrasing key story structure information and then report this information on a Book Report Cube (Figure 7.15).

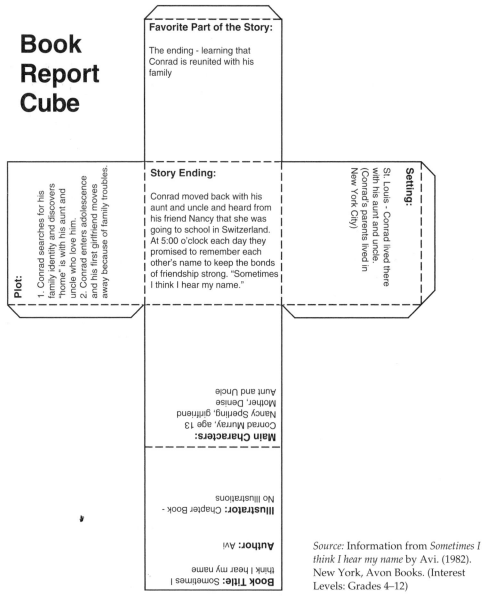

FIGURE 7.15   Book Report Cube with Paraphrased Information about Story Grammar

Surveying

Surveying is the guided exploration of the structure and content of the text material which is well suited to instructional strategies with basal readers.

Summarizing

According to the National Reading Panel Report (2000), the teaching of summarizing needs to involve rules and procedures for single and multiple passages where students generalize and integrate information found in text. Instruction in summarizing helps to improve memory for what was read in regard to free recall and answering questions. Summarizing is integral to reciprocal teaching (see p. 303) and other approaches that rely on the teaching of multiple strategies to enhance comprehension. In student summaries, teachers need to look at whether most of the important ideas were included as well as supporting details, facts, and vocabulary from the reading. C., Jr., tenth-grade

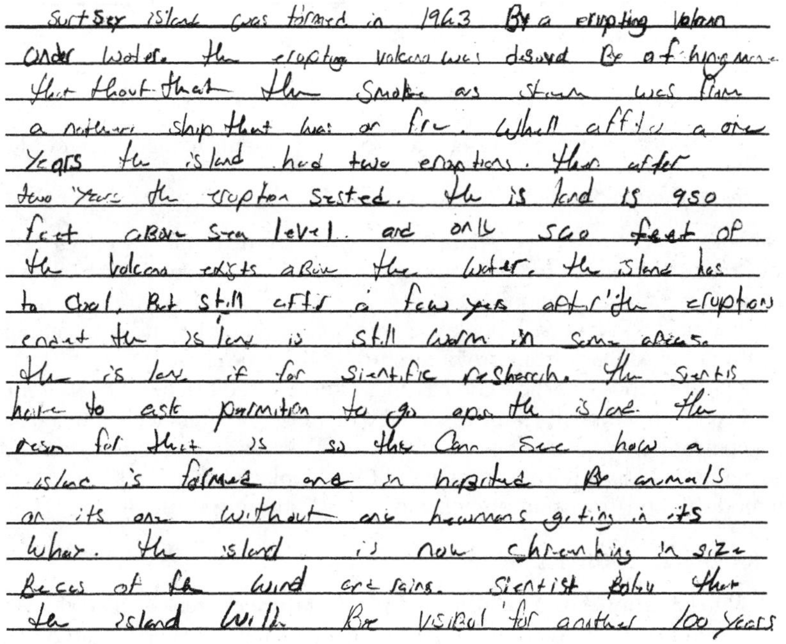

FIGURE 7.16 Example of Summarizing

student with dyslexia, wrote the summary shown in Figure 7.16 to a prompt on the subject of "Surtsey—Birth of an Island" (Beaver & Carter, 2003; DRA Grades 4–8 Pearson Education, Inc.,/Celebration Press/Pearson Learning Group, 2003). C., Jr. included the important ideas, supporting details and facts, as well as key vocabulary. Summarizing in writing nonfiction information as in this sample allows the learner to organize his or her thoughts on the subject with a reference later for study or report writing. For the student with dyslexia, if the purpose of the writing summary is for study purposes or note taking, language mechanics need not be emphasized or necessarily corrected (e.g., spelling and grammar).

The ability to summarize social studies and science text for students with dyslexia is crucial to comprehension and study notes. C., Jr. applied what is more commonly known as the SQ3R study skills method (see Chapter 10) to create his summary. As a secondary student, and with classroom assignments, it would be expected that C., Jr. would have access to a word processor to assist with language conventions and work legibility.

Some key summary points provided by C., Jr. in Figure 7.16.:

1. Surtsey Island was formed in 1963 by an erupting volcano.
2. The island is 950 feet above sea level and only 560 feet of the volcano exists above water.
3. The island has to be cool. But still a few years after another eruption the island is still warm in some areas.
4. Scientists have to ask permission to go to the island. The reason for that is so they can see how a island is formed and inhabited.
5. The island is now shrinking in size because of the wind and rain.
6. Scientists believe that the island will be visible for another 100 years.

Students can practice summarizing in literature circles or book study groups/book clubs. Table 7.6 was adapted from the work of Harvey Daniels (2002) and explains how to establish literature circles, even when scheduling can't be arranged during the regular school day. For students who are dyslexic or struggling readers, it

TABLE 7.6   Literature Circles or Book Study Groups/Books Clubs

Books: Minimum = 5 copies of 6 different books (30 books) representing a range of reading levels and genres

Group Size = 4 to 5 students in a group with designated roles; 4 students in a group would be ideal

Providing Book Choices to Engage Students

(1) Teacher displays books or articles for several days; students can read first few pages, talk to other students who have read the book, or read a summary of the book (e.g., from the back cover of the book, a library catalogue card, or a magazine book review).

(2) The teacher has a "book chat" about each book with reference to the plot and connections to any themes or material being studied. Feedback from previous students may be shared.

(3) Students list their top three book or article choices and submit to the teacher who will form groups of 4 (ideal number) or 5 children who will read the same book. Look for "balance" in the groups—e.g., numbers of boys versus girls, numbers of proficient readers versus struggling readers. For students who are dyslexic or struggling readers, it is recommended they be placed in groups with some proficient readers who can model "good" metacomprehension and questioning strategies.

Scheduling of Time for Literature Circles to Meet

Plan A (daily time of 30 to 45 minutes can be allocated for literature circles)—Schedule two days a week (T TH) for students to read and take notes (reading logs); for students with dyslexia, shared reading would be appropriate; the other three days would be devoted to literature circle group meetings (M W F). Students collaboratively discuss the reading with group members assuming various roles (see below).

Plan B—(only once per week can be devoted to literature circles)—Schedule readings and the taking of notes (reading logs) for homework after students have been taught the processes/procedures for literature circles. Students would use weekly meeting times for the literature circles (Mondays or Fridays).

Plan C—(scheduling can't be arranged for literature circles during the school day)—Schedule literature circles during recess time, study halls, or after school. If these times don't work, teach the entire class the process and procedures for literature circles and rotate small groups of literature circles who would meet in an area of the classroom that wouldn't interfere with the rest of the class working with the teacher.

Teacher's Role (5 minutes = mini-lessons; timekeeper thereafter: 20–30 minutes = students read independently [students with dyslexia could buddy read, participate in a shared reading, listen to a book on tape] and take some notes or literature circles meet; 5–10 minutes = group share or debriefing): Conduct a full group mini-lesson (5 minutes) eventually covering all of the following literature circle processes/procedures: (1) the process of selecting a good book, (2) how to divide the book up into sections for literature circle meetings, (3) how to maintain a reading log or notebook for literature circles, and (4) how to maintain a checklist of "need to do things" to periodically review before participating in literature circles as a way to self-monitor active, constructive, positive participation ("I need to pause and listen while others are talking," "When I disagree with someone's point, I need to give examples and refer to the book to validate my perspective," etc.). Continue with mini-lessons that focus on author's craft and story grammar or structure (e.g., "How did the author's use of language or development of character engage the reader?" "How much did the book title reveal what actually happened in the story?" "What major literary devices did the author use?" "Was the story resolution believable?" "Make sense?" etc.).

Suggested Roles of Literature Circle Group Members (consider appropriateness based on genre/type of reading; adapt or substitute with a new role as needed): Four Basic Recommended Roles (provide students with summary of roles; students rotate roles each meeting time)

1. **Questioner:** Probes to deepen thinking about the author's craft, story grammar or structure (e.g., "Why did the character act that way?" "What do you think will happen next [related to plot]?" "What kind of feelings does that illustration evoke?").

2. **Word Wizard:** Clarifies terminology (with access to a dictionary, teacher-made book glossary, word walls, etc.); points out author's use of language.

3. **Connector:** Makes connections to previous learning, books by the same author, real-life situations.

4. **Summarizer:** Summarizes sections of text or the passage read for the day; uses a retelling format.

Source: Adapted from the work of Harvey Daniels (2002).

is recommended they be placed in balanced groups with some proficient readers who can model good metacomprehension and questioning behaviors.

Silent Reading Comprehension

For oral reading activities, see Chapter 8, pages 199–201.

Sustained Silent Reading (SSR)   **Sustained silent reading** (SSR) activities are meant to foster/reinforce literate behavior and to encourage reading for enjoyment. These are independent reading activities that utilize literature and leisure types of reading materials. The independent reading level of the student with dyslexia needs to be identified so that sustained silent reading times can be relatively fluent and enjoyable. As an example, the DEAR (Drop Everything and Read) programs have become common SSR experiences in many schools. Teachers, principals, and students literally "drop everything and read" at specified times during the school day (usually 15 minutes). Tierney, Readence, and Dishner (1990) give three suggestions for SSR activities: (1) Everyone reads, (2) there are no interruptions, and (3) no one will be asked to report on readings.

Students with dyslexia should be able to manage SSR reading material. Support could be provided by the type of materials used: listening tapes of books with headsets; high-interest low-vocabulary library books; leisure-type activities with high-interest low-vocabulary content such as newspapers, National Geographic books for children, wordless books, comic books (remember SSR is supposed to be enjoyable), sports magazines; hobby books; and even books with accompanying tapes. Students who also experience attention problems will need to be accommodated during SSR times.

Students with Attention Problems.   Students with attention problems may find SSR times difficult at best. Students who are highly distractible need to be strategically seated during SSR times so that interruptions to other students are kept at a minimum. Certainly giving students with attention problems a job or special duty during SSR times can help channel energies constructively. As examples, the classroom teachers could (1) appoint such students to be timekeepers during SSR times and provide a stopwatch or clock—very simply a student could give the teacher a silent hand signal at each 5-minute interval (the student is alternating reading behaviors with keeping track of the time); and (2) inattentive students could shift gears every so often by changing reading materials (allowing the student to move about by selecting a new book, magazine, or other reading material).

Even more useful would be the use of self-monitoring training before and after SSR times so that inattentive students "are taught to effectively self-monitor their on-task behavior, the chances are good that their academic productivity [reading behaviors] will increase" (deBettencourt, 1990, p. 462).

Hallahan's Self-Monitoring of Inattentive Behavior.   Hallahan and his associates (see Hallahan, Kauffman, & Lloyd, 1985) have developed a self-monitoring procedure for dyslexic students (and those with other learning disabilities) who have attention problems. The procedure is as follows: (1) The teacher operationally defines desired on-task behaviors for the student (SSR as an example) and then gives the student examples; (2) the teacher models the desired behaviors (SSR) along with the student who must self-check if he or she is on task; (3) the student periodically receives a cue from the teacher and at that very moment must self-record whether he or she was on task; (4) the cueing and self-recording behaviors are diminished until the desired behaviors become somewhat acquired. Notice we say somewhat. One can't expect perfect on-task behaviors for students with attention difficulties. That is why it would be important to establish baseline behaviors and reasonable objectives before self-monitoring occurs. If a student is able to attend to SSR for only 2 minutes before instruction, a 5- to 6-minute attention span might be extremely favorable following instruction. The key is to establish reasonable expectations based on the nature of the problem and the perceived stamina of the individual.

The quality of comprehension during silent reading depends on one's metacognitive awareness or knowledge of one's own cognitive processes (Flavell, 1976). Flavell (1987) proposes that readers must be aware of self (e.g., an individual's assessment of cognitive strengths and weaknesses), task (e.g., different tasks require different kinds of information processing), and strategy (e.g., self-monitoring and self-evaluation) variables related to knowledge of cognition.

Self-Monitoring during Reading   Children need to learn at an early age that they need to keep track of the reasons why (purpose) they are reading as well as their understanding of the material read. Young children can be instructed early on to look at picture cues, context cues, initial word sounds, titles, and predictable words to assist in the comprehension of reading materials. Older students can be assisted with specific questioning techniques and study skills strategies discussed later in Chapter 10. Individuals with dyslexia and other learning disabilities do not have as sophisticated self-monitoring abilities and other metacognitive strategies as good readers do and there is a "... need to teach them metacognitive skills in reading in addition to decoding and comprehension skills ..." (Wong, 1991). All students need to be encouraged to ask questions when they do not understand what is presented. One of the best ways to develop metacognitive skills is to teach via an interrogative reading format.

Interrogative Reading

There is an old saying to the effect that our knowledge is better measured by the questions we raise than by the answers we give. It has been shown that students who develop their own questions about textual material better comprehend what is read than those who do not (Palinscar & Brown, 1984). Students with dyslexia typically approach text in a passive manner and may need direct modeling and practice to develop interrogative strategies. Certainly activities that involve students as active participants and encourage learning by the inquiry-based approach (e.g., hands-on learning in science during such science units as magnetism, electricity, exploring the characteristics of rocks and minerals, etc.) can result in improved comprehension gains (Scruggs, Mastropieri, Bakken, & Brigham, 1993). "Because most students with LD have difficulty learning from reading and workbook assignments, and benefit from concrete examples, activity-based science instruction may be preferable to textbook-based instruction" (Scruggs et al., 1993, p. 3). The questioning generated from such endeavors encourages students to self-monitor while learning and to develop better metacognitive awareness. Examples in Figures 7.17 and 7.18 emphasize the active role the reader must assume when interacting with the printed page.

Self-Monitoring of Comprehension during Reading   Questioning strategies provide the individual with dyslexia opportunities for critical thinking, summarizing major portions of text, predicting for later reading that will be confirmed or not confirmed, filling in the blanks for unknown words and concepts, and understanding the selection at hand (e.g., rereading). Additionally, questioning/self-questioning strategies allow the teacher/student to assess critical deficit areas along with other assessment measures (Wallace, Cohen, & Polloway, 1987; Wallace, Larsen, & Elksnin, 1992). There are specific questioning strategies one can use even in the content area subjects in order to facilitate learning for the student with dyslexia. *Cognitive apprenticeships* and *framing questions* are two such methods. Figure 7.18 shows how students must assume a greater role in the comprehension process if self-monitoring procedures are to be effective.

A questioning strategy is an important component of "active" reading. The inner dialogue that accompanies proficient reading needs to be modeled and practiced and can involve question generation and question answering.

Grade 4 (related to District Art Standards: e.g., strand = art critique; content area = design; major concepts = evaluation/analysis

The Importance of Art

Art has played an important role in people's lives for centuries. It has allowed people to communicate ideas and thoughts visually "without words" so that people of all ages can enjoy and understand "art's messages."

Art and art experiences can only grow from reading about and actually seeing art works first-hand. Expanding one's knowledge about art can be exciting with the discovery of and discussions about artists.

Individual art work can be personally evaluated and analyzed to develop a respect for individual artists and their expressive art works. Positive feelings for what has been created by others can result in ideas for creating one's own original art works.

The study of artists in various cultures from different continents can help further understandings and appreciations for many cultures.

Teacher models inner dialogue (question generation)

Why is art important?

Where and When can I learn more about art?

What painting could I view and evaluate for use of color, space, line, shape and composition to create my own artwork?

I wonder who some important artists are from by own cultural heritage and from that of my friends?

Source: Adapted from *Wentzville, Wisconsin R-IV School District Art Guide* (Kraus Curriculum Development Library) (18th edition), 1998. Lanham, MD: Bernan.

FIGURE 7.17   The Five Ws: Interrogative Reading

Cognitive Apprenticeships   "The central focus of much research in reading instruction is on the teacher's explanations to students of the cognitive activities engaged in by good readers" (Ross, Bondy, & Kyle, 1993, p. 89). Cognitive apprenticeships are one way to provide models for good reading behaviors (Collins, Brown, & Newman, 1989) in an interactive questioning type of format. The student with reading disabilities is coached by the teacher, who provides suggestions, feedback, appropriate reading materials, and scaffolding. Scaffolding is the way in which the teacher implements

Teachers need to model the strategies that govern skilled questioning. Gradually students take on a greater role in developing their own inner dialogue.

Self-Questioning Procedure (Question Generation)		Inner Dialogue (Question Answering)
1. Why am I reading this?	[Purpose]	To learn about the Japanese culture.
2. What will I be learning?	[Skim]	The pictures show all different parts of the Japanese culture.
3. How is this organized?	[Preview]	Each letter of the alphabet tells me about Japan.
4. What do I already know about this?	[Schemata]	I saw "Sushi" on restaurant menus.
5. Does this make sense as I read? Do I understand?	[Active Reading]	Yes. The pictures help me make a person-to-text connection.
6. Is there new information here? Should I slow down? Reread?	[Metacognitive Strategy]	Yes. The pronunciations in italics help me pronounce the words. Slow down. I should read this part again.
7. How am I doing? Am I learning as I read?	[Metacognitive Monitoring]	Yes. These words make sense because the picture images make Japan real. I'll add Japanese words to my thesaurus.

Source: Information from *A to Zen* by Ruth Wells; Illustrator, Yoshi. (1992). Saxonville, MA: Simon & Schuster.

FIGURE 7.18   Self-Monitoring during Reading

support or specific helpful hints. The student with reading disabilities is gradually withdrawn from assistance as he or she becomes more proficient.

Reading–Writing Connections

Writing activities are involved in many specific comprehension activities (e.g., prediction) and questioning methods as one must take notes or record answers, write reports, and so on. There are a number of techniques that can assist the student with dyslexia in acquiring necessary writing skills while constructing knowledge and interacting with the printed page. In any case, writing activities need to be integrated across the curriculum. Students with dyslexia and other learning disabilities have been found to be lacking in such written expressive areas as handwriting, spelling, and thematic development (Hallahan, Kauffman, & Lloyd, 1985).

Good writers pay attention to the communicative aspects of writing such as expressing one's thoughts in a clear, logical, and organized manner. Good writers can also focus on the *ideas* expressed in writing because the *mechanics* (e.g., punctuation, grammar, spelling, capitalization) are automatic. As good role models, adults can communicate to less able writers by written correspondence in forms such as letters, notes, and diaries. The letter to a student (see Figure 7.19) is a good example of how writing can be used to communicate on a personal level while modeling effective idea and topic development using standard language conventions.

The Writers' Workshop

The writers' workshop is an instructional approach to writing that engages students with each other and their teacher in a series of interactive writing activities, the final outcome of which is a published writing composition (Calkins, 1994; Graves, 1994). Often, read-aloud books (from a variety of genres) previously used for whole-class readings are used in writers' workshops. According to Marilyn Jager Adams (1991), "the most important activity for building the knowledge and skills eventually required for read-

Dear Greg,

On your high school Graduation Day, congratulations on your accomplishment. An accomplishment is an achievement, by definition a quality or ability that equips you for society. Your greatest achievement is that you found inner resources to enable you to, when necessary, persevere and withstand the moment and cope with the potential challenges school often presents. By so doing, you have developed inner resources and a core of faith in your own ability that is your hidden wealth.

You told me what a difference teachers make in developing a sound foundation from which you learn to act and react. When they help you develop confidence in your ability to learn, set goals, choose values and contribute positively, they are enhancing your self-esteem for life. One consistently essential ingredient for encouraging a student to seek the best of what is within him is to nurture these abilities until the traits become as expansive as they can be.

If a teacher wishes to oppress a student, he or she would be hard put to come up with a more effective plan than to have one standard, the traditional learning approach, that all students must measure up to. As you so aptly stated, "that's too much pressure on a little kid!" We know that the unique nature of being human means that we all have differences in character and attitude, and that many people learn most effectively by alternate methods; not traditional approaches. And some of those people are among the most accomplished—once they are viewed from the perspective that we are all different. In the end, a learning pattern, no matter how it differs from the ideal, is not the only factor in deciding what we'll be able to do or to be. It is our intelligence that shapes our world and is our most powerful edge. When you give your best effort in applying your individual skills, you show that it isn't really how smart you are that makes you accomplished, it's *how* you are smart!

Mimi

FIGURE 7.19   A Graduation Letter of Accomplishments

ing is that of reading aloud to children . . . it is not just reading to children that makes the difference, it is enjoying books with them" (pp. 86–87). Reading aloud to children on a daily basis also helps develop a firm foundation for varying story structures and lets children know how language works—both requisites for writing proficiency.

Celebrating and Enjoying the Reading and Writing Process with Students Diane E. Bushner, Sharon I. Tave, and Jean Young (1989) believe connected reading and writing activities need to invite children to "celebrate" or have a "good time" during the writing process. For students with learning disabilities who often see reading and writing as arduous tasks, motivation to pick up a book or a writing tool will remain an ongoing challenge. Bushner and her colleagues recommend bringing the writing process to levels of cooperative group collaborations as in writing scripts for readers' theatre or collectively celebrating writing accomplishments through a class newspaper. Writers' workshops help students with and without disabilities develop final published writing pieces they can proudly use in a theatre production, publish in a class or social newspaper, or display on school or family (the refrigerator!) bulletin boards.

Inspiring Student Authors through Literature Festivals and Author Receptions These types of literary events put the reader in contact with authors and literature. Frequently, workshop sessions or informal meetings are held that allow for interactions between those interested in the literature and, at times, with the author himself or herself. Letters to authors (see Figure 7.20) connect students further to literature works and inspire students to use the writing process to become "authors" and "poets."

First-Hand Accounts from Successful Dyslexics Inspire All Writers How did Avi, award-winning author of more than twenty-five well-known books for children and adolescents and severely dyslexic, achieve at the highest levels of accomplishment in writing, having been awarded the Newbery Medal in 2003 for *Crispin*, Newberry

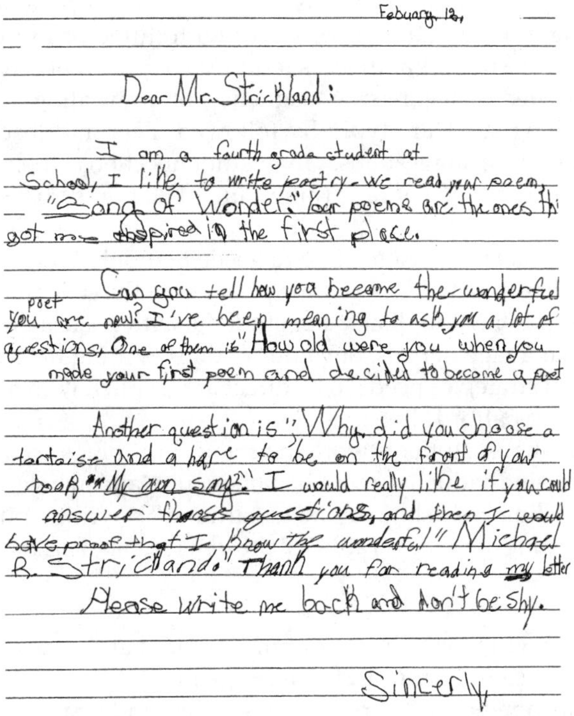

Febuary 12,

Dear Mr. Strickland:

I am a fourth grade student at School, I like to write poetry. We read your poem, "Song of Wonder." Your poems are the ones that got me inspired in the first place.

Can you tell how you became the wonderful poet you are now? I've been meaning to ask you a lot of questions. One of them is "How old were you when you made your first poem and decided to become a poet

Another question is "Why did you choose a tortoise and a hare to be on the front of your book "My own song?" I would really like if you could answer those questions, and then I would have proof that I know the wonderful "Michael R. Strickland." Thank you for reading my letter Please write me back and don't be shy.

Sincerly,

FIGURE 7.20 Letter to Michael Strickland, Author

Honors (*The True Confession of Charlotte Doyle, Nothing But the Truth*), the Scott O'Dell Award (*The Fighting Ground*), and ALA Best Booklist recognition (*Wolf Rider*), among others? Visiting Avi or other authors via Internet sites, school visits, written biographies, and teacher shares from conference attendance provide us answers to this question through *first-hand accounts*.

Avi and most authors of "popular" books share in common the tenacity or perseverance to succeed despite academic (dyslexia) and life obstacles—strongly resilient personalities (see Chapter 4 on developing resiliency). What helped Avi and other successful writers *the most*? *Reading-to-write with stories!*

Reading-to-Write with Stories! Avi (2002)

Stories soothe, bond us, entertain and perhaps save us . . . I can still feel the book in my hands that I was given at age three . . . mom read to me every day . . . we often walked to the public library . . . my first identity card was a library card . . . every holiday I received a book for a gift . . . I loved comic books . . . at age 16 my father brought me to a bookstore and gave me $35.00 to spend any way I wanted—I bought a collection of plays . . . a passion. I listened to radio stories dramatized that could be read in narrative . . . I recall the laughter stories brought to me . . . stories gave me ideas and starting points for writing my own stories . . . all stories are emotional maps which allow us to find our way through life . . . I experience life as a story . . .

Avi read and wrote extensively as a child. As an adult, Avi has written in all genres because he didn't learn one writing style or way of writing. He was exposed to many types of story structures through "wide" (various genres) reading. According to Avi, we are all storytellers but a "story doesn't become a story until it has a writer and a reader." As Avi has shown us, good writers best learn their craft by reading stories, reading often and reading extensively—this is especially true for individuals with dyslexia or other learning disabilities!

Goals of Writing Workshops   Writers' workshops help students to: (1) achieve proficiency in writing according to benchmarks or standards, (2) develop creativity and their voice in writing, (3) familiarize themselves with different forms of writing, (4) write for different purposes and audiences, and (5) communicate to others personal ideas/thoughts/knowledge/feelings. A sequence of prewriting, writing, editing, revising, and publishing steps are typically followed. Peer and teacher conferences center on ideas and editing suggestions. Often students choose their own topics and write daily for sustained periods of time (minimum of 30 minutes).

Writing Workshop Framework   According to Leslie Mandel Morrow (2003), the writing workshop should be a daily block of time planned in the schedule just for writing activities; she suggests a one-hour block. For students with dyslexia who often experience severe written language deficits, one hour of daily writing time would be a minimum. The teaching of strategies needs to be direct and explicit with modeling, guided practice and feedback (Spafford, 1999).

In writers' workshops, students work in various groupings according to instructional writing levels—individually, pairs, small groups and whole class. There is a framework for the writing workshop organized around (1) writing purposes, (2) writing forms, and (3) writing activities. Table 7.7 presents some ideas for topics.

Writing Purposes
- Students learn to write for a variety of purposes and audiences.
- Students learn to read-to-write and write-to-read.
- Students acquire a repertoire of procedures, skills, and strategies to use depending on the writing purpose and audience.

TABLE 7.7   Ideas for Writer's Workshop

"Think about" . . . "writing or writing about" . . .

- one's strength in a particular area
- one's metacognitive abilities or "metacognition"
- explaining or teaching something to someone in which the writer is an expert
- "how to" manual about something
- a "thumbnail sketch" of a person, place, or thing
- stories to accompany collages, mobiles, story boxes, posters, bulletin boards
- poems
- plays or choral theatre productions
- dialogue for characters
- dialogue for cartoon sequences
- the text for a video, overhead, or slide presentation
- word search puzzles and other language games with "how-to-play-the-game" instructions
- penpal letters, business letters, personal letters, letters to authors, persuasive letters
- thank you notes, invitations
- a request for something
- written messages for greeting cards
- environmental/national/state/local concerns or issues
- a reply or rebuttal to something found on TV or in the popular press
- taking a position on an issue
- a book or movie review
- an essay, biography, or autobiography
- a historical piece
- story recollections or retellings
- another culture; responding to cultural presentations
- a song
- notes for test taking
- maps, charts, graphs, tables—for content area study with written explanatory pieces
- an outline for an oral presentation
- a lab report
- personal assessments of progress in an area of study
- an interview
- a case study
- a character study
- a resumé
- completing the process for a driver's license application
- completing the process for a job application
- the directions to get somewhere and construct a reading road map
- a contribution for a school or class newspaper, program, yearbook
- a submission for a writing contest
- good citizenship

Source: Spafford, Pesce, & Grosser (1998).

- Students learn to value writing as a vital way to communicate ideas, knowledge, opinions, expertise, feelings, and so on. (Morrow, 2003)

Writing Genre Forms
- **Descriptive** (purpose: explain a person, place, thing or idea focusing on one thing and its components; sample key words: *also, this, that, for instance, in fact*)
- **Narrative** (purpose: to tell a story; narratives tend to summarize and describe actions and typically have elements such as characters, setting, plot)
- **Persuasive** (purpose: to persuade the reader to agree with one side of an issue or argument; in long composition writing both sides are presented and one side is favored; counterarguments are discussed; sample key words: *therefore, even though, you must admit, granted, desired*)

- **Expository** (purpose: informational or descriptive often to convey factual information, explain ideas, or present an argument; this book was written as an expository piece with a specific text outline and headings that reflect key ideas for each section. To contrast, descriptive and persuasive writing forms are much more narrow in focus; narrative writing involves story structure.) (Harrison & Cullinan, 1999; Mason & Au, 1990; Zwiers, 2004)

Writing Activities in Writer's Workshops
- Students need to first "experience" the craft of writing by seeing or hearing about how successful writers develop proficiency as writers.
- Writing assignments are explained and clarified with rubrics distributed or collectively created to guide idea and topic development as well as the use of language conventions (see pp. 165–167).
- Donald McFeely (2002) suggests including poetry, reading-aloud, music, humor, magic and delight of words, and reader's theatre to invest reluctant writers.
- Teacher crafts mini-lessons (see box) based on formal or informal observations/assessments of students' needs in writing. A mini-lesson may be a continuation of previous mini-lessons or a series of discrete, separate lessons. Example: Design a series of mini-lessons focused on acquiring proficiency in responding to open response questions.

The Design of a Mini-Lesson

Amount of time that will be devoted to the mini-lesson: 5 to 10 minutes

Preplanning
- Identify a topic for the mini-lesson and specific content.
- Reflect on, How will I teach the content or strategy so that it will have a lasting impact on students as readers and writers?
- Focus planning efforts on *designing the method* of teaching the content rather than the content itself.

Mini-lesson Implementation
- Begin the mini-lesson making a connection. How does this mini-lesson connect with previous learning? Personal lives as readers and writers?
- Teach something that you want your students to try as readers or writers. Teachers and/or students model, demonstrate, or tell what needs to be done.
- Provide all children an opportunity to "try out" the new learning or strategy for just a few minutes. Students can work independently or with partners.

And the End of the Mini-lesson
- Link the mini-lesson to the work in the writers' workshop (typically one hour) for that particular day and the students lives as readers and writers.
- At the end of the writers' workshop, follow up on the mini-lesson. What's next? How can we apply this new learning to future reading and writing?

Source: Calkins (2001, pp 84–85)

To summarize, the writers' workshop is a systematic instructional approach to writing that engages students with each other and their teachers in a series of interactive writing activities, the final outcome of which is a published writing composition. Joetta Beaver (2002) reminds us to allow children to take time with preplanning writing activities as they require time to "envision . . . they need to incubate ideas." Graphic organizers have proven to work well in this regard (Spinelli, 1999; Witherell

& McMackin, 2002). The writers' workshop requires direct and explicit teaching and modeling, conferencing, and journal writing. Marjorie Lipson (2002) emphasizes the reason for the direct and explicit teaching of mini-lessons—"we have to be explicit in what we want children to pay attention to so they can use the new learning again." To revisit new learning, and as the writers workshop concludes, Lipson (2002) suggests prompting children with "How will this help you the next time (in your writing)?" Similarly, Shelley Harwayne (1992) tells teachers to ask themselves, "How can we extend the activities once they've begun?" Harwayne also wants teachers to consider how writing projects can succeed without direct teacher support . . . "What structures can I put in place so that the project succeeds without me?" (p. 100).

Modeled Writing

There are various ways to model the writing process. Thinking aloud and sharing what good writers do during the act of writing (on chart paper or an overhead) provide students with both the process and a sample writing product. Sandra J. Stone gives three examples of modeled writing strategies in Table 7.8.

Completing the Writing Process

Showcasing published or completed student work can be done in a number of ways. Students can make their own books (see Figure 7.21). Creating bulletin board artwork to highlight writing accomplishments conveys to students the idea, "I value your work as an author."

TABLE 7.8 Modeled Writing Strategies

Strategy 1: Collaborative Writing	Strategy 2: Teacher Writing with Errors (especially helpful for students with dyslexia who need practice in finding writing errors to self-correct)	Strategy 3: Teacher Writing Using a Correct Model
■ Teacher chooses a short writing piece to model and verbalizes aloud thinking about writing strategies and the writing process. ■ Teacher writes words and sentences, and children help by choosing letters for words, showing spacing, identifying punctuation, or actually composing some of the words, sentences, or paragraphs. ■ Teacher and students read the final writing piece aloud. ■ Students write in their journals for practice.	■ Teacher verbalizes thinking about writing strategies and the writing process. ■ Teacher writes sentences on chart paper or an overhead projector that contain errors— the students read silently. ■ Teacher and students chorally read the writing piece. ■ Students collectively correct "writing errors." ■ Students write in their journals for practice.	■ Teacher verbalizes thinking about writing strategies and the writing process. ■ Teacher writes sentences that model correct writing— students read silently. ■ Teacher and students chorally read the writing piece. ■ Students circle or highlight focus skills.* ■ Students write in their journals for practice.

*Focus skills: For students with dyslexia, it is recommended that teachers abstract one or two teaching points per mini-lesson to focus on—what Stone (1996) refers to as "focus skills." The focus could be on idea or topic development and/or language conventions. Be very specific (e.g., practice writing topic sentences; practice finding colorful adjectives in the dictionary; practice correctly spelling a few high-frequency sight words; practice writing exclamatory sentences and so on). For students with dyslexia, practice, practice, and more practice are essential to develop writing proficiency.

Source: Stone (1996), p. 122.

Cloud Crystal Ball

Look into your "Cloud Crystal Ball." What can you do in the future to make this a better world? Dr. Martin Luther King, Jr. made this a better world by living "I Have A Dream."

You can also dare to make your dreams come true. Write about your dream for a better world inside the "Cloud Crystal Ball."

Teachers: Use the Cloud Crystal Ball writing pieces for this bulletin board.

FIGURE 7.21   Cloud Crystal Ball

Spelling

Don't Forget Followup Spelling Instruction!

According to Elena Boder (1970), there is a direct correlation between spelling and reading performance for children with dyslexia. Boder's research has been supported in that how a child reads and how a child spells are mutually predictive, and with dyslexics, spelling achievement is consistently below that of reading achievement. Teachers who work with students who are learning disabled are urged by George S. Grosser and Carol Spafford (2000) not to forget spelling! There needs to be some emphasis on the direct, explicit teaching of spelling based on a structured sequence of word analysis (e.g., including phonics) with some focus on irregular spellings. This can occur during the language portion of the language arts or literacy block (see p. 314).

Most Popular and Productive Word Wall Activities in Reading and Writing

Set aside 10 minutes per day to use word-wall activities—according to Cunningham, the real "power" of a word wall comes from using it!

(1) **Easy Rhyming:** Show children how words on the word wall help them pronounce and spell words (e.g., *day, pay, play, may, way*). Use the word wall words in context and have students refer to the word wall when they encounter the words in reading. For spelling, the present authors suggest word games where children learn to spell high-frequency words like *daylight* and *Wednesday*.

(2) **Easy Ending Activity:** Children work with five word-wall words; teacher helps with adding suffixes [e.g., Add *s* to the five words listed under (1) and discuss how the meaning changes.]

(3) **Harder Ending Activity:** Children work with five word-wall words. Create sentences where children have to pick one of the words and add an ending to have the sentence make sense. [e.g., How many _____ are there in a year? Choose *day* from (1) and add the suffix *s*]

(4) **Combine Rhyme and Endings:** Create a short sentence that has a word or part of a word that rhymes with a word-wall word (say or write the sentence). Show how the student can find a rhyming word on the word wall. Then change the part of the word that needs to change for the word-wall word to become the rhyming word. Students can spell words aloud before writing them. [e.g., for example: "Please say thank you." The word *may* is on the word wall. Change the *m* in *may* to a *s* and the word *say* is formed. Students can think aloud as they go through the process of letter changes.]

(5) **Mind Reader:** Students or teachers can think of a word on the word wall. Write the word on a piece of paper. Then give the rest of the class five clues to figure out the word. Have students write a word they think is the right word after each clue. By the fifth clue, all students should have read the mind of the "word magician." Example: 1. It's a word on the second list of the word wall. 2. The word has eight letters. 3. The word ends with -*ness*. 4. You can hear a vowel say its name in the word. 5. You can use the word in this sentence: Students should show _____ and respect to each other.

Variations That Can Also Be Used:

- Harder Rhyming
- Prefix Activities

Source: Cunningham (2000, p. 64).

Word Walls and Spelling

Word walls are particularly helpful during the writing process. However, students with dyslexia require practice using word walls, and Cunningham (2000) suggests "the most popular and productive activities" (p. 64) in the box.

Spelling Accommodations

Less skilled writers have difficulty with the mechanics of writing and communiating ideas both at the elementary (Birnbaum, 1982) and secondary (Pianko, 1979) levels. Spelling in particular can be problematic as the task itself requires visualization of a correct word form with no visual cues present. Additionally, English irregularities present a special problem for the student with dyslexia.

Students with dyslexia should be allowed to use *spelling assists* when necessary such as poor spellers' dictionaries, spelling computers, glossaries, and computer spell checks. Spelling games can make the learning of spelling words fun as this can be a very rote, dry task. Cued spelling can be used with a peer or parent collaborating and providing valuable feedback.

Schunk's Cued Spelling for Parent/Peer Tutoring

Schunk (1987) first introduced the format for "Cued Spelling." Students work in pairs with an individual designated as the tutor. There are ten basic steps:

1. Student with dyslexia chooses a word to spell.
2. Both the student and the tutor check the spelling of the word by using a dictionary, poor speller's dictionary, or spell check. Then the student places the word in a "spelling diary" or log.
3. Both read the word together and then the dyslexic student reads alone.
4. The dyslexic student then chooses spelling cues/assists/rules from a list, appropriate to the age and developmental level of the student (e.g., look at the base word and then see what prefixes or suffixes have been added; "i" before "e" except after "c"), provided by the teacher.
5. Both say the cues aloud.
6. The dyslexic student says the cue and the tutor then writes the word (e.g., use the chalkboard, a separate paper, the computer, and so on).
7. The tutor says the clue and the dyslexic student writes the word.
8. The dyslexic student says the cue and then writes the word independently.
9. The dyslexic student tries to write the word quickly and then says the word aloud.
10. Repeat any steps as necessary so that cues and spellings are correct. (adapted from Topping, 1995)

Spelling and the Language Experience Approach

Spelling can also be practiced within the context of language-experience stories (Stauffer, 1970, 1980). Language experience stories have been proven to be effective with students who are learning disabled and also with students who are second-language learners. With language experience stories, students develop their own stories individually with the teacher, who serves as the "secretary" or scribe. The teacher scribes the story using the exact words of the child as well as the child's grammar or syntax but *with correct spelling.* The language experience story serves as a basis for a reading activity and word study. The student writes down new words or "favorite" words on index cards to learn. The words can be matched to pictures or sentences and can be reviewed at later times for recognition (e.g., identify as a sight word) and spelling. Children are encouraged to take their language experience stories home to reread for practice. Since the words in the stories are used by the children in oral language, there is the motivation to learn to read the words, learn how to spell the words, and then use the words again in future writings.

Considerations for Students with Learning Disabilities

■ *During writing conferences teachers can share their spelling and writing "toils" and successes using various writing forms. According to Don Landry (1989) teachers could also be personally invested in the same writing task—"Poems are written by poets and that includes me!" . . .

■ *Students need to work on drafts and revisions of work, time permitting. A dictionary should be handy for spelling checks.

Spelling Fortune Teller

Prepare paper for students by having it cut in squares. (A paper cutter makes this preparation quick.)

1. Fold the square of paper into a triangle. Then fold it once again into a smaller triangle so that when the square is opened again, there is an "X" folded across it to mark the center on the paper.

2. Fold each corner of the square into the center as exactly as you can. This will make a smaller square.

3. Turn the folded paper over so that the flaps are on the bottom, and the plain side faces upward. Again, fold the corners of the square into the center. This side gives you 8 spaces on which to write spelling words. Vary the word lengths that are next to each other on the flaps. Turn the Fortune Teller over and you have 4 more flaps to put words on.

4. Slide your index fingers and thumbs into the 4 square flaps to make a 3-dimensional figure.

5. Alternately pinch your fingers and spread your 2 hands, and then bring 2 hands together and spread finger and thumb. Make one move for each letter of the word as you spell it aloud. One student chooses the word, the other spells it out, once on outer flap, three times on inner flaps.

Source: Cabana (1994)

FIGURE 7.22   Spelling Fortune Teller

- *Students need access to word walls with high-frequency words used in writing.
- *Students with dyslexia could write troublesome words on a chart to access while writing or create a "Spelling Fortune Teller" (Figure 7.22) (Cabana, 1994).
- *The teacher conferences with individual students or small groups of students and takes anecdotal records to document writing and spelling progress over time. Peer editing also occurs in mini-conferences.
- *Students reflect on their work according to the writing rubrics (see pp. 165–167) and complete a final "published" piece. Ideas or topics have been developed and language conventions appropriate to the grade level and writing purpose have been addressed—this includes spelling.
- *Writers' workshops involve schools as communities of writers (Mary O. Pottenger School). When entire schools invest in *The Writer's Workshop* on a daily basis with the collective understanding, "We are a *community* of writers," the motivation to succeed as writers and good spellers is enhanced! (e.g., Kennan, Solsken, Negroni, Kennedy, Harris, Moriarty, Santa, Williams, Cox, Lak, Radding, Silvestri from Mary O. Pottenger School, Springfield, MA, 1994).
- *Keep in mind that even students with dyslexia differ in linguistic, cognitive, and motor development so "one size fits all" instruction needs to be differentiated based on the writing needs and levels for all students (Dudley-Marling, 2002). Spelling instruction should be differentiated in some way based on the learner.
- *Use computer word processing with grammar and spell checks but don't forget spelling instruction during the school day!
- Scribe (teacher writes) oral responses for students with severe disabilities; scaffold to independence in writing without scribing (also for kindergarten and first-grade students who are emerging writers or second-language learners who are beginning transition to another language). Students see correct spelling modeled.
- *Segment writing assignments or projects into smaller chunks that will be manageable for the student. Work on spelling within each segment.

- *Focus initially on idea and topic development—this conveys to the student that the development of ideas and topics in writing are the priorities. Spelling is important but not the priority.
- Some writing formats require more emphasis on spelling than others. For one-paragraph open response writing and journal writing, the writer needs to focus on the content or "quality" of the message. In long-composition writing, however, the writer needs to focus both on topic or idea development and language mechanics or conventions (spelling, grammar, punctuation).
- *Request frequent writing conferences—these can be brief. Writing conferences are particularly important for struggling writers because they are opportunities to "check in" with the writer to offer encouragement and to determine specific areas of strength and weakness (Calkins, 1994; Graves, 1994). Atwell (1998) frames one-to-one writing conferences by having the writer first explain what he or she expects or wants from the conference. *The role of the peer or teacher is to be a good listener and respond in ways that will help the writer improve his or her writing.*

Open Response Writing Format

Students with learning disabilities need practice with spelling within many different forms of writing. One type of writing that is commonly problematic for students with and without learning disabilities is the open response writing format. This type of writing can be taught and students with dyslexia can achieve proficiency, even surpassing nondisabled peers in performance.

What Is Open Response Writing?

Open response questions are questions that require the writer to express an opinion, description, explanation, relationship (e.g., compare and contrast; cause and effect), procedure, sequence of events, and so on based on a reading (Boyles, 2001, 2002). Most high-stakes tests in grade 3 through college require students to demonstrate content understandings in reading, language arts, math, science, social studies, and other areas through open response question formats among others (e.g., multiple choice format is another type of questioning frequently used). In mathematics, students are now required to explain procedures or processes used to arrive at answers with graphs, charts, and tables with open response writing formats—simply giving the right answer is not sufficient to demonstrate mastery of mathematics in current programs. In fact, Calkins, Montgomery, Santman, and Falk (1998) estimate 50 to 85 percent of all reading passages to be informational text, with open response questions popular formats for demonstrating content understanding.

According to Sharon Benge Kletzien and Mariam Jean Dreher (2004), informational text or factual text is written for the purpose of persuading or informing the reader. Common types of informational text are autobiographies, biographies, reference books, social studies and science texts, newspapers, and magazines. According to Kletzien and Dreher, common text structures used are cause-effect (see p. 142), comparison-contrast (see p. 141), sequence (see p. 141), descriptions (see p. 140), problem-solution (see p. 142), question-answer (presents who, what, why, where, when, how questions with answers) and generalization-example (a general statement is provided with examples).

Proficiency, then, in responding to open response questions is essential in academics and subsequently the workplace. Job applications frequently request responses to

---

*Applicable to all students

open response questions ("Why are you the best candidate for this job?" "What is your philosophy of education?") with writing proficiency required for the job itself. Being able to construct a topic sentence with supporting details and a concluding sentence (open response format) is foundational to most writing forms. Long compositions and written reports require what would be considered an "expanded" open response writing format.

To Highlight

- Open response questions require students to think and respond to content they have read to demonstrate an understanding of that content.
- Open response questions allow students to return to the text to find specific details to support their answers. With well-written open response questions, there will be more than one way to answer the question.
- For clarity, it is recommended that the first word of the open response question or prompt state what essential type of writing needs to be done (e.g., describe, explain, discuss, list, etc.) as well as the expected number of supporting details or facts if relevant (Diaz, 2003).

Open Response Paragraph Structure

- Topic sentence—restate the question or writing prompt
- Three or four details/examples—support the answer
- Concluding sentence—relates back to the topic sentence (Lak, 2003)

Sample Open Response Questions/Prompts (students read a selection or segment of text before responding to the open response questions):

- **Prompt:** *Discuss* briefly three ways that show how the first Olympics in Greece differed from the present day Olympics (students would read a text selection related to the prompt).

  Sample Response: (*topic sentence restates the prompt*) The ancient Olympics in Greece differed from present day Olympics in who participated, the number of events, and how winners were honored. In ancient Greece, just men from all over Greece participated in one event, the *stade*, which is like one of the short track events in modern Olympics. Today, men and women from many countries around the world compete in a large number of events. Winners in the ancient Olympics received woven wreaths, but today athletes receive gold, silver, and bronze medals in addition to woven wreaths. There are many other differences but similarities as well.

- **Prompt:** *Describe* how Shel Silverstein's use of language made the poem "OOPS!" intriguing. Use two or three examples from the poem to support your answer.

  Sample Response: Shel Silverstein made the poem "OOPS!" intriguing by his unique use of language. The poem "OOPS!" can be read from top to bottom or bottom to top and is fun to read both ways. Two sets of rhyming words are used to open and close each stanza. There is only one piece of punctuation, a quotation mark!, and that is in the title of the poem. That's how Shel Silverstein made the poem, "OOPS!" intriguing.*

---

*Source of information: Liza Charlesworth (May/June 2004), "Ring in Spring with Shel Silverstein." *Instructor Magazine, 119*(8), p. 38.

Varied Content and Genres Used in Open Response and Other Writing

Arelys Diaz (2003) recommends providing students with repeated practice in using open response question formats that vary both the content (e.g., math, science, social studies) and the genres used. Diaz advises educators use the following genres as part of a well-balanced reading–writing program; informational, autobiography, biography, fantasy, traditional folklore (fairytales, fables, legends, myths), memoirs, poetry, historical fiction, realistic fiction, and science fiction. Most state or district language arts frameworks or standards require coverage of all these genre beginning in the elementary grades.

Adaptations for Students with Learning Disabilities or Developing Writers

Students with dyslexia or other learning disabilities may benefit from writing strategy assists that provide the framework needed to effectively complete open response questions. Margaret Ashe (2003), as an example, has found success with general response strategy bookmarks or cards that can be laminated for repeated uses (see Figure 7.23).

Additionally, struggling writers need to use computer technology to facilitate the writing process in the earliest elementary grades (Cook, 1991). Spell and grammar checks, thesauruses, and other language tools provide structural support especially as students work toward writing independence. Internet access to writing sites and resources is recommended under structured or adult "guided" situations. There is an implicit Internet social protocol children must be familiar with before independent use—that is, we use the same courtesies on the Internet that we use in polite conversations. Additionally, children with learning disabilities need a note-taking system and an outline or planner when researching topics on the Internet (see Chapter 11: note-taking preparations, p. 330; TAKE CARE Planner—Internet Research Guide on p. 330).

The open response 5-layer birthday cake seen in Figure 7.24 can be used to organize a written response to an open response question. Other graphic organizers can be used as well.

Graphic Organizers and Second-Language Learners

If students who are second-language learners have adequate writing skills in their home language but lack sufficient vocabulary (e.g., English) to write in the school language, then teaching "the students to use graphic organizers to plan a writing task is not likely to be successful unless students *also have access to a bilingual dictionary*" (Smith & Qi, 2003, pp. 58–59). Practice is using bilingual dictionaries is required especially in regard to "quickly" finding alphabet letters and guide words.

	Read and reread the question or prompt
Read	Everything before you respond
Look for	Specific key words and ideas
Think of each	Part of the question
	Organize your thoughts
Make	Notes of keywords and ideas
	Support your answer with facts
	Edit and revise your answers

Source: Ashe (2003)

FIGURE 7.23   Open Response Strategy Card or Bookmark Sample

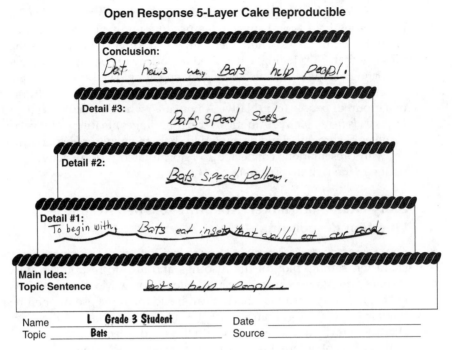

FIGURE 7.24   Filled-In Open Response 5-Layer Birthday Cake Reproducible

Reformulation with Second-Language Learners

Second-language learners will need *additional* preparations or methods to further clarify and organize thoughts during the writing process, especially when given open response questions. For example, *reformulation* is a writing method that has been successfully used to increase writing proficiency for second-language learners. In this method, a proficient speaker of the school language (e.g., English) rewrites the second-language learner's (e.g., home language is Spanish) work in the manner in which the second-language learner would have written the piece (if proficient in language conventions) but without changing the content. The writer/learner (e.g., ELL or English language learner) compares the original work with the reformulated work to notice differences and gain writing insights about the school's language, especially in regard to conveying knowledge of content clearly and concisely.

Culturally Responsive Pedagogy—Creating Individual, Neighborhood, and Group Connections   When the method of reformulation is used, it is motivating for students to make *individual* cultural connections to the text presented. As an example, The Intercultural Center for Research in Education (INCRE—www.incre.org), Arlington, Massachusetts, publishes a series of multicultural books based on a science and environmental education curriculum for elementary students. One of the books, *Mónica (from Puerto Rico) and the Summer Party*, authored by Nancy Carmen Barra (2002), was written in both English and Spanish. For Hispanic students transitioning into written English work, such picture books provide not only personal connections, but also develop a student's sense of cultural identity. Barra includes extensive, authentic portrayals of the Puerto Rican culture to accomplish this.

Individual readings or author studies can be used to make *neighborhood* cultural connections. For example, Norah Dooley's books *Everybody Cooks Rice* and *Everybody*

Bakes Bread, published by Carolrhoda Books, Inc., a division of Lerner Publishing (www.lernerbooks.com), make reference to friendly neighbors from Barbados, China, Haiti, Italy, Puerto Rico, and Vietnam, illustrating commonalities that can bring peoples together. Storytelling, when used to portray or convey cultural legacies connected to writing activities, can also be highly engaging. Walks in Peace, an Abenaki Native American, believes this art form can bring children to deeper cultural understandings of a group of people (e.g., Native Americans) when intracultural (similarities and differences *between* Native American tribal heritages) features of a people are explored. Families of students could be invited to share their cultural experiences as guest speakers with presentations connected to reformulated writing activities (families participating in the writing process).

Story Grammar Marker: Adapting to Open Response Question Responding

The *story grammar marker* can be used to facilitate acquisition of the story structure (e.g., character, setting, plot) of the readings and also to respond in writing to the open response questions. Created by Maryellen Rooney Moreau and Holly Fidrych-Puzzo (1994), the story grammar marker can be adapted for use in open response question planning. The story grammar marker is a hands-on organizational tool with a "fuzzy" character attached to a long yarn with threaded objects representing character, setting, initiating event, internal response, plan, attempts to resolve, direct consequences and resolution. The story grammar marker has been successfully used with all students, including students with learning disabilities, to help summarize story structure via a concrete, motivating cueing system. Moreau (2004) provides an open response adaptation with a sample prompt, "List three ways birds use feet in flight and use information from the article to support your answer."

In addition to a reading about how birds use their feet in flight, the student would have a *key word card* of sentence starters and connectors with words such as: *for example, also, list, for instance, and, besides, furthermore, in addition to, another, also, more, some,* and so on (Mendes, 2004). For secondary students a keyword card of writing transitions would involve time, space, and summative terminology (see Table 7.9). To scaffold the learning process, the teacher and students could initially brainstorm together possible topic sentences to begin the open response paragraph, similar to "Birds use their feet in flight in different ways." Students could then use the story grammar marker to guide thinking about story structure. Instead of "figuring out" attempts to resolve the main story line, students would attempt to find at least three details to complete the open response question. The direct consequences yarned ribbon could be a reminder to restate the topic sentence and the ending pink heart could be a cue to reread the paragraph—"Did I resolve or complete what the question asked of me?" Moreau (2004) recommends using a rubric to evaluate the quality of the work, making this available to students to ensure writing or learning expectations are clear.

Open Response Assessment: Rubric Scoring Explanations for Teachers

Open response questions are often evaluated by either general rubrics or rubrics that also reference specific content.

General Rubric for Scoring Open Response Answers   Answers can be defined as a written one-paragraph response to a content selection that shows literal (surface) and inferential (deep) levels of understanding. The *language* of a general rubric would be adapted to individual grade levels and would be accessed by students before and then

---

TABLE 7.9   Prompts to Support Higher Level Thinking/Use of Transitions in Writing, Grades K–12

Time Words:	Adding Information to Text:
first, at first, second, last, at last	and, in addition to
before, after	but, however
now, soon, later	also, another, another point
during the morning/afternoon/evening, at twilight, at dawn, at dusk	for instance, as an example
next, after	nevertheless, moreover
for a second, for a minute, for a moment	similarly, in contrast to
to begin with, to conclude with	in conclusion, to sum it up, generally speaking
rarely, never, frequently, ordinarily,	therefore, thus
usually, morning hour, noon hour,	in fact, in as much as, another point
supper time	because, the reason for
	consequently, furthermore

Space Words:
at/to the left, right, center
above, below
beneath, underneath, lower
next to, beside, opposite
nearby, within sight, in the distance, straight ahead
beyond, out of sight, within sight, within reach
at the rear/front
surrounding, around

Source: Adapted from Chamberlain, Fitzgerald, Flanagan, Hamer, Hunter, O'Callaghan, & Paleologopoulos, 1988.

during self-reflective stages in work revisions. It is recommended that the same rubric framework be used across the curriculum with additions reflecting specific content if needed. In open response question formats, the essence or purpose is for the writer to convey an understanding of content read. Typically, the writer is not required to provide details from memory but has access to the text referred to. Although language mechanics (sentence structure, grammar, spelling) are important, they are not the guiding considerations when evaluating the quality of the work. This is especially true of second-language learners who are struggling with the language conventions of a school language (e.g., English). "Superficial errors, such as faulty spelling or grammar, are very noticeable and can easily draw the teacher's attention away from the merits of a piece of writing, such as sincere attempts to pay close attention to the topic or to express a complex point with limited vocabulary" (Smith & Qi, p. 63).

Many general rubrics used to evaluate open response question answers or responses involve a four-point scale:

4 Writing response clearly shows a *thorough* understanding of the content with a topic sentence, three relevant details from the text, and a concluding sentence. Details are quoted and/or paraphrased and fully support the topic sentence (i.e., restated question) or, as an example, "details provide a complete description of at least three ways birds use their feet in flight," which is specific to a text reading (see p. 164). Deep and/or surface understandings are evident depending on the question type (5 sentences equals a minimum for the paragraph).

3 Writing response shows a *good* understanding of the content with a topic sentence, two to three relevant details from the text, and a concluding sentence.

Details are quoted and/or paraphrased and *solidly* support the topic sentence (i.e., restated question) or, as an example, "details provide a good description of two or three ways birds use their feet in flight," which is specific to the text reading (see p. 164). Deep and/or surface understandings are evident depending on the question type (4 or 5 sentences equals a minimum for the paragraph).

2 Writing response shows *gaps* in understanding of the content with supporting details not complete explanations or partially irrelevant explanations. A topic sentence or concluding sentence may be missing. Details quoted and/or attempts to paraphrase may be unclear or inadequate or, as an example, "details provide some description of ways birds use their feet in flight, "which is specific to the text reading" (see p. 164). Deep and/or surface understandings are partially evident depending on the question type—OR—The written response is less than half complete.

1 Writing response shows a *limited understanding* of the content with supporting details either unclear, inadequate, and/or most irrelevant to the question. A topic sentence or concluding sentence may be missing. Deep and/or surface understandings are not evident or are partially evident because the writing lacks clarity and/or shows irrelevance to the question presented—OR—The writing response included only a topic or concluding sentence [and/or a supporting detail], or, as an example, the writing showed "very limited or no reference to how birds use their feet in flight," specific to the text reading or an opinion related to the question given but not directly responsive to the question.

0 *No attempt* (blank) *or* response is *totally* (100%) *unrelated* to the question.

The *language* of a general student rubric (see below for an example) reflects grade or developmental expectations and needs to be accessed by students before and also during self-reflective stages in work revisions. Written responses that show *any* "good" attempt to connect writing to the reading in open response formats should receive a minimum score of 1. Students who have obviously misinterpreted an open response question and who are not responding as part of a testing situation should be given the opportunity to try again. The teacher may have to model responding in writing with a similar example but with different content or may need only to clarify expectations until he or she is confident the student has a clear understanding of the assignment. Chart paper or an overhead can be used. It is recommended that the same rubric framework be used across the curriculum.

Sample Open Response Writing Rubric for Students

4 ■ Writing response shows a *thorough understanding of the content.*
  ■ A topic sentence is well developed.
  ■ Three relevant details are included from the text (details are paraphrased or quoted).
  ■ A concluding sentence relates to the topic sentence.

3 ■ Writing response shows a *good understanding of the content.*
  ■ A topic sentence is developed.
  ■ Two or three relevant details are included from the text (details are paraphrased or quoted).
  ■ A concluding sentence relates to the topic sentence.

2 ■ Writing response shows *important information is missing* to show understanding of the content.
  ■ A topic sentence is not fully developed.
  ■ Details listed do not adequately help answer the question or prompt.
  ■ A concluding sentence is not fully developed.

1 ■ Writing response shows *almost all important information is missing* to show understanding of the content.
   ■ A topic sentence is not fully developed.
   ■ Details listed to not adequately help answer the question or prompt.
   ■ A concluding sentence is not fully developed.

0 ■ *No attempt* (blank) *or* writing response is *totally* (100%) *unrelated* to the question.

Expanding Open Response Formats to Long Composition Writing

Charlotte Lak (2003) recommends using expository writing forms when developing proficiency in long composition writing. Lak states this writing form allows students to express opinions based on personal knowledge or experiences while they thoroughly develop a topic. Supporting details relevant to the topic can also be drawn from the child's own experiences. Long composition writing requires control of language mechanics and conventions—these are not heavily emphasized in open response paragraph writing where the focus is on comprehension or understanding. In long composition writing, there needs to be an organized continuity or a flow framed by three major writing sections—the beginning, middle, and end of the writing.

1. Beginning (sample prompt—also a personal recount: "Think of an interesting school field trip you had. Tell the where, when, who, why, and what you liked best about this field trip.")

   ■ Topic paragraph: Initial sentence restates the topic/question/prompt with an opinion.

2. Middle

   Supporting paragraphs (minimum of three paragraphs with topic sentences for each paragraph)

   ■ Reason #1   Detail/Example
                  Detail/Example
                  Detail/Example

   ■ Reason #2   Detail/Example
                  Detail/Example
                  Detail/Example

   ■ Reason #3   Detail/Example
                  Detail/Example
                  Detail/Example

3. End

   ■ Concluding paragraph: serves to restate the initial topic paragraph, summing up key points. (Lak, 2003)

McREL (Mid-continent Research for Education and Learning) Standards (2003) According to national standards enumerated by McREL (www.mcrel.org), students must become proficient in using a paragraph form in writing with topic sentences, introductory and concluding paragraphs, and several related paragraphs. Use of descriptive and interesting language that clarifies and enhances ideas and transition words are also essential. Students with dyslexia often need work transitioning between major ideas or paragraphs in writing. There are several common time, space, and "adding information" words students can practice using that help make those necessary transitions in writing to make a composition flow. See Table 7.9 on page 165. Students with dyslexia can use bookmarks or cards with frequently used transition words they can reference as needed.

Journal Writing

Using Response Journals in Content Area Subjects

Crawford (1993) suggests that students can use response journals to express how they feel about content or ideas stated by relating ". . . what the information means to them, what they think about the information, and their reactions as they studied the information . . ." (p. 268). The role of the teacher is to respond to student questions without keying in on spelling or structural details. The teacher should also raise questions and give personal reactions. The focus of journal responses is on questioning, the sharing of ideas, and exploring different ways to think about the material read. The example in Figure 7.25 illustrates how teacher prompts can be useful.

Journal Writing Adaptations

We would suggest that some journal writing adaptations might need to be made for individuals with dyslexia with severe writing/spelling difficulties:

1. The teacher can be a student's secretary on occasion.
2. Encourage the use of a word processor with a spell check, although spelling should not be heavily emphasized.
3. Arrange journal partners so that one partner has more proficient writing skills.
4. Provide writing prompts and assists or a structured format to begin with.

Learning Webs in Journal Writing

Concept webs can be used to clarify language before writing. The poetry web in Figure 7.26 provides an opportunity to web an outline for an English report.

Dialogue Journals

Dialogue journals have become popular in English and reading classrooms. Students write to one another dialoguing what they are reading in a sort of book-chat format (Atwell, 1987). Learning logs are a type of dialogue journal teachers can use with students with dyslexia.

Student	*Teacher Response to Deeper Thinking and Extend Hearing*
Prompt: How can I use water more effectively?	
■ Turn water faucets on and off only as needed. Don't run water unless it will be used. Fix leaky faucets.	■ Draw pictures to show how water travels from a reservoir to the home. What happens to the reservoir when water demands exceed to replenishment of water?
■ Use the washing machine when you have full loads.	■ Illustrate the life cycle of a plant and show why water is an important nutrient.
■ Water gardens and the lawn only as much as needed. However, turn timers off during rainstorms.	

FIGURE 7.25   Response Journals

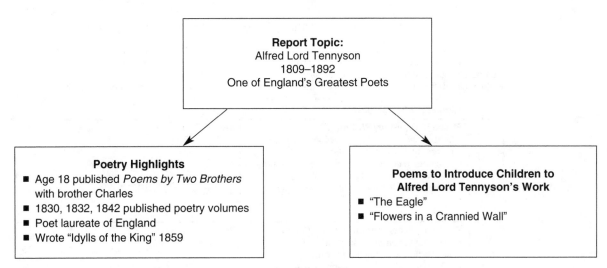

FIGURE 7.26 Web to Outline a Topic for Report Writing

Learning Logs

Learning logs can be kept by students with dyslexia as a measure of growth, performance, and learning. Glaze (1987) suggests four key questions: (1) What am I going to predict will happen in this activity, book, exercise? (2) What have I learned? (3) What do I need to learn? and (4) How do I feel about what I learned?

Continuums of Writing Development

In considering the proficiency level of student writers, continuums of writing development (see Figure 7.27) provide benchmarks that can be used to inform teaching. The continuum of writing development shown in Figure 7.27 can be used for grades K–12.

The writing process can also be viewed in stages or levels. Stice, Bertrand, and Bertrand (1995) propose three levels for emerging young writers who are dyslexic (see p. 171, *Primary Considerations for Young Authors with Dyslexia*).

Handwriting in Writers' Workshop According to Ruddell and Ruddell (1995), the goal of handwriting instruction should be to guide the child to a legible and consistent style of writing. During writers' workshop, time should be given to modeling the craft of handwriting with practice on a daily basis until the child's handwriting is legible. For manuscript print, regular text provides a good model or writing format, especially Big Books for emerging writers. There are also many commercial manuscript print models. For cursive writing, the Zaner-Bloser model among many others is widely used.

Which Handwriting System Should Be Taught to Students with Learning Disabilities—Manuscript or Cursive? According to Janet Lerner (1971), there are different schools of thought regarding which system of writing to initially teach students with learning disabilities. Some practitioners believe manuscript printing should be taught because it is easier for the child to learn since it is made up of only a sequence of circles and straight lines and is closely aligned to book print. Other practitioners feel students with learning disabilities should begin with cursive writing because it reduces spatial judgment difficulties for the child with a "rhythmic continuity and wholeness" not found in manuscript writing (Lerner, 1971, p. 190). There is a third school of thought that believes students with learning disabilities should begin with manuscript print because it is modeled continuously for students through book print. When the student has mastered the manuscript style, a series of curves and loops can be attached to the

Continuum of Writing Development Assessment

Adapted From: Writing Developmental Continuum (First published 1994). *The Writing Developmental Continuum* was researched, developed, and written by Glenda Raison, Education Department of Western Australia, in collaboration with Judith Rivalland, Edith Cowan University. Publisher: Longman Cheshire; Melbourne, Australia. Grade expectations are approximate and vary according to grade-level benchmarks.

Date   Highlight when achieved.

	Phase I - Role-Play Writing (K) • Letters and letter approximations are used to represent words and sentences. • Attempts to convey a message by stringing a series of letters or letter approximations. • Attempts to read back written messages.	SAMPLE 
	Phase II - Experimental Writing (Grade 1) • Uses some sentence structure but inconsistently (subject and verb). • Invented spelling is used and focuses on beginning/ending consonant sounds. • Is able to use a few different writing forms (e.g., recent recounts of nonfiction and fiction read-alouds, letters, lists, and so on).	SAMPLE 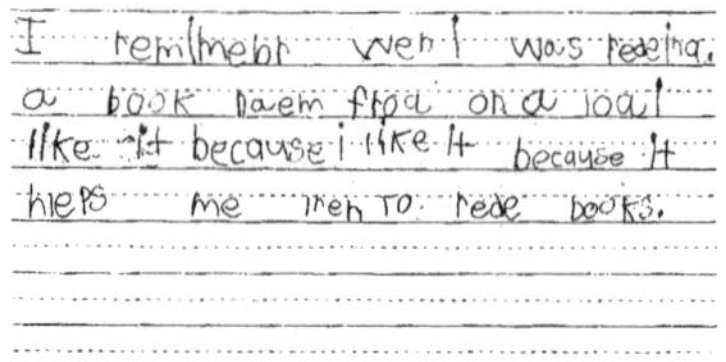
	Phase III - Early Writing (Grade 2) • Uses a basic sentence structure (subject and predicate) but may have run-on sentences and no paragraphing. • Conventional spelling emerges and use of editing skills. • Begins to use ending and other punctuation editing skills and additional writing forms.	SAMPLE 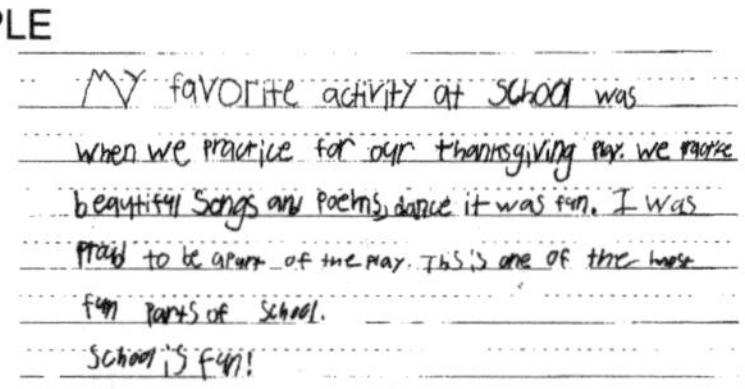
	Phase IV - Conventional Writing (Grades 3-5) • More elaborate language conventions are used: simple, compound, and extended sentences to create paragraphs. • Control of sentence structure, spelling, and punctuation may change depending on the writing format and difficulty of the writing task. • Begins to use some vocabulary specific to a topic or field and conventional proofreading and editing skills.	SAMPLE 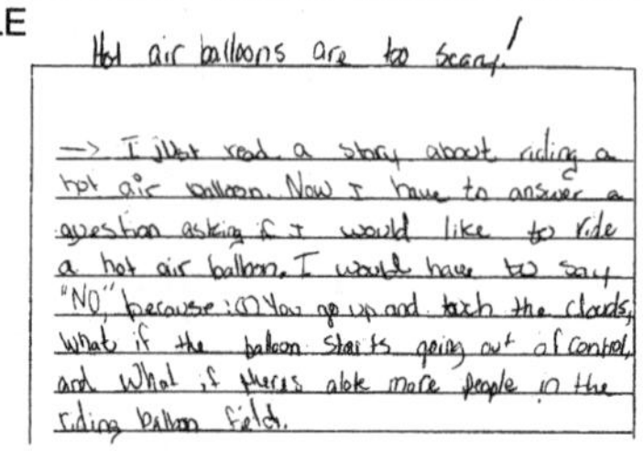
	Phase V - Proficient Writing (Grades 6-12) and Adults with Writing Proficiency • Develops cohesive and complete writing pieces using standard language conventions (spelling and grammar) and self-edits during and after composing phases. • Researches or is able to locate information and appropriate resources to synthesize, take notes from, and reference in writing. • Can write with proficiency using different forms or structures depending on audience and purpose.	SAMPLE 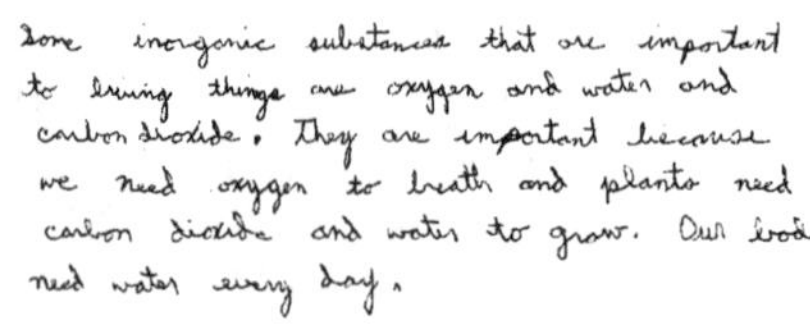

FIGURE 7.27 Continuum of Writing Development Assessment

Primary Considerations for Young Authors with Dyslexia

Stice, Bertrand, and Bertrand (1995) describe how teachers can create an environment for young authors by gently guiding preschool and primary level students through the writing process. Their approach would be appealing for those who work with students with dyslexia and is modified as follows:

Level I
"Write-Alouds"—the teacher scribes what the students dictate. Teachers could accept tape recorded versions. The teacher models good writing behaviors.

Level II
"Guided Writing"—the teacher provides for group-dictated or created stories whereby vocabulary usage, syntax, and sentence structure are negotiated by the group. An overhead, chart paper, or chalkboard should provide feedback every step of the way. The teacher should provide everyone with a printed story the next day and solicit constructive feedback. The student with dyslexia could use a writer's editing guide.

Guided writing could be complemented by expressive forms of the printed page. For example, Purves, Rogers, and Soter (1995) suggest the use of drama and dramatic activities to "expand the forms and functions of language in the classroom" and to nurture enthusiasm and style in writing. We would suggest puppetry and casting students in different roles in order to appreciate and empathize with characters. Purves et al. (1995) suggest first placing the teacher in a role, interviewing characters in pairs, with interrogative questioning about the events in a work.

Level III
"Independent Writing" (SSW or Sustained Silent Writing)—the teacher provides time for students to create and explore different writing options on their own; Stice et al. (1995) recommend writing letters (e.g., penpals), maintaining dialogue journals and observation logs, creating writing projects from thematic units covered in class, and creating original works (e.g., stories, poems).

---

various letters to scaffold the student to cursive writing. When the child has mastered these two forms of writing, he or she can then choose which is most comfortable.

To answer the question centered on which handwriting system should be taught to students with learning disabilities, probably both. The student can then choose a preferred way of writing—either manuscript or cursive are acceptable in most school situations. Having *practice with cursive writing helps* with *reading cursive writing* when necessary. Word processing subsequently needs to be taught to enhance writing presentations—spell and grammar checks and thesaurus usage are available for the writer as well.

Janet Lerner's (1971) suggestions for helping students with learning disabilities to develop proficiency in handwriting are still applicable and widely used. Charlotte Larson (1968, as quoted in Lerner, 1971) has researched the sequence of cursive letters that can be taught to students with learning disabilities (shown in the box on page 172).

In summary, handwriting practice is essential in developing a student's ability to effectively communicate in writing to others. Affirming and modeling good handwriting conveys to the student the importance of completing the writing process in writer's workshop with attention to the content of the final work as well as the writing presentation.

Janet Lerner's (1971) Considerations for Developing Handwriting Proficiency with Students with Learning Disabilities

(1) *Writing posture and position*—The student needs to be comfortably seated with the nonwriting hand holding the paper at the top. Many students need to be shown how to hold a writing utensil. Clay has sometimes been used to help a child hold a writing utensil in place.

(2) *VAK-T methods* such as fingerpainting or writing in sand or clay pans provide practice in writing movements for geometric shapes (lines and circles), numbers, and letters for beginning writers.

(3) *Chalkboard activities*—Practice with geometric shapes (e.g., circles and lines), numbers, and letters can be done on lined paper. The teacher can also make dot-to-dot lines on the board to guide letter formation.

(4) *Tracing*—An overhead projector can be used where letter images are projected on the chalkboard or large paper with the student tracing the images. Tracing with reduced cues can also be done with parts of letters or words written for the student. The student traces what was written with a felt-tip pen or marker and then completes the letter or word.

(5) *Stencils and templates*—Letters, numbers, and geometric shapes can be traced with stencils or templates. Clipping the stencil to the paper prevents the paper from moving. The student can use his or her finger to trace the letters or use a pencil, marker, or crayon.

(6) For children who have spatial difficulties fitting letters on lines, *windows* can be cut from construction paper that can be taped to the top and bottom of lines. Practice with one-line letters such as a, e, m can precede practice with two-line letters such as b, k, l.

Larson's Sequence of Introducing Cursive Letters

(1) Beginning letters—a, o, c, m, n, t, i, u, w, r, s, l, e
(2) More difficult letters—v, x, z, y, j, p, h, b, d, k, f, g, q
(3) Combination of letters—e.g., me, be, go, etc.

Source: Charlotte Larson (1968), Teaching Beginning Writing, *Academic Therapy Quarterly (4)*, 61–66.

Gifted Children

Nurturing the Writing Development of Gifted Students with and without Dyslexia

There are more independent writing approaches that assist students who have mastered the writing process and need to be challenged to extend learning and achieve greater independence as writers.

Inquiry Reading and Writing Approach   Jack Cassidy (1981) developed an inquiry-based reading-writing approach that is also systematic and requires explicit teaching. It was originally developed as a four-week instructional sequence for gifted students in grades 3 to 6, but it can be adapted for all students at all grade levels. Dyslexic and gifted students alike benefit from the preplanning stage, structured note-taking, establishment of timelines, the clearly articulated sequence of expectations, practice in multitasking, and practice speaking before groups. The sequence is summarized:

Week 1

- Operationalize the term *inquiry* until students thoroughly understand the term.
- Establish requirements for conducting a project-based inquiry to span four weeks.
- Brainstorm topics.
- Collaboratively establish one research-based inquiry question for each student.
- Brainstorm references and resources.
- Connect students with experts on topics and preplan interview questions.
- Identify how research results will be shared.
- Establish a timeline to complete various segments of the project.
- [Perhaps develop a rubric with expected report standards.]

Weeks 2 and 3

- Review note-taking (see p. 305) procedures.
- Begin library searches for resources.
- Use file cards to summarize (see p. 284) references and information.
- Have students create folders to organize materials.
- Student share sessions—students confer with each other about research successes and problems.
- Teacher individually conferences with each student—makes adjustments to individual timelines as needed.
- Students begin to put projects together.

Week 4

- Students complete projects with teacher feedback; revise original plans as needed.
- Hold a dress rehearsal for the project presentation; members of the dress rehearsal audience provide constructive feedback; presentation formats vary— speaking from an outline or notes or extemporaneously, reading a portion of the report with reference to where the full report can be located, etc. The point of the presentation is to share an original work in a scholarly manner.
- Present to an outside audience; invite family members among others.
- Reflection—teacher and students evaluate the inquiry; refer back to the student's original plans, timelines, and the report rubric. Discuss what went well and perhaps what could be handled differently in the future.

Other Gifted Considerations

Abraham J. Tannebaum (1997) proposes that giftedness "denotes . . . potential for becoming critically acclaimed performers or exemplary producers of ideas in spheres of activity that enhance the moral, physical, social, intellectual, or aesthetic life of humanity" (p. 27). Gifted students, representing approximately 1 percent of the population, are generally thought to be individuals who can make significant contributions to society. Typically, IQ tests are given and gifted children often fall at the high end of the IQ range (above IQs of 120 to 130). Robert J. Sternberg (1985) views giftedness in terms of "triarchic" multidimensionality. He theorizes that there are three different types of giftedness—*analytic* (people who do well on conventional IQ tests), *synthetic* (people who are creative, intuitive, or able to cope with novelty), and *practical* (people who can apply analytic and synthetic abilities to pragmatic or practical situations; people who are good problem solvers). Although gifted individuals do not possess one type of giftedness to the exclusion of another, Sternberg believes gifted individuals tend to fall in one of the three categories mentioned.

Gifted readers and writers have what Linda Kerger Silverman (1997) terms "asynchronous development," meaning their intellectual skills are advanced but social skills are typically age-appropriate. Contrary to the adage "all parents believe their children are gifted," parental judgment regarding whether children are gifted is very accurate, with reported accuracy ranging from 47 to 90 percent (Louis & Lewis, 1992; Silverman, 1997). This is especially true after age 4 when assessment is relatively easy for parents who spend a great deal of time with gifted children. There are several "early" signs parents can look for as seen in Figure 7.28.

Parents and Gifted Children

According to Benjamin Bloom (1984, 1985) parents are the most influential factor in the development of giftedness and creativity. The enormous impact parents can make on the development of gifted children was seen in a five-year study conducted by several researchers under Benjamin Bloom (of Bloom's Taxonomy) (1985) for a group of individuals who had achieved extraordinary levels of accomplishment in concert piano, sculpture, sports, mathematics, research, and other academic fields. Patterns were identified across families studied—consistently it was reported that early identification of and then nurturing of special gifts and talents by parents was a critical determinant of high achievement and accomplishment.

According to Lauren A. Sosniak (1997), a child "grows into a person of extraordinary talent" with "considerable exposure to and experience with field-specific content"—these are crucial over a long period of time. For example, pianists, at the urging of parents, began taking lessons around age 6 and by age 13 or 14 were competing in contests. Additionally, although the research is lacking in this area, it would appear that gifted children who live in literacy-rich home environments and develop as "precocious readers" remain superior in reading achievement throughout elementary school years (Pikulski & Tobin, 1989), or longer. Perhaps some gifted children develop those resiliency factors of persistence and stick-to-it-ness to achieve extraordinary accomplishments because of the early reading headstart. It would naturally follow that for children with special needs or at risk for reading problems, there would also be

---

- Less need for sleep as infants.
- Unusual "alertness" as infants.
- Recognizes caretakers early and "smiles" a lot.
- Reaches language milestones early, like talking and using complete sentences.
- Speaking vocabulary is above developmental expectations.
- Possesses an "incredible" memory.
- Is fascinated with books, learning, and exploring the environment.
- Enjoys learning and progresses at rapid rate.
- Sustains focus of attention easily.
- Prefers novel or new situations.
- Is curious about everything.
- Is astutely observant.
- Shows inferential or "deep" thinking early on.
- May have an excellent sense of humor.
- Displays intense reactions to noise, pain, and frustration.
- Empathizes with and is sensitive to the feelings of others.
- Enjoys "regular kid" activities; socializes with a small circle of peers.
- Is a good problem solver.

Source: Silverman, 1997, p. 384.

FIGURE 7.28   Early Signs of Giftedness

academic benefits derived from a headstart in reading—this has been documented to a much greater extent (see Jackson & Roller, 1993).

Gifted children who are learning disabled (LD) evidence the same warning signs as other learning disabled children with additional characteristics related to learning styles and rate of development for gifted children mentioned on page 221. It's difficult for parents to sort through what to do for gifted children, because many gifted children with and without learning disabilities are underachievers. The good news is that testing procedures are available to identify gifted underachievers. Parents need to contact local school systems for referrals if they suspect their child is a gifted underachiever. According to Silverman (1997), a major reason why families of gifted children seek counseling or support is "their children's underachievement." Parents should collaboratively consider the suggestions mentioned below with school staff, all looking more closely at grade acceleration, enrichment, and other curriculum adaptations if needed. Many school districts do not have formal programs for gifted children, making individual curriculum adaptations even more essential.

Grade or Content Acceleration

One of the most consistent recommendations for education adaptations for gifted students is acceleration (advancing through the education levels—e.g., "skipping grades"—or advancing in a particular course such as math but remaining in other age-appropriate coursework). Often students with extremely high IQs are accelerated a grade or two with little research evidence to substantiate anything other than positive effects, contrary to some discussion on this issue in the popular press. In fact, Sayler and Brookshire (1993) identified a group of gifted accelerated students and a randomly selected sample of average achieving students from a base of 25,000 eighth-grade students from the National Education Longitudinal Study and found, for the most part, the accelerated students to be successful, well-liked, and possessing positive self-concepts.

What about students accelerated more than a grade or two? Similarly, Gross (1992) reported students with "radical" accelerations to be "more" stimulated intellectually while possessing healthy self-esteems and close, productive social relationships.

Teachers and Underachieving Gifted Students

The strategies mentioned throughout the book to assist the academic and social progress of individuals with dyslexia and other disabilities also pertain to gifted individuals with learning disabilities. Gifted students who are underachieving or not achieving to their potential require additional considerations.

Silverman's Strategies for Reversing Underachievement with Gifted Children Linda Kreger Silverman, Gifted Development Center and the Institute for the Study of Advanced Development, Denver, Colorado (1997), proposes the following considerations: individual tutoring, counseling groups for underachievers, group counseling in which parents are matched with someone else's children, increasing and making better communications between the home and school, discussion groups that include underachievers, role-playing, *acceleration in content or grade advancement*, special class placement with accompanying appropriate interventions, alternative schools that specialize in teaching the gifted, individual academic plans, curriculum adaptations that address the student's learning style (e.g., curriculum enrichment), teaching to the strengths of the student, bibliotherapy (interactive therapeutic approach using literature—e.g., student explores and resolves a problem through a similar such situation found in a high-quality literature book), and building on student's interests to make school interesting and relevant. According to Silverman (1997), underachievement can be reversed!

Summary of Recommended Curriculum Adaptations for Gifted Underachievers

The present authors believe the curriculum adaptations offered by Gallagher and Gallagher (1994) pertain to all gifted underachievers, with or without LD: (1) *Acceleration*—advancing through educational coursework or grade levels as previously mentioned; (2) *Enrichment*—extending the regular curriculum with different units and projects (see *Inquiry Reading and Writing Approach*, page 172), content, examples, and so on; (3) *Sophistication*—direct and explicit instruction in complex networks of ideas such as specific theories relative to a particular field (e.g., teaching the theoretical underpinnings to musical chord formation and then applying that knowledge during composition of music pieces); and (4) *Novelty*—introducing unique ("novel") ideas or content into the curriculum (e.g., introduce international perspectives in various content presentations). Also endorsed is VanTassel-Baska's (1992) research to show gifted learners are served best by an approach that allows for *both enrichment and acceleration.* As gifted underachievers and students with dyslexia or other learning difficulties acquire the writing proficiency needed to complete written compositions more independently, inquiry reading and writing projects can be assigned.

Adults and Secondary Students with Dyslexia: Additional Comprehension Considerations

The International Dyslexia Association (IDA) has identified (2002) three major areas of difficulty that continue to present a problem for adults with dyslexia (see also Chapter 11, pp. 323–325):

1. Slower than average reading rates—it takes longer to complete reading.
2. Poor spelling.
3. Writing proficiency is often below level. The individual will avoid writing, a tedious task, or may not be able to write extensively.

All Secondary Students: Reading and Writing Volume Needs to Increase

The National Reading Report Card (1992) records an alarming drop in the amount of reading at the secondary level. Almost half of all fourth graders read something for pleasure every day with that percentage declining to 24.4 percent by senior year. Sally Shaywitz (2003) and others document that older students and adult dyslexics need the same research-based, systematic, and small group literacy instruction as younger people with the "need to integrate solid interest-based approaches as a centerpiece of instruction" (Rosalie Fink, 1998, p. 312).

Richard L. Allington (2001) says that given the decline in the volume of reading and writing that begins around the middle-school level, planning for increasing this volume needs to occur. Less reading and writing equate to declines in rates of achievement, with the failure to keep up with reading and writing requirements in college a primary concern. According to Allington (2001), even the most proficient reader-writer has difficulty keeping up with college reading and writing demands. On a positive note, Janice A. Magno (2004) reports that the 2001 American Council on Education is finding more students with disabilities are entering colleges and universities. These students will need the same types of comprehension and study skills teaching mentioned in this chapter and throughout the book.

Teaching Reading Content at the Secondary Level for All Learners

Vicki Jacobs, noted secondary literacy expert, prepares secondary teachers to teach content reading in a three-step strategy approach based on schema theory. This approach promotes deep structure understandings of text. For students at the secondary level, "teachers must help prepare students for and guide them through the texts so that they will learn from them most efficiently" (Jacobs, 1999, p. 4). For the secondary student with dyslexia, the prereading stage, in particular, will help to clarify unfamiliar concepts and vocabulary while *promoting student engagement and interest* in the text reading. Figure 7.29 outlines a three-step strategy approach for secondary students.

Interest-Based Secondary Reading-Writing Approaches   In addition to regular curricula approaches, four additional interest-based learning activities, among others could be considered. These have been documented to work well with older students with dyslexia and will help increase the volume of reading and writing: (1) guided journal writing, (2) student-created learning logs, (3) integrating technology with writing, and (4) project learning.

Guided Journal Writing   Bernice Y.L. Wong and her colleagues (2002) suggest the use of question frames or similar structures to guide the student's response to the text reading with interest-based approaches such as journal writing. This will have the effect of developing reader-based interactive dialogue with text. Three general questions abstracted from the work of Wong et al. (2002) are recommended for guided journal writing in response to literature selections, (1) "What do you observe?" (2) "What do you question?" and (3) "What do you feel?" A question frame or series of questions would be developed by the teacher under each of these as related to the story's structural elements. For example, if reading a biography, under general question (1), the following could be framed: "What kind of person was . . . ?" "Can you

---

Teachers actively scaffold acquisition of text knowledge through the following guided steps and activities.

(1) Prereading: Prior to the reading on text, the *purpose* of the reading is explicitly stated. Students *brainstorm* and discuss *what they know* about the topic and *organize their brainstorms into categories*, webs, outlines, or clusters with graphic organizers. Students (through directed writing or interactive discussion) *prepare to ask and answer questions* before the reading. Two essential prereading questions: What do I already know about this topic? What do I need to know before reading? (see also Ogle, 1986, K-W-L). *As a comprehension builder,* the teacher can create or make use of a *cloze passage* (by deleting important words or concepts rather than every "nth" word) *to prepare students to actively engage in the text reading.*

(2) Guided Reading: During the text reading stage, students work with reader-response journals (see also guided journal writing in this chapter) and study guides to lead them beyond surface understandings to deeper probing of text. Multiple perspective taking is emphasized as well as the search for information related to prereading text questions (with revision of preliminary text questions as needed). Students gather, organize, analyze, and synthesize text information and begin to formulate initial opinions, inferences, and generalizations about the reading.

(3) Postreading: The teacher guides students to articulate and share their understandings of the reading. This is a time when students can demonstrate deeper thinking by discussing how this new knowledge can be applied to novel situations, by presenting suppositions and arguments for and against, and so on.

Source: Jacobs (1999).

FIGURE 7.29   Jacobs's Three-Step Strategy Approach to the Teaching of Reading at the Secondary Level for All Curricular Areas

relate to this character?" "How?" "What was . . . 's contribution to humanity? Provide examples from the reading." Wong et al. (2002) conclude that "journal writing guided by a question frame that dovetails with the story structure may lead to more emotional involvement and subsequent enjoyment of the story and main characters among the students" (p. 186).

Student-Created Learning Logs   Ruth D. Farrar (1999) has successfully used learning logs (see Figure 7.30) as a form of self-assessment with college students both with and without learning disabilities. Steps 6 through 8 are reflective and help students identify how they are learning, thus facilitating the ongoing cycle of academic goal setting.

Integrating Technology with Writing   According to Bernice Y.L. Wong (2001), students with dyslexia and other learning disabilities need considerable practice with computer keyboard training, word processing, and the writing process, and in combination, to increase the quantity and quality of writing pieces. Wong (2001) suggests providing students with planning sheets or other such frameworks to guide planning and writing stages. Word processing encourages students to be attentive to language conventions with spell and grammar checks. Thesaurus options provide opportunities for students to expand their writing vocabularies and to add a more in-depth, descriptive dimension to their writings.

The use of Internet resources with students who are dyslexic will require the explicit teaching of Internet vocabulary beforehand in addition to Internet protocol and procedures (see Chapter 11, pp. 327–331). Most major educational organizations provide ideas and resources to motivate secondary learners. For example, the American Library Association (ALA) at http://www.ala.org sponsors a "Teen Read Week" in October. Suggestions for this week include (1) giving teens time to read "for the fun of it," (2) allowing teens to choose their own reading material, and (3) encouraging teens to get in the habit of reading regularly and often. Additional ideas and information are available on site.

Project Learning   Jack Cassidy (see pp. 172–173) created a project-based *Inquiry Reading and Writing Approach* that can be used with dyslexic and gifted students alike. There is a preplanning stage, structured note-taking, establishment of timelines, a clearly articulated sequence of expectations, and practice in multitasking and speaking before groups. Projects should be based on individual student hobbies or interest areas with connections to art, music, dance or drama. Howard Gardner's research (see pp. 128–130) for discussion on multiple intelligences) has shown that people will be motivated to learn when they undertake activities for which they have some talent.

(Places for students to record when and how learning takes place)

(1) Identify a reading or learning event to reflect on.

(2) Establish the purposes for learning in the form of a question or problem.

(3) Cite reference sources.

(4) Outline or list the major ideas during the reading.

(5) Describe briefly what you learned.

(6) Express how you learned.

(7) Explain how this information can be used.

(8) Identify goals for what you want to work on next.

Source: Farrar (1999).

FIGURE 7.30   Learning Logs

Summary

Comprehension begins at the level of the word and its components (letters and sounds). All students need to develop some word recognition proficiency before any degree of reading proficiency is achieved. Because dyslexics initially struggle at the level of the word, there is an emphasis on using *systematic phonics instruction,* which incorporates synthetic or analytic types of phonics instruction with synthetic approaches favored in the current research. The National Research Panel (2000) has determined, however, that it is not the type of phonics approach that matters—what matters is that systematic phonics approaches include the explicit teaching of a predetermined set of letter-sound relations with students applying what they learn in the reading of connected text. Prominent researchers (e.g., Beck & McCaslin) have worked out carefully determined letter-sound sequences; examples can be found on pages 190–191.

According to the National Reading Panel (2000) Report, the following individual comprehension strategies appear to be most effective for classroom instruction when used in combination: (1) comprehension monitoring, (2) cooperative learning, (3) graphic and semantic organizers including story maps, (4) question answering, (5) question generation, and (6) summarization. Comprehension monitoring is vital to reading because "it allows the reader to notice when a particular comprehension strategy should come into play." Self-questioning methods as suggested by Bernice Y.L. Wong and others help to develop an *awareness of* and *ability to* monitor one's own comprehension. Several of the comprehension building and study skills approaches or methods offered in this book include a self-questioning component.

In *The Disciplined Mind: What All Students Should Understand,* Howard Gardner reminds educators and parents to consider the theory of multiple intelligences because children are motivated to learn when they undertake activities for which they have some talent. Until dyslexics acquire the fluency (Chapter 8), they need to make encounters with the printed page comfortable (versus tedious and laborious), they are more likely to pick up a book and engage in learning activities that are of interest and tap into *their strengths* or *talents.*

Older students and adults with dyslexia need the same research-based, systematic, and small group literacy instruction as younger people with a concerted effort to integrate interest-based approaches. Given the decline in the volume of reading and writing that begins around the middle-school level, additional learning activities are needed to increase the volume of reading and writing to maintain equivalent achievement gains seen during the elementary school years.

Jacobs's three-step strategy approach to the teaching of reading at the secondary level in all curricula areas was cited with prereading stage activities designed to actively engage students in text readings. In addition to structured curricula approaches, five additional interest-based learning activities, among others, could be considered to increase the amount of reading and writing students complete on a daily basis: (1) guided journal writing, (2) dialogue journals, (3) student-created learning logs, (4) integrating technology with writing, and (5) project learning. With more reading and writing, dyslexics acquire additional knowledge structures (e.g., schemata) and opportunities to try out specific comprehension and writing strategies while self-monitoring learning and achievement.

Word walls are particularly helpful to use in reading and writing activities for all students. Students with dyslexia need explicit and directed practice in using word walls. Patricia Cunningham's (2000) listing of the most popular and productive practice in using word-wall activities in both reading and writing were cited in this chapter.

Writing activities were presented that connect to several comprehension activities mentioned in this chapter and throughout the book. Students with dyslexia tend to have writing and spelling deficiencies throughout their lifespan. The research over-whelmingly supports the belief that combining instruction in reading with writing enhances students' literacy learning. Arelys Diaz recommends using the same varied genres in writing that comprehensive and balanced reading programs rely on. Proficient writers need to demonstrate the craft of writing for students with learning disabilities as they need much modeling and practice—teachers, parents, peers and authors alike. Avi, severely dyslexic and internationally acclaimed author, says the secret to becoming an accomplished writer is this—*learn to become an author by reading stories, reading often, and reading extensively.* Writers like Avi who share their toils, struggles, and "long" journeys to becoming successful authors, leave children and adults alike with the impression that "I can do this too!"

The major focus of this chapter, as with the entire book, is on providing strategic academic and social support systems to our most struggling readers and writers to bring them to levels of proficiency to prepare them for future career and life successes. However, in 1993 the U.S. Secretary of Education Richard Riley identified the education of our brightest or gifted children as a "quiet crisis" (see Ross, 1993). Tannenbaum (1997), the present authors, and many other researchers argue for more effective identification procedures and appropriate education programs because gifted children, as with all children, with realized potential can be outstanding contributors to the arts, sciences, letters, and the general well-being of fellow humankind.

We would agree with Brennan (1995) that the use of ". . . language is something to be treasured, caressed, nurtured, above all used . . ." For students with dyslexia, repeated exposure to interactive and cooperative language-based learning activities is needed with opportunities to apply strategies, knowledge, and skills, and deepen and extend understandings. Chapter 8 covers the areas of fluency in which PACE factors (*P*hrasing, *A*ccuracy in word recognition, *C*omprehension, *E*xpression) are discussed in the context of developing proficient and strategic readers.

8 Fluency

> *There are four keys to learning: (1) breaking complex skills into subskills, (2) teaching subskills to accuracy, (3) practicing beyond accuracy to develop **fluency**, and (4) motivating the learner to keep on task. (Samuels, 2003).*
>
> *The critical test of fluency is the ability to decode a text and comprehend it at the same time. (Samuels, 2002)*

Fluency Defined

What Is Reading Fluency?

The National Reading Panel (2000, p. 3–1) has defined fluency as "reading text with speed, accuracy, and proper expression." Harris and Hodges (1995) and Samuels (2003) extend the definition to include comprehension. Proficient readers can be considered "fluent readers" because they can and do approach the printed page with ease and understanding. They establish a reading purpose and achieve their reading goals with a variety of reading strategies and a firm literacy base of age or developmentally appropriate vocabulary/multiple vocabulary meanings. Typically, proficient, fluent readers are "engaged" readers—that is, they consider reading as a means to an end, i.e., reading for information, to achieve goals, to excel academically, or to enjoy leisure time.

Is Fluency Fundamental to Achieving Reading Proficiency? PACE Model

Reading fluency is considered of major fundamental importance to achieving proficiency as a reader. Think of reading fluency in relation to successful completion of a musical piece with an instrument. The musician needs to be able to play the notes accurately (A) using proper phrasing (P) and expressive (E) interpretations while adjusting the speed or timing in playing as needed. Comprehension (C) of the composer's message or theme is achieved with successful playing of the music (= PACE). Fluency in reading also demands PACE (see Figures 8.1 and 8.2).

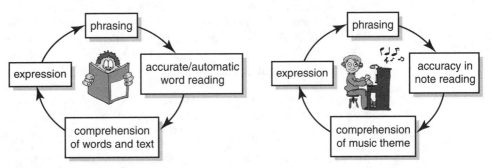

FIGURE 8.1 Fluency Factors in Reading—**P**(phrasing) **A** (accuracy) **C** (comprehension) **E** (expression)

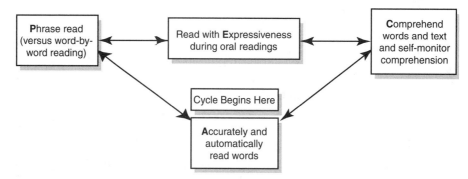

FIGURE 8.2   PACE Fluency Factors

Phrasing (P)   When students are fluent in reading text, they will read in long phrases while attending to punctuation that may impact comprehension. When critical reading is required, fluent readers will adjust their reading pace and will read in shorter phrases or word by word if needed. Students with dyslexia who are struggling with automaticity in word recognition tend to read word by word or in short phrases and often ignore punctuation marks, important times to pause in the reading. As word recognition improves, students are able to read longer phrases but need teacher modeling to show what fluent, flexible reading looks like. The *Neurological Impress Method* (NIM) was designed for struggling readers (Heckelman, 1969) and is a good fluency phrase builder. A student sits with the teacher, and they prepare to read a passage in unison with no prior preparations before the reading. It is best to use reading materials just slightly below the student's independent reading level (word recognition should be around 95%). The teacher sits just behind the student and either the student or the teacher points to the words as he or she reads. The teacher essentially leads the reading, slowing down when appropriate, picking up the pace at other times with changes in voice intonation, inflection, and stress. There is no attempt to teach word recognition or monitor comprehension during the reading—the focus is on having the student practice fluent, flexible reading as it is modeled.

Accuracy (A)   Effective reading is reading in which students can read *accurately* and *quickly*, making few reading errors or miscues when presented with materials on their independent reading levels. Efficient reading of text is accompanied by automaticity with the simultaneous decoding of text with comprehension. Accurate reading of text *without* automaticity is characterized by readings with a high percentage of words read correctly and with expression. However, comprehension of text does not occur simultaneously with the decoding. Automaticity in reading is important to word accuracy just by the nature of the world we live in—there are so many things to do and not enough time to do everything. High stakes testing in our schools/workplaces and technical or comprehensive/expert on-the-job requirements require automaticity from effective readers (Samuels, 2002, 2003). Measuring accurate and fluent reading of text can be done with running records that assess (1) reading rate or words per minute (efficient reading of text) and (2) word miscues analyses to look at the effective reading of text (pp. 187, 233–234).

Going beyond Word Accuracy to Automaticity   "We learn best to read by reading" is probably the most fundamental of all reading principles and "it works." According to Samuels (2002, 2003), practice will get the reader beyond accuracy to automaticity.

Speed in Word Recognition   Speed or automaticity in word reading impacts reading rate—the number of words correct per minute a student can read. Reading rates are typically slower for the student with dyslexia who has difficulty adjusting to different reading situations.

Types of Reading and Speed Required   Richardson and Morgan (1994) list several factors that impact reading speed or rate such as the type of material used, familiarity with content, reader's motivation and purpose, size of type, and physical conditions (e.g., lighting, lack of sleep, presence of directions, and so on). Adults need to learn to adjust to different reading situations—a speed range of 100–200 words per minute (WPM) is needed for reading materiel that requires a careful analysis of highly technical content (e.g., science texts) and poetry; a speed range of 600–800 wpm is needed for speed reading of newspapers, magazines, etc. Most reading material of the study-type nature requires 200–300 wpm (Richardson & Morgan, 1994).

Rauding   Carver (1992) has described "rauding" as the merging of reading (by looking and understanding) with auding (listening and understanding) into what is considered the reading process. For middle school students, and average rauding rate is 190 words per minute with a typical average of 300 words per minute for college students (see Table 8.1). A student with dyslexia would read below these rates, meaning that the amount of reading materials a student with dyslexia could accomplish would be less than the proficient reader (Richardson & Morgan, 1994). Teachers need to reduce reading assignments accordingly and teach specific strategies for adjusting reading rates.

Expected Oral Reading Rates: Guide by Grade Level

(Low = Beginning of Year, High = End of Year)

Gr. 1   (50–80 wpm)   Gr. 4   (100–120 wpm)
Gr. 2   (50–90 wpm)   Gr. 5   (100–130 wpm)
Gr. 3   (80–115 wpm)

Silent Reading Rates (Comprehension is adequate)

Gr. 1:	<80	Gr. 5:	150–160	Gr. 9:	200–210
Gr. 2:	80–110	Gr. 6:	160–175	Gr. 10:	210–225
Gr. 3:	110–130	Gr. 7:	175–185	Gr. 11:	225–240
Gr. 4:	130–150	Gr. 8:	185–200	Gr. 12:	240–255

Rate Determined By:

1. Count number of words read (circa 300 words)
2. Multiply by 60 = dividend $\overline{)*}$
3. Compute reading time in seconds (= divisor $*\overline{)}$)
4. Compute = wpm (words per minute)

Repeated Readings Approach   According to the National Reading Panel Report (2000), repeated readings have a clear and positive effect on reading fluency positively impacting reading rate. With struggling readers, repeated readings with feedback or guidance are more beneficial than repeated readings alone. According to Samuels (2002), the repeated reading method was developed in the early 1970s simultaneously at the University of Minnesota (David LaBerge and S. Jay Samuels) and Harvard University (Carol Chomsky). Essentially, students reread meaningful passages of text until a satisfactory

TABLE 8.1   Average Reading Rates for College Students

Reading Style	Example	For the Dyslexic	Proficient Readers
Scanning	Finding Cue Words	400–500 wpm	600 wpm
Skimming	Proofreading	300–350 wpm	450 wpm
Rauding	Comprehension of Text	200–250 wpm	300 wpm
Text Mastery	Oral Report Prep	100–150 wpm	200 wpm
Memorizing	Essay Exam	75–100 wpm	150 wpm

level of fluency is achieved. How does the teacher know when fluency has been achieved? CWPM, or correct words per minute, could be calculated (see also pp. 185–186 with attention to expected norms for a grade level or "reading like talking" could simply be the goal. That is, the student would reread the passage until it sounded like someone talking with attention to phrasing and expression. A consistent finding in the research has been that repeated readings significantly improve accuracy in word recognition, reading speed, and oral reading expression and with all readers (Samuels, 2002).

Comprehension (C)   Deriving optimal meaning from the printed page becomes a challenge when the student with dyslexia needs to place cognitive resources on **decoding,** or word reading. For proficient readers, the decoding process is automatic and therefore cognitive energies can be spent on *strategic reading* (making sense of the printed page) and monitoring one's own comprehension. For many individuals with dyslexia, picking up another book to read is an academic chore. Samuels (2003) stresses the use of positive human relations to purposefully keep a reader on task or engaged to get beyond struggles with word recognition to the point of *automaticity.* He refers to the *bonding* that must occur between the teacher and student to nurture the motivation or desire to pick up "that book" again to reread or read another new book.

Samuels (2002) recommends two informal ways of assessing comprehension fluency: determining listening comprehension and then oral reading comprehension levels. Teachers select two passages (1/2 to 2 pages) with unfamiliar topics determined to be on a student's independent reading level. One passage needs to be used to measure listening comprehension; the other passage, the student's comprehension after an oral reading of the text. Retellings can be used to evaluate the student's comprehension. For the oral reading passage, the student is told beforehand that after the reading he or she will be asked to tell all about the story or everything that "you can remember." With both passages, there is no background building and no prereading of the text before the oral reading.

Expression (E)   Spoken language is communicated with pauses, pitch variations, and intonation, providing information necessary to understand the message (Schreiber, 1987). Students with dyslexia, who struggle with word reading, typically lack expressiveness and phrasing. According to Samuels (2002), students are missing an essential link to fluent oral reading if expressiveness is limited or missing during the reading. This takes practice. The repeated reading method mentioned above allows the reader to reach the point of "reading like talking."

Dyslexics may need explicit instruction in attending to the purpose of punctuation marks in creating meaning for the reader. In Figure 8.3, commas are used two dif-

---

"The mayor then appointed **William Schwartz,** his best advisor, to serve on the important commission." The meaning in this sentence conveys that William Schwartz emphatically is the mayor's best advisor.

or

"The mayor then appointed **William Schwartz,** his best advisor to serve on the important commission." The meaning in this sentence could convey that the mayor appointed William Schwartz to do something and identified him later as the best advisor to serve on the commission.

FIGURE 8.3   PACE: Expression and Phrasing Matter

ferent ways with the same sentence, resulting in two different meanings. When read with expression, sentence meaning is clarified.

Fluency Assessment

Snow, Burns, and Griffin (1998) have identified word recognition accuracy and reading fluency as necessary for achieving, "adequate progress in learning to read . . . both . . . should be regularly assessed in the classroom permitting timely and effective instructional response when difficulty or delay is apparent" (p. 7).

The *Dyslexia Checklist* on page 225 can be referenced when evaluating word fluency factors for struggling readers. A majority of the following would be checked if the individual was diagnosed as dyslexic because one of the primary presenting problems is difficulty with fluent reading.

- Limited sight vocabulary.*
- Word-by-word or short phrase reading or poor phrasing.
- Slower than expected reading rate (reference charts with expected reading rates).
- Lack of expression especially in conversational text.
- Poor enunciation.
- Reliance on just a few strategies to identify unknown words.
- Less than satisfactory comprehension of the reading.*

(*=should test with standardized assessments, criterion-referenced tests, or research-based benchmarks)

Related Word Recognition Skills/Strategies Required for Fluent Reading*

- Ability to make accurate sound-symbol correspondences.
- Knowledge of the names of pictures beginning or ending with the same sound.
- Phonemic awareness proficiency in isolating phonemes, identifying phonemes, categorizing phonemes, blending phonemes, segmenting phonemes, and deleting phonemes.
- Ability to flexibly apply various word recognition strategies when encountering difficult words or flexible word problem solving.

(*see *Dyslexia Checklist* on p. 225 and *diagnostic word recognition checklist* on p. 99)

Measuring Efficient and Effective Reading of Text

Measuring accurate and fluent reading of text over time involves looking at (1) reading rate or correct words per minute (or efficient reading of text) and (2) word miscues to determine word recognition accuracy (of effective reading of text). Calculating correct words per minute (CWPM) and comparing progress over time through running records is important for students with dyslexia. The goal would be to automatize or make efficient word analysis strategies with cognitive processing focused on comprehension and self-monitoring of text understandings. The following guide can be used for calculating CWPM (*correct* words per minute).

Calculating Correct Words per Minute (CWPM) for Dyslexics and Proficient Readers (see also p. 183)

1. Select three passages (if constrained by time, two passages) from an instructional level text (grade level text for students who are not disabled).
2. Students read each passage for one minute.
3. Tally the number of words read for each passage and calculate the average number of words read per minute (number of words read + number of words read + number of words read, then divide by 3 = average number of words read per minute).

4. Tally the number of errors read on each of the three passages and calculate the average number of errors per minute (number of errors + number of errors + number of errors, then divide by 3 = average number of errors per minute).
5. Subtract from the average number of words read per minute the average number of errors read per minute (average number of words read minus average number of errors read).
6. The final number is the average number of correct words per minute (CWPM). Then check the student's reading rate (CWPM) against a chart with expectations for various grade levels (e.g., Dyslexia Checklist—p. 229). Keep in mind what is being compared. If a student with dyslexia is assessed at his or her instructional level, the reading rate comparison would reflect a comparison for the grade level tested. Grade-level comparisons are certainly helpful—however, if a student is unable to read with any degree of efficiency using grade-level text, the information obtained for a grade-level comparison would be of little instructional benefit. It is already known the student cannot read on grade level; CWPM would then be assumed to be below grade level as well.
7. Calculating CWPM should occur at regular intervals (e.g., each marking term). Charting a student's progress helps to determine improvement in reading fluency for this fluency factor: accurate and efficient reading of text.

Maintaining Running Records

Maintain running records of students' reading behaviors to include CWPM. Fountas and Pinnell (1996) suggest using the miscue analysis running record coding system in Figure 8.4 to assess oral reading errors. This recording method allows teachers to main-

Reading Action	Code	Additional Information (Miscue = error)
"Accurate" reading	✔ ✔ one saturday	Student made 1:1 speech-to-print match
"Substitution" Miscue*	mom (child) mother (text)	Substitution can change meaning or not (in this example = no change in meaning)
"Omission" Miscue	— (child) let's (text)	a dash is inserted indicating the word omission
"Insertion" Miscue	some (child) — (not in text)	sometimes shown (∧ some) above text where the insertion occurred
"Told" Miscue	— | A family | T {A = appealed T = told}	The teacher or adult "told" the word. If the child asked for the word "A" or appealed is noted. Appeals can also be nonverbal (the child is stuck and won't continue reading).
"Repetition" (not a miscue)	✔R ✔ one saturday R lunch for the	R = single word repeated; repeated text phrases – draw a line to where child returned
"Self Correction" (not a miscue)	Mom SC mother	SC = child self corrected

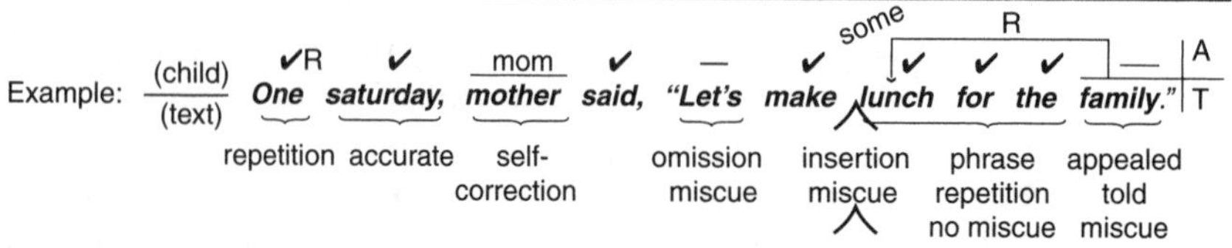

FIGURE 8.4 Running Record Coding System (Fountas & Pinnell, 1996) (see p. 233)

tain a word accuracy running record over time. Using a student's current reading materials allows the teacher to see how the student is applying both word knowledge and learned reading strategies with familiar text.

According to Fountas and Pinnell (1996, p. 78), running records have various uses—teachers are able to (1) find the appropriate level of text for children to read, (2) group students for reading instruction, (3) check on text selection and on teaching, (4) document progress in reading, (5) add to the teacher's knowledge of the reading process, (6) suggest ways to help struggling readers, (7) determine whether students are meeting proficiency targets or satisfactory progress, (8) summarize the results of a guided reading program, and (9) provide information about the student's use of meaning to guide reading.

Word Strategy Bookmark: Self-Assessment

The word strategy bookmark shown in Figure 8.5 could be used by students during reading times with the teacher noticing strategies students favor and strategies that need to be developed.

Miscue Analyses: Language Dialects

When analyzing the oral reading miscues of students with "dialects," educators need to view these dialectical differences in the context of a "standard for a cultural group" and not "incorrectly variable from the language norm." For example, some students

---

Word Strategy Bookmark

1. Sound it out. Slide your finger over the word.

2. Chunk the word or find a word part.

3. Reread the sentence or phrase.

4. Read on for meaning and go back.

5. Look at picture clues.

6. Use the dictionary.

7. Ask a friend.

8. Ask the teacher.

9. Skip the word if you can.

10. Finally, does the word make sense in this sentence?

Word Strategy Bookmark

1. Sound it out.

2. Look at the pictures.

3. Read the sentence again.

4. Does the word make sense?

5. Ask for help.

FIGURE 8.5   Word Strategy Bookmarks

speak a dialect of English in the United States sometimes referred to in the popular press as "nonstandard."

Benjamin Swan, noted educator, historian, and civic leader, feels that dialects often have systematic, rule-governed syntactical structures. According to Swan (2002), cultural literacy related to dialects has been formalized and is not random, as the term "nonstandard" would convey. Dialects can be functional in both communication and learning. In looking at dialects, educators need to consider such language variations as *standard for a cultural group.* Then consider the relevance to the learner, syntactical and semantic consistency, and effectiveness in "communicating the message."

In conducting reading miscue analyses, dialectical variations in language should not be viewed as incorrect or wrong if appropriate to the context (Brown, 2004) and the message is effectively communicated. In examples during oral readings by some U.S. black students, some endings of words may be dropped or changed (*be* for *been*); the possessive form of a word may be deleted (e.g., *they school* for *their school*); or changes in verb form may be made (student reads *she goin'* for *she is going*). The acceptance of dialectical differences without correction "puts into words" a subtler, more important message, "you, your family, and your language are valued."

Instructional Implications   The use of culturally relevant, engaging text is particularly essential for students who don't often encounter stories closely connected with their language (i.e., dialect) or cultural experiences. Some children experience the problem of "not finding themselves in books." James Banks (1991) recommends that both teachers and parents seek culturally relevant books that include realistic portrayals of characters. When dialect is spoken, they should ask, "Is it appropriate to the characters?" Figure 8.6 lists some additional considerations.

The following "questions as considerations" were abstracted from the work of Bena R. Hefflin and Mary Alice Barksdale-Ladd (2003):

■ Does the story have a memorable character of similar age to the students? Similar background?

■ Will the story plot or theme be of interest to the students? Easy to follow?

■ Are character images realistic and positive?

■ Does the story language convey clear, concrete images of the characters, actions, and setting? Natural, vivid language? Authentic and accurate?

■ Do the illustrations represent reality?

■ If dialect is presented, does it accurately portray the characters' dialect?

■ Does the story include a "motif or authentic aspect" of the culture represented by the characters?

■ Does the book contain current and accurate information about the culture represented by the characters in regard to values, beliefs, traditions, and other cultural systems?

The current authors add:

■ Was the book chosen by the student from a variety of similar books that includes books authored by individuals from similar backgrounds?

■ If other students read the book who were of similar age, did they enjoy the book? If so, could these students give a book chat or preview to establish interest and a reading purpose?

■ Can the book be used in school or taken home for read-aloud, repeated readings, shared readings, and the like?

FIGURE 8.6   Important Questions to Consider When Choosing Culturally Relevant Text: Teacher Self-Assessment

Phonemic Awareness and Fluency

Current linguists and researchers have found that students with dyslexia across languages and cultures and those dyslexics with dialectical variations all seem to have the lack of sufficient phonemic awareness in common. Phonemic awareness is causally related to reading achievement and can be considered a strong predictor of reading ability.

What Is Phonemic Awareness?

Phonemic awareness is a metalinguistic awareness of (1) "those smaller-than-a-syllable speech sounds that correspond roughly to individual letters or grapheme units" (Adams, 1991, p. 65) and (2) "spoken language consist(ing) of a sequence of phonemes" (Yopp & Yopp, 2000, p. 131) (for any particular language). Phonemes are the smallest units of sound in spoken language that, when combined, comprise words. "What is important is the awareness that they exist as abstractable and manipulative components of language" (Adams, 1991, p. 65). The English language has approximately 44 phonemes (see Table 8.2 on p. 190). Proficient readers are fluent, in part, because of a strong phonemic awareness knowledge foundation.

What Isn't Phonemic Awareness?

Phonemes differ from graphemes (graphemes are units of written language that represent phonemes in the spellings of words). Phonemic awareness also differs from phonological awareness (knowledge) in that phonological awareness is a more inclusive term covering knowledge of the smallest units of sound in spoken language (phonemes) and larger language units as well (e.g., knowledge of syllables and rhyming words). To provide additional clarification in regard to terminology in the field, a morpheme is the smallest unit of language that conveys meaning (whole words and inflectional endings and affixes)—phonemes are not morphemes. However, phonemes are "the smallest units of speech sounds that makes a difference in communication" (Yopp & Yopp, 2000, p. 131). The **alphabetic principle** in essence is an understanding that graphemes represent phonemes and not units of meaning. According to Perfetti (1985), inadequate phonemic awareness knowledge makes it difficult to acquire the alphabetic principle, essential to reading fluency.

Why Is Phonemic Awareness Important?

In a review of the research, Marilyn Jager Adams (1991) concludes, "an absence or lack of phonemic awareness appears to be characteristic of children who are failing or have failed to read" (p. 328), indicative of students who have dyslexia. Phonemic awareness can be taught. According to the National Reading Panel Report (NRPR) (2000), phonemic awareness instruction improves students' abilities to read and spell with both positive short- and long-term effects, especially in teaching children to manipulate phonemes and segment, blend, and delete phonemes.

What to Teach?

According to the NRPR (2000), the teaching of phonemic awareness tasks needs to be appropriate to the developmental level of the child. The National Reading Panel surveyed the literature and found at-risk students for reading failure showed larger effect sizes in acquiring phonemic awareness (d = 0.95) and transferring these skills to

---

TABLE 8.2   Developmental Presentation of Phonemic Awareness Tasks

---

The 44 phonemes in English: consonants = b, d, f, g, h, j, k, l, m, n, p, r, s, t, v, w, y, z, ch, sh, "th" as in *thimble*, "th" as in *the*, "hw" as in *wheel*, "zh" as in *measure*, and "ng" as in *wing*; vowels = ă, ĕ, ĭ, ŏ, ŭ, ā, ē, ī, ō, yo͞o, ə as in *arm*, o͞o, o͝o, ou, oi, ô as in *ball*, û as in *stir*, â as in *pair*, and ä as in *far*.

(1) **First sound comparisons (K)**—identify the names of pictures beginning with the same initial consonants (*this draws the young readers attention to the fact that words are comprised of sounds in addition to meanings*)

(2) **Blending onset-rime units (K)** into real words

(3) **Blending phonemes into real words**

(4) **Deleting a phoneme and saying the word that remains**

(5) **Segmenting words (K–1)** into phonemes (*this also helps young writers generate closer approximations to correct and complete spellings*)

(6) **Blending phonemes (grade 1)** into nonwords (*this helps first graders and older struggling readers decode words*)

Source: Schatschneider, Francis, Foorman, Fletcher, and Mehta (1999).

---

reading (*d* = 0.86) and spelling (*d* = 0.76) than students who were not judged to be at risk. Samuels (1973) and others point to the importance of showing students the specific feature or features of letters that make them unique to all others—knowledge children need when making first sound comparisons.

It is helpful to know what phonemic awareness tasks should be taught and which are easier than others so that teaching progresses in a developmental sequence. According to Schatschneider, Francis, Foorman, Fletcher, and Mehta (1999), phonemic awareness tasks are ordered from easiest (1) to most difficult (6) in Table 8.2.

Although, the phonemic awareness tasks mentioned are typically taught in grades K and 1, older students who have not yet mastered the concepts associated with the tasks need additional teaching and training. The amount of time devoted to the teaching of phonemic awareness should be dictated by "how long it takes students to acquire phonemic awareness skills that are taught" (NRPR, 2000, p. 2-31). It is clear from the research that phonemic awareness tasks are more difficult for students with dyslexia to acquire. There are a number of commercial programs that have a scope and sequence of phonemic awareness skills that need to be taught with manipulatives (e.g., phoneme cubes) for children to use to "blend words together" and "segment" or "pull words apart." Yopp and Yopp (2000) emphasize that phonemic awareness activities should be playful and engaging, social and interactive—stimulating curiosity and experimentation with language. According to Adams (1991), the outcome needs to be that the reader establishes a clear link between the sounds (phonemes) and letters (graphemes).

What Grapheme Correspondences Should Be Taught?

Beck and McCaslin (1978) suggest that the number of grapheme correspondences that should be taught by the end of grade 2 for the English language is 170. Adams (1991) excludes some consonant clusters, which reduces the number to 110. According to Adams (1991), the correspondences most important to teach are cited in the Beck and McCaslin (1978) research in Table 8.3.

TABLE 8.3   Thirty-Five Grapheme Units to Teach by the End of Second Grade

---

Single consonants (teach in initial word positions first): b, l, r, h, j, c, f, y, n, d, qu, t, v, m, s, w, p, z, g, k, x

Short vowels: a, e, i, o, u

Long vowels: a-e (*cake*); i-e (*rice*)

Vowel digraphs and diphthongs: ee (*meet*)

l-controlled vowels: *all* as in *call*

Initial consonant clusters: sl, br

Initial consonant digraphs: sh, ch

Final consonant digraphs: ck

Source: Beck and McCaslin (1978).

In summary, the teaching of phonemes must "be a part of a broader literacy program that includes development of the student's vocabulary, syntax, comprehension, strategic reading abilities, decoding abilities, and writing across all the content areas" (Yopp & Yopp, 2000, p. 143).

Segmenting and Blending Phonemes—Critical to Reading Fluency

As shown in the Dyslexia Checklist in Figure 8.7 for R, a grade 4 severely dyslexic student, phonemic blending and segmentation continue to be problematic, impacting fluency factors. R has limited sight vocabulary, reads word by word or in short phrases, has a relatively slow reading rate, lacks expression in conversational text, relies on just a few strategies to identify unknown words, and has less than satisfactory comprehension of a reading without extensive probing by the teacher.

Although R has a limited sight vocabulary relative to his peers, he has mastered many grade 1 through 3 high-frequency sight words and some word recognition strategies required for effective reading of connected text. This is in large part due to (1) an intensive literacy program (three-hour literacy block), (2) consistent literacy support in the home and frequent home-school communications, (3) speech and language therapy, and (4) individual tutoring by a learning disability specialist who uses a phoneme sequencing program, a spelling patterns component of a word recognition program and a K–6 sight word recognition program where R is developing images of sight words to facilitate recognition and use in decoding and spelling.

Due to R's reading disability or dyslexia, he lacks automaticity in sight word recognition (= sounds out sight words versus identifying automatically by sight) with an oral reading rate of approximately 35 wpm with grades 2 and 3 text. As stated previously, the automatic detector in the left occipito-temporal area of the brain "breaks down" in children with dyslexia. A neurological anomaly prevents their brains from gaining automatic access to the word analyzer and phoneme producer areas of the brain (Shaywitz, 2003). Children of similar age and developmental level would be expected to read approximately 100+ words per minute. Although R's reading rate will improve, he probably will read at reduced reading rates even as an adult reader. This translates into needing extra time to complete reading tasks.

The good news is that R will be a proficient reader because of early intervention efforts with early progress indicators confirming this observation. For example, a year

Dyslexia Checklist - Case Study

Name _____ Date _____ Examiner _____

School _____ Grade _4_ DOB _Age 10_

Teacher _____ Parents/Guardian _____

Second Language Learner: ☐ Yes ☑ No (If yes, test in home language if appropriate.) *Grade K - Screening score of 20 on ESI - K (Revised) at age 6-0 (Rescreenings with at-risk status; language delays)*

"Dyslexia" definition = *dys* and *lexia* or inability to effectively read words. This is the most prevalent specific learning disability (at least 50% of the LD population). It is thought to have a neurological basis because the disability is unexpected in relation to other cognitive abilities and access to effective classroom instruction. There are specific difficulties with fluent reading and the phonological processing components of language. Secondary issues may include other academic and non-academic difficulties (e.g., reading comprehension); difficulties in socialization (e.g., more negative peer interactions) and co-existing disabilities or disorders (e.g., ADD or ADHD with 25% of those with dyslexia). With intensive literacy support in reading and writing, a social-academic network of support, and the development of individual resiliency, individuals with dyslexia can lead successful and fulfilling lives. *NOTE: 1/02 (Developmental Reading Assessment) DRA2; 1/03 DRA 10; 6/03 DRA 18; 3/04 DRA 18 receiving intensive literacy support

Independent Reading Level: Word recognition 95-99% with > 90% comprehension   Gr: 2 (indicate grade level)   DRA Level 20 (November 2003 and March 2004)
Instructional Reading Level: Word recognition 90-95% with >75-80% comprehension   Gr: 3 (indicate grade level)   BRI (Basic Reading Inventory) (Grade 3 passages 70% - 90% comprehension)

Necessary: (assuming participation for 2-3 years in standards-based reading classes where peers achieved reading proficiency)
✓ Overall, individual is approximately one to two years behind age or grade level (instructional reading level) in reading achievement, based on benchmarks for grade level; standardized or criterion-referenced assessments can be used.   * High stakes Grade 3 testing - passed the full reading test (top 50% of district) and writing scores were proficient (with test accommodations).
✓ The individual has difficulty with fluency and the phonological components of language.

MAJORITY CHECKED:
Fluency (oral reading):
* ✓ limited sight vocabulary
✓ word by word or short phrase reading or poor phrasing
✓ slower than expected reading rate (see chart) 35 wpm with grade 2&3 text
✓ lack of expression especially in conversational text
☐ poor enunciation (received speech therapy)
✓ reliance on just a few strategies- (context & configuration cues only) to identify unknown words
* ✓ less than satisfactory comprehension of the reading

(* = Should test with standardized assessments, criterion - referenced tests or research - based benchmarks)

Expected Oral Reading Rates: Guide by Grade Level
(Low = Beginning of Year, High = End of Year)
Grade 1 (50 - 80 wpm)
Grade 2 (50-90 wpm)
Grade 3 (80 - 115 wpm)
Grade 4 (100 - 120 wpm)
Grade 5 (100 - 130 wpm)

Rate Determined By:
1. Count number of words read (circa 300 words)
2. Multiply by 60=dividend ⊛
3. Compute reading time in seconds (= divisor ⊛)
4. Compute = wpm (words per minute)

Silent Reading Rates (Comprehension is adequate)
Gr. 1: <80
Gr. 2: 80 - 110
Gr. 3: 110 - 130
Gr. 4: 130 - 150
Gr. 5: 150 - 160
Gr. 6: 160 - 175
Gr. 7: 175 - 185
Gr. 8: 185 - 200
Gr. 9: 200 - 210
Gr. 10: 210 - 225
Gr. 11: 225 - 240
Gr. 12: 240 - 255

MAJORITY CHECKED:
Phonological Processing Checks:
Word or Letter Knowledge Problems with:
___ Identifying sound - symbol correspondences
___ Identifying the names of pictures beginning or ending with the same sound
✓ Writing conventions appropriate to age or developmental level
✓ Spelling appropriate to age or developmental level

Phonemic Awareness Deficiencies In:
___ Isolating Phonemes (e.g., Tell me the first sound in "kind")
___ Identifying Phonemes (e.g., Tell me the sound that is the same in "say" and "see")
___ Categorizing Phonemes (e.g., Tell me another word that you can add to this group with the same beginning sound - "play," "plant")
✓ Blending Phonemes (e.g., Tell me what word is /k/ /i/ /n/ /d/) for grade level
✓ Phoneme Segmentation (e.g., How many sounds are there in "kind"?)
___ Phoneme Deletion (e.g., What is "kind" without the /d/ sound?)

ADDITIONAL CORRELATING FACTORS/INFORMATION:
Some Checked:
✓ Family history of dyslexia (dad)
✓ Delayed language development and/or language related problems
✓ Late talker (grade appropriate - strength)
___ Listening comprehension deficits (strength)
✓ Serial order and sequencing problems
✓ Time and directional confusions
✓ Problems with attention, on-task behavior, and follow-through
___ ADD/ADHD
✓ Memory (processing deficits)
✓ WISC-R and WAIS-R Verbal - Performance Discrepancies or ACID/AVID profiles (Higher 20ptV/P Discrepancy/Performance)
✓ Problems with organization and study skills
___ Social behavioral problems to include more negative peer interactions, diminished self-concept, learned helplessness and external locus of control (Very Well Adjusted)
___ Resilient with support systems
___ Other:

FIGURE 8.7 Dyslexia Checklist—Case Study (Dyslexic Fourth-Grade Student)

ago R's performance on the grade 3 high stakes state reading test (as a third grader) was passing (proficient status for reading and writing) placing him in the top 50 percent of the entire district for reading performance (and for all readers). Although he had test accommodations (e.g., clarification of instructions and directions, extra testing time, testing done in short periods with frequent breaks, and with use of a place marker), the reading test (with written open response questions) was taken independently and is the state's benchmark reading test for grade 3 students. Continued focus on sight word recognition will continue to be an important part of R's literacy program. Individuals with dyslexia need intensive practice with frequently encountered/used words in reading and writing so that these words are learned as sight words, thus facilitating the ease with which they read and write.

Sight-Word Recognition

There are a number of words that students frequently encounter in reading that, once learned, facilitate the speed or rate at which reading proceeds. One of the major reasons why the decoding task has become easier for proficient readers is that they automatically recognize approximately 300 common words that comprise approximately 80 to 90 percent of the words in our day-to-day reading (Samuels, 2003). The majority of the common words Samuels and other researchers make reference to can be found in *The Dolch Basic Sight Vocabulary List* (1942). The *Dolch* list was developed by Edward W. Dolch in the 1930s and is the most frequently cited sight vocabulary list of 220 words (excludes nouns). According to Johns (1981), thirteen of the Dolch words account for up to 25 percent of words in text: *a, and, for, he, is, in, it, of, that, the, to, was, you.*

Individuals with dyslexia have less extensive sight vocabularies as compared to proficient readers. This finding has been consistently documented. Allington (1977) has found that struggling readers in actuality spend the least amount of time engaged in reading activities and therefore have fewer opportunities to acquire expansive sight vocabularies. Determining what sight words individuals with dyslexia need to learn then becomes a priority. In addition to determining what sight words students need to learn, consideration should be given to how students are learning these sight words. Karlin and Karlin (1987) have overviewed the sight-word research, concluding that students (1) use the beginning and final elements of words and (2) rely on the initial position of the word and context to determine the rest of the word. Students with dyslexia will often rely on the context of the sentence to determine unknown words without adequate attention to ending sounds.

Lipson and Wixson (2003) recommend assessing high frequency sight-word recognition both in isolation and in context because individuals with dyslexia rely more heavily on context to facilitate word recognition than proficient readers. Sight-word recognition is typically assessed in isolation. This can be accomplished by comparing student's word recognition during actual readings of connected text with the reading of isolated sight-word lists. Various sight-word lists have been published by researchers, past and present, and by commercial publishers of basal series. The *Essential 500 Word Reading List* (Spafford & Grosser, 2005) shown in Figure 8.8 was developed based on the foundation work of (1) Edward W. Dolch (1942), whose 220 Dolch words continue to be cited as those critical "high-frequency" words children need to learn by the middle of second grade, and the more recent work of (2) Eldon E. Ekwall (1985) and Albert J. Harris and Milton D. Jacobson (1982) (please see p. 194 for information on the development of the list).

The **Essential 500 Word Reading List** was created by the authors as a sight vocabulary reference and incorporates the work of:

(1) Edward W. Dolch (1942)—220 Dolch high-frequency words to learn by the middle of second grade. These words frequently occur in basal series and literature books at the first and second grade levels.

(2) Eldon E. Ekwall (1985)—36 sight words that can be used as a quick check of a student's knowledge of high-frequency basic sight words. These were taken from Ekwall's Basic Sight Word List.

(3) Albert J. Harris and Milton D. Jacobson (1982)—60 selected non-Dolch sight words from Harris and Jacobson's *First Reader List.* These high-frequency words, initially presented in first- and second-grade texts, can be learned as sight words in second and third grade to facilitate reading fluency.

(4) Carol A. Spafford and George S. Grosser—Additional high frequency words:

Examples: number names zero through nine, twenty, thirty, forty, fifty, hundred, and thousand; basic colors not listed as sight words—purple and orange; basic operations and measurement mathematics terms (e.g., inch, gram, hour, month, ounce and cent); frequently encountered contractions in basals and texts; school-based "sight" words, class, school, office, fire-drill, nurse, secretary, principal, and teacher; social studies "resource" or "leadership" terms, police, leader, congress, emperor, empress, king, president, prime minister, prince, princess, queen, and senate; high-frequency environmental words (e.g., street, danger, and emergency); family and "people" words, mom, mother, dad, father, sister, brother, aunt, uncle, cousin, children, family, and citizen; and additional courtesy words, respect and polite. Some "tricky" word clusters frequently encountered in print were included as these can slow the reader down—quiet, quick, quite and tough, though, thought, and through. Additionally, the list was completed so that all letters of the English alphabet were represented at least twice (initial word positions).

Most Important Sight Word Question (relevant to teachers and parents):
Should the teaching of sight words be done in isolation or within the context of running or connected text? The answer is "yes" to both—practice teaching and learning sight words in isolation and in phrases and sentences. Research shows that combining both methods of teaching sight words optimizes the likelihood a student will acquire designated sight words. Students can create personal dictionaries of sight words with index cards and large rings. A sight word can be listed on one side of an index card (isolation) with a phrase or sentence using the sight word on the other sight of the card (in context). The personal dictionary could be referenced during writing times (reading-to-write). At home, families could review a few sight words a day using a sight word calendar. The *Essential 500 Word Reading List* could be used as a reference.

Includes: 220 Dolch// EKWALL Quick// Harris-Jacobson First Reader// Sight Word Lists

Name _____ Grade _____ School _____

(GE = grade equivalent) (Dolch words should be learned by grade three; if learning disabled, focus the teaching of "sight words" with the full Dolch List first)

GE List 1.0	List 1.5	List 1.5–2.0	List 2.5	List 2.5–3.0	List 3.0	List 3.5
(1)						
a*	again*✓	about*	alone	almost	addition	against
add	am*	across	also✓	along	afternoon	another×
all*	are*	after*	always*✓	aunt	already	answer
an*	as*	art	around*	began×	aren't	area
and*✓	away*	ate*	ask*	between	beautiful×	believe
any*	back	because*	best*	each	below	citizen
at*	begin	been*	bring*	easy	beside	congress
be*	better*	before*	brown*	face	bottom	country×
big*	call*	being	buy*	family	build	decide
(10)						
boy	city	black*	can't	father	children×	decimal
but*	class	blue*	carry*	fill×	couldn't×	divide
by*	come*	both*	clean*	flower×	different	division
came*	could*	brother	cold*	food×	earth	either
can*	down*✓	care	cut*	foot	easily	emergency
dad	find*	cent	drink*	friend	ever×	emperor
day	full*	danger	dry	front	fifty	empress
do*	funny*	did*	fall*	great	forty	entrance
eat*	going*	does*	fast*	home	gallon	everyone×
fire drill	gone	done*	fly*✓	hour	guess	everywhere×
(20)						
for*	grow*	don't*	found*	I'll	half	example
get*	happy✓	draw*	gave*	inch	hear×	exit
girl	have*	eight*	house	it's	high	fraction
go*	her*	end✓	hurt*✓	knew	hungry×	government
goes*	here*✓	every*	laugh*	last	inside×	gram
had*	he's	far*	left	let's	I've×	happen
has*	him*	first*✓	less	life	leaf	hard
he*✓	his*✓	five*	light*✓	month	low	heard×
I*✓	how*	four*	live*	more	making×	however
if*	its*	from*	made*	mother	mayor×	hundred
(30)						
in *	king	give*	many*	move×	metric	important
is*	little*	good*	much*	named×	might×	leader
it*	love	got*	myself*	near×	mile	learned
jump*	new*	green*	never*×	next	minute	listen
let*	nine	help*✓	once*	nice×	miss×	liter
like*	one*	hold*	open*	noise×	mix×	meter
look*	other	hot*✓	orange	nose×	multiply	million
make*	out*	I'm	plant	number	music	mountain
man	pick*	into*	please*	nurse	ounce	multiplication
me*	pull*✓	just*	present✓	office	pint	neither
(40)						
mom	same	keep*	pretty*✓	part×	pound×	nothing×
Subtotals _____	_____	_____	_____	_____	_____	_____
(also: 32 Dolch; 3 Ekwall)	(28 Dolch; 6 Ekwall)	(31 Dolch; 4 Ekwall)	(30 Dolch; 7 Ekwall)	(11 Harris-Jacobson)	(14 Harris-Jacobson)	(6 Harris-Jacobson)

(continued)

FIGURE 8.8 Essential 500 Word Reading List (Spafford & Grosser, 2005)

Includes: 220 Dolch//EKWALL Quick// Harris-Jacobson First Reader// Sight Word Lists (Spafford & Grosser, 2005)

Name _____ Grade _____ School _____

(color coding by date; progress over time running records—below)

(Page 2)

GE List 1.0	List 1.5	List 1.5– 2.0	List 2.5	List 2.5– 3.0	List 3.0	List 3.5

(GE = grade equivalent) (Dolch words should be learned by grade three; if learning disabled, focus the teaching of "sight words" with the full Dolch List first)

GE List 1.0		List 1.5	2.0	List 2.5	3.0	List 3.0	List 3.5
(41)	my*	saw*✓	kind*	right*	place	quiz	ourselves
	no*	she's*	know*	round*	police	real×	peace
	not*	six*	long*	shall*	prince	second	people
	of*	sleep*	math	should✓	princess	shape	picture×
	off*	small*	may*	slow	principal	sign×	polite
	on*	some*	must*	start*	purple	sound×	president
	or*	such✓	night	street	room×	state	prime minister
	over*	sure✓	now*	than✓	school	store×	quart
	play*	ten*	old*	thank*✓	shoe×	suppose	quarter
(50)	put*	that*	only*✓	thing✓	side×	there's	question
	ran*	their*	our*	think*	smell×	they'd	quick
	red*	them*	own*	today*	smile×	they're	quiet×
	said*	then*	queen	together*	snow	third	quit
	sat✓	there*	read*	town	song×	thirty	quite
	say*	they*	ride*	under*	sorry×	tonight×	rather
	see*	this*✓	run*	upon*	subtraction	true	really
	sing*	three*	seven*	use*✓	thought	until×	respect
	sit*	time	show*	walk*	told×	value	science
	sky	too*	sister	warm*	tried×	wasn't×	secretary
(60)	so*	try*	soon*	wash*	trip×	we'll×	senate
	sun	two*	stop*	well*✓	turn×	we're×	sentence
	the*✓	us*	subtract	where*	uncle	what's×	stem
	to*	very*	take*	which*	wet×	whole	talked
	tree✓	want*	tell*	while✓	windy	wide	teach
	up*	went*	these*	white*	without×	window	teacher
	was*	were*	those*	wish*	won't×	within	they'll
	we*	why*	twenty	work*	worker×	wouldn't	though
	when*	with*	what*	would*	world	year	thousand
	will*	your*	who*	write*	yard	you'll	through
(70)	you*✓	yes*	yellow*	yet	zero	zone	tough
Subtotals	_____	_____	_____	_____	_____	_____	toward
	(also: 26 Dolch; 4 Ekwall)	(27 Dolch; 4 Ekwall)	(24 Dolch; 1 Ekwall)	(22 Dolch; 7 Ekwall)	(16 Harris-Jacobson)	(10 Harris-Jacobson)	usually
							village
							watch×
							where's
							whether
							woman
							x-ray
							young
							you've (80)
							_____
							(3 Harris-Jacobson)

Color Coding *(highlighting known words)*	Progress Over Time Running Record
_____ date color _____	Date _____ Total Sight Words Recognized _____
_____ date color _____	Date _____ Total Sight Words Recognized _____
_____ date color _____	Date _____ Total Sight Words Recognized _____
_____ date color _____	Date _____ Total Sight Words Recognized _____
_____ date color _____	Date _____ Total Sight Words Recognized _____
_____ date color _____	Date _____ Total Sight Words Recognized _____
_____ date color _____	Date _____ Total Sight Words Recognized _____

* = 220 Dolch Sight Words; Dolch, E.W., (1942). *Basic Sight Word List.* Champaign, IL: Garrard Press. The Dolch list has been the fields' major sight word resource for over 6 decades.

✓ = 36 Sight words from the Ekwall, "Quick Check for Basic Sight Word Knowledge." (see: Ekwall, E.E., 1985, *Locating and Correcting Reading Difficulties,* Columbus, OH: Charles Merrill. This is the complete "Quick Check" list of 36 words).

× = 60 Selected words from the Harris-Jacobson, *First Reader List* (1982). Copyright by Macmillan Publishing Co., NY.

FIGURE 8.8 *(Continued)*

The following student list for level would be the protocol used during the assessment of sight-word recognition. This 1.0 (beginning first grade) list and the other levels 1.5, 1.5–2.0, 2.5, 2.5–3.0, 3.0, and 3.5 shown on pages 199–200 are reproducibles in Appendix II (seven separate student lists). Color coding allows teachers and parents to chart progress over time (running record) using only those lists the student is developmentally able to work with. The master list of 500 words can be used as a running record of sight-word progress across grade levels.

Essential 500 Word Reading List   Student Copy (1.0)(Spafford & Grosser, 2005)

Includes: **Dolch//EKWALL Quick// Harris-Jacobson First Reader// Sight Word Lists**

Name _____ Grade _____ School _____ Teacher _____

Sight Words	Check if Mastered ✓ (Date)	Sight Words	Check if Mastered ✓ (Date)	Sight Words	Check if Mastered ✓ (Date)
a* (1)		had* (25)		play* (49)	
add		has*		put* (50)	
all*		he*3		ran*	
an*		I*✓		red*	
and*✓		if*		said*	
any*		in* (30)		sat✓	
at*		is*		say*	
be*		it*		see*	
big*		jump*		sing*	
boy (10)		let*		sit*	
but*		like*		sky	
by*		look*		so* (60)	
came*		make*		sun	
can*		man		the*✓	
dad		me*		to*	
day		mom (40)		tree✓	
do*		my*		up*	
eat*		no*		was*	
fire drill		not*		we*	
for* (20)		of*		when*	
get*		off*		will*	
girl		on*		you*✓ (70)	
go*		or*			
goes* (24)		over* (48)			

Subtotal _____   Subtotal _____   Subtotal _____

(18*Dolch 1 Ekwall)   (22*Dolch 2 Ekwall)   (18*Dolch 4 Ekwall)

Color Coding *(highlighting known words)*
_____ date   color _____
_____ date   color _____
_____ date   color _____
_____ date   color _____
_____ date   color _____
_____ date   color _____
_____ date   color _____

Progress Over Time Running Record
Date _____   Total Sight Words Recognized _____
Date _____   Total Sight Words Recognized _____
Date _____   Total Sight Words Recognized _____
Date _____   Total Sight Words Recognized _____
Date _____   Total Sight Words Recognized _____
Date _____   Total Sight Words Recognized _____
Date _____   Total Sight Words Recognized _____

* = based on 220 Dolch Sight Words; Dolch (1942), *Basic Sight Word List.*

✓ = based on 36 sight words from the Ekwall (1985), "Quick Check for Basic Sight Word Knowledge."

Source: Carol A. Spafford & George S. Grosser, *Dyslexia and Reading Difficulties: Research and Resource Guide for Working with All Struggling Readers.* Copyright © 2005 by Pearson Education. May be reproduced for noncommercial purposes.

FIGURE 8.8 *(Continued)*

Sight-Word Recognition and Automaticity

The student with dyslexia as with all students must not only be able to decode but will need to have a repertoire of sight words that do not require sounding out phoneme by phoneme. Admittedly, the following approaches do require some decoding on the part of the reader. However, the main thrust of these sight-word methods is to develop as many sight words as possible to improve speed and accuracy of word recognition. For students with dyslexia, sight words need to be presented isolation and in context. In context, the student can use background knowledge to eliminate incorrect word choices.

A basic sight-word approach involves having students memorize certain words by sight without sounding out the word parts. It is estimated that from 200 to 300 sight words (e.g., *was, about, the*) comprise up to 80 to 90 percent of the reading material in the elementary grades. Bender (1985) has found that students with reading disabilities have more limited sight vocabularies than nondisabled peers. Sight-word approaches specifically stress the use of configuration (word shape) cues with little emphasis on decoding letter sounds. One's sight vocabulary (i.e., words that are recognized instantly and have meaning) needs to include high-frequency words found in literature and content area subjects. The *Dolch Basic Sight Word List* (Dolch, 1942) and the *New Instant Word List* (Fry, 1980) provide excellent resource listings of commonly used sight words, with the *Essential 500 Word Reading List* was discussed in the previous section.

Instructional Strategies to Build Sight Vocabularies

Several teacher-directed activities can be used to teach sight words to students with dyslexia. These include:

1. Modeling, in which the teacher presents a sight word in an oral context and then in written form (e.g., labels placed on objects around the room). The initial letter(s) could be emphasized to cue the student.
2. Word bank cards—students can be paired to quiz each other on sight-word identification with the teacher serving as a consultant when needed. Word bank cards should have sight words defined or used in a sentence on one side of the card.
3. Writing—students create and read sentences with new sight words with immediate feedback for sight-word errors; rereadings may be necessary.
4. Reading in context—students read stories under the direction of the teacher with the new sight words to be learned; the teacher can point out or ask the students about new words in the story.
5. Games—students can use word games (e.g., acrostics and picture-word matches), bingo games, etc., to reinforce new sight words; these activities should be structured with the goal of 90 percent success for sight-word identification.

Multiple rereadings and language experience approaches also provide good sight-word recognition practice.

Additional Teaching Considerations to Increase Reading Fluency

Providing Reading Choices

For students with dyslexia, reading tends to be tedious and dysfluent, therefore less reading typically occurs relative to peers and for a group of students who actually need more reading practice and sustained reading times. When readers have a choice, they are more apt to pick up a book or other reading for informational purposes, enjoyment, or to learn about something.

Motivation

Proficient readers are engaged readers who read regularly and enthusiastically and for a variety of purposes (Guthrie & Anderson, 1999). Applegate and Applegate (2004) define "intrinsically motivated readers" as engaged readers who will read for reading's own sake and often to enjoy satisfying their own curiosity. *Intrinsically motivated readers spend more time reading* than other students and as a result attain higher levels of achievement and perform better on standardized reading tests (Applegate & Applegate, 2004). Motivating students to read more requires teachers to provide opportunities for extensive reading and student choice. Mosenthal, Lipson, Sortino, Russ, and Mekkelsen (2002) identified several factors in schools that were unusually successful in literacy instruction. These researchers found that in successful schools teachers devoted extensive amounts of time devoted to reading and reading instruction with expansive and inviting (motivating) book collections displayed and accessible to children.

For students with dyslexia and other learning disabilities, it is especially challenging to motivate them to want to read for pleasure and lifelong learning. Gambrell (1996) cites research comparing reading motivation for struggling readers versus above-average readers with surprising results—struggling readers are motivated by the same three major factors that also motivate highly proficient readers: (1) choice in reading materials, (2) sharing readings aloud, and (3) receipt of affirmation or positive recognition for reading accomplishments. Having lots of books to choose from and from various genres (both fiction and nonfiction) provides valuable choice options.

Teacher's Endorsement

Gambrell (2004) and others have found that whatever teachers do to make books special (even just placing a book upright in full view of the classroom) impacts how children respond to choosing books. Children are more apt to choose books the teacher recommends or endorses.

To summarize, "Think of reading as both a social and private affair that calls on the emotions of the reader. Therefore, students need to be involved in making choices about what to read, how to read, and with whom to read" (Cullinan & Galda, 1998, pp. 48–49).

Culture, Fluency, and Making Real-Life Connections

When students make real-life connections to reading and writing activities, they will place more value on the learning process. Many researchers and organizations (e.g., Hooks, 1994; NCTM, 2000; Stanley & Spafford, 2002) support the idea that teachers need to consider the role of culture in literacy planning whether it be reading, mathematics, or computer science. Relating student life experiences (Ladson-Billings, 1995) and culture to lessons empower teachers to create a context for learning (Luna, Solsken, & Kutz, 2000), resulting in purposeful, engaged participation. Rosenbusch (1997) stresses including literature where students can identify with the culture because this offers "settings for learning in which students can relate more easily to topics that are of common interest (and) relate to prior knowledge" (p. 21).

Oral Reading Activities and Fluency

According to Harris and Sipay (1990), oral reading activities are necessary components of a literacy program to develop fluency. For the student with reading disabilities, these authors recommend taking turns in small groups during oral reading, to the extent that the oral reading activities allow (1) the teacher to assess reading skills such as word identification, phrasing, and self-monitoring/correction strategies and (2) the students to engage in character portrayal and story dramatization to assess and develop expressiveness.

Individuals with dyslexia require extra time to become familiar with text before oral reading. Additionally, "on-the-spot" oral readings can be frustrating and anxiety-provoking for many students. There are structured oral reading activities that can be used to aid students with dyslexia in gaining oral reading skills and confidence if done in a nonthreatening atmosphere. it should be noted that we are *not* encouraging "round-robin" or "circle" reading, which involves each student taking a turn reading a small portion of text to a group while the others in the class follow silently. There is a body of research that negates the instructional usefulness of round-robin exercises (see Allington, 1984; Brulnsma, 1981). The following four oral reading methods can be useful in developing fluent readers.

Choral and Choral Repeated Reading   These are whole-class reading activities that involve active student participation. The teacher first models good oral reading behaviors by phrasing properly, changing tempos, and varying voice intonation and expression. We recommend practicing choral reading parts with students with dyslexia before the class reading. More able readers could also be paired with struggling readers in a helping role.

Radio Reading   This approach (Searfoss, 1975) focuses on radioing or communicating a message. Essentially, a script is given to (a) designated radio announcer(s) who deliver(s) a script to an audience of listeners who respond by discussing the program. The teacher can help clarify unclear messages. There is no correction of oral reading errors during the broadcast, although opportunities for prior rehearsal and practice should be provided. It is up to the listener to fill in when errors are made. Again, the student with dyslexia will need to read, rehearse, and review reading material before a broadcast. Discussions should follow each broadcast in order to ensure comprehension.

Paired Reading   **Paired reading** (Greene, 1970; Rasinski, 2003b) simply involves placing students (buddies) together in pairs to read side by side. The teacher could pair the student with dyslexia with a more proficient reader who could assist with the pronunciations of difficult words. It is recommended that students try to self-monitor comprehension by asking themselves, "Does this make sense?" as they read. As each reader finishes a part, he or she should retell what was read to the listener. Then both readers can engage in a dialogue about what was read. Both read the passage three to five times together to help attain automaticity and encourage expressiveness while reading. Although suggested times for paired reading activities vary from 10 to 15 minutes in the primary grades and 20 to 30 minutes in the intermediate grades, we would recommend 5- to 10-minute turns for the student with dyslexia.

Neurological Impress Method (NIM)   Heckelman (1969) developed the neurological impress method (NIM). Heckelman believed that traditional oral reading methods allow students to make too many errors, which become deeply imprinted and difficult to correct. His method relies on high-interest material that is at a level slightly easier that what can be adequately handled by the individual with dyslexia. The teacher and student in essence read together side by side and in unison for 15 minutes daily. The teacher does not correct oral reading errors. In the beginning, the teacher reads louder and slightly faster than the student. Once the student learns the material, the teacher can lag behind the student in a softer voice. The teacher's finger follows the line of print during the reading in beginning sessions with the student taking over this function as he or she becomes comfortable with the print. The focus is on seeing the printed word and hearing it at the same time to produce a "neurological memory trace." Attention is not given to pictures or illustrations nor to word recognition and text comprehension. However, comprehension checks can follow the complete readings. This method has been criticized by a few researchers for placing too much emphasis on word identification and not enough on critical thinking. Certainly, this method *can* be adapted to include comprehension checks after each page of print with varying types of question asked (e.g., alternate between literal and inferential types of questions).

Readers' Theatre **Readers' theatre** allows students to choose passages from plays, dialogue in books, or favorite poems that can be acted out or dramatized (e.g., reading poems selected from Michael Strickland's *My Own Song and Other Poems to Groove to* [Wordsong Boyds Mills Press, 1997] set to music and using favorite dance motions).

Other Techniques for Building Fluency

Finding "Just Right Books" for Reading Practice and Use of Strategies Dysfluent or struggling readers will move toward proficiency with as much reading practice and support as possible. Consider the process involved in learning how to play a musical instrument. Accomplished musicians practice, practice, practice in order to be confident and fluent note and chord readers and instrumentalists. Similarly, fluent readers are confident about their abilities to identify words, read in phrases and with expression, and derive meaning from print for knowledge applications.

Students need to be guided to books for reading practice and use of strategies that can be "managed" during independent readings—these are "just right books" or books determined to be on a child's independent reading level (word recognition = 95–99% proficiency with 90% comprehension of connected text). Allington (2004) describes "just right books" as books that pose a little bit of a challenge. A word or two will pose a vocabulary challenge; a few sentences may be relatively complicated; or the use of a literary structure may require the use of a specific reading strategy (p. 12). When a student's independent reading level is determined, then appropriate leveled books can be used during independent and sustained silent readings, shared readings, and guided readings to develop word recognition and comprehension strategy usage.

Strategy Instruction and Comprehension Fluency Strategic readers are able to engage in sustained, coherent reading drawing upon and integrating prior knowledge while actively interacting with the text—a complex task! Students with dyslexia and disabled readers consistently experience word identification and fluency difficulties with secondary issues (e.g., impaired comprehension fluency and social misperceptiveness) often emanating from these problem areas. Current research shows that strategy instruction focused on improving comprehension fluency is effective for struggling and low-achieving readers and requires explicit teaching especially in content area subjects with highly technical vocabulary (e.g., math and science). "Despite a significant body of research in the 1980s suggesting the effectiveness of strategy instruction, especially for lower-achieving readers, strategy instruction has not been (fully) implemented in many American classrooms" (Taylor, Graves, & Van Den Broek, p. 62). Pearson (2000) and other researchers have shown that when teachers share the cognitive strategies used for successful reading performance as well as the "secrets" of their own cognitive successes and failures, students are more likely to develop and use these deep structure thinking approaches when confronted with difficult text. In order to accomplish this, teachers should provide enough cognitive scaffolding (that which is just within their reach) to help students acquire desired comprehension strategies.

Goals and purpose setting precede explicit strategy instruction:

- Students need to be instructed regarding *goals/purpose* setting for content area text reading (e.g., to first understand new content on a specific science topic and then synthesize and apply knowledge in answering open response questions [see p. 160]).
- The *strategies* students access will depend on the purpose of their reading. Example purposes: (1) To understand new science content and (2) to go back into the text to locate specific information to complete open response science questions. Strategy 1: frequent pauses to integrate and reflect on the information presented [to understand the new content] and to take marginal paragraph summary notes; strategy 2: quickly skim text taking few pauses; then go back into the text and look for "key words" that will identify sections of text with information needed to complete the open response questions] while recording information in a graphic organizer.

Framework for Strategy Instruction   Nebedum-Ezeh and Spafford (2001) offer a generic *framework for strategy instruction* based on the work of Taylor, Graves, and Van Den Broek (2000):

- (a) **Select one or two appropriate strategies** for students to utilize before text is presented (e.g., strategy applied during the reading of a high school science text: use frequent pauses and reflect on and self-question to determine understanding; strategy: clarify "unknowns" by effectively using glossaries, marginal glosses, teacher input, and so on).
- (b) **Explain, demonstrate, and model these strategies** (especially self-questioning strategies) with similar text before the reading. As an example, read together a few paragraphs of science text and then model a few appropriate strategies to use to discern meaning. Devote an *entire* class or one hour to these few paragraphs so that the text can be fully processed within the context of successful strategy usage.
- (c) Implement a few opportunities for **guided practice** to use the selected strategies.
- (d) **Introduce the content/text** selection.
- (e) **Actively engage students** in the material presented (purpose setting).
- (f) Build or **activate prior knowledge**.
- (g) Interactively ask and respond to questions where **students need to use the identified strategies**; encourage self-questioning.
- (h) **Reflect** on the reading and student understandings based on strategy usage.
- (i) **Evaluate** progress/understandings to guide future lessons/learning experiences.

Guided reading is an approach at the elementary level that scaffolds reading strategy use. Lyons and Pinnell (2001) suggest professional collaborations or peer coaching to learn this model.

Guided Reading   Guided reading instruction allows teachers to prompt struggling readers to strategies good readers use, prompt for word problem solving, point to natural stopping points during reading, and provide reading extensions for continued

Basic Resources/Materials Needed for Guided Reading Groups

- Comfortable areas for small group work
- Leveled book collections appropriate to each grade level with enough book copies for small groups (4–6 students)
- Clipboard with running records and other observation materials
- Independent reading book boxes
- Writing easel with chart paper
- Whiteboard/felt board/other to illustrate how words work
- Student literacy folders
- Tubs of letters for word work; place in organized containers

Guided Reading Fluency Points

- Prompt struggling readers with strategies good readers use (e.g., "read it like you are talking")
- Prompt for word problem solving (e.g., finding word chunks)
- Point to natural stopping points (punctuation) and groups of words that can be read as phrases
- Provide reading extensions such as readers theatre and choral reading

Guided Reading Instruction = Providing small group reading instruction to students who have similar reading needs and strategies.

Steps:

- **Select** "leveled text" based on assessments and observations; students in small groups have the same text.
- **Introduce** the text with background building allowing students to make connections. Look at text organization and explain or introduce a few unfamiliar words or concepts.
- **Read** text. All students read the entire text; students in K and first grade and dyslexic students (as needed) read aloud to themselves in soft voices; older students and more proficient dyslexic students read silently.
- **Teacher** interacts with individual students to see how they are processing text and **makes one or two teaching points.**
- **Discuss** text following the reading. Students come together to discuss something about the reading.
- Teach a **Strategy** after text discussion. Make a teaching point about strategies good readers use based on observations of the students reading behaviors (e.g., good readers pause at the end of sentences; they think about the meaning of what was just read).

Source: Adapted from I.C. Fountas & G.S. Pinnell. (1996). *Guided Reading: Good First Teaching for all Children.* Portsmouth, NH: Heinemann.

FIGURE 8.9   Guided Reading Basics

reading practice (guided reading fluency points). Students are placed in small groups according to similar reading processes and strategies used. The teacher selects and introduces new books, supports children reading the entire text to themselves, and makes teaching points during and following the reading (Ohio State University Literacy Collaborative Framework as cited in Fountas & Pinnell, 1996). The guided reading basics (see Figure 8.9) are used to achieve the . . .

Goal of guided reading instruction: To develop independent, flexible readers (and problem solvers) who comprehend what they read across genres and curricula.

Grade Level (Basal)	Guided Reading Levels (Fountas-Pinnell)	Early Intervention & Reading Recovery® Levels	Developmental Reading Assessment Level (DRA) (Joella Beaver)	First Steps Reading Stages (1-5)
Kindergarten	*Emerging* A, B	1, 2	A, 1, 2	1. Role Play (non-readers) / 2. Experimental
Pre-Primer	C, D, E	3-4, 5-6, 7-8	3, 4, 6-9	2. Experimental
Primer	*Early* F, G	9-10, 11-12	10, 12	3. Early
1st Grade	H, I	13-14, 15-16	14, 16	3. Early
2nd Grade	*Transitional* J-K, L-M	17-19, 20-22, 23-30	18-20, 24-28	4. Transitional / Early Fluency
3rd Grade	*Self-Extending Readers* N, O-P	—, —	30, 34-38	5. Fluent (Independent)
4th Grade	Q-R	—	40	5. Fluent (Independent)
5th Grade	T-U-V	—	44	5. Fluent (Independent)
6th Grade	WXYZ	—	—	5. Fluent (Independent)

Sources:

1. Fountas, I.C., & Pinnell, G.S. (2000). *Guiding Readers and Writers, Grades 3-6; Teaching Comprehension, Genre, and Content Literacy,* Portsmouth, NH. Heinemann.
2. Guided Reading Levels = *Guided Reading; Good First Teaching for All Children* (1996) by Irene C. Fountas & Gay Su Pinnel. Portsmouth, NH; Heinemann.
3. Early Intervention Levels = Based on: *Reading Recovery®* a registered trademark of the Ohio State University.
4. *DRA Level = Developmental Reading Assessment Resource* Guide. Joetta Beaver, Celebration Press: Pearson Learning, 1997.
5. *First Steps Reading: Developmental Continuum* by Diana Rees in Collaboration with Bruce Shortland-Jones (1994). First Steps was developed by the Education Department of Western Australia under Alison Dewsbury. Portsmouth, NH: Heinemann.

FIGURE 8.10   Textbook Leveling (K–5)

Leveled Books   Students reading levels are assessed to determine independent reading levels, those "just right levels." Standardized or criterion-referenced tests, which include formal and informal reading inventories, can be used. Developing an extensive leveled book collection for guided reading also results in providing students with many reading choices, a variety of genres, and developmentally appropriate and interesting book selections. This requires a great deal of time and organization. Fortunately, most publishers now provide listings of book levels to inform teachers as to the guided reading levels of individual books and book collections. The textbook leveling and reading stages chart for grades K through 5 (shown in Figure 8.10) includes guided reading, early intervention (Reading Recovery), and DRA-correlated levels along with the *First Steps* stages of reading.

Building Fluency at Home

Family Paired Readings   Family paired readings are strong fluency builders and involve children and parents reading together. For 15 minutes per day a child and parent read simultaneously from a book selected by the child. When the child feels he or she can read independently, he or she gives the parent a signal (e.g., a nudge) to show readiness to read alone or independently. When the child makes a mistake, the parent rejoins in the reading. Topping (1989) documented significant gains in reading from students who participated in family paired readings.

Family Paired Reading Times

- Your child chooses a book that is relatively comfortable to read. You can help your child choose a book. Have your child read one page. Your child shouldn't miss more than 1 to 2 words on a page.
- You and your child read together until your child signals you (maybe a nudge) that he or she is ready to read alone or independently.
- Your child continues to read independently until he or she makes a mistake. Then you rejoin your child in the reading. Again, your child can signal you (maybe a nudge) when he or she is ready to read independently again. Continue this cycle of reading for about 15 minutes.
- Praise your child for signaling when appropriate, trying hard to decode words, and reading fluently.
- After you finish reading, talk about what was read.

Have your child retell what was read. You can gently clarify if your child misunderstood what was read. You can also expand upon what your child tells you. Encourage your child to tell you about favorite story parts, favorite characters, and favorite illustrations, and why these are favorites.

(adapted from Topping, 1989)

Reading Aloud to Develop Fluency   Reading aloud to children is thought to be one of the most powerful types of reading activities teachers and families can provide to children and students of all ages. When we read aloud to students, we help them develop an idea of what fluent, expressive, and meaningful reading is all about (Rasinski, 2003a). Reading aloud helps build knowledge or schema (Chomsky, 1972; Durkin, 1976) and especially benefits students with reading challenges (e.g., second-language learners and students with reading disabilities) in developing a more expansive vocabulary and knowledge of story structure. Reading aloud also introduces children to new titles, genres, authors, and illustrators, inviting children "into the world of literature. . . . it is both a gift and a responsibility" (Johnson & Giorgis, 2003, p. 704). As such, Watkins (2001) and Freeman (1995) discuss the importance of providing read-aloud books that allow children to reevaluate their opinions and prejudices to nurture intolerance to injustice and to foster the development of empathy, a sense of fairness and a social conscience. Similarly, Pieronek (2001) emphasizes choosing books free of cultural bias—i.e., culturally sensitive or responsive books. The following sequence is recommended in structuring read-aloud experiences:

Ten-Step Read-Aloud Planning Sequence

1. Select a book that is age appropriate.
2. Determine if the book is conceptually understandable.
3. Review the book to ensure that it is free of cultural bias.
4. Practice reading the book before the read-aloud time.
5. Activate the children's schema beforehand—brainstorm and web ideas on chart paper or the board for all to see and reference during the reading.
6. Discuss the book title and the book cover; stimulate thinking about story possibilities—who? what? why? where? when?
7. Make some story predictions.
8. During the reading, share pictures and illustrations.
9. Read with enthusiasm—bring the story "to life."
10. After reading, discuss predictions and what actually happened. (Pieronek, 2001)

Families can have fun retelling stories in homemade read-aloud books. Figure 8.11 shows how to make your own read-aloud books.

Summary

Fluency is considered one of the five essential teaching of reading elements cited in the research and in the National Reading Panel Report (2000): (1) phonemic awareness, (2) phonics, (3) fluency, (4) vocabulary development, and (5) text comprehension and strategic reading. Word recognition is placed central to PACE (**p**hrasing, **a**ccuracy, **c**omprehension, and **e**xpressiveness) fluency factors with comprehension always the

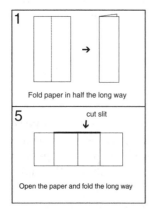
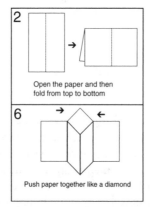
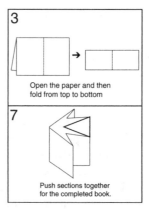
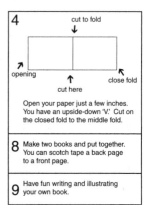

FIGURE 8.11   Making Your Own Read-Aloud Book

goal. Fluent readers can decode and comprehend at the same time. They recognize words accurately and relatively quickly and are able to read with phrasing and expression. A reader cannot be considered fluent if any one component is impaired or not developed. Individuals with dyslexia often experience difficulties decoding the printed page, which impairs reading fluency. The end result is word-by-word or short phrase readings, slower than average reading rates, and a lack of expressiveness as compared to proficient-reading peers.

Table 8.4 summarizes the characteristics of fluent versus nonfluent readers. Many individuals with dyslexia are considered "dysfluent," or not fluent in reading, due primarily to the lack of automaticity in word recognition with specific difficulties with the phonological components of language, left hemispheric types of functioning. According to Shaywitz (2003), the automatic detector in the left occipito-temporal area of the brain "breaks down" in children with dyslexia. A neurological anomaly prevents their brains from gaining automatic access to the word analyzer and phoneme producer areas of the brain (see Chapter 1 for extensive discussion on these neurophysiological implications). However, "What to Do" recommendations in Table 8.4 center on educational interventions as medical or noneducational remedies to help improve reading fluency have not been substantiated by current research.

The repeated readings method is one of the most powerful ways to build reading fluency. The teacher simply has the student reread a text passage until word accuracy, a good pace, and expressiveness are attained. The reading should sound like someone talking. Word recognition and comprehension skills are not emphasized, just as they are not in the NIM (Neurological Impress Method) created by Heckelman (1969). Another instructional approach proven to increase language fluency is reading aloud to children. On a daily basis, reading aloud improves not only fluency but also results in the acquisition of valuable print and book knowledge.

When we read aloud to students, we:

■ Help children develop an idea of what fluent, expressive, and meaningful reading is all about.
■ Introduce children to new titles, genres, authors, and illustrators.
■ Build knowledge or schemata.
■ Develop a more expansive vocabulary.
■ Provide knowledge of story structure.
■ Guide children through literature to reevaluate opinions and prejudices, demonstrate intolerance to injustice as well as empathy, a sense of fairness, and a social conscience.

Because word recognition accuracy is necessary to build reading fluency, students need to acquire an expansive sight word vocabulary and a repertoire of word identification strategies. The *Essential 500 Word Reading List* contains essential sight words frequently encountered in print. The *Diagnostic Word Recognition Checklist* on page 99 can be used as a general fluency check.

Measuring accurate and fluent reading of text requires a close examination of effective reading (i.e., accuracy in word reading with adequate comprehension) and efficient reading (i.e., an adequate reading rate with attention to phrasing and expressiveness). Running records should be maintained for students with dyslexia of reading miscues to determine if students are meeting proficiency benchmarks, to decide on guided reading levels, and to inform other instructional planning decisions especially during the word study portion of the language arts block. A coding system by Fountas and Pinnell is applicable to all grade levels. Reading rate was calculated as correct words per minute (CWPM) instead of the traditional wpm, because students with dyslexia frequently miscue, necessitating adjustments to reading rates.

TABLE 8.4 Characteristics of Fluent versus Nonfluent Readers

Fluent Readers	Why	Nonfluent Readers (Many Dyslexics)	What to Do
Decode effortlessly, with automaticity and with average reading rates or better for age and/or grade level.	Fluent readers read more, more extensively, and with a variety of printed materials.	Decode laboriously, without automaticity and with lower than expected reading rates for age and/or grade level.	✓ Provide many meaningful opportunities to read and reread (repeated readings method) a variety of leveled books and other materials chosen by the student. ✓ Provide intensive literary support two- to three-hour literacy blocks (see Chapter 11 for details).
Place a reading emphasis on comprehending words within the context of phrases, sentences, and paragraphs.	Fluent readers have acquired a variety of word recognition strategies that make word reading for the most part effortless.	Place a reading emphasis on identifying or decoding words in isolation before discerning meaning because of word recognition difficulties.	✓ Provide intensive word study support within the context of meaningful text as part of a reading workshop or activity within an intensive literacy block.
Have extensive sight vocabularies.	Fluent readers have more exposure to print and reading practice.	Have limited sight vocabularies as compared to fluent readers of similar age or developmental level.	✓ Practice learning frequently encountered reading words as sight words (see Essential 500 List on pp. 195–196). ✓ Oral reading activities (choral reading, radio reading, paired reading, NIM or Neurological Impress Method, echo reading, readers' theatre, reading aloud).

Are able to effectively handle miscues or errors in word reading.	Fluent readers have acquired a variety of strategies for fixing miscues or errors in word reading.	Often rely on one or two "fix-it" strategies when problem-solving during word recognition.	✓ Model and explicitly teach a variety of word strategies to use when encountering unfamiliar or new words. ✓ Word strategy bookmarks cue the reader and should be consistently used until fluency is adequate or satisfactory. ✓ Guided reading times provide opportunities for teaching flexible and varied use of word strategies
Can effectively decode and comprehend text simultaneously.	Fluent readers effectively key in on main ideas and important information when reading; they can accurately summarize or paraphrase readings; they are able to self-monitor comprehension and organize information learned from readings as needed.	Experience a diminished ability to comprehend text because more cognitive energies are spent on decoding and identifying words.	✓ Choose a segment of text to reread until it sounds like "people talking." ✓ Provide story grammar frameworks. ✓ Use marginal notes. ✓ Explicitly teach self-questioning strategies to use when reading. ✓ Use graphic organizers before/after readings. ✓ Routinely request story or text retellings. ✓ Practice summarizing/paraphrasing sections of text.
Adjust reading rates according to reading demands.	With frequent and extensive reading practice and feedback, fluent readers become flexible readers, adjusting reading rates as needed.	Have difficulty adjusting reading rates according to reading purpose and text difficulty.	✓ Model various ways to adjust reading rate and link to the reading purpose and text difficulty including scanning, skimming, rauding, text mastery, memorizing.

The *Dyslexia Checklist* on page 225 allows the practitioner to see average or expected rates by grade level for both silent and oral reading. Then the teacher can judge whether the student's reading rate is average for a particular grade level. Word strategy bookmarks on page 187 cue the student with dyslexia to important word study strategies for rapid word identification.

At the secondary level, there is a more intense focus on comprehension strategy instruction versus word identification strategies. Strategy instruction in content area subjects with highly technical vocabulary (e.g., math and science) is essential for struggling and low-achieving readers and requires explicit teaching. A framework for strategy instruction was offered by Nebedum-Ezeh and Spafford based on the work of Taylor, Graves, and Van Den Broek. At the elementary level, the guided reading approach scaffolds comprehension strategy use with leveled books. For all students with dyslexia, access to books on their reading levels will be necessary during independent reading times.

According to the National Reading Panel (2000), repeated reading and other methods that require students to read aloud several times while receiving feedback from teachers, peers, or family members are successful in developing reading skills. Most do not require special programs or training and are easy to use. At home, family paired reading times were recommended as well as reading aloud books to children. Finally, reading often and widely with a variety of reading materials improves reading fluency. Chapter 9 now covers the assessment process in which fluency is considered an important component.

Assessment to Inform
Instructional Practice

> *Dyslexia, in whatever form it takes—mild, moderate, or severe—is one of the most complicated central nervous system problems there is . . . it demands thoughtful, interdisciplinary diagnostic efforts. The absence of diagnosis, leads to insurmountable hurdles to successful life adjustment for the individual"*
> *—(Pavlidis & Fisher, 1986, p. xiv).*
>
> With *appropriate* assessment tools, we can . . .
>
> *Catch a falling reader, put him in your pocket, and never let him get away. . . . Imagine the power behind the ability to catch a falling reader before signs of frustration, poor habits, and low self-esteem take root and grow.*
> *—(Hebert, 2004, p. i)*

That power Connie Hebert refers to brings us to how we can use assessment to diagnose and inform instructional practice—assessment tools that can empower educators to efficiently and effectively identify those struggling students who require additional literacy support. Additionally, we can find those resilient factors that need to be nurtured and developed with each student. The goal in all of this is to bring all students to levels of proficiency in academics—capable students who are self-efficacious, confident self-starters and problem solvers who are flexible, reflective, caring individuals able to seek critical support systems and willing to advocate for others when needed (resilient learners).

Dyslexics do experience reading and writing difficulties and literacy programs naturally focus on developing proficiency in these areas. It is a given that children and adults who experience dyslexia vary in quantity and quality of manifest academic and social characteristics and require to some extent individualized literacy programs; keep in mind that there is no "magic cure-all" for dyslexia (Grosser & Spafford, 2000).

The present authors have identified "resiliency" as the third "R" in the "Reading, 'Riting, Resiliency" intervention program equation, believing it to be the critical link to successful academic and social adjustments for individuals with dyslexia (i.e., resiliency is the ability to quickly bounce back or recover from stressors, frustrations, and failures due to a personal resolve to persevere in spite of academic/social obstacles). Chapter 3 provides an in-depth look at the impact of (1) individual protective factors (traits or characteristics), (2) environmental factors (familial and community-oriented), (3) stressors, and (4) coping styles in developing resilient personalities. The QUART (QUalitative Analysis of Resilient Traits assessment (Spafford, 2004; Spafford & Grosser, 2004) can evaluate an individual's resiliency with specific instructional implications for educators to consider as assessment terminology is operationalized.

Early diagnosis and accompanying *effective early interventions* are critical to future academic and social successes and adjustments for individuals with learning problems and learning disabilities (Strickland, 2002). There are groups of students who have been diagnosed "late" in their school program. For example, boys traditionally have been diagnosed earlier as learning disabled in greater numbers than girls in many U.S. districts not because more boys are learning disabled than girls, but for reasons related to diagnostic screening that is less than effective. Additionally, often second-language learners with dyslexia and learning disabilities are diagnosed later than their peers in the dominant culture (e.g., English-speaking) or until they obtain some linguistic competence in the dominant language before being tested, again for reasons related to less than effective screening.

How Do Students View Assessment Practices or Testing?

Do we need to know the answer to the above question before delving into all of the specifics about assessment, evaluations, and diagnosis? Yes! After all, the student is the "client" when an evaluation or assessment is conducted. Establishing a positive mind-set before any testing would involve the student's or client's knowing the "what" and "why so important" of any testing.

It Depends How You Ask the Question

An entire fourth-grade group of students in a small urban elementary school (N = 32; 2 are SPED students) were asked to give their opinions about testing (Spafford, 2004b). Students in one classroom (group 1; n = 17) were asked, "Do you like taking tests?" and "Why do tests help teachers teach and students learn?" The other fourth-grade students (group 2; n = 13) were asked, "How do you feel when you do well on tests?" and "Why do tests help teachers teach and students learn?" The entire student population of Special Education (SPED) students (4% of school population—all with reading disabilities) serviced outside of the regular classroom for any part of the day (N = 12) were asked both sets of questions but at different times on two different days.

When asked, "Do you like tests?" 37 percent of the fourth graders in group 1 (n = 7) said "no," but all students indicated that tests help teachers teach and students learn. When the question was asked in a more positive way to the other group of fourth-grade children (group 2), "How do you feel when you do well on tests?" all (100%) said "good" in some way and that tests help teachers teach and students learn—the students didn't mention not liking test-taking. One fifth-grade dyslexic student dictated to the teacher, "I feel proud about myself because I take the time to study." This same student when asked, "Do you like tests?" replied, "I do not like taking tests because I feel uncomfortable." A surprising finding was for the group of seven grade 4 students who indicated they did not like testing, most were at the top of their class on a recently administered reading mid-term.

For the SPED students (twelve students—three grade 3 students; two grade 4 students; seven grade 5 students), three of the twelve students did not like taking tests, but when asked the same question the following day in a more positive way—"How do you feel when you do well on tests?"—all twelve students responded "good" in some way. For the two grade 4 students, both were very positive about taking tests. This was not surprising because both grade 4 SPED students scored in the top 50 percent of the district and their class on the grade 3 high-stakes reading tests (with accommodations). One of the grade 4 students, a student with severe dyslexia, was one of only two students to score proficient on the tryout for both open response questions on the high-stakes grade 3 state reading tests. The other grade 4 student with dyslexia scored proficient on one open response question on the high-stakes grade 3 reading test and was close to proficiency on the other question. Both students achieved overall proficiency on the grade 3 reading tests with vital standard test accommodations (small group testing with frequent breaks, extra time, clarification of directions, use of a place-marker, and teacher monitoring placement of responses in the test booklet).

For the eight grade 4 LEP (limited English proficient) students, two students indicated they did not like testing (25%). The LEP students who liked testing (the majority) responded with similar comments, "I love to take tests and I love to do good on tests and the teachers help the students." Unexpected was the test attitude for the two LEP (limited English proficient students) who did not like testing—one student scored in the top one-third of the grade 3 class on the high-stakes reading tests (still a top student) and the other student scored in the lowest quartile.

Overall, the majority of fourth graders had good testing attitudes (78%). All of the students believed that tests help teachers to teach and students to learn for the following reasons; "tests check where you are at," "tests help teachers know you are learning well and they can keep teaching," "the teachers see where most of the students got the answers wrong and she or he can go over it," "the tests help you understand how to learn . . . it helps you to be so smart . . . it's really good to have good tests," "it helps you be smart so you can go to college," and "it helps the teacher to know what students need help in." The positive test attitudes shown by the grade 4 students can be attributed to (1) purpose setting before testing—"what?" "why so important?" and "what for?"; (2) personalized notes and typed handouts sent to families before major testing to explain the purpose of testing (in essence to provide information to inform instructional practices) and test-taking tips (both in English and in Spanish); (3) individual recognition for meeting proficiency or benchmarks standards; and (4) distribution of incentives for good attendance and trying one's best regardless of performance outcomes. The responses for three students with dyslexia shown in Figure 9.1 reflected a "good" attitude toward testing. It can also be observed from the writing that students with dyslexia vary in the degree to which their disability impacts spelling and writing proficiency.

Establishing a Positive Testing or Assessment Attitude

When students are aware of a test's purpose and can relate that purpose in a positive way to learning, then a rationale is established that shows the student this is a "helping situation." Asking children how they feel when they do well on tests followed by test preparations and incentives to help them do well assists in establishing good "test" attitudes.

Determining the Presence of a Learning Disability

If the individual has a learning disability such as dyslexia, his or her need for special education and related services must be determined through a comprehensive assessment that requires individual testing of the student. The school must evaluate instructional needs to determine if specially designed instruction is necessary.

For students with dyslexia and other learning disabilities, programs must involve . . . "the planning, design, and implementation of appropriate service options and instructional strategies . . . predicated upon all concerned professionals having a clear understanding of what learning disabilities are, and the manner in which these different disabilities modify how an individual learns" (NJCLD, 1993). The assessment process will provide the information needed to plan appropriate literacy programs and support systems.

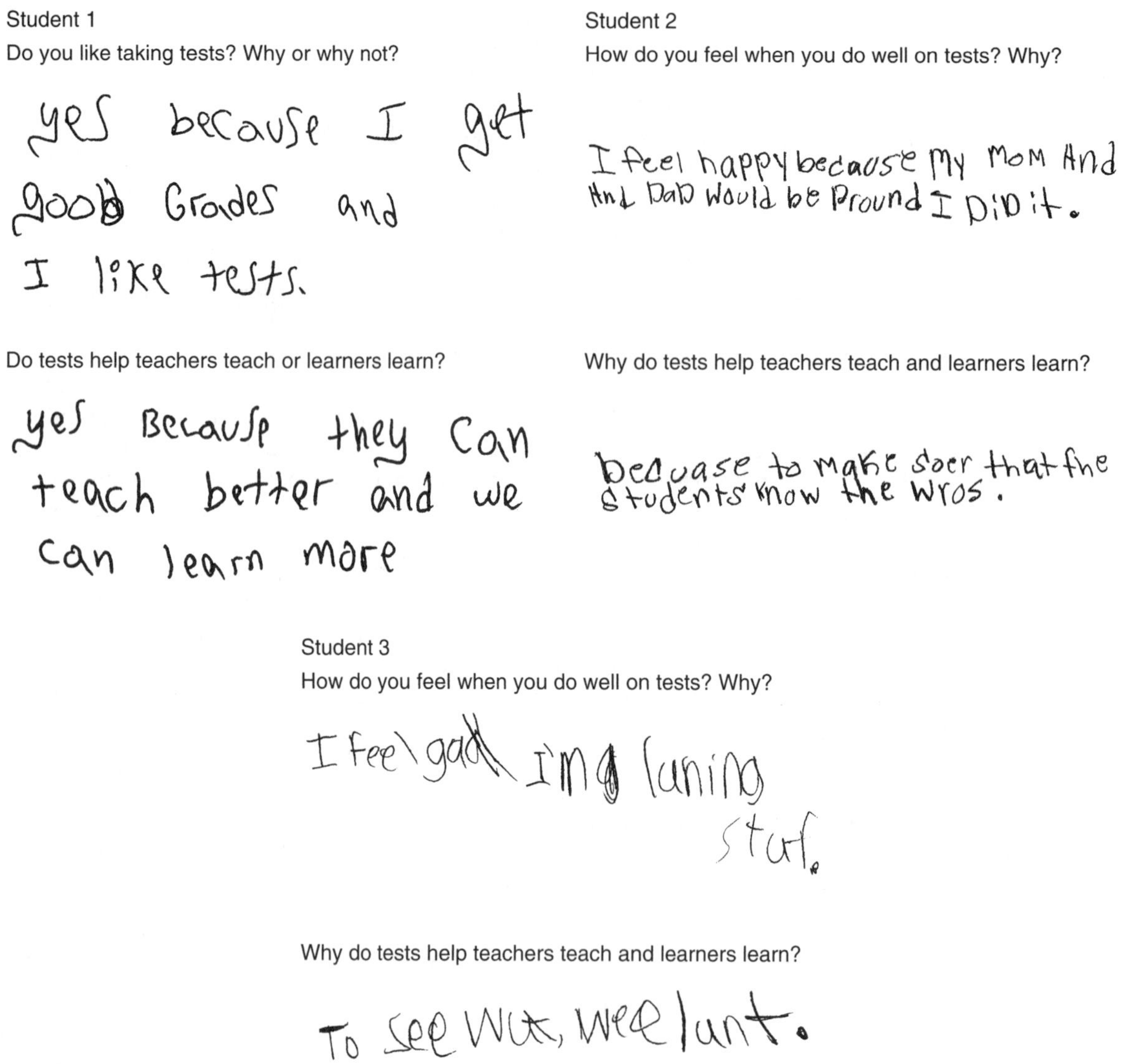

Student 1

Do you like taking tests? Why or why not?

yes because I get good Grades and I like tests.

Do tests help teachers teach or learners learn?

yes Because they can teach better and we can learn more

Student 2

How do you feel when you do well on tests? Why?

I feel happy because my mom And And Dad would be Pround I DiD it.

Why do tests help teachers teach and learners learn?

becuase to make soer that the students know the wros.

Student 3

How do you feel when you do well on tests? Why?

I feel gad I'm luning stuf.

Why do tests help teachers teach and learners learn?

To see Wut, wee lunt.

FIGURE 9.1   Responses of Students with Dyslexia

Considerations for Dyslexia Screening and Evidence-Based Instruction

Dyslexia definition = *dys* and *lexia,* or inability to effectively read words, is the most prevalent specific learning disability (at least 50% of the LD population). It is thought to have a neurological basis, and the disability is unexpected in relation to other cognitive abilities and access to effective classroom instruction. There are specific difficulties with fluent reading and the phonological components of language (i.e., phonemic awareness). Secondary issues may or may not include other academic problems (e.g., reading comprehension, difficulties in socialization (e.g., more negative peer interactions), and co-existing disabilities or disorders (e.g., ADD or ADHD with 25% of those with dyslexia). With intensive literacy support in reading and writing, a social-academic network of support, and the development of individual resiliency, individuals with dyslexia can lead successful and fulfilling lives (Spafford & Grosser, 2005).

Why So Much Testing?

Testing is an important part of the assessment process for students with learning disabilities. The screening process itself requires schools and districts choose **achievement** and **aptitude tests** as well as **criterion-referenced measures** (e.g., checklists, rubrics) to evaluate a student's proficiency in reading, writing, and spelling (to determine if the disability is unexpected in relation to other cognitive abilities and if there are specific difficulties with fluent reading and the phonological components of language). Additionally, schools and districts must consider how well a student performs relative to peers with evidence-based instructional programs (the disability is unexpected because of access to effective classroom instruction). Secondary issues for students with dyslexia may or may not include other academic problems (e.g., reading comprehension) and co-existing disabilities or disorders (e.g., ADD or ADHD). These areas need to be assessed or tested if determined to be problematic as well.

Test Selection

According to Janet Lerner (1993), a test is only one sample of a student's behavior or achievement at one moment in time. Comprehensive testing involves the use of both informal and formal assessments.

Informal Assessments   Informal assessments are nonstandardized indicators of how well students are progressing relative to curriculum standards or other learning benchmarks. Informal assessments include **curriculum-based assessment (CBA), criterion-referenced tests,** and **portfolios** (a type of authentic assessment). With CBA, teachers review the scope and sequence of skills/knowledge/strategies of the current curriculum to be learned by students and develop (or use a commercial version) a way to assess student mastery of these skills/knowledge/strategies. Student progress is continuously assessed. Criterion-referenced tests are tests that evaluate a student's performance relative to a standard or learning benchmark, in contrast to standardized tests, which measure student performance relative to group performance or the performance of other students. Checklists (see pp. 99, 132, 225, 240) and rubrics (see pp. 165–167) are more commonly used criterion-referenced measures.

Portfolios, as informal **authentic assessments,** include student work products and learning outcomes over time. Work samples often are completed or assessed with rubrics. According to Karen A. Waldron (1996), portfolios will provide strong indicators of the performance levels of students with disabilities. They provide teachers the opportunity to compare individual students' work with that of peers and to determine basic skills that may need to be addressed. Cheryl Stanley and Carol Spafford (1998) suggest portfolios include "authentic purpose setting" where students establish learning objectives and goals that will be connected to learning outcomes. Stanley and Spafford stress the need for students to highlight their growth as learners within portfolio entries (ongoing reflective statements), with personalization of the portfolio reflected in artifacts that express learning styles, cultural identities, and family and personal experiences. Interdisciplinary linkages to the arts and other subject areas can showcase academic and personal accomplishments.

Formal Assessments   Formal assessment involves the use of **standardized** tests to determine proficiency or achievement in a particular area. Standardized tests have been normed (norm: average or typical performance) with proven reliability and validity. Test manuals for standardized tests contain information on age and grade norms including percentile ranks and grade equivalents. **Standard scores** are provided so educators are able to compare performance relative to average performance for a particular group. Standardized tests are helpful in diagnosing learning disabilities and are also required under state and national regulations. **Aptitude** and **achievement tests** are examples of formal assessments.

Students with dyslexia are required to participate in the same local and state assessments as their nondisabled peers but perhaps with accommodations (see pp. 261–264) as specified in an Individualized Education Plan or IEP (see p. 254). This provides valuable evidence to school systems regarding the progress of students with dyslexia and other learning disabilities relative to district, state, and national standards and curriculum frameworks. Annual testing for all students in grades 3 through 8, and at least once in grades 10 through 12, has been legislated as part of state accountability assessment systems under *No Child Left Behind (NCLB)*. The goal in all of this is to bring all students to levels of proficiency with testing used to inform instructional practices to accomplish this end.

Section 602 of IDEA, *The Individuals with Disabilities Education Act* of 1990, reauthorized in 2003, specifies "In determining whether a child has a specific learning disability (SLD), the district 'shall not be required to take into consideration whether the child has a severe discrepancy between achievement and intellectual ability. . . .' In determining whether a child has an SLD, the district "may use a process which determines if a child responds to scientific, research-based intervention."

Scientific or Research-Based Intervention Assessment   To be considered scientific or research-based (also known as evidence-based), instructional programs/program components or methods must use procedures and assessments in which statistical evidence or research is collected to show whether the instructional program (e.g., a commercial VAK-T program), program component (e.g., phonemic awareness), or intervention/teaching method (e.g., SQ3R) works for a particular group of students. "High-quality" statistical evidence or research requires "field testing" of an instructional method of program using **experimental designs for research** studies similar to those cited in the National Reading Panel Report (2000). There must be steps to maximize the rigor of experimental designs that address as many threats to "internal and external" validity as possible.

This allows researchers to detect treatment effects (treatment effect example: positive testing results were due to the Hawthorne effect or extra attention the students received as opposed to the particular method of teaching or program) when they exist. Reliability and validity statistics are used to objectify the process for pre- and post-tests used to determine whether the program or method is effective. According to Margaret W. Matlin (1992), a "good" test must be standardized, valid, and reliable.

Key Concepts in Choosing or Creating Appropriate Tests

Standardization and Reliability   A standardized test is a test that was normed according to standards of performance for the test. The test would have been pretested with a large, representative sample of people so that average performance scores were determined for the entire group and for various subgroups (e.g., subgroups: students with learning disabilities, second-language learners, and so on). The performance for an individual who takes the test is compared to those standards. **Reliability** is the consistency or stability of a person's test scores. In other words, an individual who takes the test should perform in an equivalent manner on subsequent occasions. There are three major ways to evaluate the reliability of a test: (1) test-retest reliability, (2) alternate-form reliability, and (3) split-half reliability.

Typically reliability is reported in the form of a **correlation coefficient** (0 to ± 1.0). Positive correlation coefficients show direct or parallel relationships [e.g., *increasing* daily reading time (variable X) results in *increased* acquisition of vocabulary (variable Y), while negative correlations point to inverse (*not negative*) relationships [*increased* school attendance (variable X) results in *decreased* failure rates (variable Y) on state tests]. Correlation coefficients of ±1.0 are rare. The closer the correlation coefficient is to ±1.0, the stronger the relationship. Generally, results are interpreted in relation to the strength of the correlation coefficient or relationship between or among the variables studied as opposed to inferring direct cause-and-effect relationships (which may or may not exist). Values falling between ±.20 and ±.40 generally show a low correlation or slight relationship; ±.40 to ±.70, a moderate relationship, and above ±.70, a strong relationship between the scores/factors.

Correlation Coefficients: Pearson Product Moment Correlation Coefficient   The correlation coefficient cited in most test/program manuals is the Pearson Product Moment Correlation Coefficient. The scores on each variable (X and Y) will have a mean (X_M and Y_M,) and a standard deviation (SD_X and SD_Y). The following formula (Cohen, 1988) can be used:

$$ r = (1/n) \quad \sum \left(\frac{X_i - X_M}{SD_x} \right) \left(\frac{Y_i - Y_M}{SD_y} \right) = \sum \frac{(Z_X Z_Y)}{N} $$

Where Σ = the sum of the following numbers; N = the number of pairs of scores (e.g., number of persons measured on two variables, X and Y; example, phonemic awareness ability test scores = variable X, and reading achievement test scores = variable Y); X_i = one person's test scores on variable X; Y_i = one person's score on variable Y (note that these follow Σ, the summation sign, so that all the scores contribute to the final result); X_M and Y_M, and SD_X and SD_Y are defined above; Z_x and Z_y are standard scores on X and Y, respectively. The formula requires that each person's standard score on X be multiplied by his or her standard score on Y. These products are added up and divided by the number of persons. Thus, the Pearson *r* is the average of the products of the two sets of standardized scores. Test reliability is reported in relation to correlation coefficients.

Types of Test Reliability   *Test-retest reliability* involves administering the same test to an individual on different occasions. The test-retest reliability is high if the individual performs in a similar manner on both testings.

   Alternate-form reliability refers to two or more alternate or different forms of the same test. Alternate-form reliability is high if the individual performs in a similar manner when given different forms of the test. Educators generally give alternate forms of the same test when repeated testing is necessary. This helps to reduce the "practice effect," or the effect of improved performance on a test because of familiarity with the content and questions.

   Split-half reliability requires the test items be split into halves (even-numbered questions and odd-numbered questions). Split-half reliability is high if the individual's performance is similar on the even-numbered questions to performance on the odd-numbered questions. The Spearman-Brown split-half reliability coefficient can be used to compute split-half reliability. All of the odd-numbered test items are treated like one form of the test. The even-numbered items are treated as another form of the test. The correlation is calculated between the two halves of the test.

Spearman-Brown Split-Half Reliability Coefficient   The Spearman-Brown coefficient of reliability uses r_{oe}, the product moment correlation of the odd-numbered test items (first, third, fifth, etc.) with the even-numbered test items (second, fourth, sixth, etc.).

$$ \left(r_{xx} \text{ or Spearman - Brown Statistic} \right) = \frac{2r_{oe}}{1 + r_{oe}} $$

Often a correction for attenuation is used with the Spearman-Brown quotient to correct for splitting of the test in half, or altering the test's length.

Test Validity   **Validity** is the degree to which a test measures what it is designed to measure. It is typically expressed as a correlation coefficient computed between the test and some criterion measurement of the behavior or ability that is meant to be measured. A test with low reliability can never have high validity but a test with high reliability may or may not be valid.

Types of Test Validity   There are various ways validity can be established:

(1) The results of one test can be correlated with the results of another known, valid test already proven to measure the same concepts/knowledge/abilities = *construct validity*. A test that has construct validity correlates highly with other such measures and will also show small correlations with tests that measure different constructs.

(2) A test could be reviewed by specialists in the field = *content or face validity*. On the face of it, the test appears to be a valid measure of what it says it is designed to measure.

(3) The degree to which a test's ability (e.g., comprehension test) can predict a person's performance on another independent criterion (e.g., phonemic awareness test) = *criterion-related validity*.

(4) The test could be given (e.g., a phonemic awareness test) with a reading test or measurement of reading given at a later date. If there is a significant correlation shown between the two sets of scores, it could be shown the test has *predictive validity*. (See *Correlation Coefficient, Reliability* in Glossary).

Effect Size Statistics Determine How Effective   Measurements of reliability and validity are not in and of themselves enough to assure us that a given program or intervention is effective enough to provide the desired improvements in a person's behavior or achievement (e.g., improved reading comprehension). We may gather statistical evidence that a program "works," i.e., "after" intervention or training scores (e.g., comprehension scores) are significantly better than "before" intervention or training scores. The question remains, "by how much?" In statistical analyses, this is the matter of *effect size*. Statistical tools have been developed to estimate effect size. One of these is the effect size index, $\underline{d}$. For a comparison of a post-intervention or treatment set of scores and a pre-intervention or treatment set of scores,

$$\underline{d} = \frac{M_t - M_c}{0.5(sd_t + sd_c)}$$

M_t represents the mean of the group receiving the program/*treatment*/intervention, M_c is the mean of the *control* group (group not receiving the program/treatment/intervention), sd_t is the standard deviation of the first group, and sd_c is the standard deviation of the second group. If $\underline{d}$ turns out to be 0.1, the means differ by one-tenth of a standard deviation. If $\underline{d}$ turns out to equal 2.0, the means differ by two standard deviations. When $\underline{d} = 0$, the two sets of measures overlap perfectly, and the effect is negligible. The effect size statistic can be transformed into the more familiar correlation statistic r, by the formula:

$$r = \underline{d} \text{ divided by the square root of } \underline{d}^2 + 4 \text{ or } r = \frac{\underline{d}}{\sqrt{\underline{d}^2 + 4}}$$

The National Reading Panel (NRP) (2000) relied on effect size statistics when reviewing the scientific research literature on reading and its implications for reading instruction to determine the types of individuals for whom reading programs and program components are most and least effective. The NRP incorporated the statistics procedures outlined in Cooper and Hedges (1994; see also Cohen, 1988). According to the National Reading Panel (2000), for a program to be considered research-based or evidence-based, there needs to have been a stringently controlled **experimental** or **quasi-experimental** research design to determine effectiveness. The present authors offer a checklist of questions in Chapter 11 (pp. 319–321) to consider when educators are trying to sort out whether a program is evidenced-based and appropriate for a particular group of students.

Back to Evidence-Based Practices—How Did We Get There?

In summary, educators are concerned about the reliability and validity of achievement tests and other education tests such as classroom tests. Testing is particularly helpful in determining the effectiveness of instructional methods, programs and program components. There is always the consideration, "Is the test I am using measuring what it is suppose to measure?" (content validity). "Can a test be used to predict performance in another domain?" (criterion-related validity). For example, "Do phonemic awareness tests accurately predict performance on reading achievements tests?" If so, how can this information be used to inform instructional practices? In the instance of phonemic awareness, students with dyslexia perform relatively poorly on phonemic awareness tests and this correlates with performance on reading achievement tests where performance is also depressed.

The National Reading Panel (NRP) (2000), as an example, found a strong relationship or correlation between phonemic awareness and reading/spelling proficiency and decided to examine whether phonemic awareness training or interventions were effective teaching methods for beginning readers and for at-risk and disabled readers. If so, improved reading and spelling performance would be expected. The NRP found teaching phonemic awareness helps many different groups of students learn to read, including preschool children, children in grades K and 1, and at-risk children for reading disabilities (e.g., at-risk children showed large effect sizes in transferring these skills to reading, d = .86 and spelling, d = 0.76). Older students with reading disabilities also benefit from phonemic awareness training (moderate effect sizes). To determine the strength of the relationship between the instruction or training and an achievement measure (e.g., spelling or reading achievement), the following scale can be used (Cohen, 1988): 0 to .20 indicates no or negligible effect on learning; .20 to .50, small effects; .50 to .80, moderate effects; .80 or above, large or substantial effects. It can be concluded, then, that phonemic awareness training is an **evidence-based practice** based on well-designed studies where significant effect sizes were shown on standardized tests as well as on experimenter-designed tests.

Dyslexia/Learning Disabilities Assessments

A comprehensive evaluation should include, but is not limited to, the following components:

    I. History
    II. Interview (*teachers, parents, and student when appropriate*)
    III. Cognitive Assessment (*a comprehensive profile of cognitive abilities, including verbal and nonverbal processing and performance skills*)

A. Individuals with dyslexia should be identified through an evaluation process that addresses the following subskills of language literacy (reading and writing):
 (1) Phonemic awareness (oral)
 (2) Spelling (isolated and applied)
 (3) Phonic decoding and word identification or word analysis skills
 (4) Fluent and accurate word reading
 (5) Fluent and accurate text reading
 (6) Oral language comprehension
 (7) Reading comprehension
 (8) Written expression
B. Academic achievement (performance assessment)
C. Cognitive processing and language problems in mathematics
IV. **Social and Behavioral Functioning** (*adaptive functioning*)
 [e.g., resiliency = QUalitative Analysis of Resilient Traits (QUART)]
V. **Test Accommodations and Report Formats** (IDA, 2002, pp. 13–21)

The current authors have added:

VI. **Portfolio Assessment: Showcasing Academic Accomplishments**
VII. **Professional Development** (*What needs to be done to support educators to best implement recommendations that emanate from evaluations?*)

The comprehensive assessment components will now be described with recommendations relevant to students who have dyslexia or other learning disabilities or other disabilities. Flippo (2001) suggests that educators consider the complexity of the reading process itself—there are no easy answers that can be applied to all children and situations. With that in mind, educators need access to a repertoire of assessments in order to maintain flexibility in both assessment efforts and subsequent program planning.

Comprehensive Assessments for Students with Learning Disabilities and Other Disabilities

I. *History*

Background information should be obtained that relates directly to instructional programming and provision of services. For individuals with dyslexia, it is helpful to have knowledge of a family history of dyslexia, delayed language development or related problems, "late" talking, listening comprehension deficits, lack of resiliency (i.e., resiliency = the ability to quickly bounce back or recover from stressors, frustrations, and failures due to a personal resolve to persevere in spite of academic/social obstacles), social-behavioral issues, and so on. The Dyslexia Checklist on page 225 can be used as a guide.

Cognitive-Learning Styles: How Do Students Learn Best?   Educators can look at learning styles and cognitive styles when discussing a student's learning history. One's cognitions (thought processes) follow ongoing process development. Memory processes, as an example, are more highly developed in older children than in younger children, probably because of increased language proficiency and the neurological maturing of the cerebral cortex. Cognitive development is viewed more in terms of process than as separate stages of development with distinct breaks (Morris, 1993).

Piaget (1952) specifically ties the development of one's thought capacities to teaching presentations. Concrete presentations are more appropriate for younger children because their experiences have not resulted in many opportunities for higher order thinking (e.g., making inferences). Certainly environmental influences have a *great* impact on how one responds to learning situations. Discussions of cognitive/behavioral responsiveness to the environment during learning situations have focused on: (1) *learning styles* or how students respond to various environmental influences—an individual's *external* responsiveness to the conditions under which learning occurs, and (2) **cognitive-learning styles** or how individuals *internally* process information. Harris and Sipay (1990) have reviewed the literature and have concluded that there is little consensus as to what a learning style is or how one addresses learning styles in academic settings. We have chosen to combine the terms *cognitive* and *learning styles* into one encompassing descriptor, *cognitive-learning styles*. Cognitive-learning styles are really cognitive/behavioral correlates that are readily identifiable and overtly observed and characterize how students internally and externally respond to environmental influences in a learning environment. Table 9.1 provides an overview of cognitive-learning styles and accommodations for dyslexic students.

TABLE 9.1 Cognitive-Learning Styles for Dyslexic Students with Unique Education Challenges: Applicable to All Students

Cognitive/Behavioral Characteristics	Strategic Environmental Accommodations
Dyslexic Students with Attention Deficits (see Chapter 1 for an in-depth discussion)	
Distractible	Provide environmental experiences that minimize visual/auditory distractions; modify classroom setup if need be.
Lack of follow through	Break tasks down into small steps; provide written step-by-step directions whenever possible; allow students to self-monitor progress by logging successes/completed tasks; modify expectations when necessary.
Difficulty listening for sustained time frames	Minimize lengthy verbal exchanges; summarize whenever possible; be clear; repeat, rephrase, review to ensure understanding; encourage interactive, positive, and personally relevant exchanges for short time frames; ask the student to move to another part of the classroom, shift gears, or change activities whenever you see attention is waning.
Impulsive	Work on self-reflecting and self-monitoring behaviors and have students review the consequences of quick decision making; slow the individual down by using writing activities to summarize what needs to be done.
Disorganized in planning for school and study as well as planning activities in personal life	Develop study skills/organizational skills, use assignment notebooks, calendars, notebooks, folders, chore charts, refrigerator reminders, bulletin board clips; encourage cooperative activities where good role models can emulate desired behaviors and outcomes.
Difficulties in reading and written expressive language areas	Same techniques for other students with dyslexia mentioned in Chapters 7 though 11.
Dyslexic Students with Special Gifts and Talents	
Intellectually superior in reasoning ability, analytical and holistic thought, metacognitive processing, and divergent thinking	Encourage sharing of learning outcomes and demonstrations to others; develop areas of giftedness and talent by providing enrichment activities that are highly personalized to the student's interests, aptitudes, and social/emotional/psychological needs; provide problem-solving situations (e.g., mathematics problems, science experiments, analogies, etc.) that require divergent thinking.

(continues)

TABLE 9.1   (Continued)

Cognitive/Behavioral Characteristics	Strategic Environmental Accommodations
Inquisitive to the point of being irritating at times	Encourage positive interactive dialogues with others; develop questioning strategies, work on timing and appropriateness in questioning.
Disorganized in planning for school and study as well as planning activities in personal life	Same as above.
Prefers to work on independent assignments; likes to be alone; introverted	Balance independent activities with group assignments; encourage cooperative learning activities where the individual can serve as a coach or tutor.

II.   *Interview* (*teachers, parents, and student when appropriate*)

Student and teacher interviews can be used to obtain information necessary to planning assessments and educational interventions. A sometimes forgotten area to consider is "sociocultural" background. It is recommended that practitioners use the interview process to help determine preferred learning styles, family literacy strengths and potential contributions to literacy development, and family access to vital literacy and community services (i.e., Does the family have transportation to attend IEP meetings? child care availability?

Caution in Labeling Mislabeling Children from Diverse Backgrounds   The U.S. Department of Education (USDOE, 2003b) cites the need for greater efforts to prevent the intensification of problems connected with mislabeling children from diverse backgrounds with disabilities. There is also the problem of limited resources when identifying second-language learners with learning disabilities delaying identification and the provision of appropriate educational services. The present authors suggest testing be conducted in the home language if appropriate and by professionals who relate well to children from diverse backgrounds, understand cultural implications, and are well-versed in using "culture-fair" testing. Since nearly one of every three persons in the United States in 2003 was a member of a minority group or was limited English proficient, the means to assess, and ensure the effectiveness of efforts to educate all children with disabilities, remains a priority.

Recommendations:

1. *Incorporate culturally relevant principles in assessment and instruction* (USDOE, 2004):
   - Link assessments of student progress to instructional planning and the curricula.
   - Evaluate the individual child AND his or her instructional environment with direct observational data.
   - Develop and establish family-friendly practices to create and maintain collaborative partnerships.
   - Create classroom environments that reflect different cultural heritages and backgrounds and accommodate varying styles of communication and learning—culturally responsive classrooms.

2. *Creating culturally responsive classrooms:* Classroom management also requires cultural responsiveness on the part of teachers and students. Weinstein, Tomlinson-Clarke, and Curran (2004) suggest five essential components in building culturally responsive classrooms:
   - Reflecting on one's own ethnocentrism.
   - Possessing knowledge of one another's cultural backgrounds.
   - Understanding the broader social, economic, and political contexts.
   - Incorporating culturally responsive management strategies across the curriculum,
   - Mutually committing to building caring classrooms. Teachers recognize their values and biases and reflect on how these biases and values impact expectations for behavior and how they interact with students.

3. *Specifically, teachers can:*
   - Nurture connectedness, a sense of community and collaboration (Nieto, 2000).
   - Define and teach expectations for behavior (Weinstein, Tomlinson-Clarke, & Curran, 2004).
   - Have an organized plan for conflict resolution; don't allow minor conflicts to escalate behavior (Weinstein, Tomlinson-Clarke, & Curran, 2004).
   - Establish "families as partners" relationships with all families.

Exploring Students' Cultural Backgrounds. In regard to exploring and understanding students' cultural backgrounds, teachers can work to acquire understandings regarding the cultural heritages of the different ethnic groups represented by their students. These include, "how a specific cultural group sanctions behavior and celebrates accomplishments, and the rules of decorum, deference, and etiquette. Teachers need to understand the values orientations, standards for achievements, relational patterns, communication styles, motivation systems, and learning styles of different ethnic groups. These should be employed in managing the behavior of students, as well as teaching them" (Sheets & Gay, 1996, p. 92).

Robert T. Jiménez (2004) recommends using dictations, cloze tests, retellings, and think-alouds to evaluate the home language of second-language learners to learn more about their literacy identity (see p. 96). All students need to know how literacy connects us to others. Burke (1999) challenges all community members to be "risk takers" in helping children to reach their maximum potentials in reading and writing. In order to accomplish this, teachers can maintain family communications, make home visits, consult with parents and community members, and read related books and journals.

III. *Cognitive Assessment (a comprehensive profile of cognitive abilities including verbal and nonverbal processing and performance skills and academic achievement with running records used to show growth and development in a number of areas over time)*

Anecdotal records (records of observed behaviors over time) could be maintained if necessary, because checklists are not "all inclusive." Anecdotal records are generally notes intended to be helpful in measuring progress over time or to inform teaching practices. It is recommended that checklists be used in conjunction with anecdotal records. For example, a student with dyslexia may be disorganized in study skills and homework completion. The following anecdotal records might be kept to assess the effectiveness of the homework incentive program:

1/1 Didn't complete homework—"forgot" assignment pad.
1/2 Completed homework—well done—incentive given (5 minutes of "free reading" time).

1/3 Completed homework—didn't understand the assignment—incentive was still given as a good effort was made (5 minutes of "free reading" time).

1/4 Called parent—let parent know of homework assignment and to please help with the specifics as this topic is conceptually challenging.

Running record help teachers gather data to follow the progress of individual students and to evaluate "the impact of instruction" (Fountas & Pinnell, 1996, p. 39). Running records are important sources of information regarding what students know and can do.

A running record of a text reading is documentation of what the student actually read. A page or two of connected text (100 words) could be photocopied with the teacher making a check mark if the student correctly identifies a word, notating when substitutions, omissions, insertions, and deletions are made (miscues or word recognition errors). Self-corrections and word and phrase repetitions are noted but not counted as miscues. Also part of the running record would be an indication as to whether words were "told" or given to the student. Many informal inventories have standard ways of recording miscues. The teacher can then determine the typical or high-frequency miscues for instructional purpose, also noting how the student word-problem-solves. The number of miscues would help determine independent and instructional reading levels. The Dyslexia Checklist on page 225 provides a guide for considering independent and instructional reading levels. Generally, if a student is recognizing words with 95 to 99 percent proficiency with greater than 90 percent comprehension, this would be considered a good independent reading level. Word recognition of text with 90 to 95 percent proficiency and greater than 75 to 80 percent comprehension would help determine an appropriate instructional reading level.

A. Subskills of Language Literacy (reading and writing)

Individuals with dyslexia should be identified through an evaluation process that addresses the following literacy subskills involved in reading and writing: (1) phonemic awareness (oral), (2) spelling (isolated and applied), (3) phonic decoding (word identification), (4) fluent and accurate word reading, (5) fluent and accurate text reading, (6) oral language comprehension, (7) reading comprehension, and (8) written expression.

(1) Phonemic (phoneme = smallest unit of speech sound) Awareness

It is a well-documented finding that individuals with dyslexia have poor phonemic awareness (Bradley & Bryant, 1983; Fawcett & Nicholson, 1995). The Dyslexia Checklist in Figures 9.2 and 9.3 allows a teacher or evaluator to key in on specific phonemic awareness deficiencies in the areas of (1) isolating phonemes, (2) identifying phonemes, (3) categorizing phonemes, (4) blending phonemes, (5) segmenting phonemes, and (6) deleting phonemes. The ability to segment and *blend phonemes* is perhaps the most important skill requisite to decoding efforts especially when encountering new words. Often proficiency will be measured by the reading of nonwords.

The following tasks are directly related to phonemic awareness and should be assessed quarterly until students are proficient in these areas.

- Identifying all letters of the alphabet and corresponding short and long vowel sounds.
- Breaking words into onset (first consonant sound) and rimes (the vowel sound with the rest of the word).
- Using phonemic awareness knowledge to spell, including invented spelling.

Dyslexia Checklist

Name _____ Date _____ Examiner _____

School _____ Grade _____ DOB _____

Teacher _____ Parents/Guardian _____

Second Language Learner: ☐ Yes ☐ No (If yes, test in home language if appropriate.)

"Dyslexia" definition = *dys* and *lexia* or inability to effectively read words. This is the most prevalent specific learning disability (at least 50% of the LD population). It is thought to have a neurological basis because the disability is unexpected in relation to other cognitive abilities and access to effective classroom instruction. There are specific difficulties with fluent reading and the phonological processing components of language. Secondary issues may include other academic and non-academic difficulties (e.g., reading comprehension), difficulties in socialization (e.g., more negative peer interactions), and co-existing disabilities or disorders (e.g., ADD or ADHD with 25% of those with dyslexia). With intensive literacy support in reading and writing, a social-academic network of support, and the development of individual resiliency, individuals with dyslexia can lead successful and fulfilling lives.

Independent Reading Level: Word recognition 95-99% with > 90% comprehension _____ (indicate grade level)

Instructional Reading Level: Word recognition 90-95% with >75-80% comprehension _____ (indicate grade level)

Necessary: (assuming participation for 2-3 years in standards-based reading classes where peers achieved reading proficiency)

____ Overall, individual is approximately one to two years behind age or grade level (instructional reading level) in reading achievement, based on benchmarks for grade level; standardized or criterion-referenced assessments can be used.

____ The individual has difficulty with fluency and the phonological components of language.

MAJORITY CHECKED:

Fluency (oral reading):

* limited sight vocabulary
  ____ word by word or short phrase reading or poor phrasing
  ____ slower than expected reading rate (see chart) 35 wpm with grade 2&3 text
  ____ lack of expression especially in conversational text
  ____ poor enunciation
  ____ reliance on just a few strategies to identify unknown words
* ____ less than satisfactory comprehension of the reading

(* = Should test with standardized assessments, criterion -referenced tests or research-based benchmarks)

Expected Oral Reading Rates: Guide by Grade Level
(Low = Beginning of Year, High = End of Year)

Grade 1 (50 - 80 wpm)
Grade 2 (50-90 wpm)
Grade 3 (80 - 115 wpm)
Grade 4 (100 - 120 wpm)
Grade 5 (100 - 130 wpm)

Rate Determined By:
1. Count number of words read (circa 300 words)
2. Multiply by 60=dividend ⊛
3. Compute reading time in seconds (= divisor ⊛)
4. Compute = wpm (words per minute)

Silent Reading Rates (Comprehension is adequate)

Gr.1: <80	Gr. 5: 150 - 160	Gr. 9: 200 - 210
Gr.2: 80 - 110	Gr. 6: 160 - 175	Gr. 10: 210 - 225
Gr.3: 110 - 130	Gr. 7: 175 - 185	Gr. 11: 225 - 240
Gr.4: 130 - 150	Gr. 8: 185 - 200	Gr. 12: 240 - 255

MAJORITY CHECKED:

Phonological Processing Checks

Word or letter knowledge problems with:

____ Identifying sound-symbol correspondences
____ Identifying the names of pictures beginning or ending with the same sound
____ Writing conventions appropriate to age or developmental level
____ Spelling appropriate to age or developmental level

Phonemic awareness deficiencies in:

____ Isolating phonemes (e.g., Tell me the first sound in "kind")
____ Identifying phonemes (e.g., Tell me the sound that is the same in "say" and "see")
____ Categorizing Phonemes (e.g., Tell me another word that you can add to this group with the same beginning sound - "play," "plant" _____)
____ Blending Phonemes (e.g., Tell me what word is /k/ /i/ /n/ / d/) for grade level
____ Phoneme Segmentation (e.g., How many sounds are there in "kind"?)
____ Phoneme Deletion (e.g., What is "kind" without the /d/ sound?)

ADDITIONAL CORRELATING FACTORS/INFORMATION:

Some checked:

____ Family history of dyslexia
____ Delayed language development and/or language related problems
____ Late talker
____ Listening comprehension deficits (strength)
____ Serial order and sequencing problems
____ Time and directional confusions
____ Problems with attention, on-task behavior, and follow-through
____ ADD/ADHD
____ Memory processing deficits
____ WISC-R and WAIS-R. Verbal - Performance Discrepancies or ACID/AVID profiles
____ Problems with organization and study skills
____ Social behavioral problems to include more negative peer interactions, diminished self-concept, learned helplessness and external locus of control
____ Resilient with support systems
____ Other: _____

Source: Carol A. Spafford & George S. Grosser, *Dyslexia and Reading Difficulties: Research and Resource Guide for Working with All Struggling Readers.* Copyright © 2005 by Pearson Education. May be reproduced for noncommercial purposes.

FIGURE 9.2 Dyslexia Checklist

225

Dyslexia Checklist - Case Study

Name **R (dyslexic fourth-grade student)** Date _____ Examiner _____

School _____ Grade **4** DOB **Age 10**

Teacher _____ Parents/Guardian _____

Second Language Learner: ☐ Yes ☑ No (If yes, test in home language if appropriate.) *Grade K - Screening score of 20 on ESI - K (Revised) at age 6-0 (Rescreenings with at-risk status; language delays)*

"Dyslexia" definition = *dys* and *lexia* or inability to effectively read words. This is the most prevalent specific learning disability (at least 50% of the LD population). It is thought to have a neurological basis because the disability is unexpected in relation to other cognitive abilities and access to effective classroom instruction. There are specific difficulties with fluent reading and the phonological processing components of language. Secondary issues may include other academic and non-academic difficulties (e.g., reading comprehension); difficulties in socialization (e.g., more negative peer interactions) and co-existing disabilities or disorders (e.g., ADD or ADHD with 25% of those with dyslexia). With intensive literacy support in reading and writing, a social-academic network of support, and the development of individual resiliency, individuals with dyslexia can lead successful and fulfilling lives. *NOTE: 1/02 (Developmental Reading Assessment) DRA2; 1/03 DRA 10; 6/03 DRA 18; 3/04 DRA 18 receiving intensive literacy support

Independent Reading Level: Word recognition 95-99% with > 90% comprehension **Gr. 2** (indicate grade level) DRA Level 20 (November 2003 and March 2004)
Instructional Reading Level: Word recognition 90-95% with >75-80% comprehension **Gr. 3** (indicate grade level) BRI (Basic Reading Inventory) (Grade 3 passages 70% - 90% comprehension)

Necessary: (assuming participation for 2-3 years in standards-based reading classes where peers achieved reading proficiency)
✔ Overall, individual is approximately one to two years behind age or grade level (instructional reading level) in reading achievement, based on benchmarks for grade level; standardized or criterion-referenced assessments can be used. * High stakes Grade 3 testing - passed the full reading test (top 50% of
✔ The individual has difficulty with fluency and the phonological components of language. district) and writing scores were proficient (with test accommodations).

MAJORITY CHECKED:
Fluency (oral reading):
(* = Should test with standardized criterion - referenced tests or research-based benchmarks)
*✔ limited sight vocabulary
✔ word by word or short phrase reading or poor phrasing
✔ slower than expected reading rate (see chart) 35 wpm with grade 2&3 text
✔ lack of expression especially in conversational text
— poor enunciation (received speech therapy)
✔ reliance on just a few strategies- (context & config-to identify unknown words uration cues only)
*✔ less than satisfactory comprehension of the reading

Expected Oral Reading Rates: Guide by Grade Level
(Low = Beginning of Year, High = End of Year)
Grade 1 (50 - 80 wpm)
Grade 2 (50-90 wpm)
Grade 3 (80 - 115 wpm)
Grade 4 (100 - 120 wpm)
Grade 5 (100 - 130 wpm)

Rate Determined By:
1. Count number of words read (circa 300 words)
2. Multiply by 60=dividend ⊗
3. Compute reading time in seconds (= divisor ⊘)
4. Compute = wpm (words per minute)

Silent Reading Rates (Comprehension is adequate)
Gr. 1: <80   Gr. 5: 150 - 160   Gr. 9: 200 - 210
Gr. 2: 80 - 110   Gr. 6: 160 - 175   Gr. 10: 210 - 225
Gr. 3: 110 - 130   Gr. 7: 175 - 185   Gr. 11: 225 - 240
Gr. 4: 130 - 150   Gr. 8: 185 - 200   Gr. 12: 240 - 255

MAJORITY CHECKED:
Phonological Processing Checks:
Word or Letter Knowledge Problems with:
____ Identifying sound - symbol correspondences
____ Identifying the names of pictures beginning or ending with the same sound
✔ Writing conventions appropriate to age or developmental level
✔ Spelling appropriate to age or developmental level

Phonemic Awareness Deficiencies In:
____ Isolating Phonemes (e.g., Tell me the first sound in "kind")
____ Identifying Phonemes (e.g., Tell me the sound that is the same in "say" and "see")
____ Categorizing Phonemes (e.g., Tell me another word that you can add to this group with the same beginning sound - "play", "plant"____)
✔ Blending Phonemes (e.g., Tell me what word is /k/ /i/ /n/ /d/) for grade level
✔ Phoneme Segmentation (e.g., How many sounds are there in "kind"?)
____ Phoneme Deletion (e.g., What is "kind" without the /d/ sound?)

ADDITIONAL CORRELATING FACTORS/INFORMATION:

Some Checked:
✔ Family history of dyslexia (dad)
✔ Delayed language development and/or language related problems
✔ Late talker (grade appropriate)
— Listening comprehension deficits (strength)
✔ Serial order and sequencing problems
✔ Time and directional confusions
✔ Problems with attention, on-task behavior, and follow-through
____ ADD/ADHD
✔ Memory (processing deficits)
✔ WISC-R and WAIS-R Verbal - Performance Discrepancies or ACID/AVID profiles Discrepancy/Perfor.
✔ Problems with organization and study skills Higher
— Social behavioral problems to include more negative peer interactions, diminished self-concept, learned helplessness and external locus of control (Very Well Adjusted)
— Resilient with support systems
____ Other: _____

Source: Carol A. Spafford & George S. Grosser, Dyslexia and Reading Difficulties: Research and Resource Guide for Working with All Struggling Readers. Copyright © 2005 by Pearson Education. May be reproduced for noncommercial purposes.

FIGURE 9.3 Dyslexia Checklist—Case Study (Dyslexic Fourth-Grade Student)

Phonemes are combined to form syllables and then words with the skill of segmenting these phonemes important to spelling. *Phonemic segmentation* ability helps spellers choose letters to represent phonemes. There are 26 letters to record, approximately 44 phonemes in English (see p. 190).

Predictors of Dyslexia: Phonemic Awareness and Letter Knowledge
Phonemic awareness skills mentioned on the Dyslexia Checklist will be strong predictors of later reading. The National Reading Panel (2000) specifically identified phonemic awareness and letter knowledge as the best predictors of how well children will learn to read during their first two years of schooling. At age 4, however, language measures such as average sentence length may be better predictors for later reading proficiency (Muter, 2003).

(2) Spelling (isolated and applied)
According to Marjorie Lipson and Karen K. Wixson (2003), proficient spelling goes beyond "sounding out words." Correct spelling requires knowledge of sight words, morphemic and structural analysis, and an awareness of spelling patterns. The knowledge of spelling patterns needs to be built on a "foundation of experiences in reading and writing" (Lipson & Wixson, 2003). The National Reading Panel (2000) identified phonemic

awareness (PA) training as beneficial to at-risk students for learning disabilities and older students with reading disabilities who are able to transfer this phonemic awareness knowledge to reading and spelling.

Individuals with Dyslexia Benefit from Phonemic Awareness Instruction
Overall, phonemic awareness training does help students who are learning to acquire a language, whether it be English or other languages. There are a number of programs available to help instruct students in the various subskills (see Chapter 6). According to Leong (1986), beginning readers and struggling readers (i.e., students with dyslexia) "need instruction to codify their spoken language and to understand the spatial-temporal correspondence of symbols and sounds and their internal representation" (p. 143). Some students acquire this knowledge easily while others need intensive teaching (see Table 9.2 for description of some intervention strategies).

Spelling Remains a Lifelong Problem for Dyslexics   Spelling continues to be problematic throughout a dyslexic's life. The nature of the spelling task is such that the individual does not have "visual cues" to rely on as in the reading task. Although dyslexics learn how to read and read efficiently, visual cuing systems (the printed word; the printed word in context; pictures, illustrations, and other graphics; configuration cues) assist the reader especially when the individual is word or text problem solving. With the common use of computers and spell checks in the work and school environment, students with dyslexia should be able to use these learning tools in addition to pocket dictionaries, handheld computer dictionaries, poor spellers' dictionaries, and the like.

For young children who are struggling spellers, word walls and access to the printed page to resource spelling words are important. Figure 9.4 shows the formation of a sentence for a struggling writer from memory ("I like to is and sii and fna"). However, once the student was given the reading to refer to for spelling, a correctly spelled sentence was constructed ("I like to slide and swing and run"). Once students learn spelling words, these words need to be used over and over again in context. Commercial spelling programs contain scope-and-sequence skills development and high-frequency spelling words used in writing; these can be helpful in classwork and homework assignments. Typically, words are studied in isolation and in context—students with dyslexia need both. There are also commercial handheld computers that students can use for spelling and writing purposes with some having the capacity to connect to one of the school's computers for printing if needed.

Is Systematic Phonics Instruction Important in Developing Dyslexics' Spelling Ability?   The National Reading Panel (2000) found that systematic phonics instruction resulted in "much growth" in spelling for young children in kindergarten and first grade, but not for older students who were poor readers. As children move up in the higher grades, it was hypothesized that more complex knowledge of orthography is needed, especially for an alphabetic system, than just that covered in phonics programs.

How to Analyze a Student's Misspellings   Richard Gentry (1996) suggests that the teacher

1. Review a child's spelling for each word. Determine the type of error that best matches the child's spelling.
2. Categorize spelling errors according to developmental level.

TABLE 9.2 Identifying Phonological/Phonemic Awareness Factors/Intervention Strategies for Students with Minimal Conventional Print Skills and Spelling Difficulties (based on Grosser & Spafford, 2000, p. 427)

Academic Symptom	Example(s)	Some Intervention Strategies

Generally Lack of phonemic awareness	—problems with the sound structure of words
	  a) alphabetic knowledge
	  b) phoneme awareness
	  c) rhyme awareness
	  d) awareness of onset and rhyme (onset = the consonant sounds that precede a vowel in a syllable; the onset is followed by the rime
		—teach the alphabetic principle
		—provide opportunities for repeated readings and read-alouds to enhance the acquisition of patterns, rhythm, and sounds of language using literature books; use "big" books in read-alouds, shared readings; buddy readings.
		—use predictable, patterned books in writing activities

Specifically Doesn't fully understand the alphabet principle (= written letters and words represent sounds of spoken words) Phoneme awareness is lacking	—unable to give the names and sounds of letters in isolation and in the context of words —unable to break words down into consonants and vowels	—practice saying and writing the alphabet —teach the sounds of letters both alone in the context of words —create phoneme identification and word segmentation games at the level of the phoneme —use blocks, tiles, cut-up words to take words apart and to create words —practice oral syllabication activities
Lack of rhyme awareness	—not knowing "hat" rhymes with "sat," and also "mat" and "that"	—show rhyming patterns by reading poetry, singing songs, etc. —categorize sounds —identify or tap syllables
Lack of awareness of onset and rhyme in word recognition	—unable to break words down into onset and rimes (e.g., kind; k = onset, ind = rime)	—segment words orally in onset and rime positions

After phonemic awareness training, continue to have students make connections between letters in spellings of words and sound pronunciations (Chall, 1967). Lipson and Wixson (2003) stress that students do not need to know labels for phonic elements used in spelling (e.g., blends, digraphs), nor do they need to "think aloud" or provide a rationale (e.g., spelling rule) in order to become proficient spellers. Good spellers internalize spelling patterns and possess what Lipson and Wixson (2003) describe as a tacit knowledge that typically cannot be described in terms of rules.

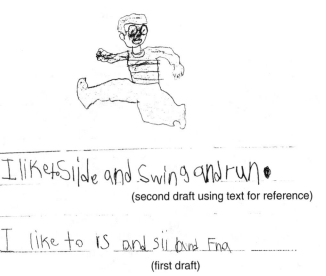

FIGURE 9.4 Example from a Struggling Speller

3. Look for error patterns or errors that appear most frequently according to the following developmental spelling continuum (Gentry, 1996):

   a. **Precommunicative level:** Spelling errors are random (example: "zs" for *and*).

   Sample: Precommunicative spelling for entering K student: (Spelling of name: Tanisha)

   b. **Semiphonetic level:** Spelling generally consists of small consonant clusters (e.g., the beginning and ending consonant sounds in a word—"kd" for *kind*). Kindergarten and grade 1 students would be expected to display *semiphonetic spelling*. E, T, and S are "semiphonetic" spellers with excellent letter formation and use of consonants in key word positions.

   c. **Phonetic level:** Spelling consists of phonetic approximations to the target word ("understaon" for "understand"). The transition to phonetic spelling involves students correctly spelling high-frequency sight words with increased accuracy to phonetic spellings of words. F and M are transitioning to the phonetic level still showing some "semiphonetic" spellings.

F.

> Draw Wlom ps The Basc
> Pem Bool Pn The wed.

M.

> Dor wen is the bas
> Pisn Pob in the ward.

W's and A's writing samples below are examples of students who are on a "phonetic" spelling level.

W.

> Dr wirR png is
> The Best pring Ph
> the wodr.

A.

> X Docker wilum is The Best Pinsabr
> in The Wuld.

Many dyslexics are stuck at this stage. The following writing sample of N, a severely dyslexic student, shows how an extremely bright student works hard to apply sound-symbol correspondences but is unable to utilize language rules and structural analysis skills effectively. This writing piece took 20 minutes, also characteristic of dyslexics who struggle to translate thoughts to writing.

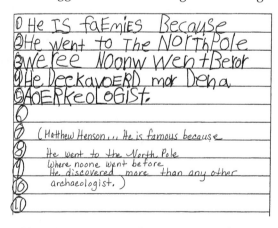

d. **Transitional level:** Spelling closely approximates the targeted word (e.g., "matereal" for *material*).

> Dr. Williams is the best princeabel
> in the world.

e. **Proficient spelling** would involve detailed knowledge of the language system as well as the ability to access multiple word analysis strategies when word problem solving. D, grade 3 honor student, demonstrates that correct spelling usage can be accomplished in early elementary schooling.

D. _____X____Dr. Williams___is___the___best___principal_____

_____in___the___world._____

_____   __

In summary, "Reading words and spelling words are not separate, distinct processes but rather processes that draw upon the same types of underlying word knowledge. The type of alphabetic information that readers use to read words is the same type of information they use to spell words" (Chard, Pikulski, & Templeton, 2003, p. 6).

Assessing spelling proficiency would also involve evaluating the ability of the student to spell words relevant to age and grade expectations (percent correct using grade level word lists). Standardized tests provide norms for spelling performance—all helpful in lesson planning efforts.

Beginning readers and students with dyslexia need practice examining written words, pronouncing words as they look at the spelling of words (making connections between letters and sounds). Templeton and Morris (2000) show how through examination of words with the same roots—as an example *sign/signature*—students will use meaning clues to remember the spellings.

(3) *Phonic Decoding and Word Analysis Skills*

The ability to encode phonological representations is an underlying difficulty of poor readers (Blachman, 1997). Decoding, therefore, is problematic for struggling readers and dyslexics. According to Ehri (1994), decoding is one approach of four in which readers analyze words: (1) *decoding,* where readers convert letters into sounds and then blend them into words; can be individual letters, digraphs like "th" and "oi," phonograms like "er," "ou," and spellings of common rimes like "-ap" and "ick"; (2) *sight* words that readers can automatically retrieve from memory after being previously learned; (3) *analogy* involving accessing from memory learned words and using information or word parts to apply to new words with similar spellings (e.g., use "nice" to discern *nicety* or knowing "oy" in *toy* to pronounce *joy*); and (4) *prediction* allowing readers to use context/picture cues, language and general background knowledge, and familiarity with text to guess or predict unknown words. Processing words through (1) and (3) helps to create sight words in memory (Ehri, 1992).

"Readers need to learn how to read words in the various ways to develop reading skill. The primary way to build a sight vocabulary is to apply decoding or analogizing strategies to read unfamiliar words. These ways of reading words help the words to become familiar" (National Reading Panel Report, 2000, p. 2–107). The ability to make connections between segmented phonemes and graphemes also helps to develop "word memory" important to proficiency in sight word reading (Ehri, 1992).

Assessing a student's sight word knowledge could be done using the Essential 500 Word Reading List (described in Chapter 8 and shown in Figure 9.5) (Spafford & Grosser, 2005).

Name _____ Grade _____ School _____

(GE = grade equivalent) (Dolch words should be learned by grade three; if learning disabled, focus the teaching of "sight words" with the full Dolch List first)

GE List 1.0	List 1.5	List 1.5–2.0	List 2.5	List 2.5–3.0	List 3.0	List 3.5
(1) a*	again*✓	about*	alone	almost	addition	against
add	am*	across	also✓	along	afternoon	another×
all*	are*	after*	always*✓	aunt	already	answer
an*	as*	art	around*	began×	aren't	area
and*✓	away*	ate*	ask*	between	beautiful×	believe
any*	back	because*	best*	each	below	citizen
at*	begin	been*	bring*	easy	beside	congress
be*	better*	before*	brown*	face	bottom	country×
big*	call*	being	buy*	family	build	decide
(10) boy	city	black*	can't	father	children×	decimal
but*	class	blue*	carry*	fill×	couldn't×	divide
by*	come*	both*	clean*	flower×	different	division
came*	could*	brother	cold*	food×	earth	either
can*	down*✓	care	cut*	foot	easily	emergency
dad	find*	cent	drink*	friend	ever×	emperor
day	full*	danger	dry	front	fifty	empress
do*	funny*	did*	fall*	great	forty	entrance
eat*	going*	does*	fast*	home	gallon	everyone×
fire drill	gone	done*	fly*✓	hour	guess	everywhere×
(20) for*	grow*	don't*	found*	I'll	half	example
get*	happy✓	draw*	gave*	inch	hear×	exit
girl	have*	eight*	house	it's	high	fraction
go*	her*	end✓	hurt*✓	knew	hungry×	government
goes*	here*✓	every*	laugh*	last	inside×	gram
had*	he's	far*	left	let's	I've×	happen
has*	him*	first*✓	less	life	leaf	hard
he*✓	his*✓	five*	light*✓	month	low	heard×
I*✓	how*	four*	live*	more	making×	however
if*	its*	from*	made*	mother	mayor×	hundred
(30) in *	king	give*	many*	move×	metric	important
is*	little*	good*	much*	named×	might×	leader
it*	love	got*	myself*	near×	mile	learned
jump*	new*	green*	never*×	next	minute	listen
let*	nine	help*✓	once*	nice×	miss×	liter
like*	one*	hold*	open*	noise×	mix×	meter
look*	other	hot*✓	orange	nose×	multiply	million
make*	out*	I'm	plant	number	music	mountain
man	pick*	into*	please*	nurse	ounce	multiplication
me*	pull*✓	just*	present✓	office	pint	neither
(40) mom	same	keep*	pretty*✓	part×	pound×	nothing×
(41) my*	saw*✓	kind*	right*	place	quiz	ourselves
no*	she's*	know*	round*	police	real×	peace
not*	six*	long*	shall*	prince	second	people
of*	sleep*	math	should✓	princess	shape	picture×
off*	small*	may*	slow	principal	sign×	polite
on*	some*	must*	start*	purple	sound×	president
or*	such✓	night	street	room×	state	prime minister
over*	sure✓	now*	than✓	school	store×	quart
play*	ten*	old*	thank*✓	shoe×	suppose	quarter
(50) put*	that*	only*✓	thing✓	side×	there's	question
ran*	their*	our*	think*	smell×	they'd	quick
red*	them*	own*	today*	smile×	they're	quiet×
said*	then*	queen	together*	snow	third	quit
sat✓	there*	read*	town	song×	thirty	quite
say*	they*	ride*	under*	sorry×	tonight×	rather
see*	this*✓	run*	upon*	subtraction	true	really
sing*	three*	seven*	use*✓	thought	until×	respect
(60) so*	try*	soon*	wash*	trip×	we'll×	senate
sun	two*	stop*	well*✓	turn×	we're×	sentence
the*✓	us*	subtract	where*	uncle	what's×	stem
to*	very*	take*	which*	wet×	whole	talked
tree✓	want*	tell*	while✓	windy	wide	teach
up*	went*	these*	white*	without×	window	teacher
was*	were*	those*	wish*	won't×	within	they'll
we*	why*	twenty	work*	worker×	wouldn't	though
when*	with*	what*	would*	world	year	thousand
will*	your*	who*	write*	yard	you'll	through
(70) you*✓	yes*	yellow*	yet	zero	zone	tough
Totals _____	_____	_____	_____	_____	_____	toward
						usually
						village
						watch×
						where's
						whether
						woman
						x-ray
						young
						you've (80)
						_____

Color Coding
(highlighting known words)

	date	color	
_____	date	color	_____
_____	date	color	_____
_____	date	color	_____
_____	date	color	_____
_____	date	color	_____
_____	date	color	_____

Progress Over Time Running Record

Date _____ Total Sight Words Recognized _____
Date _____ Total Sight Words Recognized _____
Date _____ Total Sight Words Recognized _____
Date _____ Total Sight Words Recognized _____

Source: Carol A. Spafford & George S. Grosser, *Dyslexia and Reading Difficulties: Research and Resource Guide for Working with All Struggling Readers.* Copyright © 2005 by Pearson Education. May be reproduced for noncommercial purposes.

Note: Pages 195 and 196 can be used in the classroom.

FIGURE 9.5 Essential 500 Word Reading List

Word Identification and Meaning Miscues (see p. 186 for miscue coding system) Yetta Goodman (Goodman & Burke, 1972) and others have promoted the idea that word identification miscues in reading in actuality are not "mistakes" but rather clues to how the reader is processing print. In regard to comprehension miscues, "In one sense, it is impossible for any child to make a 'wrong' response to literature. Each reader's own feelings and interpretations are valid, because each reader is different. . . . But some responses that readers make, although they may reflect true feelings, contradict the evidence of the text . . ." (Huck, Hepler, Hickman, & Kiefer, 1997, p.68). Huck et al. (1997) suggest teachers can intervene most effectively to help children "clarify their thinking" if they recognize the origins of their interpretations. There are several types of miscues that students with reading disabilities frequently make, especially word substitutions, insertions, and omissions. These can be observed and noted during oral readings. Gillet and Temple (1990) suggest posing five general questions about any oral reading miscue that relates to these types of miscues: (1) Do the miscues *mean* about the same as the word(s) in the text? Is meaning substantially changed? (2) Does the miscue *function* syntactically in nearly the same way? Is the miscue a word "chunk" or word "part"? (3) Does the miscue *look* or *sound* like the word in the text? (4) If the reader has a dialect, would the miscue be considered consistent with the dialect? (5) Did the reader attempt to self-correct the miscue? Was the reader successful in self-correcting the miscue?

For students with dyslexia who experience difficulties with fluency and the phonology of language, reading every word correctly in a passage is not the goal of fluent reading. For independent reading, word recognition should be in the range of 95 to 99 percent and instructional readings 90 to 95 percent. When working with student's miscues, focus on one or two teaching points, carefully selecting words or word families to work on. Students with dyslexia need to know that it's ok to skip some words if meaning can be abstracted from text but to attempt to identify "most" words. The number of miscues a student makes at a particular developmental level needs to be considered when choosing independent reading books. Many informal inventories provide miscue analysis templates and running records formats that are especially helpful in analyzing the word recognition difficulties experienced by dyslexics.

Using Miscues to Determine Independent Reading Levels If a student encounters more than five troublesome words (words that would be miscues if read aloud) on a full page of text, the text is probably too difficult. For independent reading, students should be encouraged to look at the title of the book, type of book (genre), and content of the book to see if it would be of interest. The student could also randomly pick a page of the text and read the entire page, placing one finger down on the table each time a problem word is encountered. If the student places more than five fingers or the entire hand on the table before the entire page is read, the text is probably too difficult. Generally, for students who keep book bags for independent reading times, it is a good idea to include (1) some "easy" books to build reading confidence, (2) some previously read books to read over and over again to build fluency, (3) "just right books" (books on a student's *independent reading level;* word recognition is 95 to 99 percent and comprehension of the text greater than 90 percent in proficiency) and (4) a few "challenge" books—books that can be read at the student's *instructional reading level* (word recognition is 90 to 95 percent and comprehension of the text greater than 75 to 80 percent in proficiency).

(4) Fluent and Accurate Word Reading

Reading fluency is considered of major fundamental importance to achieving proficiency as a reader. Think of reading fluency in relation to successful completion of a music piece with an instrument. The musician needs to be able to play the notes accurately (A) using proper phrasing (P) and expressive (E) interpretations while adjusting the speed or timing in playing as needed. Comprehension (C) of the composer's message or theme is achieved with successful playing of the music (= PACE). Fluency in reading also demands PACE (see Chapter 8 for in-depth study of fluency factors and assessment). There are word reading difficulties associated with different "types" of dyslexia, although in a dyslexia diagnosis most practitioners will identify only the condition of dyslexia and not a subtype. However, it is helpful in instructional planning efforts to consider the nature of the word reading difficulties.

Considering Dyslexia Subtypes   The present authors (Grosser & Spafford, 2000) proposed three basic subtypes of dyslexia similar to those presented by Boder (1970, 1973) and Manzo and Manzo (1993) with recommendations for teaching support based upon a current review of the literature. The identification of Grosser and Spafford's (a) *visual dysphonetic type* (individuals display a poor or unsatisfactory understanding of phoneme-grapheme correspondences and poor phonological awareness knowledge), (b) *dyseidetic type* (individuals show poor or unsatisfactory ability to recognize sight words with some intact phonological processing abilities), and (c) *dysphonetic-dyseidetic type* (exhibit poor or unsatisfactory phonological processing/sight word knowledge) is based on specific word recognition deficiencies observed for each type.

The three-type dyslexia conceptualization can be used to plan additional teaching strategies as seen on the top of page 235.

(5) Fluent and Accurate Text Reading

(See Dyslexia Checklist and Comprehension Diagnostic Checklist on pp. 225 and 132)

(6) Oral Language Comprehension

This would be an assessment of listening comprehension. Typically, an evaluator will read passages from tests or text aloud, followed by questions or a request for a retelling to assess comprehension. Often, the listening comprehension level of an individual with dyslexia is higher than independent and instructional reading levels. As noted on R's dyslexia checklist on page 226, listening comprehension is noted to be grade appropriate. This is important information because R needs to be present in any grade-level content area oral presentation because his listening comprehension is good.

(7) Reading Comprehension (Chapter 7)

The Comprehension Diagnostic Checklist on page 132 can be used as a running record—the teacher can check and date progress in the areas of affective dimensions, fluency, reading-writing, reference usage, story grammar knowledge, and linguistic awareness. This check can be used when writing progress reports as required under IEP regulations. The *cloze*

Grosser and Spafford's Dyslexia Subtypes: Instructional Implications at the Word Level

(1) If *visual-dysphonetic type,*
. . . practice in speedier processing of consonants may be helpful.
. . . . phonetic training programs are needed (e.g., direct teaching of sound separations, phonemic matching, finding sound/word differences, etc.).
. . . . use both visual and auditory modalities (i.e., shared oral readings).
. . . .writing process programs with access to word processors /spell checks/poor spellers' dictionaries (peer/teacher editing).
. . . .explicit spelling instruction with a strong phonics base.

(2) If the *dyseidetic type,*
. . .practice in coordinating all of the senses is in order so that in the recognition of letters, phonological processing can be as fast as lexical processing.
. . .multisensory instruction such as in the Orton-Gillingham and Slingerland programs (work on phonemic segmentation, sound blending, and so on).
. . . .writing process programs with access to word processors/ spell checks/poor spellers' dictionaries (peer/teacher editing).
. . . .explicit spelling instruction with a focus on irregular English spellings; incorporate phonics.
. . . .use of larger-type fonts if helpful to provide more success in reading.

(3) If *combined/dysphonetic-dyseidetic type,*
. . .both sets of treatments discussed in (1) and (2)
. . .the student has a relatively severe disability and will require some one-to-one instruction and on a daily basis.
. . . books on tape/access to tutors/individuals who can transcribe dictated materials.
. . . access to tutors or individuals who can prepare/review content (orally) for quizzes/tests.

TABLE 9.3   **Issues to Check for Assessment: Considerations for Teaching Based on Diagnosed Subtypes**

Does the primary problem appear to be phonetic?

(1) Grosser & Spafford's *visual-dysphonetic type*

Yes, if   a) auditory analysis ability is impaired (i.e., segmenting and blending aurally presented words)
   and b) nonwords or pseudowords cannot be decoded phonetically
   and c) spelling errors have no relation to phonics principles
   and d) irregularly spelled words do not provide additional problems
   and e) comprehension is impaired

(2) *Dyseidetic* type* (visual processing problems as opposed to phonological processing problems; comprehension is also impaired in this type of dyslexia)

No,   if   a) auditory analysis ability is adequate (i.e., can segment and blend aurally presented words)
   and b) nonwords or pseudowords can be decoded phonetically
   and c) spelling errors do have a relation to phonics principles
   and d) irregularly spelled words are misspelled due to the misapplication of phonic principles
   and e) reading accuracy is improved when large-type font is used

*dys = difficulty with; *eidolon* = an image.

(3) If patterns in both (1) and (2) appear to be equally present, with a concomitant comprehension (severe) deficit, this type of dyslexia is referred to as a *Combined* or *Dysphonetic-dyseidetic type.*

procedure and story retellings can be used for measuring comprehension of selected classroom text readings.

The Cloze Procedure—Developing an Expanded Vocabulary   Taylor (1953) fist introduced the term "cloze" in reference to the Gestalt principle of "closure," or the ability to complete an incomplete stimulus. It is assumed that readers fill in the gaps when needed because of prior experiences with text and background knowledge. For the student with dyslexia, the knowledge "background gaps" must be filled in with the assistance of the teacher, parent, or peer tutor. Although the "exact word must be inserted" method of assessment is sometimes used, the present authors would recommend accepting synonyms for the student with dyslexia. If students with dyslexia can fill in the gaps for at least 40 percent of the material presented, an instructional level can be established, meaning the student is comfortable with that particular grade level textual material.

Summary of Cloze for Students with Dyslexia

1. Select a passage of 200–250 words.
2. Leave a few key sentences intact (especially main idea sentences) to provide context/meaning cues for the student.
3. Delete every fifth word and make a key of exact missing words and/or corresponding synonyms for the key words.
4. Accept synonyms or words that make sense in the blanks provided.
5. Students with dyslexia may need a "read through." That is, the teacher and student can read the selection orally with the student filling in the blanks during the oral reading. The teacher can provide clues or cues when the student is "stuck." Repeated readings will help with fluency and content. Then the student is ready to read and write independently.
6. In order to determine a student's proficiency in completing the cloze exercise (which helps to assess vocabulary and comprehension proficiency), the teacher need only to double the number of correct responses and divide the number of correct responses by the number of errors or blanks and multiply by 100 (for a proficiency percentage). Richardson and Morgan (1994) suggest that students who score below 40 percent on instructional/diagnostic cloze exercises reach a frustration level where the material is inappropriate and too difficult for the student.

Story Retellings: Assessment of Story Comprehension   The reading of stories aloud to children does promote comprehension and emerging reading skills because children now have to use concepts about print in an organized manner in order to derive meaning from the printed page. Kapinus, Gambrell, and Koskinen (1988) have found that children who are poor readers gain strategic comprehension skills by retelling stories. These authors believe that teachers must first establish a purpose for the retelling and why retelling helps understanding. Kapinus et al. (1988) recommend the use of short passages at first of 50 to 100 words that can be retold in just a paragraph or less. The teacher should model some retellings of various stories or text material before students are required to do so.

Jerry L. Johns and Susan Davis Lenski (2001) provide an in-class model to use for written retellings:

(1) Students choose a favorite piece of literature.
(2) Students read the story several times and think about the sequence of action in the plot.

(3) Students summarize the story without the text with attention to the story line or main ideas.

(4) Students read their retelling.

The same format can be used for oral retellings prompting students with, "read the story, and after the story you will retell everything that happened in the story. Use your story structure guide as you read the story."

(8) Written Expression

Student at risk or students who need assistance early on in writing are readily identified when rubrics or benchmarks (standards indicators) are used to determine writing proficiency (see p. 170, Continuum of Writing Development Assessment). The writing samples of first graders in Figure 9.6 show evidence of "experimental writing" after responding to the prompt. "What do hippos do after they eat?" Children convey meaning in the writings with simplified oral language structures, and there is a one-to-one correspondence between the written and spoken word. However, the student at risk is experiencing difficulty with the phonology of language after copying the question ("under" = "adar"; "winter" = "what"; "rest" = rasd"; "their eyes" = "th is"). This is an early warning sign of dyslexia.

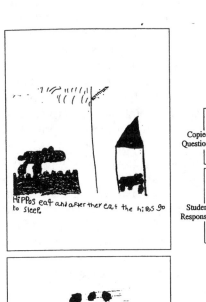

FIGURE 9.6   Using Writing Samples to Identify At-Risk Students

Although the student at risk is able to effectively place thoughts in writing using inventive spelling, additional intensive writing support may or may not be needed depending on writing benchmarks for first graders. At the beginning of first grade, inventive spellings with phonetic approximations would be expected (first assessment term benchmark). However, by the end of first grade, students are expected to use conventional spelling with high-frequency words (end of the year writing benchmark for first graders). Since this was a beginning of the year writing sample, the student falls within average writing benchmarks for first graders. Running records (p. 241) and other writing assessments could be used to monitor writing growth and development throughout the year with a close "watch" for any other signs of reading disabilities or dyslexia.

Using Rubrics and Continuums to Evaluate Writing Proficiency   Writing rubrics are used in both the holistic and analytic scoring of individual writing pieces. *Holistic scoring* involves looking at the overall quality of a writing piece and arriving at one score/grade that reflects how well the student completed the work according to pre-established standards or criteria. *Analytic scoring* involves evaluating various writing components such as topic development, content, word usage, use of language conventions, and so on and then weighting predetermined areas for an overall writing score or grade. Long composition writing is sometimes analytically evaluated with writing rubric scores given for idea or topic development (1- to 4- or 1- to 6-point scale) and also the use of language conventions (1- to 4-point scale). According to Lipson and Wixson (2003), rubrics provide a systematic structure teachers can use across grades or classrooms to evaluate and discuss student work where there is a common vision and uniform set of standards. Garcia and Verville (1994) define a rubric as a hierarchy of acceptable responses with identified qualities at several points along a scale. Most writing rubrics follow a 4-point scale and with long composition writing, 6-point scales are often used. On a 4-point scale, rubric scores of 4, 3, and sometimes 2 indicate the writer demonstrated proficient writing, with 4 representing highly proficient writing. Rubric scores of 1 and 0 (sometimes 2) show writing deficits and the need for additional writing instruction. When teachers are required to provide grades for writing pieces, 4-point rubric scales lend themselves well to grading (4 = A, 3 = B, 2 = C, 1 = D, 0 = E). Teachers who evaluate a writing piece in which the student did not know how to communicate an understanding of the topic in writing but observed a concerted effort by the student to complete the assignment, typically will not assign rubric scores of 0.

The writing continuum on page 170 is a holistic assessment of writing progress across expected developmental stages and grade levels and is adapted from the *First Steps™ Writing Developmental Continuum* (1994). In addition to a writing sample, general indicators on the continuum at each of five writing phases (role-playing writing, grade K; experimental writing, grade 1; early writing, grade 2; conventional writing, grades 3–5; proficient writing, grades 6–12) help teachers identify student placement/ progress relative to these phases or stages of writing. Grade level expectations are close approximations but may vary according to curriculum and program standards.

The self-assessment writing check on page 240 can be used by students before a teacher "rubrics" or evaluates the work. For students with dyslexia and English language learners (ELL) who are transitioning from

Spanish to English, keywords have been highlighted in both English and Spanish to cue the writer to the important writing skill or point to reflect on.

The 4-point writing rubric found on pages 166–167 can be used in both open-response and long-composition writing. Both idea and topic development and the use of language conventions are assessed. For students with dyslexia, language conventions often present a problem and should be assessed separately from idea and topic development. This will help pinpoint those areas in the use of language conventions where a student needs continued writing instruction.

Recommended Types of Writing for Students with Dyslexia

Independent Writing.   Independent writing involves setting aside or planning writing times when students can apply language conventions while developing ideas and topics that draw on personal experiences and knowledge. The goal should be to develop a final "published" writing piece—that is, a piece of writing that is the writer's best work and can be understood and enjoyed by another reader. During independent writing times, *students write for different purposes and audiences using different writing forms furthering the development of their "author's voice" and creative expressiveness.* The use of graphic organizers, rubrics, and the editing process help students to organize, refine, and further develop their writing. Often independent writers will keep a journal to jot down notes/ideas beforehand or may web ideas to refer to during the actual writing of a piece. Independent writers are good researchers; that is, they locate appropriate resources and information to complete a written work. Students with dyslexia may tape record ideas or use a word processor during the various stages of writing. Consistent engagement in independent writing activities builds fluency in writing and the writing habit. With independent writing and other writing forms, students need to check on various writing dimensions. Figure 9.7 can be used as a self-assessment writing check. The writing assessment running record in Figure 9.8 can be a quick check for the teacher on general writing progress across writing forms.

Interactive Writing.   Interactive writing is similar to shared writing in that a teacher or adult works with a student to compose a written work versus scribing the entire written piece. There is a "shared pen" in that the child and adult take turns writing. The adult brings attention to the "writing process" and how to form letters, words, and sentences. Interactive writing conveys to the student that his or her ideas have value or worth in the context of learning how writing works. Written pieces can be used in subsequent reading activities.

Reformulation.   This is a type of writing support for individuals learning a school language that is different from the home language (e.g., ELL or English Language Learners in the United States) where a speaker of the mainstream language (e.g., English) rewrites or reformulates the learner's written work to conform more to the language conventions of the school's language without changing content. The writer/learner (e.g., ELL student) compares the original work with the reformulated work to notice differences and gain writing insights about the school's language.

Shared Writing.   Teachers or adults work with students to compose a writing piece with the adult "scribing" or assuming the role of "secretary" for the student. The adult brings attention to the "writing process" and how to

Name _____ Date _____

Things I Need to Check   *OK?, ✓ or Yes or No, or Highlight*

Handwriting	Neat	_____
	Readable	_____
Spacing	Between letters	_____
	Between words	_____
Spelling—checked with	The dictionary	_____
	A thesaurus	_____
	Computer spell check	_____
	A proofreader	_____
	The teacher	_____
Ending punctuation	Periods	_____
	Question marks	_____
	Exclamation marks	_____
Other Punctuation	Commas	_____
	Quotation marks	_____
	Apostrophes	_____
	Foreign language symbols	_____
	Other	_____
Grammar/other mechanics	Complete sentences	_____
	Sentences make sense	_____
	Paragraphed	_____
Quality of my work	Fully developed a topic	_____
	Researched a topic	_____
	Interesting vocabulary	_____
	Supporting details	_____
	Interesting to others	_____
	My own work	_____
	My work flows	_____
	My best efforts	_____
Proofreading	Number of drafts	_____
	I re-read	_____
	A peer reviewed	_____
	The teacher reviewed	_____
	A family member reviewed	_____
Publishing	Ready to publish	_____
	Published work	_____

Self-Evaluation: I deserve a(n) _____ grade or rubric score on this writing piece because

_____

_____

FIGURE 9.7   Elementary through Secondary Writing Guide: Student Check

Writing Assessment: Running Record for _____

Teacher: _____   Grade: _____

School: _____   Date(s): _____

Mechanics	Writing Process
✓ = Good quality * = Problem area N/A = Not Applicable	✓ = Can do * = Problem area N/A = Not Applicable
_____ Spelling	_____ Can set a purpose
_____ Punctuation	_____ Can select a topic
_____ Capitalization	_____ Can research a topic
_____ Handwriting legibility	_____ Can seek assistance when needed
_____ Grammar	_____ Can work cooperatively with peers
_____ Spacing between letters	_____ Can proofread and revise work (drafts)
_____ Spacing between words, paragraphs	_____ Can share work
_____ College level: Can use APA style	_____ Can adjust style to task
_____ High school level: Report format & bibliography	**Qualitative Components**
_____ Typewriter or word processor	✓ = Good quality * = Problem area N/A = Not Applicable
_____ Proofreading independently	_____ Effective topic development
_____ Proofreading by peers/the teachers	_____ Logical writing sequence
	_____ Interesting or varied vocabulary
	_____ Effective dialogue (if relevant)
	_____ Character development (if relevant)
	_____ Plot development (if relevant)
	_____ Sentence sense (flows)
	_____ Paragraph sense (flows)
	_____ Adequate supporting details
	_____ Ready to publish or published work

Writing conference notes:

Instructional focus for future writing:

FIGURE 9.8   Writing Assessment Running Record

form letters, words, and sentences. Shared writing conveys to the student that his or her ideas have value or worth in the context of learning how writing works. Shared writing also provides an opportunity for teachers and students to problem-solve different writing challenges, such as when to use various punctuation marks. *Shared writing is appropriate across grade levels* and subject areas depending on the writing purpose and audience. Writing pieces can be used in subsequent reading activities ("writing-to-read").

The children are playing basketball and running to the hoop.

Writers' Workshop or Guided Writing.   This is a type of writing instruction where students are guided to proficiency through minilessons and conferences that provide feedback regarding the components to various writing structures or forms; "how to" expand topics and ideas (e.g., modeling, providing rubrics or exemplars) with practice using appropriate language conventions (e.g., grammar and spelling). Consistently providing time for guided writing activities helps students to: (1) achieve proficiency in writing according to benchmarks or standards, (2) develop creativity and their voice in writing, (3) familiarize themselves with different writing forms, (4) write for different purposes and audiences, and (5) communicate to others personal ideas/thoughts/knowledge/feelings. The goal is to have students "publish" or showcase a final written piece after much interactive dialogue (conferencing) with the teacher/peers following a sequence of (1) prewriting, (2) writing, (3) revising, (4) editing, and (5) publishing. Peer conferences center on providing ideas and editing suggestions. Often students choose their own topics and write daily for sustained periods of time (minimum of 15 to 30 minutes). The role of conferencing during writers' workshop is important when guiding students to levels of proficiency and to identify problem areas in writing.

The Role of Conferencing in Writers' Workshop to Identify Writing Problems

In addition to analyzing final student writing pieces to create future mini-lessons, conferencing can provide a closer look at student problem areas in writing.

Writers' Workshop Goal: to have students publish or showcase a final written piece after much interactive dialogue (conferencing) with the teacher/peers following a sequence of (a) prewriting, (b) writing, (c) revising, (d) editing, and (e) publishing.

What Is Writers' Workshop?

(1) Students write for sustained period of times; 30 minutes daily is necessary for struggling readers and writers.
(2) Students are very involved in writing choices (e.g., the topic).
(3) Students work to become proficient in using various writing forms/genres.
(4) Students conference with the teacher and one another for ideas, editing, and revising.
(5) Conference questions used by teachers can be constructed beforehand; for example, Shelley Harwayne (1992) created the following guides to generate questions for students who were learning how to write in response to different reading genres: . . . "(a) does the student understand literary stance? (b) does the student appreciate the genre? (c) does the student imagine possibilities? (d) does the student need closer genre study? (e) has the student attempted a draft? (f) is the student making deliberate decisions? (g) is the student ready to edit? publish?" (p. 234).
(6) Students pair or work with "writing buddies" to share work.
(7) Teachers use final writing pieces to create mini-lessons for idea and topic development (e.g., if the student was experiencing difficulty with writing topic sentences, the teacher would create a mini-lesson on how to write a topic sentence) and language conventions (e.g., related to grammar, syntax, and spelling).

Students can also be encouraged to create writing rubrics, templates, checklists and the like to self-assess their own writing pieces. Cooperative learning groups can work to develop frameworks or drafts for evaluation tools with full class discussion used to come to a "meeting of the minds." In this way, students can take some ownership in assessments. The following writing guide was developed by a third-grade student to check on open response writing.

An edited writing piece by a grade 5 student with severe dyslexia followed the steps mentioned for the writing process to include editing.

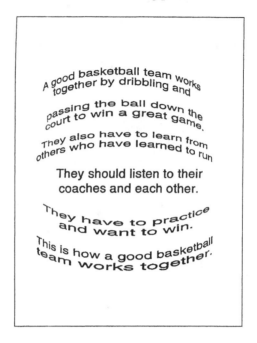

Benefits to Cooperative Learning Activities   According to research cited in the National Reading Panel Report (NRPR) (2000), cooperative learning activities lead to greater engagement in or motivation for learning, improved academic performance, and more time on task.

B. Academic Achievement (performance assessment)

Where Should Practitioners Begin Testing Students with Dyslexia or Learning Disabilities to Determine Achievement in Any Academic Area?   Typically, if a mild disability is thought to be present, testing could begin with grade-level appropriate assessments. However, for students with moderate and severe forms of dyslexia or other learning disabilities, testing needs to begin at their current known performance levels consistent with the Council for Exceptional Children (CEC) position on this issue.

Effective Assessments of Academic Achievement Consider School and Classroom Grouping Practices   According to Lipson and Wixson (2003), it is particularly important to identify the way in which students are grouped, especially for students who are struggling in the classroom. Teachers can consider such grouping options as one-to-one instruction, guided reading groups, and flexible groups.

Grouping Students   *One-to-one instruction* or tutorial instruction allows for "total concentration on a single student" where instruction can be meshed "exactly with student needs at any given time" (McCormick, 1995, p. 206). McCormick cites research that showed middle school students who received one-to-one instruction scored as much as two standard deviations higher than group-instructed students. Student attitudes are judged to be more positive in one-to-one instruction, a type of tutorial situation. The research is overwhelming in favor of research-based programs that allow for individual tutoring with students who are dyslexic—one or two teaching points per lesson are recommended, allowing for opportunities for teacher clarifications, questions back to the teacher that might not be asked in a group setting, and time to practice or try out reading strategies with feedback. The opportunity to try out new strategies in a "no-risk" (i.e., no risk for peer rejection) situation is particularly helpful to struggling readers who already have lower self-esteems and a lack of confidence in their abilities as readers and writers. Two one-to-one instruction program models that have consistently demonstrated achievement gains for struggling readers are *Reading Recovery* (Clay, 1979, 1988) and *Success for All* (Madden et al., 1991).

Reading Recovery has been widely used with first-grade children and many second-grade children with the purpose of preventing "reading failures" in children who are in the lowest 20% of their reading classes (Clay, 1979, 1988). This program seeks to empower struggling readers with multiple strategies to use when word-problem-solving and to become fluent readers and writers. Lessons focus on (1) *fluent writing practice*—writing familiar words on the chalkboard as quickly as possible to enhance memory for later story writing, (2) *rereading a "little book"* from the previous day until it "sounds like people talking" (this develops reading fluency), (3) *letter identification and word analysis* by "working with learned words" (e.g., putting letters together to form words on magnetic chalkboards), (4) *writing a short story* using learned words (spelling is facilitated with word boxes—students sound out words that are written), (5) working with *cut-up sentences* from student-generated stories. The teacher cuts up the students' stories into sentences—the student puts his or her story back together, and (6) *attempting to read a new "little book" with the teacher modeling and discussing what good readers* do to become successful readers. Interactive questions build on comprehension—the lesson sequence begins again the next day. Pinnell and colleagues (1994) found that one of the variables accounting for the success in Reading Recovery programs with at-risk readers was the one-to-one lessons in addition to the lessons themselves and the intensive training teachers must receive before becoming Reading Recovery teachers. Additionally, Lipson and Wixson (2003) note the extensive amount of reading and writing in this program provides ample practice for students to apply their knowledge and skills.

The Success for All program (Madden et al., 1991) was developed for inner-city communities for grades K–3, and one-to-one instruction has been cited as critical to the program's success. In Success for All, group instruction is balanced with one-to-one tutoring based on students' needs. Instruction in reading centers on: (1) systematic phonics instruction, (2) phonemic awareness training, (3) discussion of text structure, (4) frequent oral readings of connected text in the early stages of the program, (5) development of oral language proficiency, (6) the use of repeated readings to increase fluency, (7) writing-to-read, (8) process writing, (9) the development of metacomprehension and metacognition skills, and (10) cooperative reading ventures to further understanding (e.g., paired reading). In this approach, stories written to emphasize word analysis understandings taught in class are used in conjunction with basal reading materials. Parent support teams work together to further literacy in the home, overseeing 20 minutes of reading each night. In a review of the research, McCormick (1995) concludes that excellent results have been obtained with the Success for All program.

It should be noted that in both the Reading Recovery and Success for All programs, the five essential teaching of reading elements cited in the research and in the National Reading Panel Report (2000) are included: (1) phonemic awareness, (2) phonics, (3) fluency, (4) vocabulary development, and (5) text comprehension/strategic reading.

A *Guided Reading group* is an example (see pp. 202–203) of a type of reading instruction where students are placed in small groups according to similar reading processes and strategies used (4 to 6 students). The teacher selects and introduces new books, supports children as they read the entire text to themselves, and makes teaching points during and following the reading. Teachers prompt struggling readers to strategies good readers use and word-problem-solving. Leveled books are used and instruction is scaffolded. The goal of guided reading instruction is to develop independent, flexible readers and problem solvers who comprehend what they read across genres and curricula.

Flexible grouping, or the *flex group*, is a type of grouping that is widely used in reading classes because individual learning styles/characteristics can be considered. Flex groups are dynamic—students are typically separated into learning groups based on some level of achievement or level of academic performance with the movement of students between groups based on the needs of the students. Temporary instructional groups could be created to address a particular learning need (e.g., how to summarize) with the grouping no longer existing once the students have achievement proficiency (Spafford, Pesce, & Grosser, 1998). According to Matthews (2003), flexible groupings allow for "maximum achievement."

Continuous Assessment to Monitor Reading Performance. Lapp and Flood (2003) offer a portable assessment model for teachers who work with struggling readers (those readers who cannot read grade-level materials with fluency and comprehension) involving a diagnostic teaching cycle, ". . . essential to the literacy growth of all children" (p. 14). In essence, Lapp and Flood suggest ongoing assessment to monitor reading performance using the following portable assessment sequence:

Assess:
- Literacy behaviors where children demonstrate proficiency using performance instruments such as running records (Clay, 1979), retellings (Morrow, 1988), and questioning (Rafael, 1982) to collect data about student reading performance.
- Identify reading areas where children are struggling.

Diagnose/Analyze:
- Review the data to key in on reading strengths and areas of need to inform instruction.

Teach:
- Plan next instructional steps based on identified strengths and needs (Lapp & Flood, 2003).

Anecdotal and running records allow for continuous assessment of reading and other performance.

Participatory Action Research When Viewing the Data Participatory action research is a type of research approach where the evaluator (e.g., test administrator within a school/district) collaborates with the potential beneficiary of the data (e.g., teacher of student with dyslexia) to study data generated from research. Hyun-Sook Park and her colleagues (1998) have studied participatory action research concluding that the process empowers teachers to take "ownership" of data that can generate new strategies and ideas in implementing successful programs. The key to all of this is establishing *trusting and respectful* relations between the teacher practitioners and evaluators (CEC, 2003).

C. Assessing Cognitive Processing and Language Problems in Mathematics

Students with dyslexia have been reported to excel in mathematics, especially in computational proficiency relative to reading and writing proficiency. However, it is recommended that error analysis be conducted on a regular basis because computational errors may be based on "incorrect processing" of numbers or math concepts.

Error Pattern Analysis in Mathematics

Earlier Studies Error pattern analysis was utilized by Myers in 1924 and Brueckner and Elwell in 1932 as a reliable diagnostic tool. Grossnickle (1935) discussed two mathematics error types, constant errors (recurring incorrect responses related to specific number combinations) and careless errors. Roberts (1968), as cited by Cox (1975a, 1975b), refined and expanded Grossnickle's work to four categories: (1) use of wrong operations, (2) computational errors, (3) defective algorithms or procedures, and (4) random errors. Since these initial works, several error pattern classification types have been offered (Cox, 1975a, 1975b).

An Efficient Diagnostic Tool Error pattern analysis is considered "the most efficient tool for diagnosing [mathematics] learning difficulties" (Nunes, 1991, p. 26) and as such provides constructive instructional directions (Ashlock, 1994; Ackerman, Anhalt, & Dykman, 1986; Borasi, 1987; Humphery, 1981; McEntire, 1981). There are various error pattern classification systems. Tatsuoka (1984) points to some 200 "erroneous rules of operation" (p. 120) relating to faulty math algorithms. It would be helpful for an educator to designate an error pattern system that closely coincides with the school curriculum and the needs of the children served.

Error Patterns Experienced by Children with Learning Disabilities Bley and Thornton (1989), Ashlock (1994), and others have found that students with dyslexia and other learning disabilities may experience problems in writing numbers, recognizing number patterns, understanding the concepts of greater than and less than, and understanding the language of math. Enright (1983) has identified seven error patterns that frequently emerge with students who have learning problems in math: regrouping, process substitution, omission, directionality, placement, attention to sign, and guessing. Samples of each error pattern can be seen in the following examples:

1. Regrouping Errors:

$$\begin{array}{r} 880 \\ -229 \\ \hline 660 \end{array}$$

The student failed to regroup the tens and ones columns. The improper use of 0s is frequently seen in students with math problems.

2. Process Substitution Errors:

$$\begin{array}{r} 134 \\ \times\ 12 \\ \hline 268 \end{array}$$

The student failed to complete the process by multiplying the 1 times 134 for the second step. This type of error could involve omitting steps or substituting incorrect steps or algorithms.

3. Omissions:

$$\begin{array}{r} 21 \\ 6\ \overline{)1206} \end{array}$$

The student failed to add a 0 in the quotient. Omissions include leaving out parts of answers or a step in completing a problem.

4. Directional Errors:

$$\begin{array}{r} 129 \\ +\ 678 \\ \hline 7917 \end{array}$$

The student completed the problem from left to right instead of right to left. Directional errors involve the wrong direction or order when problem solving.

5. Placement Errors:

$$\begin{array}{r} 35 \\ +\ 17 \\ \hline 412 \end{array}$$

The student doesn't regroup the ones into tens.

6. Attention to Sign:

$$\begin{array}{r} 9 \\ \times\ 3 \\ \hline 12 \end{array}$$

The student used the wrong operation and did not follow the multiplication sign. Sign errors involve calculating an incorrect answer because the correct sign was not used.

7. Guessing:

$$2 + 4 + 5 = 1000$$

The student randomly gave an answer. This kind of error is merely a wild guess, in which the reasonableness of the answer is overlooked.

Error analyses can be done formally (i.e., testing) or informally by using the student's work (see Figure 9.9). However, there are times when . . . "it is necessary to conduct a more formal diagnosis using tests . . . " (D'Augustine & Smith, 1992, p. 21).

Examples

$\begin{array}{r} \$2.74 \\ -1.37 \\ \hline \$1.47 \end{array}$	$\begin{array}{r} 2\,\text{ft.}\ \ 7\,\text{in} \\ +1\,\text{ft.}\ 8\,\text{in} \\ \hline 4\ \ \text{ft.}\ 5\,\text{in} \end{array}$
Regrouping Error	**Process Substitution Error**
Child A has forgotten that in borrowing from the tens column, the 7 is changed to a 6.	Child B is applying a base-ten addition algorithm to measurement units based on 12.

FIGURE 9.9   Error Analysis

Focusing Intervention Efforts after Analyzing Math Errors   Instructional efforts need to consider:

a. Build self-esteem and confidence in math.
b. Task-analyze the skills necessary to perform a particular math problem.
c. Provide concrete representations to provide a conceptual base.
d. Understand the individual's math strengths and weaknesses with work on both.
e. Relate math to everyday life situations when possible.
f. Provide high-interest challenging problems of the day in order to stimulate problem-solving abilities.
g. Provide many opportunities for problem solving, frequently reworking and rewording the problems.
h. Build math vocabulary through reading and other content area subjects; using math word walls and math dictionaries based on classroom activities.
i. Provide immediate feedback and reinforcement.
j. Consistently analyze errors in math work.

SQRQCQ   SQRQCQ was developed by Leo Fay (Forgan & Mangrum, 1989) and involves six steps of (1) *S*urvey, (2) *Q*uestion, (3) *R*ead, (4) *Q*uestion, (5) *C*ompute, and (6) *Q*uestion. Students must carefully survey word problems for an understanding of the language and what the problem is looking for. Questioning at every step provides time for self-reflection, assessment, and rethinking new strategies. The final question must reflect on the answer at hand—does it make sense and is it reasonable?

Probing Children's Thinking during Math   During math lessons, Marilyn Burns (2004) suggests probing "children's thinking. Ask: 'Why did you think that? Why does that make sense? Convince us. Prove it. Does anyone have a different way to think about the problem? Does anyone have another explanation?' " According to Burns (2004), when children have to explain their math reasoning, they necessarily organize their ideas with an opportunity to further math understandings. Burns also suggests "partner talk," sometimes called "turn and talk" or "think-pair-share," where students are given a minute or so to turn and talk to a peer to "get ready" to contribute to group discussions about math.

Multisensory Approach (VAK-T)   The coordination of visual, auditory, language, kinesthetic, and motor coordination (touch) allows for optimal learning as shown in Figure 9.10 on page 250.

The Language of Math   Math terminology is not easily understood because it does not appear in conversational context or in most other subject area textbooks or library readings (with the exception of counting numbers). Rittner (1982) emphasizes how problems in language can seriously impact math learning. Certainly the language problems of dyslexics could impact math performance, but this is not always the case.

Teaching Mathematical Vocabulary Comprehension   Cangelosi (1992) recommends that math communication involve the use of general, special, and technical vocabulary terms. The special-usage terms present special learning problems, and Cangelosi suggests identifying and presenting these terms before using them in problem-solving situations. General-usage terms include terms known to everyone (e.g., circle, number, addition, and so on). Special-usage terms involve words and symbols whose meaning can change depending on the context used (e.g., "more" in two contexts: "Add 5 more to your number" and "How much more is 20 than 10?"). Technical-usage terms involve words and

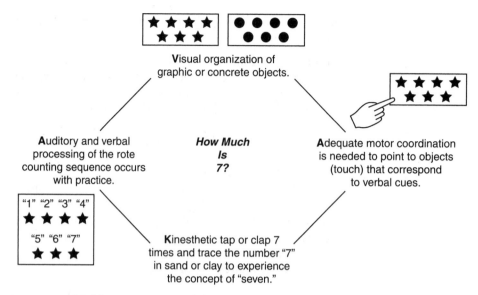

FIGURE 9.10   Multisensory Approach (VAK-T)

symbols that have meaning only in mathematics (e.g., quadrilateral, sine, and vector space). The examples in Figures 9.11 and 9.12 show several ways to develop important math vocabulary knowledge.

Teachers need to spend time with math symbols, an important part of mathematics vocabulary. The presentation of symbols and formulas can be teacher-directed or a cooperative interactive investigative format can be used. Math applications depend not only mastering math vocabulary, but also on estimating the reasonableness of an answer.

Example: Note cards can be used to collect and practice the relevant terms in a particular area of math. Students are instructed to:

1. Put the term on the front of the card.
2. Put an example on the back.—or—
3. Write a definition on the back to help remember what the term means.

Fractions
(Student Responses on Reverse Side of Note Cards)

like fractions	$\dfrac{1}{4} + \dfrac{2}{4} = \dfrac{3}{4}$
lowest terms	$\dfrac{3}{6} = \dfrac{1}{2}$
quadrilateral	any closed 4-sided figure

FIGURE 9.11   Developing Math Vocabulary

The symbols used in algebra require thorough introduction and understanding in order to serve as a working foundation for higher level skills.

For example:

Parentheses tell us that everything inside is to be treated like one number. The parentheses below show some ways of working with parenthetical terms.

$$8 + (4 \times 3) = 8 + 12$$

$$(7 - 4) + 6 = 3 + 6$$

$$8 + (x + x) = 8 + 2x$$

$$(3y - y) + 4 = 2y + 4$$

$$(3x)^2 = 3x \cdot 3x \cdot 3x$$

FIGURE 9.12   Spending Time with Symbols: Special Math Vocabulary

IV. *Social and Behavioral Functioning* (adaptive functioning)

Specific characteristics/behavioral manifestations of the social problems of dyslexics (see Table 9.4) were identified through a comprehensive research study (i.e., over 100 studies) (see Grosser & Spafford, 2000; Spafford & Grosser, 1993). Many researchers have concluded that social-academic strategies need to be explicitly taught and modeled as students with dyslexia often lack what proficient learners use to be successful in school (e.g., Deshler & Schumaker, 1993; Gersten, 1998).

TABLE 9.4   **Social/Behavioral Correlates of Dyslexia and Positive Environmental Actions**

Areas of Impaired Social Adjustment in Some Students with Dyslexia/Learning Disabilities

Characteristic:	*Results in:*
More negative peer interactions	More peer rejection
Lower social standing in the eyes of significant adults	More teacher rejection
Misinterpretations of facial expressions, body language, voice inflections/tone	More social rejection/ignoring/neglect
Diminished self-concept	Increased feelings of rejection
Lowered self-esteem	A more negative attitude toward oneself
School avoidance because of repeated failures	Episodes of anxiety; severe cases = school phobia
Few to several episodes of depression	Fewer coping skills
Learned helplessness & diminished self-efficacy	An external locus of control (i.e., one doesn't control one's own destiny—others do)
Unawareness of developmentally appropriate social conventions	Socially inappropriate behavior

*Not all individuals with dyslexia have social skills deficits; those who experience social-behavioral difficulties do so on a continuum from mild to severe with severe instances requiring counseling services. Many individuals with LD display positive self-concepts with corresponding positive feelings of self-efficacy (Meltzer, Roditi, Houser, & Perlman, 1998; Winne, Woodlands, & Wong, 1982).

(Grosser & Spafford, 2000, p. 435)

Some Recommended Environmental Actions to Alleviate Some of the Social Problems Experienced by Students with Dyslexia and other Learning Disabilities

- Try to understand the needs of the student with dyslexia before beginning efforts at teaching social skills to that child, including sociocultural considerations.
- Teach social coping strategies (i.e., teach ways to participate constructively in various aspects of social activities; creative problem solving).
- Reduce unnecessary ambiguity in the classroom by setting up procedures for such "administrivia" as leaving the classroom and so on (Kline, 1999) because disruptive behaviors could interrupt classroom instruction/social acceptance.
- Teach academic stress management behaviors (Knapp & VandeCreek, 1994) (i.e., how to reduce test anxiety, how to overcome anxiety or fears about school [e.g., math anxiety, school phobia], time management, study skills strategies, the importance of having a sense of humor). Also teach being on time, respecting and being interested in what other students have to say, following directions, and completing assignments.
- Teach positive assertive actions and behaviors that foster independence and an internal locus of control.
- Teach other students in the classroom how to attend to and respond to students who need help (e.g., explaining directions, finding one's place in reading, etc.) when the teacher is unable to assist; peer tutoring can be very effective (Hall, 1997).
- Encourage families of children with dyslexia to reinforce and support their personal growth and independence.
- Increase the level of communication between the student with dyslexia and the student's family by giving them tips and communication strategies (i.e., set aside 15 minutes per day—at the same time if possible—for special time with that child so that the child can "expect" a special family conference time).
- Encourage parental involvement with outside institutions and activities such as churches (if appropriate), recreation, team sports, and the arts. These should be extended to the student with dyslexia; the cohesiveness of the family unit could thus be increased.
- Allow the student to participate in decision-making processes that impact his or her social well-being.
- Provide counseling services or recommendations for appropriate counseling services if needed.
- Provide consistent positive reinforcement every time an improved behavior is exhibited; this will yield more positive social adjustments. A running record could be maintained to show what incentives work in addition to other major social and behavioral performance dimensions.

*The **B**ehavior**A**l **S**trategy **I**ntervention **C**hecklist (BASIC)*   The **B**ehavior**A**l **S**trategy **I**ntervention **C**hecklist (BASIC) (Figure 9.13) was developed to be used as an assessment and instructional tool to measure the four major dimensions related to social and behavioral functioning important to school or academic settings and success therein: (1) student resolution or behaviors related to an internal locus of control, (2) family connectedness and support of school progress and behaviors, (3) academic accommodations to provide social supports and address learning style and needs, (4) opportunities to develop peer collaborations and leadership, and (5)—other, those special instances particular to an individual student (e.g., provision of medical interventions to address ADHD). The teacher, parent, or clinician can mark with a check mark to suggest an intervention or with an "X" to indicate

Code: ✔ = Suggest	**B**ehavior**Al** **S**trategy **I**ntervention	Name _____
✗ = Initiated (Circle Progress Indicator and Date)	**C**hecklist (BASIC)	Grade _____
Progress Indicators:	Reason(s) for BASIC Intervention(s)	School _____
E=Excellent F=Fair		Teacher _____
G=Good P=Poor	_____	Family Contact _____
		Family Phone _____

✔	**Student Resolution**	✗	✔	**Family Intervention**	✗	✔	**Educational**	✗	✔	**Peer Collaboration**	✗	✔	**Other**	✗
	Behaviors to Modify: _____ _____ _____ Progress Indicators E G F P			Weekly or monthly school contacts (phone/progress reports) to support school initiatives Progress Indicators E G F P			Academic Support (List) Progress Indicators E G F P			Peer Tutoring Progress Indicators E G F P			Medical (List) Progress Indicators E G F P	
	With School Counselor (Specify) Progress Indicators E G F P			Incentive Program (Specify) Progress Indicators E G F P			Extra Help Sessions (Specify) Progress Indicators E G F P			Peer Buddy Progress Indicators E G F P			Counseling (Specify) Progress Indicators E G F P	
	Behavior Modification System (specify—e.g., behavior contract, tier system of rewards or consequences): Progress Indicators E G F P			Consultation with a Specialist for _____ _____ _____ Progress Indicators E G F P			Academic Accommo-dations (check) ___ seating change ___ small group or 1:1 instruction ___ daily conferencing ___ Progress Indicators E G F P			Leadership Opportunities (specify) Progress Indicators E G F P			Other: Progress Indicators E G F P	
	Self-Evaluation or Reflection Strategies (specify—e.g., journal, behavior chart): Progress Indicators E G F P			Extracurricular Activities (specify—e.g., music lessons, sports) Progress Indicators E G F P			Incentive Program (specify) Progress Indicators E G F P			Clubs, School Organiza-tions (specify) Progress Indicators E G F P			Other: Progress Indicators E G F P	

FIGURE 9.13   BASIC

progress with a qualitative progress indicator circled (excellent, good, fair, poor). This reproducible can be replicated from year to year and used as a running record and placed in a student's cumulative record or portfolio.

V. Additional Recommendations (e.g., test accommodations)

Test Accommodation Guide in English and Spanish for Parents and Teachers The accommodation guide in English and Spanish can be used for students with learning disabilities and attached to an individualized education plan or IEP, 504 plan, or placed in the student's cumulative folder. This guide covers test setting, test preparation, student responses, learning tools, and other types of accommodations.

Parents or guardians should be notified when test accommodations are recommended and should sign their child's IEP (individual educational plan) indicating agreement to any specified accommodations. Other accommodations can be made by appropriate IEP team members based on an individual child's learning profile/style.

The Impact of Test Accommodations The impact of accommodations is especially critical when using exit exams for students with dyslexia and other learning disabilities. All states have test accommodations for students with dyslexia and other disabilities but the options vary widely from state to state (CEC, 2003). Frequently used test accommodations for students with dyslexia are shown in Table

(Can be attached to Individual Education Plan or IEP; 504 Plan; Student Cum Folder)

Students with Learning Disabilities: Checklist Accommodations for Standardized and Classroom Tests

✔	Test Setting	✔	Test Presentation	✔	Student Responses	✔	Learning Tools	✔	Other - Write In
	Requires small group test administration		Requires larger print test copy		Needs a word processor, typewriter or other similar device		Mathematics calculator		
	Requires one-to-one test administration		Requires enlargement or magnifying equipment		Need to use computer spell and grammar checks		Computer to record responses		
	Needs front seating or other specified room area		Sign language interpreter or/and scribe requested to communicate (e.g., directions)		Records answers on audiotape recorder		Dictionary or poor speller's dictionary or computer spell check		
	Administer test in carrel or enclosed or partitioned area		Requires amplification equipment		Needs to review scribe's recording of work if necessary		Internet for a specific purpose		
	Test in area of school or room separate from classroom		Test administrator scribes answers verbatim onto an answer sheet or booklet		Needs someone to monitor placement of test responses		Highlighters		
	Circle: Test in AM Test in PM Test in AM or PM		Placemarker is needed to follow text answer sections and computer recording sheets		Needs to have extra time and break times		Circle: graphic organizers, templates, checklists		
	Test in short periods with breaks as needed Circle: Snacks if available and approved		Teacher rereads and clarifies instructions		Needs someone to scribe answers		Rubrics to evaluate quality work		

Adapted from: ***Massachusetts Comprehensive Assessment System: Requirements for Participation of Students with Disabilities in MCAS*** (Spring 2004 Update). Malden, MA; Massachusetts Department of Education.

FIGURE 9.14 Accommodation Guide (English Version)

(Puede ser adjuntada al Plan de Educación Individual o IEP; Plan 504; Record Acumulativo del Estudiante)

Estudiantes con necesidades especiales: Acomodo para pruebas estandarizadas y pruebas en la sala de clases

✔	Lugar a tomar la prueba	✔	Presentación de la prueba	✔	Respuestas de estudiantes	✔	Instrumentos de aprendizaje	✔	Otro Escriba en espacios
	Requiere tomar la prueba en un grupo pequeño		Requiere copia de la prueba con letras agrandadas		Necesita procesador de palabras, maquinilla u otro equipo similar		calculador matemático		
	Requiere administración de prueba uno a uno		Requiere equipo para agrandar ó magnificar		Grabar respuestas en grabadora		Computadora para grabar respuestas		
	Necesita asiento en frente o en otra área especifica		Intérprete de lenguaje de señas o alguien que escriba		Necesita repasar notas si es necesario para mejorar gramática		Diccionario o programa para revisar gramática en la computadora		
	Administrar prueba en un área preparada		Requerido para comunicarse (e.j. direcciones) Requiere equipo de amplificación		Necesita alguien que observe que el estudiante escriba las respuestas en el lugar correspond-iente en un examen		Internet para un propósito específico		
	Administrar prueba en área fuera de el salón de clases		Requiere alguien que escriba las contestaciones en la hoja ó folleto para contestar		Necesita utilizar computadora y revisador de gramática		Resaltadores		
	Circula: prueba en AM prueba en PM prueba en AM ó PM		Marcador es necesario para seguir texto o contestar secciones de la prueba. Maestra necesita releer o clarificar instrucciones		Necesita tiempo adicional y tiempo de receso		Circula: organizadores gráficos, tablas, listas de cotejo		
	Prueba en periodos cortos con recesos necesarios. Circula: Merienda si está disponible y aprobada		Necesita equipo de amplificación		Necesita alguien que escriba las respuestas		Rúbricas par evaluar calidad de trabajo		

Adapted from: ***Massachusetts Comprehensive Assessment System: Requerimientos para participacion de estudiantes con impedimentos en MCAS*** (Revisado en primavera 2004). Malden, MA; Massachusetts Departamento de Educación.

FIGURE 9.15 Accommodation Guide (Spanish Version)

9.5. A sample listing of accommodations in the format that should be recorded on an IEP plan or Section 504 plan is shown in Table 9.6 for an elementary school-age student with dyslexia. In regard to high school graduation, it is especially relevant to consider the accommodations necessary to passing high-stakes graduation tests early on as it is commonly accepted in the research that students with disabilities drop out of high school in higher numbers than students without disabilities. Test and teaching accommodations can sometimes make the difference in succeeding on tests versus performing below expectations or even failing.

As an example, R, the fourth-grade student diagnosed as dyslexic on the Dyslexia Checklist shown on page 226 was noted to pass the grade 3 reading test on his state's high-stakes Comprehensive Assessment Test in Reading. Because of an early dyslexia diagnosis, R received both teaching and testing accommodations beginning in grade 2. These accommodations are considered standard and apply to many students with dyslexia and reading disabilities. In part, these accommodations prepared R to score in the top 50 percent of his district with proficiency (a passing score) in reading and proficiency in responding to the open response questions in writing. At home, there was additional support for many of the accommodations (i.e., provide wait "think" time; repeat and clarify directions as needed

---

TABLE 9.5 Frequently Used and Routine Test Accommodations for Students with Reading Disabilities or Dyslexia

---

Preplanning:
  (1) Ensure students who have reading disabilities or dyslexia receive accommodations by having them written into IEPs or individualized educational plans.
  (2) Inform all teachers who work with involved students and prepare the teachers through professional development, conferencing, and the like.
  (3) Be certain that students and parents understand the reason/importance of testing.
  (4) Provide suggestions to parents beforehand in the language of the home to include getting a good night's rest, eating a substantive breakfast on the day(s) of testing, and reviewing content/strategies to be covered on tests.
  (5) Provide incentives for students who put forth their best efforts—let them know beforehand what incentives they can work toward.

Accommodations:
  (1) Ensure the test **administrator is** someone **familiar to the student;** ideally, someone the student is comfortable with.
  (2) Test at a **time of day** that considers the individual needs of the child.
  (3) Test in **1:1** or **small group** situations.
  (4) Test in an **alternative location** to the classroom so that frequent breaks and time extensions can be given if needed; if in classroom, testing could be done in a partitioned area, the student could wear noise buffers, or the testing could be done in another specified area of the room (e.g., the student could sit in the front seat).
  (5) **Verbally clarify or restate test instructions** or directions.
  (6) If permissible/necessary, **read the test** to the student (when not measuring reading ability per se).
  (7) If permissible/necessary, have answers dictated to a **scribe** where the scribe doesn't change responses in any way.
  (8) If permissible/necessary, use **assistive technology** to record answers.
  (9) Provide **various assists** if approved in your school district—examples: placemarkers, highlighters, scrap paper, graphic organizers, dictionaries, computer technology, amplification devices, large-print editions of the test, or a Braille edition of the test.
 (10) **Monitor** the student during test taking to ensure **correct placement of responses** on test papers or booklets.

TABLE 9.6   Teaching and Testing Accommodations Example (for an elementary school-age student with dyslexia)

Teaching Accommodations:
- Ensure preferential seating.
- Use examples following modeling whenever possible.
- Provide extra time for processing of verbal information.
- Connect verbally presented information with visuals when possible.
- Repeat and rephrase directions and information as needed.
- Develop lesson vocabulary previews.
- Explicitly teach organizational strategies with charts, timelines, and graphic organizers.
- Include opportunities for shared readings, peer partnering, peer tutoring.
- Provide frequent praise and encouragement for accomplishments.

General Testing Accommodations:
- Administer district, school, and classroom tests in small group settings with frequent breaks.
- Provide extra time to complete tests.
- Clarify test directions and procedures until full understanding is achieved.
- Read aloud portions of tests permitted under test guidelines/policies.
- Monitor use of a placemarker during all phases of testing.
- Distribute a predrawn graphic organizer for written responses.

and so on) as R's mother was completely familiar with her son's IEP. An information conference or session for families to explain and elaborate upon teaching and testing accommodations extends the work of the school to the home and strengthens the home-school connection.

Relevant Assessment Considerations for Adults with Dyslexia

  I. Previous History (with interviews)
  II. Resiliency (QUalitative Analysis of Resilient Traits [QUART, Spafford & Grosser, 2005])
  III. Reading and writing evaluations to include the following subskills using one or more of many scientifically based (valid and reliable measures) literacy assessments available to educators, psychologists, and clinicians:
- Phonic decoding (word analysis skills)
- Fluency factors: PACE (Phrasing, Accuracy, and efficiency (reading rate) in word recognition, Comprehension, Expressiveness)
- Spelling (isolated and applied)
- Oral language comprehension
- Written expression

  IV. Cognitive Assessment (a comprehensive profile of cognitive abilities, including verbal and nonverbal processing and performance skills); i.e., IQ assessment
    A. Reading and writing evaluations
    B. Academic achievement (performance assessments)
  V. Social and Behavioral Functioning (adaptive functioning)
  VI. Test Accommodations and Report Formats

    The current authors have added:

  VII. Portfolio Assessment: Showcasing Academic Accomplishments
  VIII. Surveying Reading Interests

The usefulness of a comprehensive assessment would be the extent to which it can inform instructional practice and better the academic and life circumstances for the individual with dyslexia. The addition of reading preference, or "likes," is a critical component to assessments for older dyslexics. The National Reading Report Card of 1999 as cited by Campbell, Hombo, and Mazzeo (1999) shows 45.7 percent of fourth-grade students reading for pleasure every day with the percentage dropping to 24.4 percent for twelfth-grade students. The case study on pages 258–261 highlights observed strengths and problem areas for "typical" resilient dyslexic adults. Characteristics of resiliency for successful adult dyslexics will first be presented.

Characteristics of Resilient Adults

Typically, resilient adults with dyslexia demonstrate similar strengths:

- Have strong resilient personalities: the ability to quickly bounce back or recover from stressors, frustrations, and failures due to a personal resolve to persevere in spite of academic/social obstacles.
- Can read proficiently as adults with prior intensive literacy support.
- Experience successes with most aspects of reading fluency especially <u>P</u>hrasing, <u>A</u>ccuracy (only a few oral reading miscues), <u>C</u>omprehension and <u>E</u>xpressiveness in reading.
- Have particular talents (e.g., art and design) in the visuospatial field that involve such traits as multidimensional thinking, originality, awareness of patterns, and heightened perception, right-hemispheric types of functioning.
- Can appropriately articulate knowledge of a particular topic or subject.
- Can effectively monitor their own thinking (metacognition) and comprehension of text (metacomprehension).
- Are socially perceptive (evaluate social situations accurately and determines appropriate actions based on those perceptions) with good self-concepts and self-esteems.
- Can advocate for self and others (work in an informed manner to obtain better academic or social opportunities or services for self and others).

Typically, resilient adults with dyslexia still experience difficulties, including:

- Issues with some aspects of reading fluency, especially depressed reading rates (sometimes one-half) relative to peers, meaning "less" (quantity, not quality) material can be read.
- Relying on fewer reading strategies than proficient readers to problem solve unknown words.
- Less motivation to pick up a book for enjoyment or for other reasons because of persistent reading difficulties (e.g., reading rate). Less reading results in fewer vocabulary words acquired.
- Free writing problems, including spelling difficulties because "visuals" are not present to cue the writer in regard to organization, form, and word formation.
- Confidence in abilities as a learner because of continued academic difficulties (e.g., reduced reading rates, spelling and writing problems).
- Problematic or nonfunctional organization and study skills.
- Difficulties/reluctance in testing (may need accommodations to include extended time limits and word processors to record written responses).
- Difficulties emanating from ADD/ADHD (for 25% of dyslexics) to include problems with sustained, focused attention on a task or academics (i.e., inattentiveness and lack of follow-through).

Case Study of a Typical Resilient Young Adult with Dyslexia   C., Jr. is a 15-year-old student with severe dyslexia who was diagnosed at an early age. He currently attends the public schools as a ninth-grade student. His most current grades are: Reading, A; English, B; Math, D; Science, A; Geography, B; Computers, B; and Band, A. Effort grades are excellent. C., Jr. plays in the high school band and considers reading to be a hobby. He likes classical music and history books and biographies. He also enjoys building ships and airplanes.

Typically, resilient adults with dyslexia demonstrate similar strengths and have strong resilient personalities, with the ability to quickly bounce back or recover from stressors, frustrations, and failures due to a personal resolve to persevere in spite of academic/social obstacles.

Assessment: QUalitative Analysis of Resilient Traits (QUART)
Individual Protective Factors
Noted strengths for C., Jr.: persistence (stick-to-it-ness); self-efficacy (beliefs in one's ability to plan and complete actions to reach a goal or desired levels of performance); positive self-esteem (positive evaluation of oneself in regard to personal worth, life and school successes); optimistic (anticipates the best, hopeful); overall positive temperament (characteristic "frame of mind" is positive).

QUART Coping Style
Noted strengths: **Self-starter** (takes the initiative when needed); **has an internal locus of control** (assumes much responsibility for learning or achievement and attributes many successes to motivation, effort, and resourcefulness); **self-reflective** (able to plan, self-monitor, and evaluate his own thinking, learning, comprehension, and social actions); **socially perceptive** (evaluates social situations accurately and determines appropriate actions based on those perceptions); **good reasoning ability** (able to make inferences, draw conclusions, and problem-solve appropriate to age or developmental level); **advocates for self** (works in an informed manner to obtain better academic or social opportunities or services), and **seeks critical support systems as needed** (support from peers, teachers, family, other community members).

Relative weakness: Confidence in abilities as a learner due to continued academic difficulties (i.e., math, spelling, and writing problems). C., Jr. needs to work on self-confidence. This is in part due to problems in the area of mathematics—C., Jr. is able to articulate that he has substantial difficulties in this area with the need for continued support—he will seek extra help at school when needed.

Reading Ability
Typically, resilient adults with dyslexia can read proficiently as adults with prior intensive literacy support.

Assessments
Basic Reading Inventory; Developmental Reading Assessment; Informal reading materials
C., Jr.'s Word Recognition (in isolation) = proficient at grade level (ninth grade)

	Sight	*Analysis*
Grade 5	85%	
Grade 6	90%	
Grade 7		80%
Grade 8		65%
Grade 9		70%
Grade 10		70%

Comprehension (Basic Reading Inventory)
Grade 8 (oral reading) = 80% comprehension with 97% word recognition; 90 words per minute
Grade 9 (silent reading) = 100% comprehension
Grade 10 (silent reading) = 80% comprehension

Independent Reading Level: word recognition 95 to 99% (running text) with > 95% comprehension = estimated to be grade 8

Instructional Reading Level: word recognition 90 to 95% (running text) with 75–80% comprehension (estimated to be grade 10)

Developmental Reading Assessment

Achieved	= grade 8 placement (highest placement on test)
Word recognition	= 98%
Reading rate	= 92.6 wpm (slow for grade); expected reading rate for grade 9 students = 200 to 210 wpm
Miscues	= generally consisted of words that were visually similar. Advanced structural analysis and phonetic analysis skills were evident.

Typically, resilient adults with dyslexia

- *have particular talents (e.g., art and design) in the visuospatial field that involve such traits as multidimensional thinking, originality, awareness of patterns, and heightened perception, right-hemispheric types of functioning.*

Strengths: C., Jr. can construct intricately designed models of planes and ships and pursues a hobby in this area.

Typically, resilient adults with dyslexia

- *can appropriately articulate knowledge of a particular topic or subject.*

Strengths: C., Jr. is able to effectively communicate with age and developmentally appropriate vocabulary his knowledge of a subject or topic. He is willing to take risks (i.e., spell words the way they sound when without access to a dictionary) in communicating this knowledge in writing.

Typically, resilient adults with dyslexia

- *effectively monitor their own thinking (metacognition) and comprehension of text (metacomprehension).*

Strengths: (1) C., Jr. made several **thoughtful written predictions and questions** directly related to a text reading beforehand [e.g., "What caus an island to forme? (What causes an island to be formed?)" "What are the names of the sections of the earth?" "How long it will take for an island to get life?" "The reson for sientic to wont to study the beerth of an ilend? (The reason for scientists to want to study the birth of an island).

(2) **Ability to summarize or paraphrase**—example, "What do you think is the most significant thing about Surtsey? Tell why." "I think that the most significant thing is that it gives sientis a chans to study a island land mass that was just formed. It coud give them an idea as how the contonents evolved log a go (I think that the most significant thing is that it gives scientists a chance to study an island land mass that was just formed. It could give them an idea as how the continents evolved long ago)."

Fluency Assessment (considering PACE factors while administering Basic Reading Inventory and Developmental Reading Assessment)

C., Jr.:

<u>P</u>hrasing = reads in short and long phrases with appropriate attention to punctuation.

<u>A</u>ccuracy (no more than 5% miscues in reading for text at grade levels 8 through 10) and *Reading Rate in Word Recognition* (approximately 90 words per minute, which is about half of the expected reading rate for a student in grade 9; students in grade 9 are expected to read 200 to 210 words per minute).

<u>C</u>omprehension = good for text at his independent and instructional reading levels. *Metacomprehension Awareness*—C., Jr. had checked that he had used the comprehension strategies of background knowledge, (2) determining importance, (3) inferring, and (4) visualizing. However, C., Jr. also used (5) questioning and (6) making connections to prior knowledge and text without realizing he used these strategies.

<u>E</u>xpressiveness in reading = good; appropriate to the text reading.

C., Jr. likes to read, reads often, and will read history and other books for enjoyment.

Writing Ability

Typically, resilient adults with dyslexia . . .

can experience free writing problems to include spelling difficulties because "visuals" are not present to cue the writer in regard to organization, form, and word formation.

Writing Level = estimated to be more than three years behind grade level based on open response and long composition writing. C., Jr.'s learning disability is most evident in his spelling and writing abilities (and reading rate).

Idea and Topic Development

Regarding writing ability, C., Jr.:

- Shows **some organization.**
- Uses **a few transitions** or transition words.
- Shows **some understanding of the topic,** but there needs to be more work on topic development (writing an introductory paragraph with supporting details; developing subsequent paragraphs with related topic sentences; using a concluding paragraph to summarize the writing).
- Includes **many specific details** or support for the topic.

Language Conventions

Regarding writing ability, C., Jr.:

- Uses **sentence grammar, capital letters, and punctuation marks** correctly some of the time.
- Spells many high frequency monosyllabic words correctly but misspells multisyllabic words (e.g., "observashons" for "observations" and some sight words (e.g., "wher" for "where" "whay" for "way")) using phonetic approximations.
- Attempts to use **much variety in vocabulary words** (e.g., "I think the morning was cool and crisp the pine trees were still frosted" and "when I wolk for a mille to get to the flag. And the map that I draw is topographe. The closer the lines are the steeper it is. The distenc between each line is twonty feet." C., Jr. drew a topographic map to illustrate his point).
- Writing pieces need **editing** and **some reorganization** before considered published works.

Organization and Study Skills

C., Jr. has developed excellent study habits—he is a self-starter and will follow through with assignments. His report card grades reflect this with high marks for motivation and effort. Regarding long-range planning: When given an assignment requiring extensive writing (tedious work for C., Jr.), C., Jr. paces himself within the timeframe allowed, putting forth his best efforts from beginning to end. He is able to establish learning goals to meet his career goal, which he has already established.

Summer Recommendations

■ Continue to build C., Jr.'s confidence in himself as a reader and an author. He is highly intelligent, motivated to learn, and shows much resiliency in school and social endeavors. His reading proficiency is age and developmentally appropriate (except for reading rate), a tribute to consistent engagement in reading and much hard work and effort by C., Jr. C., Jr. has also been fortunate in that he has had a strong network of academic and social support. With consistent literacy support in reading and writing to graduation, a social-academic network of support, and continued development of individual **resiliency,** C., Jr. will continue to lead a very successful and fulfilling life.

■ Summer writing and reading program to maintain current literacy levels and to further writing development. Writing proficiency is more than three years behind grade level due to C., Jr.'s learning disability. C., Jr. has expressed an interest and willingness to commit to such a program. His family will be able to seek a tutor who will individualize a program for C., Jr. A two-tier summer literacy program is recommended.

    ■ *Journal writing:* Guided journal writing is recommended following the independent reading of district recommended grade 10 books for summer programs. Provide question frames to focus C., Jr.'s responses to the literature readings. This will have the effect of helping C., Jr. to further develop his own interpretations of stories (reader-based interactive dialogue with text). The tutor could pose three general questions for each journal entry: (1) What do you observe? (2) What do you question? and (3) What do you feel? Provide a question frame or series of questions under each as related to each story structure. Example, if reading a biography, under (1), What kind of person was . . . ? Can you relate to this character? how? What was . . .'s contribution to humanity? Provide examples from the biography.

    ■ *Technology and writing:* Provide C., Jr. with keyboard training, word processing, and the writing process, all in combination to increase the quantity and quality of his writings. Currently, C., Jr. does not word-process compositions. He needs to see the advantages of using word processing such as the neatness and professional presentation word processing can provide.

Recommendations for Grade 10

■ Writing rubrics could be used as guides during open response and long composition writing activities throughout the school year. C., Jr. could access these to self-assess the quality of a writing piece before submission.

■ A grade 10 (C., Jr.'s entering grade) *English Language Arts Guide* (Composition and Language and Literature) from prior state testing could be used as a teaching tool during the school year. C., Jr. actually could read the passages and respond to the questions. He would encounter several reading genres with attention to grade 10 English Language Arts learning standards. Writing areas needing further work could be identified relative to these grade 10 ELA standards.

■ Leisure type readings should be encouraged that relate to C., Jr.'s hobbies—reading "just for fun" or to learn something of interest.

Using Assessments to Create Education "Action" Plans: The IEP (Individualized Education Plan) Process*   Students who are moderately to severely dyslexic and who require services from specialists in addition to or in place of the regular classroom teacher must have an Individualized Education Program (IEP) in the United States (also for some students with mild disabilities). IEPs are individually designed,

---

*Source for IEP information: United States Department of Education (July 2000). *My child's special needs: A guide to the individualized education program.* From the Regulations: Statement of Transition Service Needs—34 CFR §300.347(b)(1) Washington DC: Office of Special Education and Rehabilitative Services, U.S. Department of Education. http://www.ed.gov/parents/needs/speced/iepguide/index.html

and the process and document itself provide an opportunity for evaluators, teachers, parents, school staff, related services personnel, and students (depending on age-appropriateness) to work together to improve educational outcomes for children with disabilities. The goal of developing proficiency in academics is implicit during the development of the IEP. The U.S. Department of Education (USDOE, 2000) has identified ten steps to guide educators in the development of a child's IEP.

Developing Individualized Education Plans (IEPs) for Students with Dyslexia or other Disabilities

Step 1. Identifying children who possibly require special education and related services.

Each state must locate, identify, and evaluate all children with disabilities in the state who may need special education and related services. Parents are notified that an evaluation needs to take place and parents or guardians must give their consent before the evaluation commences. School professionals may initiate a process to have a child evaluated to determine the presence of a disability. Typically, schools have prereferral teams that meet to discuss implementing regular classroom strategies or interventions before the referral is actually made. This is especially helpful for students who are mildly dyslexic because the additional support from the regular classroom teacher may be enough to eliminate the need for additional special services. Evaluations need to be completed within a reasonable time after the parent gives consent—the reality is typically a wait of a month or more, because comprehensive evaluations and report writing limits the number of students who can be tested at one time. The evaluation of C., Jr. in this chapter, as an example, required four hours of testing and additional followup. The report writing and resources research involved several more hours of time.

Step 2. Student is evaluated.

The evaluation must assess the child in all areas related to the student's suspected disability. The evaluation results are used to decide eligibility for special education and related services and to make decisions about appropriate educational program planning for the student. Parents may disagree with an evaluation, and they have the right to request, at the school system's expense, an Independent Educational Evaluation (IEE).

Step 3. Presence of a learning disability or disability is confirmed or not confirmed.

School system and other professionals and parents/guardians (i.e., IEP team) meet to discuss the child's evaluation results. Together, the team decides if the student is a "child with a disability," as defined by IDEA. Parents may request a meeting to discuss or challenge the eligibility decision.

Step 4. Eligibility for special services is determined.

When a student is determined to be a "child with a disability," as defined by IDEA, he or she **is** eligible for special education and related services. The IEP team must meet to write an IEP for the child within 30 calendar days after the team met. If a student is not eligible for special education services under IDEA, he or she may be eligible for 504 services. Schools should have section 504 of the U.S. Rehabilitation Act contacts.

Step 5. Individual Education Plan (IEP) meeting is scheduled.

The school system schedules and conducts the IEP meeting. School staff must:

- Contact the participants, including the parents/guardians.
- Notify parents well in advance to ensure they had an opportunity to attend.
- Schedule a mutually agreeable meeting time.

- Inform the parents of the meeting purpose, who will be attending, and the time and location of the meeting.
- Inform the parents that they may invite people to the IEP meeting who have knowledge or special expertise about the child.
- As a courtesy, provide written information in the language of the home if possible.

Step 6. IEP meeting is convened and the IEP is developed.

Typically, a school facilitator coordinates the meeting specifics as well as the writing of the IEP. The team meets and discusses the student's learning style and needs and cooperatively writes the student's IEP. When appropriate, students are invited to be part of the team. In all instances, the parent/guardian should be part of placement decision meetings.

The student begins to receive services after informed parental consent is obtained and in a timely manner following the IEP writing meeting.

Parents may not agree with the IEP and placement. It is in the best interests of the student for parents/guardians to have a discussion of concerns with other members of the IEP team. The team will work with the parents/guardian to try and work out a mutually agreeable education action plan.

Step 7. Implementation of services.

The school ensures the IEP is followed as written. Parents receive a copy of the IEP. Each of the child's teachers and service providers must have access to the IEP and be aware of his or her specific responsibilities for implementing the IEP. This necessarily involves accommodations, modifications, and other supports consistent with the IEP. Typically, test accommodations are listed that are consistent with accommodations allowed during state high-stakes testing.

Step 8. Progress is reported to parents.

The child's progress toward the annual goals is evaluated according to provisions in the IEP. His or her parents are regularly notified and are informed regarding whether progress is sufficient for the child to achieve the goals by the end of the year. Progress reports must be given to parents at least as often as parents with nondisabled children.

Step 9. IEP is periodically reviewed: minimum, yearly.

The student's IEP is reviewed by the IEP team at least once a year, or more often if needed. Parents or teachers may also request a review. The IEP may be revised if necessary but only if parents/guardians are included in the IEP meeting where anticipated changes will be recommended. Parents can voice suggestions for changes, agree or disagree with the IEP goals, and agree or disagree with the placement. If parents do not agree with the IEP and placement, they may discuss their concerns with other members of the IEP team to try and reach agreement. There are several options available to parents and teachers should IEP agreement not be in place—these include additional testing and an independent evaluation.

Step 10. Three-year reevaluations.

The student with an IEP must be reevaluated at least every three years or more often if needed. The purpose of the reevaluation is to find out if the student continues to be a "student with a disability," with special educational needs as defined by IDEA. The student must be reevaluated more often if conditions present themselves or if the child's parent/guardian or teacher requests a new evaluation.

What Does the IEP Include?   IEPs are required to include current performance levels, annual goals, and an educational program that is designed to meet the student's learning style and needs. Addendums can be written to accommodate changes before major reevaluations. Major IEP components are as follows:

- **Current performance levels.** The IEP must state how the child is currently performing in school (known as present levels of educational performance) relative to peers. This information usually originates from evaluation results relying on classroom tests and assignments, individual tests (formal and informal) administered to decide eligibility for services or to consider during a reevaluation, and observations made by parents, teachers, related service providers, and other school staff. There must be a statement about "current performance" and how the child's disability impacts his or her involvement and progress in the general curriculum.

- **Annual goals.** These are academically related or social/behavior goals that the student can be expected to accomplish within a year. Short-term objectives or benchmarks are written for each goal. The goals stated must be measurable so that it is possible to determine whether the student has achieved the stated goals.

- **Special education and related services.** The IEP must list special education and related services the student will receive. This includes supplementary aids and services that the child needs to succeed in the school setting. Modifications (changes) to the program must be listed as well as supports for school personnel (e.g., training or professional development that will support provision of services).

- **Participation with children without learning disabilities.** The IEP must explain the extent to which (if any) the learning disabled student will ___not___ participate with nondisabled students in the regular class and other school activities.

- **Participation in state- and districtwide tests.** The IEP must state what modifications in the administration of regular classroom and district/national tests the child will need. These should be consistent across all testing. If a test is not appropriate for the child, the IEP must state why a particular test is not appropriate and how the child will be tested instead (e.g., a graduation requirement may be a state exam; for a severely disabled student, an alternate assessment may be more appropriate such as the presentation to a committee of teachers of an academic portfolio that is assessed with specific criteria or benchmarks).

- **Dates and places.** The IEP must state when services will begin, how often and where they will be provided, and how long they will last. This is subject to change based on the child's learning needs and addendums can be written before major reevaluations.

- **Transition service needs.** Beginning at age 14 (or younger, if determined to be appropriate), the IEP must address (within the various, applicable parts of the IEP) the courses the student needs to take to reach his or her post-school goals. A statement of transition services needs to be included in each of the student's subsequent IEPs.

- **Needed transition services.** Beginning when the child is age 16 (or younger, if determined to be appropriate), the IEP must state what transition services are needed to help the child prepare for high school graduation and beyond.

- **Measuring progress.** The IEP must state how student progress will be measured and how parents or guardians will be informed of that progress (e.g., progress reports).

There are sometimes situations that necessitate recommendations for special school placements. The IEP reflects such recommendations.

Special Schools for Individuals with Dyslexia   Sometimes individuals with dyslexia may benefit from participation in schools for students with dyslexia both at the K–12 levels and at the post-secondary level. Such programs can provide an education that is designed specifically to meet the needs of students with dyslexia. Special schools can provide: (1) one-to-one tutorial assistance daily; (2) small classes; (3) trained faculty members, including the tutors in the education of students with dyslexia; (4) the use of a diagnostic approach that follows the student from the admissions process to post-secondary placements; (5) the teaching of reading/language strategies and study skills within an integrated curriculum; (6) a liberal arts curriculum that involves the integration of various subjects into a program that would allow the student with dyslexia to pursue a college career; and (7) classes, special lectures, meetings with advisors, and interactions with other students with dyslexia. Social as well as academic activities round out an entire program. Counseling services are available to address the social problems and stresses that many times characterize the student with dyslexia. Special schools for dyslexics require tuition payments that generally equate to an average college tuition, regardless of level. However, many of the professional services available in private schools and clinics are also available in public schools.

Reporting Formats   A grade-level literacy running record can be used for grades 1 through 12 with major reading and writing benchmarks noted: sight-word recognition, phonic/word analysis/spelling proficiency, reading level and open response writing, and long composition writing proficiency. Grade 12 reporting also needs to include graduation information. Individual schools would decide on the particular tests or benchmarks to use. This reporting format condenses multipage assessments to a two-page handout that can follow the student throughout his or her school career in a cumulative record folder or literacy folder. A grade-level literacy running record can also be used for IEP or other team meetings. The teacher or specialist would record proficiency levels in reading and writing and then photocopy the pages needed for the meeting. With literacy information from previous grades, educators are able to visually chart progress from year to year using consistent benchmarks.

"The Proficiency Assessment for School Language (e.g., English) for Second Language Learners" (e.g., Spanish is the home language) (see Figure 9.16) is a suggested type of assessment reporting format based on the Massachusetts "Requirements for the Participation of Students with Limited English Proficiency—Mandated Assessments—2004." For second-language learners who are dyslexic or learning disabled, additional literacy information is needed for instructional planning (e.g., speaking proficiency, more formal evaluation of listening comprehension).

VI. *Portfolio Assessment: Showcasing Academic Accomplishments*

According to Spafford, Pesce, and Grosser (1998), portfolios are a type of authentic assessment and are typically included in comprehensive assessments (see Figures 9.17, 9.18, and 9.19). This is the perfect opportunity for teachers and students to showcase academic and personal accomplishments (e.g., a proficiency in art—include artwork or pictures of artwork). Authentic assessments are assessments "of student learning based on a comparison to practical and real-world situations." Outcomes and achievements are measured in relation to the style or way a student learns. Portfolios can be

> used to reveal progress in school as well as reflect student growth and development in a number of areas (e.g., type of participation in the school community, content-area progress, proficiency in written language skills . . . artistic and musical talent). Portfolio projects can encourage students to evaluate their own subject-area reading/knowledge . . . in many instances teachers periodically share . . . portfolios with parents in the course of the school year so as to justify grades/performance evaluations and to share/demonstrate growth and development in a number of areas. (pp. 24, 214)

Proficiency Assessment for School Language (e.g., English) for Second Language Learners (e.g., Spanish is home language)
Sample Reporting Format

Name of Student: _____ Dates of Testing: _____

Student Identification Number: _____ School _____ District Address _____

Literacy Evaluation (speaking, listening, reading, writing)

Massachusetts English Language Assessment-Oral (MELA-O)		Language Assessment Scales Reading/Writing (LAS R/W)										
		Reading (R) Subscore				Reading Total (45)	Writing (W) Subscore		Writing Total (30)	*R/W Results Summary		
Speaking (5)	Listening (5)	Voc (10)	Fluency (10)	Inf (10)	Mec (15)		F.S. (15)	W.H. (15)		R/W Total (75)	R/W Level BL, SL, P	Tested Status

Interpretive Information for School Language Proficiency Tests

LAS R/W Results (Reading & Writing) Source: **Language Assessment Scales for Reading and Writing** published by CTB/McGraw-Hill.

Voc: the student's ability to match illustrations to words.

Fluency: overall language fluency and the ability to infer a missing word based on a knowledge of language usage and semantics.

Inf: the ability to identify information.

Mec: Mechanics and Usage evaluates skills in language mechanics (capitalization and punctuation) and grammar usage.

F.S.: Finishing Sentences measures at the student's ability to complete a sentence correctly.

W.H.: What's Happening has prompts to elicit a written sentence.

MELA-O (Listening and Speaking) Source: **Massachusetts English Language Assessment-Oral** is a classroom assessment instrument developed by the Department of Education in collaboration with the Center for Applied Linguistics at George Washington University in 1992.

Speaking: Oral grammar, pronunciation, vocabulary and fluency. Student performance is evaluated on a scale of 0-5.

Listening: Listening comprehension. Student performance is evaluated on a scale of 0-5.

Highest Possible Score
Highest possible score shown in parentheses for various subscores.

Other Possible Reporting Formats for "School Language" Proficiency Levels (e.g., English)
Beginning
Early Intermediate
Intermediate
Transitioning

R/W Level
I. No or Beginning Level of Language Proficiency
II. Some Language Proficiency
III. Proficient in Reading and Writing

TEACHING CONSIDERATIONS
- Sheltered English Strategies
- Graphic Organizers
- Manipulatives / Visual Aids
- English Language Learning Dictionaries
- Vocabulary Rings
- Word Walls

Source: **Requirements for the Participation of Students with Limited English Proficiency in State - Mandated Assessments** (2/25/04). Massachusetts Department of Education (Massachusetts Comprehensive Assessment System).

FIGURE 9.16 Proficiency Assessment for School Language (e.g., English) for Second-Language Learners

DIAGNOSTIC PORTFOLIOS

Possible Inclusions—Using Portfolios as Diagnostic Tools:

Reading Interviews

Reading Attitude Inventory

Miscue Analysis, or

Running Records

Spelling Analysis

Check-off Lists

Holistic and Analytical Scoring of Writing

Anecdotal Records Kept by Teacher on Labels

Journal Entry Comparisons

Writing Interviews

Parent-Teacher-Student Assessment of Student as Learner

Teacher Assessment of Writing Conference

Assessment of Use of Time during Writing Workshops

Assessment of Student Performance during Writing Workshop

Silent Reading and Retelling Guide Assessment

Child as a Reader/Writer Survey: Parent, Teacher, Child

FIGURE 9.17   Portfolios Collections—Diagnostic and Reflective

Diagnostic Portfolios   Tierney, Carter, and Desai (1991) believe that portfolios are a more "rich source of information about a student's literacy achievement, progress, and ongoing development than other, more formal sources" (p. 51). These authors have found that the use of portfolios has guided many *teachers and children* into considerable awareness of their own goals, growth, and accomplishments. Additionally, reports from teachers and administrators after portfolio use

Reader self-analysis of running records

Questionnaire of metacognitive strategy use

Assess best writing piece and why

Assess writing piece that demonstrates the most growth

Analyzing book logs:

Most challenging book, why/how did you handle the reading

Easiest book to read and why

The book you enjoyed the most and why

Writing that illustrates critical thinking about reading:

Notes from individual reading and writing conferences

Writings that are evident of development of style:

Organization
Voice
Sense of audience
Choice of words
Clarity

Writing that shows growth in language conventions:

Growing ability in self-correction
Growing ability in use of punctuation
Growing ability in use of correct spelling
Growing ability in use of proper grammar
Growing ability in appropriate form
Growing ability in legibility

Samples in which ideas are modified from first draft to final product:

Unedited first draft
Revised first draft, and subsequent drafts
Edited final draft
Final copy

Evidence of effort:

Improvement noted on pieces
Completed assignments
Personal involvement noted

Self-evaluations

Source: Courtney (1995).

FIGURE 9.18   Using Portfolios as Self-Reflection Instruments

Students unacquainted with the portfolio process may require considerable direction and support in developing their portfolios into authentic, personalized vehicles of growth. Sentence starters, reflective guides, or notecard comments can be modeled and developed by direct instruction.

Reflecting

1. Explain what your entry is: _____
   _____
   _____

2. I chose this entry because _____
   _____
   _____

3. The best part of doing this project was _____
   _____
   _____

4. This entry is an example of my growth because _____
   _____
   _____

5. When I think back on earlier work like this, I realize _____
   _____
   _____

6. Next time I do a similar project, I _____
   _____

FIGURE 9.19   Portfolios—"A Format for Reflection"

point to a clearer understanding of where each child is at (with an emphasis on strengths). Tierney and his associates (1991) find that portfolio evaluation procedures generally rely on a collaboration between teachers and administrators, teachers and students, and students and peers, which enhance ongoing processes involved in self-evaluation and growth.

Value of Using Portfolio Assessments at Annual IEP Meetings   Turnbull, Turnbull, Shank, and Leal (1995) discuss the value using portfolio assessments at annual IEP meetings to show progress in literacy. As an example, pieces of writing can be placed in the portfolio at the beginning of the year and at the end of the year to show progress based on predetermined benchmarks or proficiency targets. The writing rubrics provided in this chapter provide ideas and language convention benchmarks across grade levels. A rubric could be attached to each writing piece. The student may want to include graphic organizers, drafts, and editing to show the writing process he or she used to complete written work. Some schools allow portfolio projects as alternative assessments to standardized tests for exit criteria from high school if the student is judged to have disabilities so severe that standard formalized testing cannot best determine the student's proficiency levels in academics. Schools would record the name or type of testing used to determine proficiency levels.

VII. Professional Development: School Accountability and Students' Literacy Successes

The school accountability movement stresses the importance of using research and other data to improve delivery of instruction with systemic change requiring the understanding that teachers continually reflect on instructional practices and ways to effect change as situations present themselves. In addition, the importance of professional exchanges and the sharing of research, experiences, and reflections among teachers will necessarily involve professional development participation (Spafford, 2002/2003). An important venue for such interchange is conferences devoted in some part to reading and literacy instruction and learning how best to meet the needs of all learners. State-level reading conferences such as the Massachusetts Reading Association (MRA) annual conference provide many options to assist "in planning comprehensive and balanced literacy programs to help meet the needs of our diverse populations of learners" (Spafford, 2003).

IEPs and Professional Development   The U.S. Department of Education (see USDOE, 2000), through legislative mandates and the IEP process, encourages schools and districts to engage in professional development efforts to ensure the delivery of appropriate services to students with learning disabilities and other disabilities. The No Child Left Behind Act of 2001 "includes a call for more professional development in literacy for teachers." Professional development efforts can "give all of us new insights into literacy development, extend our knowledge of recent research in reading and writing, deepen our understandings of the cultural contexts of learning, and broaden our conceptualization of instruction informed by authentic assessment" (Harris-Sharples, 2002, p. 2). A student's IEP may list supports for school personnel related to professional development that will support provision of services for students with dyslexia or other learning disabilities/disabilities.

   If systemic school reform is truly a shared and owned process, it will emphasize inclusion, knowledge building, and a common purpose or vision. In this paradigm, schools are constantly changing and improving to meet the needs of their students. The change that schools look for in their students—improved literacy in the broadest sense—is reflected by parallel changes in teachers and in school leadership. The necessary knowledge building that is part of change requires both content and process. Professional development efforts therefore build . . .

1. A critical mass of individuals with the knowledge and disposition to effect change.
2. A strong professional ethos by teachers.
3. Program coherence.
4. An adequate amount of appropriate resources.
5. Effective and shared leadership in the learning community. (Roberts, 2004)

   Marr (2004) points out that with continually evolving federal and state mandates and standards across the curriculum, teachers must continually update their knowledge and adapt teaching styles with the understanding that "every teacher is a reading teacher." Colwell, Aucoin, Berg, and Steckel (2002/2003) indicate that professional development can help to accomplish this, and, as a "multifaceted endeavor," needs to receive the full commitment of both administrators and staff. According to these researchers, professional development needs to be "shared, ongoing, and supported in a number of ways." In a Vermont study, commissioned by the State of Vermont (cited by Colwell, Aucoin, Berg & Steckel, 2002/2003), Marjorie J. Lipson (2002) found that for high-performing and successful schools, "success" was largely dependent on teachers' knowledge and expertise, as well as commitment. All of the successful schools mentioned by Lipson provided balanced literacy instruction in all major areas of literacy with "expert teachers" who shared a common vision. Ongoing professional development played a major role in all of this.

Cooperative Learning and Developing Reading Comprehension and Text Strategies
The Cornerstone approach described in Figure 9.20 encourages the use of cooperative learning activities. According to the National Reading Panel Report (NRPR, 2000),

Example: Cornerstone National Literacy Initiative Professional Development Model

The Cornerstone National Literacy Initiative believes that on-site professional development is highly effective with trained "coaches" (training = ongoing through seminars and participation on review teams with other Cornerstone schools) who help staff to *establish literacy goals; model and coach in classrooms; disseminate professional readings and research; and organize book study groups, extended day workshops, and consultation.* Cornerstone staff provides a cadre of education mentors or consultants who work on site with staff and coaches. The goal is to facilitate the development of learners who acquire strategies to become independent readers and writers so they can improve their speaking, reading, and writing proficiency through practice using high-quality literature. By means of scaffolding and practice, students learn to take responsibility for their own learning (acquire an internal locus of control, building resiliency). Students working independently allow teachers time for individualized instruction for review and extension.

Cornerstone balances surface structure skills students need to read and write fluently—phonics, spelling, and syntax—with the deeper thinking (metacomprehension skills) students need to master comprehension of what they read and to write with content and meaning. Teachers provide their students with a scaffolding structure that enables them to read with deeper understanding.

Cornerstone seeks to develop the highest level of engagement of the children (sustained learning episodes), clear teaching intentions, teacher and coaching modeling episodes and conferencing, and the use of high-quality literature. These techniques have been proven to work well with all students especially struggling students and/or at-risk students.

Collectively, Cornerstone schools work to have everyone embrace *the vision that all children can and will learn while building scientifically based comprehensive literacy programs based on the understanding that, to be literate, students must learn to read and to understand what they read.* Teachers, as lifetime learners, continue to seek more approaches to achieve this goal of developing strategic readers who are also proficient writers.

Sources: Prigohzy (2004); Roberts (2004).

FIGURE 9.20 Professional Development Model Example

"when students as peers tutor or instruct one another or interact over the use of reading strategies, the evidence is that they learn reading strategies. They engage in intellectual discussion, and they increase their reading comprehension . . . students gain more control over their learning. Cooperative learning can be a part of a natural reading program where peers as well as the teacher engage in a transaction over the meaning of text . . ." (p. 4-101). According to the NRPR, this is one of the most effective types of instruction for text comprehension instruction. The NRPR (2000) also found teachers can more effectively implement cooperative learning activities or approaches if trained in these methods through preservice or inservice workshop development.

Teachers as Learners

Peer Coaching and Conferencing—Assessing Lesson Effectiveness   Teachers, as learners, continue to seek more approaches especially in lesson planning to achieve the goal of developing strategic and proficient readers and writers (Marona & Palazzi, 1991; Resnick & Hall, 1998). Analysis of student performance involves a number of "interdependent steps," including "the scheduling and administration of tests, analysis and interpretation of test results, identification of instructional needs and priorities based on test data analysis" with enabling strategies to address those needs (Spillane, Halverson, & Diamond, 2001, p. 24). Peer conferences are one way to help teachers more effectively use data to inform instructional practice. As an example, discussions could be initiated before and after a lesson is implemented with attention to lesson design and assessment for a recommended approach listed in a student's IEP or a new approach being tried with a dyslexic student (see Figure 9.21). Conferring questions established beforehand can serve as discussion guides to facilitate the collaborative exchanges.

Lesson Design (before a lesson is presented)

- How are you using prior assessments to drive instruction for this lesson?
- How is your lesson connected to district goals? Standards?
- What do you anticipate to be the timing/pacing for your lesson? Why?
- How does this lesson connect to previous lessons?
- How is the lesson activity specifically going to advance student learning?
- What difficulties might you anticipate?
- How will you be able to differentiate instruction? What modifications are necessary for students with learning disabilities or other learning challenges?
- How will you model?
- What materials are needed? Other resources? Be specific.
- How will the students reflect on and self-monitor learning?
- How will you ensure all students are actively engaged?

Assessment (following the lesson)

- How will you assess prior student knowledge?
- What completed student products or desired learning outcomes are expected?
- How do your assessments align with your anticipated outcomes and district standards/benchmarks?
- How will you know that all students have learned what was taught?
- How will students self-assess or evaluate their own learning?
- Pedagogical strategies—How do you know that all students are learning from this strategy?
- How will you know that students will be able to apply the knowledge, skills, and strategies taught?
- What kind of running record are you maintaining to measure student progress across time?
- Based on your assessment of the lesson, what's next?

Source: Information from Annette Seitz (March 17, 2004). Institute for Learning: University of Pittsburgh. *Facilitation skills for embedded professional development.* Co-designed with Linda Abbott, Diann Cohen, Kate Fenton, and Tom Paleologopoulos. Workshop presentation: Springfield Schools, Springfield, MA, p. 5.

FIGURE 9.21 Sample Conferencing Questions before and after Lesson Implementation

Professional collaborations can involve teachers coming together for a particular purpose using models or protocols to facilitate discussion. For example, the Collaborative Assessment Conference (Figure 9.22) provides a structure where a small group of teachers (e.g., grade-level team) can meet to review student work (e.g., a writing piece) to (1) see what the writing reveals about a student and his or her work and (2) make suggestions to support the student in future instruction (Thompson-Grove & Graham, 2003).

Darling-Hammond and McLaughlin (1996) have found that effective teaching involves professional development through ". . . sustained, ongoing, and intensive work supported by modeling, coaching, and collective problem solving" around specific issues of practice (p. 203). Peer coaching is a powerful way to bring new ideas and perspectives to teachers as they practice and develop their "art" within the classroom as seen in the box on page 272.

Forming Teachers as Readers Study Groups to Reflect on Instructional Practices to Effect Change (Self-Assessment) A recent trend in professional development has centered on forming school literacy study groups to discuss readings and research in the context of helping learners to achieve proficiency across the curriculum. The *Council for Exceptional Children* (CEC) and the *International Reading Association* (IRA), as examples, offer staff development kits, mini-libraries, and modules with established goals (e.g., to help challenged learners become successful readers and writers)—resources can be purchased directly through these organizations, among others.

Overall goal: To be better observers of student work.

(1) Getting Started

- Choose a facilitator and establish a time frame (45 minutes to 1 hour and 15 minutes).
- A presenting teacher distributes copies of a student's written work without comment until step 5 (e.g., a student of concern).
- Other group members read the work in silence and make brief notes.

(2) Describe the Work of the Student

- Facilitator to group, "What do you see?" (e.g., three paragraphs without transitions, sentences that change verb tense, semi-phonetic and phonetic word spellings, etc.).
- Group members respond without reference to the quality of the work or personal preferences (e.g., "this student has really improved").
- If personal judgments are made, the facilitator asks for evidence to support the judgments.

(3) Pose Questions

- Facilitator: "What questions does this work raise for you?"
- Group members pose questions related to the work, the child, the assignment, the circumstances in which the work was completed, etc.

(4) Hypothesizing What the Student Is Working On

- Facilitator: "What do you think the student is working on?"
- Group members make suggestions about the difficulties or issues the student may have been focused on while completing the assignment.

(5) The Presenting Teacher Speaks

- Facilitator to the presenter, "What is your perspective of the student's work?"
- Presenter responds and adds additional information he or she feels is important to the group.

(6) "Big Picture" Conversation

- Facilitator, "Could everyone please share any thoughts about your own related teaching practices, children's learning, or ideas to support this particular child in future lessons or instruction?"

(7) Collaborative Assessment Conference Reflection

- Facilitator to the group, "How did the conference go?"
- Group members discuss experiences or reactions to parts of the conference or the conference as a whole.
- Facilitator paraphrases and summarizes collective responses.

(8) Thank You

- The presenting teacher and group members are thanked for their various roles.

Role of Facilitator (Thompson-Grove & Graham, 2003)

(1) Allow or offer any questioning format.
(2) Move the group through the stages.
(3) Actively engage in discussions.

Benefit to Conference: Looking at one piece of work through multiple perspectives helps in planning future instruction for that particular student and others as well.

FIGURE 9.22 The Collaborative Assessment Conference Protocol Model: Steve Seidel and Colleagues at Harvard Project Zero, Authors (1988; cited in Blythe, Allen, & Powell, 1999)

Literacy Peer Coaches Supporting Other Teachers as Life-Long Learners

Cohen et al. (2003/2004) advocate for literacy peer coaches to support teachers' learning as they practice and develop their "art" within the classroom. Literacy peer coaches are other teachers within a school who have more extensive or different teaching experiences. Often, a literacy coach is provided "blocks" of time during the day or week to assist colleagues before, during, or after classroom experiences but continues to maintain a regular teaching schedule. Consistent with Lyons and Pinnell (2001), Cohen et al. stress a major goal for literacy coaches—to empower teachers to expand their conceptual knowledge in ways they can continuously learn from their own teaching.

According to Cohen et al. (2003/2004), the role of *literacy coaches* includes but is not limited to the following:

- First, become knowledgeable of the coaching process, coaching protocols, district requirements and standards, reading and writing processes, and literacy assessments appropriate to the various grade levels.

- Create a trusting relationship with teachers who will be "coached," building on the teachers' backgrounds and strengths with the guiding question for conversations "How can I support your teaching?"
- Create a common language and mutual understandings regarding the school system's vision and mission statements.
- Use knowledge of district literacy requirements, standards, and benchmarks to help establish a coaching purpose (i.e., the teacher will try a new technique or strategy to improve reading and would like feedback) that will result in new learning within the context of an action plan to further effective teaching practices.
- Keep coaching sessions relatively brief and constructive with a specific agenda related to student learning—the focus is on bringing students to levels of proficiency in reading and writing.
- Use coaching sessions to problem-solve in a "risk-free" environment (e.g., How can I bring my struggling readers to the next level?—I'm stuck.).
- Mutually look at the available data relative to literacy benchmarks in reading and writing to inform instructional practice. What are the texts and other assessments telling us about children's learning? What is it that we want children to know and be able to do?
- Mutually consider relevant research-based educational practices that will facilitate children's learning.
- Model or demonstrate lessons or provide opportunities to observe other teachers as they teach. Analyze and discuss what occurred and what might be personally relevant.
- Provide resources, readings, and research as needed.
- Reflect on and learn from coaching episodes—reciprocal reflection and dialogue will also focus on What's next? How can I extend this new learning?
- Literacy coaches take the lead in a supportive manner in some schoolwide professional development sessions, book study groups, and the like because this shows a commitment to schoolwide staff development.
- Literacy coaches need opportunities to meet and network with other literacy coaches to become more skilled in the art of coaching.

Source: Cohen, Ashe, Brown, Chamberlain, Diaz, Fenton, Kelliher, Lak, Motto, Paleologopoulos, Panico, Rice (2003/2004).

Guides and related readings are used in self-directed, on-site Teachers as Readers study groups—teachers meet to discuss readings and their relatedness to instructional design and delivery. Schools or districts purchase professional books and related resources for teachers who include them in a "professional library" of resources in the classroom, easily accessible before, during, and after teaching.

Ways for Administrators to Support TAR Study Groups   The sustained momentum for Teachers as Readers study groups can be maintained through direct and indirect administrative support. As an example, Jamie Sussell Turner, principal of Viola L. Sickles School in Fair Haven, New Jersey, says that working time into the schedule for teachers to meet and form study groups is key—scheduled faculty meetings can allow for half-hour time blocks on a regular basis. Turner, who published "When Teachers Are Readers" in the online *Principal* (May/June 2004), also directly participates in staff discussions when teachers review the various strategies learned from study groups in previous faculty meetings. At the end of the year, teachers write about the study group experiences with the principal reading reflections, using the teachers' perspectives to help guide future faculty meetings and program planning efforts.

Ongoing Direct and Indirect Administrative Support through Teaming   Gloria Williams (2004), principal of Frank H. Freedman School in Springfield, Massachusetts, establishes weekly meeting times for grade-level teams of teachers to meet. Additionally, School Improvement Planning (SIP) team members and the principal collectively review test assessment data, school needs assessment information and feedback from teachers and parents, and then priorities are established for on-site professional development, including literacy study groups. The SIP team creates a timeline, identifies resources needed, determines who will facilitate study groups, and engages in pre-planning activities.

Massachusetts Reading Association (MRA) TAR Book Discussion Groups

> . . . Teachers as Readers "book discussion groups" offer teachers the opportunity to come together to discuss children's literature, young adult literature, and professional books. Teachers use the exchange of experiences and ideas to create richly literate classrooms and foster the development of life long readers. (Thompson & Fischer, 2001/2002)

Why Form a Teachers as Readers Book Discussion Group?

- Provide opportunities to share quality literature.
- Learn from the ideas and experiences of others.
- Reflect upon personal experience.
- Become exposed to a wider range of literature and authors.
- Model strategies for guiding students on their journeys to becoming lifelong readers.

Guidelines for Organizing a TAR Book Discussion Group

- Establish a group of approximately ten interested members, breaking large faculty meetings into smaller groups.
- Select a discussion facilitator for each meeting.
- Determine meeting location and dates.
- Select books to be read.
- Encourage participants to prepare for group meetings.
- Agree upon expectations for meetings.

Focus Study Groups   Another type of teacher study group is the "focus study group." Focus groups are small groups of individuals who meet for a particular purpose with collective problem solving centered on a particular issue or topic. There isn't necessarily a professional reading to consider. A focus group may decide, as an example, to assess the effectiveness of an intervention program for students with dyslexia or "the next step" after collecting data centering on student work. Leibowitz (2003) and Keene (2003) offer suggestions for such focus groups in Figure 9.23.

Building Learning Communities: A Vision to Promote and Sustain Increased Learning for All   Jonathan D. Saphier and the Research for Better Teaching, Inc. (RBT) (2004) offer a two-part vision statement with best general practices that promote and sustain increased student learning and achievement—these can be extended to the entire school community: *Teachers and staff* will (1) communicate to all students that they can achieve at high levels of performance, (2) assist students in developing positive academic identities, (3) use multiple sources of data when making decisions about teaching, (4) be continuously reflective about teaching practices, and (5) "provide expert instruction" in every classroom. *School leaders* will: "cultivate, support, and sustain expert instruction" by (1) "sharing a common language and concept system about teaching and learning with teachers, (2) collaboratively create professional communities that believe in continual improvement and engage in the study of teaching and learning, (3) distribute leadership throughout the school or organization, (4) develop structural mechanisms and resources that nurture organizational effectiveness, and (5) ensure shared respon-

Focus group example: Evaluate an intervention program for students with dyslexia—Consider:

(1) Including students with dyslexia in the focus group if age and developmentally appropriate.

(2) Crafting questions carefully beforehand and include open-ended questions.

(3) Limiting the size of the group to 6–8.

(4) Ensuring the "comfort factor"—(e.g., trusted facilitator).

(5) Limiting time to 30–45 minutes.

Source: CEC (Fall 2003), "Views from the Field," by Marion Leibowitz.

Focus group example: Hold before or after school study (focus) groups to discuss data gathered from work with students—Consider the following questions:

(1) What does the data suggest for instruction?

(2) Does the data suggest any strengths or areas of weakness for all of the students tested or sampled?

(3) What does the data suggest to create a set of goals for children and teachers?

(4) What types of professional development would be assistive considering the data?

(5) Do you have suggestions for extended day workshops, summer institutes, or learning forums?

Source: "Student Assessment Overview" (July 3, 2003) by Ellen Keene from *Tool Kit At-A-Glance.* Cornerstone.literacy.org

FIGURE 9.23 Examples of Suggestions for Focus Study Groups

sibility and accountability for student learning and achievement" (Saphier, Bigda-Peyton, & Pierson, 2004). Building learning communities necessarily involves families.

Empowering Parents to Support Their Children's Learning Parents also take a lead role in linking home to school to support the literacy successes of their children. In order to facilitate this, schools need to (1) provide activities, workshops, and materials to help parents/guardians in their role as their children's "first literacy teacher"; (2) invite parents to become members of the school's leadership team, develop school-community partnerships, apply for grants, and the like; (3) find ways to include the home language for second-language learners; and (4) through parent involvement in various school activities, pinpoint issues for community building (Fraley, 2004).

As an example, Lamson T. Lam, grade 4 teacher, collected data over a period of four years in which parents attended Public School 198 in New York City to help their children do well on tests. Families (students and parents/guardians) participated in after-school workshop test preparation sessions. At the workshop session, families received a folder with a corrected practice test and individualized checklist of "trouble spots." Teachers also passed out abbreviated practice tests and invited parents to watch their children complete these tests or take the practice test themselves. Then parents were asked to go over test mistakes with their children at home. Lam found that parental involvement in test preparations resulted in dramatic increases in performance on the state English and math tests (Keller, 2004).

To conclude, when teachers involve parents in student learning, "teach to the big ideas," participate in ongoing content-based professional development, receive support in the classroom from colleagues, and use specific assessment information to inform instruction, their students will learn and achieve more (Foster & Noyce, 2004, p. 374).

Summary

Some assessment practices have resulted in the mislabeling of children who are dyslexic or learning disabled. Correct identification of students with learning disabilities is critical in that there are proven instructional practices that can bring learning-disabled students to levels of proficiency in reading and writing. Before testing begins, establishing a positive testing or assessment attitude was stressed. For students who are moderately to severely dyslexic and who require services from specialists outside of the regular classroom teacher, an Individualized Education Program (IEP) can be developed; this process was discussed in depth.

Consistent with the International Reading Association (2000), it is recommended that students with dyslexia or reading disabilities: (1) have access to assessments (i.e., state and national) that evaluate their literacy levels and in ways that can be used by teachers to plan and design instruction that leads to proficiency in reading and writing and (2) be provided accommodations and alternative assessments appropriate to their developmental levels and educational and social needs without changing the essence of the tests in regard to content and strategy usage requirements.

Discussion in this chapter centered on what a comprehensive evaluation should include with reference to the *International Dyslexia Association* (IDA) approved standards as of January 7, 2002 (pp. 13–21). For individuals with dyslexia a comprehensive evaluation would include:

I. History
II. Interview (teachers, parents, and student when appropriate)
III. Cognitive Assessment (a comprehensive profile of cognitive abilities, including verbal and nonverbal processing and performance skills)
   A. Individuals with dyslexia should be identified through an evaluation process that addresses the following subskills of language literacy (reading and writing):
      (1) Phonemic awareness (oral)
      (2) Spelling (isolated and applied)
      (3) Phonic decoding and word identification or word analysis skills
      (4) Fluent and accurate word reading
      (5) Fluent and accurate text reading
      (6) Oral language comprehension
      (7) Reading comprehension
      (8) Written expression
   B. Academic achievement (performance assessment)
   C. Assessment of cognitive processing and language problems in mathematics
IV. Social and Behavioral Functioning (adaptive functioning) (e.g., resiliency = QUalitative Analysis of Resilient Traits [QUART])
V. Test Accommodations and Report Formats

The current authors have added:

VI. Portfolio Assessment: Showcasing Academic Accomplishments
VII. Professional Development (What needs to be done to support educators to best implement recommendations that emanate from evaluations?)

Literacy assessments should be designed to provide substantive information to the teacher, pupil, and family that can be used to guide and improve instruction and learning. A Dyslexia Checklist on page 225 was offered with the suggestion to affix the test accommodation grid found on page 254 to assessments.

The **B**ehavior**A**l **S**trategy **I**ntervention **C**hecklist (BASIC) was developed as an instructional tool to measure the four major dimensions related to social and behavioral functioning important to school or academic settings and success therein: (1) student resolution or behaviors related to an internal locus of control, (2) family connectedness and support of school progress and behaviors, (3) academic accommodations to provide social supports and address learning style and needs, and (4) opportunities to develop peer collaborations and leadership. The miscue analysis running record format offered by Irene Fountas and Gay Su Pinnell allows teachers to maintain an ongoing informal assessment of progress in word recognition to inform instructional practices.

When analyzing the oral reading miscues of students with "dialects," it was recommended educators view these dialectical differences in the context of "standard for a cultural group" and not "incorrectly variable from the language norm." According to Benjamin Swan, noted educator, historian, and civic leader (2002), dialects are not necessarily nonstandard; rather, many have systematic, rule-governed syntactical structures. The acceptance of dialectical differences without correction puts into words a subtler, more important message, "you, your family, and your language are valued."

The case study of C., Jr., a dyslexic adult, was presented and is typical of resilient "dyslexic" adults who read on grade level, shows persistence (stick-to-it-ness), self-efficacy (beliefs in one's ability to plan and complete actions to reach a goal or desired level of performance), positive self-esteem (positive evaluation of oneself in regard to personal worth, life and school successes), optimism (anticipates the best, hopeful), and an overall positive temperament (characteristic frame of mind is positive). C., Jr. has been fortunate in that he has had a strong network of academic and social support. In C., Jr.'s situation, as with so many other struggling students who achieve literacy successes, caring families and exemplary teachers effect this positive change and growth.

Exemplary teachers engage in ongoing reflective teaching practices or self-assessment and professional development. Currently, many professional development program models as outlined in this chapter are designed to assist staff in establishing literacy goals; disseminating and discussing professional readings and research; and organizing book study groups, extended day workshops, and consultation. A recent trend in professional development has centered on forming Teachers as Readers groups and School Literacy Study Groups in the context of helping learners to achieve proficiency across the curriculum.

With consistent literacy support in reading and writing to graduation, a social-academic network of support, and ongoing reinforcement of individual resiliency, C., Jr. and other individuals who experience the sometimes debilitating condition of dyslexia will lead successful and fulfilling lives. Chapter 10 will cover study skills and those ways educators can provide specific strategy instruction to develop good study habits. Establishing school–home partnerships will be discussed within the context of homework support and preparations for test taking.

CHAPTER

10 Study Skills

According to Ellin Oliver Keene and Susan Zimmerman (1997), proficient readers and learners "purposefully use synthesis to better understand what they have read. Syntheses are frequently an amalgam of all comprehension strategies used by proficient readers" (p. 185).

What Are Successful Dyslexics and Proficient Learners Able to Do Well in the Area of Study Skills?

On the hierarchy of cognitive learning, Benjamin Bloom (1956) places synthesis as the critical cognitive ability before deriving abstract relations, producing communications, and formulating plans. According to Bloom, knowledge, comprehension, and analysis precede *synthesis* in a hierarchical taxonomy of cognitive learning, followed by evaluation. Synthesis, or "putting it all together," is exactly what students who have good study habits are able to do. Students with good study habits are able to summarize knowledge, whether it be in notetaking, creating graphic organizers, engaging in systematic text study, or preparing for homework and tests. A "good" summary is really an effective synthesis or synopsis of major concepts, ideas, and content from text.

Good study habits can be taught, and Bloom and his colleagues (1984) persuade the reader through their research to believe that most students can learn study skills or any other skill or concept. Instruction must be individualized as needed, and dyslexic students, especially, require enough explanations, illustrations, and demonstrations with practice, reinforcement, and corrective feedback/additional teaching (direct or explicit teaching/master learning).

According to Armbruster and Osborn (2001), the steps for explicit teaching include (1) **direct explanation**, (2) **modeling** by the teacher with think-alouds, (3) **guided practice** (assisting students with how and when to apply strategies), and (4) **application** (scaffolding learning until students achieve independence). You will find with the study skills techniques mentioned in this chapter that there is explicit teaching of skills in a step-by-step format, necessary for dyslexics who tend to lack good study skills without direct or explicit instruction. Actually, most students benefit from direct or explicit teaching of study skills.

What helps students most with study skills both in the classroom and at home? What do the experts tell us?

I. *Strategy instruction* that includes *self-questioning instruction.*
II. Direct teaching and modeling of *paraphrasing* and *summarizing strategies* during the reading process provides students with valuable study skills strategies.
III. Direct teaching of *mnemonic, keyword strategies,* and *other vocabulary interventions* to improve vocabulary comprehension and information retention. Knowledge of

important vocabulary and related concepts for a subject (e.g., math) at a particular developmental level (e.g., preschool) is crucial in identifying appropriate vocabulary words and terms to target for learning.

IV. Use of *graphic organizers* to diagram or outline the main structure of material to be read or material read (e.g., main concepts or ideas, key terminology, and concepts) improves comprehension and is an assistive study guide—key concepts and terms are used to create the graphic organizer.

V. *Practice, practice, and more practice* are important, especially repeated practice after new strategies and knowledge are acquired. Practice needs to occur in a variety of formats and contexts. Students with dyslexia need opportunities to apply knowledge and to "try out" newly learned strategies. According to grade 2 student "expert," J, he gets better in school learning when he practices.

> I Practice Spell I Practice to read over and over.

Y, grade 2 student, discusses practicing words (aloud) and writing them on paper.

> I Practice doin the words and writing on a Paper

S, grade 2 student, emphasizes the importance of continued practice both at home and at school.

> You study and Pratice at home and at school many time and in th Morning.

VI. *Homework* is important, *and parent involvement in the child's homework assignments* is directly related to school achievement and developing personal attributes that contribute to school achievement such as self-regulation, ability to manage time, and positive self-concepts of ability (Delgado-Gaitan, 1992).

At home, N shares how family "teaming" with mom helps with homework.

> Fist my mom reads my test then we read it together and I also read my test by my self.

J shows how siblings can help one another on homework assignments:

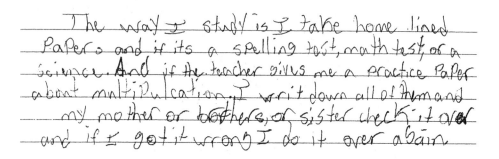

I Study with my Sister
She tells me and I Spell them.

Fifth-grade honor student T wants to "get it right," so he has other family members review his work for accuracy:

The way I study is I take home lined Papers and if its a spelling test, math test, or a science. And if the teacher gives me a practice Paper about multiplication. I writ down all of them and my mother or brothers, or sister check it over and if I got it wrong I do it over again.

L, grade 5 honor student, also reminds us to ensure students have the "right homework" learning tools such as assignment pads, pencils, notebook paper, resource books, a dictionary, and so on.

VII. Increasing *peer collaboration time* through cooperative learning groups, pairings during reading times, and *peer tutoring* are an effective ways to improve academic achievement for students with dyslexia. In essence, peer tutoring involves pairing a student with dyslexia with a student who is a proficient reader and writer. Sometimes the reverse occurs in "reverse-role tutoring" where the student with dyslexia would serve as the tutor in an area of strength.

VIII. Direct teaching, modeling, and consistent use of *specific study skill strategy models or systems* such as K-W-L, Reciprocal Teaching, SQ3R, ReQuest, QAR, and DRTA.

IX. Direct teaching and modeling of *note taking, systematic textual study,* and *test taking strategies.*

Strategy Instruction

The *strategies* students access will depend on the purpose of their reading (e.g., *purpose,* to understand new science content; *strategy,* frequent pauses to integrate and reflect on the information presented and to assist with comprehension).

Georgina Nebedum-Ezeh and Carol Spafford (2001) suggest a basic *framework for strategy instruction* based on the work of Barbara Taylor, Michael Graves, and Paul Van Den Broek (2000):

1. Select one or two appropriate strategies for students to utilize before a selected science text is presented (e.g., *strategy,* use frequent pauses and reflect on and self-question to determine understanding; *strategy,* clarify "unknowns" by effectively using marginal glosses).

2. Explain, demonstrate, and model these strategies (especially self-questioning strategies) with other text—as an example, read together a few paragraphs of difficult text and then model appropriate strategies to develop an understanding of the text. Devote the *entire* class or one hour to these few paragraphs so that the text can be fully processed within the context of successful strategy usage.
3. Implement a few opportunities for guided practice.
4. Introduce the content/text selection.
5. Build or activate prior knowledge,
6. Actively engage students in the material presented.
7. Interactively ask and respond to questions; self-question.
8. Reflect on the reading and student understandings.
9. Evaluate progress/understandings to guide future lessons/learning experiences.

Provide explicit instruction/practice and advance organizers to help students acquire new learning strategies (Schumaker & Deshler, 1992; Swanson & Deshler, 2003) (advance organizers examples = to provide particular or prior information about a task beforehand, to direct the individual to focus on particular information, to present learning objectives, and so on).

Swanson and Deshler (2003) summarize eight instructional stages that ensure acquisition and full mastery of a learning strategy: (1) pretest and making commitments, (2) description, (3) modeling, (4) verbal practice, (5) controlled practice and feedback, (6) advanced practice and feedback, (7) posttest, and (8) generalization. Dyslexics, however, typically have difficulty with "task completion" (Shapiro, 1982) and need to learn to manage assignments within timeframes (Palladino, Poli, Masi, & Marcheschi, 2000). Wong and Jones (1982) suggest teaching steps (see Figure 10.1) regarding a specific study skills strategy important to metacomprehension or the ability to monitor one's own comprehension of text—self-questioning.

Self-Questioning

Courtney and Montano (2002/2003) have shown that strategies can be directly taught even to the youngest readers (grade 1). These researchers found that although strategy instruction for first graders can be "challenging and confusing, the investment of time and planning will result in children acquiring and using multiple strategies." Their first-grade readers were able to use the following reading strategies as they constructed meaning from text by the end of the school year: pictures cuing, making use of the first sounds in words, thinking about what "makes sense," going back to reread, skipping words and then going back, skipping words and reading to the end of a sentence, looking for chunks, stretching the sound, and sounding out if needed.

Students can be provided self-questioning prompts to support their use of literacy strategies while reading. DePierro (2004) offers question prompts related to analyzing a book cover (see Figure 10.2) before reading, and Fountas and Pinnell (1996) suggest that teachers prompt students with questions related to reading miscues (see Figure 10.3) These guide students to metacognitive monitoring of their own reading miscues.

According to Johns and Berglund (2002), teachers need to share with students how learning strategies will help them become better readers. During the modeling stage, Johns and Berglund recommend thinking aloud to describe what one is thinking as the strategy is being used. These researchers also stress developing strategies over time with reminders to students to use learned strategies in a variety of contexts. The use of prompts to support the use of strategies can also be modeled.

Method	Authors	Sources	Teaching Steps for Implementation (Samples)

Modified Self-Questioning Instruction (metacomprehension monitoring or developing an awareness of and ability to monitor one's own comprehension of text)	Bernice Y.L. Wong and Wayne Jones	Wong, B.Y.L. & Jones, W. (1982). Increasing metacomprehension in learning disabled and normally achieving students through self-questioning training. *Learning Disability Quarterly, 5,* 228–239.
		
		Pruit, P. (1997). Study skills strategy instruction. In Buchanan, Weller & Buchanan, *My Special Education Desk Reference.* San Diego, CA: Singular Publishing Group.
			I. Identify main concept or ideas for reading text: Practice finding main ideas or concepts for paragraphs and full selections to proficiency (80% accuracy or greater)
			
			II. Develop questions from the main concepts or ideas (intense two-day preparation), including how to develop good questions. Establish:
			
			  A. Purpose setting and explanation of metacomprehension strategy learning
			  B. Suggested sequence for direct instruction
			    1. "Why are you studying this information (or book or [passage])?"
			    2. "Locate the main idea for each (paragraph, page, passage) and draw a line underneath each one or highlight."
			    3. "Think of a question about each main idea and try to remember the steps used in forming good questions."
			    4. "Respond to your questions thoughtfully and in writing."
			    5. "Review and reflect on each of your own questions and responses."
			    6. "How was your understanding of the reading improved when you monitored your own comprehension or understanding?"

FIGURE 10.1 Study Skills Method to Improve Comprehension and Information Retention: From Research to Practice

Example with Story Characters:

(1) What characters are on the book cover?
(2) Describe how each character looks using details from the book cover.
(3) What else appears on the book cover?
(4) What mood or tone did the book illustrator want to convey?
(5) What is unique about the artwork?
(6) What main idea is the illustrator trying to tell the reader through the book cover artwork?
(7) Do you like the book cover for this particular book? Why or why not?
(8) Can you compare this book cover to another? Be specific.

Source: DePierro, 2004

FIGURE 10.2   Analyzing a Book Cover through Question Prompts to Begin Comprehension Scaffolding

Fountas and Pinnell (1996) suggest using prompts to support the use of strategies. For example, to support the reader's use of all sources of information (a good reading strategy), sample prompts offered by Fountas and Pinnell include:

"Check the picture.

Does that look right?

Does that sound right?

You said _____. Does that make sense?

Try that again and think what would make sense.

What can you do to help yourself?

You're nearly right. Try that again.

I like the way you worked that out." (p. 161).

These prompts can be listed on a card for the individual with dyslexia and referred to when problem solving unknown words.

FIGURE 10.3   Instructional Application—Using Prompts to Support the Use of Literacy Strategies

Direct Teaching and Modeling of Paraphrasing and Summarizing Strategies

Paraphrasing Words and Meanings

Rephrasing or paraphrasing the words, sentences, and inferred meanings of what children communicate to adults orally connects syntactically correct and elaborated vocabulary structures with "personally relevant speech"—the words of children. Explaining to children, "We know you are bright enough to manage the complexity of abstract ideas . . . as a teacher, I'm giving you the language to verbalize the complexity of your thinking," creates a context for "deep structure" learning and reflection (Keene, 2004).

Students need opportunities to correct the teacher's rephrasing if necessary and to take more time to elaborate upon their thinking. Explicitly model and teach, "the language of thought" using "thinking words" like "schema," "infer," "I wonder," "imagine," "feel," and other phrases as seen in the following box.

"Thinking Vocabulary" Requires Explicit Teaching and Modeling

Examples

- "My schema for this is"
- "An inference is" "I will infer"
- "I wonder" "I'm thinking about"
- "I hypothesize" "I predict"
- "I imagine"
- "My feeling is"
- "It appears to be"
- "My analysis of this is"
- "In synthesizing the information, I conclude that"
- "After evaluating"
- "Upon reflection"

Effective Paraphrasing with Second-Language Learners   Gersten and Jiménez (1994) studied effective reading practices with second-language learners and determined that paraphrasing students' statements was particularly helpful. For example, the teacher asks, "What did you learn today about 'metacognition'?" The student replies, "making connections." The teacher could paraphrase and elaborate, "Yes, you learned to make personal connections to the story we read—you had to think about if you were similar in some way to the story character." There could be a followup question, "What personal connection did you make to the story character?"

When rephrasing or paraphrasing, define sophisticated vocabulary parenthetically during conversation. Rename or label vocabulary for the purpose of definition (Saskatchewan, Canada, Education Government Website, 2004).

Restructuring and rephrasing key story structure information have been shown to improve comprehension with marked improvement observed for students with dyslexia and "less able readers" (National Reading Panel Report, 2000). With narrative material, teachers can initiate discussions of the content and organization of stories through question answering and generation strategies. Summarizing, or providing a synopsis, outline, or abstract of the entire reading, requires explicit teaching for students with dyslexia.

Summarizing

Students can be given rules and procedures to summarize single and then multiple paragraph selections. This requires being able to integrate and then generalize information found in the reading. According to the National Reading Panel Report (2000), the instruction of summarizing improves "memory for what is read, both in terms of free recall and answering questions" (p. 4-113).

The NRPR (2000) states four general rules readers can be taught to apply when summarizing text (with repeated practice and feedback):

1. Delete unnecessary information or trivia.
2. Delete text that is redundant.
3. Use the principle of "superordination"—replacing a list of examples or exemplars with a "superordinate" term.
4. Find or create a topic sentence that will scaffold the summary.

When summarizing multiple paragraphs, readers synthesize the information in individual paragraphs first and then construct a "summary" of the "summaries." This can be accomplished using an outline format. The plot map with silhouette example in Figure 10.4 provides an outline format for an entire story where students must organize events in the story as they unfold.

Similarly, the character map silhouette shown in Figure 10.5 allows the reader to summarize important information about a story's main character(s) to use in summaries.

Other semantic maps can be used to help summarize important story information such as an expansion or cause-and-effect map and a brainstorming or topic map (see Figure 10.6).

Entire books or topics can also be summarized via expanded charts and semantic maps. In Figure 10.7, important math vocabulary is summarized by topic. This can be used as a study guide, in conversations about math, and to reference during math journal writing. This is a type of vocabulary scaffolding to improve comprehension when such terms are encountered in print and in math conversations.

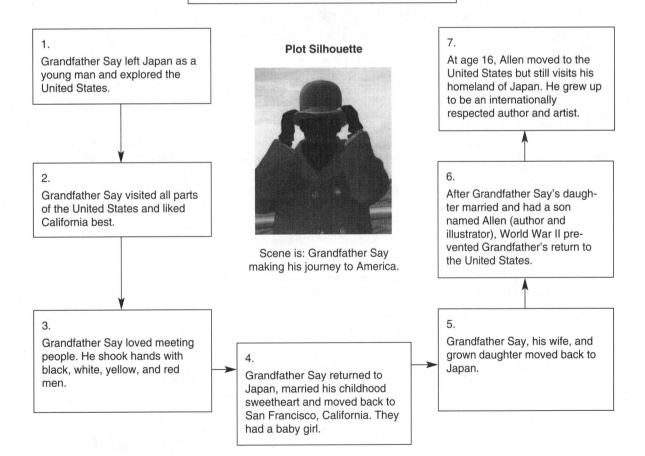

This book is mainly about:
Allen Say's loving memories of his grandfather and his parents' journeys between Japan and America.

Genre: Nonfiction
Narrative Picture Book

Plot Silhouette

Scene is: Grandfather Say making his journey to America.

1. Grandfather Say left Japan as a young man and explored the United States.

2. Grandfather Say visited all parts of the United States and liked California best.

3. Grandfather Say loved meeting people. He shook hands with black, white, yellow, and red men.

4. Grandfather Say returned to Japan, married his childhood sweetheart and moved back to San Francisco, California. They had a baby girl.

5. Grandfather Say, his wife, and grown daughter moved back to Japan.

6. After Grandfather Say's daughter married and had a son named Allen (author and illustrator), World War II prevented Grandfather's return to the United States.

7. At age 16, Allen moved to the United States but still visits his homeland of Japan. He grew up to be an internationally respected author and artist.

Source: Grandfather's Journey by Allen Say (1993). New York: Houghton Mifflin. (Illustrated by Allen Say)

FIGURE 10.4 Plot Map with Silhouette Example

SAMPLE

Character Studied: Queen Elizabeth I of England

Why: To learn more about a remarkable world leader.

Genre: Historical Biography

Setting Information

Lived (place)

1. Grew up in Palace of Hatfield
2. As Queen—moved from palace to palace for safety
3. Visited her people all over the country

Lived (time)

1. Born September 7, 1533
2. Died March 24, 1603
3. "Elizabethan Age of England"

Family Information

1. Mother—Queen Anne
   Father—King Henry VIII
2. Brother—King Edward VI (was King—age 9, died age 15)
3. Princess Mary—half sister; was Queen for 5 years

Character Silhouette
Queen Elizabeth

Trace of photocopy and then use a marker to darken.

Did What?

1. Became Queen of England at age 25
2. Kept the country at peace
3. Initiated a cultural revolution

Is important to the story because . . .

1. She's the main character
2. She ruled England for 45 years
3. Queen Elizabeth I or Bess's rule = Elizabethan Age of England; resulted in new theaters, artwork, music, and world explorations

Looks Like

1. Young (only 25 when Queen)
2. Elegant (clothes/hair)
3. Stately/regal (poise/presentation)

Acts Like

1. World leader
2. Caretaker of a nation for 45 years
3. Humble servant of her people

Considered a good character because . . .

1. Devoted to her people
2. Ruled with a firm, kind hand
3. Provided the best cultural and social opportunities possible for people during turbulent times

Considered a bad character because . . .

1.
2.
3.

Source: Good Queen Bess: The Story of Elizabeth I of England by Diane Stanley and Peter Vennema. (1990). New York: Harper Collins. (Illustrated by Diane Stanley).

FIGURE 10.5   Character Map with Silhouette

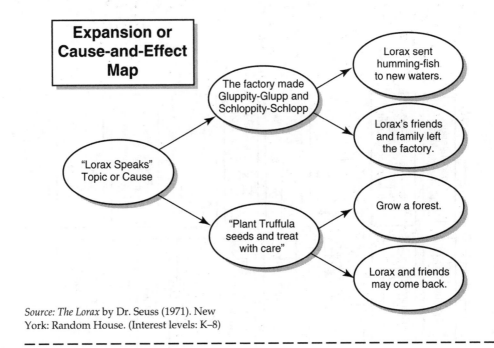

Source: The Lorax by Dr. Seuss (1971). New
York: Random House. (Interest levels: K–8)

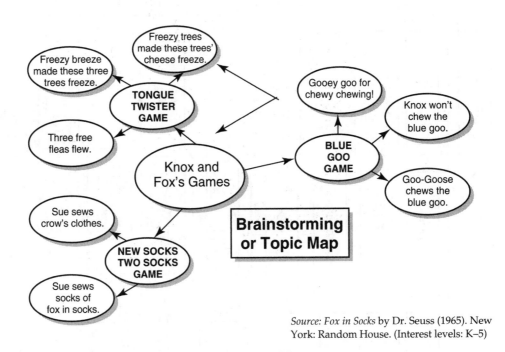

Source: Fox in Socks by Dr. Seuss (1965). New
York: Random House. (Interest levels: K–5)

FIGURE 10.6 Cause-and-Effect and Brainstorming Maps

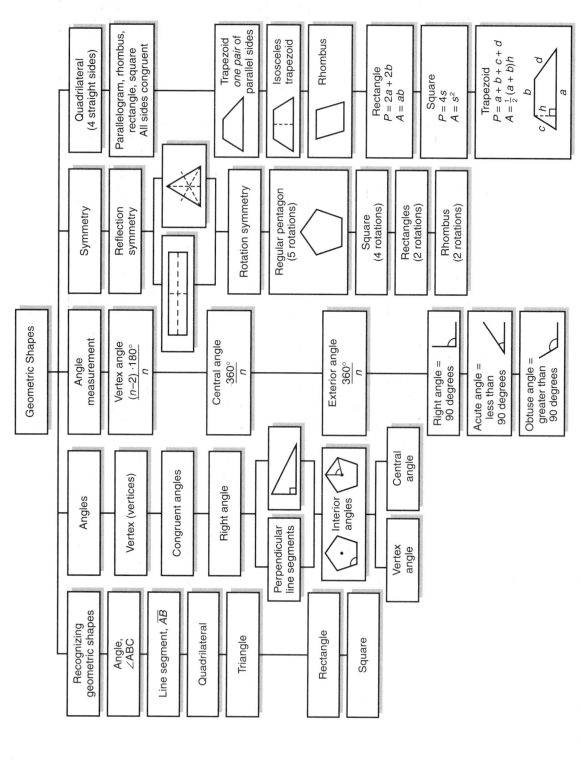

FIGURE 10.7 Vocabulary and Comprehension Scaffold

288

Teaching of Mnemonics, Keyword Strategies, and Other Vocabulary Interventions

The use of mnemonics, keywords, and mental imagery strategies to improve information recall involves "mental imagery instruction." Grosser (1995) summarizes some research-based and proven specific mnemonic devices. Active Reader Reports also improve comprehension and information retention for important vocabulary (see Figure 10.8)

Specific Mnemonic Devices*

Letters. Some more frequently cited mnemonic devises include ROY G. BIV (colors of the visual spectrum—red, orange, yellow, green, blue, indigo, and violet) and HOMES (the Great Lakes—Huron, Ontario, Michigan, Erie, and Superior). Keep in mind that each letter in the mnemonic is a cue for a word to be recalled. Such mnemonics are also referred to as acronyms.

Phrases. Mnemonic phrases are also helpful: I before E, except after C (i/e vowel rule); *every good boy does fine* (the lines on the treble clef; E G B D F); when the "mites" go up, the "tites" go down (directional differences between stalagmites and stalactites); thirty days hath September, April, June, and November—all the rest have 31 except February, which has 28 (the number of days in each month); "On old Olympus' towering top, a Finn and German viewed some homes" (first letter of each word cues the twelve cranial nerves—olfactory, optic, oculomotor, trochlear, trigeminal, abducens, facial, auditory, glossopharyngeal, vagus, spinal accessory, and hypoglossal).

"*My very educated mother just served us nine pizzas*" is an example of a sentence that can be used to remember the nine planets (in sequence from nearest to the sun to outermost: Mercury, Venus, Earth, Mars, Jupiter, Saturn, Uranus, Neptune, and Pluto). The sentence, "*All eager children must play yet always be happy*" can assist memory of the nine standard United States time zones: Atlantic, Eastern, Central, Mountain, Pacific, Yukon, Alaska, Bering, and Hawaii. In mathematics, "*Please excuse my dear Aunt Sally,*" can be used to explain the order of operations in solving equations: p = parenthesis; e = exponent; m = multiplication; d = division; a = addition; and s = subtraction. "Acrostics" is also the term used when the first letter of each word in the mnemonic represents an item to be learned.

Sometimes a short phrase can be used to trigger more lengthy information. For example, the "right hand" rule in physics for determining the flow of a magnetic field around an electrical current can be remembered as follows: ". . . place the thumb of the right hand in the direction of the current—the curl of the fingers around the conductor will show the direction of the magnetic field . . ." (Glover, Ronning, & Bruning, 1990, p. 188). Rhyming phrases also enhance memory such as "one, two, buckle my shoe; three, four, shut the door; five, six, pick up sticks; seven, eight, lay them straight; nine, ten, we see Ben."

Semantic mapping can be used for preplanning activities to introduce a unit or topic of study so as to further or expand content subject vocabulary (see Figure 10.9).

Knowledge of important vocabulary and related concepts for a subject (e.g., math) at a particular developmental level (e.g., preschool) is crucial in identifying appropriate vocabulary words and terms to target for learning (see Figure 10.10).

---

*by George S. Grosser

Proficient Learners and Readers	Students with Reading Disabilities	Technique for Major or Important Vocabulary Terms	Supporting Research	Techniques for Learning Groups of Words
• Possess effective metacognitive awareness, processing, and use of variable strategies to word-problem-solve. • Are able to use metacomprehension strategies to correct reading problems. • Can effortlessly recall information during word-problem-solving.	• Rely on one or two metacognitive strategies to word-problem-solve. • Are frequently unable to correct reading problems. • Sometimes experience problems with information recall.	**Active Reader Report** (Boyles, 2004, adapted) After encountering major vocabulary in content area subjects, immediately check: ✔ Do I have a good **picture** of the word in my mind? ✔ What **connection** can I make to my own life, another book, things in the world? ✔ What did I **figure out** about the new word the author didn't tell me? ✔ Is there something I **don't understand?** ✔ What will I do to **problem solve?** ✔ What am I still **wondering** about?	Boyles (2004).	*Utilize effective vocabulary instruction principles* (Stahl, 2004; Stahl & Fairbanks, 1986) by: 1. Providing definitional and contextual information about words to be learned. 2. Engaging the individual in deep processing or thinking about the new words and make connections to previous knowledge. 3. Providing multiple exposures or contexts to show how words change.
• The use of mnemonics and keywords helps to organize and retain information. • Explicit teaching of mnemonic and keyword strategies needs to occur even with highly proficient readers for optimal learning.	• All students need explicit teaching of mnemonic and keyword strategies with guided practice, repetition, multiple exposures to word meanings. Experiencing words in different contexts (sentences, with pictures or definitions and in elaborated contexts) also needs to occur.	Mnemonics, keywords, and mental imagery strategies to improve memory or information recall. Examples: 1. *Mnemonics* - "I before E, except after C (i/e vowel rule)." 2. *Keywords* - take unfamiliar term (dahlia = flower) and recode to acoustically similar keyword such as **doll**; remember **dahlia** by having a **doll** smell a flower. 3. *Mental imagery* - picturing the shape of Italy on a map as a boot.	Atkinson (1975); Grosser (2005); Levin, Levin, Glasman, & Nordwall (1992); Veit, Scruggs, & Mastropieri (1986).	*Teaching Tier Two Words – High Frequency Words for Mature Language Users.* (Beck, McKeown, & Kucan, 2002) 1. Identify approximately 400 words per year across a variety of domains where students understand the general concept but lack precision and specificity in describing the concept (e.g., "fortunate" = "lucky"). These are words students will be reading from text. 2. Create a student-friendly definition for each word by thinking about what elements make an identified word "different" and relevant to daily language usage. 3. Develop instructional contexts. 4. Engage students in purposeful activities where the words' meanings appear.

Source: Carol A. Spafford & George S. Grosser, *Dyslexia and Reading Difficulties: Research and Resource Guide for Working with All Struggling Readers.* Copyright © 2005 by Pearson Education. May be reproduced for noncommercial purposes.

FIGURE 10.8 Acquisition of Study Skills and Strategies: Recommended Vocabulary Interventions to Improve Comprehension and Information Retention

290

Proficient Learners and Readers	Dyslexics and the Learning Disabled	Technique	Example	Implementation
Proficient readers learn an average of 2,500 to 3,000 words per year and high-achievers, 5,000 words per year (Nagy, Anderson, & Herman, 1987; Beck, McKeown, & Kucan, 2002). In other words, children who are achieving are learning about 7 new words a day.	**Proficient readers** read at least 3,000 words per day encountering 10,000 unknown words per year (Nagy, Anderson, & Herman, 1987). **Low-achieving and dyslexic students** have been reported in various studies to read fewer than 1,000 words per day, learning fewer than 1,000 words per year.	**Semantic Mapping -** For content subject area preplanning activity to introduce a unit or topic of study (e.g., topics in science) so as to further or expand content subject area vocabulary.	Art Moderne Victorian Gothic Beaux-Arts Romanesque Neoclassical **Architectural Study of the History of Urbanism** | **Philadelphia, Pennsylvania** | **Founding Father, Benjamin Franklin** Inventor Statesman Diplomat Businessman Founded first library, Published *Poor Richard's Almanac* Established Penn. Hospital (first city hospital in USA) Invented Franklin stove Discovered electricity	**Semantic Mapping** (McKenna, 2004) **1. Brainstorming** Teachers and students collectively brainstorm words and ideas related to a topic. The teacher may clarify, explain, or elaborate upon words or concepts generated by the students. The teacher scribes these ideas or words on the board or chart paper. **2. Mapping** Teachers and students can draw or use predrawn semantic maps to arrange words and categories. **3. Reading-Related Activity Following the Mapping** A reading focused on the semantic map topic furthers word and concept understandings. **4. Reflect, Revise, Elaborate** Teachers and students revisit completed semantic maps following the topic reading and revise or elaborate based on the discussion.

FIGURE 10.9   Acquisition of Study Skills and Strategies: Recommended Vocabulary Intervention to Improve Comprehension and Information Retention—Vocabulary Semantic Mapping

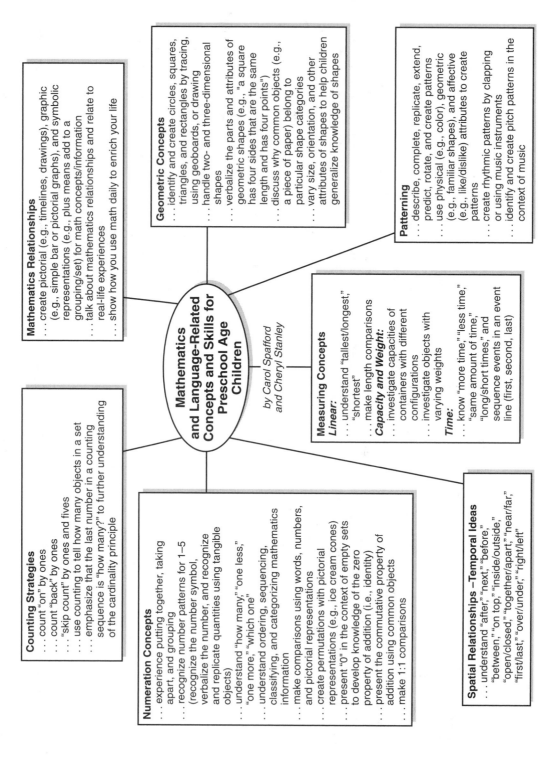

Counting Strategies
... count "on" by ones
... count "back" by ones
... "skip count" by ones and fives
... use counting to tell how many objects in a set
... emphasize that the last number in a counting sequence is "how many?" to further understanding of the cardinality principle

Numeration Concepts
... experience putting together, taking apart, and grouping
... recognize number patterns for 1–5 (recognize the number symbol, verbalize the number, and recognize and replicate quantities using tangible objects)
... understand "how many," "one less," "one more," "which one"
... understand ordering, sequencing, classifying, and categorizing mathematics information
... make comparisons using words, numbers, and pictorial representations
... create permutations with pictorial representations (e.g., ice cream cones)
... present "0" in the context of empty sets to develop knowledge of the zero property of addition (i.e., identity)
... present the commutative property of addition using common objects
... make 1:1 comparisons

Mathematics and Language-Related Concepts and Skills for Preschool Age Children

by Carol Spafford and Cheryl Stanley

Mathematics Relationships
... create pictorial (e.g., timelines, drawings), graphic (e.g., simple bar or pictorial graphs), and symbolic representations (e.g., plus means add to a grouping/set) for math concepts/information
... talk about mathematics relationships and relate to real-life experiences
... show how you use math daily to enrich your life

Geometric Concepts
... identify and create circles, squares, triangles, and rectangles by tracing, using geoboards, or drawing
... handle two- and three-dimensional shapes
... verbalize the parts and attributes of geometric shapes (e.g., "a square has four sides that are the same length and has four points")
... discuss why common objects (e.g., a piece of paper) belong to particular shape categories
... vary size, orientation, and other attributes of shapes to help children generalize knowledge of shapes

Patterning
... describe, complete, replicate, extend, predict, rotate, and create patterns
... use physical (e.g., color), geometric (e.g., familiar shapes), and affective (e.g., like/dislike) attributes to create patterns
... create rhythmic patterns by clapping or using music instruments
... identify and create pitch patterns in the context of music

Measuring Concepts
Linear:
... understand "tallest/longest," "shortest"
... make length comparisons
Capacity and Weight:
... investigate capacities of containers with different configurations
... investigate objects with varying weights
Time:
... know "more time," "less time," "same amount of time," "long/short times," and sequence events in an event line (first, second, last)

Spatial Relationships –Temporal Ideas
... understand "after," "next," "before," "between," "on top," "inside/outside," "open/closed," "together/apart," "near/far," "first/last," "over/under," "right/left"

FIGURE 10.10 Mathematics and Language-Related Concepts and Skills for Preschool Age Children

Using Graphic Organizers

Venn Diagrams

What were the first graphic organizers used for educational purposes? Educators who use graphic organizers extensively most likely would respond, "Venn diagrams!" Venn diagrams are graphic organizers that are used across all subject areas and are easy to construct and use. They essentially consist of overlapping circles (typically two or three) to allow for compare and contrast of information (see p. 294). Does the reader wonder if there was an individual named Venn we can credit for this "ingenious" way to diagram information? Your present authors wondered this very point and discovered that John Venn was the originator in 1880. Venn actually extended the work of Leonhard Euler (1770) to create what is commonly known as the Venn diagram. Originally, Euler used circles for checking the validity of syllogisms. Venn continued this systematic way to present logic representations using three overlapping circles. The practice of condensing information to a visual, graphic organizer, easily read and understood, has its roots with Euler and then Venn, more than two centuries ago!

Venn diagrams assist readers, especially those readers with reading disabilities, to synthesize information for more ready analysis and deeper understanding (see pp. 114–116 and 134–142 for several examples of graphic organizers). Analysis of the printed page depends on reading purpose, but in essence one is acquiring and building on word knowledge to make text connections, infer, draw conclusions, and critique.

Spinelli (1999) encourages using a number of graphic organizers especially in regard to writings that rely on text readings. Spinelli suggests cause/effect, sequence, and pro/con graphic organizers for content area subjects; models (see birthday cake graphic organizer on p. 163) to summarize main concepts and supporting details and Venn diagrams to compare and contrast. As one type of graphic organizer, Venn diagrams are easy to construct, can be used across the curriculum, and require "deep structure" or critical thinking about comparisons and contrasts.

Cinderella Stories

Instructional Application: The Use of Venn Diagrams

Venn diagrams can be used to model and organize thinking about similarities and differences or compare and contrast with cultural variants; these diagrams can be used as study guides. The "Multicultural Cinderella Venn Diagram" compares and contrasts some cultural variants for two Cinderellas—an Algonquin (from Lake Ontario Region) and a Mexican Cinderella (see Figure 10.11). Presenting the model or exemplar provides the "how to." Blank Cinderella Venn diagrams can be used to compare and contrast two "new" Cinderella stories after the student has had some practice with the model or has had guided teacher-directed instruction in completing a Venn diagram. For students with dyslexia, scaffolding the learning process via models or exemplars provides the language and processes needed for successful completion.

Providing Opportunities for Diverse Learning

Sloan and Vardell (2004) and Shepard (2002) encourage teachers to provide opportunities for students to respond to the type of cultural variants listed within the Venn diagrams when reading Cinderella stories. This will help children develop an appreciation of cultures they are not familiar with. As a caution, teachers and families would need to preview books for considered readings to look for prejudicial, stereo-

Name _____ Date _____ Grade _____

Multicultural Cinderella Venn Diagrams to Compare and Contrast Cultural Variants

Names of Cinderella and Countries _____

_____

Sources_____

_____

_____

Example: (Interest Levels: K–12)
Names of Cinderellas and Countries: Domitila from Mexico and the Rough Faced Girl from the Lake Ontario region. Sources: *The Rough-Faced Girl* by R. Martin (1998). Illustrated by D. Shannon. New York: Philomel. *Domitila: A Cinderella Tale from the Mexican Tradition* (2000) adapted by Jewell Reinhart Coburn. Illustrated by Connie McLennan.

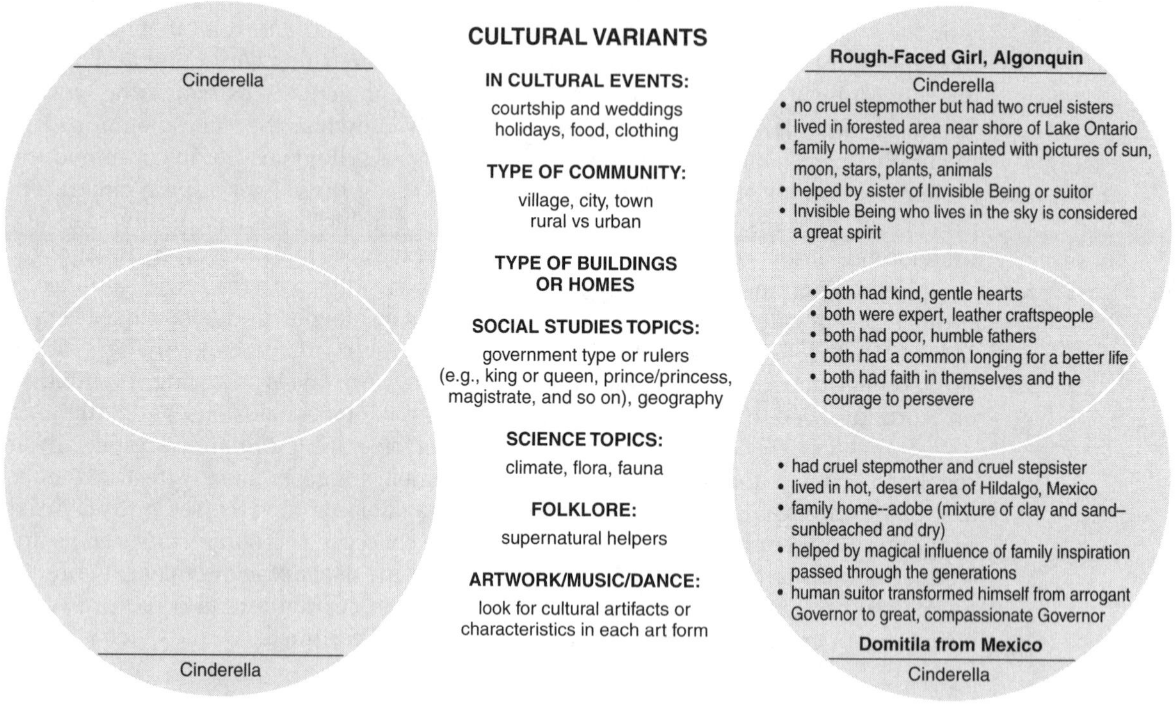

CULTURAL VARIANTS

IN CULTURAL EVENTS:

courtship and weddings
holidays, food, clothing

TYPE OF COMMUNITY:

village, city, town
rural vs urban

**TYPE OF BUILDINGS
OR HOMES**

SOCIAL STUDIES TOPICS:

government type or rulers
(e.g., king or queen, prince/princess,
magistrate, and so on), geography

SCIENCE TOPICS:

climate, flora, fauna

FOLKLORE:

supernatural helpers

ARTWORK/MUSIC/DANCE:

look for cultural artifacts or
characteristics in each art form

Cinderella (circle labels)

Rough-Faced Girl, Algonquin
Cinderella
• no cruel stepmother but had two cruel sisters
• lived in forested area near shore of Lake Ontario
• family home--wigwam painted with pictures of sun, moon, stars, plants, animals
• helped by sister of Invisible Being or suitor
• Invisible Being who lives in the sky is considered a great spirit

• both had kind, gentle hearts
• both were expert, leather craftspeople
• both had poor, humble fathers
• both had a common longing for a better life
• both had faith in themselves and the courage to persevere

• had cruel stepmother and cruel stepsister
• lived in hot, desert area of Hildalgo, Mexico
• family home--adobe (mixture of clay and sand– sunbleached and dry)
• helped by magical influence of family inspiration passed through the generations
• human suitor transformed himself from arrogant Governor to great, compassionate Governor

Domitila from Mexico
Cinderella

FIGURE 10.11   Multicultural Cinderella Venn Diagram

typical, biased, and offensive language and unrealistic or inappropriate portrayals of cultural groups or cultures. The listing of Cinderella books in the following box is offered for grades K–12, since most of the books could be read aloud to students of all ages.

Common elements emerge in all of the Cinderella stories—"a persecuted, poor, humble, kind heroine" with "jealous sisters or stepsisters," "a supernatural helper," and a royal or noble "suitor" who loves Cinderella for her good, kind ways. At one time or another, the reader of a Cinderella story can relate in some way to some of the situations such as "rising above" the cruel ways of negative others by being that "good example" as do the Cinderella heroines or "believe in yourself" and "don't give up" when you set a goal or "have a dream."

Reasons for Using Cinderella Stories in the Classroom

■ Multiple cultural variants can be compared and contrasted.
■ Cultural identity and cultural sensitivity can be developed and nurtured.
■ As folktales, Cinderella stories have a basic, "formulaic" structure with the likable "heroine" overcoming "evil" or cruelty by being resourceful, perseverant, good, and kind—this type of story has universal appeal.
■ There are many cultural versions of Cinderella with almost every culture represented in one of the versions.

Multicultural Cinderella Story References

African

Climo, S. (1989). Illustrated by R. Heller. *The Egyptian Cinderella*. New York: HarperCollins.

Onyefulu, O. (1994). Illustrated by E. Safarewicz. *Chinye: A West African Folk Tale*. New York: Viking.

Sierra, J. (2000). Illustrated by R. Ruffins. *The Gift of the Crocodile: A Cinderella Story*. New York: Simon & Schuster.

Steptoe, J. (1987). *Mufaro's Beautiful Daughters*. New York: Lothrop, Lee & Shepard.

Asian

Climo, S. (1996). Illustrated by R. Heller. *The Korean Cinderella*. New York: HarperTrophy.

Coburn, J.R. (1998). Illustrated by E. Flotte. *Angkat: The Cambodian Cinderella*. Arcadia, CA: Shen's.

Coburn, J.R., & Lee, T.C. (1996). Illustrated by A.S. O'Brien. *Angkat: Jouanah: A Hmong Cinderella*. Arcadia, CA: Shen's.

De la Paz, M. (2001). (Adapted by). Illustrated by Y. Tang. *Abadeha: The Philippine Cinderella*. Auburn, CA: Shen's Books.

Louie, A. (1982). (Retold by). Illustrated by E. Young. *Yeh-Shen: A Cinderella Story from China*. New York: Puffin.

Lum, D. (1994). Illustrated by M. Nagano. *The Golden Slipper: A Vietnamese Legend*. New York: Puffin.

Yen Mah, A. (1999). *Chinese Cinderella*. New York: Delacorte Press (for high school students and adults).

European

Brown, M. (1954). *Cinderella* (French version). New York: Atheneum.

Daly, J. (2000). *Fair, Brown & Trembling: An Irish Cinderella Story*. New York: Farrar, Straus & Giroux.

Latin American

Coburn, J.R. (2000). (Adapted by). Illustrated by C. McLennan. *Domitila: A Cinderella Tale from the Mexican Tradition*. Auburn, CA: Shen's Books.

Hayes, J. (2000). Illustrated by G.O. Perez and L.A. Perez. *Estrellita de Oro/Little Gold Star: A Cinderella Cuento*. El Paso, TX: Cinco Puntos.

San Souci, R.D. (2000). (Retold by). Illustrated by S. Martinez. *Little Gold Star: A Spanish American Cinderella Tale*. Singapore: Harper Collins.

San Souci, R.D. (1998). Illustrated by B. Pinkney. *Cendrillon: A Caribbean Cinderella*. New York: Simon & Schuster.

Native American

Martin, R. (1998). Illustrated by D. Shannon. *The Rough-Faced Girl*. New York: Philomel.

Pollock, P. (1996). Illustrated by E. Young. *The Turkey Girl: A Zuni Cinderella*. Boston: Little Brown & Co.

San Souci, R.D. (1997). *Sootface: An Ojibwa Cinderella Story*. New York: Bantam.

Middle Eastern

Climo, S. (1999). Illustrated by R. Florczak. *The Persian Cinderella*. New York: HarperCollins.

Hickox, R. (1998). Illustrated by W. Hillenbrand. *The Golden Sandal*. New York: Holiday House.

Jaffe, N. (1998). Illustrated by L. August. *The Way Meat Loves Salt: A Cinderella Tale from the Jewish Tradition*. New York: Henry Holt & Co.

- Cinderella stories provide cultural "snapshots" that can be used in discussions, writings, art and music, and dramatizations.
- The genre type (fairytales) and rich vocabulary make them ideal "tools" to use in the teaching of reading. (Shepard, 2002; Sloan & Vardell, 2004)

Worthy and Bloodgood (1998) found language in Cinderella stories that can be used to identify some of the stylistic features of fairy tales: common language ("once upon a time," "happily ever after"), themes (goodness is rewarded, wrongdoing is punished), and motifs (impossible gifts, supernatural elements, events happening in threes, disguises) (p. 253). The language and stylistic features can be replicated by students when creating their own fairy tales. After reading Cinderella stories, Phillips (1986) observed improved writing with diverse vocabulary, including sensory language, and vigorous action words with first-grade children.

For the student with dyslexia, a graphic organizer with a sequence of common story plot cues helps organize the story from beginning to end and can be referenced for a retelling. Worthy and Bloodgood (1998) have found that after identifying and analyzing the story structure in Cinderella stories, students became more adept at observing and discussing similarities and differences.

In addition to graphic organizers, a book report cube (see p. 144) could be used to summarize key story structure information from Cinderella stories.

Authentic Books to Create Multicultural Cinderella Stories   Intricate and culturally authentic book forms could be used in bookmaking. According to Gaylord (1994), there are six basic book forms: scrolls, accordion, palm leaf, slat, Asian stitched binding, and Western stitched binding. Gaylord suggests seven bookmaking steps:

Gaylord's (1994) Seven Multicultural Bookmaking Steps

(1) Determine materials needed such as paper in specific sizes, beads, yarn and
(2) Tools like scissors, markers, hole punchers and
(3) Materials per student and then
(4) Prepare ahead before
(5) Making the book with step-by-step instructions and use
(6) Variations or vary the content, construction and size of the books with
(7) The teacher providing suggested readings for specific cultural connections and ideas.

Learning Assessment   In regard to assessment, a daily exit slip (see Figure 10.12) could be used at the end of the day to evaluate new learning (e.g., new vocabulary) as well as to organize *thoughts about homework* and what needs to be done the next day.

Artwork Can Facilitate Learning Retention

Using pictures and graphics to reflect understandings is natural for young children as most children can draw what they know before they can write what they know. Building on the natural tendency of children to use artwork, teachers can encourage the use of visual representations mentioned in this chapter and throughout the book such as concept maps, diagrams, cause-and-effect graphics, comparison-contrast charts, timelines, and so on to represent information (Kletzien & Dreher, 2004). For students with

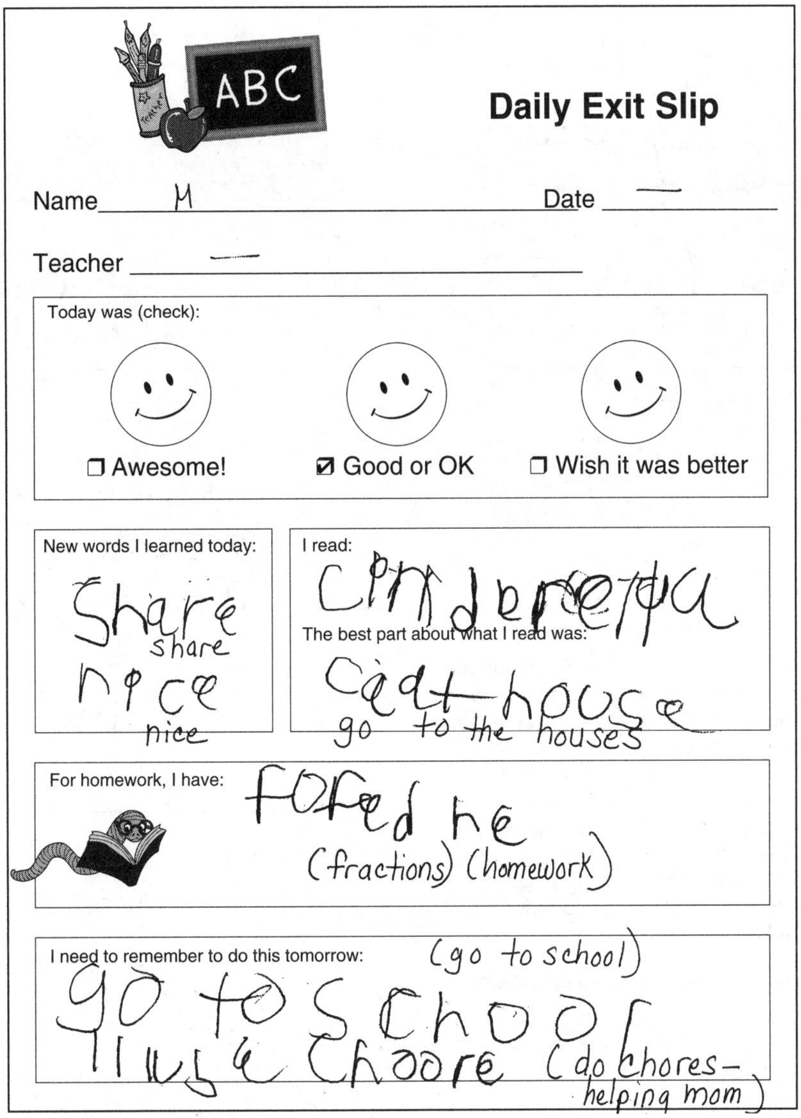

FIGURE 10.12   Daily Exit Slip

dyslexia and other learning disabilities, graphics and artwork provide valuable learning and reference frameworks.

Sometimes it is helpful to reproduce or draw the work of an artist because this may provide motivation to explore various art dimensions and help the individual with dyslexia to remember the work. For students in grades K–5, the painting "Central Railway of Brazil (created with geometric shapes)," by Tarsila do Amaral, could be presented with the works of other Latin American artists (e.g., source: Alma Flor Ada and Isabel Campoy's children's book, *Blue and Green*, 2000). Tarsila created a figurative scene with geometric shapes. Another example for older students would be Russian artist Marc Chagall's work "The Promenade." This work could be used to explore visionary images within layers of geometric shapes, or students could collaboratively select weekly cultural art pieces to write about in dialogue journals (Chira, 1999). Written responses to artwork can be highly motivating, especially for young students with dyslexia or struggling readers, as seen in Figure 10.13.

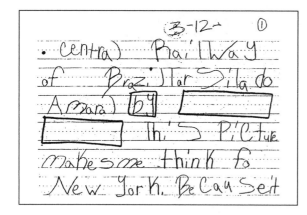

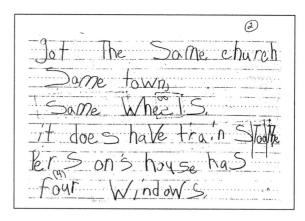

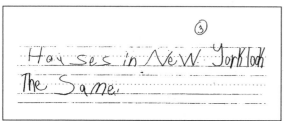

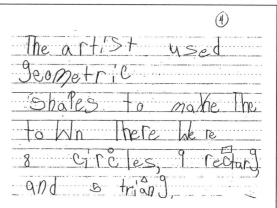

A struggling first-grade reader and writer, A, responded to *The Central Railway of Brazil.* A language experience format was used. The student dictated the response to a scribe, then copied the work for continued reading and word study. After several rereadings for fluency, the student was able to read the work (with some picture cues) to others. The size of the box for the student's name, the highlighting of the name, the meticulous formation of letters and words, and the completeness of the work (3 pages), give an indication as to how the student felt about this written piece.

FIGURE 10.13   Making Art-Literacy Connections

Practice, Practice, Practice

Individuals with dyslexia need to "read, read, read," and then read some more. Struggling readers need consistent opportunities to apply or practice the strategies and methods they acquire through intensive instruction—this is best accomplished within the context of "regular reading." According to Allington (2001), very beginning readers would benefit from reading at least ten titles per day (counting rereadings of previous books), and grade 5 and above should read at least one title per week (chapter books). Repeated readings of the same book (up to 200 words) serve to build fluency (accurate, fluid reading with understanding) in reading (Samuels, 2002) and *confident, resilient readers.* Ekwall and Shanker (1988) suggest placing emphasis on word accuracy first and then on speed. Goal setting (e.g., read two books per day) needs to be taught because many students with dyslexia need assistance with establishing goals. (Hallahan & Kauffman, 1991; Silverman, Zigmond, & Sansone, 1981). Practice or repetition of learning episodes can include connections made to the arts.

Homework

According to Warton (2001), "there is little research that convinces us that students recognize the purposes of homework that adults nominate" (p. 162). Purpose setting could be done on the homework assignment itself. The following example provides explicit purpose setting, a questioning format to guide reflections and a followup assignment to establish deeper personal connections.

A Learning Opportunity to Further School Achievement

Warton (2001) and others have studied the relationship between homework and academic achievement. Some important observations: (a) There is a positive correlation between the amount of time spent on homework and academic achievement with strong evidence for homework at the secondary level especially for high school seniors. (b) Students need to recognize adult purposes for homework and understand that the "purposes apply to them" (Warton, 2001, p. 161). Since homework is a valuable learning tool, *The Springfield Teacher* (2003) cautions educators not to use homework as a punishment but rather as a learning opportunity to further student achievement.

Chen and Ehrenberg (1993) found a stronger correlation when the achievement measure used to determine homework effectiveness is teacher grades versus standardized tests. This would be expected because most homework assignments extend knowledge and learning from the school day versus preparing students for standardized tests.

Establishing Homework Purposes

Epstein (1988) defines seven purposes for homework at the elementary level:

1. To fulfill school system requirements.
2. To practice learned skills.
3. To enhance learning-task involvement.
4. To nurture personal development of study habits and competence as a learner (e.g., time management, self-confidence).
5. To establish communications between parents and their children about schoolwork.
6. To inform parents of school learning.
7. To extend learning and classroom requirements for students at home.

Figure 10.14 shows a sample homework assignment. Warton (2001) emphasizes that teachers need to ensure that homework is "enjoyed, valued, and not seen as a disliked, solitary activity" (p. 164). Homework purposes, according to Warton, need to include developing "learning autonomy." For students with dyslexia and other learning disabilities, this can only occur if homework purposes are clearly articulated and even shared with the students, including a framework for study. Frameworks can include posing questions that students need to consider as they complete an assignment. The homework example in the box on page 300 seeks to develop deeper understandings of personal self-identity, a factor to consider when nurturing learning autonomy.

Parent involvement is strongly related to homework completion and the quality of the work. Suggestions are provided in Figure 10.15 to establish family practices that nurture "homework successes."

Establishing Goals or Purposes for Homework and a Framework for Study

Sample Homework Assignment Theme: "Developing Personal Self-Identity"

Goals: (1) To understand that personal self-identity is not just self-constructed but also influenced by others such as family, friends, peers, society, and individuals in other social settings; and (2) To understand that self-identity is affected by each individual's social characteristics (e.g., gender, age, race, where one lives, and so on).

(1) Paraphrase in your own words the "plain prose meaning" of the poem "Silence" by Tu-Uyen Nguyen.

(2) Think about how the author used imagery.

 • How did imagery enhance this poem? Do images add to the "emotional color" or associations to the "plain sense" of the poem.

 • Is the use of imagery consistent in the poem? Is this important?

(3) Consider how the author views herself.

 • Did the author's perception of herself change by the end of the poem?

 • How did the author's personal experiences shape her identity?

 • How do the author's experiences impact with whom or which group(s) she identified?

 • How do others view the author in this poem?

 • What environmental factors influenced the author's identity?

(4) How does imagery used in the poem relate to the theme of identity?

(5) Paraphrase, web, or outline the overall tone or mood of the poem (the feeling communicated to the reader of the poem) using words or phrases from the poem.

(6) Can you make a personal connection?

Homework Assignment 2 (a followup)

Create a collage that visually depicts or expresses your identity. Be creative and use magazines, newspapers, construction paper, markers, colored pencils, paint, and so on. As an example, your collage may include pictures that look like friends or the ethnic communities to which you belong; pop culture items like favorite bands, clothing brands of choice that reflect your clothing style, and so on. Your collage should reflect not only how you see yourself but how others view you as well.

Based on: "An Exploration of Silence" (*Vietnamese Americans: Lessons in American History,* 2004, p. 35)

FIGURE 10.14   Sample Homework Assignment with Goal Setting, and Questions to Guide Reflections

---

Parental involvement in a child's homework assignments is directly related to school achievement and developing personal attributes in children that contribute to school achievement such as self-regulation, ability to manage time, and positive self-concepts of ability (Delgado-Gaitan, 1992)—these are also considered resiliency factors (developing an internal locus of control, self-confidence, and positive self-esteem). Hoover-Dempsey, Battiato, Walker, Reed, DeJong, and Jones (2001) discuss several family practices that will contribute to "homework successes" and how these are directly related to school achievement:

 • Consistently interact with the teachers at school about homework expectations and student outcomes,

 • Generally oversee the homework process—check for understanding of the assignments and quality and completeness,

 • Respond to homework performance in the form of praise, reference to "family standards" and incentives or extrinsic rewards,

 • Actively engage in homework assignments (e.g., tutoring, assisting, "doing homework" with the child),

 • Use strategies that "fit" a child's skill level as well as the demands of the task itself (e.g., breaking a homework task into manageable components),

 • Clarify, model, and demonstrate to enhance understandings (e.g., discuss a problem-solving strategy and model using this strategy).

FIGURE 10.15   Parent Involvement in Facilitating Homework Successes

Increasing Peer Collaboration Time

Cooperative Learning Ventures

Cooperative learning ventures involve students working with other students and teachers working with other teachers. According to the National Reading Panel Report (2000), "when students as peers tutor or instruct one another or interact over the use of reading strategies, the evidence is that they learn reading strategies" (p. 4-101). Cooperative learning or peer tutoring can be an integral part of any literacy program.

Teacher-Assistance Teaming (Cooperative Teacher Consultation) Teacher-Assistance Teaming very simply involves a consultation model whereby teacher assistance teams within a school building (e.g., special educators and literacy specialists) are available to network with the teacher who has a student with dyslexia in dealing with any academic, social, or behavioral problems. This model has been in use for several years (e.g., see Chalfant, Pysh, & Moultrie, 1979). Problem solving would center on accommodating the student with dyslexia within the regular classroom before other program options are considered.

Slavin (1992) cites the importance of cooperative learning ventures when students with disabilities are mainstreamed. Cooperative learning groups can include the teaming of two or three students or slightly larger groups if necessary. Slavin (1992) suggests that cooperative learning groups can be involved in partner readings, story-related writing, math activities, story retellings, spelling, and partner checking in all areas. One of the most important side effects of this approach is the development of friendships among students who can grow to respect and nurture the unique differences and similarities among them in regard to learning, ethnicity, and so on.

Cooperative learning skills are not easily taught by teachers nor are the skills presented easily learned by students. Cooperative learning will not work with just the grouping of students. Teachers must take the time to develop appropriate attitudes on the part of the students and an interdependent frame of reference (Ryder & Graves, 1994). It is recommended that teachers consult tried and proven cooperative learning models (see Slavin, 1992).

Student Teams-Achievement Divisions (STAD) Slavin offers the Student Teams-Achievement Divisions (Slavin, 1992) as a cooperative learning model. This approach uses groups of four with differing abilities, ethnicity, gender, and social class (SES) working together. After the teacher presents a lesson, students work together to ensure that each member of the group learns the material presented. Group members share answers, encourage each other, problem solve, present alternative solutions, and quiz each other. After students accomplish their learning goals, they individually demonstrate what was learned and receive points based on learning gains from a previous performance. Individual points are totaled for team scores.

Jigsaw Jigsaw is another cooperative learning model that was developed by Aronson, Blaney, Stephan, Sikes, and Snapp (1978). Essentially, with Jigsaw, groups of six students are formed. Lesson material is broken down into sections with each student in a group learning a section of the material being studied. For example, students might be studying the solar system. One student in each group might investigate the planets, another the sun, another the moon, and so on. Each member of the group becomes an expert on his or her topic and then must return to the group to share information about that topic. Students show what they learned from their own research and what they learned from the group. This approach can only be used with material that is easily broken into topics/units/areas of study (e.g., especially in science and social studies).

Peer Tutoring

Peer tutoring is an effective way to improve academic proficiency and social skills for students with dyslexia. The empirical evidence is convincing (Fuchs, 1997), especially for children who experience behavior difficulties. In essence, peer tutoring involves pairing a student with dyslexia with a student who is a proficient reader and writer. Sometimes the reverse occurs in "reverse-role tutoring," where the student with dyslexia would serve as the tutor in an area of strength. According to Tournaki and Criscitiello (2003), there is limited evidence regarding the effectiveness of reverse-role tutoring, but the current authors believe there is enough research (e.g., Brown, 1993; Cook, Scruggs, Mastropieri, & Castro, 1986) to support its use. The advantages of reverse-role tutoring (i.e., dyslexics serve as the tutors) are presented in the box below.

Tournaki and Criscitiello (2003) suggest two types of pair assignments based on the academic need and type of assignment: random pairs and choosing partners based on academic, social, and behavioral factors or considerations. Choosing partners for students with dyslexia has to be done with caution, especially considering the depressed self-esteem and self-images frequently experienced by students with dyslexia due to repeated academic failures and sometimes social difficulties. Often children with dyslexia experience more negative peer interactions and what has been termed as the "social misperception syndrome." That is, individuals with dyslexia sometimes have impaired social awareness that interferes with positive peer interactions attributable to impaired communications or impaired perceptual skills. Empathic or understanding adults and peers are critical to the development of self-confident, socially perceptive, and personally resilient individuals. Peer tutoring provides opportunities for students not only to improve academic proficiency in reading and writing but also to develop and maintain "good social interaction skills" and resiliency. When individuals with dyslexia serve as tutors, further positive social change can occur.

Peer tutoring should involve (1) a predictable schedule and (2) some type of journal activity where the tutor and or tutee log content or activity covered and some reflective comments. Teacher and family feedback commenting on the positive accomplishments of the tutoring would be recorded in the journal as well. Using stickers or other positive incentives could be used as well to maintain and continue the tutoring program.

Use of Specific Study Skill (Cognitive) Strategy Models or Systems

Research shows that when readers are provided with specific study skill or cognitive strategy models and instruction, they improve significantly in reading comprehension versus students who do not receive such instruction (Palinscar & Brown, 1987; Rosenshine & Meister, 1994).

Advantages of Reverse-Role Tutoring

1. Because the individual with dyslexia or other learning disabilities assumes a *"prestigious role,"* a change in status may lead to more *positive social interactions* and a *higher self-esteem.*
2. The focus of attention is placed on the *student's strengths* rather than on the student's weaknesses.
3. Both the tutor and tutee *are engaged in an activity with a positive learning purpose* implicitly and explicitly stated.
4. The improved social changes may *generalize to the classroom setting.*

Source: Tournaki & Criscitiello (2003)

Reciprocal Teaching

Reciprocal teaching is a method where students take turns with the teacher, reading segments and formulating questions about the reading. They switch roles during some or all parts of the reading. Reciprocal teaching has been offered by Palinscar and Brown (1984) and is particularly useful with students with learning disabilities in providing an understanding of difficult text, new or unfamiliar vocabulary terms, difficult concepts, and unclear referent words. Students learn that "reciprocal" means shared— teachers and students will take turns "leading" the lesson.

1. The teacher chooses text (e.g., expository text) and explains sections of the beginning section of the book that have difficult concepts or are difficult to understand.
2. The teacher shows how to summarize the information from the selected section of text.
3. The teacher demonstrates how to ask good questions about the selected text.
4. The teacher makes a prediction about the next section of text.
5. A student is assigned a section of text (e.g., a paragraph) and assumes the teacher's role for (1)–(4).
6. The teacher's role is then given to another student(s) for another section of text.
7. If students show difficulty summarizing, then rereading occurs and the teacher clarifies and models meaningful summaries.
8. Teachers and students provide feedback to each other regarding the process. (Palinscar & Brown, 1984, 1987).

K-W-L

The K-W-L (Ogle, 1986) as a graphic organizer facilitates comprehension building by connecting (personalizing) prior knowledge to the present topic (K), establishing a reading purpose (W), and reflecting on and then summarizing what was learned (L). The following boxed example centers on the life of Gandhi. A read-aloud using the book *Gandhi* (interest level: Grades 3–12) by Demi (2001) (New York: Margaret K. McElderry Books) could be preceded by the "K" and "W" from KWL developed through interactive discussion. The teacher could scribe class responses on chart paper for reference during the read-aloud. An example is presented in the box on Gandhi.

Gandhi

K (What I already know)	W (What I want to learn)	L (What I learned)
■ Gandhi is one of the most respected and revered social activists and humanitarians of all time.	■ What groups of people did Gandhi advocate for?	■ Poor Black and Indian people, women, sick people, lepers, and the dying
■ Gandhi was born in India and was a strong voice in advocating for the rights of "common people."	■ What is the "Karma" Gandhi refers to?	■ Karma is the idea that to keep a pure soul one needs to pray, be disciplined, be honest, harm no one, and have few possessions.
■ Gandhi spoke of change through nonviolent means and inspired Dr. Martin Luther King Jr.'s nonviolent civil rights movement in the United States.	■ Did Gandhi inspire any other major human rights movements?	■ Gandhi inspired Nelson Mandela's anti-apartheid movement in South Africa.

Teaching Steps for K-W-L

Step 1 Preparation—the teacher determines the content.

Step 2 Group Instruction—Pre-reading activities.

   K a. The group brainstorms to determine what they already know about the topic.

   b. After discussion, the group categorizes information and might develop semantic maps.

Step 3 Individual Reflection.

   W a. Students develop questions about what they want to know (or learn) and set a purpose for reading.

   b. Students predict what they might learn to answer their generated questions.

Step 4 Reading.

   The actual reading of text can be broken into sections or read as a whole.

Step 5 After Reading—Learning Assessment.

   L Students identify new information they have learned. They can add this information to their semantic maps to illustrate how the new information fits into existing knowledge. (Ogle, 1986)

Direct Teaching and Modeling of Other Study Skills

SQ3R

The SQ3R method of study was developed by Robinson in 1946 and is one systematic approach to studying textual material. The purpose of this study method is to guide students through content area subjects by using the text format. This technique is more suited for secondary-level students. The SQ3R format is actually five steps: (1) surveying the chapter content by reading and thinking about chapter headings, topic sentences and headings, the concluding paragraph, and end-of-chapter questions; (2) questioning by restating chapter headings in the form of a question; (3) reading the material after each topic and formulating answers to questions along the way; (4) reciting answers to questions in one's own words (repeating steps 2–4 throughout the chapter reading); and (5) reviewing notes and trying to recall main points after each main heading in the chapter. Interrogative reading is critical to the acquisition and retention of knowledge for all students.

There have been some adaptations to the SQ3R method that have been used to enhance study skills acquisition. Simpson, Hayes, Stahl, Connor, and Weaver (1988) offered the PORPE method, which focuses students on *p*redicting, *o*rganizing, *r*ehearsing, *p*racticing, and *e*valuating study material. It would be particularly important for the teacher at the secondary level to model time management skills (Manganello, 1994) as part of study skills training.

ReQuest

Reciprocal questioning (Manzo, 1985) occurs with the teacher first modeling how to ask good questions. A reading purpose is established and then sections of text are read. Teachers and students alike take turns asking and answering questions.

Question-Answer Relationships—QAR

In QAR (Rafael, 1986), students are taught to identify types of information needed to answer questions, the sources for the information, and how to retrieve the information.

According to Rafael (1986), students can be taught there are two sources of information (1) "in the book" and (2) "in my head." Students need to understand the difference between prior knowledge and text information. Students learn that "in the book" sources can be subdivided into (a) "right here" information that is explicitly stated in the text and (b) "think-and-search" information that is implicitly stated. Additionally, students learn they may have to combine textual information with prior knowledge ("author" and "you") or the reading may be passage independent with only prior knowledge needed ("on my own"). Harris and Sipay (1990) reviewed the research and point out that learning the QAR strategy results in improved ability to respond to questions with average and stuggling students showing considerable improvement. Harris and Sipay also have found that fourth and fifth graders can acquire the QAR strategy in approximately one week with six to eight weeks of practice needed thereafter.

Directed Reading-Thinking Activity—DRTA

According to Russell Stauffer (1969), the DRTA calls for teachers who are adept at encouraging students to ask questions to stimulate deep-thinking processes. According to Stauffer, "the reading-thinking process must begin in the mind of the reader. He must raise questions and to him belongs the challenge and responsibility of judgment. The teacher keeps the process active."

Rubin (1991b, p. 331) outlines the process:

I. Pupil actions
   A. Predict (set purposes)
   B. Read (process ideas)
   C. Prove (test answers)
II. Teacher actions
   A. What do you think?
   B. Why do you think so?
   C. Prove it

Note Taking

Many students with dyslexia are overwhelmed with the task of taking notes. ". . . this is not surprising since note taking requires simultaneous listening, comprehending, synthesizing, and/or extracting main ideas, while retaining them long enough to formulate and write a synopsis . . ." (Vogel, 1987, p. 253). Note taking can be facilitated by

Survey, Question, Read, Recite, Review—SQ3R

Sample Application:

(1) Teacher and students choose a "new" reading selection.
(2) **S**urvey the reading to see what it is all about.
(3) Prepare some **Q**uestions to set reading purposes (4–5 questions).
(4) Students **R**ead the text.
(5) Students **R**ecite or state the answers to the questions to themselves either subvocally or through underlining, highlighting, note taking, or outlining.
(6) Teacher **R**eviews the text and questions/answers immediately following the reading to see if the text was understood. (Robinson, 1946)

ReQuest

Outline

(1) Prior to the reading, the teacher models how to ask good questions and how to answer these questions (e.g., restating the question to begin the answer).
(2) A purpose for a "new" reading is established.
(3) Students and the teacher examine the book cover (see Figure 10.2 on p. 283), read the book title, read the first sentence in the story, and then discuss any illustrations on the first page of the book.
(4) Students ask the teacher questions about the introductory information in the book; the teacher answers these questions.
(5) The teacher tries to focus the students on the "big picture" or main ideas; reading purpose.
(6) A small portion of text is read with the students and teachers questioning each other about the text.
(7) The interchange continues for about 10 minutes.
(8) Students complete the reading silently. At the end of the story, the teacher asks, "Did we read for the right reading purpose?" with additional questions about the story. (Manzo, 1985; Manzo & Manzo, 1993)

having good students in the same classes photocopy and share their notes. Tape-recorded lectures (with the permission of the instructor) allow students to listen to the cues that teachers provide that might signal main ideas, important information, and summary statements. Teachers can word-process their notes in a *guided* format for students to use if and when appropriate (time permitting).

Guided Notes   Lazarus (1988) developed a study skills approach called Guided Notes, which involves an incomplete outline of material to be studied. Teachers create an outline of material from lectures and reading assignments. Space is allowed for students to fill in as the teacher speaks or fill in after reading textual material. Figure 10.16 provides some ideas as to how students can organize key concepts abstracted from lecture notes. Guided notes can be used to prepare for tests and quizzes. The use of guided notes should include the main ideas of presented material and key terms on student copies; a consistent format that parallels lecture/text material; and a review tally if

Question-Answer Relationship—QAR

Farrar (1999, p. 7) outlines the process:

(1) Preread the material.
(2) Survey the questions to be answered.
(3) Read to find the answers.
(4) Discuss the relationship.
(5) Point out the role of the readers' prior knowledge (educated guess).
(6) Right there: Answers are right there, literally and straightforwardly stated.
(7) Think and search: Answers require a search and putting together information.
(8) Author and me: The author has supplied clues, but you must link them with what you know.
(9) On my own: The answer is not in the selection, you must rely on prior knowledge. (Rafael, 1986)

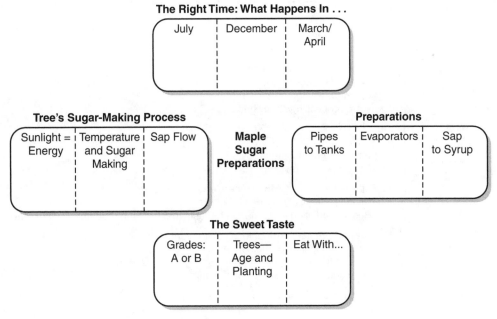

The Right Time: What Happens In . . .

July	December	March/April

Tree's Sugar-Making Process

Sunlight = Energy	Temperature and Sugar Making	Sap Flow

Maple Sugar Preparations

Preparations

Pipes to Tanks	Evaporators	Sap to Syrup

The Sweet Taste

Grades: A or B	Trees—Age and Planting	Eat With...

Source: Sugaring Time by Kathryn Lasky (1983). New York: Macmillan.

FIGURE 10.16 Guided Notes

needed (Lazarus, 1988). A review tally could consist of a small box in the right-hand corner of the first page of a student's guided notes that is divided into several squares. Students can check and date review dates or tally key concepts reviewed/learned. Lazarus and McKenna (1991) have found that the use of guided notes along with a subsequent review of the material result in best learning results. McKenna and Robinson (1993) believe that this format is especially useful for the struggling reader. In fact, providing the entire class with guided notes should enhance the learning experience for all.

Test Taking Strategies

First and foremost, students need to sleep well before an exam. Cramming all night at the last minute does not serve to benefit any student. Certain pretesting strategies can increase the likelihood of successful performance for students with dyslexia:

1. Determine the test format (e.g., multiple choice versus essay).
2. Be certain of the material to be covered on an exam.
3. For college students, ask students who have had a particular course about the nature of the teacher's expectations for exams.
4. Students and parents or tutors can anticipate questions to be asked and practice answering those questions.
5. Multiple choice exams will require recognition abilities and therefore close attention to details when studying.
6. Essay exams require more emphases on main ideas with supporting details.
7. Review material for an exam every day for ten 30-minute time segments as opposed to lengthy study just before the exam.

For the student in college, the study skills tips in Figure 10.17 can be referenced.

1. Be a time manager by organizing
   -Study schedules
   -Planning calendars

2. Develop appropriate accommodations by using:
   -Pass/fail grades
   -Untimed testing
   -Word processing/spell checking
   -Tutoring
   -Taped text notes

3. Form study groups that provide:
   -Repetition and review

4. Establish a rapport with teachers and professors:
   -Request clarification when needed
   -Request additional assistance for tests, papers, and research assignments

5. Always do repeated reading of assignments by:
   -First time looking for main ideas
   -Second time looking for subtopics
   -Third time looking for essential details

6. Always thank those who assist you!

Source: Susan Guay, Tutor, and Joann McClain, Student

FIGURE 10.17   Study Skills for the Individual with Dyslexia in College

Culturally Responsive Educational Practices

Familiarity with students' cultural practices, values, and beliefs, as well as an understanding of the realities of urban and suburban community living, provide foundations for culturally responsive teaching in all contexts. Rueda, Monzó, and Higareda (2004) use the term *sociocultural scaffolding* to describe a type of culturally responsive teaching in which educators use their cultural and community knowledge in interactions with students to scaffold learning, especially during the literacy block. Cultural exchanges are one way to help students feel more comfortable in the learning environment while positively impacting learning (Stanley & Spafford, 2001, 2002). Engaging students in activities that foster social collaborations where students must communicate with one another (Piaget, as cited in Ripple & Rockcastler, 1964) will lead them to more meaningful and deeper understandings that can be personalized.

Weiss (1994) stresses the importance of learning about students' home lives and experiences. These combined with pedagogical skills and "a critical consciousness toward serving . . . students, can make an important contribution to the development of effective learning contexts" (Rueda, Monzó, & Higareda, 2004, p. 56). Additionally, Tatum (1997) advises educators to pay close attention to the development of personal self-identities and concerted efforts need to occur to give positive messages to all (Comer, 1997). Teachers need to empower both themselves and their students with the necessary content knowledge to achieve proficiency in school while considering background relevant to the cultural context of families. This would necessarily include knowing about and interacting with families to inform instruction (Stanley & Spafford, 2001, 2002).

Summary

The current authors explored what helps students most with study skills both in the classroom and at home and summarized some research in eight major areas with instructional suggestions offered for use with all students:

I. Strategy instruction that includes self-questioning instruction.
II. Direct teaching and modeling of paraphrasing and summarizing strategies during the reading process provide students with valuable study skills strategies.
III. Direct teaching of mnemonic, keyword strategies, and other vocabulary interventions to improve vocabulary comprehension and information retention (see Grosser, 2005).
IV. Use of graphic organizers to diagram or outline the main structure of material to be read or material read (e.g., main concepts or ideas, key terminology, and concepts).
V. Practice, practice, and more practice are important, especially repeated practice after new strategies and knowledge are acquired.
VI. Homework and parent involvement in their child's homework assignments as these are directly related to school achievement and developing personal attributes that contribute to school achievement, such as self-regulation, ability to manage time, and positive self-concepts of ability, also considered resiliency factors.
VII. Increasing peer collaboration time through cooperative learning groups, pairings during reading times, and peer tutoring are effective ways to improve academic achievement for students with dyslexia. In essence, peer tutoring involves pairing a student with dyslexia with a student who is a proficient reader and writer. Sometimes the reverse occurs in "reverse-role tutoring," where the student with dyslexia would serve as the tutor in an area of strength.
VIII. Direct teaching, modeling, and consistent use of specific study skill and test taking strategies.

Several study skills models or approaches were overviewed with direct and explicit teaching steps: Reciprocal Teaching, K-W-L, SQ3R, ReQuest, QAR, and DRTA. How to summarize text needs to be systematically taught through general teaching principles and the use of outlines and graphic organizers. Of the seven most effective comprehension strategy teaching approaches cited by the National Research Panel Report (2000), summarizing is the most essential to developing effective study skills.

Warton (2001) and others have studied the relationship between homework and academic achievement with some important observations: (a) There is a positive correlation between the amount of time spent on homework and academic achievement with strong evidence for homework at the secondary level especially for high school seniors and (b) students need to recognize adult purposes for homework and understand that the "purposes apply to them." Students with dyslexia need to have homework purposes clearly articulated and a framework for study—a sample homework assignment was given that makes reference to both of these points.

Parent involvement in homework → positive student perceptions about school and school effort→ increased likelihood of homework completion → better homework performance → more positive school behavior → increased student learning and school successes.

Various cooperative learning ventures were discussed. According to the National Reading Panel Report (2000), "when students as peers tutor or instruct one another or interact over the use of reading strategies, the evidence is that they learn reading strategies" (p. 4-101). Cooperative learning or peer tutoring can be an integral part of any literacy program and involves teachers working with teachers as well.

Chapter 11 now presents what the complete literacy block should look like with some attention given to extending support systems to adults with dyslexia. Internet resourcing, as a powerful technology to support literacy learning for teachers and students, is discussed.

11 The Complete Literacy Block and Internet Resourcing

According to dyslexia pioneer Grace Fernald (1943),

- Students with serious reading problems have tremendous potential if they receive appropriate instruction.
- These students need intensive, small group instruction.
- Multisensory methods are successful.
- The language experience approach is useful.
- Repeated reading methods are effective.
- Integrating oral language, reading and writing enhances all language components . . .

(*Source:* Lerner, 2003)

■

Teach [all] your students to present themselves as well-behaved, bright, and able (Comer, 1988, p. 221). . . . Incorporate a cultural approach to literacy education where "school climate, physical environment, curriculum, and relationships among teachers and students and community" are consistently and positively impacted (Nieto, 1996, p. 315) . . .

■

The goal: to bring all students to levels of proficiency in academics—capable students who are self-efficacious, confident self-starters and problem solvers who are flexible, reflective, caring individuals able to seek critical support systems when needed and willing to advocate for others when needed as well (resilient learners).

According to Dorothy Strickland (2001), student achievement will be advanced "by establishing clear and challenging goals in specific subject areas for each grade, focusing teaching on helping students achieve these goals" (p. 20). Lipson and Wixson (1997) also stress the importance of goal setting while communicating to struggling readers the value of becoming literate within a supportive environment that minimizes those factors that produce performance anxiety or stress. As discussed in Chapter 4, an individual's resiliency, or ability to quickly bounce back or recover from stressors, can be impacted in a positive way by supportive environmental "protective factors." The QUART survey (see p. 69) can help pinpoint these factors.

Exemplary Teaching Characteristics

Exemplary classroom teachers are able to establish caring, safe, supportive, and nurturing classroom environments where students are engaged and motivated to reach high levels of achievement.

Exemplary Teachers . . .

1. *Create classroom cultures* and "communities of learners" where "deep or higher level thinking" is nurtured through pro-learning, pro-reading, and pro-writing discourse, and high expectations are communicated with many opportunities for reflective learning and teaching (Cambourne, 1995).

2. *Connect with families* in terms of comprehensive and long-lasting involvement to further student learning and academic achievement; emphasize the importance of "reading to children" consistently (Edwards, 2003; Vukelich, 1984)

3. Engage in *culturally responsive teaching* by first demonstrating respect, care, and concern for all students. Require all students "meet high academic and behavioral standards" (Tatum, 2003). According to Tatum, a culturally responsive approach involves talking to struggling readers from diverse backgrounds (e.g., African American students) about "personal value, the collective power, and the political consequences of choosing academic achievement"—cooperation is emphasized over competition and learning is structured as a social activity" (Tatum, 2003, p. 99). Ladson-Billings (1994) emphasizes *using a student's culture for a vehicle of learning* and broadening all students' "sociopolitical consciousness" so they can critique those institutions and systems, values, and norms that perpetuate inequalities.

4. Consider the *role of culture in direct lesson planning* efforts. Relating student life experiences and culture to lessons empowers teachers to create a context for learning where students will listen to and become engaged in the learning process (Stanley & Spafford, 2002).

5. *Engage readers* so that they become "lost in a book," "have a virtual experience with a book," or "identify with a character in a book." Teachers can use narrative fiction to create enthusiastic and interested readers (Galda & Liang, 2003).

6. Provide *choices in reading materials* for children; "choice leads to ownership" (Thomas & Barksdale-Ladd, 1995).

7. Develop *opportunities for students to activate schemata* or prior knowledge (Pearson & Dole, 1987) so they can connect that knowledge with what they encounter on the printed page (Vacca, 2002).

8. *Integrate skills instruction with holistic literacy activities using mini-lessons* followed by direct applications (Pressley, Allington, Wharton-McDonald, Block, & Morrow, 2001).

9. Use *multiple and varied teaching strategies and skills* through demonstration and modeling in structured lessons (Morrow, Tracey, Woo, & Pressley, 1999).

10. *Provide opportunities for much reading of* connected text and many writing responses to connected text (Spafford, 2001).

11. Are *multitask oriented*; that is, do more than one thing at a time. They teach and observe; model and coach; plan and remain flexible (Richgels, 2003).

12. *Have carefully organized classrooms* to support learning with easy accessibility to materials within a literacy-rich environment (Ruddell & Ruddell, 1995).

13. Meet all literacy needs with *high expectations* and *learning goals* set for the teacher and student (Rizzo, 1999).

There is no one program for developing reading and writing proficiency for individuals with dyslexia, but many current best methods/strategies/resources and research-based programs have shown documented successes. Research has demonstrated that schools that incorporate (A) *comprehensive or balanced reading programs* within (B) an extended *literacy block* and (C) rely on *evidence-based* specific *instructional practices* best meet the academic needs of students with dyslexia and other learning disabilities. Adaptations to the literacy block need to be made for students who are second-language learners.

Comprehensive or Balanced Reading Programs

Comprehensive or balanced reading programs:

- Contain the five essential teaching of reading elements: (1) phonemic awareness, (2) phonics (with systematic explicit instruction), (3) fluency, (4) vocabulary development, and (5) text comprehension.
- Incorporate academic content standards and achievement standards (expected levels of performance students should achieve).
- Rely on evidence-based instructional materials and methods.
- Use assessments to evaluate how well students achieve mastery of the standards or instruction benchmarks while guiding future instructional practices.
- Require a daily extended time "block" (minimum suggested time: two to three hours per day).
- Involve students in reading and writing choices to enhance learning engagement and motivation.
- Link writing to reading with a strong focus on reading-to-write and using writings to read and share.
- Utilize guiding questions for continuous reflections on teaching such as (1) "What content or strategies do we want students to know?" or "What is it that we want students to know?" (2) "What level of performance do we expect relative to the standards or benchmarks?" and (3) "How well did the students learn?"
- Continue the learning process beyond the school day with study skills preparations and family literacy outreach.

The Responsive Classroom

The following "responsive" teaching considerations are recommended to parallel implementation of the language arts block (Denton & Kriete, 2000):

- *Create a classroom environment of warmth and safety.*
- *Articulate and post classroom routines and expectations* for scholars and responsible school citizens.
- *Familiarize students with the school environment and resources* so they feel a sense of ownership and pride.
- *Regularly convey expectations for high-quality work,* provide models of exemplary work, and state benchmarks and standards for both the processes and products of learning.

It is the responsive classroom teacher who will bring a dyslexic student to levels of proficiency. According to Cathy M. Roller (2001), "it is what teachers actually do in the classroom with curriculum materials themselves that produce high reading achievement" (p. 198).

Complete Literacy Block

The present authors recommend the following comprehensive literacy block, shown in Figure 11.1 on page 314.

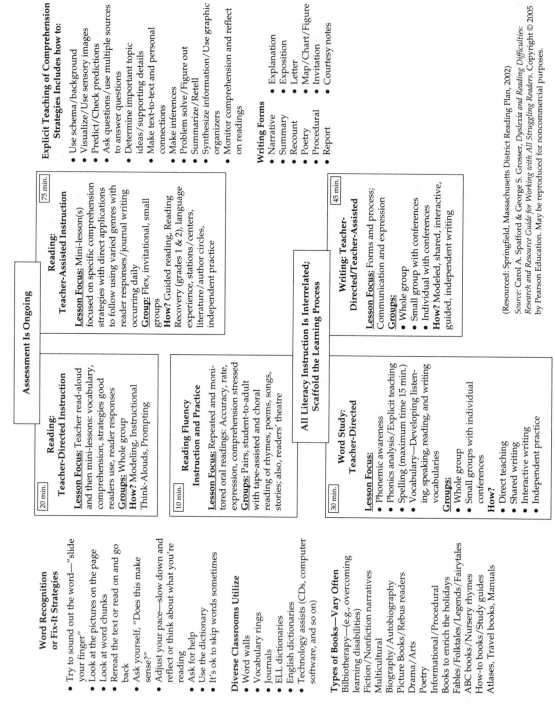

FIGURE 11.1 Three-Hour Language Arts Instructional Block

Considerations for Second-Language Learners

Attention should be given to the 1997 TESOL (Teachers of English to Speakers of Other Languages, Inc.) *ESL (English as a Second Language) Standards for Pre-K to 12 Students* (as cited in Valdés, 2001) or other such standards if the home language for the student with dyslexia or learning disabilities is different than the school language (if the school language happens to be English).

The TESOL standards specify that (1) the second language to be learned (e.g., English) is used to communicate in social settings, (2) the second language is used to achieve academically, and (3) the second language is used in socially and culturally appropriate ways. Sheltered English strategies will provide the language experiences for students with dyslexia who are also second-language learners.

As seen in the language arts block adapted for second-language learners in Figure 11.2, additional sheltered subject matter teaching includes language builders that need to be used to personalize instruction: graphic organizers, manipulatives/visual aids, ELL dictionaries, vocabulary rings, and word walls. The level of English language proficiency determines the percentage of time spent teaching English and the content area subjects the students will participate in (specifying which subjects will be taught in the home language and which subjects will be taught in English). For students with dyslexia who are second-language learners, there is the need for access to the same instructional materials dyslexics receive who are not second-language learners.

Sheltered English Strategies

Additional sheltered English strategies need to be incorporated within the Language Arts Literacy Block to build oral and written language proficiency.

Echevarria, Vogt, and Short (2000) recommend that the following considerations be in place for sheltered planning, pointing out that not all elements will be present for each lesson. Sheltered English planning is applicable to students who are determined to be Limited English Proficient (LEP). These are students whose home language is a language other than English and who are unable to complete routine classroom work in English (if English is the language of the school).

Instructional Considerations

Lesson Planning

- Choose age-appropriate vocabulary and concepts to introduce
- Preplan lesson objectives
- Plan to use language builders especially to clarify new terms and concepts (e.g., graphic organizers, word walls)

Lesson Implementation

- Convey lesson objectives to the students and introduce key concepts through the use of the overhead projector, flipcharts, and the chalkboard
- Introduce new vocabulary—highlight or write words as they are introduced for reinforcement; link to prior learning
- Provide opportunities to use reading strategies and metacognitive processing skills especially predicting, synthesizing, evaluating, and paraphrasing
- Scaffold learning through verbal prompts, clarification, and elaboration
- Make personal connections, text-to-text connections, and self-to-text connections
- Extend and clarify text knowledge by outlining, rewriting, or paraphrasing

English Language Levels of Proficiency

Phase I

Mainstream Classes: Art, Music, Physical Ed (PE)

Sheltered English: Language Arts (LA) and Math

Home Language: LA, Science, Social Studies (Soc St)

Time Spent Teaching in English: 40 to 50% of day

Phase II

Mainstream Classes: Art, Music, PE

Sheltered English: L.A., Math, Science

Home Language: L.A., Soc St.

Time Spent Teaching in English: 60 to 70%

Language Builders to Personalize Instruction:
- Graphic organizers
- Manipulatives/Visual aids
- ELL dictionaries
- Vocabulary rings
- Word walls

Phase III

Mainstream Classes: Art, Music, PE, Math, Science

Sheltered English: LA, Math, Science, Social Studies

Home Language: LA

Time Spent Teaching in English: 80–90%

Mainstream Classes: All

Sheltered English: Reading support all year

Home Language: Discretion of Teacher—LA

Time Spent Teaching in English: 100%

Teacher-Directed: Reading Flex Groupings and Guided Reading Groups

- KWL—to build interest and purpose for reading
- Prereading schema building and collaborative talk in peer groups
- Build a repertoire of comprehension strategies to develop students' abilities to synthesize knowledge and critically analyze information
- Student choices and extended times for silent reading using grade level and comfort level books
- Use thematic approach
- Use graphic organizers, marginal glosses, highlighters

Teacher-Assisted Reading Instruction

- Paraphrase the meaning of what was read—make personal connections to students' experiences and past learning
- Engage in repeated readings to develop fluency
- Show there are many ways to use language both in reading and in writing—purpose setting
- Frequently question and do comprehension checks
- Model how to self-question to develop understanding

Word Study: Teacher-Directed

- During opening/routines (A.M., lunch, changes between classes) provide opportunities for students to use words/knowledge they have recently learned (e.g., shared experiences, weather, current events)
- Present vocabulary from whole to part, then in context
- Provide many opportunities for students to use new words in writing (journals), oral presentations (e.g., writing shares), and other expressive domains (e.g., art and music)

Teacher-Directed, Teacher-Assisted Writing

- KWL
- Design writing activities designed so students can relate to a theme, to themselves, and to others
- Form small discussion groups and then develop a quick write (5–10 minutes)
- Use literature to prompt writing pieces
- Use Language Experience Approach to personalize reading and writing
- Focus on content/meaning building and not form in social studies, science, and math before mainstreaming has fully occurred

Additional considerations for students with dyslexia and learning disabilities who are second-language learners: Second-language instruction (e.g., English) should be for same amount of time as nondisabled peers—IEP specifies if instruction is in regular or SPED setting. Dyslexics who are second-language learners need access to same instructional materials recommended for dyslexics who are not second-language learners.

Source: Adapted from 2002–2005 *English Language Learning Program for Grades Pre K through 12* Editor: Edgardo L. Reyes, Director of ELL Program, Springfield Schools, Springfield, MA. From: Carol A. Spafford & George S. Grosser, *Dyslexia and Reading Difficulties: Research and Resource Guide for Working with All Struggling Readers.* Copyright © 2005 by Pearson Education. May be reproduced for noncommercial purposes.

Suggestions during the L.A. Block for **Second-Language Learners** (SSMT Approach was developed by Stephen Krasner and was inspired by Canadian immersion approaches)

FIGURE 11.2 Additional Sheltered Subject Matter Teaching (SSMT)

Conversational Issues

To Improve Communicative Comprehensibility

- When conversing, adjust rate of speech to a slower rate to allow pause or thinking time for students to process between languages
- Show expressiveness in speech using gestures and body language
- Repeat vocabulary and show how vocabulary is used in different contexts

During Interactive Classroom Dialogue and Exchange

- Use cooperative learning pairs or groups where students are able to converse using learned vocabulary and concepts
- Prove for elaborated responses or deeper thinking—Examples: "Can you tell me more?" "Why do you think . . . ?" "What do you mean by that?" and so on

Gerry Morgan (2003) stresses the need to continue sheltered English strategies when English language learners (ELL) are mainstreamed with English-speaking peers in all subject areas. Relying on prior research and experience, Morgan (2003) recommends (1) summarizing information for the ELL student on a regular basis; (2) making a point to review basic literary elements; (3) providing opportunities for the ELL students to acquire and use critical thinking skills, especially text presentations that allow students to readily make inferences and generalizations; (4) stressing the need for older students to use conventional spelling in written work and providing ELL dictionaries that have word-to-word translations (from the home language to English); and (5) providing leveled books on student's independent reading levels and many opportunities for sustained silent reading where students can use the "strategies" they have learned to "integrate language effectively and automatically."

Evidence-Based Instructional Practices

Instructional Emphases within the Literacy Block

Research indicates that some students with learning disabilities need a multisensory phonics approach (see Chapter 6), with instruction in phonological awareness [and fluency] (see Chapter 8) . . . while other students need interventions to address comprehension problems (see Chapter 7). For many students a combination of approaches is effective. LDA EMPHASIZES THAT NO SINGLE READING METHOD WILL BE EFFECTIVE FOR ALL STUDENTS WITH LEARNING DISABILITIES. (Learning Disabilities Association of America, 2001)

There is no one best way to teach within the literacy block; rather there are a large number of successful, evidence-based approaches, strategies, and methods available to educators and practitioners. Choice often depends on what works best according to district, state, and national standards and requirements, resources, developmental levels, and individual learning styles and needs.

Figure 11.3 includes recommendations that were discussed throughout the book and have been proven to work well with individuals who are dyslexic. This figure also includes some recommended phonics programs whose effectiveness was evaluated in at least three different control-treatment group comparisons with acceptable experimental designs according to the National Reading Panel Report (NRP) (2000). *Synthetic phonic approaches* are cited as they were determined to have the largest effect size ($\underline{d}$ = 0.45) or impact on reading achievement as compared to other types of phonic instruction (e.g., *analytic*). See page 320 for discussion on interpreting effect size statistics.

Program Component	Recommended Instructional Approach/Strategy/Method (small group or one-to-one instruction) (see index for chapter locations of descriptions and examples) (Spafford & Grosser, 2005)
Five Essential Teaching of Reading Elements:	
(1) Phonemic Awareness	Teach all the letters of the alphabet and how letters can be used to manipulate phonemes; the names and sounds of letters need to be overlearned; identify difficulties (Dyslexia Checklist) and teach to that skill (e.g., especially phoneme segmentation and blending); practice breaking words into onset and rimes; in written work, promote the use of invented spellings before guiding to conventional rules.
(2) Phonics (tutorial instruction is most effective followed by small group work and then whole class instruction) (Note: Systematic phonics instruction is explicit with systematic teaching of predetermined associations between letters and sounds with practice using these associations in connected text.)	**Systematic phonics instruction** to include analytic and synthetic approaches. *Synthetic approaches* cited by the National Reading Panel Report (2000); DISTAR and Reading Mastery (1988) ($\underline{d}$ = 0.48, p < .05); Lovett's adaptation of Direct Instruction (1994) ($\underline{d}$ = 0.41, p < .05); Lovett's adaptation of the Benchmark Word Identification Program (1994) ($\underline{d}$ = 0.48, p < .05); The Lippincott Basic Reading Program (1981) ($\underline{d}$ = 0.68, p < .05); Beck and Mitroff's New Primary Grades Reading System (1972) ($\underline{d}$ = 0.47, p < .05); Orton Gillingham Programs (1940–1984) ($\underline{d}$ = 0.23, p < .05); Sing, Spell, Read, and Write (1972) ($\underline{d}$ = 0.35, p < .05) (NRP, 2000, p. 2-160) Additionally: VAK and VAK-T approaches, intensive structural analyses programs, decodable text
(3) Fluency	Increasing time spent reading, read-alouds; repeated readings; sight word practice (Essential 500 Word Reading List); oral reading activities—Neurological Impress Method (NIM); reader's theatre, radio reading, peer and family paired reading; use of word strategy bookmarks when reading
(4) Vocabulary development	Read-alouds, language experience, vocabulary overview guides, vocabulary concept circles, vocabulary maps, semantic maps, Vocabulary Self-Collection Strategy (VSS), charting word features, combined feature analysis and informational charting, keyword strategies, word games, dictionary/thesaurus use
(5) Text comprehension	Metacomprehension instruction, reading aloud, strategy instruction, schema building, background building, interrogative reading, working groups or cooperative learning, mnemonics, K-W-L, graphic organizers (anticipation guides, semantic maps, guide-o-ramas, reading road maps, marginal glosses, text structure guides), story grammar mapping/frameworks, Story Grammar Marker, paraphrasing (reformulation for second-language learners), summarizing, literature circles
Additional:	
(6) Study skills	Family involvement; graphic organizers (brainstorming or topic maps and charts, cause-and-effect maps, Venn diagrams, chain-of-events outlines); cooperative learning ventures—jigsaw, peer tutoring, reverse-role tutoring; reciprocal teaching; K-W-L; SQ3R; ReQuest, QAR; DRTA; guided notes; TAKECARE Internet Planner
(7) Considerations for second-language learners who are dyslexic	Sheltered English strategies; reformulation
(8) Writing	Writers' workshop; journal writing; double-entry journals, prompted writing; modeled writing; interactive writing; shared writing; collaborative writing; language experience approach; use of graphic organizers prior to and during writing activities; open response writing strategy card; inquiry reading/writing activities; word walls/activities; use of writing rubrics before, during, and after writing; use of word processors and scribes

FIGURE 11.3 Teaching during the Literacy Block: Recommended Instructional Approaches/Strategies/Methods for Struggling Readers

Choosing the Right Reading Program
or Component for the Literacy Block

How does one choose a particular phonemic awareness, phonics, word analysis, or reading program to use within the literacy block for students with moderate to severe reading disabilities or dyslexia? According to Sally Shaywitz (2003), well-balanced, research or evidence-based programs implemented by well-trained teachers are ALL highly effective and "produce remarkably comparable results." "According to the research, no one program is head and shoulders above the rest" (p. 267).

What is research-based? According to Shanahan (2002), the term *research-based* is reserved for those instances "when there was strong evidence that a particular type of instructional intervention . . . had worked in the past" (p. 12). These would be programs shown to be successful in experimental studies. Research-based interventions rely on systematic data collection and analyses using formal methods that address reliability and validity issues. These should be clearly articulated in a program guide or manual. According to the National Reading Panel (2000), "high-quality" research must involve steps to maximize the rigor of experimental designs that address as many threats to "internal and external" validity as possible. This allows researchers to detect treatment effects (e.g., for a treatment effect, the positive results were due to the Hawthorne effect or extra attention the students received as opposed to a particular method of teaching) when they exist.

Scientific Basis for Research-Based or Evidence-Based According to the National Reading Panel (2000), for a program to be considered research-based or evidence-based, there needs to have been stringently controlled *experimental* or *quasi-experimental* research designs to determine program effectiveness. In the following box, the present authors offer the following questions to consider when educators are trying to sort out whether a program is evidence-based and appropriate for a particular group of students.

Evaluating Evidence-Based Educational Programs: A Checklist

(1) *What type of program is needed?* Why or what is the need? Example: A more intense phonics program is needed because students are experiencing difficulty with word recognition (dyslexic, struggling readers, at-risk readers).

(2) *Does the proposed reading program or program component match identified needs* from assessments? For example, "yes"; testing with the Dyslexia Checklist on page 225 shows phonemic awareness deficiencies and phonological processing difficulties for the students with reading disabilities who need this program.

(3) *What is the focus area* for the proposed program? What does the program propose to do in regard to the focus area? For example, with Program X, there is a focus on phonemic awareness training for three months followed by explicit and systematic phonics instruction similar to the comprehensive phonics program studied by Benita Blachman and her colleagues in 1999.

(4) *What prior research is available to show that this type of program works well* with the students we are trying to help? For example, the National Reading Panel reported in 2000 that systematic phonics instruction improves the reading performance for students with reading disabilities.

(5) *How much time is needed* to implement the proposed program? *Do we have the staff?* For example, by the end of Program X, students are expected to know all letter-sound correspondences with proficiency in segmenting and blending phonemes. Students will know the basic six syllable types (closed syllables, final E, open, vowel team, vowel + r,

and consonant le) with proficiency in applying this knowledge to word reading in the context of sentences in decodable books. For Program X, running records are maintained in regard to student progress. The students' reading levels are determined at the beginning and at the end of the programs using benchmark books (see leveling chart on page 204). In regard to formal or standardized assessments or testing, the issues of validity and reliability become very important.

(7) *How does the proposed program manual show that this particular program* (e.g., Systematic Phonics Program X) *is effective* and/or more effective than a program without such instruction or with a different type of instruction? What type(s) of experimental or quasi-experimental design was (were) used to determine program effectiveness? What statistical procedures were used? For example, the average **effect size** (using an effect size statistic) for Program X with groups of students who were determined to be dyslexic or reading disabled was $\underline{d}$ = .57. This is a moderate or very good effect size showing improved performance for the students with reading disabilities who received this systematic phonics training program in comparison to control groups (groups of students with reading disabilities who did not receive this training).

According to the National Reading Panel (NRP) (2000), an appropriate statistic to use to evaluate reading program or reading program component effectiveness is *effect size*. Effect size measures how much the mean (average) of a group receiving a particular type of instruction or training differs from the mean of a control group of students or group of students who do not receive similar instruction in units of standard deviation. With effect sizes of 0.0 to 0.20, the instructional program is determined to not have a significant impact on learning or achievement. To determine the strength of the program's impact on learning, the following scale can be used (Cohen, 1988): .20 to .50, small effects; .50 to .80, moderate effects; .80 or above, large or substantial effects. The NRP (2000) found that systematic phonics instruction was most effective in improving children's ability to decode regularly spelled words ($\underline{d}$ = 0.67), and with younger children, to comprehend (text processing) what they read ($\underline{d}$ = 0.51). For groups of disabled readers, statistically significant effect sizes were reported by the NRP (2000). Even small effect sizes in the range of .20 to .50 are significant because systematic phonics instruction (as part of a balanced reading instruction) increases reading achievement more than programs without systematic phonics instruction.

(8) *Are there variations in performance* when this proposed program is introduced at different grade levels? Most appropriate grade level? The program manual should publish the specifics in regard to what groups of students have benefited from the use of the program (e.g., early elementary versus older students, nondisabled versus disabled students).

(9) If the proposed program stresses a particular component of reading (e.g., systematic phonics instruction), *are the other essential reading components or elements addressed with other program materials/resources/instruction?* As previously stated, individuals with dyslexia will require both intensive and comprehensive reading programs that balance all of the five essential teaching of reading elements cited in the research and in the Reading First legislation: (a) phonemic awareness, (b) phonics (with systematic explicit instruction), (c) fluency, (d) vocabulary development, and (e) text comprehension/strategic reading.

(10) Do you know of schools or teachers who used the proposed program *who can provide first-hand knowledge of how well the proposed program worked with students with similar learning needs?*

(11) *Does the proposed reading program require special training?* Who can provide the training? The publisher of the program may have consultants who can assist in this regard. Parents and teachers, is it possible to *observe a classroom* where the proposed reading program/component being considered is used with students of similar age and learning needs?

(12) *Does the reading program have a family literacy component?* What kind of parent training or support would be involved?

(13) *How do program outcomes fit into district or state standards* or benchmarks? For example, Standard 7 from the Language Arts Strand of the *English Language Arts Scope-and-*

Sequence for the Springfield, Massachusetts, Public Schools (2001) refers to the expectation that all students will understand the nature of written English and the relationship of letter and spelling patterns to the sounds of speech in grades 1 and 2. Students need to demonstrate an understanding of all letters and letter patterns and be able to combine single letters, consonant blends, consonant diagraphs, and vowel digraphs and diphthongs into recognizable words; in other words, students need to be able to use letter-sound knowledge to decode written English one syllable and multisyllable real words and nonsense words as well.

Resource: National Reading Panel. (2000). *Teaching children to read: An evidence-based assessment of the scientific research literature on reading and its implications for reading instruction.* Reports of the subgroups. (National Institute of Health Pub. No. 00-4754). Washington, DC: National Institute of Child Health and Human Development)

District and State Standards: Reading and Writing Benchmarks

States provide reading and writing standards to teachers in the areas of reading and writing that are used as benchmarks or indicators of performance for each grade level. Families and students alike need to be informed of these standards when goal setting and preparing for academics throughout the school year. Many teachers post important standards or expectations for student reference throughout the year. There are three critical times before high school graduation when literacy standards need careful review for the student with dyslexia so that appropriate interventions are in place if students are not proficient in meeting the standards: (1) kindergarten (reading readiness), (2) grade 3 (grade at which all students should be proficient and fluent readers), and (3) grade 8 (exiting elementary educational experiences). Figure 11.4 on page 322 provides an example of these standards.

Interpreting Research Results for Reading Tests and Programs

Reviewing program or test manuals requires background and practice in interpreting effect sizes and other relevant statistics beyond what a publisher may overtly state in advertisements and summaries. For example, in a recent advertisement, a publisher claimed "research proves this program accelerates fluency gains by 70%." How does the publisher define and measure fluency (**construct validity**)? Keep in mind the checklist just previously mentioned when considering this fluency program. A teacher or school administrator may also want to review some of the commonly used terminology found in statistics sections of publishers' manuals: mean, mode, median, standard deviation, raw score, percentile score, normal frequency distribution, reliability, validity, effect size, correlation coefficient, levels of significance or levels of confidence, standard score, *t* test, F test, chi square, and independent and dependent variables.

What's next after traditional K–12 schooling for dyslexics who have benefited from the aforementioned evidence-based literacy support throughout their elementary and secondary education programs? Are children with dyslexia entering adolescence and adulthood problem-free? No, dyslexia is not cured in the sense that all of the symptoms of childhood disappear. Difficulties with reading rate, spelling, and writing are the primary presenting problems that persist into adulthood.

Grade Level	Reading	Writing
Kindergarten [*Sources: (1) Springfield, Massachusetts English Language Arts Scope and Sequence: Kindergarten through Grade 5; (2) Massachusetts English Language Arts Curriculum Frameworks, 2001; (3) First Steps™ Developmental Reading and Writing Continuums, 1994*]	• Students will have an awareness of the concepts of print. • Students will understand orally that phonemes exist and will be able to isolate and manipulate phonemes to create words. • Students will recognize letter-sound correspondences by naming and identifying each letter of the alphabet. • Students will be able to ask questions about important story characters, settings, and events. • Students will make predictions using prior knowledge, pictures, and text. • Students will read and retell a main event and important facts from a text read or heard.	• Students will assign messages to their own symbols. • Students will understand that writing and pictures are different. • Students will use letters or letter approximations to represent written language. • Students will rely on the most obvious sound or sounds of a word. • Students will attempt to read back their own writing.
Grade 3 (*Sources: (1) Put Reading First: The Research Building Blocks for Teaching Children to Read: Kindergarten through Grade 3, Armbruster & Osborn, 2001; (2) First Steps™ Developmental Reading and Writing Continuums, 1994; (3) Massachusetts Department of Education Supplement to the Massachusetts English Language Arts Curriculum Frameworks, 2004; Grades 3, 5 and 7 for vocabulary, reading, and literature; McREL K–8 National Standards for Language Arts, 2003*]	• Students will be able to coordinate and adjust several strategies to facilitate comprehension (four comprehension strategies should be in place at this level: asking questions about the text students are reading, summarizing or paraphrasing parts of text, clarifying words and sentences students don't understand, and predicting what might occur next in text). • Students will identify basic facts and main ideas from a text and use this information as the basis for interpretation. • Students will identify, analyze, and apply knowledge of the characteristics of different genres.	• Students can use writing and other methods (e.g., telling, creating illustrations) to tell about experiences, persons, places, or objects. • Students can respond in writing to literature readings (e.g., summarize main ideas and supporting details; relate personal ideas to writing; advance opinions and support opinions with references to the reading and background knowledge).
Grade 8 [*Sources: (1) Pennsylvania Academic Standards for Reading, Writing, Speaking, and Listening, 8th grade, 2002; (2) First Steps™ Developmental Reading and Writing Continuums, 1994*]	• Students will read and understand essential content from informational texts and in all academic areas (reading critically in all content areas). • Students will locate appropriate texts for an assigned purpose before reading (learning to read independently). • Students will locate information using appropriate sources (including a variety of media) and strategies (researching to read and write).	• Students can write multi-paragraph informational pieces. • Students can write with a clear, distinct focus. • Students can write using well-developed content appropriate for the topic.

FIGURE 11.4   Some Essential Reading and Writing Standards or Benchmarks for Grades K, 3, and 8

Adults with Dyslexia or Reading Disabilities

Characteristics of Adult Dyslexia Consistent with IDA

Adults with dyslexia:

- Experience slower than average reading rates—it takes longer to complete readings.
- Often are very verbal in oral language—a strength.
- May be self-conscious about reading problems and deny or hide the problem.
- Often are poor spellers—they will need spelling assists such as poor spellers' dictionaries, spell checks on word processors, and the like.
- Will avoid writing, which is tedious work; may not be able to write.
- Rely on memory; may have excellent memories.
- Often show good social skills but may on occasion misinterpret social situations (e.g., social misperception).
- Often have visuospatial gifts and talents that lend themselves well to professions in architecture, engineering, art and design work, mathematics, and careers in the medical field.

However,

- Often seek jobs working below their intellectual capacity because of literacy "obstacles" in reading and writing.
- May have problems with time management and organization of materials and tasks.
- Often are entrepreneurs who can rely on others to complete written work and other tasks presenting difficulties. (IDA, http://www.interdys.org, 4/25/04)

The National Council on Disability (NCD) commissioned the 2004 *Improving Education Outcomes for Students with Disabilities* report, paying close attention to how IDEA (Individuals with Disabilities Education Act) and NCLB (No Child Left Behind) are impacting outcomes for adults with disabilities. The NCD mentioned concern for (1) reducing the number or percentage of students with disabilities who drop out of high school, (2) increasing the number of students with disabilities who receive a diploma as opposed to a certificate of attendance, and (3) increasing the availability of resources and strategies to help students with disabilities remain connected to postsecondary education outcomes (Frieden, 2004).

Supporting Students with Dyslexia in High School and Beyond

According to Lehr, Hansen, Sinclair, and Christenson (2003), students with disabilities will persist in their high school studies with continued reading support, counseling services, tutoring, attendance monitoring, and participation in afterschool clubs. According to the NCD (Frieden, 2004), these are critical factors because more than 36 percent of high school students with learning disabilities do not obtain a high school diploma at the end of high school with dropout rates of 27 percent, much higher for students with learning disabilities than for students without learning disabilities. Sally Shaywitz (2003), international researcher and dyslexia expert, documents that older students and adult dyslexics need the same research-based, systematic, and small-group literacy instruction as younger people with dyslexia. Many programs rely on the same basic teaching tenets but are restructured in some way to meet the learning needs and interests of adults (e.g., see p. 32 for specific VAK-T programs recommended for adults).

Comprehension Monitoring   Bernice Wong (1979) was one of the first researchers to suggest the teaching of comprehension must include direct, explicit teaching of comprehension monitoring to improve information retention and understandings and this needs to continue with older students and adults who are dyslexic. Linda Kucan and Isabel L. Beck (2003) looked at comprehension monitoring using "student talk" with older students and found improved test scores when students were engaged in talk or discussions about text. Comprehension also increased when students summarized and paraphrased text aloud in a variety of formats. As an example, Chi and her colleagues (Chi, de Leeuw, Chiu, & LaVancher, 1994), worked with a group of college students who were asked to read text, stop after each sentence, and explain and paraphrase what was just read. Students who explained or paraphrased what was read were significantly better in responding to literal and inferential questions about the text than students who just reread the same text. Additionally, the Reciprocal Teaching Method (page 304), K-W-L (page 303), SQ3R (page 304), DRTA (page 305), ReQuest (page 304), and QAR (page 305) are all evidence-based instructional study-skills methods that use questioning or probing to deepen thinking processes to increase comprehension and work well with older students with dyslexia.

Supporting Students with Dyslexia after High School   Students with disabilities need continued support as they transition into college and postsecondary education. Benz, Lindstrom, and Yovanoff (2000) found that developing self-determination skills (self-advocacy and goal setting) to be of major importance. The present authors would agree that there needs to be emphasis placed on developing those positive characteristics shown by resilient (i.e., the ability to quickly bounce back or recover from stressors, frustrations, and failures due to a personal resolve to persevere in spite of academic/social obstacles) and successful individuals with dyslexia. Involvement in transition planning (e.g., career awareness, job search) and other programs that take into consideration personal social skills, problem solving, and community living skills (e.g., how to access services) will be necessary as well.

Transitioning Students with Dyslexia to College   Hart, Zafft, and Zimbrich (2001) created a checklist to prepare students with disabilities for college:

1. Establish postsecondary education and career goals.
2. Collaboratively review college catalogues—does the college service students with learning disabilities? how? jobs on campus?
3. Continually update a folder with information related to the student's learning disability—how does the student learn best? what teaching and testing accommodations are needed?
4. Meet with the college's disability service office to learn more about the college's accommodations for students with learning disabilities.
5. Attend summer orientation sessions at the college to become better acquainted with the college and its services.
6. Work with the financial aid office to learn how to take care of funding for tuition; books, transportation, fees, and the like; scholarships available for students with learning disabilities?
7. What services are available through local human services agencies? jobs off campus? transportation? The National Council on Disability (NCD) (Frieden, 2004) believes workplace preparation or paid work experience after high school regardless of disability or severity of disability provides students with valuable work experience and employers can also help individuals meet their human resources needs.

Help for Adults with Dyslexia

Adults with dyslexia who need continued literacy support can contact their local education agency for post-high school programs or a local community college. The International Dyslexia Association (IDA) provides links to resources for adults with dyslexia at http://www.interdys.org/servlet/adults. The Learning Disabilities Association (LDA) is another organization whose purpose is to advance the education and general welfare of adults (and children) who manifest disabilities. LDA's website provides alerts and bulletins, links to other organizations, publications, and contact information [http://www.ldanatl.org/].

Local libraries may offer tutorial services through programs such as Project Read.

Adult Literacy Programs through Libraries

Example: Project Read in San Francisco
http://sfpl.lib.ca.us/librarylocations/

Since 1983 Project Read at the San Francisco, California, Library has provided free one-on-one tutoring, workshops, and ongoing instructional support to English-speaking adults who seek to improve their basic reading and writing skills. Volunteers help adult learners identify personal literacy goals and improve their literacy skills to enhance their lives. Project Read tutors are estimated to contribute over 10,000 volunteer hours each year. Project Read is a public service of the San Francisco Public Library System, funded by the City and County of San Francisco, federal and state grants, and contributions from the private sector.

Learner and Tutor Services
- Free one-to-one tutoring
- Professional training for tutors
- Instructional resources for tutors and learners
- Continuous evaluation and instructional support
- Referrals to other educational programs as needed
- Computer learning lab
- Skills-based workshops

Family literacy services are provided to encourage reading in the home.

The Legal System and Individuals with Dyslexia

Federal Legislation*

Three U.S. laws protect adults and children with dyslexia and disabilities from discrimination in school and in the workplace (1) IDEA, (2) Section 504, and (3) ADA.

Individuals with Disabilities Education Act (IDEA)   [P.L. 101-476 of 1990, which had renamed the Education of the Handicapped Act (EHA) or P.L. 94-142 of 1975] specified special education and related services for children and young people with disabilities be provided up to an individual's 22nd birthday. IDEA provides for a Free and Appropriate Public Education (FAPE) and for an Individualized Education Program (IEP). See pages 261–263 for the IEP process especially for parents of children with dyslexia and other learning disabilities.

---

*See pages 40–41 for more in-depth discussion.

Section 504 of the Rehabilitation Act (P.L. 93-112)   of 1973, as amended through 1998, prohibits discrimination against children and adults with disabilities. It guarantees that persons with disabilities have equal access to all programs and services receiving federal funding. This includes public and private schools and colleges and employers who receive federal funds.

> **Sec. 504.(a)** No otherwise qualified individual with a disability in the United States, as defined in section 7(20), shall be subjected to discrimination under any program or activity receiving Federal financial assistance. The standards used to determine whether this section has been violated in a complaint alleging employment discrimination under this section shall be the standards applied under Title I of the American with Disabilities Act of 1990 (42 U.S.C. 12111 et seq.) and the provisions of sections 501 thourgh 504, and 510, of the American with Disabilities Act of 1990 (42 U.S.C. 12201-12204 and 12210), as such sections relate to employment (see pages 00 for a 504 referral form for school systems to use in written in both Spanish and English).

Americans with Disabilities Act (ADA)   of 1990 (P.L. 101-336) was created to protect children and adults with disabilities from discrimination in employment, public, and private settings. The law applies to all public and most private schools and colleges, testing institutions, and licensing authorities. It is also applicable to state and local governments and to private employers who have fifteen or more employees.

Requesting Advocates for Adults and Children with Dyslexia

Importance for Adolescents and Adults   Sometimes parents or guardians who have children with dyslexia request support especially in regard to program planning for their children. This is a critical issue as the dropout rate for students with learning disabilities was 28 percent in the school year 1999–2000, which compares to a national dropout rate of 11 percent for students without disabilities. Although dropout rates vary from state to state for both general and special education populations, the fact remains that teens and young adults with dyslexia drop out of school at higher rates than their nondisabled peers. If parents are unable to attend school meetings or IEP meetings where program services are discussed and recommended, they can choose an advocate who can represent them. In regard to the workplace, adults with dyslexia frequently take jobs or positions that underutilize their expertise or talents. Advocates can help individuals with dyslexia realize their potentials by helping them seek work opportunities and services that tap into their strengths and needs.

Who Are Advocates?   Dyslexia or learning disabilities advocates are individuals who "advocate" for a good education and work situations for individuals with disabilities and work with families in positive, constructive ways. Public policy advocates work with legislators and other policy makers to create, amend, or delete relevant legislation.

National Center for Learning Disabilities (NCLD)   The *National Center for Learning Disabilities (NCLD)* [http://www.ld/org/] promotes public awareness and understanding of the rights of individuals with learning disabilities. The NCLD website includes information about "Legal Rights" for individuals with learning disabilities and other topics such as, "Do I have LD?" "LD on the Job" and "Resources."

NCLD Advocates Guide   The *LD Advocates Guide* is one example of a resource and is available online through the National Center for Learning Disabilities (NCLD) [http://www.ld.org/advocacy/tutorial_profiles.cfm]. School systems and local social service agencies will provide the names of advocates when needed.

The First Step to Being an Effective Advocate *The first step to being an effective LD advocate is to honestly connect with families to understand the presenting issue* (in addition to understanding the nature of learning disabilities or dyslexia) *and how to talk about it.* For example, if an advocate is representing a parent or guardian with parent permission at an IEP meeting and the topic is test accommodations, the advocate needs to learn about the types of test accommodations available to students with learning disabilities before the meeting. The test accommodations checklists, as examples, on pages 254 and 255 could be reviewed and brought to the IEP meeting.

Other Steps Advocates Can Take: Facilitating Parent–School and Parent–Community Partnerships At the beginning of the school year, it is particularly important for families to inform incoming teachers about the learning styles, strengths, and needs of students with learning disabilities. How can parents facilitate this collaboration? The Charles Schwab Learning Foundation, a nonprofit organization, provides suggestions through a website devoted to furthering the academic and social progress of individuals with learning disabilities—http://www.schwablearning.org (downloaded 4/25/04). Advocates can seek tips for families from such websites as well as from publications on the subject matter of learning disabilities, brainstorming together how to use suggestions.

Charles Schwab Foundation (2004) *ten tried-and-true steps to foster positive, supportive relationships between families and teachers*—parents take the lead:

1. Help your child's teacher to get to know your child.
2. Show a collaborative communication style and
3. Communicate, communicate, communicate!
4. Try to be even-tempered.
5. Put information and requests in writing.
6. "Join forces to help your child get organized," especially in regard to homework.
7. Participate in school and classroom activities.
8. "Sweeten the relationship."
9. "Stretch the teacher's awareness" of dyslexia and learning disabilities.
10. Make a point to learn about your rights and responsibilities.

Based on: Robbie Fanning's List, compiled in collaboration with parents who participated in Schwab Foundation projects.

In regard to parent-community partnerships, advocates can help seek out services (e.g., a local library reading program), tutorial or summer reading programs that can accommodate the financial means of the family, community clubs (e.g., Boys and Girls Clubs, YMCA and YWCA, sports teams, chess clubs, and the like), or individual/family counselors (e.g., to work with a high school student and his or her family who is at risk for dropping out of high school) with extensive experiences working with families of children who have learning disabilities.

Internet Resourcing

Making resources available for adult dyslexics necessarily involves use of the Internet. This section on Internet resourcing was developed to help teachers more fully explore a most valuable resource for teaching and learning.

Leu (2001) and Leu and Leu (2000) describe the Internet in terms of a richly networked technology for communication and information and argue that it is a powerful technology available to teachers to support reading and writing experiences. Teachers will want to make use of the ITEA (International Technological Education Association) (2000, 2002) standards for technological literacy and a variety of program approaches such as self-paced modules, programs that make interdisciplinary connections and programs that offer different ways to problem-solve (Boser, Palmer, & Daugherty, 1998; Hill, 2004).

Go Right to the Experts: Teacher Recommendations for Internet Sites

Teachers often have excellent recommendations for Internet websites in addition to professional journals, newsletters, books on the subject, and the like. In fact, larger education associations publish newsletters with "tried and proven" Internet sites on a regular basis. Smaller education associations without this benefit could establish a collaboration or professional exchange of resources. Timothy Collins, Springfield, Massachusetts, Education Association (SEA) President, as an example, publishes monthly Internet notes and encourages his teachers to participate in Read Across America (www.nea.org/readcross) during the month of March providing suggested website-sponsored events, web-based activities, and so on (Collins, 2003, p. 10).

To facilitate accessing information on the Internet for a particular purpose (e.g., to obtain information and references to complete a research paper or writing piece), the following suggestions are offered (adapted from Frank, 2000 and Tuttle, 2002, 2003):

1. Narrow areas to research on a selected topic as much as possible by a cognitive think-aloud.
2. Show how to phrase key terminology to use with search engines that will help locate relevant websites.
3. Show how to access search engines that allow one to ask a question.
4. Show how to access online reference materials that will help with word and content understandings such as dictionaries, thesauruses, and encyclopedias.
5. Demonstrate how to navigate through a website to find desired information.
6. Use a preplanning guide for students with dyslexia (adaptable for use with all students; see Figure 11.5 on page 330).
7. Print relevant pages and show how to take notes with index cards with appropriate references (see Figure 11.6 on page 331).
8. Model how to integrate the information found into a written piece (see writing process in Chapter 7).

According to Bertram Bruce (2003), the ability to use the Internet and computers is a requirement of the "knowledge work" we need to bring to the workplace. The "new literacies" that Internet technology has brought about include video, digital, multimedia, and hypertext literacies, in addition to the reading and writing literacies required for successful navigation. Leu and Leu (2000) cite required new literacies for locating, evaluating, and using information found on the Internet and new writing strategies to structure text and other media forms.

Cushla Kapitzke (2003) emphasizes the interplay between social and technological change and the notion of "socioethical" competence in regard to the proper use of print and electronic materials. This includes, but is not limited to, issues regarding copyright, plagiarism, system access, and standard social conventions of respectful and polite interchange. Practice in accessing and using cybraries or cyberlibraries is one way to develop the social conventions desired and educational expertise needed for efficient and effective use of Internet resources. Cybraries or cyberlibraries serve as electronic library portals for college students where students can check out and peruse journals, newspapers, and books, request resources, and download information as needed.

Developing "Cybrary" Literacies

For the individual with dyslexia, and consistent with the new information computer literacies cited by Kapitzke (2003), it is recommended that an informational Cybrary literacy program focus on giving the student opportunities to:

- Learn about the structures of information (e.g., headings and the arrangement of data records).
- Learn about the physical organization of information (the Dewey Decimal System or Library of Congress Classification Systems).
- Practice structured information problem solving.
- Apply search strategies.
- Determine appropriate and valid information sources.

(example: homepage of the cybrary at the University of Queensland, Australia— http://www.library.uq.edu.au)

How we construct from and share information on the Internet is a complex social literacy that requires practice, knowledge of the process and procedures, and access. There is the implicit "social literacy protocol" that one follows in Internet communications where what we communicate may not be as important as how we communicate the message.

Sensitivity to the "Digital Divide" for Computer Availability

Educators need to be sensitive to the issue of computer availability, especially for African American and Latino students who experience what has been termed as the "digital divide"—more than twice as many white students have access to home computers for practice and use (Bruce, 2003). Poverty is also a factor—in 1999, students who attended schools in which up to 11 percent of students were eligible for reduced or free lunches had approximately twice as much access to the Internet as peers from poorer schools in which 71 percent or more of the students were eligible for free or reduced lunch (National Center for Educational Statistics, 2000).

Explicit Internet Vocabulary Instruction with Dyslexics

Individuals with dyslexia will need explicit instruction regarding the vocabulary associated with the Internet as well as practice and modeling regarding its use. Teaching children to use Internet vocabulary and "technology is challenging due to time constraints in the school day . . . . Some students will need instruction in how to use software programs, access the Internet, do searches, and use word processing" (Morrow, Barnhart, & Rooyakkers, 2002, p. 219). For students with dyslexia and other learning disabilities, the teaching of web vocabulary and Internet usage and applications will need to be ongoing. Students with dyslexia will also need specific instruction and practice in preplanning research work and efficient ways to take notes once on the Internet. Figure 11.5 shows a planner that can be used for Internet research.

Name _____ Date _____

Teacher _____ Grade _____

Internet Research Guide
TAKECARE Planner

Topic and purpose—What am I researching and why?

Areas to research—What am I looking for on my topic?

Keywords—What are the keywords I need to use to access the websites I need?

Evaluate resources that will help in my search—What are the reference book sites I can use? What search engines can I use?

Conduct the web research

Always look for additional web links

Read, read, read

Evaluate and reflect on the information found on the Internet. Is the information accurate? Useful? Confirmed by other resources?

Notes:

FIGURE 11.5 Internet Research Guide: TAKECARE Planner

Using Index Cards for Guided Note Taking on the Internet

An index card template (see Figure 11.6) can be helpful for the student with dyslexia with a completed sample provided beforehand. The teacher and student could then complete an index card together on a topic chosen by the student. Afterwards, the student can practice completing an index card independently with the teacher available for feedback and clarifications. Students with dyslexia may need repeated practice before an actual research assignment is undertaken.

Note Taking Preparations   According to Buss and Karnowski (2002), teachers need to:

- **Provide** a mini-lesson on the importance of not copying word for word from resources.
- **Practice** with students creating index cards and organizing index cards by topics.
- **Model** how to list references.

```
┌─────────────────────────────────────────────────────────┐
│                                                         │
│   Topic:                                                │
│                                                         │
│   Internet Source for Reference:                        │
│                                                         │
│                                                         │
│   Key Concepts:                                         │
│                                                         │
│                                                         │
│   Quotes with page numbers:                             │
│                                                         │
│                                                         │
└─────────────────────────────────────────────────────────┘
```

FIGURE 11.6   Index Card Sample—Internet Note Taking

Summary

Keeping in mind the words of Grace Fernald: All teachers share one vision—the desire to increase the academic achievement of all children; that is, until "no child is left behind" (No Child Left Behind Act, 2002). The *Reading First* Program is providing necessary assistance to states to establish research-based or scientifically proven reading programs during the first decade of the new millennium, providing tools for appropriate and effective, evidence-based literacy instruction.

The National Reading Panel (NRP) (2000), chaired by Donald N. Langenberg, conducted an exhaustive, in-depth study of the scientific research on reading and its implications for reading instruction as related to comprehensive or balanced literacy programs. Comprehensive or balanced literacy programs contain the five essential teaching of reading elements: (1) phonemic awareness, (2) phonics, (3) fluency, (4) vocabulary development, and (5) text comprehension. Academic content standards need to be addressed at the same time. Reading and writing standards benchmarks were listed in the chapter for grades K, 3, and 8, critical transition times.

A suggested literacy block (two to three hours per day is recommended for struggling readers) was presented with a chart of several instructional strategies, methods, and approaches to address each of the five essential teaching of reading elements. How to determine whether a reading program or program component is evidence-based was covered extensively. The types of assessments that will be required to evaluate student proficiency in reading and writing and how well they achieve mastery of learning standards or instructional benchmarks were discussed in Chapter 9 (e.g., the Dyslexia Checklist).

For the student with dyslexia or learning disabilities, the question isn't "different curriculum?" or "different literacy instruction?" Rather, the questions are "where to focus?" and "how do we provide additional support, resources, and instruction?" For many students with dyslexia, there is the need for additional teaching in the areas of phonemic awareness, phonics, and fluency because the primary presenting academic problems for dyslexics and reading-disabled students involve reading fluency and the phonological components of language. Students who are proficient readers are fluent readers who have internalized the phonetic components of language with little instruction needed in these areas. However, research also shows that struggling readers tend to read less, have less expansive vocabularies, are less able to monitor their own comprehension of text, and have less organized study skills. Evidence-based instructional approaches to help in these areas are mentioned throughout the book.

Four basic "responsive" classroom teaching practices offered by Denton and Kriete (2000) were recommended to parallel implementation of the literacy block:

- *Create a classroom environment of warmth and safety.*
- *Articulate and post classroom routines and expectations* for scholarly work and responsible school citizenship.
- *Familiarize students with the school environment and resources* so they feel a sense of ownership and pride.
- *Regularly convey expectations for high-quality work,* provide models of exemplary work and convey benchmarks and standards for both the processes and products of learning.

For students who are second-language learners, an adaptive literacy block is offered on page 332 based on a sheltered English-Canadian model with additional literacy suggestions and information relevant to the teaching of second-language learners. Attention to the 1997 TESOL (Teachers of English to Speakers of Other Languages) *ESL Standards for Pre-K–12 Students* (as cited in Valdés, 2001) is necessary if the home language for the student with dyslexia or learning disabilities is different from the school language. Recommendations for sheltered English teaching by Echevarria, Vogt, and Short (2000) focused on language building with recommendations in the areas of lesson planning and interactive exchanges in the classroom. Morgan (2003) stressed the need to continue sheltered English strategies when English-language learners (ELL) are mainstreamed with English-speaking peers in all subject areas.

Families are considered literacy partners who continue school learning in the home environment. Several relevant literacy extensions and supports for families can be found throughout the book. Students with learning or other disabilities are more apt to continue their high school studies with ongoing family involvement, reading support, counseling services if needed, tutoring, attendance monitoring, and participation in afterschool activities/clubs. These have been found to be critical school retention factors as approximately one-third of high school students with learning disabilities do not obtain a high school diploma at the end of high school. Sally Shaywitz (2003), international researcher and dyslexia expert, documents that older dyslexics need the same research-based, systematic, and small group literacy instruction as younger people with dyslexia. Several recommendations were offered for adults with dyslexia because reading disabilities are not cured in the sense that all of the symptoms of childhood disappear. Assistance with personal goal setting and the development of self-advocacy are of primary importance.

Technology experts (e.g., Leu and Leu, 2000) and education leaders alike (e.g., LEA President Timothy Collins, 2003) show how technology and Internet resourcing help us to think more effectively about teaching. Any Internet addresses were surveyed during the writing stage of the book. The URLs for websites do sometimes change when websites are updated. If the URL changes, typing the name of the website in an Internet search should result in finding the new website. Strategies regarding how to narrow Internet searches, acquire Internet social conventions or protocols, pre-plan research work (TAKECARE Planner) and take guided notes were offered.

According to Dorothy Strickland (2002) and other researchers, *early diagnosis* with accompanying *effective interventions* are critical to future academic and social successes and adjustments for individuals with learning disabilities. With consistent literacy support in reading and writing to graduation, a social-academic network of support, and ongoing reinforcement of individual resiliency, individuals who experience the sometimes debilitating condition of dyslexia will lead successful and fulfilling lives.

REFERENCES

Aaron, P.G., & Baker, C.A. (1991). *Reading disabilities in college and high school.* Parkton, MD: York Press.

Ackerman, P.T., Anhalt, J.M., & Dykman, R.A. (1986). Arithmetic automatization failure in children with attention and reading disorders: *Associations and sequela. Journal of Learning Disabilities, 19,* 222–232.

Ada, A.A., & Campoy, F.I. (2000). *Blue and green.* Miami, FL: Santillana Publishing.

Adams, A.D., Carnine, D., & Gersten, R., (1982). Instructional strategies for studying context area texts in the intermediate grades. *Reading Research Quarterly, 18,* 27–55.

Adams, M.J. (1991). *Beginning to read: Thinking and learning about print.* Cambridge, MA: MIT Press.

Aksornkool, N. (Ed.). (2002). *Gender sensitivity: A training manual for sensitizing educational managers, curriculum and material developers and media professionals to gender concerns.* France: United Nations Educational, Scientific and Cultural Organization.

Allen, J. (1999). *Words, words, words: Teaching vocabulary in grades 4–12.* Portland, ME: Stenhouse.

Allen, J. (2000). *Yellow brick roads: Shared and guided paths to independent reading 4–12.* York, ME: Stenhouse.

Alley, G., & Deshler, D. (1979). *Teaching the learning disabled adolescent: Strategies and methods.* Denver: Love.

Allin, J. (2003). Untying the knot of time constraints: Using technology to extend student writing beyond the classroom. In S. Peterson (Ed.), *Untangling some knots in K–8 writing instruction* (pp. 88–95). Newark, DE: International Reading Association.

Allington, R. (1977). If they don't read much, how they ever gonna get good? *Journal of Reading, 21,* 57–61.

Allington, R. (2004, January/February). Fluency: A vital key to comprehension. *The Arts of Teaching: Supplement to Instructor, 113* (5), 12–13.

Allington, R.L. (1984). Oral reading. In P.D. Pearson, R. Barr, M.L. Kamil, & P. Mosenthal (Eds.)., *Handbook of reading research.* New York: Longman.

Allington, R.L. (2001). *What really matters for struggling readers: Designing research-based programs.* New York: Longman.

American Psychiatric Association. (1994). *Diagnostic and statistical manual of mental disorders (DSM-IV)* (4th ed.) Washington, DC: Author.

American Psychiatric Association Task Force on Vitamin Therapy in Psychiatry. (1973). *Megavitamin and orthomolecular therapy in psychiatry.* Washington, DC: American Psychiatric Association.

Americans with Disabilities Act of 1990. (PL 101-336). (1991, July 26). Equal Employment Opportunity Commission. Regulations of the Americans with Disabilities Act of 1990.

Anderson, R.C., Hiebert, E.H., Scott, J.A., & Wilkinson, I.A.G. (1985). *Becoming a nation of readers: The report of the Commission on Reading.* Champaign-Urbana, IL: Center for the Study of Reading.

Anderson, R.C., Shirley, L.L., Wilson, P.T., & Fielding, L.G. (1984). *Interestingness of children's reading material* (Report No. 323). Urbana-Champaign, IL: Center for the Study of Reading.

Angiulli, A., & Siegel, L.S. (2003). Cognitive functioning as measured by the WISC-R: Do children with learning disabilities have distinct patterns of performance? *Journal of Learning Disabilities, 36,* 1, 48–58.

Applegate, A.J., & Applegate, M.D. (March 2004). The Peter Effect: Reading habits and attitudes of preservice teachers. *The Reading Teacher, 57* (6), 554–563.

Aram, D.M. (1997). Hyperlexia: Reading without meaning in young children. *Topics in Language Disorders, 17* (3), 1–13.

Armbruster, B.B., & Osborn, J. (2001, September). *Put reading first: The research blocks for teaching children to read.* Washington, DC: National Institute for Literacy, NICHHD, and USDOE.

Arnold, L.E., Christopher, J., Huestis, R.D., & Smeltzer, D.J. (1978). Megavitamins for minimal brain dysfunction: A placebo controlled study. *Journal of the American Medical Association, 240,* 2642–2643.

Aronson, E., Blaney, N., Sikes, J., Stephan, C., & Snapp, M. (1975). The jigsaw route to learning and liking. *Psychology Today, 8,* 43–50.

Aronson, E., Baney, N., Stephan, C., Sikes, J., & Snapp, M. (1978). *The jigsaw classroom.* Newbury Park, CA: Sage.

Arzarello, F. (1996). Tendenze attuali della ricera italiana in didattica della matematica [Trends in Italian research on mathematical teaching]. *Notiziario* UMI, 1–2, 68–78.

Ashe, M. (2003). *Student response strategies for success in responding to open response questions.* Workshop presentation. Springfield, MA: Meline Kasparian Professional Development Center.

Ashlock, R.B. (1994). *Error patterns in computation* (6th ed.). New York: Merrill.

Atkinson, R.C. (1975). Mnemotechnics in second-language learning. *American Psychologist, 30,* 821–828.

Atwell, N. (1987). *In the middle: Writing, reading and learning with adolescents.* Portsmouth, NH: Heinemann.

Atwell, N. (1998). In the middle: New understandings about writing, reading, and learning. Portsmouth, NH: Heinemann-Boynton/Cook.

Au, K.H. (1998). Social constructivism and the school literacy learning of students of diverse cultural backgrounds. *Journal of Literacy Research, 30,* 297–319.

Au, K.H. (2002). Multicultural factors and the effective instruction of students of diverse backgrounds. In A.E. Farstrup & S. Jay Samuels (Eds.), *What research has to say about reading instruction* (pp. 392–413). Newark, DE: International Reading Association.

Aukerman, R.C. (1984). *Approaches to beginning reading.* New York: Wiley & Sons.

Ausubel, D. (1960). The use of advance organizers in learning and retention of meaningful verbal material. *Journal of Educational Psychology, 51,* 267–272.

Avi. (2002, March). *For the love of story.* Keynote presentation at the 33rd annual conference of the Massachusetts Reading Association (MRA), Sturbridge, MA.

Baker, L., & Brown, A. (1984). Cognitive skills and reading. In P.D. Pearson (Ed.), *Handbook of Reading Research*. New York: Longman.

Baker, S.K., Simmons, D.C., & Kameenui, E.J. (1995). *Vocabulary acquisition: Synthesis of the research*. Technical Report No. 13. Eugene: University of Oregon: National Center to Improve Tools for Educators.

Banks, J.A. (2000). *Teaching strategies for ethnic studies* (5th ed.). Boston: Allyn and Bacon.

Banks, J.A. (2000). Series foreword. In G. Gay, *Culturally responsive teaching: Theory, research, and practice*. New York: Teachers College Press.

Baroody, A.J. (1991). Teaching mathematics developmentally to children classified as learning disabled. In D.K. Reid, W.P. Hresko, & L.L. Swanson, *A cognitive approach to learning disabilities*. Austin, TX: Pro-Ed.

Barsch, R. (1965). *A movigenic curriculum* (Bulletin No. 25). Madison, WI: Department of Public Instruction, Bureau for the Handicapped.

Barsch, R. (1967). *Achieving perceptual-motor efficiency* (Vol. 1). Seattle, WA: Special Child Publications.

Barsch, R. (1968). *Enriching perception and cognition* (Vol. 2). Seattle, WA: Special Child Publications.

Bartlett, F.C. (1932). *Remembering*. Cambridge, UK: Cambridge University Press.

Bartlett, F.C. (1932). *Remembering: A study in experimental and social psychology*. Cambridge, England: Cambridge University Press.

Bastian, H.C. (1898). *A treatise on aphasia and other speech defects*. London: H.K. Lewis.

Beaver, J. (1997). *Developmental reading assessment*. Glenview, IL: Celebration Press. Pearson Learning.

Beaver, J.M. (2002). *The power of linking assessment with classroom instruction*. Keynote presentation at the 33rd annual conference of the Massachusetts Reading Association (MRA), Sturbridge, MA.

Beaver, J.M., & Carter, M.A. (2003). *Developmental reading assessment: Grades 4–8: In collaboration with classroom teachers*. Glenview, IL: Celebration Press: Pearson Learning Group.

Beck, I.L., McKeown, M.G., & Kucan, L. (2002). *Bring words to life: Robust vocabulary instruction*. New York: Guilford Press.

Beck, I.L., McKeown, M.G., & Omanson, R.C. (1987). The effects and uses of diverse vocabulary instructional techniques. In M.G. McKeown & M.E. Curtis (Eds.), *The nature of vocabulary acquisition* (pp. 117–156). Hillsdale, NJ: Erlbaum.

Belmont, L., & Birch, H.G. (1965). Lateral dominance, lateral awareness and reading disability. *Child Development, 36*, 59–71.

Bender, W.N. (1985). Differential diagnosis based on task related behavior of learning disabled and low-achieving adolescents. *Learning Disability Quarterly, 8*, 261–266.

Benton, A.L. (1987). Mathematical disability and the Gerstmann syndrome. In G. Deloche & X. Seron (Eds.), *Mathematical disabilities: A cognitive neuropsychological perspective* (pp. 111–120). Hillsdale, NJ: Lawrence Erlbaum.

Benton, A.L. & Pearl, D. (Eds.). (1978). *Dyslexia: An appraisal of current knowledge*. New York: Oxford University Press.

Benz, M.R., Lindstrom, L., & Yovanoff, P. (2000). Improving graduation and employment outcomes of students with disabilities: Predictive factors and student perspectives. *Exceptional Children, 66* (4), 509–529.

Berg, R., & McCarthy, J. (2002/2003). Senator Edward Kennedy Honored in Worcester. *MRA Connection, 8* (1), 6–7.

Berger, C.F. (1994). *The efficacy of the Benchmark School Word Identification Program as an instructional method for teaching word recognition skills to learning disabled students*. Unpublished doctoral dissertation, American International College, Springfield, MA.

Bermejo, V., Lago, M.O., Rodríguez, P., Dopico, C., & Lozano, M.J. (2002). *El PEI: un programa de intervención para la mejora del rendimiento matemático [The Instrumental Enrichment Program: An intervention program to improve mathematics Performance]*. Madrid: Complutense.

Bettleheim, B. (1976). *The uses of enchantment: The meaning and importance of fairy tales*. New York: Knopf.

Birnbaum, J.C. (1982). The reading and composing behaviors of select fourth- and seventh-grade students. *Research in the Teaching of English, 16*, 241–260.

Bishop, D.V.M., Jancey, C., & Steel, A.Mc.P. (1979). Orthoptic status and reading disability. *Cortex, 15*, 659–666.

Blachman, B. (1997). *Foundations of reading acquisition and dyslexia: Implications for early intervention. New York: Lawrence Erlbaum*.

Blachman, B., Tangel, D., Ball, E., Black, R., & McGraw, D. (1999) Developing phonological awareness and word recognition skills: A two-year intervention with low-income, inner-city children. Reading and Writing: An Interdisciplinary Journal, 11, 273–293.

Bley, N.S., & Thornton, C.A. (989, 1995). *Teaching mathematics to the learning disabled* (2nd and 3rd eds.). Austin, TX: Pro-Ed.

Blinco, P. (1991). Task persistence in Japanese elementary schools. In E. Beauchamp (Ed.), *Windows on Japanese education* (pp. 127–138). New York: Greenwood Press.

Block, C., & Pressley, M. (2002). *Comprehension instruction: Research-based best practices*. London: Guilford Press.

Bloom, B. (1956). *Taxonomy of educational objectives* (pp. 6–8) New York: Longmans, Green.

Bloom, B. (1984). The search for methods of group instruction. *Educational Leadership, 42* (9), 5.

Blythe, T., Allen, D., & Powell, B.S. (1999). *Looking together at student work*. New York: Teachers College Press.

Boder, E. (1970). Developmental dyslexia: A diagnostic approach based on the identification of three subtypes. *Journal of School Health, 40*, 289–290.

Boder, E. (1973). Developmental dyslexia: A diagnostic approach based on three atypical reading-spelling patterns. *Developmental Medicine and Child Neurology, 15*, 663–687.

Borasi, R. (1987). Exploring mathematics through analysis of errors. *For the Learning of Mathematics, 7*, 2–8.

Boser, R.A., Palmer, J.D., & Daugherty, M.K. (1998). Students' attitudes toward technology in selecting technology education programs. *Journal of Technology Education, 10* (1), 4–19.

Boyles, N. (2001). *Teaching written response to text: Constructing quality answers to open-ended comprehension questions.* Gainesville, FL: Maupin House Publishers.

Boyles, N. (2004). *Kid-friendly comprehension strategy instruction.* Workshop Packet. Ct. by author.

Bradley, L. (1988). Making connections in learning to read and spell. *Applied Cognitive Psychology, 2,* 3–18.

Bradley, L., & Bryant, P.E. (1983). Categorizing sounds and learning to read—A causal connection. *Nature, 301,* 419–421.

Brennan, J. (1995). *America: Land of Opportunity.* Unpublished manuscript. Springfield, MA.

British Columbia, Ministry of Education. (2002, August). http://www.bced.gov.bc.ca/specialed/ppandg/planning_4.htm downloaded, *Special Education Services: A Manual of Policies, Procedures and Guidelines,* 3/10/04.

Broca, P. (1865). Remarques sur le siege de la faculte du language articule. *Bulletin de la Societe d'Anthropologie, 6,* 18–28.

Brown, B., Haegerstrom-Portnoy, G., Yingling, C.D., Herron, J., Galin, D., & Marcus, M. (1983). Dyslexic children have normal vestibular responses to rotation. *Archives of Neurology, 40,* 370–373.

Brown, J.A. (1993). Reverse-role tutoring: An alternative intervention for learning disabled students. *B.C. Journal of Special Education, 17* (3), 238–243.

Brown, R. (2004). *Analyzing the miscues of struggling readers.* Workshop packet/presentation. Springfield, MA: Meline Kasparian Professional Development Center.

Bruce, B.C. (2003). (Ed.). *Literacy in the information age: Inquiries into meaning making with new technologies.* Newark, DE: International Reading Association.

Brueckner, L.J., & Elwell, M. (1932). Reliability of diagnosis of errors in multiplication of fractions. *Journal of Education Research, 26,* 175–185.

Brulnsma, R. (1981). A critique of "round-robin" oral reading in the elementary classroom. *Reading-Canada-Lecture, 1,* 78–81.

Brumback, R.A. (1996). Nonverbal learning disabilities, Asperger's syndrome, pervasive developmental disorder—Should we care? *Journal of Child Neurology, 11,* 427–429.

Buehl, D. (2001). *Classroom strategies for interactive learning.* Newark, DE: International Reading Association.

Burke, G. (1999). The habits that bind. *MRA (Massachusetts Reading Association) Connection, 5,* 2, 4.

Burns, M. (April 2004). 10 Big math ideas. *Instructor, 113* (7), 16–19.

Bush, G.W. (January 8, 2002). *No child left behind* [Online]. Available: edworkforce.house.gov/press/press107/NoChildLeftBehind.pdf.

Bushner, D.E., Tave, S.I., & Young, J. (1989, April). *Celebrating reading and writing.* Paper presentation at the 22nd annual conference of the Massachusetts Reading Association, Sturbridge, MA.

Buss, K., & Karnowski, L. (2002). *Reading and writing: Nonfiction genres.* Newark, DE: International Reading Association.

Cabana, N. (1994). *Spelling fortunes.* Unpublished paper. Springfield, MA.

Calkins, L. (1986). *The art of teaching writing.* Portsmouth, NH: Heinemann.

Calkins, L. (1991). *Living between the lines.* Portsmouth, NH: Heinemann.

Calkins, L.M. (1994). *The art of teaching writing* (2nd ed.). Portsmouth, NH: Heinemann.

Calkins, L.M., Montgomery, K., Santman, D., & Falk, B. (1998). *A teacher's guide to standardized reading tests.* Portsmouth, NH: Heinemann.

Cambourne, B.L. (1995). Toward and educationally relevant theory of literacy Learning: Twenty years of inquiry. *The Reading Teacher, 49,* 182–190.

Campbell, J.R., Hombo, C.M., & Mazzeo, J. (1999). *NAEP 1999 trends in academic progress: Three decades of student performance,* U.S. Department of Education (Washington, DC: National Center for Educational Statistics, 2000).

Canadian definition of Learning Disabilities (2002). http://www.ldac-taac.ca/english/defined/jan02eng.pdf (downloaded 3/10/2004)

Cangelosi, J.S. (1992). *Teaching mathematics in secondary and middle school.* New York: Merrill.

Cardinal, D.N., Griffin, J.R., & Christenson, G.N., (1993). Do tinted lenses really help students with reading disabilities? *Intervention in School and Clinic, 28,* 275–279.

Carlisle, J.F. (1993). Selecting approaches to vocabulary instruction for the reading disabled. *Learning Disabilities Research and Practice, 8,* 97–105.

Carr, E. (1985). The vocabulary overview guide: A metacognitive strategy to improve vocabulary, comprehension, and retention. *Journal of Reading, 21,* 684–689.

Carroll, T.A., Mullaney, P., & Eustace, P. (1994). Dark adaptation in disabled readers screened for scotopic sensitivity syndrome. *Perceptual and Motor Skills, 78,* 131–141.

Carver, R.P. (1992). Reading rate: Theory, research, and practical implications. *Journal of Reading, 36,* 84–95.

Casalis, S., Colé, P., & Sopo, D. (2004). Morphological awareness in developmental dyslexia. *Annals of Dyslexia, 54* (1), 114–138.

Casas, A., & Castellar, R. G. (2004). Mathematics education and learning disabilities in Spain. *Journal of Learning Disabilities, 37*(1), 62–73.

Cassidy, J. (1981). Inquiry reading for the gifted. *The Reading Teacher, 35* (1), 17–21.

Castelnuovo, E. (1965). L'oggetto e l'azione nell'insegnamento della geometria intuitive [Object and action in intuitive geometry teaching]. *Il Materiale per l'Insegnamento della Matematica* (10), 41–65.

Catts, H.W., Hu, C.F., Larrivee, L., & Swank, L. (1994). Early identification of reading disabilities in children with speech-language impairments. In. R.V. Watkins & M.L. Rice, *Specific language impairments in children* (pp. 145–160). Baltimore, MD: Paul D. Brookes.

CEC. (2003, November/December). Service learning—Students with disabilities give to others. *CEC (Council for Exceptional Children) today.* Vol. 10 (4), 1,7.

Chalfant, J.C., Pysh, M., & Moultrie, R. (1979). Teacher assistance teams: Findings of an introspective study. *Learning Disability Quarterly, 6*, 321–333.

Chall, J.S. (1967). *Learning to read: The great debate.* New York: McGraw-Hill.

Chall, J.S. (1983). *Learning to read: The great debate (rev. ed.).* New York: McGraw-Hill.

Chamberlain, M., Fitzgerald, K., Flanagan, K., Hamer, C., Hunter, P., O'Callaghan, D., & Paleologopoulos, T. (1998). *The art of persuasive writing: Teacher's resource guide.* Springfield, MA: Springfield Public Schools.

Chan, D.W., Suk-Han Ho, C., Tsang, S-M., Lee, S-K., & Chung, K.K.H. (2003). Reading-related behavioral characteristics of Chinese children with dyslexia: The use of the teachers' behavior checklist in Hong Kong. *Annals of Dyslexia, 53*, 300–323.

Chapman, J.W. (2002, Summer). Learning disabilities around the world. *Thalamus Updates: A Newsletter of the International Academy for Research in Learning Disabilities. Vol. 4 (2).* http://www.iarld.net/thalamus/vol_21_01.htm—(downloaded 4/3/04).

Chard, D.J., Pikulski, J.J., & Templeton, S. (2003). *From phonemic awareness to fluency: Effective decoding instruction in a research-based reading program* (Current research in reading/language arts booklet). New York: Houghton Mifflin.

Charlesworth, L. (2004, May/June). Ring in spring with Shel Silverstein. *Instructor Magazine, 113* (8), 38.

Cheek, E.H., Flippo, R.F., & Lindsey, J.D. (1989). *Reading for success in elementary schools.* Chicago, IL: Holt, Rinehart, & Winston.

Chen, C.S., Lee, S.Y., & Stevenson, H.W. (1996). Long-term prediction of academic achievement of American, Chinese, and Japanese adolescents. *Journal of Educational Psychology, 18*, 750–759.

Chen, M., & Ehrenberg, T. (1993). Test scores, homework, aspirations and teachers' grades. *Studies in Educational Evaluation, 19*, 403–419.

Cheng, K., Fujita, H., Kanno, I., Miura, S., & Tanaka, K. (1995). Human cortical regions activated by wide-field visual motion: An H2(15) O PET study. *Journal of Neurophysiology, 74* (1), 413–427.

Chi, M.T.H., de Leeuw, N., Chiu, N., & LaVancher, C. (1994). Eliciting self-explanations. *Cognitive Science, 18*, 439–477.

Chira, D. (1999). *Teaching and reaching every child: Equity education theory and practice.* Unpublished master's thesis, American International College, Springfield, MA.

Chomsky, C. (1972). Stages in language development and reading exposure. *Harvard Educational Review, 42*, 1–33.

Clay, M.M. (1979). *The early detection of reading difficulties* (2nd ed.). NH: Heinemann.

Clay, M.M. (1979). *Reading: The patterning of complex behavior* (2nd ed.). Auckland, New Zealand: Heinemann.

Clay, M.M. (1988). *The early detection of reading difficulties.* Auckland, New Zealand: Heinemann Educational Books.

Cohen, D., Ashe, M., Brown, R., Diaz, A., Chamberlain, M., Fenton, K., Kelliher, M., Lak, C., Motto, C., Paleologopoulos, T., Panico, D., & Rice, T. (2003–2004). *Professional development presentations: Empowering literacy coaches to support teachers' learning.* Meline Kasparian Professional Development Center for Teachers, Springfield, MA.

Cohen, J. (1988). *Statistical power analysis for the behavioral sciences* (2nd ed.). Hillsdale, NJ: Lawrence Erlbaum.

Colangelo, N., & Davis, G.A. (1997). *Handbook of gifted education.* Boston: Allyn and Bacon.

Collins, A., Brown, J.S., & Newman, S.W. (1989). Cognitive apprenticeship: Teaching the craft of reading, writing, and mathematics. In L.B. Resnick (Ed.), *Knowing, learning and instruction: Essays in honor of Robert Glaser* (pp. 453–494). Hillsdale, NJ: Lawrence Erlbaum.

Collins, T. (2003, February). Notes from the President (President of the Springfield Education Association), Springfield, Massachusetts. *The Springfield Teacher,* XXIV (6), 10.

Colwell, M., Aucoin, M., Berg, R., & Steckel, B. (2002/2003). A report on research reviewed by the Massachusetts Reading Association (MRA) Studies and Research Committee: Literacy report card. *MRA Primer: The challenge of teaching comprehension, 31* (2), 3.

Comer, J.P. (1988). *Maggie's American dream: The life and times of a black family.* New York: The Free Press.

Comer, J.P. (1993). *School power: Implications for an intervention project.* New York: The Free Press.

Comer, J.P. (1997). *Waiting for a miracle: Why schools can't solve our problems—and how we can.* New York: Penguin.

Connors, G.K., Goyette, C.M., Southwick, D.A., Lees, J.M., & Andrulonis, P.A. (1976). Food additives and hyperkinesis: A controlled double-blind experiment. *Pediatrics, 58*, 154–166.

Cook, L. (April 9, 1991). *A teaching recipe for your elementary classroom computer.* Paper presentation at the 22nd annual conference of the Massachusetts Reading Association (MRA), Sturbridge, MA.

Cook, S.B., Scruggs, T.E., Mastropieri, M.A., & Castro, G.C. (1986). Handicapped students as tutors. *Journal of Special Education, 19*, 483–492.

Coon, D. (1994). *Essentials of psychology: Exploration and application.* St. Paul, MN: West Publishing.

Cooper, H., & Hedges, L.V. (1994). *The handbook of research synthesis.* New York: Russell Sage Foundation.

Cordeiro, P. (1993). *Whole learning-Whole language and content in the upper elementary grades.* New York: R.C. Owen.

Cornoldi, C., & Lucangeli, D. (2004). Arithmetic education and learning disabilities in Italy. *Journal of Learning Disabilities, 37* (1), 42–49.

Corson, D. (1995). *Using English words.* Dordrecht, Netherlands: Kluwer Academic Publisher.

Cott, A. (1977). *The orthomolecular approach to learning disabilities.* San Rafael, CA: Academic Therapy.

Cott, A. (1985). *Help for your learning disabled child: The orthomolecular treatment.* New York: Times Books.

Council for Exceptional Children (CEC). (2003, Fall). Views from the field: Using data from participatory action research to support change and innovation. *Research Connections in Special Education, 13*, 6–7.

Courtney, A.M., & Montano, M. (2002/2003). Direct teaching of comprehension strategies in one first grade classroom. *MRA Primer: The challenge of teaching comprehension, 31* (2), 9–17.

Cox, L.S. (1975a). Systematic errors in the four vertical algorithms in normal and handicapped population. *Journal for Research in Mathematics Education, 6,* 202–220.

Cox, L.S. (1975b). Using research in teaching. *Arithmetic Teacher, 22,* 151–157.

Crawford, L.W. (1993). *Language and literacy learning in multicultural classrooms.* Boston: Allyn and Bacon.

Critchley, M. (1970). *The dyslexic child.* London: Heinemann.

Critchley, M. (1981). Dyslexia: An overview. In G. Pavlidis & T. Miles (Eds.), *Dyslexia research and its application to education* (pp. 1–11). New York: J. Wiley & Sons.

Cullinan, B.E. & Galda, L. (1998). *Literature and the child.* New York: Harcourt Brace.

Cunningham, P.M., & Allington, R.L. (1999). *Classrooms that work* (2nd ed.). New York: Longman.

Cunningham, P.M., (2000). *Phonics they use: Words for reading and writing* (3rd ed.). New York: HarperCollins.

Cunningham, R., & Shablak, S. (1975). Selective reading guide-o-rama: The content teacher's best friend. *Journal of Reading, 18,* 380–382.

DaFontoura, H.A., & Siegel, L.S. (1995). Reading, syntactic and working memory skills of Portuguese-English bilingual children. *Reading and Writing, 7,* 139–153.

Dahl, K.L., Scharer, P.L., Lawson, L.L., & Grogan, P.R. (2001). *Rethinking Phonics: Making the best teaching decisions.* Portsmouth, NH: Heinemann.

Daniels, H. (2002). *Literature circles: Voice and choice in book clubs and reading groups.* Markham, Ontario, Canada: Stenhouse.

Darling-Hammond, L., & McLaughlin, M.W. (1996). Policies that support professional development in an era of reform. In M. McLaughlin & I. Oberman (Eds.), *Teacher learning: New policies, new practices* (pp. 202–218). New York: Teachers College Press.

D'Augustine, C., & Smith, C.W. (1992). *Teaching elementary school mathematics.* New York: Harper Collins.

Davey, B. (1983). Think-aloud: Modeling the cognitive processes of reading. *Journal of Reading, 27,* 44–47.

David, O.J., Hoffman, S., McGann, B., Sverd, J., & Clark, J. (1976). Low lead levels and mental retardation. *Lancet, 6,* 1376–1379.

deBettencourt, L.U. (1990). Cognitive strategy training with learning disabled students. In P.I. Myers & D.D. Hammill (Eds.), *Learning disabilities* (pp. 453–466). Austin, TX: Pro-Ed.

DeFries, J.C., Alarcon, M., & Olson, R.K. (1997). Genetic etiologies of reading and spelling deficits: Developmental differences. In C. Hulme & M.J. Snowling (Eds.), *Dyslexia: Biology, cognition and intervention* (pp. 20–37). London, UK: Whurr.

DeFries, J.C., Olson, R.K., Pennington, B.F., & Smith, S.D. (1991). Colorado reading project—An update. In D. D. Duane & D.B. Gray (Eds.), *The reading brain* (pp. 53–87). Parkton, MD: York Press.

Dejerine, J. (1892). Contribution a l'etude anatomopathologique et clinique des differents varietes de cecite verbale. *Comptes Rendus des Seances de la Societe de Biologie, 4,* 61–90.

Delacato, C.H. (1963). *The diagnosis and treatment of speech and reading problems.* Springfield, IL: Charles C. Thomas.

Delgado-Gaitan, C. (1992). School matters in the Mexican-American home. Socializing children to education. *American Educational Research Journal, 86,* 277–294.

Demb, J.B., Boynton, G.M., Best, M., & Heeger, D.J. (1998). Psychophysical evidence for a magnocellular pathway deficit in dyslexia. *Vision Research, 38,* 1555–1559.

Denton, P., & Kriete, R. (2000). *The first six weeks of school.* Greenfield, MA: Northeast Foundation for Children.

DePierro, M. (March 26, 2004). *Using children's choices in the classroom.* Paper presentation at the 32nd annual conference of the Massachusetts Reading Association, Sturbridge, MA.

Deshler, D.D., Alley, G.R., & Carlson, S.C. (1980). Learning strategies: An approach to mainstreaming secondary students with learning disabilities. *Education Unlimited, 2,* 6–11.

Deshler, D.D., & Shumaker, J.B. (1986). Learning strategies: An instructional alternative for low-achieving adolescents. *Exceptional Children, 52,* 583–590.

Deshler, D.D., & Shumaker, J.B. (1993). Strategy mastery by at-risk students: Not a simple matter. *Elementary School Journal, 94,* 153–167.

Deshler, D.D., & Shumaker, J.B., Lenz, B.K., & Ellis, E.S. (1984). Academic and cognitive interventions for learning disabled students: Part II. *Journal of Learning Disabilities, 17,* 170–187.

Desoete, A. (2001). *Off-line metacognition in children with mathematical learning disabilities.* Unpublished doctoral dissertation, RUG University, Ghent, Belgium.

Desoete, A., Roeyers, H., & De Clercq, A. (2004). Children with mathematics learning disabilities in Belgium. *Journal of Learning Disabilities, 37* (1), 50–61.

Diagnostic and Statistical Manual of Mental Disorders (4th ed.) (1994). Washington, DC: American Psychiatric Association.

Diaz, A. (2003). *Student response strategies for success in responding to open response questions.* Workshop presentation. Springfield, MA: Meline Kasparian Professional Development Center.

Dickman, G.E., Hennessy, N.L., Moats, L.C., Rooney, K.J., & Harley, T. (2002, January 7). *Response to OSEP Summit on Learning Disabilities.* Approved by The International Dyslexia Association—January 7, 2002. URL: http://www.interdys.org, (downloaded 3/20/04).

Doig, B. (1991). *Diagnostic mathematics profile (DIAMAP).* Melbourne: Australian Council for Educational Research.

Dolch, E.W. (1942). *Basic sight word list.* Champaign, IL: Garrard Press.

Dolch, E.W. (1942. *The basic sight word test part 1 and 2.* Champaign, IL: Garrard.

Doman, R., Spitz, E., Zucman, E., Delacato, C., & Doman, G. (1960). Children with severe brain injuries (neurological organization in terms of mobility). *Journal of the American Medical Association, 174,* 257–262.

Drake, W.E. (1968). Clinical and pathological findings in a child with a developmental learning disability. *Journal of Learning Disabilities, 1,* 486–502.

Drew, A.L. (1956). A neurological appraisal of familial congenital word-blindness. *Brain* (79), 440–460.

Duane, D.D., (1991). Biological foundations of learning disabilities. In J.E. Obrzut & G.W. Hynd (Eds.), *Neuropsychological foundations of learning disabilities* (pp. 7–27). San Diego, CA: Academic Press.

Dudley-Marling, C. (2002). *Current issues in language arts: Threats to the professionalism of teachers.* Featured speaker at the 33rd annual conference of the Massachusetts Reading Association (MRA), Sturbridge, MA.

Duin, A.H., & Graves, M.F. (1987). Intensive vocabulary instruction as a prewriting technique. *Reading Research Quarterly, 22,* 89–96.

Durgunoglu, A.Y. (2002). Cross-linguistic transfer in literacy development and implications for language learners. *Annals of Dyslexia, 52,* 189–228.

Durkin, D. (1976). *Strategies for identifying words.* Boston: Allyn and Bacon.

Durkin, D. (1993). *Teaching them to read* (6th ed.). Boston: Allyn and Bacon.

Eakle, A.J., & Garber, A.M. (2004). International reports on literacy research. *Reading Research Quarterly, 39* (1), 114–118.

Echevarria, J., Vogt, M.E., & Short, D. (2000). Making content comprehensible for English language learners: The SIOP model. Boston: Allyn and Bacon.

Eden, G.F., & Zeffiro, T.A. (1998). Neural systems affected in developmental dyslexia revealed by functional neuroimaging. *Neuron, 21,* 279–282.

Edwards, P.A. (2003). Introduction to chapter 7. In P.A. Mason & J.S. Schumm (Eds.), *Promising practices for urban reading instruction.* Newark, DE: International Reading Association.

Ehri, L. (1992). *Reconceptualizing the development of sight word reading and its relationship to recoding.* In P. Gough, L. Ehri, & R. Treiman (Eds.), Reading acquisition (pp. 107–143). Hillsdale, NJ: Erlbaum.

Ehri, L. (1994). Development of the ability to read words: Update. In R. Ruddell, M. Ruddell, & H. Singer (Eds.), *Theoretical models and process of reading* (4th ed., pp. 323–358). Newark, DE: International Reading Association.

Ehri, L.C. (1991). Development of the ability to read words. In R. Barr, M.L. Kamil, P. Mosenthal, & P.D. Pearson (Eds.), *Handbook of reading research* (2nd ed., pp. 383–417). New York: Longman.

Ekwall, E.E. (1985). *Locating and correcting reading difficulties.* Columbus, OH: Charles Merrill.

Ekwall, E.E., & Shanker, J.L. (1988). *Diagnosis and remediation of the disabled reader.* Boston: Allyn and Bacon.

Elkins, J. (2002). Numeracy. In A.F. Ashman & J. Elkins (Eds.), *Educating children with diverse abilities* (pp. 436–469). Frenchs Forest, NSW, Australia: Pearson Education.

Elkonin, D.B. (1963). The psychology of mastering the elements of reading. In B. Simon & J. Simon (Eds.), *Educational psychology in the U.S.S.R.* (pp. 165–179). London: Routledge & Kegan Paul.

Elkonin, D.B. (1973). U.S.S.R. In J. Downing (Ed.), *Comparative reading* (pp. 551–579). New York: Macmillan.

Elly, W.B. (1992, July). How in the world do students read? *Hamburg: International association for the evaluation of educational achievement.* Newark, DE: International Reading Association.

Enright, B.C. (1983). *Enright Diagnostic Inventory of Basic Arithmetic Skills.* North Billerica, MA: Curriculum Associates.

Epstein, J.L. (1988). *Homework practices, achievements, and behaviors of elementary school students.* Baltimore, MD: Center for Research on Elementary and Middle Schools, John Hopkins University. (ERIC Document Reproduction Service No. PS 017 621).

Farnham-Diggory, S. (1987, July). *From theory to practice in reading.* Paper read at the Annual Conference of the Reading Reform Foundation, San Francisco, CA.

Farr, R. (1969). *Reading: What can be measured?* Newark, DE: International Reading Association.

Farr, R. (1988, April 11). *Strategies and not skills produce better readers and better thinkers.* Keynote Address at the 19th annual conference of the Massachusetts Reading Association (MRA), Sturbridge, MA.

Farrar, R.D. (1999, March 25). *Teaching for concepts in content area reading.* Paper presentation at the 30th annual conference of the Massachusetts Reading Association, Sturbridge, MA.

Farstrup, A.E., & Samuels, S. J. (Eds.). (2002). *What research has to say about reading instruction.* Newark, DE: International Reading Association.

Fawcett, A., & Nicholson, R. (1995). Persistence of phonological awareness deficits in older children with dyslexia. *Reading and Writing: An Interdisciplinary Journal, 7,* 361–376.

Federal Register. (1977, December 29). *Procedures for evaluating specific learning disabilities.* Washington, DC: Department of Health, Education and Welfare.

Feingold, B.F. (1975). *Why your child is hyperactive.* New York: Random House.

Feingold, B.F. (1976). Hyperkinesis and learning disabilities linked to the ingestion of artificial food colors and flavors. *Journal of Learning Disabilities, 9,* 551–559.

Feingold, B.F. (1977). A critique of "Controversial medical treatments of learning disabilities." *Academic Therapy, 13,* 173–183.

Feingold, B.F., & Feingold, H. (1979). *The Feingold cookbook for hyperactive children and others with problems associated with food additives and salicylates.* New York: Random House.

Ferguson, W.E. (2004). Dyslexia in Kenya. In I. Smythe, J. Everatt, & R. Salter (Eds.), *The international book of dyslexia: A guide to practice and resources* (pp. 152–154). West Sussex, England: John Wiley & Sons.

Fernald, G.M. (1943). *Remedial techniques in basic school subjects.* New York: McGraw-Hill.

Fernald, G.M (1988). *Remedial techniques in basic school subjects* (L. Idol, Ed.). Austin, TX: Pro-Ed. (Original work published in 1943).

Ferreri, C.A., & Wainwright, R.B. (1984). *Breakthrough for dyslexia and learning disabilities.* Pompano Beach, FL: Exposition Press.

Fink, R.P. (1998). Literacy development in successful men and women with dyslexia. *Annals of Dyslexia, 48,* 311–346.

Fink, R.P. (Dec. 1995/Jan. 1996). Successful dyslexics: A constructivist study of passionate interest reading. *Journal of Adolescent & Adult Literacy, 39* (4), 268–280.

First Steps (see: G. Raison, 1994; D. Rees, 1994).

Fischer, M.M., & Thompson, J.A. (Eds.) (2002/2003). Teachers as readers, a literacy journey of wealth and inheritance. *MRA Primer, 31,* (1), 3.

Flavell, J.H. (1976). Metacognitive aspects of problem solving. In L.B. Resnick (Ed.), *The nature of intelligence* (pp. 231–235). Mahwah, NJ: Lawrence Erlbaum.

Flavell, J.H. (1987). Speculations about the nature and development of metacognition. In R.H. Kluwe & F.E. Weinert (Eds.). *Metacognition, motivation and learning* (pp. 21–39). Mahwah, NJ: Laurence Erlbaum.

Flippo, R.F. (Ed.). (2001). *Reading researchers in search of common ground.* Newark, DE: International Reading Association.

Foertsch, M.A. (May 1992). *Reading in and out of school.* Educational Testing Service/Educational Information Office (pp. 6–7, 35–36). Washington, DC: U.S. Department of Education.

Forgan, H.W. & Mangrum, C.T. (1989). *Teaching content area reading skills* (4th ed.). Columbus, OH: Merrill.

Foster, D., & Noyce, P. (2004, January). The mathematics assessment collaborative: Performance testing to improve instruction. *Phi Delta Kappan, 85* (5), 367–374.

Fountas, I.C., & Pinnell, G.S. (1996). *Guided reading: Good first teaching for all children.* Portsmouth, NH: Heinemann.

Fountas, I.C., & Pinnell, G.S. (2000). *Guiding readers and writers, Grades 3–6: Teaching comprehension, genre, and content literacy.* Portsmouth, NH: Heinemann.

Fraley, S. (2004). *Cornerstone: You, your children, and literacy.* Pamphlet. Philadelphia: Cornerstone Foundation.

Fraley, S. (2004). *Cornerstone: You, your children, and literacy.* Pamphlet published by the Cornerstone Foundation. Philadelphia, PA.

Frank, J., & Levinson, H.N. (1977). Seasickness mechanisms and medications in dysmetric dyslexia and dyspraxia. *Academic Therapy, 12,* 133–153.

Frank, M. (2000). Tech for learning, Q and A on . . . smooth surfing. *Creative Classroom, 15* (2), 68.

Freeley, M.E. (1987, August/September). Teaching to both hemispheres. *Teaching K–8,* 65–75.

Freeman, J. (1995). *More books kids will sit still for.* New Providence, NJ: R.R. Bowker.

Freeman, J. (2001, January/February). Book Talk. *Instructor Magazine, 110* (5), 19–23.

Frieden, L. (Chairperson) (2004, May 26). *Improving educational outcomes for students with disabilities.* Washington, DC: National Council on Disability.

Frith, U., & Snowling, M. (1983). Reading for meaning and reading for sound in autistic and dyslexic children. *British Journal of Developmental Psychology, 1,* 329–342.

Frostig, M. (1968). Education for children with learning disabilities. In H. Myklebust (Ed.)., *Progress in learning disabilities* (pp. 234–266). New York: Grune & Stratton.

Fry, E.B. (1980, December). The new instant word list. *The Reading Teacher, 34,* 284–289.

Fuchs, D. (1997). Peer-assisted learning strategies: Making classrooms more responsive to diversity. *American Educational Research Journal, 34* (1), 174–206.

Gaddes, W.H. (1985). *Learning disabilities and brain function: A neuropsychological approach* (2nd ed.). New York: Springer-Verlag.

Galaburda, A. (1999). Developmental dyslexia: a multi-level syndrome. *Dyslexia, 5* (4), 183–192.

Galaburda, A.M. (1988). The pathogenesis of childhood dyslexia. In P. Plum (Ed.), *Language, communication and the brain* (pp. 127–137). New York: Raven Press.

Galda, L., & Liang, L.A. (2003). Literature as experience or looking for facts: Stance in the classroom. *Reading Research Quarterly, 38,* 2, 268–275.

Gallagher, J., & Gallagher, S. (1994). *Teaching the gifted child* (4th ed.). Boston: Allyn and Bacon.

Gambrell, L. (1996). Creating classroom cultures that foster motivation. *The Reading Teacher, 50,* 14–25.

Gambrell, L. (2004, January/February). Motivating kids to read. *The Arts of Teaching: Supplement to Instructor, 113* (5), 10–11.

Garcia, M.W., & Verville, K. (1994). Redesigning teaching and learning: The Arizona state assessment program. In S.W. Valencia, F. Hiebert, & P.P. Afflerbach (Eds.), *Authentic reading assessment: Practices and possibilities* (pp. 228–246). Newark, DE: International Reading Association.

Gardner, H. (1983). *Frames of mind.* New York: Basic Books.

Gardner, H. (1993). *Multiple intelligences.* New York: Basic Books.

Gardner, H. (1999). *The disciplined mind: What all students should understand.* New York: Simon & Schuster.

Gaskins, I.W., Downer, M.A., Anderson, R.C., Cunningham, P.M., Gaskins, R.W., Schommer, M., & the Teachers of Benchmark School. (1988). A metacognitive approach to phonics: Using what you know to decode what you don't know. *Remedial and Special Education, 9,* 36–41.

Gaylord, S.K. (1994). *Multicultural books to make and share.* New York: Scholastic Professional Books.

Geary, D.C. (1993). Mathematical disabilities: Cognitive neurological, and genetic components. *Psychological Bulletin, 114,* 362.

Geary, D.C. (2004). Mathematics and learning disabilities. *Journal of Learning Disabilities, 37* (1), 4–15.

Geiger, G., & Lettvin, J.Y. (1987). Peripheral vision in persons with dyslexia. *New England Journal of Medicine, 316,* 1238–1243.

Geitelson, D., & Goldstein, Z. (1986, May). Patterns of book ownership and reading to young children in Israel school-oriented and nonschool oriented families. *The Reading Teacher,* 924–930.

Genest, M. (1996). *A study of social and academic factors important to the academic successes of college students with attention deficit disorder both with and without learning disabilities.* Unpublished doctoral dissertation, American International College, Springfield, MA.

Gentry, R. (1986). *My kid can't spell: Understanding and assisting your child's literacy development.* Portsmouth, NH: Heinemann.

Gersten, R. (1998). Recent advances in instructional research for students with learning disabilities: An overview. *Learning Disabilities Research & Practice, 13* (3), 162–170.

Gersten, R., & Jiménez, R.T. (1994). A delicate balance: Enhancing literature instruction for students of English as a second language. *The Reading Teacher, 47,* 438–447.

Geschwind, N. (1962). The anatomy of acquired disorders in reading. In J. Money (Ed.), *Reading disability.* Baltimore, MD: Johns Hopkins Press.

Geschwind, N. (1982). Why Orton was right. *Annals of Dyslexia, 32,* 13–30.

Geschwind, N., & Levitsky, W. (1968). Human brain: Left-right asymmetries in temporal speech region. *Science, 161,* 186–187.

Geva, E., Yaghoub-Zadeh, Z., & Schuster, B. (2000). Understanding individual differences in word recognition of ESL children. *Annals of Dyslexia, 50,* 121–154.

Gillet, J., & Temple, C. (1990). *Understanding reading problems: Assessment and instruction.* Glenview, IL and London, England: Scott, Foresman/Little, Brown.

Gillingham, A., & Stillman, B.W. (1940, 1966). *Remedial training for children with specific disability in reading, spelling, and penmanship.* Cambridge, MA: Educators Pub.

Ginbayashi, K. (1984). *Mathematics education achievement of AMI.* Tokyo, Japan.

Ginsburg, H. (1977). *Children's arithmetic: The learning process.* New York: Van Nostrand.

Glaze, B. (1987). *"Learning logs," Plain talk about learning and writing across the curriculum.* Richmond, VA: Virginia Dept. of Education, Commonwealth of Virginia.

Glover, J.A., Ronning, R.R., & Bruning, R.H. (1990). *Cognitive psychology for teachers.* New York: Macmillan.

Goldman, S., Hasselbring, T., & the Cognition and Technology Group at Vanderbilt. (1997). Achieving meaningful mathematics literacy for students with learning disabilities. *Journal of Learning Disabilities, 30,* 198–208.

Goodman, K., & Goodman, Y. (1978). *Reading of American children whose language is a stable rural dialect of English or a language other than English.* (NIE-C-00-3-0087). Washington, DC: U.S. Department of Health, Education, and Welfare.

Goodman, K., & Goodman Y. (1982). A whole language comprehension centered view of reading development. In L. Reed & S. Ward (Eds.), *Basic skills: Issues and choices* (pp. 125–134). St. Louis, MO: CEM-REL.

Goodman, K.S. (1976). Reading: A psycholinguistic guessing game. In H. Singer & R. Ruddell (Eds.), *Theoretical models and processes of reading* (pp. 497–501). Newark, DE: International Reading Association.

Goodman, K.S., Bird, L.B., & Goodman, Y.M. (1992) *The whole language catalog: Supplement on authentic assessment.* New York: SRA Macmillan.

Goodman, Y.M. (1996). Revaluing readers while readers revalue themselves: Retrospective miscue analysis. *The Reading Teacher, 49* (8), 600–609.

Goodman, Y., & Burke, C.L. (1972). *Reading Miscue Inventory.* Chicago, IL: Richard C. Owen.

Gorman, G. C. (2003, July 28). Why some children struggle so much with reading used to be a mystery. Now researchers know what's wrong—and what to do about it. *Time, 162* (4), 53–59.

Goswami, U. (2002, June 27). *Phonology, reading development and dyslexia: A cross-linguistic study.* Keynote address at the Multilingual & Cross-Cultural Perspectives on Dyslexia Conference, Washington, DC.

Goswani, U., & Bryant, P. (1990). *Phonological skills and learning to read.* East Sussex: Lawrence Erlbaum.

Gough, P. (1972). One second of reading. In J. Kavanaugh & I. Mattingly (Eds.), *Language by ear and by eye: The relationship between speech and reading.* Cambridge, MA: MIT Press.

Gough, P.B. (1983). Context, form, and interaction. In K. Rayner (Ed.), *Eye movements in reading* (pp. 203–211). New York: Academic Press.

Goulandris, N. (Ed.). (2003). Consultant in dyslexia: Professor Margaret Snowling. *Dyslexia in different languages: Cross-linguistic comparisons.* London, England: Whurr Publishers.

Grammaticos, E., & Cooreman, A. (2004). Dyslexia in Belgium. In I. Smythe, J. Everatt, & R. Salter (Eds.), *The international book of dyslexia: A guide to practice and resources* (pp. 24–28). West Sussex, England: John Wiley & Sons.

Graves, D. (1994). *A fresh look at writing.* Portsmouth, NH: Heinemann.

Graves, D. (1996). Teaching writing. If you write, they will too. *Instructor, 105* (5), 40–41.

Gray, D.B., & Kavanagh, J.F. (1985). *Biobehavioral measures of dyslexia.* Parkton, MD: York Press.

Greaney, K., Tunmer, W., & Chapman, J. (1997). Effects of rime-based orthographic analogy training on the word recognition skills of children with reading disability. *Journal of Educational Psychology, 89,* 645–651.

Greene, F.P. (1970). *Paired reading.* Unpublished paper. New York: Syracuse University.

Grigorenko, E.L., Wood, F.B., Meyer, M.S., Hart, L.A., Speed, W.C., Shuster, A., & Pauls, D.L. (1997). Susceptibility loci for distinct components of developmental dyslexia on chromosomes 6 and 15. *American Journal of Human Genetics, 60,* 27–39.

Gross, M. (1992). The use of radical acceleration in cases of extreme intellectual precocity. *Gifted Child Quarterly, 36,* 91–99.

Grosser, G.S. (2005). *The teaching of neurophysiology.* Unpublished manuscript.

Grosser, G.S., & Spafford, C.S. (1989). Perceptual evidence for an anomalous distribution of rods and cones in the retinas of dyslexics: A new hypothesis. *Perceptual and Motor Skills, 68,* 683–698.

Grosser, G.S., & Spafford, C.S. (1990) Light sensitivity in peripheral retinal fields of dyslexics and proficient readers. *Perceptual and Motor Skills, 71,* 467–477.

Grosser, G.S., & Spafford, C.S. (1993a, April). *The relationship between particular visual deficits and reading problems.* In J. Donatelle (Chair), The Massachusetts Society of Optometrists. Western district meeting notice, W. Springfield, MA.

Grosser, G.S., & Spafford, C.S. (1993b, May). *A closer look at the learning disabled child.* In C. Spafford (chair), The Massachusetts Division of Learning Disabilities. Spring symposium meeting, Springfield, MA.

Grosser, G.S., & Spafford, C.S. (1998). *Contrast sensitivity responses of dyslexics and proficient readers to luminance gratings of various spatial frequencies.* Paper presentation: American International College, Springfield, MA.

Grosser, G.S., & Spafford, C.S. (2000). Dyslexia: Overview and treatment. In L. VanderCreek & T. Jackson, (Eds.), *Innovations in clinical practice: A source book,* Vol. 18, pp. 417–440. Sarasota, FL: Professional Resource Press.

Grosser, G.S., Spafford, C.A., Donatelle, J., Squillace, S., & Dana, J. (1995). *Contrast sensitivity responses of reading-disabled and proficient readers to chart-displayed luminance gratings of various spatial frequencies.* Paper presentation at American International College, Springfield, MA.

Grosser, G.S., & Trzeciak, G.M. (1981). Duration of recognition for single letters, with and without visual masking, by dyslexics and normal readers. *Perceptual and Motor Skills, 53,* 991–995.

Grossnickle, F.E. (1935). Reliability of diagnosis of certain types of errors in long division with a one-figure divisor. *Journal of Experimental Education, 4,* 7–16.

Gross-Tur, V., Shalev, R.S., Manor, O., & Amir, N. (1995). Developmental right-hemisphere syndrome: Clinical spectrum of the nonverbal learning disability. *Journal of Learning Disabilities, 28,* 80–86.

Guidance for the Reading First Program, (2002, April). Washington, DC: U.S. Department of Education, Office of Elementary and Secondary Education.

Guthrie, J.T. (1973). Models of reading and reading disability. *Journal of Educational Psychology, 65,* 9–18.

Guthrie, J.T., & Anderson, E. (1999). Engagement in reading: Processes of motivated, strategic, knowledgeable, social readers. In J.T. Guthrie & D.E. Alvermann (Eds.), *Engaged reading: Processes, practices, and policy implications* (pp. 17–45). New York: Teachers College Press.

Guthrie, J.T., Wigfield, A., Metsala, J.L., & Cox, K.E. (1999). Motivational and cognitive predictors of text comprehension and reading amount. *Scientific Studies of Reading, 3,* 231–256.

Haggard, M.R. (1986a). The vocabulary of self-collection strategy: An active approach to word learning. In E.K. Dishner, T.W. Bean, J.E. Readence, & D.W. Moore (Eds.), *Reading in the content areas: Improving classroom instruction* (2nd ed.; pp. 179–183). Dubuque, IA: Kendall/Hunt.

Haggard, M.R. (1986b). The vocabulary of self-collection strategy: Using student interest and word knowledge to enhance vocabulary growth. *Journal of Reading, 29,* 634–642.

Hall, E.C. (1997). *Inclusion is here to stay.* Unpublished master's thesis. Springfield, MA: American International College.

Hall, S.R. (1829). *Lectures on school-keeping.* Boston: Richardson, Lord, & Holbrook.

Hallahan, D., & Kauffman, J.M. (1991). *Exceptional children: Introduction to special education.* Englewood Cliffs, NJ: Prentice-Hall.

Hallahan, D.P., Kauffman, J.M., & Lloyd, J.W. (1985). *Introduction to learning disabilities* (2nd ed.). Englewood Cliffs, NJ: Prentice-Hall.

Hammill, D.D. (1990). on defining learning disabilities: An emerging consensus. *Journal of Learning Disabilities, 23,* 74–84.

Hammill, D.D, Goodman, L. & Wiederholt, J.L. (1974). Visual-motor processes: Can we train them? *Reading Teacher, 27,* 469–478.

Hammill, D.D., Leigh, J.E., McNutt, G., & Larsen, S.C. (1981). A new definition of learning disabilities. *Learning Disability Quarterly, 4,* 336–342.

Harnois, V.D., & Furdyna, E.J.H. (1994). *The Harnois program: Decoding skills for dyslexic readers.* Pittsburgh, PA: Dorance Publishing.

Harris, A.J., & Jacobson, M.D. (1982). *First Reader List.* New York: Macmillan Publishing Co.

Harris, A.J. & Sipay, E.R. (1990). *How to increase reading ability* (9th ed.). New York: Longman.

Harris, T.L., & Hodges, R.E. (Eds.). (1981). *A dictionary of reading and related terms.* Newark, DE: International Reading Association.

Harris, T.L., & Hodges, R.E. (Eds.). (1995). *The literacy dictionary. The vocabulary of reading and writing.* Newark, DE: International Reading Association.

Harrison, D.L., & Cullinan, B.E., (1999). *Easy poetry lessons that dazzle and delight.* New York: Scholastic.

Harris-Sharples, S. (2002). A message from the MRA (Massachusetts Reading Association). President. *MRA 33rd annual conference book.* Milford, MA: MRA.

Harvey, S., & Goudvis, A. (2000). *Strategies that work: Teaching comprehension to enhance understanding.* York, ME: Stenhouse.

Harwayne, S. (1992). *Lasting impressions: Weaving literature into the writing workshop.* Portsmouth, NH: Heinemann.

Hart, D., Zafft, C., & Zimbrich, K. (Winter 2001). Creating access to college for all students. The *Journal for Vocational Special Needs Education, 23,* 19–31.

Hauser, S.T. (1999). Understanding resilient outcomes: Adolescents lives across time and generations. *Journal of Research on Adolescence, 9* (1), 1–24.

Healy, J.M. (1982). The enigma of hyperlexia. *Reading Research Quarterly, 17,* 319–338.

Hebert, C. (2004). *Catching a falling reader.* In press.

Heckleman, R.G. (1969). A neurological-impress method of remedial-reading instruction. *Academic Therapy, 4,* 277–282.

Hefflin, B.R. & Barksdale-Ladd, M.A. (2003). African American children's literature that helps students find themselves: Selection guidelines for grades K–3 (pp. 203–219). In P.A. Mason & J.S. Schumm (Eds.), *Promising practices for urban reading instruction.* Newark, DE: International Reading Association.

Hellinckx, W., & Ghesquière, P. (1999). *Als leren pijn doet: Opvoeden van kinderen met een leerstoornis* [When learning hurts: Education children with learning disabilities]. Leuven, Belgium: Acco.

Helveston, E.M., Billips, W.C., & Weber, J.C. (1970). Controlling eye-dominant hemisphere relationships as a factor in reading ability. *American Journal of Ophthalmology, 70,* 96–100.

Hendrick, J. (1990). *Total learning—Curriculum for the young child.* Columbus, OH: Merrill.

Hennessy, N. (2003, Winter). Free and appropriate = Free and effective. *Perspectives, 29*(1), 2.

Henning, W. (1936). *The fundamentals of chromeorthoptics.* Actino Lab, Inc.

Heward, W.L., & Orlansky, M.D. (1984, 1988, 1992). *Exceptional children*. Columbus, OH: Merrill.

Hill, J.A. (December/January 2004). Teaching an old project new tricks: Incorporating multiple standards in a seventh grade technology classroom. *The Technology Teacher*, 7–14.

Hinshelwood, J. (1896). A case of dyslexia: A peculiar form of word-blindness. *The Lancet*, 1451–1454.

Hinshelwood, J. (1917). *Congenital word blindness*. London: H.K. Lewis.

Holland, A.L., & Reinmuth, O.M. (1982). Aphasia in adults. In G.H. Shames & E.H. Wiig (Eds.), *Human communication disorders: An introduction* (pp. 561–593). Columbus, OH: Merrill.

Honert, D.V.D. (1985). *Reading from scratch/RFS*. Cambridge, MA: Educators Publishing.

Hooks, B. (1994). *Teaching to transgress: Education as the practice of freedom*. New York: Routledge.

Hoover-Dempsey, K.V., Battiato, A.C., Walker, J.M.T., Reed, R.P., DeJong, J.M., & Jones, K.P. (2001). Parent involvement in homework. *Educational Psychologist*, 36 (3), 195–209.

Howell, E., & Stanley, G. (1988). Colour and learning disability. *Clinical & Experimental Optometry*, 71, 66–71,

Huck, C.S., Hepler, S., Hickman, J., & Kiefer, B. Z. (1997). *Children's literature in the elementary school* (6th ed). Madison, WI: Brown & Benchmarks.

Hughes, A. (2004). Dyslexia in Ireland. In I. Smythe, J. Everatt, & R. Salter (Eds.), *The international book of dyslexia: A guide to practice and resources* (pp. 132–135). West Sussex, England :John Wiley & Sons.

Humphery, J.M.H. (1981). *Persistent error patterns on whole number computations and scores on Piagetian tasks as they relate to mathematics achievement of adolescents*. Unpublished doctoral dissertation, University of Texas, Austin, TX.

Hynd, G., & Cohen, M. (1983). *Dyslexia: Neuropsychological theory, research, and clinical differentiation*. Boston: Allyn and Bacon.

Hynd, G.W., & Cohen, M. (1983). *Dyslexia: Neuropsychological theory research and clinical differentiation*. New York: Grune & Stratton.

Hynd, G.W., & Semrud-Clikeman, M. (1989). Dyslexia and neurodevelopmental pathology: Relationships to cognition, intelligence, and reading skill acquisition. *Journal of Learning Disabilities*, 22, 204–216.

International Dyslexia Association (IDA). (2000). Website: www.interdys.org

International Dyslexia Association (IDA). (2003). *Finding the answers (pamphlet)*. Baltimore, MD: Author.

International Reading Association. (2000, May). *Assessment in the U.S. for children in special education experiencing reading difficulties. Summary of a board resolution*. Newark, DE: Author.

International Reading Association. (2001). *Second-language literacy instruction: A position statement of the International Reading Association*. Newark, DE: Author.

International Technological Education Association (2000, 2003). *Standards for technological Literacy: Content for the study of technology*. Reston, VA: Author.

Irlen, H. (n.d.). Irlen Institute information on Scotopic Sensitivity Syndrome [correspondence].

Jackson, J.H. (1874). On the nature of the duality of the brain. *Medical Press and Circular, 1*.

Jackson, N.E., & Roller, C.M. (1993). Reading with young children. *Research-based decision making series, No. 9302*. Storrs, CT: National Research Center on the Gifted and Talented.

Jacobs, V.A. (1999, July/August). What secondary teachers can do to teach reading. *Harvard Education Letter*, 4.

Jenkins, J.R., Matlock, B., & Slocum, T.A. (1989). Two approaches to vocabulary instruction: The teaching of individual word meanings and practice in deriving word meaning from context. *Reading Research Quarterly*, 24, 215–235.

Jimenez, J.E., & García, A. I. (2002). Strategy choice in solving problems: Are there differences between students who have learning disabilities, G-V variety performance, and typical achievement students? *Learning Disability Quarterly*, 25, 113–122.

Jiménez, J.E., Siegel, L.S., & López, M.R. (2003). The relationship between IQ and reading disabilities in English-speaking Canadian and Spanish children. *Journal of Learning Disabilities*, 36, 1, 15–23.

Jiménez, R.T. (2004, March). More equitable literacy assessment for Latino students. *The Reading Teacher*, 57 (6), 576–578.

John, P., George, S.K., & Mampilli, A.B. (2004). Dyslexia in India. In I. Smythe, J. Everatt, & R. Salter (Eds.), *The international book of dyslexia: A guide to practice and resources* (pp. 122–127). West Sussex, England: John Wiley & Sons.

Johns, J. L. (1981, Spring). The development of the Revised Dolch List. *Illinois School Research and Development*, 17, 15–24.

Johns, J.J., & Lenski, S.D. (2001). *Strategies for content area learning*. Dubuque, IA: Kendall/Hunt Publishing.

Johns, J.L., & Berglund, R.L. (2002a). *Fluency: Questions, answers, evidence-based strategies*. Dubuque, IA: Kendall/Hunt Publishing.

Johnson, D.J. (1968, February 1–3). *Clinical teaching of children with learning disabilities*. Proceedings of the Fifth Annual International Conference of the ACLD. Successful programming—Many points of view. Boston, MA.

Johnson, D.J. & Myklebust, H.R. (1967). *Learning disabilities: Educational principles and practices*. New York: Grune & Stratton.

Johnson, N.J., & Giorgis, C. (2003). Literature in the reading curriculum. *The Reading Teacher*, 56 (7), 704–712.

Kapinus, B.A., Gambrell, L.B., & Koskinen, P.S. (1988). *The effects of practice in retelling upon readers*. Thirty-sixth yearbook of the National Reading Conference. Rochester, NY: National Reading Conference.

Kapitzke, C. (2003). Information literacy: The changing library. In B.C. Bruce (Ed.), *Literacy in the information age: Inquiries into meaning making with new technologies*. Newark, DE: International Reading Association.

Kaplan, R. (1983). Changes in form visual fields in reading disabled children produced by syntonic (colored light) stimulation. *International Journal of Biosocial Research*, 5, 20–33.

Karlin, R., & Karlin, A.R. (1987). Teaching elementary reading: Principles and strategies. San Diego, CA: Harcourt Brace Jovanovich.

Kavale, K.A., & Forness, S.R., (1985). *The science of learning disabilities.* San Diego: College-Hill Press.

Kavale, K.A., Forness, S.R., & Bender, M. (1988). *Handbook of learning disabilities: Volume II: Methods and intervention.* Boston: Little, Brown & Co.

Kavale, K., & Mattison, P.D. (1983). One jumped off the balance beam: Meta-analysis of perceptual-motor training. *Journal of Learning Disabilities, 16,* 165–173.

Keenan, J.W., Solsken, J., Negroni, P., Kennedy, J., Harris, H., Moriarty, C., Santa, L., Williams, G., Cox, T., Lak, C., Radding, L., Silvestri, N. (1994, April 8). *The future is now: The learning community of the Mary O. Pottenger School, Springfield, MA.* Workshops at the 25th annual conference of the Massachusetts Reading Association (MRA), Sturbridge, MA.

Keene, E. (2003, July 3). Student assessment overview. *Tool Kit At-A-Glance: Enhancing: Monitoring Progress.* Sourced on Internet: Cornerstone.literacy.org.

Keene, E. (2004, February 22–24). *Looking for language.* Presentation at the Cornerstone Northern Regional Annual Conference, Bridgeport, CT.

Keene, E., & Zimmerman, S. (1997). *Mosaic of thought: Teaching comprehension in a reader's workshop.* Portsmouth, NH: Heinemann.

Keller, B. (2004, April 14). Teacher taps parents to help with test prep. *Education Week, XXIII* (31), 6.

Keller, C.E., & Sutton, J.P. (1991). Specific mathematics disorders. In J.E. Obrzut & G.W. Hynd (Eds.), *Neuropsychological foundations of learning disabilities* (pp. 549–571). San Diego, CA: Academic Press.

Kennedy, K.M., & Backman, J. (1993). Effectiveness of the Lindamood Auditory Discrimination In Depth Program with students with learning disabilities. *Learning Disabilities Practice, 8,* 253–259.

Kephart, N.C. (1960). *The slow learner in the classroom.* New York: Merrill.

Kephart, N.C. (1963). *Perceptual-motor problems of children.* Proceedings of the First Annual Meeting of the ACLD Conference on Exploration into the Problem of the Perceptually Handicapped Child. Chicago, reprinted in S.A. Kirk & J.M. McCarthy (Eds.). *Learning disabilities: Selected ACLD papers* (1975) (pp. 27–32). Boston: Houghton Mifflin.

Kershner, J.R., Cummings, R.L., Clarke, K.A., Hadfield, A.J., & Kershner, B.A. (1986). Evaluation of the Tomatis Listening Training Program with learning disabled children. *Canadian Journal of Special Education, 2,* 1–32.

Kinsbourne, M., & Warrington, E.T. (1963). The developmental Gerstmann syndrome. *Archives of Neurology, 8,* 490–501.

Kintsch, W. (1980). Learning from text, levels of comprehension, or: Why anyone would read a story anyway. *Poetics, 9,* 87–89.

Kirk, S.A. (1963). *Behavioral diagnosis and remediation of learning disabilities.* Proceedings of the annual meeting of the Conference on Exploration into the Problems of the Perceptually Handicapped Child, Chicago, IL, Vol. 1

Kirk, S.A, & Chalfant, J.C. (1984). *Psycholinguistic learning disabilities: Diagnosis and remediation.* Chicago, IL: University of Illinois Press.

Kleffner, F.R., (1964). Teaching aphasic children. In J. Magary & J. Eichorn (Eds.), *The exceptional child* (pp. 330–337). New York: Holt, Rinehart & Winston.

Kletzien, S.B., & Dreher, M.J. (2004). *Informational text in K–3 classrooms.* Newark, DE: International Reading Association (IRA).

Kline, J.E. (1999). President's message. *MRA Primer, 28* (1), 2.

Kling, B. (2000, January/February). Assert yourself: Helping students of all ages develop self-advocacy skills. *Teaching Exceptional Children, 32*(3), 66–70.

Knapp, M.S., with Adelman, N.E., Marder, C., McCollum, H., Needels, M.C., Padilla, C., et. al. (1995). *Teaching for meaning in high-poverty classrooms.* New York: Teachers College Press.

Knapp, S., & VandeCreek, L. (1994). *Anxiety disorders: A scientific approach for selecting the most effective treatment.* Sarasota, FL: Professional Resource Press.

Koenig, A., & Spafford, C.S. (2001). *Dyslexia: The myths and the realities.* Unpublished manuscript.

Kolker, B., & Terwilliger, P.N. (1981). Sight vocabulary learning of first and second graders. *Reading World, 20,* 251–258.

Konopak, B.C., & Williams, N.L. (1988). Using the key word method to help young readers learn content material. *The Reading Teacher, 41,* 682–687.

Kosc, L. (1974). Developmental dyscalculia. *Journal of Learning Disabilities, 7,* 164–177.

Krashen, S.D. (1987). *Principles and practice in second language acquisition.* Englewood Cliffs, NJ: Prentice-Hall.

Kroesbergen, E. (2002). *Mathematics education for low-achieving students: Effects of different instructional principles on multiplication learning.* Doetinchem, Netherlands: Gravant Educatieve Uitgaven.

Kucan, L., & Beck, I.L. (2003, Spring). Inviting students to talk about expository texts: A comparison of two discourse environments and their effects on comprehension. *Reading Research and Instruction, 42* (3).

Kussmaul, A. (1877). Disturbance of speech. *Cyclopedia of Practical Medicine, 14,* 581–875.

LaBerge, D., & Samuels, S. (1974). Toward a theory of automatic information processing in reading. *Cognitive Psychology, 6,* 293–323.

Ladson-Billings, G. (1994). *The dreamkeepers: Successful teaching of African American children.* San Francisco: Jossey-Bass.

Ladson-Billings, G. (1995). New directions for equity in mathematics education. In W.G. Secada, E. Fennema, & L.B. Adajian (Eds.), *Making mathematics meaningful in a multicultural context.* New York: Cambridge University Press.

Lak, C. (2003). *Student response strategies for success in responding to open response questions.* Workshop presentation. Springfield, MA: Meline Kasparian Professional Development Center.

Laker, M. (1982). On determining trace element levels in man: The uses of blood and hair. *The Lancet, 2,* 259–262.

Landesman-Dwyer, S., Ragozin, A.S., & Little, R.E. (1981). Behavioral correlates of prenatal alcohol exposure: A four-year follow-up study. *Neurobehavioral Toxicology and Teratology, 3,* 187–193.

Landmark College. http://www.landmark.edu/about/index.html (Downloaded 7/12/04)

Landry, D.L. (1989, April 6). *Poems are written by poets and that includes me!* Paper presentation at the 20th annual conference of the Massachusetts Reading Association, Sturbridge, MA.

Lapp, D., & Flood, J. (2003). Understanding the learner: Using portable assessment. In R.L. McCormack & J.R. Paratore (Eds.), *After early intervention, then what? Teaching struggling readers in grades 3 and beyond* (pp. 10–24). Newark, DE: International Reading Association.

Lauritzen, C. (1982). A modification of repeated readings for group instruction. *The Reading Teacher, 36,* 456–458.

Lazarus, B.D. (1988). Using guided notes to aid learning disabled students in secondary mainstream settings. *The Pointer, 33,* 32–36.

Lazarus, B.D., & McKenna, M.C. (1991, April). *Guided notes: Review and achievement of mainstreamed LD students.* Paper presented at the meeting of the Council for Exceptional Children, Atlanta, GA.

Learning Disabilities Association of America (LDA). (Approved June 1996 and updated April 2001). *Reading and learning disabilities position paper of the Learning Disabilities Association of America.* Author: http://ldanatl.org/positions/reading.html.

Lefly, D.L., & Pennington, B.F. (1991). Spelling errors and reading fluency in Compensated adult dyslexics. Annals of Dyslexia, 41, 143–162.

Lefroy, R. (1975). Some remedial techniques for severe learning disabilities. In M. White, R. Lefroy, & S.D. Weston (Eds.), *treating reading disabilities* (pp. 21–54). San Raphael, CA: Academic Therapy Publications.

Lehr, C.A., Hansen, A.L., Sinclair, M.F., & Christenson, S.L. (2003). Moving beyond dropout toward school completion: An integrative review of data-based interventions. *School Psychology Review.*

Leong, C.K. (1986). The role of language awareness in reading proficiency. In G.T. Pavlidis & D.F. Fisher (Eds.), *Dyslexia: Its neuropsychology and treatment* (pp. 131–148). Chichester, England: John Wiley & Sons.

Leong, C.K. (1999). What can we learn from dyslexia in Chinese? In I. Lundberg, F.I. Tonnessen, & I. Austad (Eds.), *Dyslexia: Advances in theory and practice* (pp. 117–139). Dordrecht: Kluwer Academic Publishers.

Leong, C.K. (2004). Editor's commentary. *Annals of Dyslexia, 54* (1), 1–8.

Leong, C.K., & Tan, L.H. (2002). Phonological processing in learning to read Chinese: In search of a framework. In E. Helmquist & C. von Euler (Eds.), *Dyslexia and literacy* (pp. 126–150). London: Whurr Publishers.

Leppänen, U., Niemi, P., & Nurmi, K.A.J. (2004). Development of reading skills among preschool and primary school pupils. *Reading Research Quarterly, 39* (1), 72–93.

Lerner, J.W. (1971). *Children with learning disabilities.* Boston: Houghton Mifflin.

Lerner, J.W. (1993). *Learning disabilities: Theories, diagnosis, and teaching strategies* (6th ed.). Boston: Houghton Mifflin.

Lerner, J.W. (2003). Grace Fernald: A remembrance by a student. *Learning Disabilities: A Multidisciplinary Journal, 12* (1).

Lerner, J.W., Lowethal, B., & Lerner, S.R. (1995). *Attention deficit disorders: Assessment and teaching.* Boston: Houghton Mifflin.

Leu, D.J., Jr. (2001). Internet project: Preparing students for new literacies in a global Village. *The Reading Teacher, 54,* 568–572. Also available on *Reading Online*: http://www.readingonline.org/electronic/elec_index.asp?HREF=/electronic/RT/ 3–01_Column/index.html.

Leu, D.J., Jr., & Leu, D.D. (2000). *Teaching with the Internet: Lessons from the classroom.* Norwood, MA: Christopher-Gordon.

Levasseur, R. (1997). *Cognitive learning style profiles with Passamaquoddy Native American Indians.* Unpublished doctoral dissertation, American International College, Springfield, MA.

Levin, H., & Kaplan, E.L. (1970). Grammatical structure and reading. In H. Levin & J.P. Williams (Eds.), *Basic studies on reading* (pp. 110–133). New York: Basic Books.

Levin, J.R., Levin, M.E., Glasman, L.D., & Nordwall, M.B. (1992). Mnemonic Vocabulary instruction: Additional effectiveness evidence. *Contemporary Educational Psychology, 17* (2), 156–174.

Levinson, H.N. (1980). *A solution to the riddle dyslexia.* New York: Springer-Verlag.

Levinson, H.N. (1988). The cerebellar-vestibular basis of learning disabilities in children, adolescents and adults: Hypothesis and study. *Perceptual and Motor Skills, 67,* 983–1006.

Liberman, I.Y. (1983). A language oriented view of reading and its disabilities. In H.R. Myklebust (Ed.), *Progress in learning disabilities,* Vol. V. New York: Grunes & Stratton.

Liberman, I.Y., Liberman, A.M., Mattingly, I.G., & Shankweiler, D. (1980). Orthography and the beginning reader. In J.F. Kavanagh & R.L. Venezky (Eds.). *Orthography, reading and dyslexia.* Baltimore, MD: University Park Press.

Liberman, I.Y., Rubin, H., Duques, S., & Carlisle, J. (1985). Linguistic abilities and spelling proficiency in kindergarten and adult poor readers. In J. Kavanagh & D.G. Gray (Eds.), *Biobehavioral measures of dyslexia.* Parkton, MD: York Press.

Liberman, I.Y., Shankweiler, D., Fischer, F.W., & Carter, B. (1974). Explicit syllable and phoneme segmentation in the young child. *Journal of Experimental Child Psychology, 18,* 201–212

Liberman, J. (1986). The effect of syntonic (colored light) stimulation on certain visual and cognitive functions. *Journal of Optometric Vision Development, 17,* 4015.

Lindamood, C.H. & Lindamood, P.C. (1975). *The A.D.D. Program, Auditory Discrimination in Depth.* Hingham, MA: Teaching Resources Corp.

Lindamood, P., & Lindamood, P. (2002). *The Lindamood Phonemic Sequencing® (LiPS®, www.lblp.com) Program.*

Lindfors, J.W. (1985). Understanding the development of language structure. In A. Jaggar & M.T. Smith-Burke (Eds.), *Observing the language learner* (pp. 41–56). Newark, DE: International Reading Association.

Lipson, M. (2002). *Creating school success one school at a time: Taking responsibility for our own destiny.* Keynote presentation at the 33rd annual conference of the Massachusetts Reading Association (MRA), Sturbridge, MA.

Lipson, M.Y., & Wixson, K.K. (2003). *Assessment and instruction of reading and writing disability: An interactive approach.* New York: Longman.

Lipson, M.Y., Mosenthal, J.H., Mekkelsen, J., & Russ, B. (2004). Building knowledge and fashioning school success one school at a time. *The Reading Teacher, 57,* 6, 534–542.

Little, S.S. (1993). Nonverbal learning disabilities and socioemotional functioning: A review of recent literature. *Journal of Learning Disabilities, 26,* 653–665.

Livingstone, M. (1993). Parallel processing in the visual system and the brain: Is one system selectively affected in dyslexia? In A.M. Galaburda (Ed.), *Dyslexia and development* (pp. 237–256), Cambridge, MA: Harvard University Press.

Livingston, M.S., & Hubel, D.H. (1988). Do the relative mapping densities of the magno- and parvocellular systems vary with eccentricity? *Journal of Neuroscience, 8,* 4334–4339.

Lopez, R., Yolton, R.L., Kohl, P., Smith, D.L., & Saxerud, M.H. (1994). Comparison of the Irlen Scotopic Sensitivity Syndrome test results to academic and visual performance data. *Journal of the American Optometrics Association, 65,* 705–714.

Louis, B., & Lewis, M. (1992). Parental beliefs about giftedness in young children and their relation to actual ability level. *Gifted Children Quarterly, 36,* 27–31.

Lovegrove, W., Martin, F., & Slaghuis, W. (1986). A theoretical and dyslexic case for a visual deficit in specific reading disability. *Cognitive Neuropsychology, 3,* 225–267.

Lubs, H.A., Duara, R., Levin, B., Jallad, B., Lubs, M., Rabin, M., Kushch, A., & Gross-Glenn, K. (1991). Dyslexia subtypes—genetics, behavior and brain imaging. In D.D. Duane & D.B. Gray, *The reading brain* (pp. 89–117). Parkton, MD: York.

Lucangeli, D., & Passolunghi, M.C. (1995). Psicologia dell'apprendimento matematico [Psychology of mathematical learning]. Torino, Italy: Utet.

Luna, C., Solsken, J., & Kutz, E. (2000). Defining literacy: Lessons from high-stakes teacher testing. *Journal of Teacher Education, 51* (4), 276–288.

Lundberg, I. (2002). Second language learning and reading with the additional load of dyslexia. *Annals of Dyslexia, 52,* 165–187.

Luque, D., Romero, J., Rodríguez, J.K., & Lavigne, R. (2002). Dificultades en el aprendizaje de las matemáticas: Características en educación primaria [Learning disabilities in math: Characteristics in primary education]. In M.I. Fajardo, M.I. Ruiz, A. Díaz, F. Vicente, & J.E. Julve (Eds.), *Necesidades educativas especiales: Familia y educacíon* [Special education needs: Family and education] (pp. 197–208). Badajoz, Spain: PSICOEX.

Lyon, G.R. (1985). Identification and remediation of learning disability subtypes: Preliminary findings. *Learning Disability Focus, 1,* 21–35.

Lyon, G.R. (1988). Subtype remediation. In K.A. Kavale, S.R. Forness, & M. Bender (Eds.), *Handbook of learning disabilities* (pp. 33–58). Boston: Little, Brown & Co.

Lyons, C.A., & Pinnell, G.S. (2001). *Systems for change in literacy education: A guide to professional development.* Portsmouth, NH: Heinemann.

Lyons, C.A., Pinnell, G.S., McCarrier, A., Young, P., & DeFord, D. (1988). *The Ohio reading recovery project: Volume X and State of Ohio Year 1, 1986–1987.* Volume VIII (Technical Report). Columbus: The Ohio State University.

Madden, N.A., Slavin, R.E., Karweit, N.L., Dolan, L.J., & Wasik, B.A. (1991). Success for all: Ending reading failure from the beginning. *Language Arts, 68,* 47–52.

Maggart, Z.R., & Zintz, M.V. (1990). *Corrective reading.* Dubuque, IA: William C. Brown.

Magno, J. (June 2004). Improving outcomes for students with disabilities: A work in progress. *Mainstream: A publication for the Massachusetts Federation Council for Exceptional Children,* p. 2.

Malara, N.A., Menghini, M., & Reggiani, M. (1996). *Italian research in mathematics Education: 1988–1995.* Rome: Litoflash.

Malmquist, E. (1958). *Factors related to learning disabilities in the first grades of the elementary school.* Stockholm, Sweden: Almquist & Wiksell.

Mandler, J.M. (1984). *Stories, scripts, and scenes: Aspects of schema theory.* Hillsdale, NJ: Lawrence Erlbaum.

Manganelo, R.E., (1994). Time management instruction for older students with learning disabilities. *Teaching Exceptional Children, Winter,* 60.

Manzo, A.V. (1985). Expansion modules for the ReQuest, CAT, GRP, and REAP reading/study procedures. *Journal of Reading, 20,* 498–502.

Manzo, A.V., & Manzo, U.C. (1993). *Literacy disorders: Holistic diagnosis and remediation.* New York: Harcourt Brace Jovanovich.

Marlowe, M., Cossairt, A., Welch, K., & Errera, J. (1984). Hair mineral content as a predictor of learning disabilities. *Journal of Learning Disabilities, 17,* 418–421.

Marr, T. (2004). Welcome . . . A message from 2004 MRA (Massachusetts Reading Association) Conference Chair. *MRA 35th annual conference book.* Milford, MA: MRA.

Mason, J.M., & Au, K.H. (1990). *Reading instruction for today* (2nd ed.). Glenview, IL: Scott, Foresman.

Mason, J.M., & Au, K.H. (1990). *Reading instruction for today.* Glenview, IL: Scott, Foresman/Little, Brown Higher Ed.

Massachusetts Department of Education English Language Arts Curriculum Frameworks. (2001, June). Malden, MA: Author.

Massachusetts Department of Education Supplement to the Massachusetts English Language Arts Curriculum Frameworks (2004): Grades 3,5 and 7 for vocabulary, reading, and literature. Malden, MA: Author.

Mastropieri, M.A., Scruggs, T.E., & Levin, J.R. (1985). Memory strategy instruction with learning disabled adolescents. *Journal of Learning Disabilities, 18,* 94–100.

Matejcek, Z. (2002, Winter). Learning disabilities around the world. *Thalamus Updates: A Newsletter of the International Academy for Research in Learning Disabilities. Vol. 4 (1).* http://www.iarld.net/newsletters/winter02.htm#czechrepublic (downloaded 4/3/04).

Matlin, M. W. (1992). *Psychology.* Fort Worth, TX: Harcourt Brace Jovanovich.

Matlock, S.A. (1999). *Metamorphosis: Reflections of a first year teacher.* Self-published.

Matthews, M. (2003). Reading instruction: *Flexible grouping for maximum achievement.* Paper presentation at the 32nd annual conference of the Massachusetts Reading Association, Sturbridge, MA.

Maugh, T.H. (1978). Hair: A diagnostic tool to complement blood serum and urine. *Science, 202,* 1271–1273.

McCormick, S. (1995). *Instructing students who have literacy problems.* Englewood Cliffs, NJ: Merrill (Prentice Hall).

McEntire, E. (1981). Learning disabilities and mathematics. *Topics in Learning and Learning Disabilities, 1,* 1–18.

McFeely, D. (2002). *Snapshots of a radical teacher.* Featured IRA Session at the 33rd annual conference of the Massachusetts Reading Association (MRA), Sturbridge, MA.

McKay, R. (2004, August). *Schema: Homes in the mind: Setting the stage for the literacy block.* Workshop presentation. Springfield, MA.

McKenna, M. (2004). Teaching vocabulary to struggling older readers. *Perspectives: The International Dyslexia Association, 30* (1), 13–16.

McKenna, M.C., & Robinson, R.D. (1993). *Teaching through text: A content literacy approach to content area reading.* New York: Longman.

McKeown, M.G., Beck, I.L., Omanson, R.C., & Pople, M.T. (1985). Some effects on the nature and frequency of vocabulary instruction on the knowledge and use of words. *Reading Research Quarterly, 20,* 522–533.

McREL (Mid-continent Research for Education and Learning). (2003). *K–8 national standards for language arts.* http: www.mcrel.com.

Mehegan, C.C., & Dreifus, R.E. (1972). Hyperlexia—Exceptional reading ability in brain damaged children. *Neurology, 22,* 1105–1111.

Melikian, B.A. (1990). Family characteristics of children with dyslexia. *Journal of Learning Disabilities, 23,* 386–391.

Meltzer, L., Roditi, B., Houser, R.F., & Perlman, M. (1998). Perceptions of academic strategies and competence in students with learning disabilities. *Journal of Learning Disabilities, 31* (5), 437–451.

Mendes, M. (2004). *Keyword cards to accompany open response writing.* Unpublished guide, Springfield, MA.

Mercer, C.D. (1987, 1991). *Students with learning disabilities.* Columbus, OH: Merrill.

Miller, D. (2002). *Reading with meaning: Teaching comprehension in the primary grades.* Portland, ME: Stenhouse.

Milton, M. (2000). How do schools provide for children with learning difficulties in numeracy? *Australian Journal of Learning Disabilities, 5* (2), 23–27.

Ministry of Education. (2001). *To encourage zest for living: Special education in Japan.* Tokyo: Ministry of Education.

Ministry of Education: Education for All Japan's Action From UNESCO, EFA Global Monitoring Report on Education for All (2002). http://www.mofa.go.jp/policy/oda/category/education/action/02.html (downloaded 3/10/04).

Miranda, A., Arlandis, P., & Soriano, M. (1997). Instrucción en estrategias y entrenamiento atribucional: Efectos sobre la resolución de probelmas y el auto-concepto de los estudiantes con dificultades de aprendizaje [Instruction in strategies and attribute training: Effects on problem solving and the self-concept of students with learning disabilities]. *Infancia y Aprendizaje, 80,* 37–52.

Monroe, M. (1932). *Children who cannot read.* Chicago: University of Chicago Press.

Montague, M., Woodward, J., & Bryant, D.P. (2004). International perspectives on mathematics and learning disabilities. *Journal of Learning Disabilities, 37* (1), 2–3.

Moore, D.W., More, S.A., Cunningham, P.M., & Cunningham, J.W. (1994). *Developing readers & writers in the content areas K–12.* New York: Longman.

Moreau, M.E.R. (2004). *The story grammar marker.* Workshop Presentation: Alfred Zanetti Montessori School. Springfield, MA.

Moreau, MR., & Fidrych-Puzzo, H. (1994). *How to use the Story Grammar Marker.* Easthampton, MA: Discourse Skills Production.

Morgan, E., & Klein, C. (2003). With consultant in dyslexia: Professor Margaret Snowling, University of York. *The dyslexic adult in a non-dyslexic world.* London, England: Whurr Publishers.

Morgan, G. M. (2003, October 21). *Sheltered English in Springfield Public Schools: Prepared for Frank H. Freedman Elementary.* Workshop presentation, Springfield, MA.

Morgan, W.P. (1896). A case of congenital word-blindness. *British Medical Journal, 2,* 1378–1379.

Morris, C.G. (1993). *Psychology: An introduction* (8th ed.). Englewood Cliffs, NJ: Prentice Hall.

Morrison, J. (2000). *Coping with ADD/ADHD.* New York: The Rosen Publishing Group.

Morrow, L.M. (1988). Retelling stories as a diagnostic tool. In S.M. Glazer, L.W. Searfoss, & L.M. Gentile (Eds.), *Reexamining reading diagnosis: New trends and procedures* (pp. 128–149). Newark, DE: International Reading Association.

Morrow, L.M. (2003). *Organizing and managing the language arts block.* New York: Guilford Press.

Morrow, L.M., Barnhart, S., & Rooyakkers, D. (2002). Integrating technology with the teaching of an early literacy course. *The Reading Teacher, 56* (3), 218–230.

Morsink, C.V. (1984). *Teaching special needs students in regular classrooms.* Boston: Little, Brown & Co.

Mortimore, T. (2003). *With consultant in dyslexia: Professor Margaret Snowling, University of York.* Dyslexia and learning style: A practitioner's handbook. London, England: Whurr Publishers.

Mosenthal, J., Lipson, M., Sortino, S., Russ, B., & Mekkelsen, J. (2002). Literacy in rural Vermont: Lessons from schools where children succeed. In B. Taylor & P.D. Pearson (Eds.), *Teaching reading: Effective schools and accomplished teachers* (pp. 115–140). Mahwah, NJ: Lawrence Erlbaum.

Munroe, J. (1977). Language abilities and math performance. *Australian Journal of Remedial Education, 9* (3), 24–31.

Murdick, N.L., Gartin, B.C., & Rao, S.M. (2004, March/April). Teaching children with hyperlexia. *Teaching Exceptional Children, 36* (4), 56–59.

Muter, V. (2003). With consultant in dyslexia: Professor Margaret Snowling, University of York. *Early reading development and dyslexia.* London, England: Whurr Publishers.

Myers, G.C. (1924). Persistence of errors in arithmetic. *Journal of Educational Research, 10,* 19–28.

Myklebust, H.R. (1975). Nonverbal learning disabilities: Assessment and intervention. *Progress in Learning Disabilities, 3,* 85–121.

Nagy, W., & Anderson, R.C. (1984). How many words are there in printed school English? *Reading Research Quarterly, 19,* 304–330.

Nagy, W., Anderson, R., & Herman, R. (1987). Learning word meanings from context during normal reading. *American Educational Research Journal, 24,* 237–270.

National Center for Education Statistics. (2000, February 15). *Internet access in U.S. public schools and classrooms: 1994–1999.* Washington, DC: U.S. Government Printing Office.

National Council of Teachers of Mathematics (NCTM). (2000). *Principles and standards for school mathematics.* Reston, VA: Author.

National Institute of Child Health and Human Development (NICHD). (2000). Report of the National Reading Panel. Teaching children to read: An evidence-based assessment of the scientific research literature on reading and its implications for reading instruction (NIH Publication No. 004769). Washington, DC: U.S. Government Printing Office. http://www.nationalreadingpanel.org

National Joint Committee on Learning Disabilities. (1988). A position paper of the National Trust Committee on Learning Disabilities (Letter to NJCLD member organizations). *Journal of Learning Disabilities, 1,* 53–55.

National Joint Committee on Learning Disabilities (NJCLD). (1993). *Issues in the delivery of services to individuals with learning disabilities—A position paper of the National Joint Committee on Learning Disabilities,* February 21, 1982. In LDA (*Learning Disabilities Association*) *Items of Interest on Learning Disabilities, 28,* No. 2, 3.

National Reading Panel Report. (2000). *Teaching children to read: An evidence-based assessment of the scientific research literature on reading and its implications for reading instruction. Reports of the subgroups.* (National Institute of Health Pub. No. 00–4754). Washington, DC: National Institute of Child Health and Human Development.

Nebedum-Ezeh, G., & Spafford, C.A. (2001, March 29). *Key general components to good reading programs for all students.* Presentation at the 32nd annual conference of the Massachusetts Reading Association, Sturbridge, MA.

Needleman, H.L., Gunnoe, C., Leviton, A., Reed, R., Peresie, H., & Barret, C. (1979). Deficits in psychologic and classroom performance of children with elevated dentine lead levels. *New England Journal of Medicine, 300,* 689–695.

Newman, S.P., Karle, H., Wadsworth, J.F., Archer, R., Hockly, R., & Rogers, P. (1985). Ocular dominance, reading and spelling: A reassessment of a measure associated with specific reading difficulties. *Journal of Research in Reading, 8,* 127–138.

Nieto, S. (1996, 2000). *Affirming diversity: The sociopolitical context of multicultural education.* White Plains, New York: Longman.

Novick, B.Z., & Arnold, M.M. (1988). *Fundamentals of clinical child neuropsychology.* Philadelphia, PA: Grune & Stratton.

Nunes, R.J. (1991). *Utilization of mathematical error patterns in the differential diagnosis of various disabled subtypes.* Unpublished doctoral dissertation, American International College, Springfield, MA.

Obrzut, J.E., (1989). Dyslexia and neurodevelopmental pathology: Is the neurodiagnostic technology ahead of psychoeducational technology? *Journal of Learning Disabilities, 22,* 217–218.

Ogbu, J.U. (1987). Variability in minority school performance: A problem in search of an explanation. *Anthropology and Education Quarterly, 18,* 312–334.

Ogle, D. (1986). The K-W-L: A teaching model that develops active reading of expository text. *The Reading Teacher, 39,* 564–570.

Ojemann, G.A. (1989). Some brain mechanisms for reading. In C. von Euler, I. Lundberg, & G. Lennerstrand (Eds.), *Brain and reading* (pp. 47–59). Hampshire, UK: Macmillan.

Ojemann, G.A. (1991). Cortical organization of language. *Journal of Neuroscience, 11,* 2281–2287.

Okano, K., & Tsuchiya, M. (1999). *Education in contemporary Japan.* New York: Cambridge University Press.

Optiz, M.F. (Ed.). (1998). *Literacy instruction for culturally and linguistically diverse students.* Newark, DE: International Reading Association.

Orton, C. (2004). Dyslexia in England. In I. Smythe, J. Everatt, & R. Salter (Eds.), *The international book of dyslexia: A guide to practice and resources* (pp. 86–91). West Sussex, England: John Wiley & Sons.

Orton, J.L. (1963). Specific language disabilities. *Bulletin of the Orton Society, 13,* 3.

Orton, S.T. (1925). "Word-blindness" in school-children. *Archives of Neurological Psychology, 14,* 581–615.

Orton, S.T. (1928). Specific reading disability—Strephosymbolia. In M. Monroe (ed.), *Genetic psychology monographs* (1095–1099). (Reprinted from the *Journal of the American Medical Association, 90,* 1095–1099).

Orton, S.T. (1937). *Reading, writing and speech problems in children: A presentation of certain types of disorders in the development of language faculty.* New York: Norton.

Ozols, E.J., & Rourke, B.P. (1988). Characteristics of young learning-disabled children classified according to patterns of academic achievement: Auditory-perceptual and visual-perceptual abilities. *Journal of Clinical Child Psychology, 17,* 44–52.

Palinscar, A.S., & Brown, D.A. (1984). Reciprocal teaching of comprehension-fostering and comprehension-monitoring activities. *Cognition and Instruction, 1,* 117–175.

Palinscar, A.S., & Brown, D.A. (1987). Enhancing instructional time through attention to metacognition. *Journal of Learning Disabilities, 20,* 66–75.

Palinscar, A.S., & David, Y.M. (1992). Classroom-based literacy instruction: The development of one program of intervention research. In B.Y.L. Wong (Ed.). *Contemporary intervention research in learning disabilities: An international perspective* (pp. 65–80). New York: Springer-Verlag.

Palladino, P., Poli, P., Masi, G., & Marcheschi, M. (2000). The relation between metacognition and depressive symptoms in preadolescents with learning disabilities: Data in support of Borkowski's model. *Learning Disabilities Research & Practice, 15* (3), 142–148.

Papagno, C., & Vallar, G. (1995). Verbal short-term memory and vocabulary learning in polygots. *Quarterly Journal of Experimental Psychology, 48A,* 98–107.

Paratore, J. (2001). *How well are our children learning to read and write? Sorting out the rhetoric from the reality.* Paper presentation at the 32nd annual conference of the Massachusetts Reading Association, Sturbridge, MA.

Park, H.-S., Gonsier-Gerdin, J., Hoffman, S., Whaley, S., & Yount, M. (1998). Applying the participatory action research model to the social inclusion at worksites. *JASH, 23*(3), 189–202.

Pavlidis, G.T., & Fisher, D.F. (Eds.). (1986). *Dyslexia: Its neuropsychology and treatment.* Chichester, Great Britain: John Wiley & Sons.

Pavlidis, G.T., & Fisher, D.F. (Eds.). (1986). *Dyslexia: Its neuropsychology and treatment.* New York: John Wiley & Sons.

Pearson, P.D. (2000). *Building a literacy curriculum for tomorrow's children: What lessons can we learn from yesterday's successes?* Presentation at the 31st annual conference of the Massachusetts Reading Association, Sturbridge, MA.

Pearson, P.D., & Dole, J.A. (1987). Explicit comprehension instruction: A review of research and a new conceptualization of instruction. *The Elementary School Journal, 88,* 151–165.

Pearson, P.D., & Fielding, L. (1991). Comprehension instruction. In R. Barr, M.L. Kamil, P. Mosenthal, & P.D. Pearson (Eds.), *Handbook of reading research* (Vol. 2, pp. 815–860). New York: Longman.

Pearson, P.D., & Johnson, D.D. (1978). *Teaching reading comprehension.* New York: Holt, Rinehart, & Winston.

Pearson, P.D., & Vacca, R.T. (2003, May 5). *Opening session.* Keynote speakers at the first session of the 48th annual conference of the International Reading Association (IRA), Orlando, FL.

Pennington, B.F., Gilger, J.W., Pauls, D., Smith, S.A., Smith, S.D., & DeFries, J.C. (1991). Evidence for major gene transmission of developmental dyslexia. *Journal of the American Medical Association, 266,* 1527–1534.

Pennsylvania Department of Education. (2002, January). *Academic standards for reading, writing, speaking, and listening.* (Publication 22 Pa. code, ch. 4, appendix B, final form). Peterson, S. (Ed.). (2003). *Untangling some knots in K–8 writing instruction.* Newark, DE: International Reading Association.

Perfetti, C.A. (1985). *Reading ability.* New York: Oxford University Press.

Perino, J., & Ernhart, C. (1974). The relation of subclinical lead levels to cognitive and sensorimotor impairment in black preschoolers. *Journal of Learning Disabilities, 7,* 616–620.

Pesce, A. (1995). *Pesce's papers.* Unpublished manuscript.

Phillips, L.M. (1986). *Using children's literature to foster written language development.* (ERIC Document Reproduction Service No. ED 276 027).

Piaget, J. (1952). *The child's conception of number.* London, England: Routledge & Kegan Paul.

Pianko, S. (1979). A description of the composing processes of college freshmen writers. *Research in the Teaching of English, 13,* 5–22.

Pieronek, F.T. (2001). Inservice project: Upper primary Brunei Darussalan teachers' responses to using four specific reading strategies. *The Reading Teacher, 54,* (5), 522–532.

Pikulski, J.J., & Tobin, A.W. (1989). Factors associated with long-term reading achievement of early readers. In S. McCormick & J. Zutell (Eds.), *Cognitive and social perspectives for literacy research and instruction.* Thirty-eighth yearbook of the National Reading Conference (pp. 123–124). Chicago, IL: National Reading Conference.

Pinnell, G.S. (1985). Helping teachers help children at risk: Insights from the Reading Recovery Program. *Peabody Journal of Education, 62,* 70–85.

Pinnell, G.S., Lyons, C.A., Deford, D.E., Bryk, A.S., & Seltzer, M. (1994). Comparing instructional models for the literacy education of high-risk first graders. *Reading Research Quarterly, 29,* 9–39.

Pirozzolo, F.J. (1979). *The neuropsychology of developmental reading disorders.* New York: Praeger Press.

Polacco, P. (2001, January/February). A chance to soar. *Instructor, 110* (5), 31.

Powers, H.W.S. Jr. (1975). Caffeine, behavior and the LD child. *Academic Therapy, 11,* 5–11.

Pressley, M., Allington, R., Wharton-McDonald, R., Block, C.C., & Morrow, L.M., (2001). *Learning to read: Lessons from exemplary first-grade classrooms.* New York: Guilford.

Pressley, M., Johnson, C.J., Symons, S., McGoldrick, J.A., & Kurita, J.A. (1989). Strategies that improve children's memory and comprehension. *The Elementary School Journal, 90,* 3–32.

Pressley, M., & Levin, J.R. (1987). Elaborative learning strategies for the inefficient learner. In S.J. Ceci (Ed.), *Handbook of cognitive, social and neurological aspects of learning disabilities.* Hillsdale, NJ: Lawrence Erlbaum.

Pressley, M., Levin, J.R., & Miller, G.E. (1981). How does the keyword method affect vocabulary comprehension and usage. *Reading Research Quarterly, 16,* 213–225.

Price, L., Gerber, P.J., & Mulligan, R. (2003, November/December). The Americans with Disabilities Act and adults with learning disabilities as employees. *Remedial and Special Education, 24* (6), 350–358.

Prigohzy, S. (2004, February 22–24). *Yesterday, today, tomorrow.* Presentation at the Cornerstone Northern Regional Annual Conference, Bridgeport, Ct.

Pruitt, P. (1997). Study skills strategy instruction. In M. Buchanan, C. Weller, & C. Buchanan (Eds.), *My special education desk reference.* San Diego, CA: Singular Publishing Group.

Public Law 107-110. (2001, January 3). No Child Left Behind Act of 2001. U.S. Congress.

Rafael, T. (1982). Question-asking strategies for children. *The Reading Teacher, 39,* 186–190.

Rafael, T.E. (1986). Teaching questions-answers relationships, revisited. *The Reading Teacher, 39,* 516–522.

Raison, G. (Education Department of Western Australia, EDWA) and in collaboration with J. Rivalland, Edith Cowen University. (1994). *First Steps Writing Developmental Curriculum.* Melbourne, Australia: Longman Cheshire.

Rasinski, T. (2003a, November/December). Fluency. *Instructor,* 16–20.

Rasinski, T. (2003b). *The fluent reader.* New York: Scholastic.

Raymond, E., & Sorensen, R.E. (1998). Visual motor perception in children with dyslexia: Proficient detection but abproficient integration. *Visual Cognition, 5* (3), 389–404.

Reading First. (2002, April). Washington, DC: U.S. Department of Education, Office of Elementary and Secondary Education and (2) Public Law 107-110. (2001, January 3). No Child Left Behind Act of 2001. U.S. Congress.

Rees, D., in collaboration with B. Shortland-Jones. (1994). *Reading Developmental Continuum: First Steps.* Melbourne, Australia: Longman Cheshire.

Reid, R., Maag, J., Vasa, S., & Wright, G. (1994). Who are the children with ADHD: A school-based survey. *The Journal of Special Education, 28,* 117–137.

Reif, L. (1991). *Seeking diversity: Language arts with adolescents.* Portsmouth, NH: Heinemann.

Resnick, L.B., & Hall, M.W. (1998, Fall). Learning organizations for sustainable education reform. *Daedalus, Journal of the American Academy of Arts and Sciences, 127* (4), 89–118.

Reutzel, R.D., (1985). Story maps improve comprehension. *The Reading Teacher, 38,* 400–405.

Richardson, J.S., & Morgan, R.F. (1994). *Reading to learn in the content areas.* Belmont, CA: Wadsworth.

Richgels, D.J. (2003). The professional library: Exemplary literacy teaching. *The Reading Teacher, 56,* 8, 796–800.

Riddell, P.M., Fowler, M.S., & Stein, J.F. (1990). Spatial discrimination in children with poor vergence control. *Perceptual and Motor Skills, 70,* 707–718.

Ridder, W.H. III, Borsting, E., Cooper, M., McNeal, B., & Huang, E. (1997). Not all dyslexics are created equal. *Optometry and Vision Science, 74,* 99–104.

Ripple, R.E., & Rockcastler, V.N. (1964). *Piaget rediscovered.* Ithaca, NY: Cornell University Press.

Rittner, M. (1982). Error analysis in mathematics education. *Special Education in Canada, 56,* 4–8.

Rizzo, C. (1999). Advice to educators from past MRA presidents. *MRA Primer, 28* (1), 19.

Roberts, M. (2004, March). *The Cornerstone National Literacy Initiative.* Personal communication.

Roberts, M., Kennedy, J., Powe, T., Roberson, C., & Sutton-Obas, S. (2003/2004). *Teaching children "deep structure" thinking skills: Implementing the Cornerstone Framework.* On-site professional development. Springfield, MA.

Robinson, H.M. (1946). *Why pupils fail in reading.* Chicago, IL: University of Chicago Press.

Roller, C. (2001). (Ed.). *Learning to teach reading: Setting the research agenda.* Newark, DE: International Reading Association.

Rosenbusch, M.H. (1997). *Bringing the standards into the classroom: A teacher's guide.* Ames: Iowa State University.

Rosenshine, B., & Meister, C. (1994). Reciprocal teaching: A review of the research. *Review of Educational Research, 64* (4), 479–530.

Ross, A.O. (1976). *Psychological aspects of learning disabilities and reading disorders.* New York: McGraw-Hill.

Ross, D.D., Bondy, E., & Kyle, D.W. (1993). *Reflective teaching for student empowerment.* New York: Macmillan.

Ross, P. (1993). *National excellence: The case for developing America's talent.* Washington, DC: U.S. Department of Education.

Rostain, A.L., Power, T.J., & Atkins, M.S. (1993). Assessing parents' willingness to pursue treatment for children with attention deficit hyperactivity disorder. *Journal of the American Academy of Child and Adolescent Psychiatry, 32,* 175–181.

Rourke, B.P. (1985). Overview of learning disability subtypes. In B.P. Rourke (Ed.), *Neuropsychology of learning disabilities* (pp. 3–14). New York: Guilford.

Rourke, B.P. (1998). Significance of verbal-performance discrepancies for subtypes of children with learning disabilities: Opportunities for the WISC-III. In A. Pritiera & D. Saklofske (Eds.), *WISC-III, clinical use and interpretation* (pp. 139–156). San Diego: Academic Press.

Rourke, B.P., & Strang, J.D. (1983). Subtypes of reading and arithmetical disabilities: A neuropsychological analysis. In M. Rutter (Ed.), *Developmental neuropsychiatry* (pp. 473–488). New York: Guilford Press.

Routman, R. (1996). *Literacy at the crossroads.* Portsmouth, NH: Heinemann.

Rubin, D. (1991a). *Diagnosis and correction of reading difficulty.* Boston: Allyn and Bacon.

Rubin, D. (1991b). *Diagnosis and correction of reading instruction.* Boston: Allyn and Bacon.

Ruddell, M.R. (1993). *Teaching content reading and writing.* Boston: Allyn and Bacon.

Ruddell, R.B., & Ruddell, M.R. (1995). *Teaching children to read and write: Becoming an influential teacher.* Boston: Allyn and Bacon.

Rueda, R., Monzo, L.D., & Higareda, I. (2004). Appropriating the sociocultural resources for Latino paraeducators for effective instruction with Latino students: Promise and problems. *Urban Education, 39* (1), 52–90.

Ruijssenaars, A.J.J.W. (2001). *Leerproblemen en leerstoornissen. Remedial teaching en behandeling. Hulpschema's voor opleiding en praktijk. [Learning problems and learn-ing disabilities. Remedial teaching and treatment. Schemas for teachers and practitioners.* Rotterdam: Lemniscaat.

Rumelhart, D.E. (1977). Toward an interactive model of reading. In S. Dornic (Ed.), *Attention and performance* (pp. 573–603). Hillsdale, NJ: Lawrence Erlbaum.

Rumelhart, D.E. (1981). Schemata: The building blocks of cognition. In J. T. Guthrie (Ed.), *Comprehension and teaching: Research reviews.* Newark, DE: International Reading Association.

Rupley, W.H., & Blair, T.R. (1989). *Reading diagnosis and remediation.* Columbus, OH: Merrill.

Russell, C.L. (2004, March/April). Understanding nonver-bal learning disorders in children with spina bifida. *Teaching Exceptional Children, 36* (4), 8–13.

Rutter, M., Avshalom, C., Fergusson, D., Goodman, R., Maughan, B., Moffitt, T., Meltzer, H., Carroll, J., & Horwood, J. (April 28, 2004). Current research on gender. *Journal of the American Medical Association.* http://jama.ama/assn.org (downloaded May 1, 2004).

Ryder, R.J., & Graves, M.F. (1994). *Reading and learning in content areas.* New York: Merrill.

Samuels, S.J. (1973, April). Effect of distinctive feature training on paired associate learning. *Journal of Edu-cational Psychology, 64,* 147–148.

Samuels, S.J. (1979). The method of repeated reading. *The Reading Teacher, 32,* 403–408.

Samuels, S.J. (2002). Reading fluency: Its development and assessment. In A.E. Farstrup & S.J. Samuels (Eds.), *Reading researchers in search of common ground* (pp. 166–183). Newark, DE: International Reading Associ-ation.

Samuels, S.J. (2003). *Development and measurement of read-ing fluency.* Keynote presentation at the 34th annual conference of the Massachusetts Reading Associa-tion, Sturbridge, MA.

Samuels, S.J., & Miller, N.L. (1985). Failure to find atten-tion differences between learning disabled and nor-mal children on classroom and laboratory tests. *Exceptional Children, 51,* 358–375.

Sanders, M. (2001). *Understanding dyslexia and the reading process: A Guide for Educators and Parents.* Boston: Allyn and Bacon.

Saphier, J., Bigda-Peyton, T., & Pierson, G. (2004). *How to make decisions that stay made* (5th ed.). Acton, MA: Research for Better Teaching, Inc.

Saskatchewan, Canada, Government Education Website (February 2000 posting). Early literacy: A resource for teachers. http://www.sasked.gov.sk.ca/evergreen/ela/e_literacy/index.html.

Sato, N. (1993). Teaching and learning in Japanese ele-mentary schools: A context for understanding. *Peabody Journal of Education, 68* (4), 111–147.

Sayler, M., & Brookshire, W. (1993). Social, emotional, and behavioral adjustment of accelerated students, stu-dents in gifted classes, and regular students in eighth grade. *Gifted Child Quarterly, 37,* 150–154.

Scarborough, H.S. (1990). Very early language deficits in dyslexic children. *Child Development, 61,* 1728–1743.

Scanlon, D., & Mellard, D.F. (2002). Academic and partici-pation profiles of school-age dropouts with and with-out disabilities. *Exceptional Children, 68* (2), 239–258.

Schank, R.C. (1979). Interestingness: Controlling infer-ences. *Artificial Intelligence, 12,* 273–297.

Schatschneider, C., Francis, D., Foorman, B., Fletcher, J., & Mehta, P. (1999). The dimensionality of phonological awareness: An application of item response theory. *Journal of Educational Psychology, 91,* 439–449.

Schiff, R., & Ravid, D. (2004). Representing written vowels in university students with dyslexia compared with normal Hebrew readers. *Annals of Dyslexia, 54,* 1, 39–64.

Schmidt, H.P., Kuryliw, A.J., Saklofske, D.H., & Yackulic, R.A. (1989). Stability of WISC-R scores for a sample of learning disabled children. *Psychological Reports, 64,* 195–201.

Schmidt, M.C., & O'Brien, D.G. (1986). Story grammars: Some cautions about the translation of research into practice. *Reading Research and Instruction, 26,* 1–8.

Schreiber, P.A. (1987). Prosody and structure in children's syntactic processing. In R. Horowitz & S.J. Samuels (Eds.), *Comprehending oral and written language* (pp. 243–270). New York: Academic Press.

Schulte-Korne, G., Deimel, W., Bartling, J., & Remschmidt, H. (1998). Auditory processing and dyslexia: Evi-dence for a specific speech processing deficit. *Neu-roReport, 9,* 337–340.

Schumaker, J.B., & Deshler, D.D. (1992). Validation of learning strategy interventions for students with learning disabilities: Results of a programmatic research effort. In B.Y.L. Wong (Ed.), *Contemporary intervention research in learning disabilities: An interna-tional perspective* (pp. 22–46). New York: Springer Verlag.

Schumaker, J.B., Deshler, D.D., Alley, G.R., Warner, M.M., & Denton, P.H. (1982). Multipass: A learning strategy for improving reading comprehension. *Learning Dis-ability Quarterly, 5,* 295–304.

Schunk, D.H. (1987). Self-efficacy and motivated learning. In N. Hastings & J. Schwieso (Eds.), *New directions in educational psychology: Vol. 2, Behavior and motivation in the classroom.* (pp. 233–252). Lewes, Sussex, UK: Falmer Press.

Schwartz, E., & Sheff, A. (1975). Student involvement in questioning for comprehension. *The Reading Teacher, 29,* 150–154.

Science News (1991). *140,* 189.

Scruggs, T.E., Mastropieri, M.A., Bakken, J.P., & Brigham, F.J. (1993). Reading versus doing: The relative effects of textbook-based and inquiry-oriented approaches to science learning in special education classrooms. *Journal of Special Education, 27,* 1–15.

Searfoss, L.W. (1975). Radio reading. *The Reading Teacher, 29* 295–296.

Searfoss, L.W., & Readence, J.W. (1994). *Helping children learn to read.* Boston: Allyn and Bacon.

Seitz, A. (2004, March 17). Institute for Learning: Univer-sity of Pittsburgh. *Facilitation skills for embedded profes-sional development.* Co-designed with Dr. Linda Abbott, Diann Cohen, Kate Fenton and Tom Paleolo-gopoulos. Workshop presentation: Springfield Schools, Springfield, MA.

Shalev, R.S., Manor, O., Kerem, B., Ayali, M., Badichi, N., Friedlander, Y., et al. (2001). Developmental dyscalculia is a familial learning disability. *Journal of Learning Disability, 34,* 59–65.

Shanahan, T. (2002). What research says: The promises and limitations of applying research to reading education. In A.E. Farstrup & S.J. Samuels (Eds.), *What research has to say about reading instruction* (pp. 8–24). Newark, DE: International Reading Association.

Shankweiler, D., & Liberman, I.Y. (1972). Misreading: A search for causes. In J.F. Kavanaugh & I.G. Mattingly (Eds.), *Language by eye and by ear* (pp. 293–317). Cambridge, MA: MIT Press.

Shapiro, J. (1982). *Metamemory and learning disabled children.* Unpublished doctoral dissertation, Columbia University.

Sharma, M.C. (1986). Dyscalculia and other learning problems in arithmetic: A historical perspective. *Focus on Learning Problems in Mathematics, 8,* 7–45.

Shaywitz, B.A., Shaywitz, S.E., Liberman, I.Y., Fletcher, J.M., Shankweiler, D.P., Duncan, J.s., Katz, L., Liberman, A.M., Francis, J.J., Dreyer, L.G., Crain, S., Brady, S., Fowler, A., Kier, L.E., Rosenfield, N.S., Gore, J.C., & Makuch, R.W. (1991). Neurolinguistic and biologic mechanisms in dyslexia. In D.D. Duane & D.B. Gray (Eds.), *The reading brain* (pp. 27–52). Parkton, MD: York Press.

Shaywitz, S. (2003). *Overcoming dyslexia.* New York: Knopf.

Shaywitz, S.E., Shaywitz, B.A., Fletcher, J.M., & Escobar, M.D. (1990). Prevalence of reading disability in boys and girls. *Journal of the American Medical Association, 264,* 998–1002.

Sheets, R.H., & Gay, G. (1996). Student perceptions of disciplinary conflict in ethnically diverse classrooms. *NASSP Bulletin, 80* (580), 84–94.

Shepard, R. (2002). *Where in the world is Cinderella?* Presentation at the 33rd annual conference of the Massachusetts Reading Association, Sturbridge, MA.

Sieben, R.L. (1977). Controversial medical treatments of learning disabilities. *Academic Therapy, 13,* 133–147.

Silberberg, N.E., & Silberberg, M.C. (1967). Hyperlexia—Specific word recognition skills in young children. *Exceptional Children, 34,* 41–42.

Silberberg, N.E., & Silberberg, M.C. (1971). Hyperlexia: The other end of the continuum. *The Journal of Special Education, 5,* 233–242.

Silver, L.B. (1987). The "magic cure." A review of the current controversial approaches for treating learning disabilities. *Journal of Learning Disabilities, 20,* 498–504.

Silverman, R., Zigmond, N., & Sansone, J. (1981). Teaching coping skills to adolescents with learning problems. *Focus on Exceptional Children, 13* (6), 1–20.

Simpson, M.L., Hayes, C.G., Stahl, N., Connor, R.T., & Weaver, D. (1988). An initial validation of a study strategy system. *Journal of Reading Behavior, 20,* 149–180.

Singleton, J. (1989). Gambaru: A Japanese cultural theory of learning. In J. Shields (Ed.), *Japanese schooling: Patterns of socialization, equality, and political control* (pp. 8–16), University Park: Pennsylvania State University Press.

Slavin, R.E., (1992). *Student team learning: A practical guide to cooperative learning.* Washington, DC: National Education Association.

Slingerland, B.H. (1976). *A multi-sensory approach to language arts for specific language disability children: A guide for primary teachers.* Cambridge, MA: Educators Publishing Service.

Sloan, A., & Vardell, S.M., (2004). Cinderella and her sisters: Variants and versions. In T.A. Young (Ed.), *Happily ever after* (pp. 248–262). Newark, DE: International Reading Association.

Smith, F., & Goodman, K.S. (1971). On the psycholinguistic method of teaching reading. *Elementary School Journal, 71,* 177–181.

Smith, M., & Qi, D.S. (2003). A complex tangle: Teaching writing to English language learners in the mainstream classroom. In S. Peterson (Ed.), *Untangling some knots in K–8 writing instruction* (pp. 52–65). Newark, DE: International Reading Association.

Smythe, I., Everatt, J., & Salter, R. (Eds.). (2004). *The international book of dyslexia: A guide to practice and resources.* West Sussex, England: John Wiley & Sons.

Snow, C.E., Burns, M.S., & Griffin, P. (1998). *Preventing reading difficulties in young children.* Washington, DC: National Academy Press.

Solan, H.A. (1990). An appraisal of the Irlen technique of correcting reading disorders using tinted overlays and tinted lenses. *Journal of Learning Disabilities, 23,* 621–626.

Solman, R.T., Dain, S.J., & Keech, S.L. (1991). Color-mediated contrast sensitivity in disabled readers. *Optometry and Vision Science, 68,* 331–337.

Spache, G.D. (1976). *Diagnosing and correcting reading disabilities.* Boston: Allyn and Bacon.

Spafford, C. (2002/2003). A letter from Carol Spafford, 2002–2003 MRA (Massachusetts Reading Association) President. MRA Primer: The Challenge of Teaching Comprehension, 31 (2), 3.

Spafford, C. (2003). A message from the MRA (Massachusetts Reading Association). President. *MRA 34th annual conference book.* Milford, MA: MRA.

Spafford, C., Pesce, A.J.I., & Grosser, G.S. (1998). *The cyclopedic education dictionary.* Boston: Delmar Publishing.

Spafford, C.A. (1999, March 25). *Literacy strategies for students with reading disabilities.* Featured speaker at the 30th annual conference of the Massachusetts Reading Association, Sturbridge, MA.

Spafford, C.A. (2001). *Multiple literacy strategies for students with reading disabilities.* Paper presentation at the 32nd annual conference of the Massachusetts Reading Association, Sturbridge, MA.

Spafford, C.A. (2004a). *Developing resiliency in individuals with reading disabilities: The third "R"—reading, 'riting, resiliency.* Paper presentation at the 35th annual conference of the Massachusetts Reading Association, Sturbridge, MA.

Spafford, C.A. (2004b). *Student attitudes toward testing.* Unpublished paper.

Spafford, C.A., & Grosser, G.S. (1995). *Dyslexia: Research and resource guide.* Boston: Allyn and Bacon.

Spafford, C.A., & Grosser, G.S. (2004). *The relationship of resiliency to reading disabilities (dyslexia).* Manuscript prepared for submission.

Spafford, C.A., & Grosser, G.S. (2005). *Dyslexia and reading disabilities: Research and resource guide for working with all struggling readers.* Boston: Allyn and Bacon.

Spafford, C.S. (1989). Wechsler digit span subtest: Diagnostic usefulness with dyslexic children. *Perceptual and Motor Skills, 69,* 115–125.

Spafford, C.S. (1995). *Concurrent and predictive validity study of the TOMA in examining math grades of students at-risk for learning disabilities.* Unpublished paper.

Spafford, C.S., & Grosser, G.S. (1991). Retinal differences in light sensitivity between dyslexic and proficient reading children: New prospects for optometric input in diagnosing dyslexia. *Journal of the American Optometric Association, 62,* 610–615.

Spafford, C.S., & Grosser, G.S. (1993). The "social misperception syndrome" in children with learning disabilities: Social causes versus neurological variables. *Journal of Learning Disabilities, 26,* 178–189, 198.

Spafford, C.S., Grosser, G.S., Donatelle, J.R., Squillace, S.R., & Dana, J.P. (1995). The use of chromatic lenses during visual search and contrast sensitivity among proficient and disabled readers. *Journal of Learning Disabilities, 28,* 240–252.

Sparks, R.L. (1995). Phonemic awareness in hyperlexic children. *Reading and Writing: An Interdisciplinary Journal, 7,* 217–235.

Spaulding, R.B., with Spalding, W.T. (1957, 1962, 1969, 1986, 1990). *The writing road to reading.* Author.

Spiers, P.A. (1987). Acalculia revisited: Current issues. In G. Deloche & X. Seron (Eds.), *Mathematical disabilities: A cognitive neuropsychological perspective* (pp. 1–25). Hillsdale, NJ: Lawrence Erlbaum.

Spillane, J.P., Halverson, R., & Diamond, J.B. (2001, April). Investigating school leadership practice: A distributed perspective. *Educational Researcher, 30* (3), 23–28.

Spinelli, D. (1999). *Open response questions: Response structures/formats.* Workshop Presentation, Springfield Schools, Springfield, MA.

Spradlin, J. (1967). Procedures for evaluating processes associated with receptive and expressive language. In R. Schiefelbusch, R. Copeland, & J. Smith (Eds.), *Language and mental retardation* (pp. 118–136). New York: Holt, Rinehart, & Winston.

Spring, C., & Sandoval, J. (1976). Food additives and hyperkinesis: A critical evaluation of the evidence. *Journal of Learning Disabilities, 9,* 560–569.

Springfield, Massachusetts English Language Arts scope and sequence for kindergarten to grade 5 (2001). Springfield, MA: The Public Schools of Springfield, Massachusetts.

The Springfield Teacher. (2003, November). Tips for teachers. Vol XXV (3). Springfield, MA: Author.

Stahl, S., & Fairbanks, M. (1986). The effects of vocabulary instruction: A model-based meta-analysis. *Review of Educational Research, 56,* 72–110.

Stahl, S.H. (2004, Winter). Scaly? Audacious? Debris? Salubrious? Vocabulary learning and the child with learning disabilities. *Perspectives: The International Dyslexia Association (IDA), 30* (1), 4–12.

Stanford, L., & Hynd, G. (1994). Congruence of behavioral symptomatology in children with ADD/H,

ADD/WO, and learning disabilities. *Journal of Learning Disabilities, 27,* 243–253.

Stanley, C.A., & Spafford, C. (1998). MARC and MAPP. In C. Spafford, A.J.I. Pesce, & G.S. Grosser, *The cyclopedic education dictionary* (pp. 363–368). Albany, NY: Delmar Publishing.

Stanley, C.A., & Spafford, C.S. (2001, April). *Math activities/ideas that reinforce curriculum standards and culture for grades K–4.* Paper presented at the 79th annual meeting of the National Council of Teachers of Mathematics, Orlando, FL.

Stanley, C.A., & Spafford, C.S. (2002). Cultural perspectives in mathematics planning efforts. *Multicultural Education, 10* (1), 40–42.

Stanovich, K.E. (1980). Toward an interactive-compensatory model of individual differences in the development of reading fluency. *Reading Research Quarterly, 16,* 32–71.

Stanovich, K.E. (1986). Matthew effect in reading: Some consequences of individual differences in the acquisition of literacy. *Reading Research Quarterly, 21,* 360–407.

Stanovich, K.E. (1994). Romance and reality. *The Reading Teacher, 47,* 280–289.

Stanovich, K.E., Siegel, L.S., Gottardo, A., Chiappe, P., & Sidhu, R. (1997). Subtypes of developmental dyslexia: Differences in phonological and orthographic coding. In B. Blachman (Ed.), *Foundations of reading acquisition and dyslexia* (pp. 115–141). Mahwah, NJ: Lawrence Erlbaum.

Stauffer, R.G. (1969). *Directed reading maturity as a cognitive process.* New York: Harper & Row.

Stauffer, R.G. (1980). *The language experience approach to the teaching of reading* (2nd ed.). New York: Harper & Row.

Stein, J. (1989). Visuospatial perception and reading problems. *Irish Journal of Psychology, 10,* 521–533.

Stein, J., & Fowler, S. (1985). Effect of monocular occlusion on visuomotor perception and reading in dyslexic children. *The Lancet, 69,* 73.

Stein, N.L., & Trabasso, T. (1981). *What's in a story: An approach to comprehension and instruction* (Technical Report No. 200). Urbana-Champaign, IL: University of Illinois.

Stella, G. (2004). Dyslexia in Italy. In I. Smythe, J. Everatt, & R. Salter (Eds.), *The international book of dyslexia: A guide to practice and resources* (pp. 139–142). West Sussex, England: John Wiley & Sons.

Sternberg, R.J. (1985). *Beyond IQ: A triarchic theory of human intelligence.* New York: Cambridge University Press.

Stewart, M.T. (2003). Building effective practice: Using small discoveries to enhance literacy learning. *The Reading Teacher, 56* (6), 540–547.

Stice, C.F., Bertrand, J.E., & Bertrand, N.P. (1995). *Integrating reading and other language arts.* Boston: Wadsworth Pub.

Stone, S.J. (1996). *Multiage classroom.* Glenview, IL: Good Year Books (Addison-Wesley).

Stotsky, S. (1999). *Losing our language: How multicultural classroom instruction is undermining our children's ability to read, write, and reason.* New York: Free Press

Strauss, A.A., & Lehtinen, L. (1947). *Psychopathology and education of the brain-injured child* (Vol. I). New York: Grune & Stratton.

Strickland, D. (2001). The interface of standards, teacher preparation, and research: Improving the quality of teachers. In C. Roller (Ed.), *Learning to teach reading: Setting the research agenda* (pp. 20–29). Newark, DE: International Reading Association.

Strickland, D. (2002). The importance of effective early intervention. In A.E. Farstrup & S.J. Samuels, (Eds.), *Reading researchers in search of common ground* (pp. 69–86). Newark, DE: International Reading Association.

Struempler, R.E., Larson, G.E., & Rimland, B. (1985). Hair mineral analysis and disruptive behaviors in clinically normal young men. *Journal of Learning Disabilities, 18*, 609–612.

Swail, W.S., Cabrera, A.F., & Lee, C. (2004, June). *Latino youth and the pathway to college*. Washington, DC: Educational Policy Institute.

Swan, B. (2002, March 19). *Communication and learning: Expanding literacy within diverse populations*. Featured presentation at the 33rd annual conference of the Massachusetts Reading Association (MRA), Sturbridge, MA.

Swanson, H.L. (1988). Memory subtypes in learning disabled readers. *Learning Disabilities Quarterly, 11*, 342–357.

Swanson, H.L. (1993). Principles and procedures in strategy use. In L.J. Meltzer (Ed.), *Strategy assessment and instruction for students with learning disabilities* (pp. 61–92). Austin, TX: Pro-Ed.

Swanson, H.L., Cochran, K.F., & Ewers, C.A. (1990). Can learning disabilities be determined from working memory performance? *Journal of Learning Disabilities, 23*, 59–67.

Swanson, H.L., & Deshler, D. (2003, March/April). Instructing adolescents with learning disabilities: Converting a meta-analysis to practice. *Journal of Learning Disabilities, 36* (2), 124–135.

Taba, H. (1967). *Teacher's handbook for elementary social studies*. Reading, MA: Addison Wesley.

Talcott, J.B., Hansen, P.C., Willis-Owen, C., McKinnell, I.W., Richardson, A.J., & Stein, J.F. (1998). Visual magnocellular impairment in adult developmental dyslexics. *Neuro-ophthalmology, 20* (4), 187–201.

Tannebaum, A.J. (1997). The meaning and making of giftedness. In N. Colangelo & G.A. Davis (Eds.), *Handbook of gifted education* (p. 27–42). Boston: Allyn and Bacon.

Tatsuoka, K.K. (1984). Changes in error types over learning stages. *Journal of Educational Psychology, 76*, 120–129.

Tatum, A.W. (2003). Breaking down barriers that disenfranchise African American adolescent readers in low-level tracks. In P.A. Mason & J.S. Schumm (Eds.), *Promising practices for urban reading education*. Newark, DE: International Reading Association.

Tatum, B. (1997). *Why are all the black kids sitting together in the cafeteria?* New York: Basic Books.

Taylor, B., Graves, M., & Van Den Broek, P. (2000). *Reading for meaning*. New York: Teachers College Press.

Taylor, K.K. (1984, February). Teaching summarization skills. *Journal of Reading, 27*, 389.

Taylor, W. (1953). Cloze procedure: A new tool for measuring readability. *Journalism Quarterly, 30*, 415–433.

Teale, W.H. (1984). Reading to young children: Its significance in literacy development. In H. Goelman, A. Oberg, & F. Smith (Eds.), *Awakening to literacy*. Exeter, NH: Heinemann.

Templeton, S., & Morris, D. (2000). Spelling. In M. Kamil, P. Mosenthal, P.D. Pearson, & R. Barr (Eds.), *Handbook of reading research,* Volume 3 (pp. 525–543). Mahwah, NJ: Lawrence Erlbaum Associates.

Thatcher, R.W., & Lester, M.L. (1985). Nutrition, environmental toxins, and computerized EEGs: A mini-max approach to learning disabilities. *Journal of Learning Disabilities, 18*, 287–289.

Thomas, E., & Robinson, H.A. (1972). *Improving reading in every classroom*. Boston: Allyn and Bacon.

Thomas, K.F., & Barksdale-Ladd, M.A. (1995). Effective literacy classrooms: Teachers and students exploring literacy together. In K.A. Hinchman, D.J. Leu, & C. Kinzer, (Eds.), *Perspectives on literacy research and practice* (pp. 169–179). Chicago, IL: National Reading Conference.

Thompson, J., & Fischer, M. (2001/2002). (Teachers as Readers Committee). *Massachusetts Reading Association (MRA) teachers as reader's brochure*. Milford, MA: MRA.

Thompson, S. (1997). *The source for nonverbal learning disorders*. East Moline, IL: LinguiSystems.

Thompson-Grove, G., & Graham, B. (2003, October 1–3). *Critical friends group institute* (booklet for workshops presentation). Bloomington, IN: National School Reform Faculty (NSRF).

Tierney, R.J., Carter, M.A., & Desai, L.E. (1991). *Portfolio assessment in the reading-writing classroom*. Norwood, MA: Christopher-Gordon.

Tierney, R.J., & Cunningham, J.W. (1984). Research on teaching reading comprehension. In P.D. Pearson (Ed.), *Handbook of reading research* (pp. 609–656). New York: Longman.

Tierney, R.J., Readance, J.E., & Dishner, E.K. (1990). *Reading strategies and practices—A compendium*. Boston: Allyn and Bacon.

Todo, E. (2004). Dyslexia in Japan. In I. Smythe, J. Everatt, & R. Salter (Eds.), *The international book of dyslexia: A guide to practice and resources* (pp. 143–146). West Sussex, England: John Wiley & Sons.

Tomatis, A. (1978). *Education and dyslexia*. France-Quebec: Les Editions, AIAPP.

Topping, K. (1989). Peer tutoring and paired reading: Combining two powerful techniques. *The Reading Teacher, 42*, 488–494.

Torgesen, J.K. (1988). Studies of children with learning disabilities who perform poorly on memory span tasks. *Journal of Learning Disabilities, 21*, 605–612.

Tournaki, N., & Criscitiello, E. (2003, November/December). Using peer tutoring as a successful part of behavior management. *Council for Exceptional Children, 36* (2), 22–25.

Tovani, C. (2000). *I read it, but I don't get it: Comprehension strategies for adolescent readers*. York, ME: Stenhouse.

Traub, N. (with Frances Bloom). (1992, 1990, 1975, 1973, 1972). *Recipe for reading*. Cambridge, MA: Educators Publishing.

Trelease, J. (1982). *The read-aloud handbook*. New York: Penguin Books.

Trelease, J. (2001). *The read-aloud handbook* (5th ed.). New York: Penguin Books.

Troutman, A.P., & Lichtenberg, B.K. (1987, 1995). *Mathematics—A good beginning—Strategies for teaching children.* Pacific Grove, CA: Brooks/Cole Pub.

Tsuge, M. (2001). Learning disabilities in Japan. In D. Hallahan & B. Keogh (Eds.), *Research and global perspectives in learning disabilities: Essays in honor of William M. Cruickshank* (pp. 255–272). Mahwah, NJ: Lawrence Erlbaum.

Tunmer, W., & Hoover, W. (1993). Phonological recoding skill and beginning reading. *Reading and Writing: An Interdisciplinary Journal, 5,* 161–179.

Tur-Kaspa, H., & and Margalit, M. (2001, Winter). Learning disabilities around the world. *Thalamus Updates: A Newsletter of the International Academy for Research in Learning Disabilities.* Vol. 3 (3). http://www.iarld.net/newsletters/winter01.htm#world (downloaded 4/3/04).

Turnbull, A.P., Turnbull, H.R., Shank, M., & Leal, D. (1995). *Exceptional lives: Special education in today's schools.* Englewood Cliffs, NJ: Prentice Hall.

Turner, J.S. (May/June 2004). When teachers are readers. *On-Line Principal.* http://www.naesp.org.

Tuttle, J. (2002/2003). Using technology with a teachers as readers group. *Massachusetts Reading Association (MRA) Primer, 31* (1), 9–11.

U.S. Census Bureau. (1995). *Statistical abstract of the United States: 1995* (115th ed.). Washington, DC: U.S. Department of Commerce.

U.S. Department of Education (USDOE). (1975, November 29). *Education for All Handicapped Children Act (P.L. 94-142).* Washington, DC: U.S. Congress.

U.S. Department of Education (USDOE). (1977, August 23). *Education of handicapped children: Implementation of Part B of the Education of Handicapped Act,* Federal Register I, Part II. Washington, DC: U.S. Department of Health Education and Welfare.

U.S. Department of Education (USDOE). (2001, January 3). *No Child Left Behind Act of 2001. (Public Law 107-110).* Washington, DC: U.S. Congress.

U.S. Department of Education (USDOE). (2002). *Twenty-fourth annual report to Congress on implementation of the Individuals with Disabilities Act (IDEA).* Washington, DC: U.S. Government Printing Office.

U.S. Department of Education (USDOE). (2003a). H.R.1350. (IDEA). *Improving education results for Children with Disabilities Act of 2003.* Washington, DC: U.S. Government Printing Office.

U.S. Department of Education (USDOE). (2003b). *Interim report for the study of state and local implementation of the Individual with Disabilities Education Act (1999–2000 school year).* Washington, DC: U.S. Department of Education, Office of Special Education Programs.

U.S. Department of Education (USDOE). (2004). History: Twenty-five years of progress in educating children with disabilities through IDEA. http://www.ed.gov/policy/speced/leg/idea/history.pdf

Vacca, R.T. (2002). Making a difference in adolescents' school lives: Visible and invisible aspects of content area reading. In A.E. Farstrup & S. J. Samuels (Eds.), *What research has to say about reading instruction* (pp. 184–204). Newark, DE: International Reading Association.

Valdés, G. (2001). *Learning and not learning English: Latino students in American schools.* New York: Teachers College Press.

Valencia, S.W., & Buly, M.R. (2004, March). Behind test scores: What struggling readers really need. *The Reading Teacher, 57*(6), 520–531.

Valeri-Gold, M. (1987). Previewing: A directed reading-thinking activity. *Reading Horizons, 27,* 123–126.

Van Kraayenoord, C. (2001). Learning difficulties in Australia: Some brief notes. *Thalamus Updates: A Newsletter of the International Academy for Research in Learning Disabilities. Vol. 3 (2).* Reference: Louden, W., et al. (2000). *Mapping the territory—Primary students with learning difficulties: Literacy and numeracy* (Vols. 1–3). Canberra: Commonwealth of Australia, Department of Education, Training and Youth Affairs. http://www.gu.edu.au/school/cls/cler

van Kraayenoord, C.E., & Elkins, J. (2004). Learning difficulties in numeracy in Australia. *Journal of Learning Disabilities, 37*(1), 32–41.

Van Nest, P.E. (2003). Untangling approaches to teaching writing: A process of change in one classroom. In S. Peterson (Ed.), *Untangling some knots in K–8 writing instruction* (pp. 6–16). Newark, DE: International Reading Association.

Varnhagen, C.K., & Goldman, S. R. (1986). Improving comprehension: Causal relations instruction for learning handicapped learners. *The Reading Teacher, 39,* 896–904.

Veit, D.T., & Mastropieri, M.A. (1986). Extended mnemonic instruction with LD adolescents. *Journal of Educational Psychology, 78,* 300–308.

Vietnamese Americans: Lessons in American History. (online curriculum from Teaching Tolerance and the Orange County Asian and Pacific Islander Community Alliance—www.teachingtolerance.org/vietnamese) (2004, Spring), 25, 31–35.

Vukelich, C. (1984). Parents' role in the reading process: A review of practical suggestions and ways to communicate with parents. *The Reading Teacher, 37,* 472–477.

Waldron, K.A. (1996). *Introduction to a special education: The inclusive classroom.* Albany, NY: Delmar Publishers.

Walker-Dalhouse, D. (1992). Fostering multicultural awareness: Books for young children. *Reading Horizons, 33,* 47–54.

Warton, P.M. (2001). The forgotten voices in homework: Views of students. *Educational Psychologist, 36* (3), 155–165.

Watkins, Y.K. (1986). *So far from the bamboo grove.* New York: Beech Tree Paperback Books.

Watkins, Y.K. (2001). *The power of story: Connecting the past in the future.* Presentation at the 31st annual conference of the Massachusetts Reading Association, Sturbridge, MA.

Weinstein, C.A., Tomlinson-Clarke, S., & Curran, M. (2004, January/February). Toward a conception of culturally responsive classroom management. *Journal of Teacher Education, 55* (1), 25–38.

Wheeler, R.J., & Frank, M.A. (1988). Identification of stress buffers. *Behavioral Medicine, 14* (2), 78–89.

White, M. (1988). Dyslexia and thinking disorders. *Transactional Analysis Journal, 18,* 141–147.

Williams, C. (2000, September 20). Testimony before Congress of Ms. Carmelita Williams, Committee on Education and the Workforce. Washington, DC: Hearing on The Importance of Literacy. http://edworkforce .house.gov/hearings/106th/fc/literacy92600/w192600.htm

Williams, C. (2002). *Making it difficult for our children to fail.* Featured speaker at the 33rd annual conference of the Massachusetts Reading Association (MRA), Sturbridge, MA.

Williams, G. (2004). *School improvement planning packet: Frank H. Freedman School.* Springfield Schools: Springfield, MA.

Williams, M.C., & LeCluyse, K. (1990). Perceptual consequences of a temporal processing deficit in reading disabled children. *Journal of the American Optometric Association, 61,* 111–121.

Wilsher, C., & Taylor, J. (1987). Remedies for dyslexia: Proven or unproven? *Early Child Development and Care, 27,* 437–449.

Winne, P.J., Woodlands, M.J., & Wong, B.Y.L. (1982). Comparability of self-concept among learning disabled, proficient, and gifted students. *Journal of Learning Disabilities, 15,* 470–475.

Witherell, N., & McMackin, M. (2002). *Graphic organizers and activities for differentiated instruction in reading.* New York: Scholastic.

Wolfarth, H. & Sam, C. (1982). The effect of color psycholodynamic environmental modifications upon psychophysiological and behavioral reactions of severely handicapped children. *The International Journal of Biosocial Research, 1,* 10–38.

Wong, B.Y.L. (1979). Increasing main ideas through questioning strategies. *Learning Disabilities Quarterly, 2,* 42–47.

Wong, B.Y.L. (2000). Writing strategies instruction for expository essays for adolescents with and without learning disabilities. *Topics in Language Disorders, 20,* 29–44.

Wong, B.Y.L. (2001). Commentary: Pointers for literacy instruction from educational technology and research on writing instruction. *The Elementary School Journal, 101,* 3, 359–369.

Wong, B.Y.L., & Jones, W. (1982). Increasing metacomprehension in learning disabled and normally achieving students through self-questioning training. *Learning Disability Quarterly, 5,* 228–239.

Wong, B.Y.L., Kuperis, S., Jamieson, D., Keller, L., & Cull-Hewitt, R. (2002). Effects of guided journal writing on students' story understanding. *Journal of Educational Research, 95,* 179–191.

Woodward, J., & Ono, Y. (2004). Mathematics and academic diversity in Japan. *Journal of Learning Disabilities, 37*(1), 74–82.

Worrall, R.S. (1990a). Detecting helath fraud in the field of learning disabilities. *Journal of Learning Disabilities, 23,* 207–212.

Worrall, R.S. (1990b). Neural organization technique—treatment or torture? *Skeptical Inquirer, 15,* 40–50.

Worthy, M.J., & Bloodgood, J.W. (1998). Enhancing reading instruction through Cinderella tales. In M.F. Opitz (Ed.), *Literacy instruction for culturally and linguistically diverse students* (pp. 245–257). Newark, DE: International Reading Association.

Yin, W.G., & Weekes, B.S. (2003). Dyslexia in Chinese: Clues from cognitive psychology. *Annals of Dyslexia, 53,* 255–279.

Yopp, K.K., & Yopp, R.H. (2000). Supporting phonemic awareness in the classroom. *The Reading Teacher, 54* (2).

Zhang, C.F., Zhang, J.H., Yin, R.S., Zhou, J., & Chang, S.M. (1996). Research on reading disabilities in Chinese speaking children (in Chinese). *Acta Psychologica Sinica, 19,* 222–226.

Zhang, L. (2000). University students' learning approaches in three cultures: An investigation of Biggs' 3P model. *The Journal of Psychology, 134* (1), 37–55.

Zimbardo, P.G., & Gerrig, R.J. (1996). *Psychology and life* (4th ed.). New York: HarperCollins.

Zwiers, J. (2004). *Building reading comprehension habits in grades 6–12: A toolkit of classroom activities.* Newark, DE: International Reading Association.

INDEX